Managing Human Resources

Productivity, Quality of Work Life, Profits

Also Available from McGraw-Hill

■ Schaum's Outline Series in **Accounting, Business & Economics**

Most outlines include basic theory, definitions, and hundreds of solved problems and supplementary problems with answers.

Titles on the current list include:

Available at your College Bookstore. A complete listing of Schaum titles may be obtained by writing to: **Schaum Division, McGraw-Hill, Inc., Princeton Road, S-1, Hightstown, NJ 08520.**

Managing Human Resources

Productivity, Quality of Work Life, Profits

THIRD EDITION

Wayne F. Cascio
Graduate School of Business
University of Colorado, Denver

McGraw-Hill, Inc.
New York St. Louis San Francisco Auckland Bogotá
Caracas Lisbon London Madrid Mexico Milan
Montreal New Delhi Paris San Juan Singapore
Sydney Tokyo Toronto

Managing
Human
Resources:

Productivity,
Quality of Work Life,
Profits

4 5 6 7 8 9 0 HAL HAL 9 0 9 8 7 6 5 4 3 2 1

ISBN 0-07-010996-6

This book was set in Janson Text by Waldman Graphics, Inc.
The editors were Alan Sachs, Dan Alpert, and Linda Richmond;
the designer was Jo Jones;
cover illustration by Roy Wiemann;
the production supervisor was Richard A. Ausburn.
The photo editor was Anne Manning.
New drawings were done by Fine Line Illustrations, Inc.
Arcata Graphics/Halliday was printer and binder.

Library of Congress Cataloging-in-Publication Data

Cascio, Wayne F.
    Managing human resources: productivity, quality of work life,
profits / Wayne F. Cascio. — 3rd ed.
       p.   cm. — (McGraw-Hill series in management)
    Includes bibliographical references and indexes.
    ISBN 0-07-010996-6
    1. Personnel management.   I. Title.   II. Series.
HF5549.C2975   1992   91-25125
658.3 — dc20

About
the Author

■ Wayne F. Cascio earned his B.A. degree from Holy Cross College in 1968, his M.A. degree from Emory University in 1969, and his Ph.D. in industrial/organizational psychology from the University of Rochester in 1973. Since that time he has taught at Florida International University, the University of California-Berkeley, and the University of Colorado-Denver, where he is at present Professor of Management.

Professor Cascio is a Fellow of the American Psychological Association and a Diplomate in industrial/organizational psychology of the American Board of Professional Psychology. His editorial board memberships have included the *Journal of Applied Psychology*, the *Academy of Management Review*, *Human Performance*, *Organizational Dynamics*, and *Asia-Pacific HRM*. He has consulted with a wide variety of organizations in both the public and private sectors on HR matters, and periodically he testifies as an expert witness in employment discrimination cases. Professor Cascio is an active researcher and is the author or editor of five books on human resource management.

To Dorothy
and Joe,

the choicest blessings life has provided;
constant reminders of what really counts.

Contents

Preface

This book was not written for aspiring human resource management (HRM) specialists. It was written for the student of general management whose job inevitably will involve responsibility for managing *people*, along with other organizational assets. A fundamental assumption, then, is that all managers are accountable to their organizations in terms of the impact of their HRM activities. They also are accountable to their peers and to their subordinates in terms of the quality of work life they are providing.

As a unifying theme for the text, there is explicit linkage in each chapter of the three outcome variables—productivity, quality of work life, and profit—to the HRM activity under discussion. This relationship should strengthen the student's perception of HRM as an important function affecting individuals, organizations, and society.

Each of the six parts that comprise the text includes a figure that illustrates the organizing framework for the book. The specific topics covered in each part are highlighted for emphasis.

Each chapter incorporates the following distinguishing features:

■ A split-sequential vignette, often from the popular press, that illustrates Human Resource Management in action. Events in the vignette are designed to sensitize the reader to the subject matter of the chapter. The events lead to a climax, but then the vignette stops—like a two-part television drama. The reader is asked to predict what will happen next and to anticipate the impact of alternative courses of action.

In keeping with the general management orientation of the book, the vignette is then followed by a new section entitled, "Questions This Chapter Will Help Managers Answer." This section provides a broad outline of the topics to be covered in the chapter. Then the text for the chapter appears, replete with concepts, theories, research findings, and company examples that illustrate current practices. Ultimately we are trying to teach prospective managers to *make decisions* based on accurate diagnoses of situations that involve HRM issues. Their ability to do this is enhanced by familiarity with theory, research, and practice.

At the end of the chapter we continue the vignette introduced at the outset, to see what happened. This dynamic design allows the student to move back and forth from concept to evidence to practice—then back to evaluating concepts—in a continuous "learning loop."

■ Relevant research findings plus clippings from the popular press (Company Examples) provide real world applications of concepts and theories. It has often been said that experience is a hard teacher because it gives the test first and the lessons afterward. Actual company examples, plus numerous international applications, allow the student to learn from the experience of others.

■ Near the end of the chapter, before the summary and discussion questions, there is a section called "Implications for Management Practice," which provides concrete, no-nonsense advice on how to manage the issues that have been discussed.

HRM texts have sometimes been criticized for overemphasizing the HR practices of large businesses. There is often scant advice for the manager of a small business who "wears many hats" and whose capital resources are limited. To address this issue explicitly, I have made a conscious effort to provide examples of effective HRM practices in small businesses in almost every chapter.

This was no cosmetic revision. I examined every topic, every example, in each chapter for its continued relevance and appropriateness. Thus 11 of the 17 split-sequential vignettes are new, some topics that appeared separately in the previous editions are now combined (e.g., job analysis and human resource planning, employee and management staffing), and others that were combined now appear separately (e.g., recruitment and staffing, pay and benefits).

Above all, I have tried to make the text readable, neither too simplistic nor too complex.

New Topics in the Third Edition

■ Key characteristics of the competitive environment of business, especially increasing cultural diversity at home and international issues overseas—how these are impacting the workplace and the management of people within it (Chapter 1).

■ The development of global product and service market strategies, and how HR specialists and line managers can develop strategic partnerships to support them (Chapter 2).

■ New social and organizational realities—more women, more older workers, more people of color—and recent laws and civil rights rulings by the Supreme Court that affect the management of people at work. International applications help students put U.S. requirements into perspective (Chapter 3).

■ Succession planning in small, family-owned businesses is presented in the context of job analysis and human resource planning (Chapter 4).

- Recruiting—internal, external, and as a long-term business strategy—as well as tips on job search (i.e., how to find a job, Chapter 5).
- The impact of organizational culture on staffing decisions, as well as much new information on the effectiveness of alternative selection methods. An international application highlights the Japanese approach to staffing decisions (Chapter 6).
- Impact of the changing work force on training activities, potential pitfalls in worker retraining, new research on team training, and the use of video at small firms (Chapter 7).
- The strategic side of performance appraisal—that is, "What do I want this process to accomplish"? as well as the interpersonal aspects of the feedback process (Chapter 8).
- New research findings on the costs and benefits of company-sponsored day care, alternative strategies for dealing with plateaued workers, and legally sound ways to handle layoffs (Chapter 9).
- Thorough discussions of internal, external, and individual equity, comparable worth, linkage of internal pay relationships to market data, and the development of policies with respect to pay secrecy, compression, pay raises, and the effect of inflation (Chapter 10).
- Strategic aspects of indirect pay (employee benefits), the Older Workers Benefits Protection Act of 1990, health insurance and the small business, and Social Security in other countries (Chapter 11).
- Expanded discussion of motivation theories, especially expectancy theory and goal setting, self-managed work teams at GM's Saturn plant, and enhanced treatment of profit sharing, gainsharing, and employee stock ownership plans (Chapter 12).
- The changing nature of industrial relations in the U.S., a brief overview of industrial relations systems in other countries (especially Japan), forms of third-party involvement, and trends in labor-management cooperation (Chapter 13).
- Corporate due process in union and nonunion settings, including grievance procedures, discipline, termination, employee privacy concerns, employee searches, and whistle-blowing (Chapter 14).
- Policy choices for managers with regard to substance abuse, safety and health hazards of high technology work (video display terminals, exposure to chemicals, and repetitive motion injuries), and the costs and benefits of employee assistance and wellness programs (Chapter 15).
- The costs and benefits of HRM activities (Chapter 16) involve more than just methods and formulas. The chapter focuses on the reduction of controllable costs in areas most relevant to the competitive strategy of a business, for example, innovation, quality enhancement, or cost control.
- Greater emphasis on the role of cultural understanding in international management practice. Chapter 17 helps managers assess any culture in terms of 10 defining characteristics.

ORGANIZATION AND PLAN OF THE BOOK

The figure below provides an organizing framework for the book. It will appear again at the opening of each of the six parts that comprise the book. Each component of the organizing framework will be highlighted for the student as it is discussed. The organization of the parts is designed to reflect the fact that human resource management (HRM) is an integrated, goal-directed set of managerial functions, not just a collection of techniques.

The text is founded on the premise that three critical strategic objectives guide all HRM functions: productivity, quality of work life, and profits. The functions (employment; development; compensation; labor-management accommodation; and support, evaluation, and international implications) in turn are carried out in the context of multiple environments: competitive, social, legal, and organizational.

■ A CONCEPTUAL VIEW OF HUMAN RESOURCE MANAGEMENT ■
STRATEGIC OBJECTIVES, ENVIRONMENTS, FUNCTIONS

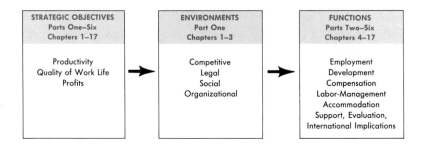

RELATIONSHIP OF HRM FUNCTIONS TO HRM ACTIVITIES

FUNCTIONS	ACTIVITIES
PART 2 EMPLOYMENT	Job Analysis, Human Resource Planning, Recruiting, Staffing (Chapters 4–6)
PART 3 DEVELOPMENT	Orientation, Training, Performance Appraisal, Managing Careers (Chapters 7–9)
PART 4 COMPENSATION	Pay, Benefits, Incentives (Chapters 10–12)
PART 5 LABOR-MANAGEMENT ACCOMMODATION	Union Representation, Collective Bargaining, Procedural Justice, Ethics (Chapters 13, 14)
PART 6 SUPPORT, EVALUATION, INTERNATIONAL IMPLICATIONS	Job Safety and Health, Costs/Benefits of HRM Activities, International Dimensions of HRM (Chapters 15–17)

Part 1, Environment, comprises Chapters 1, 2, and 3. It provides the backdrop against which to appreciate the nature and content of each HRM function. These first three chapters paint a broad picture of the competitive, social, legal, and organizational environments of HRM. They also describe key economic and non-economic factors that affect productivity, quality of work life, and profits. The remaining five parts (14 chapters) in the book are presented in the context of this conceptual framework.

Logically, Employment (Part 2) is the first step in the HRM process. Job analysis, human resource planning, and staffing are key components of the employment process. Once employees are "on board,'" the process of Development (Part 3) begins with orientation and is sustained through continuing training, performance appraisal, and career management activities.

Parts 4, 5, and 6 are all concurrent processes. That is, Compensation (Part 4), Labor-Management Accommodation (Part 5), and Support, Evaluation, and International Implications (Part 6) are all closely intertwined conceptually and in practice. They represent a network of interacting activities, such that a change in one of them (e.g., a new pay system or collective bargaining contract) inevitably will have an impact on all other components of the HRM system. It is only for ease of exposition that they are considred separately in Parts 4, 5, and 6. Chapter 17 of Part 6, International Dimensions of HRM, is a capstone chapter. That is, each of the topics we considered throughout the book is addressed in the special context of international business practices. It forces the student to consider the broad spectrum of HR activities across countries, across cultures, and across economic systems. The need to "fit" HRM practices to the company and country cultures in which they are embedded, in order to achieve the strategic objectives of enhancing productivity, quality of work life, and profits, is an important concept for students to understand and to apply.

In teaching HRM courses at both graduate and undergraduate levels, I use this model as a "road map" throughout the course. I believe that it is important for students to grasp the "big picture", as well as to understand how the topics in question fit into the broader scheme of HRM functions. I have found that by presenting the model frequently throughout the course, showing students where we have been and where we are going, students are better able to adopt a more systematic, strategic perspective in addressing any given HRM issue.

ACKNOWLEDGMENTS

Many people played important roles in the development of this edition of the book, and I am deeply grateful to them. Ultimately, of course, any errors of omission or commission are mine, and I bear responsibility for them.

Four people at McGraw-Hill were especially helpful. Management Editor Alan Sachs and Associate Editor Dan Alpert provided continual support and encouragement. Editing Supervisor Linda Richmond is a true professional and was a pleasure to work with on this, as on the second, edition of the book. As in the first two editions, I found Mike Elia's help to be indispensable. Finally, the many reviewers of various portions of the first and second editions provided important insights that helped to improve the final product. They deserve special thanks: Murray Barrick, University of Iowa; Alan Cabelly, Portland State University; Herschel N. Chait, Indiana State University; Anne C. Cowden, California State University–Sacramento; Robert W. Eder, Cornell University; Robert A. Giacalone, University of Richmond; Linda A. Krefting, Texas Tech University; Mark L. Lengnick-Hall, Wichita State University; Glenn McEvoy, Utah State University; Gregory Northcraft, University of Arizona; and Lee Stepina, Florida State University.

Wayne F. Cascio

Managing Human Resources

Productivity,
Quality of Work Life,
Profits

■ A CONCEPTUAL VIEW OF HUMAN RESOURCE MANAGEMENT ■
STRATEGIC OBJECTIVES, ENVIRONMENTS, FUNCTIONS

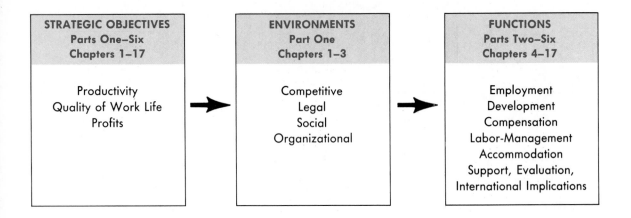

RELATIONSHIP OF HRM FUNCTIONS TO HRM ACTIVITIES

FUNCTIONS	ACTIVITIES
PART 2 EMPLOYMENT	Job Analysis, Human Resource Planning, Recruiting, Staffing (Chapters 4–6)
PART 3 DEVELOPMENT	Orientation, Training, Performance Appraisal, Managing Careers (Chapters 7–9)
PART 4 COMPENSATION	Pay, Benefits, Incentives (Chapters 10–12)
PART 5 LABOR-MANAGEMENT ACCOMMODATION	Union Representation, Collective Bargaining, Procedural Justice, Ethics (Chapters 13, 14)
PART 6 SUPPORT, EVALUATION, INTERNATIONAL IMPLICATIONS	Job Safety and Health, Costs/Benefits of HRM Activities, International Dimensions of HRM (Chapters 15–17)

Environment

n order to manage people effectively in today's world of work, it is essential to understand and appreciate the significant competitive, legal, and social issues. The purpose of Chapters 1 and 3 is to provide insight into these issues. Chapter 2 considers the historical development and current status (role, organization, and evaluation) of the human resource management function in organizations.

1

Human Resources in a Competitive Business Environment

■ **HUMAN RESOURCE MANAGEMENT IN ACTION**

MCDONALD'S EXPORTS SOMETHING NEW TO THE SOVIET UNION — JOB SATISFACTION*

It's a few minutes before 10 A.M. on a bright spring day in Moscow, and 300 people are lined up outside the locked doors of the only McDonald's in the U.S.S.R. Inside, 100 edgy crew members jostle behind the 27-station, stainless steel counter.

The doors open and a great cheer explodes from the crew. They're screaming and waving to customers to come on in, like a crowd cheering the arrival of a rock star. One of the crew, Katherine Zhurovleva, age 17, looks at the scene and beams. She says this happens every day. Spontaneously. Nobody told them to do it. It happens because all the McDonald's crew members love their jobs so much. Says Zhurovleva, grinning, "I can't imagine life without working here."

To anyone in the United States who once toiled at a McDonald's to scrape through college, this must sound more like a McDonald's on Mars. It is not,

---

*Adapted from: K. Maney, Their kind of place; job satisfaction is a new concept to Soviets; U.S. ideas creep into Soviet Union, *USA Today*, May 11, 1990, pp. 1B, 2B. Copyright 1990, USA Today. Reprinted with permission.

McDonald's is a popular place in Moscow. (*Source:* Courtesy McDonald's.)

because in the Soviet Union, a workplace where people like their jobs is rarer than a fresh fruit salad. What makes *this* McDonald's different is that it is one of the first places where a large number of Soviets are employed in an almost exact replica of a U.S. workplace. In fact, the restaurant under Moscow's golden arches is more like a theme park than a fast-food shop. The restaurant offers not only burgers and fries, but a little piece of the U.S.A., right down to the service and cleanliness. Being a part of that is what is transforming the lives of McDonald's-Moscow employees. It's also an early sign that U.S. companies could contribute something else: We could shed some sun on the U.S.S.R.'s dark attitude toward work.

Said one U.S. economist and expert on the Soviet Union: "We may not be able to inject large amounts of capital into the U.S.S.R., but one thing we can do is management training, labor relations. It's damn important to create an environment of positive contribution."* In that respect, McDonald's is an extraordinary window on what may happen in the Soviet Union.

Challenges

1. Since Soviets have almost no tradition of capitalism, or, for that matter, happy and productive workers, is all of this just a "honeymoon" effect,

*Levine, in Maney, 1990, p. 1B.

or have the crew at McDonald's-Moscow and the company's culture fused to create something unusual?

2. Does the concept of job satisfaction mean the same thing in different cultures?

3. In recent years there has been a rapid spread of democratic principles throughout Eastern Europe. In what ways might McDonald's-Moscow contribute to the trend toward democratization?

1. Given the coming changes in workforce demographics, what can our firm do to be a beneficiary, rather than a victim, of these changes?

2. What people-related problems are likely to arise as a result of a merger, take-over, or leveraged buyout? How can we avoid these problems?

3. How are the various factors of production affected by global competition? What human resource strategies can we adopt to strengthen our position in global markets?

QUESTIONS THIS CHAPTER WILL HELP MANAGERS ANSWER

THE ENTERPRISE IS THE PEOPLE

Organizations are managed and staffed by people. Without people, organizations cannot exist. Indeed, the challenge, the opportunity, and also the frustration of creating and managing organizations frequently stem from the people-related problems that arise within them. People-related problems, in turn, frequently stem from the mistaken belief that people are all alike, that they can be treated identically. Nothing could be further from the truth. Like snowflakes, no two people are exactly alike, and everyone differs physically and psychologically from everyone else. Sitting in a sports arena, for example, will be tall people, small people, fat people, thin people, black people, white people, elderly people, young people, and so on. Even within any single physical category there will be enormous variability in psychological characteristics. Some will be "screamers," others will be reserved; some will be intelligent, others will be not so intelligent; some will prefer indoor activities, others will prefer outdoor activities. The point is that these differences demand attention so that each person can maximize his or her potential, so that organizations can maximize their effectiveness, and so that society as a whole can make the wisest use of its human resources.

Some managers place greater emphasis than others on developing employees' potential. For example, Mr. Konosuke Matsushita, founder of the giant electronics firm that bears his name and markets its products under the brand names National, Panasonic, Technics, and Quasar, was a lifelong believer in the notion that "the enterprise is the people." Here is a brief excerpt from his written philosophy of management.

When my company was still small I often told my employees that when customers asked, "What does your company make?" they should answer, "Matsushita Electric is making men. We also make electrical appliances, but first and foremost our company makes men." (ref. 32, p. 45)

This book is about managing people, the most vital of all resources, in work settings. Rather than focus exclusively on issues of concern to the personnel specialist, however, we will examine human resource management issues in terms of their impact on management in general. A changing world order has forced us to take a hard look at the ways we manage people. Research has shown time and again that human resource management practices can make an important, practical difference in terms of three key organizational outcomes: productivity, quality of work life, and profit. This is healthy. Each chapter in this book considers the impact of a different aspect of human resource management on these three broad themes. To study these impacts, we will look at the latest theory and research in each topical area, plus examples of actual company practices.

In this chapter we will examine some general issues related to productivity and quality of work life. In the next chapter we will focus on the relationship between competent human resource (HR) practices and profits. Let's begin by considering some basic ideas about organizations.

ORGANIZATIONS: WHY DO THEY EXIST AND HOW DO THEY WORK?

As our wants and needs grow, so do the ways of satisfying them. Consider the growth of the home-computer industry, for example, and how the firms within it are racing to deliver software—games, puzzles, educational exercises—to meet consumer demands for such products. None of our wants and needs is satisfied randomly or haphazardly. When you go to a store that sells computers, for example, the store will be open, and you can buy the product of your choice even though the salesperson who helped you last time has the day off. In the process of satisfying needs and wants, *continuity* and *predictability* are essential in the delivery of goods and services. In modern society, continuity and predictability are made possible by *organizations*.

Some of the organizations that accommodate our wants and needs are fast-food restaurants, movie theaters, sporting goods stores, hospitals, universities, accounting firms, and antique stores, just to name a few. Each of these organizations exists because what must be done, the task to be accomplished, is too large or complex for one person to accomplish alone. So a number of people are gathered together, and each is assigned a part of the total task. It is most efficient to divide a large task (such as building a house) into its component parts so that specially qualified individuals can perform the subfunctions. *Specialization* by subfunction and *coordination* among all the tasks to be accomplished make the largest-scale task possible.

Although there are great differences among the organizations in our society, they also have much in common. Every organization is (1) comprised of people (2) who perform specialized tasks (3) that are coordinated (4) to enhance the value

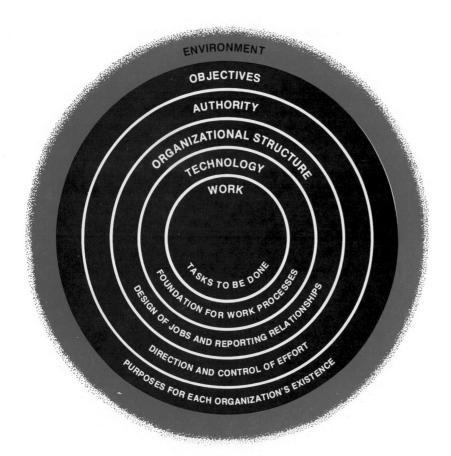

FIGURE 1-1
Key elements of formal organization, from specific to general.

or utility (5) of some good or service (6) that is wanted by and provided to a set of customers or clients.

In the simplest terms, a formal organization exists by reason of two things: the work it does and the technology it embraces to do that work. However, these are not the only elements of a formal organization. The key elements of a formal organization are related as follows (Figure 1-1). All organizations have objectives (e.g., to provide high-quality goods and services at competitive prices) that are based on some perceived unfilled demand in the outside environment. To attain these objectives, certain tasks must be done (e.g., processing canceled checks, assembling parts of an appliance, checking a patient's vital signs). Indeed, formal organizations are *defined* by the kind of work they do. Technology determines the nature of the work processes since it includes all the aspects of knowledge that are related to the attainment of a firm's objectives (e.g., employee skills, machines, and facilities). Organizational structure supports and facilitates technology by designing jobs and grouping tasks in order to optimize control, coordination, and productivity. This, for example, is why some firms are organized by function—production, marketing, sales, and distribution. To attain the benefits of specialization and efficiency, authority is used to ensure adequate role performance and direction of efforts. Some workers are bosses (in whom authority is formally vested by the organization), while others are subordinates. These concepts are best illustrated by an example.

Consider some of the problems associated with assembly line work in the making of automobiles, where the basic technology is mass production. Each worker holds a certain job, does specified actions at a regimented pace, and occupies a certain work station. The specific organizational structure of the assembly line and the content of each job are determined through industrial engineering studies. Once the job is set, the actions of the jobholder are set as well, and the worker must perform what the job dictates; the worker has no discretion to determine whether or not bumpers should be attached to the front and rear of each auto. Technology also limits permissible behavior on the job, for the assembly line worker cannot leave the workstation to take care of "personal business" unless a replacement can be found. In short, technology and organizational structure together place restrictions and requirements on workers' behavior.

When work structure is analyzed with respect to greater specialization for the purpose of producing higher efficiency, little consideration is usually given to the people who do the work and who are thus the substance of specialization and efficiency. This is a serious mistake, as we shall see in later chapters. An organizational structure designed without regard for workers is a structure that dictates behavior to these workers; it will have an adverse effect on their behavior and thus on efficiency. A structure designed with workers in mind affects them so that they contribute more favorably to efficiency. The result is that the workers play an important role in determining the overall efficiency of the organization.

Organizations Need People, and People Need Organizations

Without people, organizations could not function. Even in highly automated plants, such as the one designed and built by Yamazaki to run smoothly using only 12 workers (Yamazaki is a large Japanese company that makes machine tools), people are nevertheless required to coordinate and control the plant's operations. Conversely, people need organizations so that they can satisfy their needs and wants, so that they can maintain their standard of living (by working in organizations), and so that modern society can continue to function.

These needs (organizations for people, people for organizations) will be ever more difficult to satisfy in the context of today's competitive business environment. That environment is defined by characteristics such as the following.

Some Key Characteristics of the Competitive Environment of Business

Demand for environmentally responsible use of all resources In the face of growing worldwide concern over dwindling natural resources (oil, lumber, fish, metals, and clean air and water, for example), we recognize that nothing exists in limitless supply. Indeed, there is a growing worldwide consensus that business and society in general must abandon wasteful practices and conserve resources for use in the future, as well as for generations to come. Organizations (or nations) that ignore these pressures should expect to be roundly and publicly criticized.

In the United States, both federal and state governments are redoubling efforts to catch and punish environmental violators. If convicted, they are more likely to draw prison time now because of felony clauses added in the 1980s and also because of federal sentencing guidelines set in 1987. Before the new guidelines jail terms were rare, and typically totaled 60 to 90 days. Now similar offenses carry 2-year prison sentences.

The typical scenario for toxic turpitude is a cash-strapped firm deciding that plugging the flow of pollutants is just too expensive. Properly disposing of a 55-gallon barrel of toxic waste now costs as much as $1000. For small companies, such expenses can quickly become a make-or-break expense when business is slow.

To counter such tricks, government agencies have assembled teams of scientists, lawyers, and detectives outfitted with gear ranging from electronic sniffers to "moon suits" for poking around in sewers. Despite these efforts, however, environmental violators remain difficult to catch and to convict.[54] Natural resources are not the only types of resources in short supply, as the next section demonstrates.

Demographic changes and increasing cultural diversity From now until the end of the century, 88 percent of workforce growth in America will come from these groups: women, African Americans, and people of Hispanic or Asian origin, including immigrants. White men, meanwhile, account for most retirees and are leaving the workforce in record numbers. These trends are shown graphically in Figure 1-2.

FIGURE 1-2
The changing labor pool.

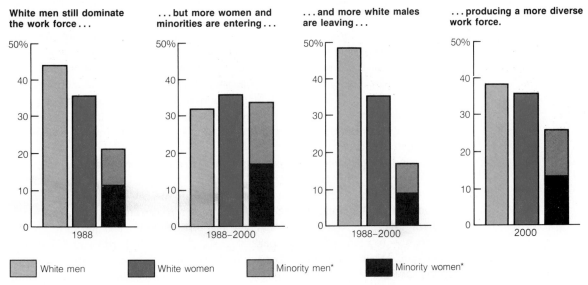

THE CHANGING LABOR POOL

Source: Bureau of Labor Statistics, Office of Employment Projections

*Includes Hispanics

In addition, the number of Americans aged 16 to 24, the age group when people typically enter the paid workforce, dropped 14 percent between 1980 and 1990. These workers all were born after the end of the post-World War II baby boom (1946 to 1964). According to the Labor Department, the effects of the "baby-bust" generation will bottom out in 1996, when the number of new entrants to the workforce aged 16 to 24 will be almost 20 percent less than the number in that age group in 1980.[59]

These trends have two key implications for managers: (1) The reduced supply of entry-level workers will make finding and keeping employees a top priority in the decade ahead. Companies that once grudgingly shoehorned women and minorities into their ranks now find them indispensable.[53] (2) The task of managing a culturally diverse workforce, of harnessing the motivation and efforts of a wide variety of workers, will present managers with one of their biggest challenges throughout the 1990s and beyond.

The crisis in education Consider this fact: between now and the year 2000 more than 50 percent of all new jobs will require an education beyond high school, and of those, 30 percent will require a college degree.[19] Unfortunately, however, drop-out rates in U.S. high schools range from 10 to over 50 percent! More than 27 million American adults are functionally illiterate, which means that they cannot even write a bank check, fill out a job application, or identify a deduction for social security on a wage statement. Some 40 million others are barely competent in those skills. If current trends continue, by the year 2000, 70 million Americans will be functionally illiterate.[55]

U.S. firms are feeling these effects now. Thus 20 to 40 percent of job applicants at Motorola flunk an entry-level exam that requires seventh- to ninth-grade English and fifth- to seventh-grade mathematics. Southwestern Bell processed more than 15,000 applications last year just to find 3700 people to test. As a manager at Absorbent Cotton Company, a small business in Valley Park, Missouri, commented: "You look at the parade of people who are completely unqualified to hold even a simple job and you think, 'This is the future?' "[47]

To deal with these problems, business is following two broad strategies. One of these is illustrated by the Boston Compact, an agreement in which 600 Boston-area companies joined with the public schools to form a compact that provides jobs to be reserved for high school graduates who meet academic and attendance requirements. Seven other cities followed Boston's example, and now have similar compacts in existence.[22]

A second strategy is in-house training for current or prospective employees. Thus Motorola spends an average of $1350 per person per year for six basic skills courses, so that the worker is at a point where he or she can be retrained. Planters Nuts in Suffolk, Virginia, spent $40,000 to improve the reading and writing skills of 48 employees. Unisys in Mission Viejo, California, spent $150,000 to teach 125 workers how to read, write, and speak English. Hewlett-Packard spent $22,000 at its Spokane, Washington, plant to teach high school mathematics to 30 production supervisors. These investments are relatively modest. Polaroid, on the other hand, spent $700,000 at its Cambridge, Massachusetts, operation to teach basic English and mathematics to 1000 new and veteran employees.[57]

Although both of these strategies are expensive, the alternative—not having a competent workforce that will enable firms to compete in world markets—is unthinkable. For American business, this is a "must-win" situation. Our standard of living and our very way of life are at stake.

Lagged effects of the merger, takeover, and leveraged buyout trend of the 1980s Mergers in general are rather risky propositions; an estimated 50 percent of domestic U.S. takeovers later end in divestitures. When a foreign business attempts a long-distance marriage with a U.S. company, the obstacles to success rise even higher, largely because of the ambivalence of U.S. workers toward their foreign bosses. In fact, 50 percent of American managers either resign or are fired within 18 months of a foreign takeover.[33] One of the major reasons for the post-merger or takeover people problems is culture shock. As one manager put it: "You don't quite know their values, where they're coming from, or what they really have in mind for you."[33]

The delayed, or lagged, people problems resulting from leveraged buyouts (LBOs) can be even more serious. In an LBO, a small group of investors that generally includes senior management borrows heavily to buy a company from public shareholders and takes it private. The debt is to be rapidly repaid from the company's own cash flow or from sales of its assets.[9]

Proponents argue that LBOs are good for business and good for America, triggering long-overdue actions in companies that have grown fat. By placing ownership in the hands of a small group of investors and managers with a powerful debt-driven incentive to improve productivity, the argument goes, companies can't help but shape up.

The LBO of Safeway Stores, Inc., is often cited as one of the most successful in this regard. It brought shareholders a substantial premium at the outset, and since then the company has raised productivity and operating profits and produced riches for the new investors and top management.

While much has been written about the supposed benefits of LBOs, little has been said about the hundreds of thousands of people directly affected by the buyout binge of the past decade: employees of the bought-out corporations. In the case of Safeway, an in-depth investigation of the buyout conducted by *The Wall Street Journal* revealed enormous human costs and unintended side effects.

More than 63,000 managers and workers were cut loose from Safeway, through store sales or layoffs. While the majority were reemployed by their new store owners, this was largely at lower wages, and many thousands of Safeway people wound up either unemployed or else forced into part-time work. In fact, a survey of former Safeway employees in Dallas found that nearly 60 percent still hadn't found full-time employment more than a year after the layoff. Across all of the laid-off workers in the survey, their average pay had fallen from $12.09 an hour to $6.50 an hour.

At company headquarters in Oakland, California, 300 people were fired immediately after the LBO. The company conceded (in a later court deposition) that many of those fired were "very good" employees. For its haste, Safeway wound up paying $8.2 million to settle a wrongful termination class action suit, and $750,000 to settle a separate suit for age discrimination.

Safeway said that organized labor was primarily to blame, especially in Dallas, and that it was paying 30 percent more than its competitors in wages, thus preventing it from cutting prices, remodeling stores, and the like. But rival Kroger was also unionized, and it found a way to prosper and expand in Dallas by renovating stores and negotiating lower wages with its union. Its market share was on the rise. What does the Kroger case imply about Safeway? The Safeway layoffs might have been made necessary as much by mismanagement as by labor costs. Even company officials conceded that Safeway had other problems besides wages in Dallas: its stores were too small, too old, and poorly designed.[9]

Global competition for high-quality workers As every advanced economy becomes global, a nation's most important competitive asset becomes the skills and cumulative learning of its workforce.[46] Globalization, almost by definition, makes this true. Virtually all developed countries can design, produce, and distribute goods and services equally well and equally fast. Every factor of production other than workforce skills can be duplicated anywhere in the world. Capital moves freely across international boundaries, seeking the lowest cost. State-of-the-art factories can be erected anywhere. The latest technologies move from computers in one nation, up to satellites parked in space, and back down to computers in another nation—all at the speed of electronic impulses. As Reich[46] has noted, it is all fungible: capital, technology, raw materials, information—all, except for one thing, the most critical part, the one element that is unique about a nation: its workforce.

Trends in world affairs, such as the unification of the European Common Market in 1992 and the growing democratization of Eastern Europe (including the Soviet Union, as the chapter opening vignette illustrates) and Asian countries, suggest that human resource management issues are important components of the success or failure of firms operating in global markets. Because all of the other factors of production can move so rapidly around the globe, a workforce that is knowledgeable and skilled at doing complex things keeps a company competitive and attracts foreign investment.

In fact, the relationship forms a virtuous circle: well-trained workers attract global corporations, which invest and give the workers good jobs; the good jobs, in turn, generate additional training and experience. Let's face it: Regardless of the shifting political breezes in Tokyo, Berlin, Washington, Beijing, or Budapest, the shrunken globe is here to stay. Today Tokyo is closer than the town 100 miles away was 30 years ago (after all, routine long-distance phone use didn't begin until the 1970s).

And tomorrow? Our networks of suppliers, producers, distributors, service companies, and customers will be so tightly linked that we literally won't be able to tell one locale from another. No political force can stop, or even slow down for long, the borderless economy. The lesson for managers is clear: be ready or be lost.[41]

We noted at the beginning of this section that people make organizations go. How the people are selected, trained, and managed determines to a large extent how successful an organization will be. As you can certainly appreciate by now, the task of managing people in today's world of work is particularly challenging in light of the changes we have discussed. Indeed, one of the most pressing concerns that organizations face is productivity improvement.

PRODUCTIVITY: WHAT IS IT?

A popular buzzword in American industry today is "productivity." Although people talk about it as though they know precisely what it means, productivity is surprisingly difficult to define and measure, especially in highly diversified firms. How can or should we compare the productivity of a secretary whose boss dictates letters that take hours to edit against one whose boss produces clean copy? How can we measure accurately the productivity of a salesperson who fills her order book every day, but with customers whose subsequent service requirements far outweigh the investment returned?[42]

Scholars generally agree that productivity concepts, definitions, and measures are arbitrary. Their relevance depends on the purpose for which they are developed—for example, to compare individuals, work groups, companies, or the competitive positions of nations.[30,43]

In general, however, productivity is a measure of the output of goods and services relative to the input labor, material, and equipment. The more productive an industry, the better its competitive position because its unit costs are lower. Improving productivity simply means getting more out of what is put in. It does not mean increasing production through the addition of resources, such as time, money, materials, or people. It is doing better with what you have. Improving productivity is not working harder, it is working smarter. Today's world demands that we do more with less—fewer people, less money, less time, less space, and fewer resources in general. These ideas are shown graphically in Figure 1-3.

The United States had led the world in annual rate of productivity improvement for decades, but as Figure 1-4 shows, since the 1950s its productivity growth rate has slowed, while Japan and other industrial nations kept gaining. Later we will consider some of the reasons for this decline, but let's first consider what it implies.

Beginning in the late nineteenth century, for example, the yearly rise in the productivity of England, then the world's foremost industrial nation, was just slightly less (1 percent) than that of its industrial rivals, mainly the United States and Germany. But by the mid-twentieth century that seemingly small difference proved to be enough to tumble England from its previously undisputed industrial prominence.[60]

Some of the increase in manufacturing productivity is undoubtedly due to widespread automation in the factory, but some of the increase may also reflect the fact that it is easier to measure the output of the blue-collar sector than it is to

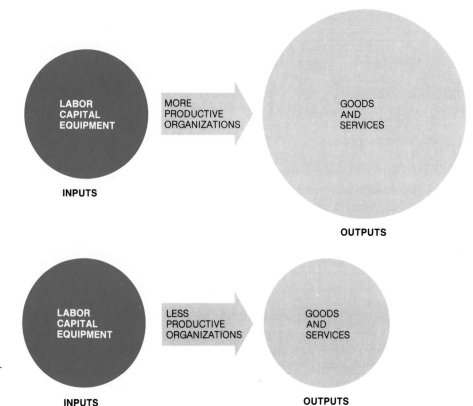

FIGURE 1-3
More productive or-
ganizations get more
goods and services out
of a given amount of la-
bor, capital, and equip-
ment than do less pro-
ductive organizations.

measure the output of the people who work in marketing, engineering, human
resources, and the rest of the white-collar population, where outputs may be less
tangible. For example, Tandem Computers, Inc., of Cupertino, California, has cut
the average design time for its semiconductors to just 4 weeks from 14 by installing
several million dollars worth of computer-aided design equipment. But Tandem
cannot identify similar savings for its largest white-collar investment, an information network that links marketing, engineering, and manufacturing divisions at
200 locations in 35 countries.[44] And it is the white-collar segment of the workforce
that is growing most rapidly.

Just 10 years ago a typical manufacturing company's workforce was made up
mostly of blue-collar workers. Today white-collar employees make up about 50
percent of a manufacturing company's workforce—about 70 percent of its payroll.
Both percentages are expected to increase in the years ahead. Getting people to
work smarter, not necessarily merely harder, is the greatest challenge facing management today.

To evaluate how to increase productivity in America, let's first consider some
of the reasons why it declined.

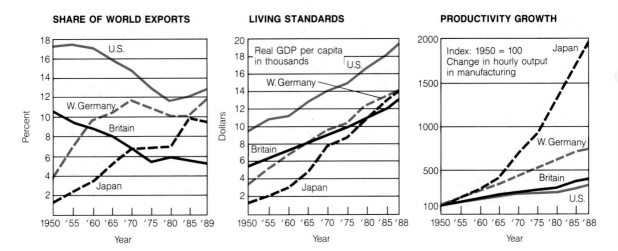

By almost any measure, the U.S. remains the country to beat. Its share of world exports has rebounded after declining for much of the postwar era. Its wealth per capita, adjusted to reflect differences in purchasing power, is unmatched by any major rival. The same goes for total productivity (see table at right): The average Japanese worker still takes until mid-afternoon to produce what the average American can before lunch. Only in productivity growth—the key to future prosperity—does the U.S. look like a country in trouble.

TOTAL PRODUCTIVITY *

	United States	Japan	West Germany	Great Britain
1950	$24,062	$ 3,655	$ 8,299	$12,932
1970	$35,670	$16,303	$22,084	$20,768
1988	$41,281	$29,678	$33,605	$29,771

*Output per employed person in 1988 U.S. dollars.

FIGURE 1-4

America's place in the competition race. [*Source:* Reprinted from Petre, P. (1990, April 23). Lifting American Competitiveness, *Fortune*, p. 59.]

PRODUCTIVITY: WHAT AILS IT?

The causes of the decline in U.S. productivity lie deep within our value, economic, and political systems. However, some of the measurable causes cited by economists include:

- In many industries, the ability to improve productivity through further improvements in technology declined.
- The supply of labor that can be directed from inefficient productive activities, such as outdated steelmills, to more productive endeavors, such as electronics or health care, has shrunk. Lacking the necessary skills and trained only as steelworkers, these people are "structurally unemployed."
- Complying with environmental and safety laws, as well as with other government regulations, adds costs to production but does not increase it.
- Increasing dishonesty and crime generate costs that are reflected in increased production costs but that do not increase productivity.
- Outlays by business and government for civilian research and development are a smaller share of the economy in the United States than in other countries (Figure 1-5).[5]
- Capital spending on new plants and modern equipment has been reduced.

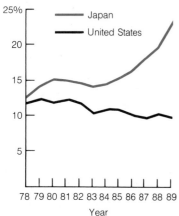

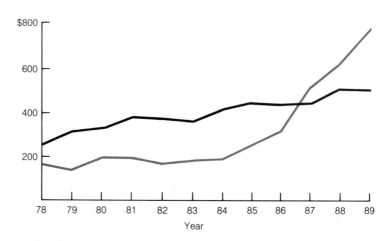

Source: Deutsche Bank   Source: Deutsche Bank

FIGURE 1-5
Japan keeps up the big spending to maintain its industrial might. (*Source:* Reprinted from the April 11, 1990, issue of *The New York Times*, pp. A1, C6. Copyright © 1990 by The New York Times Company. Reprinted by permission.)

While it is relatively easy to describe the obvious causes of productivity decline, economists admit that they cannot explain all the reasons for the decline in terms of common economic measures. In the following sections, therefore, we will consider four other causes: (1) the quality of management; (2) the government; (3) short-term planning; and (4) the growing numbers of "paper entrepreneurs," those who capitalize on legal and financial opportunities for profit rather than on improved methods of production.[8]

The Quality of Management

In 1977 a Motorola plant in Illinois was producing color television sets that regularly experienced defects at the rate of about 150 to 180 defects per 100 TV sets. Then a Japanese firm took over the plant. By 1980 the defects had dropped to only 3 to 4 per 100 TV sets produced. What changed? Not the workforce, since 80 percent of those working at the plant before 1977 were still working there in 1980. The ways people were managed, however, changed drastically. Worker participation in decision making, greater individual responsibility for quality control, and improved communication between management and the workers were the primary factors involved in the improvements in product quality. Consider another example: Four years after the Toyota–General Motors joint venture opened its New United Motor Manufacturing, Inc. (NUMMI) plant in Fremont, California, it found that its cars made in the United States were just as good as the ones made in Japan.[28] Does this mean that the NUMMI workers in California are different from those who turn out "low quality" U.S. economy cars? No, the workers are all members of the United Auto Workers. The differences are in job design, worker involvement, and management (the quality control inspector reports to a higher-level manager in Japan and has the power to shut down the plant).

While it is true that the most productive American auto plants are those that have paid the most attention to blurring the class lines between management and labor, when it comes to making steel, a positive employee attitude is not as productive as a basic-oxygen furnace. On the auto assembly line, no amount of team spirit will make a door fit more closely than it was designed to fit. When Japanese steel productivity soared during the 1970s, it could have been because workers and management felt a personal commitment to the economic welfare of their nation. But most likely it had more to do with the dozens of new mills—with continuous casters and electric furnaces—that the Japanese installed. "It's as simple as two able, willing workers, one with a power saw, and one with a hand saw," says Senator Lloyd Bentsen of Texas. "Which one do you think is going to turn out more work?" With knowledge workers (those who produce ideas and information rather than tangible products), however, it is very difficult, if not impossible, to replace worker decision making with improved technology. Besides, innovation is a social process.[20] Creating and deploying new technologies is not merely a sequence of mechanical events; it is inherently a social process that depends heavily on human factors as well as machines. Whether we are analyzing the conduct and management of research, the dissemination and marketing of new technical products, or the implementation of new manufacturing processes at the shop-floor level, we must be sure to consider the social and organizational influences involved. Social science informs us of the influence of these social and organizational factors. Human resource management focuses on how to apply them.

The Government's Role in Productivity Decline

By building inflation into the economy through such practices as cost-plus contracting, automatic cost-of-living increases in government spending, and big deficits to fight recessions, the government has been a drag on business's flexibility and on its capital investment in new plants and equipment.[8] Individually some of these steps make sense, but together they serve to increase inflation. Increased inflation discourages capital investment, which leads eventually to reduced productivity.

In addition to government-induced inflation, there are government regulations. General Motors claims that it now spends $1.9 billion per year to comply with government regulations through retooling for new safety equipment and emissions controls, reducing air and water pollution from its plants, and the unproductive activity of filling out forms to comply with regulations.

Short-Run Planning

Neither capital shortage nor government obstruction has prevented U.S. industries from being more profitable than foreign competitors. The problem is that a firm's continuing success depends on long-term productivity rather than on short-term profitability.

Unfortunately, the imperatives of the financial markets focus the attention of American firms on the short-run instead of on the long-run. "Today's financial measurements are biased against the long term," says Senator Bentsen. "When you have to make this year's annual report look as good as possible, why [should you] engage in market entry pricing in East Asia? Why accept losses for two or three years to build volume and brand recognition? I can assure you that our competition in the world of trade is more than ready to make market investments that may not pay off for a decade. They are willing to spend years positioning themselves to conquer global markets.[8] While the Japanese, Germans, and Koreans are making significant inroads on American markets, many American industries have shown an absolute inability to look toward their welfare in the long run.

Paper Entrepreneurs

The term "paper entrepreneurs" was first expressed by Robert Reich, director of the Office of Policy Planning at the Federal Trade Commission. His theory is that economic life has yielded more and more of its prizes to those who can work the legal and financial angles or who can guess right in speculation rather than to those who work at improving a product or making a sale. According to Reich:

> Paper entrepreneurs—trained in law, finance, accountancy—manipulate complex systems of rules and numbers. They innovate by using the system in novel ways: establishing joint ventures, consortiums, holding companies, mutual funds; finding companies to acquire, "white knights" to be acquired by, commodity futures to invest in, tax shelters to hide in; engaging in proxy fights, tender splits, spinoffs, divestitures; buying and selling notes, bonds, convertible debentures, sinking-fund debentures; obtaining government subsidies, loan guarantees, tax breaks, contracts, licenses, quotas, price supports, bailouts; going private, going public, going bankrupt. (ref. 8)

Paper entrepreneurs provide the necessary grease for the wheels of the capital system, but they do not, by themselves, add to production. The government is dominated by lawyers; financiers rise to the top of many of the largest corporations; many of the best students are drawn into law and business schools, and from there into consulting, accounting, and lobbying rather than into production itself. Consider that out of every 10,000 citizens in Japan and in the United States, the following are found:

	Japan	United States
Lawyers	1	20
Accountants	3	40
Engineers and scientists	400	70

In short, there is a serious "brain drain" from genuine innovation in production, marketing, distribution, and sales to paper entrepreneurialism. Consider the ways that executives are compensated, for example. Many companies follow the practice of the auto industry, in which executives are given substantial bonuses in profitable years. In theory the bonuses reward those who have been pulling their weight, but in practice so much of the business is done internally that the profit and loss for each division depends mainly on the "transfer prices" charged on purchases from other divisions of the organization. Since the financial staff sets the transfer prices, they have become quite powerful.

Several years ago, two General Motors plants were producing virtually identical automatic transmissions. The Chevrolet transmission plant "sold" directly to the Chevrolet division. The Hydramatic division sold to Oldsmobile, Cadillac, and other divisions, including Chevy. The transfer price for the Chevy transmission was $130; Hydramatic's was $185. Actual production costs at the Chevrolet plant were $7 less per transmission than at Hydramatic, but the way the financial staff allocated the profits meant astronomical bonuses for the Hydramatic officials. One year Hydramatic's manager received $250,000 in salary and bonuses. The manager of the Chevrolet plant got $80,000—for doing exactly the same job but doing it more efficiently.

Lessons We Have Learned

Many factors contribute to a decline in productivity (Figure 1-6). So what can we conclude regarding the causes of and possible solutions to our productivity decline? We can say that we need:

- Solutions designed to have some definite payoff in the long run, whether or not they pay off immediately

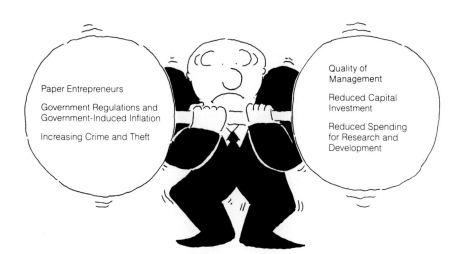

Paper Entrepreneurs

Government Regulations and Government-Induced Inflation

Increasing Crime and Theft

Quality of Management

Reduced Capital Investment

Reduced Spending for Research and Development

FIGURE 1-6
Many factors contribute to a decline in productivity. It's hard to single out any one factor as *the* primary cause.

- Steps by the government to allow and to encourage businesses to make capital investments and to be more flexible as a result of less government regulation
- To make workers aware through their unions, and managers as well, that their rewards ultimately depend on production
- Recognition that there is no "quick fix" approach. Worker training, work redesign, product reengineering—all must be linked to the priorities of the business plan and integrated into a comprehensive productivity improvement strategy.
- Recognition of the crucial importance of controlling quality (an important aspect of productivity improvement) through prevention. Doing so requires a reshaping of attitudes from the board room to the loading dock, so that quality becomes more important than simply getting a product out the door.

Behavioral science can contribute to productivity improvement through valid selection procedures, well-designed training programs, performance feedback coupled with goal setting, and a host of worker participation programs.[4] Yet we must not lose sight of the limited role that changes in employee behavior can play. Behavioral science can yield substantial improvements in the contribution of labor, but its contribution to capital or equipment is likely to be considerably more modest.

Greater productivity benefits organizations directly (e.g., it improves their competitive position relative to rivals), and it benefits workers indirectly (e.g., improved job security and pay). But many workers want to see a tighter connection between working smarter and the tangible and psychological rewards they receive from doing their jobs well. They want to see significant improvements in their quality of work life.

QUALITY OF WORK LIFE: WHAT IS IT?

There are two ways of looking at what *quality of work life (QWL)* means.[26] One way equates QWL with a set of objective organizational conditions and practices (e.g., job enrichment, democratic supervision, employee involvement, and safe working conditions). The other way equates QWL with employee's perceptions that they are safe, relatively well-satisfied, and able to grow and develop as human beings. This way relates QWL to the degree to which the full range of human needs is met.

In many cases these two views merge: workers who like their organizations and the ways their jobs are structured will feel that their work fulfills them. In such cases, either way of looking at one's quality of work life will lead to a common determination of whether a good QWL exists. However, because of the differences between people and because the second view is quite subjective—it allows, for example, that not everyone finds such things as democratic decision making and enriched jobs to be important components of a good QWL[25]—we will define QWL in terms of employees' perceptions of their physical and mental well-being at work.

Current Status of Quality of Work Life Efforts

In theory, QWL is simple—it involves giving workers the opportunity to make decisions about their jobs, the design of their workplaces, and what they need to make products or to deliver services most effectively. It requires managers to treat workers with dignity on the job. Its focus is on employees and management operating the business together.

In practice, its best illustrations can be found in the auto, steel, food, electronics, and consumer products industries, in plants characterized by self-managing work teams, flat organizational structures, and challenging roles for all. It requires a willingness to share power, extensive training for workers and managers, and considerable patience by all involved. Workers must get to know the basics of cost, quality, profits, losses, and customer satisfaction by being exposed to more than a narrowly defined job. Managers must come to understand their new role: leaders, helpers, and information gatherers. None of this is simple or easily done.

One reviewer found that QWL efforts often require 3 to 10 years or more to become fully integrated into a business.[36] Here are some other things that successful QWL efforts require:

- Management to become leaders and coaches, not bosses and dictators.
- Openness and trust. It can't be used as a tool to break unions or to keep unions out. It must remain separate from the collective bargaining contract. And it can't be used by unions as a tool against management.
- Information typically held by management only must be shared, and suggestions made by nonmanagers must be taken seriously.
- QWL must change continually and go forward from initial problem solving to an actual partnership between management and workers.
- QWL cannot be mandated unilaterally by management.

Participation: The Essence of Quality of Work Life

As we have noted, the common denominator of QWL experiments is joint worker-management participation for the purpose of identifying problems and opportunities in the work environment, making decisions, and implementing changes. Results of these undertakings are beginning to appear in the literature (e.g., refs. 16, 27, 31). Critics say that participation will not work over time because it requires managers to give up too much power; this is why 75 percent of all such programs in the early 1980s failed.[49] On the other hand, advocates point to a study which examined 101 industrial companies and which found that the participatively managed companies outscored the others on 13 of 14 financial measures.[49] The advocates argue that we are just beginning to understand what is required in order to bring about large-scale social change in organizations.

There has been widespread interest in worker participation in management decisions among U.S. organizations. This interest is not so much motivated by concern with how an organization affects the people who comprise it. Rather, it is motivated by an increasing recognition that American firms are facing a productivity crisis that threatens both our way of life and the very existence of many of our basic industries. Fearful for their own competitive viability, American business leaders are taking a close look at alternative management approaches. Japanese management style in particular has caught the attention of many of our business leaders. Japanese management has been described as highly participative and consensus-based.[39,40,52] Employees are treated with respect and concern, and in turn they are ideologically and culturally inclined to act in the best interests of the company.

Some American businesses (e.g., General Electric) are hoping that if they adopt the participative management practices of Japanese organizations, the U.S. employee will respond in a manner similar to the Japanese employee, thus reversing the trend toward declining productivity. In general, five broad types of participative methods can be identified:

1. Quality circles and other types of employee problem-solving groups
2. Union-management cooperative projects and problem-solving ventures
3. Participative work design
4. Gain sharing, profit sharing, and Scanlon plans
5. Worker ownership or employee stock ownership

The following gives a brief description of these methods, and their effectiveness is then discussed in the section "Does participation work?"

Employee problem-solving groups Of the many forms that this method takes, one is the quality-circle format that is popular in Japan. A *quality circle* is a group of employees (4 to 10) from the same department who meet on company time to solve work-related problems. These groups tend to focus on organizational efficiency issues, such as waste, damage, or equipment maintenance; on work context issues, such as facilities; and on communication problems. Sometimes a group will make changes in job design, such as at Westinghouse, where assembly line workers developed a way to reduce defective products to 1 percent of output from 16 percent. The same group also increased productivity by 30 percent.[45] In other situations, unfortunately, changes were suggested but not implemented in the work setting, and the groups became demotivated.[3,23,26] The current view is that quality circles are transitional vehicles toward other forms of participation, such as temporary task forces or self-managing work teams.[27]

Union-management cooperative projects and problem-solving ventures These methods explicitly recognize the need to bring two conflicting groups together to identify areas of mutual concern and to reduce the level of adversarial behavior in the work setting. Union-management committees often serve as sounding boards and attempt to prevent potential problems from occurring or escalating. In addition, a joint union-management committee may identify opportunities, solve problems, and guide union-management task forces dealing with specific problems.[56]

Such "jointness" efforts have spread far and wide. For example, since 1982 as many as 40 percent of Ford Motor Company's 109,000 hourly workers have taken advantage of the programs. Similar efforts are being made at General Motors, with impressive results. At its Toledo, Ohio, transmission factory, GM shaved $20 million off its production costs in 1987, and quality improved so much that the number of rejects dropped 90 percent. Certainly part of these gains resulted from GM's joint program, but without controlled research it is not possible to say exactly how much.[50]

Participative work design In this method, a team is put together specifically to redesign a job by analyzing its technical and human requirements. Jobs designed in this way have been found to be particularly effective in work settings where tasks are highly interdependent and employees have high personal growth needs.[17] A frequent outcome is the development of self-managing work teams. Each team is given primary responsibility for planning, doing, and controlling the quality of a major component of the work, and team members are cross-trained to do more than one job.

Self-managing work teams have been especially successful in conjunction with new plant start-ups, for they create an organizational setting quite different from that in the traditional plant. A comprehensive review of all studies that have used this approach found that it does improve productivity and specific job attitudes, such as responsibility, control, and job variety, but it has little effect on outcomes such as absenteeism and turnover.[14]

Gain sharing, profit sharing, and Scanlon plans These are methods for sharing profits with employees, based on some formula. They are particularly effective in situations in which workers can affect the major factors that influence economic performance, such as labor hours, materials, or damage. Not surprisingly, workers tend to focus their attention and energy on the factors that are included in the formula for determining the payout; nevertheless, the results can be impressive.[15] At Barnes Hospital in St. Louis, for example, all 5500 employees participated in a gain-sharing plan begun in 1986. One year later, the plan resulted in payments to employees of $4.3 million and in financial gains to the institution of over $4.7 million.[7]

Some plans, such as the Scanlon plan, build in several layers of committees to ensure the implementation of ideas and include training in problem solving.[35] These plans have been found to be highly successful in affecting productivity in manufacturing organizations, for their use assumes that productivity can be measured accurately and compared from year to year.

Employee participation in the ownership of a company The participation ranges from (1) partial ownership through the acquisition of company stock by employees to (2) complete ownership by employees. More than 10,000 firms in the United States now share some ownership with over 10 million employees. In at least 1000 companies, employees own the majority of the stock. Employee ownership can be found in every industry, in firms of every size, and in every part of the country.[21,48,58] In terms of bottom-line performance, companies that are mostly employee-owned generate 3 times more new jobs than do their competitors, and high-tech companies that share ownership grow 2 to 4 times as fast as those which do not. Publicly held companies that are at least 10 percent employee-owned outperform 62 to 75 percent of their competitors, depending on the measure used.

Worker ownership originally occurred in rather desperate situations, such as when workers purchased a plant rather than allow it to be sold or to go out of business. More recently, it has resulted from concessions by unions during collective bargaining (e.g., with the airlines) or has been initiated by management for financial, tax, or motivational reasons.[12]

Does Participation Work?

Although it is still premature to state which approaches are definitely effective and which are not, it is possible to detect trends in the emerging literature. Some of these are as follows:[6,34]

1. Worker participation programs that are tied directly to financial incentives for employees tend to result in productivity increases for the organization. For example, of 72 companies using Improshare[10]—production standards based on time-and-motion studies, plus a sharing of productivity gains 50/50 between employees and the company—38 companies were nonunion, and 34 were represented by 18 different international unions. The average gain in productivity over all companies using the plan after 1 year was 22.4 percent. Productivity gains tended to be larger if workers were provided with training and information; gains tended to be smaller, or none, or negative (that is, productivity deteriorated) if workers perceived that there was "nothing in it" for them. Reports show that a program intended to get workers to improve productivity without sharing with them the financial rewards of that gain will take 1.5 to 3 years to establish. And, of course, gains in productivity, specifically, and in labor relations, in general, will not be seen until after that time. In contrast, consider the following situation, as reported by Fein, in which workers will share in the financial gains that come along with gains in productivity:

In a meeting called by the management of a highly mechanized machine shop to discuss the introduction of an Improshare plan, operating managers and union committee representatives were present. In response to a question posed by the plant manager as to how long it would take for an Improshare plan to start operating in one of the large machine departments, a union steward replied, "15 minutes." This was not a flippant remark but a considered statement by a knowledgeable worker of how long it would take him to turn up his production—if he wanted to. (ref. 10)

IMPACT OF IMPROVED PRODUCTIVITY AND QUALITY
OF WORK LIFE ON THE BOTTOM LINE

Efforts to enhance worker productivity through sharing rewards and implementing joint programs may well be worth the effort. To appreciate this, consider the contrast between management actions at General Motors and at Ford during the 1980s. General Motors experienced tense relations with its workers and only modest gains in productivity, in part because management inconsistency and plunging market share undermined collaborative programs to boost quality and output. Meanwhile, Ford enjoyed placid relations with its union, the United Auto Workers, along with dramatic increases in productivity, because it made its workers feel rewarded, secure, and involved in its success. Those were two key findings in a 1990 report on the U.S. auto industry.[11]

GM began the 1980s by fighting with its union over its plan to open nonunion component plants in the south. It espoused collaborative plans slowly and at different rates in different parts of the organization. It relied heavily on symbolic joint appearances with union leaders and on wholesale reorganization of existing contracts. When GM's market share eroded, it couldn't offer workers job security or profit sharing on a par with Ford. The report also noted that GM failed to engineer products and work methods to help boost productivity, and instead launched shop-floor efficiency campaigns that to many workers resembled traditional assembly line speed-ups.

Ford, conversely, enjoyed placid relations with the UAW because the company: (1) communicated a consistent, high-level commitment to joint programs; (2) offered gain sharing in the form of steady work, profit sharing, and extensive overtime; (3) maintained clear distinctions between joint programs and traditional collective bargaining structures; and (4) achieved much of its productivity gains through product design and work method changes that in many cases did not increase the everyday workload of workers. The bottom line: Since the inception of the employee involvement process in 1980, product quality has improved more than 50 percent for cars and 47 percent for trucks.[2] High quality, in turn, has led to high profits for the company, and both employees and managers have shared in those benefits, averaging 11 percent of their annual paychecks.[51] These are some of the key factors that have contributed to the 40 percent improvement in Ford's break-even point for its North American automotive operations.

2. Participation programs are generally perceived positively by those who directly participate but negatively by workers who do not.[29,37] In one case nonparticipating union members pressured management to terminate a large union-management work redesign effort becuse of perceived salary inequities.[13]

3. Participative strategies that alter the job itself tend to have a lasting impact on attitudes and productivity if the new job involves substantial increases in responsibility and autonomy. Worker participation in problem solving that does not alter the job itself or job rotational schemes that do not add responsibility and challenge tend only to motivate employees over the short term.[23]

4. Worker participation programs die out eventually if the organization does not change in a manner consistent with the democratic values and behaviors of the participation programs. Here are some of the ways to kill worker participation:

- Middle and upper management cease their responsiveness to worker suggestions after the initial enthusiasm, if there was any, is over.
- The pay system fails to acknowledge the new activities and contributions of workers.
- Supervisors resent the increased attention to workers and undermine the program by not cooperating with the groups.
- Participating workers develop distorted perceptions of their own promotability and value to the company, and they become disillusioned when they do not advance.

Many American organizations embody a hierarchical, departmentalized structure, a set of management assumptions, and a set of norms that discourage employees from taking initiative, accepting responsibility, and cooperating with one another.[38,40] The unlearning of these assumptions and norms requires a conscious attempt to alter the culture of the organization, something that organizations such as Honeywell, Cummins Engine, and Westinghouse are systematically setting out to do.

5. Many participative programs underestimate the amount of training and learning necessary to support worker involvement. Workers need exposure to problem solving, group processes, and business concepts. Managers need training in the listening and feedback skills necessary to work with groups of workers who are taking responsibility for decision making. Both workers and managers need to learn the basic interpersonal skills necessary to treat others with dignity and respect.[1] Participation as an effort to improve QWL requires that managers treat lower-level employees as mature individuals, for participation implies a redistribution of power within the organization.

6. Workers sometimes reject the participation program. Often this reaction reflects the official position of a union, which sees a threat to its long-term strength in dealing with management. Union and nonunion employees often perceive participation programs as management manipulation in which workers are expected to contribute something for nothing.[18] Managers frequently perceive a participation program as something they are doing "for" the workers. Workers detect this attitude and judge it to be patronizing at best and deceptive at worst.

7. There are interactions among different forms of participation. Thus it appears that informal participation works best when other formal mechanisms for participation already exist.

8. Performance or productivity effectiveness is associated with participation that is direct (as opposed to indirect through representatives) and long-term.[6]

■ **HUMAN RESOURCE MANAGEMENT IN ACTION:**
CONCLUSION

MCDONALD'S EXPORTS SOMETHING NEW
TO THE SOVIET UNION—JOB SATISFACTION

McDonald's-Moscow opened on January 31, 1990. It employs 630 Soviets, each of whom makes about 1.5 rubles or $2.40 per hour (at the commercial exchange rate). For most, that comes to about 250 rubles ($400) per month—near the Soviet average wage and more than a doctor or a TV producer makes in Moscow. (Doctors and TV producers are notoriously underpaid.) The restaurant seats 700 customers, it serves about 30,000 customers a day, and the average wait in line is about 45 minutes.

One crew member says his old friends simply cannot understand how he can like his work and his bosses. It's completely against the Soviet norm. "Our attitudes are different," he says about his friends. "That is what is tearing us apart. But I feel I don't need them as badly as before. I have new friends here."* Alexander Morozov, age 26 and the father of two children, used to work loading boxes. "I was a machine for my bosses," he says. And he hated work. Now at McDonald's he's found his calling. "I had been warned that I would have to work a lot and my salary would be so much," he says. "But for me, salary is not most important. The job and the attitude toward the staff is."†

And there's one other reason that people like to work at McDonald's. As three crew members gather, one of them blurts out, "Nobody's ever been poisoned at McDonald's!" Is that different than at other Moscow restaurants? All three nod their heads vigorously and say, "Da! Da!"

SUMMARY

The competitive business environment of the 1990s will be characterized by factors such as the following: increasing demands for the environmentally responsible use of all resources; an aging and changing workforce—one with more minorities, women, and low-skilled workers—in a high-tech workplace that demands ever-increasing skill; many workers who have been scarred by the unpleasant side effects of mergers, takeovers, and leveraged buyouts; and increasing global competition in almost every sector of the economy. The challenge of managing people effectively has never been greater.

*Grishin, in Maney, op. cit., p. 2B.
†Ibid.

IMPLICATIONS FOR MANAGEMENT PRACTICE

The trends that we have reviewed in this chapter suggest that the old approaches to managing people may no longer be appropriate responses to economic or social reality. The willingness to experiment with new approaches to managing people is healthy. To the extent that the newer approaches do enhance productivity and QWL, everybody wins. The competitive problems facing us cannot simply be willed away, and because of this we may see even more radical experiments in organizations. The traditional role of the manager may be blurred further as workers take a greater and greater part in planning work, doing it, and controlling it. This change suggests that human resource management, an essential part of the jobs of all managers, will play an even more crucial role in the future.

One of the most pressing demands we face today is for productivity improvement—getting more out of what is put in, doing better with what we have, and working smarter, not harder. Some reasons proposed for the decline in American productivity are: workers with nonmarketable job skills as a result of the economic decline of their industries, excessive government regulations, dishonesty and crime, reduced spending on research and development, and reduced spending for capital improvements that would cut labor costs. However, noneconomic factors have also played a role: lazy workers and indifferent managers, a growing number of paper entrepreneurs, and an inability of American business to plan for the long run. While the effects of some of these factors are exaggerated, the solution is probably a mixed approach that includes improvements in all the preceding areas. Clearly, though, increased productivity does not preclude a high quality of work life (QWL).

QWL may be defined and operationalized in terms of employees' perceptions of their physical and psychological well-being at work. It involves giving workers the opportunity to make decisions about their jobs, the design of their workplaces, and what they need to make products or to deliver services most effectively. Its focus is on employees and management operating a business together. Joint labor-management cooperation is the very essence of QWL efforts, but participation can take several forms. The most effective of these seem to be those which combine (1) financial rewards to workers for productivity improvements, (2) job changes that involve substantial increases in worker responsibility and autonomy, and (3) substantial training of workers and managers in order to support greater worker involvement. Although there are many pitfalls associated with instituting a productivity improvement or QWL program, the potential financial gains may well justify the effort.

DISCUSSION QUESTIONS

1■1 How are the demographic trends for the 1990s, the education crisis, the lagged effects of the 1980s merger and acquisition trend, and the global competition for high-quality workers interrelated?

1■2 Discuss alternative strategies for harnessing the energies of workers concerned with QWL issues.

1■3 What common characteristics do the following organizations share: a hospital, a school, an auto repair shop, and a baseball team?

1■4 Considering all the issues we have discussed in this chapter, describe management styles and practices that will be effective for American businesses in the next decade.

1■5 In your opinion, what are three major causes of the decline in the growth rate of productivity? How would you remedy each one?

REFERENCES

1. Argyris, C., & Schon, D. A. (1978). *Organizational learning: A theory of action perspective.* Reading, MA: Addison-Wesley.

2. Banas, P. A. (1988). Employee involvement: A sustained labor/management initiative at the Ford Motor Company. In J. P. Campbell & R. J. Campbell (eds.), *Productivity in organizations.* San Francisco: Jossey-Bass, pp. 388–416.

3. Barrick, M. R., & Alexander, R. A. (1987). A review of quality circle efficacy and the existence of positive-findings bias. *Personnel Psychology,* **40,** 579–592.

4. Campbell, J. P., Campbell, R. J., & Associates (1988). *Productivity in organizations.* San Francisco: Jossey-Bass.

5. Can America compete? (1987, April 20). *Business Week,* pp. 45–47.

6. Cotton, J. L., Vollrath, D. A., Froggatt, K. L., Lengnick-Hall, J. L., & Jennings, K. R. (1988). Employee participation: Diverse forms and different outcomes. *Academy of Management Review,* **13,** 8–22.

7. Drosie, T. (1987, June 5). Gainsharing: The newest way to up productivity. *Hospitals,* p. 71.

8. Fallows, J. (1980, September). American industry: What ails it, how to save it. *The Atlantic,* pp. 35–49.

9. Faludi, S. C. (1990, May 16). The reckoning: Safeway LBO yields vast profits but exacts a heavy human toll. *The Wall Street Journal,* pp. A1, A10, A11.

10. Fein, M. (1982, August). Improved productivity through worker involvement. Paper presented at the annual meeting of the Academy of Management, New York.

11. Ford policies avoid labor strife (1990, Jan. 8). *Denver Post,* p. 3C.

12. French, J. L. (1987). Employee perspectives on stock ownership: Financial investment or mechanism of control? *Academy of Management Review,* **12,** 427–435.

13. Goodman, P. S. (1979). *Assessing organizational change: The Rushton quality of work life experiment.* New York: Wiley.

14. Goodman, P. S., Devadas, R., & Hughson, T. L. (1988). Groups and productivity: Analyzing the effectiveness of self-managing teams. In J. P. Campbell & R. J. Campbell (eds.), *Productivity in organizations.* San Francisco: Jossey-Bass, pp. 295–327.

15. Graham-Moore, B., & Ross, T. L. (1990). *Gainsharing.* Washington, DC: Bureau of National Affairs.

16. Griffin, R. W. (1988). Consequences of quality circles in an industrial setting: A longitudinal assessment. *Academy of Management Journal*, **31**, 338–358.

17. Help wanted (1987, Aug. 10). *Business Week*, pp. 48–53.

18. Jacoby, S. M. (1982). Union-management cooperation in the U.S.: 1915–1945. Working paper, Graduate School of Management, UCLA.

19. Johnston, W. B. (1987). *Workforce 2000: Work and workers for the 21st century*. Indianapolis, IN: Hudson Institute.

20. Kanter, R. M. (1989). Swimming in the new streams: Mastering innovation dilemmas. *California Management Review*, **31**, 45–69.

21. Klein, K. J., & Hall, R. J. (1988). Correlates of employee satisfaction with stock ownership: Who likes an ESOP most? *Journal of Applied Psychology*, **73**, 630–638.

22. Kruger, P. (1990, January). A game plan for the future. *Working Woman*, pp. 67–71.

23. Lawler, E. C., & Ledford, G. E. (1982). Productivity and the quality of work life. *National Productivity Review*, **2**, 2.

24. Lawler, E. E. (1982). Strategies for improving the quality of work life. *American Psychologist*, **37**, 486–493.

25. Lawler, E. E. (1973). *Motivation in work organizations*. Monterey, CA: Brooks/Cole.

26. Lawler, E. E., & Mohrman, S. A. (1985, January–February). Quality circles: After the fad. *Harvard Business Review*, pp. 65–71.

27. Ledford, G. E., Jr., Lawler, E. E., III, & Mohrman, S. A. (1988). The quality circle and its variations. In J. P. Campbell & R. J. Campbell (eds.), *Productivity in organizations*. San Francisco: Jossey-Bass, pp. 255–294.

28. Lee, B. (1988, Dec. 25). The GM-Toyota team: Worker harmony makes NUMMI work. *The New York Times*, p. 2F.

29. Macy, B., & Peterson, M. (1981, August). Evaluating attitudinal change in a longitudinal quality of work life intervention. Paper presented at the annual meeting of the Academy of Management, San Diego.

30. Mahoney, T. A. (1988). Productivity defined: The relativity of efficiency, effectiveness, and change. In J. P. Campbell & R. J. Campbell (eds.), *Productivity in organizations*. San Francisco: Jossey-Bass, pp. 13–39.

31. Marks, M. L., Mirvis, P. H., Hackett, E. J., & Grady, J. F., Jr. (1986). Employee participation in a quality circle program: Impact on quality of work life, productivity, and absenteeism. *Journal of Applied Psychology*, **71**, 61–69.

32. Matsushita, K. (1978). *My management philosophy*. Tokyo: PHP Institute, Inc.

33. McWhirter, W. (1989, Oct. 9). I came, I saw, I blundered. *Time*, pp. 72, 77.

34. Mohrman, S. A. (1982, May). The impact of quality circles: A conceptual view. Paper presented at Bureau of National Affairs conference, "Current directions in productivity—Evolving Japanese and American practices." Houston.

35. Moore, B. E., & Ross, T. L. (1978). *The Scanlon way to improved productivity: A practical guide*. New York: Wiley.

36. Moskal, B. S. (1989, Jan. 16). Quality of life in the factory: How far have we come? *Industry Week*, pp. 12–16.

37. Nurick, A. J. (1982). Participation in organizational change: A longitudinal field study. *Human Relations*, **35**, 413–430.

38. O'Toole, J. (1981). *Making America work: Productivity and responsibility*. New York: Continuum.

39. Ouchi, W. G. (1981). *Theory Z: How American business can meet the Japanese challenge*. Reading, MA: Addison-Wesley.

40. Pascale, R. T., & Athos, A. G. (1981). *The art of Japanese management: Application for American executives.* New York: Simon & Schuster.

41. Peters, T. (1989, Oct. 17). Global thinking mandatory for companies in the 1990s. *Rocky Mountain News*, p. 52.

42. Preaching the gospel of productivity (1982, March 21). *The Washington Post*, pp. F3–F5.

43. Pritchard, R. D., Jones, S. D., Roth, P. L., Stuebing, K. K., & Ekeberg, S. E. (1989). The evaluation of an integrated approach to measuring organizational productivity. *Personnel Psychology* **42**, 69–115.

44. Productivity: Why it's the no. 1 underachiever (1987, April 20). *Business Week*, pp. 54–55.

45. Quality circles can raise productivity, execs told (1982, March 21). *Atlanta Constitution*, pp. 4C–5C.

46. Reich, R. B. (1990, January–February). Who is us? *Harvard Business Review*, pp. 53–64.

47. Richards, B. (1990, Feb. 9). Wanting workers. *The Wall Street Journal*, pp. R10, R11.

48. Rosen, C., Klein, K. J., & Young, K. M. (1986). When employees share the profits. *Psychology Today*, **20**, 30–36.

49. Saporito, B. (1986, July 21). The revolt against "working smarter." *Fortune*, pp. 58–65.

50. Schlesinger, J. M. (1987, Aug. 25). Costly friendship: Auto firms and UAW find that cooperation can get complicated. *The Wall Street Journal*, pp. 1, 20.

51. Schroeder, M. (1988, Nov. 7). Watching the bottom line instead of the clock. *Business Week*, pp. 134, 136.

52. Sethi, S. P., Namiki, N., & Swanson, C. L. (1984). *The false promise of the Japanese miracle.* Boston: Pitman.

53. Solomon, J. (1989, Nov. 7). Firms grapple with language barriers. *The Wall Street Journal*, pp. B1, B12.

54. Stipp, D. (1990, Sept. 10). Toxic turpitude: Environmental crime can land executives in prison these days. *The Wall Street Journal*, pp. A1, A6.

55. Szabo, J. C., & Tait, R. (1990, January). Business writes a new lesson plan. *Nation's Business*, pp. 36–38.

56. Thacker, J. W., & Fields, M. W. (1987). Union involvement in quality of work life efforts: A longitudinal investigation. *Personnel Psychology*, **40**, 97–111.

57. The literacy gap (1988, Dec. 19). *Time*, pp. 56, 57.

58. Ungeheuer, F. (1989, Feb. 6). They own the place. *Time*, pp. 50–51.

59. Winter, R. E. (1990, March 28). Scarcity of workers is kindling inflation. *The Wall Street Journal*, p. A2.

60. Working smarter (1984, June 4). *Time*, p. 53.

CHAPTER 2

Human Resource Management: A Field in Transition

■ HUMAN RESOURCE MANAGEMENT IN ACTION

1990s CHALLENGE: MANAGING PEOPLE-RELATED BUSINESS ISSUES*

Blame it on a demographic firestorm that gathered force in the 1980s and is likely to reach full strength during the 1990s. No longer can companies rely on an endless supply of young, homogeneous workers, ready to join up for a lifetime with a single company. Now they have to worry about the working mother with day-care needs, the middle-aged executive who has to care for an elderly parent, an influx of workers who can't speak, or read, English.

If mishandled, "human resources" can be a source of corporate distress; if handled well, they can provide a competitive advantage. As a senior partner at an international consulting firm noted, "You have to be the village idiot not to see how critical these issues are to a company's future."

---

*Adapted from: J. Solomon. People power. *The Wall Street Journal*, March 9, 1990, p. R33. Reprinted by permission of *The Wall Street Journal*, © 1990 Dow Jones & Company, Inc. All rights reserved worldwide.

The upshot is that companies, inspired by fear and opportunity, are taking human resources executives more seriously. Median cash compensation among the Fortune 500 was $175,000 in 1989, with about 100 HR chiefs making over $250,000. Between 1984 and 1989, for a broader range of companies, salaries of HR executives rose 69 percent, compared with 56 percent for other top executives. Many HR executives now report directly to the chief executive officer, and serve on the executive committee.

This is not the way things always were. Rather, it was, "Let's run the business, and, by the way, we need somebody to take care of the people problem," says the vice president of human resources at Scott Paper Company. "People were viewed as a constraint to strategy and human resources as a cost in itself."

Today the challenge is to use the "human factor" creatively in planning and problem solving. HR executives are expected to be at the management table initiating ideas to make their companies more productive. Moreover, the rank and file aren't the only employees now considered to be "human resources." More and more it means "management of managers," with the top HR executive sitting in judgment on who will be the future leaders of the organization at every level.

Another familiar—yet transformed—HR role involves labor relations. At Scott Paper, the HR department traditionally had a simple task: representing management's adversarial role in contract negotiations. Now that has changed. Last summer the HR vice president and other senior executives fashioned a new agreement with Scott's biggest union. At Scott's Somerset, Maine, mill, which is introducing new machinery, the agreement gives labor a say in the promotion and training of machinery operators. And in white-collar areas, HR executives are helping traditional antagonists—such as engineers and marketers—learn to communicate.

If all this sounds a bit, well, *too perfect,* you're right. Clearly an increasing number of top executives think these changes are essential to improving productivity. But the changes aren't coming easily.

Challenges

1. What is the difference between "people issues" and "people-related business issues?" How might this affect the operation of the HR function?
2. Aside from demographic changes, what are some other reasons why "people-related business issues" are becoming more and more important to a company's long-term success?
3. Can you suggest reasons why some line managers are resisting these changes?

1. What should be the role, objectives, and responsibilities of the HR function?
2. From a strategic perspective, how should the HR function be used?
3. What key questions should be asked in evaluating the HR function?
4. What specific people-related business issues provide the greatest opportunity for HR executives to add value to the firm?

THE EVOLUTION OF HUMAN RESOURCE MANAGEMENT

To appreciate where the HRM field is going, let's consider where it has come from. Doing so will help today's line manager gain a better insight and understanding of this aspect of business. Modern HRM has emerged from nine interrelated sources:

1. Rapid technological change that increased the specialization of labor associated with the industrial revolution
2. The emergence of free collective bargaining, with constraints established for both unions and employers
3. The scientific management movement
4. Early industrial psychology
5. Governmental personnel practices growing out of the establishment of the Civil Service Commission
6. The emergence of personnel specialists and the grouping of these specialists into personnel departments
7. The human relations movement
8. The behavioral sciences
9. The social legislation and court decision of the 1960s and 1970s[9]

Let us now consider the first eight of these; the ninth is the subject of Chapter 3.

The Industrial Revolution

Three characteristics of the industrial revolution were the development of machinery, the linking of human power to the machines, and the establishment of factories in which a large number of people were employed. The result was a tremendous increase in job specialization as well as in the amount of goods that workers could produce. "Division of labor" became the rallying cry of this revolution.

Clearly the industrial revolution greatly accelerated the development of business and commerce. Owners and entrepreneurs generally did quite well for themselves, but the average citizen fared poorly in comparison to today's workers in terms of purchasing power and working conditions. Labor was considered a commodity to be bought and sold, and the prevailing political philosophy of laissez-faire resulted in little action by governments to protect the lot of workers.[9]

In the early 1900s, before the enactment of child labor laws, the employment and exploitation of children under the age of 16 was quite common. Here a young girl collects and delivers garments for tailors and cleaners.

The Emergence of Free Collective Bargaining

Because of the way they were abused, it was inevitable that workers would organize to protect themselves and to improve their lot in life. From the perspective of workers, the industrial revolution fostered specialization and fostered the need for workers within each specialization to organize themselves against its abuses. Trade unions, also called "labor unions," spread rapidly, and so did the incidence of strikes (e.g., in 1886 by employees at the McCormick Reaper Works in Chicago, who went on strike for an 8-hour day).[6]

Until 1935, courts tended to side with management, and adopted a decidedly antiunion stance. However, in that year the Wagner Act, technically called the National Labor Relations Act, was passed. The act focused largely on labor's right to organize, and it provided that a majority of employees in an appropriate "bargaining unit" (as determined and certified by the National Labor Relations Board that the act created) could obtain exclusive collective bargaining rights for all the employees in that unit. It became an unfair labor practice for an employer to coerce or restrain employees in the exercise of their rights, to dominate or interfere with a labor organization, or to refuse to bargain collectively with a legal representative of the employees. Administration of the act was the responsibility of the National Labor Relations Board. Subsequent legislation refined, broadened, and set legal limits on the scope of management and union activities.

Viewed through the perspective of labor, the development of free collective bargaining and the American labor movement created the need for what we are now coming to recognize as effective human resource management.

Scientific Management

Viewed through the perspective of management, the scientific management movement also created a need for effective human resource management. Frederick Winslow Taylor was the prophet of scientific management, and his "bible" was the stopwatch.[1]

Taylor was a pioneer in the scientific study of jobs ("time-and-motion" study). In addition, he argued that individuals selected to do the work should be as perfectly matched, physically and mentally, to the demands of the job as possible and that *overqualified* individuals should be excluded.

Employees should be trained carefully by supervisors (whose own work was also divided into specialties) to ensure that they performed the work exactly as specified by prior scientific analysis. In no case, however, should employees ever be called upon to work at a pace that would be detrimental to their health.

Finally, to provide an incentive for the employee to follow the detailed procedures specified (which were closely supervised by line supervisors on the shop floor), Taylor felt that the employee should receive an addition of from 30 to 100 percent of his or her ordinary wages whenever the task was done right and within the time limits specified—labor's first piecework incentive systems. Taylor was also interested in the social aspects of work, although he saw little good emerging from the social interaction within work groups. He felt that work groups fostered a level of individual efficiency equal to the level of the least productive worker in the group. In other words, he believed that the efficiency of the group would not be any greater than the efficiency of the least productive member.

Overall, there is little doubt that application of the principles of scientific management has resulted in much higher productivity than would otherwise have been possible. What is remarkable is not that Taylor was "correct in the context of his time," but that many of his insights are still valid today.[19]

Early Industrial Psychology

In 1913 Hugo Munsterberg's book, *Psychology and Industrial Efficiency*, described experiments in selecting streetcar operators, ship's officers, and telephone switchboard operators. His contributions to personnel management are noteworthy for his emphasis on the analysis of jobs in terms of (1) the abilities required to do them and (2) the development of testing devices.[20,23]

Paralleling these developments were advances in checking references given by workers, in the use of rating sheets for interviewers, and in statistical methods for estimating validity (the extent to which selection devices accurately forecast job performance). World War I accelerated the development of intelligence tests (the Army Alpha and the Army Beta) so that each individual could be matched more effectively with job requirements. Other kinds of psychological measures also appeared during and after World War I, such as measures of aptitude, interest, and personality.

The U.S. Civil Service Commission

The Pendelton Act of 1883 established the U.S. Civil Service Commission (today known as the U.S. Office of Personnel Management). A forerunner in progressive personnel policies, the act provided that competitive examinations be administered as a basis for employment in the public service. It also provided a measure of employment security for those selected, prohibited discharge for refusing to engage in political activity, encouraged a nonpartisan approach to appointments, and mandated that a commissioner administer the act.[28] Perhaps the major impact of this act was to foster employment promotion policies in the federal government on the basis of merit. Over the years, however, the progressive personnel policies of the Civil Service (e.g., by 1900, entrance criteria were developed for the majority of federal positions) have influenced personnel practices in state and local governments as well as in private industry.

Private Industry's Approach to Personnel Management

Historians consider 1912 the approximate date of the emergence of the modern personnel department.[8] The term "personnel," with its modern connotation of managing people in organizations, began to appear about 1909. It was used as a major item in the index of the Civil Service Commission's report of that year, and in 1910 the secretary of commerce and labor used the term in a major heading in his annual report. Between 1900 and 1920, while advances were being made in scientific management, industrial psychology, and the federal civil service, a number of *personnel specialists* emerged in companies such as B. F. Goodrich, National Cash Register, and Standard Oil of California. The specialists managed such areas as employment, employee welfare (financial, housing, medical, and educational), wage setting, safety, training, and health. This kind of specialization formed the basis for the organization of the modern human resource department.

The Human Relations Movement

Beginning in 1923, and continuing until the early 1930s, the Hawthorne Works of the Western Electric Company in Chicago provided the setting for one of the most famous behavioral research efforts of all time. The purpose of the research was to identify factors in the work situation that led to high productivity.

The results of these experiments indicated to some observers that productivity was directly related to the degree of group teamwork and cooperation. The level

FIGURE 2-1

Conclusion of the Hawthorne experiments regarding the antecedents of high worker productivity.

of teamwork and cooperation, in turn, seemed to be related to the interest of the supervisor and the researchers in the work group, the lack of coercive approaches to productivity improvement, and the participation afforded the workers in changes affecting them.[25,26] These relationships are shown in Figure 2-1. In short, the researchers came to view the organization of workers as a *social system*, in contrast to Taylor's view of the organization as a technical-economic system.

The conviction that group behavior and workers' feelings were associated with morale and productivity characterized much of the research and theorizing in the human relations movement for the next two decades. Unfortunately, these new concepts, popularized as the "Pet Milk theory," were widely misunderstood and misapplied. The Pet Milk Company advertised that it had better milk because Pet Milk came from contented cows. A similar idea, that happy workers are productive workers, provided the rationale for trying to improve the workers' social environment with company picnics, newly created status symbols, employee coffee rooms, and other gimmicks.

The "Pet Milk" approach was widely discredited during the late 1950s. The 1957 recession led to a severe curtailment of human relations training programs. Failure to find evidence that these programs made a difference in workers' satisfaction or that happy workers were productive workers helped kill this approach to human resource management.[3] Many managers seemed to use human relations for the short-term purpose of manipulating workers to increase output rather than for the long-term goal of satisfying worker needs *while* meeting organization needs. By 1960 the "happy worker" fad had largely ended.

The Behavioral Sciences

The behavioral science approach to managing people is an outgrowth of the human relations studies, although it embraces a wider base of academic and applied disciplines and is concerned with a wider range of problems.[9] *Behavioral sciences* refers to the social and biological sciences concerned with the study of human behavior (see Figure 2-2).

Much of the knowledge about HRM and many of its practical applications have come from such behavioral science disciplines as the following:

Industrial/organizational psychology. The study of the behavior of people at work
Social psychology. The study of how people affect and are affected by one another

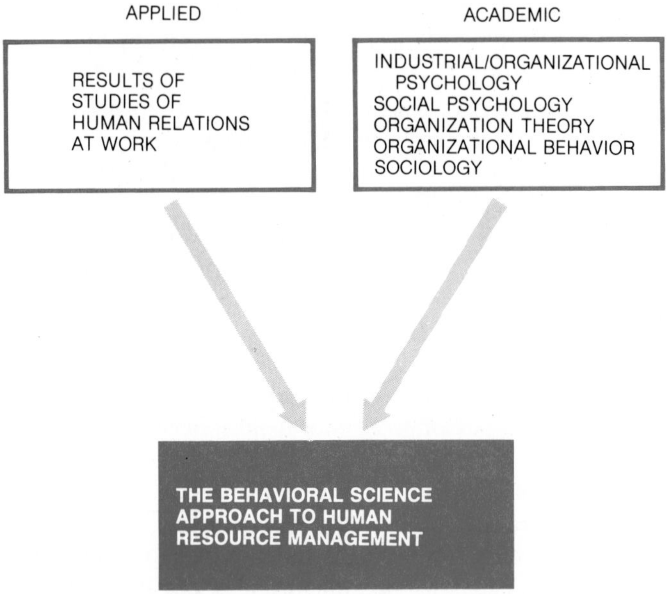

APPLIED   ACADEMIC

```
┌─────────────────────┐     ┌─────────────────────────────┐
│ RESULTS OF          │     │ INDUSTRIAL/ORGANIZATIONAL   │
│ STUDIES OF          │     │   PSYCHOLOGY                │
│ HUMAN RELATIONS     │     │ SOCIAL PSYCHOLOGY           │
│ AT WORK             │     │ ORGANIZATION THEORY         │
│                     │     │ ORGANIZATIONAL BEHAVIOR     │
│                     │     │ SOCIOLOGY                   │
└─────────────────────┘     └─────────────────────────────┘
```

THE BEHAVIORAL SCIENCE APPROACH TO HUMAN RESOURCE MANAGEMENT

FIGURE 2-2
Academic and applied disciplines that contribute to the behavioral science approach to managing people at work.

Organization theory. Basic philosophies about why organizations exist, how they function, how they should be designed, and how they can be effective

Organizational behavior. The study of the causes of individual and group behavior and of how this knowledge can be used to make people more productive and satisfied in organizational settings

Sociology. The study of society, social institutions, and social relationships

Needless to say, much behavioral science research cuts across these disciplines. As a result we now know that the ways people behave in organizations cannot be explained simply by human relationships. The organization itself, through its unique "culture," molds, constrains, and modifies human performance. The way the organization is structured, the authority attached to different positions, and job and technology requirements clearly affect behavior. Even though our present understanding of the determinants and effects of behavior in organizations is incomplete, we do have a better sense of the ways in which separate influences interact with each other to affect individuals.

THREE GROWTH STAGES OF HUMAN RESOURCE MANAGEMENT

The foundation for modern HRM rests on the nine factors listed earlier. Beyond that, HRM developed in three stages.

The first stage may be called the "file maintenance" stage, for it typified HRM activities up through the mid-1960s and the degree of emphasis placed on employee concerns. The first part of the chapter opening vignette illustrates some typical HRM responsibilities at this stage of the field's development. "Personnel" was the responsibility of a special department. These responsibilities included screening applicants, orientation for new employees, collecting and storing personal data on each employee (date of birth, years of company service, education), planning the company picnic, and circulating memos "whose impertinence was exceeded only by their irrelevance."[22]

The second growth stage of HRM began soon after the Civil Rights Act of 1964 was passed. This is considered the "government accountability" stage. Discrimination laws, pension laws, health and safety laws, federal regulatory agencies and their interpretive guidelines, and court rulings affecting virtually every aspect of employment—all of these accelerated the rise in importance of the HRM function. Class action suits and the large financial settlements of the winning suits illustrated the costs of *personnel mismanagement*. Thus at American Telephone & Telegraph, a 1973 consent agreement with the federal government to bring the starting pay of women promoted to managerial positions up to the starting pay of men who were so promoted cost the company over $30 million.

Managers outside the HRM function began to take notice because top management let it be known that ineptitude in this area simply would not be tolerated. Staying out of federal court became a top organizational priority. These trends also signaled the need for particular competence in each aspect of the HRM field.

Within HRM there began to appear specialties in compensation and benefits, affirmative action (the promotion of minority concerns in all aspects of employment), labor relations, and training and development. Considerable resources were devoted to compliance activities, for example: filing government-required reports on the numbers of minorities and nonminorities recruited, selected, and promoted by job class. Many top executives viewed these activities as nonproductive drains on overall organizational performance.

In the late 1970s and early 1980s, when many firms were struggling simply to survive, a combination of economic and political factors (high interest rates, growing international competition, shrinking U.S. productivity) led to the demand for greater accountability in dollar terms of all the functional areas of business. Human resource management activities were not exempted from this emphasis on accountability. Although methods for assessing the costs and benefits of personnel programs are available, they are not widely known.[5] In addition, social trends (more women in the workforce, as well as more minorities, immigrants, older workers, and poorly educated workers) have accelerated demands for improving the quality of work life, for managing cultural and ethnic diversity, and for continual training and retraining.

Thus in the 1980s, and continuing on into the 1990s, HRM has evolved to a third growth stage, "gaining and sustaining a competitive advantage." Top management looks to the HR department, as it does to line managers, to control costs, to enhance competitiveness, and to add value to the firm in everything it does. Consider a recent appraisal of the strategic importance of HRM by *Business Week*:

It is the most dramatic change in a managerial function since financial executives rose to power in the 1960s conglomerate era. . . . At a time when companies are constantly acquiring, merging, and spinning off divisions, entering new businesses and getting out of old ones, management must base strategic decisions more than ever on HR considerations—matching skills with jobs, keeping key personnel after a merger, and solving the human problems that arise from introducing new technology or closing a plant. (ref. 11, p. 58)

The responsibility for effective management of people, along with the effective management of physical and financial resources, is squarely on the shoulders of line managers—those directly responsible for the operations of the business (Figure 2-3). In terms of the discussion in Chapter 1 about changes in the technical and social environments, we now know that productivity improves most when all three factors of production—equipment, capital, and labor—are used most wisely; we cannot emphasize any one factor (e.g., computer equipment) to the exclusion of the rest (since, for example, it takes people who are properly selected, trained, and motivated to operate and maintain the computers). American Telephone & Telegraph found this out when an accident wiped out toll-free 800 service to tens of thousands of callers nationwide. The cause? A service technician who had forgotten to program some information on a group of 800 numbers into a network computer.[12] In the contemporary view, therefore, all managers, no matter what their line of responsibility (production, marketing, sales, or finance), are accountable to their organizations in terms of the financial impact of HRM operations and are accountable to their fellow employees in terms of the quality of work life they are providing. This suggests that the most effective approach to HRM may result from close interaction between the department charged with the administration of HRM and line managers charged with the responsibility for optimizing *all their resources*. To be sure, the HR department is still responsible for file maintenance and government accountability, but HRM in general is now viewed as a joint responsibility.

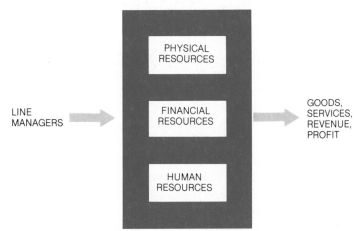

FIGURE 2-3
Line managers are responsible for optimizing the use of all three kinds of resources— physical, financial, and human—in order to generate useful output.

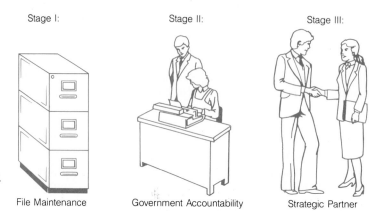

Stage I: Stage II: Stage III:

FIGURE 2-4
Development of the HR
field over the course of
the twentieth century.   File Maintenance   Government Accountability   Strategic Partner

Line managers have the authority to initiate change, and it is their responsibility to ensure that their wishes are understood clearly by the HR department. However, it is the responsibility of the HR department to communicate clearly to management what it has to offer, what it should offer, and what can be expected from it. Helped along by (1) the example of the Japanese, by (2) survey results showing that 82 percent of executives regard people problems as more important to the long-term success of a merger than financial considerations,[16] and by (3) such best sellers as *In Search of Excellence* and *The One Minute Manager* that describe the emphasis on HRM in successful firms, the chances for genuine cooperation between HR professionals and line managers have never been better.[13] A summary of the ideas presented in this section is shown in Figure 2-4.

THE RESPONSIBILITIES AND OBJECTIVES OF HUMAN RESOURCE MANAGEMENT

When it comes to managing people, all managers must be concerned to some degree with the following six activities: attraction, selection, retention, development, assessment, and adjustment.

Attraction comprises the activities of (1) identifying the job requirements within an organization, (2) determining the numbers of people and the skills mix necessary to do these jobs, and (3) providing equal opportunity for qualified candidates to apply for jobs.

Selection is the process of choosing the people who are best qualified to perform the jobs.

Retention comprises the activities of (1) rewarding employees for performing their jobs effectively and (2) maintaining a safe, healthy work environment.

Development is a function whose activities are aimed at preserving and enhancing employees' competence in their jobs through improving their knowledge, skills, abilities, and other characteristics; HR specialists use the abbreviation KSAOs to refer to these items.

Assessment involves the observation and evaluation of behaviors and attitudes relevant to jobs and to job performance.

Adjustment comprises activities intended to maintain compliance with the organization's HR policies.

Needless to say, these activities can be carried out at the individual, group, or larger organizational unit (e.g., department) level. Sometimes they are initiated by the organization (e.g., recruitment efforts or management development programs), and sometimes they are initiated by the individual or group (e.g., voluntary retirement, safety improvements). Whatever the case, the responsibilities for carrying out these activities are highly interrelated. Together they comprise the HRM system.

To illustrate how each of the major activities within HRM relates to every other one, consider the following scenario.

As a result of a large number of unexpected early retirements, the Hand Corporation finds that it must recruit extensively to fill the vacated jobs. The firm is well aware of the rapid changes that will be occurring in its business over the next 5 to 10 years, and so it must change its recruiting strategy in accordance with the expected changes in job requirements. Selection procedures must therefore be developed that will identify the kinds of KSAOs required of future employees. Compensation policies and procedures may have to change because job requirements will change, and new incentive systems will probably have to be developed. Since the firm cannot identify all the KSAOs that will be required 5 to 10 years from now, new training and development programs will have to be offered to satisfy those needs. Assessment procedures will necessarily change as well, since different KSAOs will be required in order to perform the jobs effectively. As a result of carrying out all this activity, the firm may need to discharge, promote, or transfer some employees to accomplish its mission. It is surprising, isn't it, how that single event, an unexpectedly large number of early retirees, can change the whole ball game?

So it is with any system or network of interrelated components. Changes in any single part of the system have a reverberating effect on all other parts of the system. Simply knowing that this will occur is healthy, because then we will not make the mistake of confining our problems only to the part where they occur. We will recognize and expect that whether we are dealing with problems in selection, training, compensation, or labor relations, they are interrelated. In short the *systems approach* provides a conceptual framework for integrating the various components within the system and for linking the HRM system with larger organizational needs.

As noted above, the activities of attraction, selection, retention, development, assessment, and adjustment are the special responsibilities of the HR department. But these responsibilities also lie within the core of every manager's job throughout any organization—and because line managers have authority (the organizationally granted right to influence the actions and behavior of the workers they manage), they have considerable impact on the ways that workers are actually utilized. This

■ TABLE 2·1

HRM ACTIVITIES AND THE RESPONSIBILITIES OF LINE MANAGERS AND THE HR DEPARTMENT

Activity	Line management responsibility	HR department responsibility
Attraction	Providing data for job analyses, job descriptions, and minimum qualifications; integrating strategic plans with HR plans at the unit level (e.g., department, division)	Job analysis, human-resource planning, recruitment, and affirmative action
Selection	Interviewing candidates, integrating information collected by HR department and making final decisions	Compliance with civil rights laws and regulations; application blanks, written tests, performance tests, interviews, background investigations, reference checks, and physical examinations
Retention	Fair treatment of employees, open communication, face-to-face resolution of conflict, promotion of teamwork, respect for the dignity of each individual, and pay increases based on merit	Compensation and benefits, labor relations, health and safety, and employee services
Development	On-the-job training, job enrichment, coaching, applied motivational strategies, and feedback to subordinates	Technical training, management and organizational development, career planning, and counseling
Assessment	Performance appraisals and morale surveys	Development of performance appraisal systems and morale surveys; personnel research and audits
Adjustment	Discipline, discharge, promotions, and transfers	Layoffs, retirement counseling, and outplacement services

implies two things: A *broad objective* of HRM is to optimize the usefulness (i.e., the productivity) of all workers in an organization, and a *special objective* of the HR department is to help line managers manage those workers more effectively. The HR department accomplishes this special objective through policy initiation and formulation, advice, service, and control in resonance (close communication, understanding, and aims) with line managers when it comes to managing people. To be sure, each of the responsibilities of HRM is shared both by the HR department and by the line managers, as shown in Table 2-1.

In the context of Table 2-1, note how line and HR managers share people-related business activities. Generally speaking, HR provides the technical expertise in each area, while line managers use this expertise in order to manage people effectively. In the small business, however, line managers are responsible both for the technical and managerial aspects of HRM.

For example, in the area of retention, line managers are responsible for treating employees fairly, resolving conflicts, promoting teamwork, and providing pay increases based on merit. In order to do these things effectively, however, it is the

HR department's responsibility to devise a compensation and benefits system that employees will perceive as attractive and fair, to establish merit increase guidelines that will apply across departments, and to provide training and consultation to line managers on all labor relations issues—such as conflict resolution and team building.

The Role and Mission of the HR Department: A Top-Management View

There is a perception among some people that this small department, with no revenue or profit-and-loss responsibility, somehow manages the human resources of the corporation. As noted earlier, this is not true, for *all managers*, regardless of their functional specialty, are responsible not only for managing capital and equipment, but also for managing people. Another common perception is, in effect, that "Employees should be viewed as costs, not as assets." This also is not true, for as Bruce Ellig, Pfizer's top HR executive, noted: "You cut costs; you develop assets. The renaming of the personnel function to Human Resources in most organizations is at least an outward indication of that" (ref. 10, p. 41).

Recent in-depth interviews of 71 chief executive officers (CEOs) of major corporations indicated that in general, they subscribe to neither of these views. The HR department does not have the sole responsibility for managing people, and people are seen as assets, not just as costs. CEOs see HRM as one of the most important corporate functions—one to which they look for help in forging a competitive edge for the business. They cite quality of talent, flexibility and innovation, superior performance or productivity, and customer service as key factors in accomplishing this.[29] However, the CEOs also say that they expect more of the HRM function than they are getting. Despite such advances as HR planning, improved information systems, and new approaches to compensation, the function is often viewed as following, rather than leading, change. Often it is "responsive" rather than "proactive" (that is, anticipating events, not just reacting to them).

Using the HRM Function Strategically

In order to use the HRM function most effectively as a corporate resource, top management should consider doing the following things:

1. Define the HR department's responsibility as the maximization of corporate profits through the better management and utilization of people. The key issues are time and money. Concentrate the HRM function on ways to make people more productive—especially on ways to improve the employees' job skills, to improve their motivation by improving their quality of work life (QWL), and to improve the professional skills of managers.

2. The senior HR executive should report directly to the CEO. At present this occurs in about 70 percent of companies nationwide. Consider whether any corporate resource is more important than its people: Suppose that a fire destroyed all the plant and equipment of a 1000-employee firm; how long would it take to

rebuild the plant and replace the equipment? One year? Now suppose that the same firm lost all its employees; how long would it take to replace the same level of competence and commitment? Considerably longer. Indeed, is any management function more important than managing the people who comprise the organization? HR policy cannot have any real meaning unless the CEO is intimately involved in its development.

3. Do not dilute the HRM function by saddling the HR department with unrelated responsibilities, such as the mail room and public relations. Do consider moving productivity functions, such as industrial engineering, into the HR department.

4. Require that HR executives be experienced businesspeople, for unless these executives are perceived as equals by their corporate peers, their ability to make significant contributions to the firm will be diminished. In today's climate of increased competition and cost control, there is simply no room for people who cannot have a significant impact on the firm's productivity and profitability.[18]

HR Initiatives: Consider the Possibilities

Study after study has shown that top management wants the HRM function to concentrate on people-related business issues involving productivity and cost containment. Here are some typical initiatives:[14,29]

- Containing the costs of employee health care and other benefits
- Redesigning compensation programs, tying them closer to performance
- Improving productivity through employee involvement and meaningful performance appraisal

HR staff should help plan and implement changes in organizational structure or management practices, such as:

- Staffing changes resulting from downsizing, restructuring, mergers, or acquisitions.
- Increasing the innovation, creativity, and flexibility necessary to enhance competitiveness. Proactive HR departments are doing this by designing and facilitating the application of new approaches for job design (e.g., to promote entrepreneurship), succession planning, career development, and intraorganizational mobility.
- Managing the implementation of technological changes through improved staffing, training, and communications with employees.
- Promoting changes in relations with unions, particularly those changes that will enhance cooperation, productivity, and flexibility.
- Anticipating and influencing the management impact of new legislation and court decisions.

As companies look to world markets more aggressively, they are faced with developing world class products and services at world class costs. This means changes in design, production, distribution, and marketing. There are multiple HRM implications, including developing new forms of design teams, better use of strategic sourcing, and establishing world class standards for design, service, and performance. To accomplish these objectives, it is necessary to build complementary agendas for senior line executives and senior HR executives. Here are the basic elements of each one.

Agenda for Line Executives

- Clearly articulate why "going global" is needed
- Determine what markets the firm *must* be in in order to be a strong player 10 years from now
- Identify major competitors worldwide—who the firm needs to beat, and who it needs to join (preempt)
- Define the competitive imperatives, such as mastering economies of scale, technological advantage, access to markets, distribution, and so forth.
- Identify the skills required and where they exist in the organization
- Determine how to create organizational processes that treat globalization as an ongoing experiment with deliberate learning and redirection as necessary

Agenda for HR Executives[†]

- Ensure HR involvement as an integral partner in formulating the global strategy [Adjustment]
- Develop competencies among senior HR staff in order to be a contributing partner [Development]
- Take the lead in developing processes and concepts for top management as they develop global strategy. These might include information scanning, decision making, or learning processes [Assessment]
- Develop a framework to help top management fully understand the organization structure and people implications of globalization [Assessment]
- Facilitate the implementation phase by identifying key skills required, assessing current competencies, and developing strategies for locating outside talent that may be required [Attraction and Selection]

Note how the two agendas complement each other—as they must in order to make the strategic partnership work.

---

*Adapted from: N. M. Tichy, Setting the global human resource management agenda for the 1990s, *Human Resource Management*, **27**, 1–18 (1988). Copyright © 1988 by John Wiley & Sons, Inc. Reprinted by permission of John Wiley & Sons, Inc.
[†]Comments in brackets refer to broad HR activities as shown in Table 2-1.

Key Management Questions to Ask in Evaluating the HRM Function

Just as it does when evaluating any other function, a company's management should ask tough questions, such as:

■ How many HR managers, professionals, and support staff does the company employ this year? How much does this cost the company? (Considering the total cost per person of salaries and benefits, equipment, supplies, computer time, heat, light, water, depreciation, and rent, employees cost about 3 times their annual salaries.[2])

■ How do these numbers (people and dollars) relate to company revenues and to the employee population?

■ How do these ratios compare with those of competitors and/or with national figures?

■ What trends can be identified in the HR department over the past 5 years? What ratios would it be desirable to maintain in the future?

Evaluation from the HR Perspective

It has been said many times that if HR people are to make meaningful contributions to an enterprise, they must think and act like businesspeople. To promote this sort of outlook, it is useful to ask, "How much profit must a profit center make to keep an HR department going"?

Suppose you run an HR department for a firm that makes bicycles. Last year the total cost to the company for your department's services was $1 million. How many bikes does the company have to sell to pay your way? Let's say that on a $200 bicycle, your company makes a profit of $20. Dividing this $20 into $1 million shows that 50,000 bikes must be sold to keep the HR department in business!

The point of this exercise is not to argue for the abolition of HR departments in order to save profits or to save selling more bikes. Certainly, if the HR department was not doing its work, somebody else would be doing much of it. Rather, the point is that there is an important connection between human resources management and profits. It is seldom discussed, but it should be, to promote increased awareness of how time and money are spent. Imagine an HR director asking how many bikes will have to be sold to support a new orientation program!

A second important question that management should ask and that HR people should be prepared to answer is "How much more product can be sold because of your services?" While many HR contributions are not related directly to the bottom line, it is important to promote increased awareness of how HR activities relate to the purposes of the organization. Here are some possible HR department responses in six key areas:[2]

■ "Here's what we did for you (in recruiting, say), here's what it cost, and here's what you would have done without us and what it would have cost you."

- "Here's how much money we saved you by changing insurers in our benefits package."
- "Here's an idea that workers developed in a training program we were leading. It's now working and saving you $50,000 per year."
- "If you had not asked us to do this executive search, you would have had to go outside, at a cost of $30,000. We did it for $5000."
- "You used to have an unhappy person doing this job for $40,000 per year. As a result of our job redesign, you now have a motivated person doing the same work for $20,000."
- "In working with the union on a new contract, we found a new way to reduce grievances by 30 percent, saving the company 6429 hours per year in management time."

Even though precise bottom-line numbers might be hard to come by for many HR activities, it is important to encourage HR people to think in these terms.

Current Status of HRM Activities

Progressive organizations are rotating their best managers through the various specialized HRM functions as a required part of their development and as a way of bringing line experience to HRM problems. Higher levels of education and experience are required for individuals who are given such HRM assignments. In fact, the vice president of human resources frequently reports directly to the chief executive officer and sits on the board of directors and the planning committee. As the chapter's opening vignette indicated, salaries for top HR executives also reflect this increased stature.

What are firms getting for this money? The best HR talent executes six roles well:[27]

- Business person
- Shaper of change
- Consultant to the organization and partner to line managers
- Strategy formulator and implementor
- Talent manager (i.e., networking with professional colleagues, including recruiters, line managers, and other HR professionals)
- Asset manager and cost controller (based on understanding financial and accounting procedures)

As the director of HR planning at Bank of America noted, "The perception used to be that human resources thought about the happiness of employees, and line managers thought about costs. Now both realize that the overriding concern is the yield from employees."[13]

IMPACT OF EFFECTIVE HRM ON PRODUCTIVITY, QUALITY OF WORK LIFE, AND THE BOTTOM LINE

Even a seemingly simple issue such as the quality of the work environment for office workers can affect their productivity and QWL. In a study of 1047 office workers and 209 executives commissioned by Steelcase, Inc., 74 percent gave their employers high marks for providing good working conditions. Over 70 percent felt that their QWL had improved, as compared with only 58 percent who saw improvement in the quality of life generally. Negative responses were most common from workers in "pool offices," rows of adjacent desks with no space or partitions between them. Many executives seemed unaware of how highly workers rate conversational privacy as a part of their work environment. Over 99 percent of those surveyed saw a connection between satisfaction with their work area and their productivity.[21]

IMPACTS OF EFFECTIVE HUMAN RESOURCE MANAGEMENT

For all its increased status, what impact does effective HRM have on productivity, QWL, and the bottom line? The following examples give a range of answers to this question.

Goal Setting and Feedback

Effective management of employees' goals and plans, together with constructive feedback telling them of their progress toward their goals, can produce impressive results. This was demonstrated in a study of sewing machine operators in a southwestern garment factory.[15] The 150 workers in the study assembled pairs of pants using an "assembly line" on which 34 separate operations (each requiring an average time of 18 seconds) were performed.

The quality of the work done was inspected at the end of the line by full-time inspectors. Each garment was inspected. Sewing errors were called to the attention of the operators only if the number of errors for a particular operator's segment of the total job was excessive in a 60-unit bundle of pants. Errors were mended by "menders," not by the operator who caused the error.

The plant where the study was conducted was experiencing more than twice the employee turnover normal for the garment industry at the time. When the study began, annual turnover was 216 percent, and daily absenteeism was 9.4 percent.

One purpose of the study was to determine the effects of goal setting and feedback on the operators' work. Challenging individual goals were set. The overall group goal was to reach the quality level of the best plants owned by the manufacturer. Feedback was accomplished by erecting 4- by 6-foot Plexiglas display boards on which the daily results for the workers were posted by management.

Within a month after the goal setting and feedback were established, sewing errors decreased 66 percent; 1 year later, although the turnover was still unacceptably high, it had dropped from 216 to 136 percent.

Job Redesign

Typists are a favorite target for job redesign because theirs is one of the few jobs in which so critical a function is performed by people so bored. In fact, one study found that 60 percent of all typists who quit their jobs do so because of boredom and lack of work, not because of overwork.[20]

The study's authors reported that in one division of Bankers Trust, typically bored typists were engaged in processing work that was more than typically critical—stock transfers. The problems were severe because of the consequences. In addition to the problems of high employee turnover and absenteeism, both the quality and the quantity of work were low. To deal with this situation, the following changes were introduced gradually over 6 months, and supervisors received formal training on how to cope with employee responses to the new changes:

1. Groups of customers were assigned to specific typists.
2. Individuals whose work was accurate and reliable were not required to have their work verified by checkers.
3. Other typists and checkers became teams, with each team responsible for the work done for a particular group of customers.
4. Typists corrected their own mistakes, and feedback from checkers was immediate for those whose work still required verification.

Redesigning the jobs resulted in work yielding considerably fewer errors. For the group of typists as a whole, the processing time was decreased. The speed of typists who worked without checkers and verified their own work was a bit slower, but not so slow as to take longer than if others had checked their work.

Rewards-Based Suggestion Systems

Suggestion systems designed to improve the quality or speed of goods and services have gotten quite a bad reputation of late. Most managers are convinced that they simply do not work. Perhaps they do not because of faulty suggestion-system design and implementation.

One exception is Honeywell's Defense Systems and Avionics Division, based in Minneapolis.[30] One year this company division received over 18,000 suggestions (3.66 per employee) that resulted in a savings of over $1 million. The Honeywell Suggestion System rewards employees who offer cost-saving suggestions by recognizing them and paying them an amount based on their suggestions.

Cash is awarded to employees based on one-sixth of the total first year's anticipated savings. The more valuable the suggestion, the greater the reward: a clear application of "pay for performance."

The trend in this area is for companies to provide more top prizes with higher cash awards. For example, Pitney Bowes Business Systems raised its top prize from $30,000 paid over 3 years to $50,000 paid over 2 years. Ford Motor Company now allows *groups* of hourly workers, instead of just an *individual*, to win its top award of $6000. Recently, Eastman Kodak paid $3.6 million in awards, up 8.7 percent from the previous year, and figures that it saved $16 million from the suggestions.[17]

Unique Contributions of the HR Department to Profits

As noted earlier, a staff department such as HR must be able to demonstrate that what it does is important to the success of the organization and that the procedures it suggests provide positive results; otherwise, the HR department is perceived as nothing more than one of "happiness vendors." The HR staff must be able to demonstrate the impact of its programs on that indicator of corporate health—the bottom line. It must also be able to demonstrate the efficiency of its own departments. Only with such evidence will the HR staff be able to justify the priority setting and resource allocation that favors HRM and moves it toward parity with the other functional areas of business.[4]

Contrary to common belief, *all* aspects of HRM (including morale) can be measured and quantified in the same manner as any other function in an organization. Some of the major areas in which HRM can demonstrate measurable cost savings, productivity increases, and turnover reductions are shown and described briefly in Table 2-2.

This has been just a brief glimpse into several areas where effective HRM can make a substantial contribution to the improvement of productivity, the quality of work life, and the bottom line. Although each area has been discussed separately, the overall objective is to develop a uniform financial reporting system for the entire HRM subsystem. Significant and timely information can be produced, both line managers and HR staff can see how their work is interconnected, and over time such a measurement system can become a very powerful tool.

■ HUMAN RESOURCE MANAGEMENT IN ACTION:
CONCLUSION

1990s CHALLENGE: MANAGING PEOPLE-RELATED BUSINESS ISSUES

In the opinion of many top managers, the only way to make "people-related business issues" credible is to support them with real assets—such as pay and promotions. At Scott Paper, managers are now evaluated on how their employees develop and on how well they interact with other departments.

Senior management also needs to send signals that HR issues and HR executives are major players. Unfortunately, however, some of the biggest

■ **TABLE 2·2**
THE CONTRIBUTION OF EFFECTIVE HRM TO PROFITS—
SOME AREAS AND EXAMPLES

Compensation policies. Development of a structured pay plan that accurately reflects labor market worth in each job avoids the problem of overpayment or underpayment for specific jobs.

Employee benefits administration. Finding the greatest value for the money in health and life insurance, employee assistance, and pension plans; monitoring the costs of benefits paid out against premiums contributed; requesting a dividend when premiums exceed payouts.

Personnel tax management. Monitoring federal and state unemployment tax rates. Since the rates charged are a function of claims by former employees, as turnover is reduced the rates drop—and potential savings can be significant.

Selection and training. To the extent that more valid selection procedures help to reduce the attrition and increase the retention of newly hired employees, savings may be huge. For example, at a cost of $1 million to train a Navy fighter pilot,[24] and a loss of $250,000 for each unsuccessful candidate, a reduction of five unsuccessful candidates would save the Navy $1.25 million *per year.*

Affirmative action control. Given the demographic changes looming on the horizon, affirmative action to find and retain the best talent from the pool of women, racial, and ethnic minorities makes more economic sense than ever. "Tokenism" is dead; managing cultural and ethnic diversity effectively can add genuine value to a firm. With regard to older workers, consider that the odds are 5 to 1 that a recent college graduate will leave within the first 3 years of employment. The odds of a 50-year-old recruit staying with an organization for 15 or more productive years are far better.[7]

Control of turnover costs. Using proper accounting procedures to compute the real cost of turnover (i.e., separation, replacement, and training costs) reveals that six- or seven-figure annual turnover figures are common for large firms.[5] Controlling such costs through joint HR and line management efforts (e.g., through job redesign, retraining, changes in compensation)—even to a modest degree— can represent considerable savings.

problems are the HR executives themselves—many of whom are not willing, or able, to make the leap to being major players. Thus when a new CEO took over Scientific-Atlanta, Inc., a communications company, he promptly dismissed the HR executive he inherited from the previous administration. Why? The man ran a "sleepy" department. Said the new CEO: "This can't be someone sitting in a back office looking at compensation schedules."

The new role also means unfamiliar visibility and accountability. Even more intimate contact with top management carries a price; since the fit with a chief executive is critical, job security is only as good as the boss's tenure. As a result, says one expert, "some good people just can't take the heat." Those who can "are in short supply because companies just haven't been growing this type of person."

Career tracks for the long-time HR executive also have changed. Bob Murphy, the top HR executive at Rockwell International Corporation, is typical. He went back to school to earn his master's in business administration at night, and did stints overseas and in finance. In fact, when top executives were asked to rank the ideal skills needed by their chief executive in the year 2000, the top four were strategy formulation, marketing-sales, negotiation and conflict resolution, and human resource management. People-related business skills are essential ingredients for success as a manager now, and all indications are that they will continue to be so in the future.

SUMMARY

Modern HRM has evolved from nine interrelated sources: (1) the industrial revolution, (2) the emergence of free collective bargaining, (3) the scientific management movement, (4) early industrial psychology, (5) governmental personnel practices resulting from the establishment of the U.S. Civil Service Commission, (6) the emergence of personnel specialists and their grouping into personnel departments, (7) the human relations movement, (8) the behavioral sciences, and (9) the social legislation and court decisions of the 1960s and 1970s.

HRM today involves six major areas: attraction, selection, retention, development, assessment, and adjustment. Together they comprise the HRM system, for they describe a network of interrelated components. Top management views the HRM function as an important tool to enhance competitiveness. To accomplish this purpose, the HRM function must be used strategically. Its responsibility is the maximization of productivity, quality of work life, and profits through better management of people. To fulfill this responsibility, the senior HR executive should report directly to the CEO, the HRM function should focus on productivity-related activities, and the HR people should above all be businesspeople, accountable, just as any other function, in terms of their overall contributions to enhancing productivity and controlling costs.

Finally, contributions to improved productivity, QWL, and the bottom line can come from more effective management of a number of areas. These include but certainly are not limited to improved work environments; goal setting and feedback; job redesign; rewards-based suggestion systems; compensation policies and procedures; benefits administration; personnel tax management; recruiting, training, and management development; affirmative action control; and turnover and outplacement.

DISCUSSION QUESTIONS

2▪1 Discuss the contributions of the industrial revolution, scientific management, and early industrial psychology to the development of modern HRM.

2▪2 Describe the characteristics of the new role of the HR executive—that of "strategic partner" with top management.

IMPLICATIONS FOR MANAGEMENT PRACTICE

According to Robert Galvin, Chief Executive Officer of Motorola:

> Generally we're seeing the HR manager and HR department being offered the opportunity to be transformed from a functional specialist to management team member, and it is expected that the shift from "employee advocate" to "member of the management team" will continue into the 1990s. Human resource professionals will be called upon to think and act like line managers and to address people-related business issues. Management will increasingly expect HR to think and act, and to view human resource activities from a business perspective. (ref. 27, p. 50)

If this is the role for HR professionals, what will be the role of line managers in the HRM area? Predominantly it will be a set of activities that indicate an increased awareness of the implications of the phrase "human resources." Organizations and line managers will truly consider their employees as important resources "to be invested in prudently, to be used productively, and from whom a return can be expected—a return that should be monitored as carefully as is the return on any other business investment."[4] Human resource management is not only planning and controlling, manipulating numbers, and reporting to higher management. It is also relating on a daily basis to the employees of the company. All managers must emphasize the human side of the workforce and give more than lip service to honoring and understanding that side. This is the real challenge of managing people effectively.

2•3 How do the responsibilities and objectives of HRM contribute to employee productivity and employee job satisfaction?

2•4 In what ways can effective HRM contribute to profits?

2•5 What changes do you see in HRM over the next 5 years?

REFERENCES

1. Bell, D. (1972). Three technologies: Size, measurement, hierarchy. In L. E. Davis and J. C. Taylor (eds.), *Design of jobs*. London: Penguin.
2. Bellman, G. M. (1986). Doing more with less. *Personnel Administrator*, **31**, 46–52.
3. Brayfield, A. H., & Crockett, W. H. (1955). Employee attitudes and employee performance. *Psychological Bulletin*, **52**, 396–424.
4. Briscoe, D. R. (1982, November). Human resource management has come of age. *The Personnel Administrator*, **26**, 75–83.
5. Cascio, W. F. (1991). *Costing human resources: The financial impact of behavior in organizations* (3d ed.). Boston: PWS-Kent.
6. Cohen, S. (1960). *Labor in the United States*. Columbus, Oh: Charles E. Merrill.
7. Driessnack C. H. (1979). Financial impact of effective human resources management. *The Personnel Administrator*, **23**, 62–66.

8. Eilbert, H. (1959). The development of personnel management in the United States. *Business History Review*, **33**, 345–364.

9. French, W. L. (1986). *The personnel management process* (6th ed.). Boston: Houghton Mifflin.

10. Holder, J. (1986). Regaining the competitive edge. *Personnel Administrator*, **31**, 35–41, 122, 124.

11. Human resources managers aren't corporate nobodies anymore (1985, December 2). *Business Week*, pp. 58, 59.

12. Keller, J. J. (1990, Feb. 13). AT&T's 800 service disrupted Friday, in another embarrassing breakdown. *The Wall Street Journal*, p. B4.

13. Kiechel, W. III. (1987, Aug. 18). Living with human resources. *Fortune*, pp. 99, 100.

14. Klingner, D. E. (1979, September). Changing role of personnel management in the 1980s. *The Personnel Administrator*, **23**, 41–47.

15. Koch, J. L. (1979). Effects of goal specificity and performance feedback to work groups on peer leadership, performance, and attitudes. *Human Relations*, **32**, 819–840.

16. Labor Letter (1986, Aug. 26). *The Wall Street Journal*, p. 1.

17. Labor Letter (1984, May 15). *The Wall Street Journal*, p. 1.

18. Lengnick-Hall, C. A., & Lengnick-Hall, M. L. (1990). *Interactive human resource management and strategic planning*. New York: Quorum Books.

19. Locke, E. A. (1982). The ideas of Frederick W. Taylor: An evaluation. *Academy of Management Review*, **7**, 14–24.

20. McAfee, R. B., & Poffenberger, W. (1982). *Productivity Strategies: Enhancing employee job performance*. Englewood Cliffs, NJ: Prentice-Hall.

21. Merry, R. W. (1979, Feb. 6). Office workers feel work environments have improved greatly in 10 years. *The Wall Street Journal*, p. 1.

22. Meyer, H. E. (1976, February). Personnel directors are the new corporate heroes. *Fortune*, **93**, 84–88.

23. Moskowitz, M. J. (1977). Hugo Munsterberg: A study in the history of applied psychology. *American Psychologist*, **32**, 824–842.

24. Navy worried over growing jet losses (1986, Mar. 23). *Honolulu Star Bulletin & Advertiser*, pp. A-1, A-4.

25. Pennock, G. A. (1930, February). Industrial research at Hawthorne and experimental investigation of rest periods, working conditions, and other influences. *Personnel Journal*, **8**, 296–309.

26. Roethlisberger, F. J., & Dickson, W. J. (1939). *Management and the worker*. Boston: Harvard University Press.

27. Schuler, R. S. (1990). Repositioning the human resource function: Transformation or demise? *Academy of Management Executive*, **4**(3), 49–60.

28. Van Riper, P. P. (1958). *History of the United States Civil Service*. Evanston, IL: Row-Peterson.

29. Walker, J. W. (1986). Moving closer to the top. *Personnel Administrator*, **31**, 52–57, 117.

30. Zemke, R. (1980, July). Combine recognition and reward. *Training*, pp. 12–13.

CHAPTER 3

The Social, Legal, and Organizational Contexts of Personnel Decisions

■ **HUMAN RESOURCE MANAGEMENT IN ACTION**

ON MANAGING A MULTICULTURAL WORKFORCE*

Cultural misunderstandings, usually far from overt, happen every day in the workplace. The following scenarios are not blatant cases of unlawful discrimination; rather, they represent the details of day-to-day life.

A manager from the dominant U.S. culture sees two Arab-Americans arguing—and figures he'd better stay out of it. As a result, what started as a small disagreement escalated into real conflict, with the potential for formal disciplinary action. In fact, the employees *expected* a third-party intermediary, or *wasta* in Arabic, and without one the incident blew up.

According to experts, the expectation goes back to the Koran and Bedouin tradition. While the dominant American culture is likely to assume an individualistic, win-lose approach and emphasize privacy, Arab-Americans tend to value a win-win result that preserves group harmony but often requires mediation.

---

*Adapted from: J. Solomon, As cultural diversity of workers grows, experts urge appreciation of differences. *The Wall Street Journal*, September 12, 1990, pp. B1, B12. Reprinted by permission of *The Wall Street Journal*, © 1990 Dow Jones & Company, Inc. All rights reserved worldwide.

■

In another incident, a Latino manager starts a budget-planning meeting by chatting casually and checking with his new staff on whether everyone can get together after work. His boss frets over the delay and wonders why he doesn't get straight to the numbers. Latino culture teaches that building relationships is often critical to working together, while the dominant American culture encourages "getting down to business."

A second-generation Asian woman appears for an employment interview. Deferring to authority, she keeps her eyes down, rarely meeting the interviewer's. The interviewer, a white American male, thinks "She's not assertive, not strong enough, maybe she's hiding something or is insecure." Meanwhile the Asian woman views the persistent eye contact of the interviewer as domineering, invasive, and controlling. Neither person trusts the other.

Finally, consider the reverse scenario: someone from a minority group who displays behavior common to many cultures, but is scrutinized more closely than others would be. One consultant, who is black, commented, "In a corporate setting, anything a person of color does is exaggerated. Especially at professional levels, they're usually the only one in the room. So if I show up late for a meeting once, it's noticed. If there are three [white] guys from finance, and one is late, it's not much of an issue."

As the white male corporate culture disappears, the workplace is becoming less a melting pot than a mosaic. Even now, because the workforce is growing more slowly, employees of different cultures are in a position to demand more flexibility from management.

Challenges

1. What is the objective of effective cross-cultural communication?
2. If the workplace is truly becoming more of a mosaic than a melting pot, how does this affect the way that managers relate to employees?
3. What steps can you take now in order to become more effective as a manager in a multicultural work environment?

QUESTIONS THIS CHAPTER WILL HELP MANAGERS ANSWER

1. Is there evidence that any of the five forms of unlawful discrimination exist in our organization?
2. How are our employment practices affected by the civil rights laws and Supreme Court interpretations of them?
3. What should be the components of an effective policy to prevent sexual harassment?

4. How can I maximize the potential of a multicultural workforce?
5. What can I do to accommodate women and older workers?

THE SOCIAL CONTEXT OF PERSONNEL DECISIONS

Chapters 1 and 2, as well as the opening vignette in this chapter, have addressed the coming demographic changes in the American workforce, and emphasized the need for effective organizational responses to these challenges. Yet personnel decisions are not made in a vacuum. Rather, they are embedded in social, legal, and organizational contexts. Let us begin the chapter, therefore, by considering some of the special problems associated with three large, and growing, segments of the working population: African Americans, women, and older workers.

African Americans in the Workforce

African Americans comprise 11 percent of the civilian workforce in the U.S. Comprehensive studies have shown that since the early 1970s, the economic status of African Americans, relative to white Americans, has stagnated or deteriorated.[83] Hispanics, who account for another 7 percent of the civilian labor force, experience many of the same disadvantages. Some of the reasons for this are:

1. A shift in the industrial base of the U.S. economy from blue-collar manufacturing to service industries
2. Falling employment rates among African Americans, relative to whites
3. An enormous increase in nonworkers among African American men in the prime working age
4. An increase in poverty rates associated with increases in African American families headed by females
5. Large occupational differences between African Americans and white Americans, with overrepresentation of African Americans in low-wage–low-skill jobs.

Despite these dismal statistics, dramatic improvements in earnings and occupational status were made by a younger, well-educated segment of the African American workforce. Many have gained from expanded opportunities associated with enforcement of antidiscrimination laws, litigation in the federal courts, and improvements in educational achievement. Nonetheless, only 24 percent of African American families have attained the middle-class living standards of the U.S. Bureau of Labor Statistics, as compared with 50 percent of white American families.[83]

Among the major options proposed to reduce impediments to occupational advancement among African Americans and other minorities are public- and private-sector investments in training to enhance skills and productive capabilities, facilitation of economic growth (since growth creates new job opportunities), and a reduction in discrimination and involuntary segregation.

Women in the Workforce

Feminism was the last focus of the civil rights movement and of the more general social activism of the late 1960s. Potentially its constituency was the broadest and deepest, and so were the problems it addressed. In 1972 women questioned the possibility of having a family and holding a job at the same time. By the mid-1980s more women—including some of the daughters of the past generation—took it for granted that they should be able to manage both. Five forces account for the changed attitudes:

1. *Changes in the family.* Legalized abortion, contraception, divorce, and a declining birthrate have all contributed to a decrease in the proportion of most women's lives devoted to rearing children. Women are now important providers of family income.

2. *Changes in education.* Ever since World War II, increasing numbers of women have been attending college. By the mid-1980s, about a third of law school, medical school, and MBA students were female.[7]

3. *Changes in self-perception.* Many women experience considerable conflict over the relative importance of their work and family roles and over the social costs associated with upward mobility in the organizations they work for. Thus *a major goal of affirmative action for women is to raise the consciousness level of both women and men so that women can be given a fair chance to think about their interests and potential, to investigate other possibilities, to make an intelligent choice, and then to be considered for openings or promotions on an equal basis with men.*[11]

4. *Changes in technology.* Both in the home (e.g., frozen foods, microwave ovens) and in the workplace (e.g., robotics), advances in technology have reduced substantially the physical effort and time required to accomplish tasks. Thus more women can now qualify for formerly all-male jobs.

5. *Changes in the economy.* Ever since World War II there has been a shift away from goods production and toward service-related industries (e.g., health care, banking, law enforcement). Between now and 1995, almost 9 out of 10 of the 16 million new jobs projected will be in a service-producing industry.[78] Increasing numbers of employees in all types of industry are female.

This social revolution is characterized by these statistics:

- Of families having annual incomes that reach $40,000 to $50,000, 70 percent have working wives.
- Women are expected to hold about a third of the top jobs in major concerns by the year 2001 and to head 10 percent of all companies.[56]
- The percentage of married women in the workforce is now over 55 percent.
- The number of children with mothers who work is now larger than the number of children with mothers at home.
- An affluent, consumer-oriented society has developed that depends on two wage earners to support such a standard of living.

Now for the bad news:

- Of all female workers, 80 percent hold "pink-collar" jobs (i.e., jobs dominated by women) and are paid about 68 cents for every dollar that men earn.
- About 70 percent of all classroom teachers are women, yet for the same job they make an average of $3000 less than their male colleagues.[34]
- The situation is not much brighter on the management level: Despite a 20-year boom in the number of women in the workplace, female managers are mired mostly in the middle ranks. Only 2 percent of top executives are women, even though companies with more than 100 employees average 44 percent women.[10]
- Women in paid jobs still bear most of the responsibility for housework and family care.

In many instances, however, discrimination may not be the primary reason for the earnings gap. It may be that (1) women do not commit themselves to a career as early as men; that (2) most workers remain in sexually segregated jobs, many by choice; and that (3) women may have shorter job tenure because they take time off to have children.[84]

Perhaps the major need is for imaginative, creative organizational responses to accommodate the needs of the new workforce and the flexible family. For example, there are not many executives who can appreciate or allow that the skill of time management at home might be applied to office management. Adjustments to work schedules (flextime), extended maternity *and* paternity leaves, and quality day care based near the job come a little closer to workable solutions. Wang Laboratories, Inc., and Stride Rite Corp. have begun model day-care projects that might well become blueprints for other firms to follow. Chapter 9 will consider this issue in greater detail.

The Aging Workforce

It was not too long ago that we used to hear predictions about the "greening" of America. Today organizations are more concerned about the "graying" of America and the composite effects of demographic trends, improvements in life expectancy, and changes in social legislation. Consider some demographic trends forecast by the Bureau of the Census: A middle-aged bulge is forming in the United States as a consequence of the 43 million babies born in the years immediately following World War II. Eventually the 35- to 45-year-old age group will increase by 80 percent, and by the year 2020 this group will be reaching age 65, increasing the relative size of that population from 12 to 17 percent of all Americans, a jump from 31 to 52 million people.[19]

Based on the rate of this change, the population between the ages of 62 and 64 will not be affected dramatically until the year 2000. Between 2000 and 2010 it will grow at a 48 percent rate. However, to assume that there is no cause for concern until 1999 would be an error, for this group will be moving through several critical career phases before reaching the preretirement years.

On top of all this, the 1986 amendments to the Age Discrimination in Employment Act (which eliminated mandatory retirement at any age for most employees) further heighten the concern about job performance in the later years. The actual impact of the legislation depends, of course, on how older workers respond to the opportunity to remain on the job. Labor force participation rates are dropping for workers over age 55. In view of this trend, some companies are concluding that early retirements will offset the effects of extended tenure possibilities.

Research suggests that such a trend reflects worker income, education, job conditions, and retirement security. Dissatisfied workers and those with better pension plans seem more likely to opt out earlier.

Yet, tight labor markets will put increased pressure on employers to make work more attractive than retirement, and to use older workers more effectively. Older workers have much to offer, and in a later section we will examine what managers can do to retain them.

The chapter opening vignette illustrates the difficulties associated with managing a multicultural, multiethnic workforce. Whenever heterogeneous groups must work together, the possibility of unfair discrimination exists. Civil rights laws have been passed at the federal and state levels to provide remedies for job applicants or employees who feel they have been victims of unfair discrimination. From a managerial perspective, it is important to understand the rights as well as the obligations of employers, job candidates, and employees. Ignorance in this area can turn out to be *very* expensive. Let us begin, therefore, by considering the meaning and forms of unfair discrimination.

UNFAIR DISCRIMINATION: WHAT IS IT?

Civil rights laws, judicial interpretations of the laws, and the many sets of guidelines issued by state and federal regulatory agencies have outlawed discrimination based on race, religion, national origin, age, sex, and physical disability. In short, they have attempted to frame national policy on *equal employment opportunity (EEO)*. Although no law has ever attempted to define precisely the term *discrimination*, in the employment context it can be viewed broadly as the giving of an unfair advantage (or disadvantage) to the members of a particular group in comparison to the members of other groups.[50] The disadvantage (sometimes known as an "adverse impact") usually results in the denial or restriction of employment opportunities or in an inequality in the terms or benefits of employment.

It is important to note that whenever there are more candidates than available positions, it is necessary to select some in preference to others. Selection implies exclusion. And as long as the exclusion is based upon what can be demonstrated to be job-related criteria, then that kind of discrimination is entirely proper. It is only when candidates are excluded on some basis not related to the job (e.g., age, race, sex, or any characteristic common to a particular group but not having anything to do with ability to learn and do the work required by the job) that comprises unlawful and unfair discrimination.

Despite federal and state laws on these issues, they represent the basis of an enormous volume of court cases, indicating that stereotypes and prejudices do not die quickly or easily. Discrimination is a subtle and complex phenomenon that can take at least five different forms:[50]

1. *Intentional discrimination* is an open expression of hatred, disrespect, or inequality, knowingly directed against members of a particular group, regardless of the job-relevant capabilities of individuals. Examples are:

- Minimum qualifications that exclude all members of a particular race, sex, or age group
- Help-wanted ads that list jobs under separate "male" and "female" headings

2. *Unequal treatment* is a form of discrimination that uses one set of standards, procedures, or facilities with respect to a particular group and uses some other set of standards, procedures, and facilities to treat all other groups. Examples are:

- The use of specific tests, specific test conditions, or cutoff scores for the members of a particular race, sex, or age group, with different tests, test conditions, or cutoff scores used for other groups
- Separate job classifications, salary ranges, lists of eligible candidates, or seniority lists on the basis of race, sex, or age

3. *Unequal-effect discrimination* is what you get if you could turn unequal-treatment discrimination inside out. With unequal-effect discrimination, identical standards, procedures, or facilities are applied to everyone, despite the fact that they have an adverse effect on the members of a particular group. Examples are:

- Recruitment ads placed in media that appeal predominantly to the members of a particular race, sex, or age group, with no comparable advertising being placed in other media that appeal to other groups
- Job evaluation procedures that result in different salary levels for the members of a particular race, sex, or age group

The only exception is when these standards, procedures, methods, or facilities are demonstrably legitimate business or operational necessities. Examples of allowable exceptions are:

- Recruitment ads that seek specifically to hire members of a particular religion to teach in a denominational school
- Licensure requirements, as with registered nurses, that are required by state law

4. *Continuation of past effects discrimination* exists in the form of any standard, procedure, or facility that *perpetuates* the disadvantages suffered by the members of particular groups as the result of past discrimination. Examples are:

- Word-of-mouth recruitment methods among present employees when, through past unfair discrimination, those employees are all white males

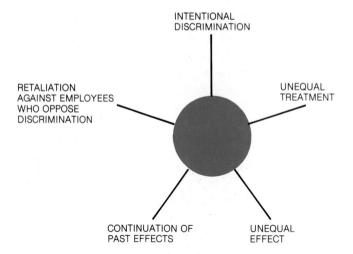

FIGURE 3-1

The various forms of unfair discrimination in employment.

- Maximum-age requirements for employment when particular groups have been denied employment previously due to discrimination on the basis of race, sex, or ethnic group (the maximum-age requirement perpetuates the disadvantages suffered by individuals in these groups)

    5. *Retaliation against people who oppose discrimination*, such as coercion, intimidation, or any other action directed against any person because she or he has opposed discriminatory practices, made charges, or in any manner participated in an investigation, proceeding, or hearing regarding alleged unlawful discriminatory practices. Examples are:

- Dismissal, suspension, transfer, or demotion of an employee who has filed discrimination complaints
- Permitting employees to intimidate or harass coworkers who have filed discrimination complaints

These five forms of unfair discrimination are illustrated graphically in Figure 3-1.

THE LEGAL CONTEXT OF PERSONNEL DECISIONS

Now that we understand the several forms that unfair discrimination can take, let us consider the major federal laws governing employment. They fall into two broad classes:

1. Laws that provide *absolute* prohibitions against unfair discrimination
2. Laws that require nondiscrimination as a *condition* for receiving federal funds (e.g., contracts, grants, revenue-sharing entitlements)

The particular laws we shall discuss within each category are:

Absolute prohibition	Conditional on federal funding
Thirteenth and Fourteenth Amendments to the U.S. Constitution	Executive Orders 11246, 11375, and 11478
Civil Rights Acts of 1866 and 1871	Rehabilitation Act (1973)
Equal Pay Act (1963)	Vietnam Era Veterans Readjustment Act (1974)
Title VII of the 1964 Civil Rights Act	
Age Discrimination in Employment Act (1967), as amended in 1986	
Immigration Reform and Control Act (1986)	
Americans with Disabilities Act of 1990	

Involuntary Servitude

The Thirteenth Amendment to the U.S. Constitution became effective on December 18, 1865; its main purpose was the abolition of slavery. In part, it states: "Neither slavery nor involuntary servitude, except as punishment for crime whereof the party shall have been duly convicted, shall exist within the United States, or any place subject to their jurisdiction." Traditionally the Thirteenth Amendment has been applied only in cases involving racial discrimination as a basis for the elimination of slavery and the "badges" (symbols) and "incidents" of slavery. However, any form of discrimination can be considered a badge or incident of slavery and is therefore liable to legal action under the Thirteenth Amendment.[32]

Equal Protection

In 1868 the Constitution was amended to require all state and local governments to provide for all people "equal protection of the laws." Discrimination against any particular person or class is therefore prohibited not only in employment but also in the provision of public services (e.g., education, zoning, police protection).

The Fourteenth Amendment was used as the legal basis for suit in the landmark Supreme Court case, *Bakke v. Regents of the University of California*.[4] The central issue in the case was the legality of the admissions policy of the University of California at Davis medical school. The Davis system set aside 16 of 100 places in its entering classes for "disadvantaged" applicants who were members of racial minority groups. Since this admissions policy was a formal, numerically based racial quota system, whites could compete for only 84 of the 100 places, while minorities could compete for all 100. The Court ruled that the Fourteenth Amendment had been violated since all individuals were not treated equally; the admissions program had disregarded the white individual's right to equal protection of the laws. Moreover, there was no previous history of racial discrimination at the school that might have justified a program of preferential selection in order to make up for past unlawful discrimination.

The Court also addressed the legality of "affirmative action" programs—*those actions appropriate to overcome the effects of past or present policies, practices, or other barriers to equal employment opportunity.*[50] The Court said that such programs are permissible as long as they consider applicants on an individual basis and do not set aside a rigid number of places for which whites cannot compete. Thus personnel selection decisions must be made on an individual, case-by-case basis. Race can be taken into account along with grades and extracurricular activities, for example, as one factor in an applicant's favor, but the overall decision to select or reject must be made on the basis of a combination of factors and not on the basis of race alone.

The Civil Rights Acts of 1866 and 1871

The Thirteenth and Fourteenth Amendments both grant Congress the power to enforce their provisions by enacting appropriate legislation. The Civil Rights Act of 1866 grants all citizens the right to make and enforce contracts for employment, and the Civil Rights Act of 1871 grants all citizens the right to sue in federal court if they feel they have been deprived of any rights or privileges guaranteed by the Constitution and laws.

Until recently, both of these laws were viewed narrowly as tools for Reconstruction era racial problems. This is no longer so. In *Johnson v. Railway Express Agency*, the Supreme Court held that while the Civil Rights Act of 1866 on its face relates primarily to racial discrimination in the making and enforcement of contracts, it also provides a federal remedy against racial discrimination in private employment.[48] It is a powerful remedy. Under this act, individuals are entitled to both equitable and legal relief, including compensatory and, under certain circumstances, punitive damages. And unlike Title VII (which will be discussed shortly), back-pay awards are not limited to 2 years. However, in *Patterson v. McLean Credit Union*[71] the Supreme Court ruled that the law does not cover cases of racial harassment or other discriminatory conduct by an employer *after* a person is hired.

The 1866 law also has been used recently to broaden the definition of racial discrimination originally applied to blacks. In a unanimous decision, the Supreme Court ruled in 1987 that race was equated with ethnicity during the legislative debate after the Civil War, and therefore Arabs, Jews, and other ethnic groups thought of as "white" are not barred from suing under the 1866 act. The Court held that Congress intended to protect identifiable classes of persons who are subjected to intentional discrimination solely because of their ancestry or ethnic characteristics. Under the law, therefore, race involves more than just skin pigment.[20]

The Equal Pay Act of 1963

This act was passed as an amendment to an earlier compensation-related law, the Fair Labor Standards Act of 1938. For those employers subject to the Fair Labor Standards Act (i.e., those engaged in interstate or foreign commerce or in the production of goods for such commerce), the Equal Pay Act requires that men and women working for the same establishment be paid the same rate of pay for work that is substantially equal in skill, effort, responsibility, and working conditions. Pay differentials are legal and appropriate if they are based upon seniority, merit, piece-rate payment systems, or any factor other than sex. Moreover, in correcting any inequity under the Equal Pay Act, employers must raise the rate of lower-paid employees, not lower the rate of higher-paid employees.

Hundreds of equal-pay suits were filed (predominantly by women) during the 1970s and early 1980s. For individual companies the price can be quite high. For example, at Chicago's Harris Trust, the company agreed to pay $14 million in back wages to thousands of female workers in order to settle a 12-year-old lawsuit. The women claimed that they were treated differently solely because of their sex. For example, female trainees were required to type, but male trainees were not.

Even before the decision, however, the bank had come a long way. When the suit was filed in 1977, Harris had five female vice presidents. By 1989, 102 out of 380 vice presidents were female.[12]

Title VII of the Civil Rights Act of 1964

The Civil Rights Act of 1964 is divided into several sections, or titles, each dealing with a particular facet of discrimination (e.g., voting rights, public accommodations, public education). Title VII is most relevant to the employment context, for it prohibits discrimination on the basis of race, color, religion, sex, or national origin in all aspects of employment (including apprenticeship programs). Title VII is the most important federal EEO law because it contains the broadest coverage, prohibitions, and remedies. Through it, the Equal Employment Opportunity Commission (EEOC) was created to ensure that employers, employment agencies, and labor organizations comply with Title VII.

Some may ask why we need such a law. As an expression of social policy, the law was passed to guarantee that people would be considered for jobs not on the basis of the color of their skin, or their religion, or their gender, or their national origin, but rather on the basis of individual abilities and talents that are necessary to perform a job.

In 1972 the coverage of Title VII was expanded. It now includes (1) both public and private employers (including state and local governments and public and private educational institutions) with 15 or more employees, (2) labor organizations with 15 or more members, and (3) both public and private employment agencies. The 1972 amendments also prohibited the denial, termination, or suspension of government contracts (without a special hearing) if an employer has and is following an affirmative action plan accepted by the federal government for the same facility within the past 12 months. Finally, back-pay awards in Title VII cases are limited to 2 years.

Elected officials and their appointees are excluded from Title VII coverage, but they are still subject to the Fourteenth Amendment and the Civil Rights Acts of 1866 and 1871. The following are also specifically exempted from Title VII coverage:

1. *Bona fide occupational qualifications (BFOQs).* Discrimination on the basis of race, religion, sex, or national origin is permissible when any of these factors are bona fide occupational qualifications for employment, that is, when any of them is considered "reasonably necessary to the operation of that particular business or enterprise." The burden of proof rests with the employer to demonstrate BFOQs. (According to one personnel director, the only legitimate BFOQs that she could think of are sperm donor and wet nurse!) Both the EEOC and the courts interpret BFOQs quite narrowly.[4] Preferences of the employer, coworkers, or clients are irrelevant and do not constitute BFOQs.

2. *Seniority systems.* As we shall see shortly, the legal status of seniority has been hotly contested in the courts. Title VII explicitly permits bona fide seniority, merit, or incentive systems "provided that such differences are not the result of an intention to discriminate."

3. *Preemployment inquiries.* Inquiries regarding such matters as race, sex, or ethnic group are permissible as long as they can be shown to be job-related. Even if not job-related, some inquiries (e.g., regarding race or sex) are often necessary to meet the reporting requirements of federal regulatory agencies. Applicants provide this information on a voluntary basis.

4. *Testing.* An employer may give or act upon any professionally developed ability test provided the test is not used as a vehicle to discriminate unfairly on the basis of race, color, religion, sex, or national origin.

5. *Preferential treatment.* The Supreme Court has ruled that Title VII does not *require* the granting of preferential treatment to individuals or groups because of their race, sex, religion, or national origin on account of existing imbalances:

> The burden which shifts to the employer is merely that of proving that he based his employment decision on a legitimate consideration, and not an illegitimate one such as race.... Title VII forbids him from having as a goal a work force selected by any proscribed discriminatory practice, but it does not impose a duty to adopt a hiring procedure that maximizes hiring of minority employees. (ref. 33)

6. *Veterans' preference rights.* These are not repealed or modified in any way by Title VII. In *Personnel Administrator of Massachusetts v. Feeney*, the Supreme Court held that while veterans' preference does have an adverse impact on women's job opportunities, this was not caused by an *intent* to discriminate against women.[73] Both men and women veterans receive the same preferential treatment, and male nonveterans are at the same disadvantage as female nonveterans.

**INTERNATIONAL APPLICATION: DOES TITLE VII COVER AMERICAN
CITIZENS WORKING IN FOREIGN OFFICES OF U.S. COMPANIES?**

According to a 1990 ruling by the Fifth Circuit Court of Appeals (upheld by the
Supreme Court in 1991), the answer is no. Such employees are governed by the
discrimination laws of the country they are working in, not by Title VII. If Congress
had wanted the statute to apply overseas, it would have specifically said so, declared
the court.

The issue is particularly important to large, multinational corporations, which must
contend with a variety of sometimes conflicting laws in different countries. According
to the Arabian American Oil Company, the defendant in the case, such coverage is
not necessary since most countries have adopted discrimination laws that protect
overseas workers. However, the plaintiff's attorney argued that few, if any, of those
laws are as strong as Title VII, and that the court's decision substantially weakens
employee protections. "If a company wants to get rid of an employee, all it has to
do is transfer him overseas and then fire him," he asserted.[37]

---

7. *National security*. Discrimination is permitted under Title VII when it is
deemed necessary to protect the national security (e.g., against members of the
Communist party).

Initially it appeared that these exemptions (summarized in Figure 3-2) would
blunt the overall impact of the law significantly. However, it soon became clear
that they would be interpreted very narrowly both by the EEOC and by the courts.

**EXEMPTIONS TO
TITLE VII COVERAGE**

BONA FIDE OCCUPATIONAL
QUALIFICATIONS

SENIORITY SYSTEMS

PREEMPLOYMENT INQUIRIES

TESTING

VETERAN'S PREFERENCE RIGHTS

NATIONAL SECURITY

FIGURE 3-2
The six exemptions to
Title VII coverage.

The Age Discrimination in Employment Act of 1967

As amended in 1986, this act prohibits discrimination in pay, benefits, or continued employment for employees over the age of 40, unless an employer can demonstrate that age is a BFOQ for the job in question. Like Title VII, this law is administered by the EEOC. A key objective of the law is to prevent financially troubled companies from singling out older employees when there are cutbacks. However, the EEOC has ruled that when there are cutbacks, older workers can waive their rights to sue under this law (e.g., in return for sweetened benefits for early retirement) as long as the waiver is voluntary and written simply.[55]

Increasingly, older workers are being asked to sign such waivers in exchange for enhanced retirement benefits. For example, at AT&T Communications, Inc., employees who signed waivers received severance pay equal to 5 percent of current pay times the number of years of service. For those without waivers, the company offered a multiplier of 3 percent. The practice is stirring an emotional and legal debate, with companies defending the waivers as a necessary business tool, and employee rights advocates arguing that they are exploitative.

Companies that require such waivers hope to insulate themselves from age discrimination lawsuits, over 15,000 of which are filed with the EEOC every year. Although only a fraction of such cases ever get to court, the stakes can be high and the defense expensive.

To date, five federal appeals courts have ruled that the waivers are valid when they are "knowing and voluntary," that is, the employee has not been coerced into signing. The courts generally consider the employee's education and business experience, whether the employee was encouraged to see a lawyer, and how much time the employee was given to think about the waiver before being asked to sign.[47]

The Immigration Reform and Control Act of 1986

This law applies to *every* employer in the United States, even to those with only one employee. It also applies to every employee—whether full-time, part-time, temporary, or seasonal. This act makes the enforcement of national immigration policy the job of every employer. While its provisions are complex, the basic features of the law fall into four broad categories:[13]

1. Employers may not hire or continue to employ "unauthorized aliens" (that is, those not legally authorized to work in this country).
2. Employers must verify the identity and work authorization of every new employee. Employers must examine documents provided by job applicants (e.g., U.S. passports for U.S. citizens; "green cards" for resident aliens, showing identity and work authorization). Both employer and employee then sign a form (I-9), attesting under penalty of perjury that the employee is lawfully eligible to work in the United States.

3. Employers with 4 to 14 employees may not discriminate on the basis of citizenship or national origin. Those with 15 or more employees are already prohibited from national origin discrimination by Title VII. However, this prohibition is tempered by an exception that allows employers to select an applicant who is a U.S. citizen over an alien when the two applicants are equally qualified.

4. "Amnesty" rights of certain illegal aliens. Those who can prove that they have resided in the United States continuously from January 1982 to November 6, 1986 (the date of the law's enactment), are eligible for temporary, and ultimately for permanent, resident status.

Penalties for noncompliance are severe. For example, for failure to comply with the verification rules, fines range from $100 to $1000 for *each* employee whose identity and work authorization have not been verified. The act also provides for criminal sanctions for employers who engage in a pattern or practice of violations.

This became obvious in 1989 when the government imposed a record fine of $580,000 against a South Carolina pillow factory accused of hiring more than 100 illegal aliens, including a 12-year-old boy. Further, the company, its owners, and nine managers were indicted by a federal grand jury on charges of illegally recruiting and harboring 117 illegal aliens. Such charges carry maximum prison terms of 653 years and fines totaling $5.1 million.[2]

Americans with Disabilities Act of 1990

Passed to protect the estimated 43 million Americans with disabilities, this law is effective in July 1992 for employers with 25 or more employees, and in July 1994 for employers with 15 or more employees. Persons with disabilities are protected from discrimination in employment, transportation, and public accommodation.

"Disability" is a physical or mental impairment that substantially limits one or more major life activities, such as walking, talking, seeing, hearing, or working. Persons are protected if they have a record of such impairment or if the employer *thinks* it is an impairment (e.g., a person with diabetes under control). Rehabilitated drug and alcohol abusers are protected, but current abusers who cannot perform their jobs or who pose a threat to their employer's property or to others are not protected under the act. The law also protects persons who have tested positive for the AIDS virus.[18] There are five practical implications for employers.

- Any factory, office, retail store, bank, hotel, or other building open to the public will have to be made accessible to those with physical disabilities (e.g., by installing ramps, elevators, telephones with amplifiers). "Expensive" will be no excuse, unless such modifications will lead an employer to go out of business or to suffer losses to the point where significant layoffs will occur.

- Employers must make "reasonable accommodations" for disabled job applicants or employees (e.g., by restructuring job and training programs, modifying work

With reasonable accommodation, disabled people can perform many different jobs.

schedules, or purchasing new equipment that is "user friendly" to blind or deaf people).

- Preemployment physicals will now be permissible only if all employees are subject to them, and they cannot be given until after a job is offered. Further, job applications can ask only if there is any reason that an applicant can't perform the job in question at the current time. They can't ask about physical disabilities in general.

- Medical information on employees must be kept separate from other personal or work-related information about them, lest a personnel decision be based upon medical information that is not relevant to the matter in question.

- Drug testing rules remain intact. An employer can still prohibit the use of illegal drugs and alcohol at the workplace, and continue to give drug and alcohol tests.

This law includes all of the remedies of Title VII of the Civil Rights Act of 1964, including reinstatement and back pay.[68] What will be the cost to employers? According to the EEOC, making such accommodations will cost employers $16 million a year, while providing productivity gains of $164 million and reduced government support payments and higher tax revenues of $222 million a year.[52]

This completes the discussion of "absolute prohibitions" against discrimination.

The following sections discuss nondiscrimination as a basis for eligibility for federal funds.

Executive Orders 11246, 11375, and 11478

Presidential Executive Orders in the realm of employment and discrimination are aimed specifically at government contractors and subcontractors. The requirements of these orders are parallel to those of Title VII.

In 1965 President Johnson issued Executive Order 11246, prohibiting discrimination on the basis of race, color, religion, or national origin as a condition of employment by federal agencies, contractors, and subcontractors.

In 1967, Executive Order 11375 prohibited discrimination in employment based on sex.

Executive Order 11478 was issued by President Nixon in 1969. It has three major parts:

Part I prescribes that employment policies in the federal government be based on merit and fitness, and not on race, color, sex, religion, or national origin. It supersedes Part I of the earlier orders and requires the head of each federal agency to establish and maintain an EEO program. The U.S. Office of Personnel Management is responsible for overall supervision of this program.

Part II of the order specifies that all federal contractors or subcontractors doing as little as $10,000 worth of government business are required to comply with the provisions of the order.

Part III makes each government agency dealing with contractors responsible for seeing that they, as well as their subcontractors, comply with nondiscrimination in employment. Unions are wholly exempt from the provisions of the order, but they still remain subject to Title VII of the 1964 Civil Rights Act.

Enforcement of executive orders Executive Order 11246 provides considerable enforcement power, administered by the Department of Labor through its Office of Federal Contract Compliance Programs (OFCCP). Upon a finding by the OFCCP of noncompliance with the order, the EEOC will be notified if it appears that Title VII has also been violated, the Department of Justice may be advised to institute criminal proceedings, and the secretary of labor may cancel or suspend current contracts as well as the right to bid on future contracts. Needless to say, noncompliance can be *very* expensive.

The Rehabilitation Act of 1973

This act requires federal contractors (those receiving more than $2500 in federal contracts annually) and subcontractors actively to recruit qualified handicapped people and to use their talents to the fullest extent possible. The legal requirements are similar to those of the Americans with Disabilities Act.

The purpose of this act is to eliminate *systemic discrimination*, i.e., any business practice that results in the denial of equal employment opportunity.[46] Hence the act emphasizes "screening in" applicants, not screening them out. It is enforced by the Employment Standards Administration of the Department of Labor.

The Vietnam Era Veterans Readjustment Act of 1974

Federal contractors and subcontractors are required under this act to take affirmative action to ensure equal employment opportunity for Vietnam era veterans (August 5, 1964, to May 7, 1975). This act is enforced by the OFCCP.

FEDERAL ENFORCEMENT AGENCIES: EEOC AND OFCCP

The Equal Employment Opportunity Commission is an independent regulatory agency whose five commissioners (one of whom is chairperson) are appointed by the President and confirmed by the Senate for terms of 5 years. No more than three of the commissioners may be from the same political party. Like the OFCCP, the EEOC sets policy and in individual cases determines whether there is "reasonable cause" to believe that unlawful discrimination has occurred. If reasonable cause is found, then the EEOC can sue either on its own behalf or on behalf of a claimant. As far as the employer is concerned, the simplest and least costly procedure is to establish a system to resolve complaints internally. However, if this system fails or if the employer does not make available an avenue for such complaints, an aggrieved individual (or group) can file a formal complaint with the EEOC. The process is shown graphically in Figure 3-3.

As Figure 3-3 indicates, complaints must be filed within 180 days of an alleged violation. If that requirement is satisfied, the EEOC immediately refers the complaint to a state agency charged with enforcement of fair employment laws (if one exists) for 60 days. If the complaint cannot be resolved within that time, the state agency can file suit in a state district court and appeal any decision to a state appellate court, the state supreme court, or to the U.S. Supreme Court. Alternatively to filing suit, the state agency may redefer to the EEOC. Again voluntary reconciliation is sought, but if this fails, the EEOC may refer the case to the Justice Department (if the defendant is a public employer) or file suit in federal district court (if the defendant is a private employer). Like state court decisions, federal court decisions may be appealed to one of 12 U.S. Courts of Appeal (corresponding to the geographical region or "circuit" in which the case arose). In turn, these decisions may be appealed to the U.S. Supreme Court, although very few cases are actually heard by the Supreme Court. Generally the Court will grant *certiorari* (review) when two or more circuit courts have reached different conclusions on the same point of law or when a major question of constitutional interpretation is involved. If certiorari is denied, then the lower court's decision is binding.

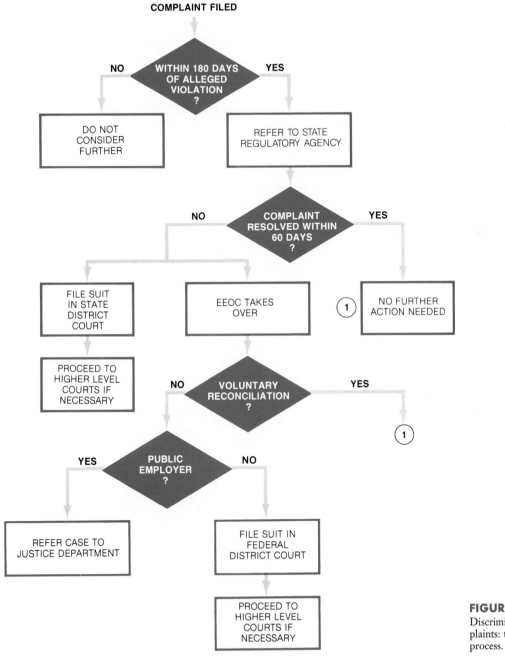

FIGURE 3-3
Discrimination complaints: the formal process.

EEOC Guidelines

The EEOC has issued a number of guidelines for Title VII compliance. Among these are guidelines on discrimination because of religion, national origin, sex, and pregnancy; guidelines on affirmative action programs; guidelines on employee selection procedures; and a policy statement on preemployment inquiries. These guidelines are not laws, although the Supreme Court indicated in *Albemarle v. Moody* that they are entitled to "great deference."[1] Violators may incur EEOC sanctions and possible court action.

Information gathering This is another major EEOC function, for each organization in the United States with 100 or more employees must file an annual report (EEO-1) detailing the number of women and minorities employed in nine different job categories ranging from laborers to managers and professionals. Over 300,000 organizations file these forms annually with the EEOC. Through computerized analysis of the forms, the EEOC is able to identify broad patterns of discrimination (systemic discrimination) and to attack them through class action suits. In any given year the EEOC typically has about 500 class action suits in progress, receives 70,000 complaints, and wins monetary awards that total over $36 million.[89]

The Office of Federal Contract Compliance Programs (OFCCP)

Contract compliance means that in addition to quality, timeliness, and other requirements of federal contract work, contractors and subcontractors must also meet equal employment opportunity and affirmative action requirements. These cover all aspects of employment, including recruitment, hiring, training, pay, seniority, promotion, and even benefits.

Companies are willing to go to considerable lengths to avoid loss of government contracts. Over a quarter of a million companies, employing 27 million workers and providing the government with over $100 billion in construction, supplies, equipment, and services, are subject to contract compliance enforcement by the OFCCP.[62] Contractors and subcontractors with more than $50,000 in government business and with 50 or more employees must prepare and implement written affirmative action programs.

In jobs where women and minorities are *underrepresented* in the workforce relative to their availability in the labor force, employers must establish goals and timetables for hiring and promotion. Theoretically, goals and timetables are distinguishable from rigid quotas in that they are flexible objectives that can be met in a realistic amount of time (Figure 3-4). Goals and timetables are not required under the handicapped workers and Vietnam veterans laws.

In its 1986 ruling in *Local 28 Sheet Metal Workers v. EEOC*, the Supreme Court found that Congress specifically endorsed the concept of non-victim-specific racial hiring goals to achieve compliance.[91] Further, the court noted the benefits of flexible affirmative action rather than rigid application of a color-blind policy that would deprive employers of flexibility in administering human resources. How do

QUOTAS: INFLEXIBLE; *MUST* BE MET IN A SPECIFIED AMOUNT OF TIME

GOALS AND TIMETABLES: FLEXIBLE; *CAN* BE MET IN A REALISTIC AMOUNT OF TIME

FIGURE 3-4
The distinction between rigid quotas and goals and timetables.

employers do in practice? One 7-year study of companies that set annual goals for increasing black male employment found that only one-tenth of the goals were achieved. Some may see this as a sign of failure, but it also reflects the fact that the goals were not rigid quotas. "Companies promise more than they can deliver, . . . but the ones that promise more do deliver more" (ref. 72, p. E5).

When a compliance review by the Office of Federal Contract Compliance Programs indicates problems that cannot easily be resolved, it tries to reach a conciliation agreement with the employer. Such an agreement might include back pay, seniority credit, special recruitment efforts, promotion, or other forms of relief for the victims of unlawful discrimination. In fiscal 1980, for example, the OFCCP collected over $9 million in pack pay.[58]

The conciliation agreement is the OFCCP's preferred route, but if such efforts are unsuccessful, formal enforcement action is necessary. Contractors and subcontractors are entitled to a hearing before a judge. If conciliation is not reached before or after the hearing, employers may lose their government contracts, their payments may be withheld by the government, or they may be debarred from any government contract work. Debarment is the OFCCP's ultimate weapon, for it indicates in the most direct way possible that the U.S. government is serious about equal employment opportunity programs. Between 1965 and 1980, 24 companies were debarred from government work.[30]

EMPLOYMENT CASE LAW: SOME GENERAL PRINCIPLES

Although Congress enacts laws, the courts interpret the laws and determine how they shall be enforced. Such interpretations define what is called *case law*, which serves as a precedent to guide future legal decisions. And, of course, precedents are regularly subject to reinterpretation.

In the area of employment, a considerable body of case law has accumulated since 1964. Figure 3-5 illustrates areas where case law is developed most extensively. Lawsuits affecting virtually every aspect of employment have been filed, and in the following sections we shall consider some of the most significant de-

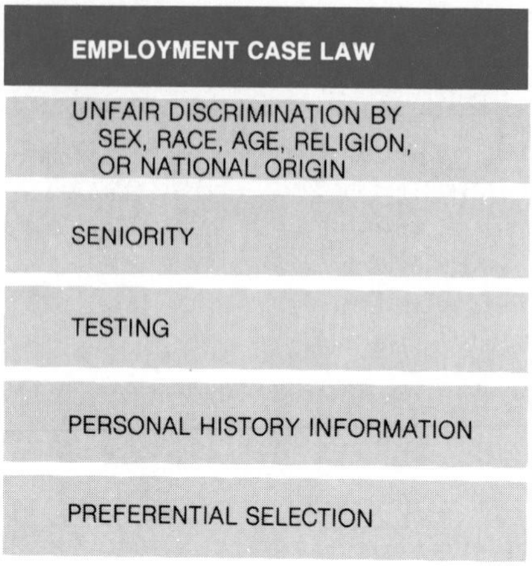

FIGURE 3-5
Areas comprising the main body of employment case law.

cisions to date. It should be pointed out that in bringing suit under Title VII, the first step is to establish a *prima facie* case of discrimination (i.e., a body of facts presumed to be true until proven otherwise). However, the nature of prima facie evidence differs depending on the type of case brought before the court. If an individual is alleging that a particular employment practice had a *disparate impact* on all members of a class that he or she represents, then prima facie evidence is presented when adverse impact is shown to exist. Adverse impact is usually demonstrated by showing that the selection rate for the group in question is less than 80 percent of the rate of the dominant group (e.g., white males). If the individual alleges that he or she was *treated* differently from others in the context of some employment practice, then a prima facie case is usually presented by satisfying a four-part test first specified in the *McDonnell-Douglas v. Green* case,[64] wherein a plaintiff must be able to demonstrate that:

1. She or he is a member of a class of persons protected by Title VII.
2. She or he applied for and qualified for a job for which the employer was seeking applicants.
3. Despite having the qualifications, the applicant was rejected.
4. After rejection, the position remained open, and the employer continued to seek applications from persons with the plaintiff's qualifications.

Sex Discrimination

Title VII explicitly states that the *individual*, not the group, is the appropriate unit to consider in discrimination proceedings. However, sex role stereotypes are deeply rooted in our society, with some jobs deemed absolutely inappropriate for members of a particular sex.

How about the job of partner in a major public accounting firm? Such was the issue in the case of *Price Waterhouse v. Hopkins*.[75] Ann Hopkins was not promoted to the rank of partner in the firm after she was evaluated by several male partners as being "too macho" and in need of a "charm school." Of the 88 candidates for partner (all but Hopkins were male), she had the best record at generating new business for the firm.

The Supreme Court ruled that the firm must show that it would not have promoted Hopkins based on purely nondiscriminatory factors. However, instead of having to present "clear and convincing evidence," the firm was required to back its claim with a "preponderance of the evidence"—a less rigorous standard. What happened to Ann Hopkins? By the time the Supreme Court issued its opinion, she had left the firm to assume a senior management position with the World Bank. Now consider another example.

Suppose you run an organization that has 238 skilled crafts positions—all filled by men. Suppose that only a 2-point difference in test scores separates the best-qualified man from the best-qualified woman. Only one promotional opportunity is available. What do you do? Until a landmark Supreme Court decision in 1987 (*Johnson v. Santa Clara Transportation Agency*[49]), if you promoted the woman you invited a lawsuit by the man. If you promoted the woman to correct past discrimination (thereby acknowledging past bias), you would invite discrimination suits by women. No longer. The Supreme Court ruled unambiguously that in traditionally sex-segregated jobs, a qualified woman can be promoted over a marginally better-qualified man to promote more balanced representation. The Court stressed the need for affirmative action plans to be flexible, gradual, and limited in their effect on whites and men. The Court also expressed disapproval of strict numerical quotas except where necessary (on a temporary basis) to remedy severe past discrimination.

Many employers are in similar positions. That is, they have not been proven guilty of past discrimination, but they have a significant underrepresentation of women or minorities in various job categories. This decision clearly put pressure on employers to institute voluntary affirmative action programs, but at the same time it also provided some welcome guidance on what they were permitted to do.

Pregnancy The Equal Employment Opportunity Commission's guidelines on the Pregnancy Discrimination Act of 1979 state:

> The basic principle of the Act is that women affected by pregnancy and related conditions must be treated the same as other applicants and employees on the basis of their ability or inability to work. A woman is therefore protected against such practices as being fired, or refused a job or promotion, merely because she is pregnant or has had an abortion. She usually cannot be forced to go on leave as long as she can still work. If other employees who take disability leave are entitled to get their jobs back when they are able to work again, so are women who have been unable to work because of pregnancy. (ref. 28)

In 1989 the EEOC received about 3600 complaints related to pregnancy (about one out of every 50 complaints the commission receives).[23] However, it is important to note that an employer is never *required* to give pregnant employees special treatment. If an organization provides no disability benefits or sick leave to other employees, it is not required to provide them for pregnant employees.[81] While the actual length of maternity leave is now an issue to be determined by the women's and/or the company's physician, a 1987 Supreme Court decision in *California Federal Savings and Loan v. Guerra* upheld a California law that provides for up to 4 months of unpaid leave for pregnancy disability.[17]

Economic pressures on employers may make legal action unnecessary in the future. Evidence now indicates that the vast majority of employers are doing their best to accommodate pregnant women through flexible work scheduling and generous maternity leave policies.[23] Given the number of women in the workforce of childbearing age, plus the tight labor markets in many areas of the country, there really is no other choice.

One large survey of company practices found that new mothers typically spend 1 to 3 months at home following childbirth, that job guarantees for returning mothers were provided by 35 percent of the companies, and that employers of 501 to 1000 employees are most likely to provide full pay.[74]

What percentage of women use disability benefits fully and then decide not to return to work? At Corning Glass, Inc., First Bank of Minneapolis, and Levi Straus & Co., over 80 percent *do* return to work. Moreover, the provision of maternity leave benefits has helped to establish good rapport with employees.[74]

How much do these extra benefits cost? The Health Insurance Association of America estimated that the extension of health insurance coverage to pregnancy-related conditions of women employees and employees' spouses would increase premiums by an average of 13 percent.[81]

Reproductive hazards Another way that sex discrimination may be perpetuated is by barring women from competing for jobs that pose occupational health hazards to their reproductive systems. In a landmark 1991 decision (*UAW v. Johnson Controls, Inc.*) the Supreme Court ruled that such "fetal protection" policies, which had been used by more than a dozen major companies, including General Motors, Du Pont, Monsanto, Olin, Firestone, and B.F. Goodrich, are a form of illegal sex discrimination that is prohibited by Title VII. At issue was the policy of Johnson Controls, Inc., a car battery manufacturer, that excluded women of childbearing age from jobs involving exposure to lead.[53] The company argued that its policy was based on the BFOQ exception to Title VII, because it was essential to a safe workplace.

The high court disagreed, and ruled that the BFOQ exception is a narrow one, limited to policies that are directly related to a worker's ability to do the job. "Women as capable of doing their jobs as their male counterparts may not be forced to choose between having a child and having a job. . . . Decisions about the welfare of future children must be left to the parents who conceive, bear, support, and raise them rather than to the employers who hire those parents," said the Court.[27,88]

What are businesses to do? Clearly they will have to provide more complete information to inform and warn female workers about fetal health risks on the job. They may also urge women to consult their physicians before starting such assignments. However, mere exclusion of workers, both unions and managers agree, does not address chemicals remaining in the workplace where other workers may be exposed. Nor are women more sensitive to reproductive hazards than men. Changing the workplace, rather than the workforce, is a more enlightened policy.

Sexual harassment In the vast majority of cases on this issue, females rather than males have suffered from sexual abuse at work. Such abuse may constitute illegal sex discrimination. It seems like only yesterday that sexual harassment was not a subject for legal concern. In 1936 one legal commentator expressed the typical (male) supervisor's attitude toward exploiting sexual consideration from female employees when he said, "There's no harm in asking!" At that time the courts found that a woman had no legal remedy unless she was actually assaulted or battered.[59] Today there is a broader view of what constitutes unacceptable behavior, but it is still surprisingly difficult to define sexual harassment.[92] Perhaps the best definition to date is that proposed by the Michigan Task Force on Sexual Harassment in the Workplace:

> Sexual harassment includes . . . continual or repeated abuse of a sexual nature including, but not limited to, graphic commentaries on the victim's body, sexually suggestive objects or pictures in the workplace, sexually degrading words used to describe the victim, or propositions of a sexual nature. Sexual harassment also includes the threat or insinuation that lack of sexual submission will adversely affect the victim's employment, wages, advancement, assigned duties or shifts, academic standing, or other conditions that affect the victim's "livelihood."

This definition specifies examples of unacceptable conduct in the workplace; it does not rely on the victim's perception of objectionable actions. Also, it limits the bringing of sexual harassment suits based on isolated incidents that are not part of a continual or repeated pattern of behavior.[59]

While there are few well-controlled studies of the incidence of sexual harassment, available data indicate that its incidence among working women ranges from about 30 to 50 percent. About 10 percent of women have quit their jobs because of sexual harassment.[42] It is perilous self-deception for a manager to believe that sexual harassment does not exist in his or her own organization.

The Equal Employment Opportunity Commission has issued guidelines on sexual harassment, indicating that it is a form of sex discrimination under Title VII of the 1964 Civil Rights Act. Courts generally have agreed with this position. However, this is true only when the harassment is a *condition of employment*. For example, consider the case of *Barnes v. Costle*: The plaintiff rebuffed her director's repeated sexual overtures. She ignored his advice that sexual intimacy was the path she should take to improve her career opportunities. Subsequently the director abolished her job. The court of appeals found that sexual cooperation was a condition of her employment, a condition the director did not impose upon males. Therefore, sex discrimination occurred and the employer was liable.[5]

The courts have gone even further, holding employers responsible even if they knew nothing about a supervisor's conduct. For example, a federal appeals court held Avco Corporation of Nashville, Tennessee, liable for the sexually harassing actions of one of its supervisors against two female secretaries working under his supervision. The court found that the employer had a policy against sexual harassment but failed to enforce it effectively. Both the company *and* the supervisor were held liable. Regarding the company's liability, the court noted: "Although Avco took remedial action once the plaintiffs registered complaints, its duty to remedy the problem, or at a minimum, inquire, was created earlier when the initial allegations of harassment were reported" (ref. 22, p. A1).

Such suits can be expensive. In November, 1982, eight women miners won a settlement from Consolidated Coal Co. in a landmark $5.5 million sexual harassment suit. Charging that their privacy had been invaded, the women claimed that male coal miners spied on them as they showered and dressed. A peephole was bored into the women's locker-room wall from a supervisor's office, and although managers knew about the hole for a year, they failed to fill it in. The company settled just before the summation of the case in federal district court.[90]

Preventive actions by employers What can an employer do to escape liability for the sexually harassing acts of its managers or workers? An effective policy should include the following features:

- A statement from the chief executive officer that states firmly that sexual harassment will not be tolerated
- A workable definition of sexual harassment that is publicized via staff meetings, bulletin boards, and employee handbooks
- An established complaint procedure to provide a vehicle for employees to report claims of harassment to their supervisors or to a neutral third party, such as the HR department
- A clear statement of sanctions for violators and protection for those who make charges
- Prompt investigation of every claim of harassment, no matter how trivial
- Preservation of all investigative information, with records of all such complaints kept in a central location
- Training of all managers and supervisors to recognize and respond to complaints, giving them written materials outlining their responsibilities and obligations when a complaint is made[69]

The courts have made it clear that employers are expected to take remedial action as soon as they become aware of sexual harassment (heterosexual by either sex or homosexual by either sex). Such action is not limited to supervisor-subordinate relationships. The EEOC's guidelines hold an employer liable even for harassment of an employee by a nonemployee, such as a customer. The grievance procedure should assist the employee in informing management of any problems. Management must then take immediate and firm action in order to avoid the legal liability possible under the EEOC's guidelines.[39]

Age Discrimination

The Equal Employment Opportunity Commission's guidelines on age discrimination emphasize that in order to discriminate fairly against employees over 40 years old, an employer must be able to demonstrate a "business necessity" for doing so. That is, it must be shown that age is a factor directly related to the safe and efficient operation of a business. To establish a prima facie case of age discrimination, an individual must show that:[77]

1. She or he is within the protected age group (over 40 years of age).
2. She or he is doing satisfactory work.
3. She or he was discharged despite satisfactory work performance.
4. The position was filled by a person younger than the person replaced.

For example, an employee named Schwager had worked for Sun Oil Ltd. for 18 years, and his retirement benefits were to be vested (i.e., not contingent on future service) at 20 years. When the company reorganized and had to reduce the size of its workforce, the average age of those retained was 35 years, while the average age of those terminated was 45.7 years. The company was able to demonstrate, however, that economic considerations prompted the reorganization and that factors other than age were considered in Schwager's termination. The local manager had to let one person go, and he chose Schwager because he ranked lowest in overall job performance among salespeople in his district and did not measure up to their standards. Job performance, not age, was the reason for Schwager's termination.

In another case, *Hodgson v. Greyhound Lines*, the Supreme Court upheld a lower court's ruling that the employer was able to show that age was related to the safe conduct of the business.[43] Greyhound contended that age was a bona fide occupational qualification and refused to hire applicants over 40. In the words of the court:

> We find ... compelling ... the statistical evidence reflecting, among other things, that Greyhound's safest driver is one who has 16 to 20 years of driving experience with Greyhound and is between 50 and 55 years of age, an optimum blend of age and experience with Greyhound which could never be attained in hiring an applicant 40 years of age or over.

To some, lifting the cap off mandatory retirements at age 70 signals a flood of age-related lawsuits. In many ways, however, it is much ado about nothing. The

INTERNATIONAL APPLICATION: AGE BIAS IN EUROPE

Unlike America, Europe lacks tough laws that outlaw age discrimination. Employers routinely run advertisements seeking workers under 40, force staffers as young as 55 to retire, and fire people simply for being too old.[61] In fact, rampant discrimination against older Europeans is just starting to decline, thanks to a scarcity of young people, and the spread of U.S.-style advocacy groups.

European units of American multinationals typically copy such local practices, long outlawed at home. The British unit of Ford Motor Company didn't ban age-specific recruitment advertising until November, 1988, when the auto giant and its unions negotiated an equal employment opportunity policy covering age bias.

Such policies are rare in corporate Britain, but age barriers are tumbling among employers who are courting older workers for vacancies. Why? The number of Britons aged 16 to 20 will plummet by a third between 1989 and 1995, and a third of the British population will be more than 50 years old by the year 2000.

average retirement age in the United States is now 63; it has been falling gradually for the last 25 years despite age protections.[15] Many workers are eager to retire well before the traditional (and arbitrary) age of 65.

Employers can still fire unproductive workers, but the key is to base personnel decisions on ability, not on age.[66] By offering truly voluntary early retirement programs (not "either accept this or your're fired"), firms can still plan for the future. For example, a federal judge recently dismissed a suit brought by four employees of the National Geographic Society challenging the company's early retirement program. The judge reasoned that since the workers had more than 2 months to decide about the plan, and that it really was a benefit, the company could not be sued.[54]

Seniority

Title VII explicitly permits bona fide seniority systems as long as they were not devised with the intent to discriminate unfairly. There has been considerable litigation over seniority (the term has been in vogue since the nineteenth century), but it was not until the Supreme Court's ruling in *California Brewers Assoc. v. Bryant* that a legal definition of the concept was issued.[16] The Court stated:

> "Seniority" is a term that connotes length of employment. A "seniority system" is a scheme that, alone or in tandem with "non-seniority" criteria, allots to employees ever-improving employment rights and benefits as their relative lengths of pertinent employment increase. (ref. 16, pp. 605, 606)

Although the prevalence of seniority clauses varies by type of industry, about 85 percent of union contracts contain such provisions.[67] They are major sources of legal and quasi-legal problems for both unions and management.[36] Legal disputes are subject to resolution by state or federal courts. Quasi-legal disputes are subject to resolution by joint union-management committees.

In the realm of quasi-legal affairs, seniority is the subject of many grievances. Collective bargaining contracts frequently require that personnel decisions regarding, for example, layoff or promotion be based upon a combination of seniority plus ability or qualifications. Grievances over such seniority provisions often are filed because the provisions are seldom precise about the manner of assessing worker ability.[21] In addition, seniority accounts for a substantial number of grievances in declining industries as workers strive to protect their rights to shrinking numbers of jobs.[65]

Unions and management have also encountered legal problems stemming from the impact of established seniority systems on programs designed to ensure equal employment opportunity. Three major seniority issues have been decided by the courts:

1. *Rightful place.* In *Franks v. Bowman Transportation Co.*, the Supreme Court ruled that Title VII does not bar relief in the form of retroactive seniority for minorities who were improperly denied employment opportunities after the effective date of the 1964 Civil Rights Act.[31] The Court concluded that without an award of seniority dating from the time of the company's refusal to hire each properly qualified minority applicant, an employee who applied for and attained such a position would never obtain his or her rightful place in the seniority hierarchy. For example, suppose a candidate applied for work and was unlawfully discriminated against in 1966, but, as a result of the time required to try the case, he or she was not authorized to reapply until 1976. Without an award of retroactive seniority, the candidate would lose 10 years' worth of seniority credit. This "rightful-place" approach has been adopted by the majority of courts evaluating seniority systems in Title VII cases.[36]

2. *Legality of "facially" neutral seniority systems that perpetuate minorities' employment disadvantage.* In 1977 the Supreme Court ruled in *International Brotherhood of Teamsters v. U.S.* that a bona fide seniority system initiated *prior* to the 1964 Civil Rights Act may apply different terms of employment if it operates in a neutral fashion and is not designed intentionally to discriminate because of race, color, religion, or national origin.[45]

A 1982 Supreme Court decision, *American Tobacco Co. v. Patterson*, extended the *Teamsters* decision to seniority systems implemented *after* 1965 (the effective date of the 1964 Civil Rights Act).[3] Unlike other measures used as a basis for staffing decisions (e.g., tests), the legality of seniority systems will not be judged in terms of adverse impact on women or minorities. The result of this ruling is to make it more difficult for civil rights groups and the EEOC to challenge seniority systems as biased.

3. *Last-hired-first-fired layoffs.* The courts have been quite clear in their rulings on the legitimacy of last-hired-first-fired layoffs (often referred to as LIFO, or last-in-first-out, layoffs) when such decisions cause a disproportionate reduction

in the number of minority and female employees. In two landmark decisions, *Firefighters Local Union No. 1784 v. Stotts*[29] (decided under Title VII) and *Wygant v. Jackson Board of Education*[91] (decided under the equal protection clause of the Fourteenth Amendment), the Supreme Court ruled that an employer may not protect the jobs of recently hired black employees at the expense of whites who have more seniority.[38]

Moreover, the court ruled in 1989 that challenges must be brought within 300 days of the adoption of a seniority system that is alleged to discriminate against blacks or women.[60]

Voluntary modifications of seniority policies for affirmative action purposes remain proper, but where a collective bargaining agreement exists, consent of the union is required. Moreover, in the unionized setting, courts have made it clear that the union must be a party to any decree that modifies a bona fide seniority system.[14]

Testing and Interviewing

Title VII clearly sanctions the use of "professionally developed" ability tests. Nevertheless, it took several landmark Supreme Court cases to clarify the proper role and use of tests. The first of these was *Griggs v. Duke Power Co.*, decided in favor of Griggs.[41] The employer was prohibited from requiring a high school education or the passing of an intelligence test as a condition of employment or job transfer where neither standard was shown to be significantly related to job performance:

> What Congress has forbidden is giving these devices and mechanisms controlling force unless they are demonstrably a reasonable measure of job performance. . . . What Congress has commanded is that any tests used must measure the person for the job and not the person in the abstract. (ref. 41, p. 428)

The ruling also included four other general principles:

1. The law prohibits not only open and deliberate discrimination but also practices that are fair in form but discriminatory in operation. For example, suppose an organization wants to use prior arrests as a basis for selection. In theory, arrests are a "neutral" practice since all persons are equally subject to arrest if they violate the law. However, if arrests cannot be shown to be job-related, and, in addition, if a significantly higher proportion of blacks than whites are arrested, then the use of arrests as a basis for selection is discriminatory in operation.

2. The employer bears the burden of proof that any requirement for employment is related to job performance. (The Supreme Court later reversed itself on this point in *Wards Cove Packing Co. v. Antonio*.[85] Plaintiffs must now identify specific policies or practices alleged as causing unlawful discrimination, and they must

also show that the employer has no legitimate business justification for the practices.)

3. It is not necessary for the plaintiff to prove that the discrimination was intentional; intent is irrelevant. If the standards result in discrimination, they are unlawful.

4. Job-related tests and other personnel selection procedures are legal and useful.

The confidentiality of individual test scores has also been addressed. In 1979 the Supreme Court affirmed the right of the Detroit Edison Co. to refuse to hand over to a labor union copies of aptitude tests taken by job applicants and to refuse to disclose individual test scores without the written consent of employees.[51]

As is well known, interviews are commonly used as bases for employment decisions to hire or to promote certain candidates in preference to others. Must such "subjective" assessment procedures satisfy the same standards of job relatedness as more "objective" procedures, such as written tests? If they produce an adverse impact against a protected group, the answer is yes, according to the Supreme Court in *Watson v. Fort Worth Bank & Trust*.[86]

As in its *Griggs* ruling, the court held that it is not necessary for the plaintiff to prove that the discrimination was intentional. If the ratings result in adverse impact, they are presumed to be unlawful, unless the employer can show some relationship between the content of the ratings and the requirements of a given job. This need not involve a formal validation study, although the court agreed unanimously that it is possible to conduct such studies when subjective assessment devices are used.[8] The lesson for employers? Be sure that there is a legitimate, job-related reason for every question raised in an employment or promotional interview. Limit questioning to "need to know," rather than "nice to know," information.

Personal History

Frequently job qualification requirements involve personal background information. If the requirements have the effect of denying or restricting equal employment opportunity, they may violate Title VII. For example, in the *Griggs v. Duke Power Co.* case, a purportedly neutral practice (the high school education requirement that excluded from employment a higher proportion of blacks than whites) was ruled unlawful because it had not been shown to be related to job performance.[41] Other allegedly neutral practices that have been struck down by the courts on the basis of non-job relevance include:

- Recruitment practices based upon present employee referrals, where the workforce is nearly all white to begin with.[26]
- Height and weight requirements.[24]
- Arrest records, because they show only that a person has been accused of a crime, not that she or he was guilty of it. Thus arrests may not be used as a

basis for selection decisions,[40] except in certain sensitive and responsible positions (e.g., police officer, school principal).[87]

■ Conviction records, unless the conviction is directly related to the work to be performed—for example, a person convicted of embezzlement applying for a job as a bank teller.[44]

Despite such decisions, it should be emphasized that personal-history items are not unlawfully discriminatory per se, but their use in each instance requires that job relevance be demonstrated. Just as with employment interviews, the employer should be collecting information on a "need to know," not on a "nice to know," basis.

Preferential Selection

In an ideal world, selection and promotion decisions would be "color-blind." That is, social policy as embodied in Title VII emphasizes that so-called reverse discrimination (discrimination against whites and in favor of minorities) is just as unacceptable as is discrimination by whites against minorities. As we saw earlier, this was decidedly not the situation in the *Regents of the University of California v. Bakke* case. However, since that case involved the legality of an affirmative action plan at a public educational institution, it did not affect private employers directly. The case of *United Steelworkers of America v. Weber* clearly did: Brian Weber, a white lab analyst at Kaiser Aluminum & Chemical Company's Grammercy, Louisiana, plant, brought suit under Title VII after he was bypassed for a crafts-retraining program in which the company and the union jointly agreed to reserve 50 percent of the available places for blacks.[82] As in *Regents of the University of California*, there was no proven record of bias at the plant on which to justify a quota. Thus the company and the union were caught in a dilemma. To eliminate the affirmative action plan was to run the risk of suits by minority employees and the loss of government contracts. To retain the plan when there was no previous history of proven discrimination was to run the risk of reverse discrimination suits by white employees. And to admit previous discrimination at the plant in order to justify the affirmative action plan was to *invite* suits by minority applicants and employees.

The Supreme Court ruled that employers can give preference to minorities and women in hiring for "traditionally segregated job categories" (i.e., where there has been a societal history of purposeful exclusion of minorities and women from the job category). Employers need not admit past discrimination in order to establish voluntary affirmative action programs. The Court also noted that the Kaiser plan was a "temporary measure" designed simply to eliminate a manifest racial imbalance.[9]

Subsequent cases have clarified a number of issues left unresolved by *Weber*. Major affirmative action cases decided by the Supreme Court from 1986 to 1989 resolved several thorny issues for employers:[29,35,49,91]

1. Courts may order, and employers voluntarily may establish, affirmative action plans, including numerical standards, to address problems of underutilization of women and minorities. However, court-approved affirmative action settlements can be reopened when white male employees allege reverse discrimination.[63]

2. The plans need not be directed solely to identified victims of discrimination, but may include general, classwide relief.

3. While the courts will almost never approve a plan that would result in whites *losing* their jobs through layoffs, the Court has apparently sanctioned plans that impose limited burdens on whites in hiring and promotions (i.e., postpones them).

4. Numerically based preferential programs should not be used in every instance, and they need not be based on an actual finding of discrimination.[76]

Numerically based programs will probably be used less in the future, since they can be challenged subsequently (see item 1 above). Instead, consent agreements will stipulate that valid selection procedures will be developed that minimize potential adverse impact. Those who would challenge such agreements cannot object to a job-relevant test, and since there is no absolute requirement that there be no adverse impact or quota, they cannot object to that part of the agreement either.[6]

The Supreme Court has not approved no-holds-barred affirmative action. In fact, its recent decisions suggest a genuine effort to provide a "more level playing field" that allows women, minorities, and nonminorities to compete for jobs on the basis of merit alone.

As Eleanor Holmes Norton, former chair of the EEOC, noted:

Affirmative action alone cannot cure age-old disparities based on race or sex. But if Title VII is allowed to do its work, it will speed the time when it has outlived its usefulness and our country has lived up to its promises. (ref. 70, p. A27)

THE ORGANIZATIONAL CONTEXT OF PERSONNEL DECISIONS

As the chapter opening vignette points out, the American workforce is becoming more of a mosaic than a melting pot, with women, minorities, and immigrants accounting for 80 percent of the growth in the labor force by the year 2000. Businesses that want to grow will have to rely on them.[25] In the following three sections, therefore, let us consider some practical steps that managers can take to prepare for the changes in the internal environments of organizations that are being wrought by multicultural workers, females, and older workers.

Multicultural Workers

The chapter opening vignette addresses this issue explicitly, but in addition, it is important to emphasize that workforce diversity cannot merely be tolerated; it must be valued. To bring about this change and to manage diversity effectively, an organization must do three things: *communicate diversity, cultivate diversity,* and *capitalize on diversity.*

Communication must get beyond the traditional public relations "hype" and focus on awareness training for all workers and managers. It should address all aspects of diversity, as well as its polar opposite, unlawful discrimination.

To cultivate diversity, workers and managers need to provide support and encouragement to each other at every opportunity. Channels for doing this include QWL (quality of work life) committees, associations of managers, women's groups, and formal and informal complaint processes. To measure progress, consider installing a feedback system (e.g., through periodic attitude surveys) that indicates how the internal environment of the organization is changing over time.

To capitalize on diversity, consider adopting a formal career management process that focuses on identifying each individual's strengths and weaknesses, options for development, and potential jobs to consider. For more on this, see Chapter 9. None of these approaches will work, however, unless a majority of employees want them to work. Reaching that objective will require a coordinated company effort that is spearheaded by top management.

Female Workers

Firms are using at least six vehicles to accommodate women's needs.[80] These include:

1. *Alternative career paths.* This is especially popular in law and accounting firms that have sanctioned part-time work for professionals.
2. *Extended leave.* IBM grants up to 3 years off with benefits and the guarantee of a comparable job on return. However, leave takers must be on call for part-time work during 2 of the 3 years.
3. *Flexible scheduling.* At NCNB employees create customized schedules and work at home. New mothers can "phase in" after 6-months maternity leave. Most who choose to cut their hours work two-thirds time and receive two-thirds pay.
4. *Flextime.* One common form allows any employee the right to shift the standard workday forward or back by 1 hour. Thousands of public and private employers now allow such flexibility.
5. *Job sharing.* Not for everyone, but may work especially well with clerical employees. At Steelcase, for example, two employees can share title, workload, salary, health benefits, and vacation.
6. *Telecommuting.* This is the high-tech answer to being a working Mom. Employers such as Pacific Telesis allow employees to limit the time they spend in the office by using personal computers, fax machines, and electronic mail at home.

IMPACT OF SOCIAL, LEGAL, AND ORGANIZATIONAL FACTORS ON PRODUCTIVITY, QUALITY OF WORK LIFE, AND THE BOTTOM LINE

There are both direct and indirect costs associated with unlawful discrimination. For example, sexual harassment can create high levels of stress and anxiety for both the victim and the perpetrator. These psychological reactions can lead to outcomes that increase labor costs for employers. Job performance may suffer, and absenteeism, sick leave, and turnover may increase. Both internal discrimination against present employees and external discrimination against job applicants can lead to costly lawsuits. Litigation is a time-consuming, expensive luxury that few organizations can afford. Lawsuits affecting virtually every aspect of the employment relationship have been litigated, and many well-publicized awards to victims have reached millions of dollars.

The legal and social aspects of the human resource management process should not be viewed in negative terms exclusively. Most of the present civil rights laws and regulations were enacted as a result of gross violations of individual rights. In most instances, the flip side of unlawful discrimination is good HR practice. For example, it is good practice to use properly developed and validated personnel selection procedures and performance appraisal systems. It is good HR practice to treat people as individuals, and not to rely on stereotyped group membership characteristics (e.g., stereotypes about women, ethnic groups, older workers, disabled workers). Finally, it just makes good sense to pay people equally, regardless of sex, if they are doing the same work. These kinds of HR practices can enhance productivity, provide a richer quality of work life, and contribute directly to the overall profitability of any enterprise.

In the seller's market of the 1990s, flexible approaches like these will be critical to attracting and retaining top female talent.

Older Workers

Here are six priorities to consider in order to manage older workers effectively.[79]

1. *Age/experience profile.* Executives should look at the age distribution across jobs, as compared with performance measures, to see what career paths might conceivably open in the future and what past performance measures have indicated about those holding these positions.

2. *Job performance requirements.* Companies should then define more precisely the types of abilities and skills needed for various posts. Clear job specifications must serve as the basis for improved personnel selection, job design, and performance appraisal systems. For example, jobs may be designed for self-pacing, may require periodic updating, or may require staffing by people with certain physical abilities.

3. *Performance appraisal.* Along with improved analyses of jobs, companies must improve their analyses of individual performance. Age biases may be reflected in the format of the appraisal instrument as well as in the attitudes of managers; this is known as *age grading:* subconscious expectations about what people ought to be doing at particular times in their lives.[57] Management training programs should be developed to address and correct both of these biases. Both Banker's Life and Casualty Co. and Polaroid have teams that audit the appraisals of older workers to check for unfair evaluations. These units have also been used to redress general age prejudice in the workplace.

4. *Workforce interest surveys.* Once management acquires a better understanding of the basic abilities that workers have, it must then determine what current workers want. Interest surveys make this possible. Such understanding is essential in reducing the harmful personal and organizational consequences of midcareer plateauing. Moreover, if management decides that it wants to encourage selectively certain types of workers to continue with the organization while encouraging turnover of other types, it must next determine what effects different incentives will have on each group.

5. *Education and counseling.* Workers are understandably concerned about the direction of their lives after terminating current employment. Not surprisingly, therefore, counseling on retirement and second-career development are becoming increasingly common. IBM now offers tuition rebates for courses on *any* topic of

To Prepare for Coming Changes in
Internal Organizational Environments

Develop an age, gender, and race/ethnic
  profile of the present workforce

Carefully assess job performance
  requirements

Check for possible unfairness in
  performance appraisals

Use interest surveys to determine
  what current workers want

Provide opportunities for employee
  training and career counseling

Explore with workers alternatives
  to traditional work patterns

FIGURE 3-6
Priority listing of suggested actions to manage effectively the internal organizational environment of the future.

interest within 3 years of retirement and continuing into retirement. To meet the needs of the workforce remaining on the job, career planning to avoid midcareer plateauing and training programs to reduce obsolescence should be developed. The educational programs must reflect the special needs of older workers (e.g., self-paced programs), for older workers can learn new tricks, but they need to be taught differently.

6. *Job structure.* Management may have more flexibility than anticipated in changing such conditions as work pace, the length or timing of the workday, leaves of absence, and challenges on the job. Nevertheless, any alternatives to traditional work patterns should be explored jointly with the workforce. Some union leaders, for example, have expressed reservations about part-time workers, whom they fear may threaten the power of organized labor.

Yes, America's workforce is aging, but America's organizations are not doomed to senility. Older workers still have much to offer, but organizations must examine their human resource policies carefully to ensure that their people are being used most effectively.

A list of actions that managers can take to deal with the issues we have discussed in this section is presented in Figure 3-6.

■ **HUMAN RESOURCE MANAGEMENT IN ACTION:**
CONCLUSION

ON MANAGING A MULTICULTURAL WORKFORCE

The objective in cross-cultural communication is not to decide "who's rational and who's irrational," but to understand both perspectives and to become comfortable with them. This is quite different from the days when the workplace was considered a melting pot. Under those circumstances, managers were taught to ignore differences, or at best to consider them as irrelevant. Today we recognize that differences across cultures exist that are both real and relevant, and that they reflect genuine cultural habits and values. So rather than suppress cultural differences at work, more and more managers are being taught how to respect them and how to deal appropriately with them in order to maximize the contribution of each employee.

Today managers and employees are encouraged to look for and to talk about such differences. Yet even in training programs, many people are frightened and uncomfortable with bringing tensions to the surface in an organization that seems to be functioning well.

Even when people do acknowledge problems, they often see them as someone else's affair. Thus when a group of executives of a large oil company received orientation kits for an upcoming training program on work force diversity, they found that the kits contained, among other things, a *Harvard Business Review* article called, "Black Managers: The Dream Deferred," describing African Americans' corporate experiences. Without reading the article, dozens of white managers sent their copies to the one African American manager in the group, thinking, with some good will, "Oh, this will interest Tom." When the group met, the African American manager chided them, "You're the ones that need to read it. Tom *knows* what it's like."

Experts caution that even when we begin to learn a bit about various cultures, we still have to be aware of differences within a culture and of personal idiosyncrasies and preferences. It may turn out that the person who wants private recognition is a blond California woman who just happens to be shy. What's the bottom line in all of this? According to many experts it's simple: Ask.

SUMMARY

The following laws were enacted to promote fair employment. They provide the basis for discrimination suits and subsequent judicial rulings:

- U.S. Constitution, Thirteenth and Fourteenth Amendments
- Civil Rights Acts of 1866 and 1871
- Equal Pay Act of 1963
- Title VII of the 1964 Civil Rights Act
- Age Discrimination in Employment Act of 1967 (as amended in 1986)
- Immigration Reform and Control Act of 1986
- Americans with Disabilities Act of 1990
- Executive Orders 11246, 11375, and 11478
- Rehabilitation Act of 1973
- Vietnam Era Veterans Readjustment Act of 1974

The Equal Employment Opportunity Commission (EEOC) and the Office of Federal Contract Compliance Programs (OFCCP) are the two major federal regulatory agencies charged with enforcing these nondiscrimination laws. The EEOC is responsible for both private and public nonfederal employers, unions, and employment agencies. The OFCCP is responsible for ensuring compliance from government contractors.

A considerable body of case law has developed, affecting almost all aspects of the employment relationship. Case law is most extensive in the following areas:

- Sex discrimination, sexual harassment, and pregnancy
- Age discrimination in employment
- Seniority
- Testing

IMPLICATIONS FOR MANAGEMENT PRACTICE

As a manager, it is easy to feel "swamped" by the gauntlet of laws, court rulings, and regulatory agency pronouncements that organizations must navigate through. While it is true that in the foreseeable future there will continue to be legal pressure to avoid unlawful discrimination against protected groups, there will be great eco-nomic pressure to find and retain top talent from these groups.[83] In short, affirmative action is a competitive necessity, and employers know it. Progressive managers recognize that now is the time to begin developing the kinds of interpersonal skills that will enable them to operate effectively in multicultural work environments.

■ Personal history (specifically, preemployment inquiries)
■ Preferential selection

Finally, it is vital that organizations devote special attention to the concerns of three large and growing segments of the working population—minorities, women, and older workers. The bottom line in all these cases is that, as managers, we need to be very clear about job requirements and performance standards, we need to treat people as individuals, and then we must evaluate each individual fairly relative to job requirements and performance standards.

DISCUSSION QUESTIONS

3∎1 If you were asked to advise a private employer (with no government contracts) of her equal employment opportunity responsibilities, what would you say?

3∎2 Putting all the laws, court rulings, and interpretive guidelines into perspective, describe to the employer the downside risks of noncompliance as well as the benefits to be gained from full compliance.

3∎3 Prepare a brief outline of an organizational policy on sexual harassment. Be sure to include grievance, counseling, and enforcement procedures.

3∎4 What steps would you take as a manager to ensure fair treatment for older employees?

3∎5 In your opinion, what specific steps should managers take to attract and retain a workforce that is more female and multicultural?

REFERENCES

1. *Albemarle Paper Company v. Moody*, 442 U.S. 407 (1975).
2. Alien workers bring factory a $580,000 fine (1989, Dec. 14). *The New York Times*, p. A32.
3. *American Tobacco Company v. Patterson*, 535 F2d 257 (CA-4, 1982).
4. *Bakke v. Regents of the University of California*, 17 FEPC 1000 (1978).
5. *Barnes v. Costle*, 561 F2d 983 (D.C. Circuit 1977).
6. Barrett, G. V. (1990). Personnel selection after Watson, Hopkins, Antonio, and Martin (WHAM). *Forensic Reports*, 3(2), 179–203.

7. Bennett, A. (1986, March 24). Following the leaders. *The Wall Street Journal*, pp. 10D, 11D.

8. Bersoff, D. N. (1988). Should subjective employment devices be scrutinized? *American Psychologist*, **43**, 1016–1018.

9. Beyond Bakke: High court approves affirmative action in hiring, promotion (1979, June 28). *The Wall Street Journal*, pp. 1, 30.

10. *Blumenthal et al. v. New York City et al.*, U.S. District Court, Eastern District of New York, 79 C 1813 (1982).

11. Boyle, M. B. (1975). Equal opportunity for women is smart business. *Harvard Business Review*, **51**, 85–95.

12. Boys' club pays its dues (1989, Jan. 23). *Time*, p. 47.

13. Bradshaw, D. S. (1987). Immigration reform: This one's for you. *Personnel Administrator*, **32**(4), 37–40.

14. Britt, L. P., III (1984). Affirmative action: Is there life after *Stotts? Personnel Administrator*, **29**(9), 96–100.

15. Cabot, S. J. (1987). Living with the new amendments to the Age Discrimination in Employment Act. *Personnel Administrator*, **32**(1), 53, 54.

16. *California Brewers Association v. Bryant*, 444 U.S. 598 (1982).

17. *California Federal Savings & Loan Association v. Guerra*, 42 FEP Cases 1073 (1987).

18. Carey, J. H. (1990, Aug. 15). Americans with Disabilities Act of 1990. *Employment Testing*, **4**(13), 629–633.

19. U.S. Bureau of the Census (1984, May). Projections of the population of the United States, by age, sex, and race: 1983–2080. *Current Population Reports*, Series P-25, No. 952.

20. Civil rights statutes extended to Arabs, Jews (1987, May 19). *Daily Labor Report*, pp. 1, 2, A-6.

21. Cohen, S. (1979). *Labor in the United States* (4th ed.). Columbus, OH: Charles E. Merrill.

22. Court holds employer liable for harassment by supervisor (1987, June 1). *Daily Labor Report*, pp. A1, D1–D5.

23. Cowan, A. L. (1989, Aug. 21). Women's gains on the job: Not without a heavy toll. *The New York Times*, pp. A1, A14.

24. *Dothard v. Rawlinson*, 433 U.S. 321 (1977).

25. Dwyer, P. (1989, July 3). The blow to affirmative action may not hurt that much. *Business Week*, pp. 49, 50.

26. *EEOC v. Radiator Specialty Company*, 610 F2d 178 (4th Cir. 1979).

27. Epstein, A. (1991, March 21). Ruling called women's rights victory. *Denver Post*, pp. 1A, 16A.

28. Equal Employment Opportunity Commission (1979, March 9). Pregnancy Discrimination Act: Adoption of interim interpretive guidelines, questions, and answers. *Federal Register*, **44**, 13,277–13,281.

29. *Firefighters Local Union No. 1784 v. Stotts*, 104 S. Ct. 2576 (1984).

30. Firestone Tire is barred from U.S. jobs as a result of job discrimination case (1980, July 16). *The Wall Street Journal*, p. 6.

31. *Franks v. Bowman Transportation Co.*, 424 U.S. 747 (1976).

32. Friedman, A. (1972). Attacking discrimination through the Thirteenth Amendment. *Cleveland State Law Review*, **21**, 161–178.

33. *Furnco Construction Corp. v. Waters*, 438 U.S. 567 (1978).

34. Gamarekian, B. (1987, July 22). Status of women rises, but pay lags, study finds. *The New York Times*, p. A23.
35. Gold, M. E. (1990). A spring of discontent. *ILR Report*, **27**(2), 3–18.
36. Gordon, M. E., & Johnson, W. A. (1982). Seniority: A review of its legal and scientific standing. *Personnel Psychology*, **35**, 255–280.
37. Green, W. E., & Brannigan, M. (1990, Feb. 5). Appeals court says job-bias law doesn't apply to citizens abroad. *The Wall Street Journal*, p. B4.
38. Greenhouse, L. (1984, June 13). Seniority is held to outweigh race as a layoff guide. *The New York Times*, pp. A1, B12.
39. Greenlaw, P. S., & Kohl, J. P. (1981). Sexual harassment: Homosexuality, bisexuality, and blackmail. *Personnel Administrator*, **26**, 59–62.
40. *Gregory v. Litton Systems, Inc.*, 472 F2d 631 (9th Cir. 1972).
41. *Griggs v. Duke Power Company*, 401 U.S. 424 (1971).
42. Gutek, B. A. (1988, August). Survey research on sexual harassment: What we have learned, what we cannot learn. In R. H. Faley (Chair), *An integrated approach to understanding sexual harassment at work*. Symposium presented at the annual convention of the Academy of Management, Anaheim, CA.
43. *Hodgson v. Greyhound Lines, Inc.*, 419 U.S. 1122 (1975).
44. *Hyland v. Fukada*, 580 F2d 977 (9th Cir. 1978).
45. *International Brotherhood of Teamsters v. United States*, 432 U.S. 324 (1977).
46. Jackson, D. J. (1978). Update on handicapped discrimination. *Personnel Journal*, **57**, 488–491.
47. Jacobs, D. L. (1989, Oct. 29). The growing legal battle over employee waivers. *The New York Times*, p. 2.
48. *Johnson v. Railway Express Agency, Inc.*, 95 S. Ct. 1716 (1975).
49. *Johnson v. Santa Clara Transportation Agency* (1987, March 26). *Daily Labor Report*, pp. A1, D1–D19.
50. Jones, J. E., Jr., Murphy, W. P., & Belton, R. (1987). *Discrimination in employment* (5th ed.). St. Paul, MN: West.
51. Justices uphold utility's stand on job testing (1979, March 6). *The Wall Street Journal*, p. 4.
52. Karr, A. R. (1991, Feb. 28). EEOC clarifies law on rights of handicapped. *The Wall Street Journal*, p. A12.
53. Kilborn, P. (1990, Sept. 2). Manufacturer's policy, women's job rights clash. *Denver Post*, p. 2A.
54. Labaton, S. (1987, Aug. 3). Retirements are challenged. *The New York Times*, p. D2.
55. Labor Letter (1987, Aug. 25). *The Wall Street Journal*, p. 1.
56. Labor Letter (1987, June 16). *The Wall Street Journal*, p. 1.
57. Labor Letter (1986, Dec. 2). *The Wall Street Journal*, p. 1.
58. Labor Letter (1980, Dec. 16). *The Wall Street Journal*, p. 1.
59. Linenberger, P., & Keaveny, T. J. (1981). Sexual harassment: The employer's legal obligations. *Personnel*, **58**, 60–68.
60. *Lorance v. AT&T Technologies*, 109 S. Ct. 2261 (1989).
61. Lublin, J. S. (1990, Aug. 14). Graying Europeans battle age bias. *The Wall Street Journal*, p. B1.
62. Lublin, J. S., & Pasztor, A. (1985, Dec. 11). Tentative affirmative action accord is reached by top Reagan officials. *The Wall Street Journal*, p. 4.
63. *Martin v. Wilks*, 109 S. Ct. 2180 (1989).

64. *McDonnell-Douglas v. Green*, 411 U.S. 972 (1973).
65. Miernyk, W. H. (1980). Coal. In G. C. Somers (ed.), *Collective bargaining: Contemporary American experience*. Madison, WI: Industrial Relations Research Organization, pp. 1–48.
66. Miller, C. S., Kaspin, J. A., & Schuster, M. H. (1990). The impact of performance appraisal methods on age discrimination in employment act cases. *Personnel Psychology*, **43**, 555–578.
67. Miller, R. U. (1980). Hospitals. In G. C. Somers (ed.), *Collective bargaining: Contemporary American experience*. Madison, WI: Industrial Relations Research Organization, pp. 373–433.
68. Mountain States Employers Council Bulletin (1990, September). Americans with Disabilities Act of 1990, p. 1.
69. Mountain States Employers Council Bulletin (1989, August). Sexual harassment, p. 1.
70. Norton, E. H. (1987, May 13). Step by step, the court helps affirmative action. *The New York Times*, p. A27.
71. *Patterson v. McLean Credit Union*, 109 S. Ct. 2643 (1989).
72. Pear, R. (1985, Oct. 27). The cabinet searches for consensus on affirmative action. *The New York Times*, p. E5.
73. *Personnel Administrator of Massachusetts v. Feeney*, 19 FEP cases, 1377 (June 5, 1979).
74. *Pregnancy and employment: The complete handbook on discrimination, maternity leave, and health and safety* (1987). Washington, DC: Bureau of National Affairs.
75. *Price Waterhouse v. Hopkins*, 109 S. Ct. 1775 (1989).
76. Replying in the affirmative (1987, March 9). *Time*, p. 66.
77. *Schwager v. Sun Oil Company of PA*, 591 F2d 58 (10th Cir. 1979).
78. Silvassy, K. (1987, Apr. 4). Jobs on horizon for 1990s. *Atlanta Constitution*, pp. 1S, 4S.
79. Sonnenfeld, J. (1980). Dealing with the aging workforce. In E. L. Miller, E. H. Burack, & M. H. Albrecht (eds.), *Management of human resources*. Englewood Cliffs, NJ: Prentice-Hall.
80. The mommy track (1989, March 20). *Business Week*, pp. 126–134.
81. Trotter, R., Zacur, S. R., & Greenwood, W. (1982). The pregnancy disability amendment: What the law provides, Part II. *Personnel Administrator*, **27**, 55–58.
82. *United Steelworkers of America v. Weber*, 99 S. Ct. 2721 (1979).
83. Wallace, P. A. (1990). Affirmative action from a labor market perspective. *ILR Report*, **27**(2), 40–47.
84. Wallis, C. (1989, Dec. 4). Onward, women! *Time*, pp. 80–89.
85. *Wards Cove Packing Co. v. Antonio*, 109 S. Ct. 2115 (1989).
86. *Watson v. Fort Worth Bank & Trust*, 108 S. Ct. 299 (1988).
87. *Webster v. Redmond*, 599 F2d 793 (7th Cir. 1979).
88. Wemiel, S. (1991, March 21). Justices bar "fetal protection" policies. *The Wall Street Journal*, pp. B1, B8.
89. Williams, L. (1987, Feb. 8). Harnessing the horses on job discrimination. *The New York Times*, p. 54.
90. Women miners win Peeping Tom suit (1982, November). *Coal Age*, pp. 11, 13.
91. *Wygant v. Jackson Board of Education*, 106 S. Ct. 1842 (1986); *Local 28 Sheet Metal Workers v. E.E.O.C.*, 106 S. Ct. 3019 (1986); *Local 93 Firefighters v. Cleveland*, 106 S. Ct. 3063 (1986).
92. York, K. M. (1989). Defining sexual harassment in workplaces: A policy-capturing approach. *Academy of Management Journal*, **32**, 830–850.

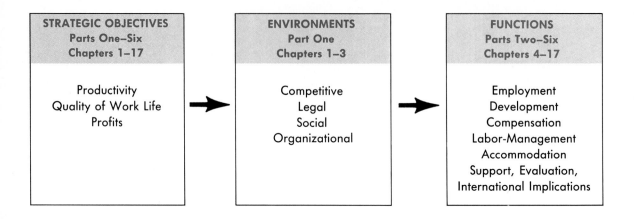

STRATEGIC OBJECTIVES Parts One–Six Chapters 1–17	ENVIRONMENTS Part One Chapters 1–3	FUNCTIONS Parts Two–Six Chapters 4–17
Productivity Quality of Work Life Profits	Competitive Legal Social Organizational	Employment Development Compensation Labor-Management Accommodation Support, Evaluation, International Implications

RELATIONSHIP OF HRM FUNCTIONS TO HRM ACTIVITIES

FUNCTIONS	ACTIVITIES
PART 2 EMPLOYMENT	Job Analysis, Human Resource Planning, Recruiting, Staffing (Chapters 4–6)
PART 3 DEVELOPMENT	Orientation, Training, Performance Appraisal, Managing Careers (Chapters 7–9)
PART 4 COMPENSATION	Pay, Benefits, Incentives (Chapters 10–12)
PART 5 LABOR-MANAGEMENT ACCOMMODATION	Union Representation, Collective Bargaining, Procedural Justice, Ethics (Chapters 13, 14)
PART 6 SUPPORT, EVALUATION, INTERNATIONAL IMPLICATIONS	Job Safety and Health, Costs/Benefits of HRM Activities, International Dimensions of HRM (Chapters 15–17)

PART TWO

Employment

N
ow that you understand the environmental context within which human resource management activities take place, it is time to address three major aspects of the employment process: analyzing jobs, determining their human resource requirements, and hiring employees. Logically, before an organization can select employees, it needs to be able to specify *what* work needs to be done, *how* it should be done, the *number* of people needed, and the *knowledge*, *skills*, *abilities*, and other characteristics required to do the work. Chapter 4 addresses these issues. Chapter 5 considers the planning, recruitment, and evaluation of recruitment operations. Finally, Chapter 6 examines initial screening and personnel selection—why they are done, how they are done, and how they can be evaluated.

Job Analysis and Human Resource Planning

■ **HUMAN RESOURCE MANAGEMENT IN ACTION**

SUCCESSION PLANNING—A PRACTICAL AND WORKABLE APPROACH*

Succession planning means different things to different organizations and executives. To some, it means occasionally thinking about who might replace whom should an opening occur in a key position. To others, succession planning may mean having a detailed, career-pathed, multiple backup group of managers in reserve to fill any position opening that might occur. Between these ends of the spectrum, there are an infinite number of intermediate positions.

One such intermediate approach focuses on identifying needs for certain managerial skills and characteristics that may be required by an organization in the future, and planning to have an inventory of appropriate people available to fill those needs if and when they occur. To implement this approach, HR staff members (or outside consultants) work directly with an organization's senior executives. In structured personal interviews, execu-

---

*Adapted from: Succession planning—a better approach. The Human Resource Consulting Group, Inc., *Newsletter*, December 1988, pp. 1–2.

tives are asked to identify the management education, experience, and skills that the organization can expect to require as it evolves over its planning horizon (usually 3 to 5 years). They are also asked to identify characteristics of managers that might make them more or less successful in performing the tasks identified.

These projections are then aggregated, and a best-guess profile of future management and executive needs is compiled. The profile becomes the inventory of senior human resource needs that the organization should be able to fill over the organization's planning horizon.

The next step is to identify those managers with the capabilities to fill projected positions or to grow to fill the positions. This can be done on a voluntary basis by managers themselves, or else the organization can use its performance appraisal system, personal interviews, or special tools (such as workshops and behavioral simulations) to identify potential candidates.

Each individual in this group is then asked to prepare a career development plan for himself or herself with the assistance and counsel of his or her superior and HR staff. This puts the responsibility for career development squarely on each individual. The organization has a responsibility to assist in the process, however. It does so by offering training in how to assess oneself and manage one's career and by providing as much information as possible about its strategy, plans, and activities. Another major piece of information is a description of the kinds of managerial skills and experience that will be required in senior-level jobs as the organization evolves. Using these tools, each individual then puts together a written, specific career development plan for himself or herself.

As individuals develop, the organization supports them by providing formal outside education, internal training programs, job rotations and reassignments, and whatever else may be necessary to assist each individual's career development.

The process of career development is monitored by HR professionals. It is their responsibility to know at any given time the state of development of each person who is part of the upwardly mobile group. It is also their responsibility to track changes in organizational strategy and other events that might potentially change the mix of HR needs the organization will require in the future.

Challenges

1. Assess the advantages and disadvantages of the approach to succession planning described above.
2. How far down the corporate ladder should HR planning extend? Should it include all managerial positions? All positions throughout the organization?
3. Traditionally, the processes of HR planning and individual career development were regarded as separate and relatively independent. The ap-

proach described above proposes a much tighter linkage. Is this something we should expect to see more or less of in the future?

1. How can job analysis information be useful to the operating manager?
2. Which methods of job analysis will be most effective for different organizational purposes?
3. How can human resource planning be integrated most effectively with general business planning?
4. What should be the components of a fair information practice policy with regard to information about employees?
5. How can human resource forecasts be most useful?
6. What control mechanisms might be most appropriate to ensure that action plans match targeted needs?

As the chapter opening vignette indicates, competent succession planning requires two types of information about an organization: (1) a description of the work to be done, the skills needed, and the training and experience required for various jobs, and (2) a description of the future direction of a business. Once these are known, it makes sense to forecast the numbers and skills mix of people required at some future time period. We consider the first of these needs, job analysis, in the sections to follow, and the second, human resource planning, in the latter part of the chapter.

ALTERNATIVE PERSPECTIVES ON JOBS

Jobs are frequently the subject of conversation: "I'm trying to get a job"; "I'm being promoted to a new job"; "I'd sure like to have my boss's job." Or, as Samuel Gompers, first president of the American Federation of Labor, once said, "A job's a job; if it doesn't pay enough, it's a lousy job."

Jobs are important to individuals: They help determine standards of living, places of residence, status (value ascribed to individuals because of their position), and even one's sense of self-worth. Jobs are important to organizations because they are the vehicles through which work (and thus organizational objectives) are accomplished. The way to manage people to work efficiently is through answers to such questions as:

Who specifies the content of each job?
Who decides how many jobs are necessary?
How are the interrelationships among jobs determined and communicated?
Has anyone looked at the number, design, and content of jobs from the perspective of the entire organization, the "big picture"?

Samuel Gompers, fiery ex-president of the American Federation of Labor. One of his most famous lines occurred in response to the question "What makes a good job?" His response: "A job's a job; if it doesn't pay enough, it's a lousy job."

What are the minimum qualifications for each job?

What should training programs stress?

How should performance be measured on each job?

How much is each job worth?

Unfortunately, there is often a tendency, even an urgency, to get on with work itself ("Get the job done!") rather than to take the time to think through these basic questions. But this tendency is changing as firms struggle to cope with such problems as stagnant productivity, deregulation, and global economic competition.

Firms in every developed country around the world are rethinking the fundamental principles that underlie the design of jobs and the required numbers and skills of people to do them. Job analysis is essential to this process.

The term *job analysis* describes the process of obtaining information about jobs. As we shall soon see, this information is useful for a number of business purposes. Regardless of how it is collected, it usually includes information about the tasks to be done on the job, and the personal characteristics (education, experience, specialized training) necessary to do the tasks.

An overall written summary of task requirements is called a *job description*. An overall written summary of worker requirements is called a *job specification*.

The result of the process of job analysis is a job description and a job specification. An abbreviated example of a job description is shown in Figure 4-1, and an abbreviated example of a job specification is shown in Figure 4-2.

Position Title: Labor Relations Specialist

Reports To: Manager, Labor Relations

ACCOUNTABILITY OBJECTIVE:

Serves as an assistant to the Manager of the Labor Relations section of the Human Resource Department by providing effective and efficient support in organizational maintenance of the labor-management relations function.

SPECIFIC ACCOUNTABILITIES:

1. Provides expert opinion on the interpretation of company policies and procedures, collective bargaining contracts, and local, state, and federal laws.

2. Assists supervisors in composing documentation when disciplinary action is pending to ensure inclusion of all pertinent facts leading to the violation of company policy and procedures.

3. Resolves grievance cases filed by the union, as well as grievance cases filed by non-bargaining-unit employees.

4. Provides monthly statistics on the number of disciplinary actions and issues.

5. Assembles data for contract negotiations by assisting in the preparation of analyses of job classifications, statistics relative to bargaining unit's turnover, pay recommendations, and benefits.

6. Assists in supervisory training through individual and group discussions of the role of the supervisor in counseling, disciplinary actions, and grievance procedures.

FIGURE 4-1
A portion of a job description.

Position Title: Labor Relations Specialist

Required Knowledges, Abilities, and Skills

1. Knowledge of fundamental human resource management principles.

2. Knowledge of basic statistical methods.

3. Knowledge of basic principles of compensation administration.

4. Knowledge of principles and laws pertaining to labor relations and collective bargaining.

5. Ability to interpret and explain company human resource policies, rules and regulations.

6. Ability to communicate effectively, both verbally and in writing.

7. Ability to assess a situation, draw valid conclusions, and make sound recommendations.

FIGURE 4-2
A portion of a job specification.

Why Study Job Requirements?

Sound human resource management practice dictates that thorough, competent job analyses always be done, for they provide a deeper understanding of the behavioral requirements of jobs. This in turn creates a solid basis on which to make job-related human resource decisions.[39] Unfortunately, job analyses are often done for a specific purpose (e.g., training design) without consideration of the many other uses of this information. Some of these other uses, along with a brief description of each, are listed below. Many of them have been incorporated into Figure 4-3.

> *Organizational structure and design.* By clarifying job requirements and the interrelationships among jobs, responsibilities at all levels can be specified, promoting efficiency and minimizing overlap or duplication.

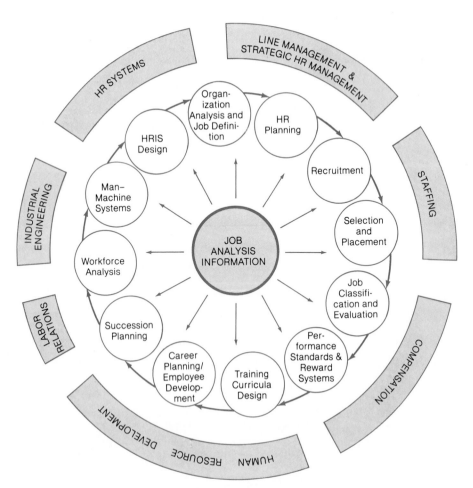

FIGURE 4-3
Job analysis is the foundation for many human resource management programs. [*Source:* R. C. Page and D. M. Van De Voort (1989), Human resource planning and job analysis. In W. F. Cascio (ed.), *Planning, employment, and placement,* vol. 2 of the ASPA/BNA *Human resource management series.* Washington, DC: Bureau of National Affairs.]

Human resource planning. Job analysis is the foundation for forecasting the need for human resources as well as for plans for such activities as training, transfer, or promotion. Frequently job analysis information is incorporated into a human resource information system (HRIS).

Job evaluation and compensation. Before jobs can be ranked in terms of their overall worth to an organization or compared to jobs in other firms for purposes of pay surveys, their requirements must be understood thoroughly. Job descriptions and specifications provide such understanding to those who must make job evaluation and compensation decisions.

Recruitment. The most important information an executive ("headhunter") or company recruiter needs is full knowledge of the job(s) in question.

Selection. Any method used to select or promote applicants must be based on a keen, meaningful forecast of job performance. An understanding of just what a worker is expected to do on the job, as reflected in job-related interviews or test questions, is necessary for such a meaningful forecast.

Placement. In many cases, applicants are first selected and then placed in one of many possible jobs. When there is a clear picture of the needs of a job and the abilities of the workers to fulfill those needs, then selection decisions will be accurate, and workers will be placed in the specific jobs where they will be the most productive. That is, selection and placement tend to go hand in hand. On the other side of the selection-placement coin, when there is a blurred picture of the needs of a job, selection decisions will not be accurate, and placement will probably be worse.

Orientation, training, and development. Training a worker can be very costly, as we shall see later. Up-to-date job descriptions and specifications help ensure that training programs reflect actual job requirements. In other words, "What you learn in training today you'll use on the job tomorrow."

Performance appraisal. If employees are to be judged in terms of how well they do those parts of their jobs that really matter, those that distinguish effective from ineffective performers, then critical and noncritical job requirements must be specified. Job analysis does this.

Career path planning. If the organization (as well as the individual) does not have a thorough understanding of the requirements of available jobs and how jobs at succeeding levels relate to one another, then effective career path planning is impossible.

Labor relations. The information provided by job analysis is helpful to both management and unions for contract negotiations, as well as for resolving grievances and jurisdictional disputes.

Engineering design and methods improvement. To design equipment to perform a specific task reliably and efficiently, engineers must understand exactly the capabilities of the operator and what he or she is expected to do. Similarly, any improvements or proposed new working methods must be evaluated relative to their impact on the overall job objectives.

Job design. As with methods improvement, changes in the way work is accomplished must be evaluated through a job analysis, focusing on the tasks to be done and on the behaviors required of the people doing the tasks.

Safety. Frequently, in the course of doing a job analysis, unsafe conditions (environmental conditions or personal habits) are discovered and thus may lead to safety improvements.

Vocational guidance and rehabilitation counseling. Informed decisions regarding career choices may be derived meaningfully from comprehensive job descriptions and specifications.

Job classification systems. Selection, training, and pay systems are often keyed to job classification systems, also referred to as "job families." Without job analysis information, it is impossible to determine reliably the structure of the relationships between jobs in an organization.

Dynamic Characteristics of Jobs

There are two basic things to keep in mind when thinking about what job analysis is and what it should accomplish:

One, as time goes on, everything changes, and so do jobs. This has been recognized only recently; the popular view of a job was that what it required did not change; a job was a static thing, designed to be consistent although the workers who passed through it were different. Now we know that for a job to produce efficient output, it must change according to the workers who do it. In fact, the nature of jobs might change for three reasons:[4]

- *Time.* For example, lifeguards, ski instructors, and accountants do different things at different times of the year.
- *People.* Particularly in management jobs but also in teaching or coaching, the job is what the incumbent makes of it.
- *Environment.* Such changes may be technological—for example, word processing has drastically changed the nature of many secretarial jobs. Or the changes may be situational, as in a recent collective bargaining agreement between Gulf Oil Corp. and the Oil, Chemical, and Atomic Workers union, in which the company has "total flexibility" in assigning work across traditional craft lines; thus welders may be assigned as helpers to pipe fitters, boilermakers, and forklift operators.

Two, job analysis comprises job specifications and people requirements that should reflect *minimally* acceptable qualifications for job holders. Frequently they do not, reflecting instead a profile of the *ideal* job holder. For example, in evaluating positions for government and industry, the EEOC found that more than 65 percent of the jobs requiring a college degree could easily be handled by workers who are not college graduates.[16]

How are job specifications set? Typically by consensus among experts—immediate supervisors, job incumbents, and job analysts. Such a procedure is professionally acceptable, but care must be taken to distinguish between required and desirable qualifications. The term *required* denotes inflexibility; that is, it is assumed that without this qualification, an individual absolutely would be unable to do the job. *Desirable* implies flexibility; it is "nice to have" this ability, but it is not a "need to have." To be sure, required qualifications will exist in almost all jobs, but care must be exercised in establishing them, for they must meet a higher standard.

How Do We Study Job Requirements?

There are a number of methods used to study jobs. At the outset it is important to note that no one of them is sufficient. Some combination of methods must be used to obtain a total picture of the task and the physical, mental, social, and environmental demands of the job. Here are five common methods of job analysis:

1. *Job performance.* With this approach, an analyst actually does the job under study to get firsthand exposure to what it demands. (In the 1980 Florida governor's race, one of the candidates actually performed 100 different jobs so that he could better identify with the workers' concerns.)

2. *Observation.* The analyst simply observes a worker or group of workers doing a job. Without interfering, the analyst records the what, why, and how of the various parts of the job. Usually this information is recorded in a standard format.

3. *Interview.* In many jobs where it is not possible for the analyst actually to perform the jobs (e.g., airline pilot) or where observation is impractical (e.g., architect), it is necessary to rely on workers' own descriptions of what is done, why it is done, and how it is done. Like recordings of observations, a standard format should be used to collect input from all workers to survey the requirements of a particular job. In this way all questions and responses can be restricted to job-related topics. But more important, standardization makes it possible to compare what different people are saying within the overall survey.

4. *Critical incidents.* These are vignettes comprising brief actual reports that illustrate particularly effective or ineffective worker behaviors. For example:

On January 14, Mr. Vin, the restaurant's wine steward, was asked about an obscure bottle of wine. Without hesitation, he described the place of vintage and bottling, the meaning of the symbols on the label, and the characteristics of the grapes in the year of vintage.

When a large number of these little incidents are collected from knowledgeable individuals, they are abstracted and categorized according to the general job area they describe. The end result draws a fairly clear picture of actual job requirements.

5. *Structured questionnaires.* With this approach, the worker is presented with a list of tasks, a list of behaviors (e.g., negotiating, coordinating, using both hands), or both. Tasks focus on *what* gets done. This is a job-oriented approach. Behaviors,

on the other hand, focus on *how* a job is done. This is a worker-oriented approach. Each task or behavior is rated in terms of whether or not it is performed, and, if it is, it is further described in terms of characteristics such as frequency, importance, difficulty, and relationship to overall performance. The ratings provide a basis for scoring the questionnaires and for developing a profile of actual job requirements.[10] One of the most popular structured questionnaires is the Position Analysis Questionnaire (PAQ).

The PAQ is a behavior-oriented job analysis questionnaire.[28] It consists of 194 items that fall into the following categories:

Information input. Where and how the worker gets the information to do her or his job

Mental processes. The reasoning, planning, and decision making involved in a job

Work output. Physical activities as well as the tools or devices used

Relationships with other persons.

Job context. Physical and social

Other job characteristics. For example, apparel, work continuity, licensing, hours, and responsibility.

The items provide either for checking a job element if it applies or for rating it on a scale, such as in terms of importance, time, or difficulty. An example of some PAQ items is shown in Figure 4-4. While structured job analysis questionnaires are growing in popularity, the newest applications use computer-generated graphics to help illustrate similarities and differences across jobs and organizational units.[47]

	Code	Importance to This Job (I)
5.3 Personal and Social Aspects	DNA	Does not apply
	1	Very minor
This section includes various personal and social aspects of jobs. Indicate by code the *importance* of these aspects as part of the job.	2	Low
	3	Average
	4	High
	5	Extreme

148　I　Civic obligations (because of the job the worker assumes, or is expected to assume, certain civic obligations or responsibilities)

149　I　Frustrating situations (job situations in which attempts to deal with problems or to achieve job objectives are obstructed or hindered, and may thus contribute to frustration on the part of the worker)

150　I　Strained personal contacts (dealing with individuals or groups in "unpleasant" or "strained" situations, for example, certain aspects of police work, certain types of negotiations, handling certain mental patients, etc.)

FIGURE 4-4
Sample PAQ items.

The preceding five methods of job analysis represent the popular ones in use today. Table 4-1 considers the pros and cons of each method. Regardless of the method used, the workers providing job information to the analyst must be knowledgeable about the jobs in question;[14,21] however, there seem to be no differences in the quality of information provided by members of different gender or race/ethnic subgroups,[38] or by high as opposed to low performers.[11] In terms of the types of data actually collected, the most popular methods today are observation, interviews, and structured questionnaires.

Analyzing Managerial Jobs

There are a number of special considerations in analyzing managerial jobs. One is that managers tend to adjust the content of their jobs to fit their own styles rather than to fit the needs of the managerial tasks to be done. The result of this is that when it comes to querying them about their work, they will describe what they actually do, having lost sight of what they should be doing. Another consideration is that it is difficult to identify what a manager does over time because her or his activity differs from time to time, whether it be one activity one month or week or day, and then some other activity the following day or week or month. Indeed, managers' activities change throughout the day. As immediate situations or general environments change, so will the content of a manager's job, and each such change will affect managers differently in different functional areas, different geographical areas, and different organizational levels (i.e., first-line supervisors versus divisional vice presidents). To analyze them, we must identify and measure the fundamental dimensions along which they differ and change. That is, we must identify what managers actually do on their jobs, and then we must specify behavioral differences due to time, person, and environmental changes.

Two methods of analyzing managerial jobs are based on questionnaires. They are the Management Position Description Questionnaire (MPDQ) and the Supervisor Task Description Questionnaire (STDQ).

The MPDQ is a 197-item behaviorally based instrument for describing, comparing, classifying, and evaluating executive positions in terms of their content.[49] An example of one portion of the MPDQ is shown in Figure 4-5.

The STDQ describes 100 work activities of first-line supervisors in seven areas:[15]

- Working with subordinates
- Organizing work of subordinates
- Work planning and scheduling
- Maintaining efficient quality and production
- Maintaining safe and clean work areas
- Maintaining equipment and machinery
- Compiling records and reports

■ **TABLE 4·1**
ADVANTAGES AND DISADVANTAGES OF FIVE POPULAR JOB ANALYSIS METHODS

Job Performance

Advantages   With this method there is exposure to actual job tasks, as well as to the physical, environmental, and social demands of the job. It is appropriate for jobs that can be learned in a relatively short period of time.

Disadvantages   This method is inappropriate for jobs that require extensive training or are hazardous to perform.

Observation

Advantages   Direct exposure to jobs can provide a richer, deeper understanding of job requirements than workers' descriptions of what they do.

Disadvantages   If the work in question is primarily mental, observations alone may reveal little useful information. Critical yet rare job requirements (e.g., "copes with emergencies") simply may not be observed.

Interviews

Advantages   This method can provide information about standard as well as nonstandard activities and about physical as well as mental work. Since the worker is also his or her own observer, he or she can report on activities that would not be observed often. In short, the worker can provide the analyst with information that might not be available from any other source.

Disadvantages   Workers may be suspicious of interviewers and their motives; interviewers may ask ambiguous questions. Thus distortion of information (either as a result of honest misunderstanding or as a result of purposeful misrepresentation) is a real possibility. For this reason, the interview should never be used as the sole job analysis method.

Critical Incidents

Advantages   This method focuses directly on what people do in their jobs, and thus it provides insight into job dynamics. Since the behaviors in question are observable and measurable, information derived from this method can be used for most possible applications of job analysis.

Disadvantages   It takes considerable time to gather, abstract, and categorize the incidents. Also, since by definition the incidents describe particularly effective or ineffective behavior, it may be difficult to develop a profile of average job behavior—our main objective in job analysis.

Structured Questionnaires

Advantages   This method is generally cheaper and quicker to administer than other methods. Questionnaires can be completed off the job, thus avoiding lost productive time. Also, where there are large numbers of job incumbents, this method allows an analyst to survey all of them, thus providing a breadth of coverage that is impossible to obtain otherwise. Furthermore, such survey data often can be quantified and processed by computer, which opens up vast analytical possibilities.

Disadvantages   Questionnaires are often time-consuming and expensive to develop. Rapport between analyst and respondent is not possible unless the analyst is present to explain items and clarify misunderstandings. Such an impersonal approach may have adverse effects on respondent cooperation and motivation.

Part 8
Contacts

To achieve organizational goals, managers and consultants may be required to communicate with employees at many levels within the company and with influential people outside of the company. This part of the questionnaire addresses the nature and level of these contacts.

Directions:

Step 1 — Significance

For each contact and purpose of contact noted on the opposite page, indicate how significant a part of your position each represents by assigning a number between 0 to 4 to each block. Remember to consider both the importance and the frequency of the contact.

0—Definitely not a part of the position.

1—Minor significance to the position.

2—Moderate significance to the position.

3—Substantial significance to the position

4—Crucial significance to the position.

Step 2 — Other Contacts

If you have any other contacts, please elaborate on their nature and purpose below.

_____
_____
_____
_____
_____
_____
_____
_____
_____
_____
_____

Purpose of Contact

Internal Contacts	Share information regarding past, present, or anticipated activities or decisions.	Influence others to act or decide in a manner consistent with your objectives.	Direct the plans, activities, or decisions of others.
1. Executives.	10	11	12
2. Group Managers (managers report to position).	13	14	15
3. Managers (supervisors report to position).	16	17	18
4. Supervisors (no supervisors report to position).	19	20	21
5. Professional/Administrative Exempt.	22	23	24
6. Clerical or Support staff (Nonexempt).	25	26	27
7. Other Nonexempt employees.	28	29	30

External Contacts	Provide/gather information or promote the organization or its products/services.	Resolve problems.	Sell products/ services.	Negotiate contracts/ settlements, etc.
8. Customers of the company's products or services.	31	32	33	34
9. Representatives of vendors/subcontractors.	35	36	37	38
10. Representatives of other companies or professional organizations and institutions.	39	40	41	42
11. Representatives of labor unions.	43	44	45	46
12. Representatives of influential community organizations.	47	48	49	50
13. Individuals such as applicants or shareholders.	51	52	53	54
14. Representatives of the media, including the press, radio, television, etc.	55	56	57	58
15. National, state, or regional elected government representatives and/or lobbyists.	59	60	61	62
16. Local government officials and/or representatives of departments such as: customs, tax, revenue, traffic, procurement, law enforcement, and environment.	63	64	65	66

FIGURE 4-5

Sample Management Position Description Questionnaire items.

Responses from 251 first-line supervisors from 40 plants yielded few differences in the supervisors' jobs regardless of technology or function. These results imply that with the exception of the technical knowledge that may be required in a first-line supervisory job, organizations should be able to develop selection, training, and performance appraisal systems for first-line supervisors that can be applied generally throughout the organization.

Job Analysis: Relating Method to Purpose

Given such a wide choice among available job analysis methods, the combination of methods to use is the one that best fits the purpose of the job analysis research (e.g., employee selection, training design, performance appraisal). Table 4-2 is a matrix that suggests some possible match-ups between job analysis methods and various human resource management purposes. The table simply illustrates the *relative* strengths of each method when used for each purpose. For example, the job performance method of job analysis is most appropriate for the development of tests and interviews, training design, and performance appraisal system design.

COSTS AND BENEFITS OF ALTERNATIVE JOB ANALYSIS METHODS

Key considerations in the choice of job analysis methods are the method-purpose fit, cost, practicality, and an overall judgment of their appropriateness for the situation in question. Comparative research based on the purposes and practicality of these seven job analysis methods has yielded a pattern of results similar to that shown in Table 4-2.[25,26] In terms of costs, the PAQ (a behavior checklist) was the least costly method to use, while critical incidents was the most costly. However, cost is not the only consideration in choosing a job analysis method. Appropriateness for the situation is another. While the PAQ is used widely, unless a trained analyst actually interviews job incumbents, the PAQ may be more appropriate for

■ **TABLE 4·2**
JOB ANALYSIS METHODS AND THE PURPOSE(S) *BEST* SUITED TO EACH

Method	Job descriptions	Development of tests	Development of interviews	Job evaluation	Training design	Performance appraisal design	Career path planning
Job performance		X	X		X	X	
Observation	X	X	X				
Interviews	X	X	X	X	X	X	
Critical incidents	X	X	X		X	X	
Questionnaires:							
Task checklists	X	X	X	X	X	X	
Behavior checklists			X	X	X	X	X

analyzing higher-level jobs since a college-graduate reading level is required to comprehend the items.[3] Related to the issue of appropriateness is an awareness that *behavioral* similarities in jobs may mask genuine *task* differences between them. For example, the jobs performed by typists and belly dancers may appear quite similar—both require fine motor movements!

A thorough job analysis may require a considerable investment of time, effort, and money. Choices among methods must be made. If the choices are based on a rational consideration of the trade-offs involved, they will result in the wisest use of time *and* effort *and* money.

As an example, consider a job analysis approach called JobScope, used by Nationwide Insurance Companies. As a result of improved accuracy in job evaluation (assessment of the relative worth of jobs to the firm), the system is saving the company more than $60,000 in salary and benefits *each year*. The company recouped the entire cost of developing JobScope during its first 2 years of operation and is using it as the basis for developing an integrated HR system.[33]

RELATIONSHIP OF JOB ANALYSIS TO HUMAN RESOURCE PLANNING

Having identified the behavioral requirements of jobs, the organization is in a position to identify the numbers and skills required to do those jobs at some future time period. This process is known as human resource planning (HRP). However, to have a meaningful impact on future operations, HRP must be integrally related to general business planning. General business plans, in turn, may be strategic or tactical in nature.

Types of Plans: Strategic, Tactical, and Human Resources

Strategic planning is the process of setting objectives and deciding on the actions to achieve them.[32,43] Strategic planning for an organization includes:

- *Defining philosophy.* Why does the organization exist? What unique contribution does it make?
- *Formulating statements of identity, purpose, and objectives.* What is the overall mission of the organization? Are the missions of divisions and departments consistent with the mission of the organization?
- *Evaluating strengths and weaknesses.* Identify factors that may enhance or inhibit any future courses of action aimed at achieving objectives.
- *Determining design.* What are the components of the organization, what should they do, and how should they relate to each other, toward achieving objectives and fulfilling the organization's mission?
- *Developing strategies.* How will the objectives, at every level, be achieved? How will they be measured, not only in quantitative terms of what is to be achieved, but also in terms of time?

■ *Devising programs.* What will be the components of each program, and how will the effectiveness of each program be measured?

Strategic planning differs considerably from short-range tactical (or operational) planning. It involves fundamental decisions about the very nature of the business. Strategic planning may result in new business acquisitions, divestitures of current (profitable or unprofitable) product lines, new capital investments, or new management approaches.[27]

It is long-range in scope, and it may involve substantial commitments of resources. Almost always it involves considerable data collection, analysis, and repeated review and reevaluation by top management.

Tactical, or operational, planning deals with the normal growth of current operations, as well as with any specific problems that might disrupt the pace of planned, normal growth. Purchasing new or additional office equipment to enhance production efficiency (e.g., word processors), coping with the recall of a defective product (e.g., defective brakes in cars), or dealing with the need to design tamper-proof bottle caps (e.g., in the pharmaceutical industry) are examples of tactical planning problems. Beyond the obvious difference in time frames distinguishing strategic planning and tactical planning, the other difference between the two is the degree of change resulting from the planning—and hence the degree of impact on human resource planning.

Human resource planning (HRP) parallels the plans for the business as a whole. HRP focuses on questions such as: What do the proposed business strategies imply with respect to human resources? What kinds of internal and external constraints will (or do) we face? For example, restrictive work rules in a collective bargaining contract are an internal constraint, while a projected shortfall in the supply of college graduate electrical engineers (relative to the demand for them by employers) is an external constraint. What are the implications for staffing, compensation practices, training and development, and management succession? What can be done in the short run (tactically) to prepare for long-term (strategic) needs?

■ **COMPANY EXAMPLE**

PHILIPS, THE DUTCH MULTINATIONAL CORPORATION

In Holland, the Philips Company recently decided to open a new plant to capitalize on its competitive advantages. One important advantage was that existing production facilities were already located in Holland. Another was that the Dutch workforce viewed Philips as an attractive place to work. Before building the new plant, elaborate strategic studies were made. Of course, one of the factors under study was the availability of qualified human resources. But the study especially focused on how to build in changes in the manufacturing technology to match the characteristics of the labor force 20 years ahead. Machines and methods used to produce the products efficiently by today's labor force may not be used efficiently as the labor force grows older. This is an important consideration because one of the cultural characteristics of Dutch workers is that they tend not to move from one location to another during their working careers. Hence it is difficult to transfer employees and almost impossible to replace them. So to maintain its competitive advantage, Philips attempted to incorporate into the production planning process the characteristics of the future labor force. Since the planners anticipated that the future workforce will be better educated and more independent, they tried to design the manufacturing process in a way that might permit improved opportunities for job rotation, job sharing, and job enrichment. This represents a true integration of planning—strategic and human resource—to optimize overall company performance.[2]

More on Human Resource Planning

Although HRP means different things to different people, general agreement exists on its ultimate objective—namely, the most effective use of scarce talent in the interest of the worker and the organization. Thus we may define HRP broadly as *an effort to anticipate future business and environmental demands on an organization, and to provide the personnel to fulfill that business and satisfy those demands.*[8] This general view suggests several specific, interrelated activities that together comprise an HRP system. They include:

- *A personnel inventory* to assess current human resources (skills, abilities, and potential) and to analyze how they are currently being used
- *A human resource forecast* to predict future personnel requirements (the number of workers needed, the number expected to be available, the skills mix required, internal versus external labor supply)
- *Action plans* to enlarge the pool of people qualified to fill the projected vacancies through such actions as recruitment, selection, training, placement, transfer, promotion, development, and compensation
- *Control and evaluation* to provide feedback on the overall effectiveness of the human resource planning system by monitoring the degree of attainment of human resource objectives (an example of a hypothetical control and evaluation procedure is shown in Figure 4-6)

RELATIONSHIP OF HUMAN RESOURCE PLANNING TO STRATEGIC AND TACTICAL PLANNING

A variety of HRP applications exists.[18] For example, HRP itself can be strategic (long-term and general) or tactial (short-term and specific). It may be done organizationwide, or it may be restricted to divisions, departments, or any common employee groups. Or it may be carried out on a recurring basis (e.g., annually) or

OBJECTIVE: INCREASE REPRESENTATION OF WOMEN BY 15% IN ENTRY-LEVEL MANAGEMENT JOBS OVER THE NEXT TWO YEARS.

STRATEGY: PROVIDE INCREASED OPPORTUNITIES FOR TRAINING IN BASIC MANAGEMENT SKILLS.

PROGRAM: BY THE END OF THE FIRST QUARTER OF THE FISCAL YEAR, PROVIDE A "CAREER ASSESSMENT" DAY FOCUSING ON INDIVIDUAL APTITUDES AND INTERESTS FOR ALL WOMEN INTERESTED IN MANAGEMENT JOBS. FOR THOSE WITH THE REQUIRED APTITUDES, PROVIDE SPECIAL COURSES IN DECISION MAKING (2ND QUARTER OF THE FISCAL YEAR), SUPERVISORY SKILLS (3RD QUARTER), AND FINANCIAL ANALYSIS (4TH QUARTER).

EVALUATION OF THE PROGRAM—TWO YEARS LATER

KEY QUESTIONS TO ASK:

1. WAS OUR INITIAL OBJECTIVE (15%) TOO AMBITIOUS?

2. WERE WOMEN IN NONMANAGMENT JOBS REALLY ENCOURAGED AND PERMITTED TO ATTEND TRAINING CLASSES?

3. WAS THE CAREER ASSESSMENT THOROUGH? DID IT PROVIDE USEFUL PLANNING INFORMATION?

4. WHAT PERCENTAGE OF THE WOMEN COMPLETED THE TRAINING COURSES SATISFACTORILY?

5. SHOULD WE CHANGE OUR EFFORTS TO RECRUIT WOMEN INTO MANAGEMENT JOBS? IF SO, HOW, IN LIGHT OF THE ANSWERS TO THESE QUESTIONS?

FIGURE 4-6
Hypothetical control and evaluation process applied to a human resource planning system.

only sporadically (e.g., when launching a new product line or at the outset of a capital expansion project). Regardless of its specific application, almost all experts agree that if HRP is to be genuinely effective, it must be linked with the different levels of general business planning, not as an end or *goal* in and of itself, but rather as a *means* to the end of building more competitive organizations. The overall process is directed by line managers. When line managers perceive that human resource practices help them achieve their goals, they are more likely to initiate and support HRP efforts. Furthermore, the process raises important human resource questions.[50] How business planning affects HRP is depicted in Figure 4-7.

The long-range perspective (2 to 5 years or longer) of strategic planning flows naturally into the middle-range perspective (1 to 2 years) of operational planning. Annual budgeting decisions provide specific timetables, allocations of resources, and standards for implementing strategic and operational plans. As the time frame shortens, planning details become increasingly specific.

At the level of strategic planning, HRP is concerned with such issues as assessing the management implications of future business needs, assessing factors external to the firm (e.g., demographic trends, social trends), and gauging the internal supply of employees over the long run. The focus here is to analyze issues, not to make detailed projections.

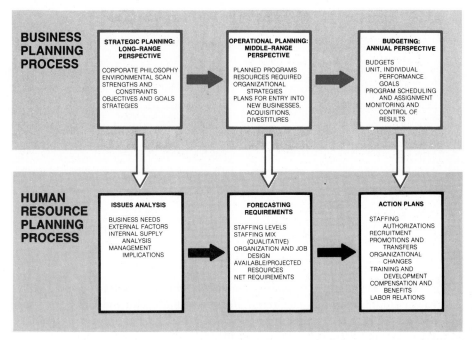

FIGURE 4-7

Impact of three levels of business planning on human resource planning.

At the level of operational, or tactical, planning, HRP is concerned with detailed forecasts of employee supply (internal and external to the organization) and employee demand (numbers needed at some future time period). Based on the forecasts, specific action plans can be undertaken. These may involve recruitment, decruitment (easing some workers out), promotions, training, or transfers. Procedures must be established to control and evaluate progress toward targeted objectives.

As Figure 4-7 shows, human resource planning focuses on firm-level responses to people-related business issues over multiple time horizons. What are some examples of such issues, and how can managers identify them?

Such people-related business concerns, or issues, might include the impact of rapid technological change, more complex organizations (in terms of products, locations, customers, and markets), more frequent responses to external forces such as legislation and litigation, demographic changes, or increasing multinational competition. In this scenario, environmental changes drive issues, issues drive actions, and actions encompass programs and processes used to design and implement them.[40] Issues themselves may be identified with the aid of an HR strategy worksheet, such as that shown in Figure 4-8.

Realistically, HR concerns become business concerns and are dealt with by the line only when they affect the line manager's ability to function effectively. Such concerns may result from an immediate issue, such as downsizing or a labor shortage, or from a longer-term issue that can be felt as if it were an immediate issue, such as management development and succession planning.[40] On the other hand,

DATA TO INCLUDE ON AN HR STRATEGY WORKSHEET

HUMAN RESOURCES ISSUE	ANALYSIS: EVIDENCE OPTIONS
What is the HR problem, gap, or opportunity identified a result of changes in the following? • Business environment • Business strategy • Organizational circumstances	What are the dimensions of the issue? • Evidence of the issue • Scope • Coverage/applicability • Potential business impact • Alternative solutions and their pros and cons

MANAGEMENT ACTIONS/RESOURCES	MEASURES/TARGETS
What course of action will be implemented? • Strategy of 1–2 years • Specific action programs • Responsibility assigned • Timing for completion • Financial and staff resources required	How will the results be measured? • Outcomes • Measures/evidence • Target levels

FIGURE 4-8

Data to include on an HR strategy worksheet. [*Source:* R. S. Schuler & J. W. Walker (1990, Summer), Human resources strategy: Focusing on issues and actions. Reprinted by permission of publisher, from *Organizational Dynamics,* © 1990 American Management Association, New York. All rights reserved.]

HR issues such as workforce diversity, changing requirements for managerial skills, no-growth assumptions, mergers, retraining needs, and health and safety are issues that relate directly to the competitiveness of an organization and threaten its ability to survive. In short, progressive firms regard HR issues as people-related business issues that will have powerful impacts on their strategic business *and* HR planning throughout the 1990s.

LABOR MARKETS: THE FOUNDATION OF HUMAN RESOURCE OBJECTIVES

Human resource objectives cannot be developed in a vacuum. First, they must be consistent with the planned future direction of the organization; that is, they must be consistent with long-range strategic plans. Second, they must be consistent with tactical business objectives (Figure 4-7). The staffing mix, staffing levels, job design, and available and/or projected resources ultimately depend on the structure and functioning of internal and external labor markets. Let us therefore discuss labor market issues first and then say more about human resource objectives.

A *labor market* is a geographical area within which the forces of supply (people looking for work) interact with the forces of demand (employers looking for people) and thereby determine the price of labor.[35] In a *tight labor market*, demand by employers exceeds the available supply of workers, which tends to exert upward pressure on wages. In a *loose labor market*, the reverse is true; the supply of workers exceeds employer demand, exerting downward pressure on wages. In recent years the labor market for electrical engineers, nurses, and aircraft mechanics has been fairly tight; wages for these jobs have been increasing steadily.[42] On the other hand, the labor market for lawyers, steelworkers, and unskilled labor has been fairly loose in recent years, reducing pressure for wage increases for these workers.

Unfortunately, it is not possible to define the geographical boundaries of a labor market in any clear-cut manner.[35] Employers needing key employees will recruit far and wide if necessary. From the perspective of job applicants, movement from a labor market in one geographical area to another is also quite restricted. There are exceptions: During 1982, in the depths of an economic recession, hundreds of unemployed auto workers left Detroit for Houston in the hope of finding work. In 1986, as oil prices plummeted, workers moved from Houston to other cities. Such movements reflect an underlying turbulence in the environment. In short, employers do not face a single, homogeneous market for labor, but rather a series of discontinuous, segmented labor markets over which supply and demand conditions vary substantially.[41] Economists focus on this fact as the major explanation for wage differences between occupations and between geographical areas.

Of practical concern to managers, however, is a reasonably accurate definition of labor markets for planning purposes. Here are some factors that are important for defining the limits of a labor market:[33,52]

- Geography
- Education and/or technical background required to perform a job
- Industry
- Licensing or certification requirements
- Union membership

Companies may use one or more of these factors to help define their labor markets. Thus an agricultural research firm that needs to hire four veterinarians cannot restrict its search to a local area since the market is national or international in scope. Union membership is not a concern in this market, but licensing and/or certification is. Typically a doctor of veterinary medicine degree is required along with state licensure to practice. Applicants are likely to be less concerned with where the job is located and more concerned with job design and career opportunities. On the other hand, suppose a hospital is trying to hire a journeyworker plumber. The hospital will be looking at a labor market defined primarily by its geographic proximity and secondarily by people whose experience, technical background, and (possibly) willingness to join a union after employment qualify them for the job.

Internal versus External Labor Markets

The discussion thus far has concerned the structure and function of external labor markets. Internal labor markets also affect HRP, in many cases more directly, because firms often give preference to present employees in promotions, transfers, and other career-enhancing opportunities. Each employing unit is a separate market. At Delta Airlines, for example, virtually all jobs above the entry level are filled by internal promotion rather than by outside recruitment. Delta looks to its present employees as its source of labor supply, and workers look to this "internal labor market" to advance their careers. In the internal labor markets of most organizations, employees peddle their talents to available "buyers."[1,5,46] Three elements comprise the internal labor market:

- Formal and informal practices that determine how jobs are organized and described
- Methods for choosing among candidates
- Procedures and authorities through which potential candidates are generated by those responsible for filling open jobs

In an open internal labor market, every available job is advertised throughout the organization, and anyone can apply. Preference is given to internal candidates by withholding outside advertising until the job has been on the internal market for several days. Finally, each candidate for a job receives an interview.

When looking at internal labor markets for HRP purposes, it is critical to anticipate the aging of the workforce, along with terminations (unavoidable or controllable), and normal employee flows through various jobs over time. The more keenly this is done, the more useful will be the estimates of the supply of workers at some future time period.

More on Establishing Human Resource Objectives

Objectives can be expressed either in behavioral terms ("By the third week of training, you should be able to do these things . . .") or in end-result terms ("By the end of the next fiscal year five new retail stores should be open, and each should be staffed by a manager, an assistant manager, and three clerks"). In the context of cost control in compensation, for example, the following questions should prove useful in setting human resource objectives:[52]

- What level will the wage rate be for an occupation?
- How many people will be employed?
- How much more will our firm have to pay to attract more employees?
- How would the number of people our company would employ change if the wage were lower? If it were higher?

HRP objectives vary according to such things as the type of environment a company operates in, its strategic and tactical plans, and the current design of jobs and employee work behaviors. As examples, consider some of McDonald's human resource objectives: Define jobs narrowly so that they are easy to learn in a short period of time; pay minimum wages to most nonmanagement employees so that the cost of turnover is low; design jobs to minimize decision making by the human operator (e.g., computer-controlled cooking operations, item labeling on cash registers).[47]

As another example of HRP objectives, consider again the Philips Company, which decided to build a futuristic plant in an area where the workforce is quite stable. The company focused its human resource objectives on minimizing turnover (since workers are so hard to replace), paying competitive wages, and designing jobs to challenge the workforce anticipated 20 years hence.

Setting human resource objectives is art as much as it is science. It requires conscious forethought based on the kind of future the firm wants to create for itself. It requires teamwork; it cannot be left to serendipity.

PERSONNEL INVENTORIES

Once objectives are set, it then becomes useful to compare the numbers, skills, and experience of the current workforce with those desired at some future time period. A personnel inventory facilitates assessment of the current workforce; HR forecasts of supply and demand help to determine future needs. In combination they provide powerful planning information for the development of action programs. In both large and small organizations, such information is often computerized. When combined with other data bases; it can be used to form a complete human resource information system (HRIS) that is useful in a variety of situations.

Personnel inventories and HR forecasts must complement each other; an inventory of present talent is not particularly useful for planning purposes unless it can be analyzed in terms of future human resource requirements. On the other hand, a forecast of human resource requirements is useless unless it can be evaluated relative to the current and projected future supply of workers available internally. Only at that time, when we have a clear understanding of the projected surpluses or deficits of employees in terms of their numbers, their skills, or their experience, does it make sense to initiate action plans to rectify projected problems. Such an integrated HRP system is shown in Figure 4-9.

Projected uses Although secondary uses of the personnel inventory data may emerge, the primary uses must be specified at the concept development stage. This will provide direction and scope regarding who and what kinds of data should be included.

Some common uses of a personnel inventory are: identification of candidates for promotion, management succession planning, assignment to special projects, transfer, training, affirmative action planning and reporting, compensation planning, career planning, and organizational analysis.

Personal Privacy

Two crucial issues that must be considered in setting up and maintaining an HRIS (human resource information system) are data security and personal privacy. Data security is a technical problem that can be dealt with in several ways, including the use of passwords and elaborate codes. Personal privacy in the information age is an ethical and moral issue.

Unfortunately, many companies are failing to safeguard the privacy of their employees. Thus a recent study of 126 Fortune 500 companies employing 3.7 million people found that:

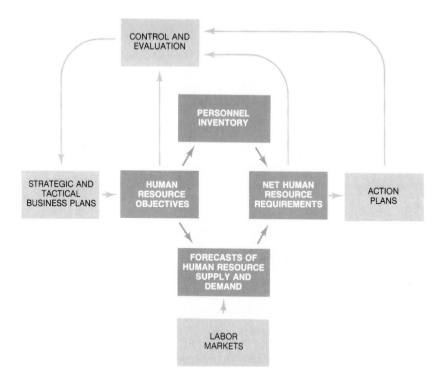

FIGURE 4-9
An integrated human
resource planning
system.

- While 87 percent of the companies allow employees to look at their personnel files, only 27 percent give them access to supervisors' files, which often contain more subjective information.
- 57 percent use private investigative agencies to collect or verify information about employees, and 42 percent collect information without telling the employee.
- 38 percent have no policy covering release of data to the government; of those that do, 38 percent don't require a subpoena.
- 80 percent of companies will give information to an employee's potential creditor without a subpoena, and 58 percent will give information to landlords.[45]

To establish a fair information practice policy, here are some general recommendations provided by one expert:

1. Set up guidelines and policies to protect information in the organization: on types of data to be sought, on methods of obtaining the data, on retention and dissemination of information, on employee or third-party access to information, and on mishandling of information.
2. Inform employees of these information-handling policies.
3. Become thoroughly familiar with state and federal laws regarding privacy.

Here are some specific recommendations:[12]

1. Avoid fraudulent, secretive, or unfair means of collecting data. When possible, collect data directly from the individual concerned.
2. Do not maintain secret files on individuals. Inform them of what information is stored on them, the purpose for which it was collected, how it will be used, and how long it will be kept.
3. Collect only job-related information that is relevant for specific decisions.
4. Maintain records of individuals or organizations who have regular access or who request information on a need-to-know basis.
5. Periodically allow employees the right to inspect and update information stored on them.
6. Gain assurance that any information released to outside parties will be used only for the purposes set forth prior to its release.

DUN & BRADSTREET'S COMPUTERIZED MANAGEMENT INVENTORY SYSTEM

■ **COMPANY EXAMPLE**

This personnel inventory program is intended to facilitate the transfer of managers among the company's various operating units. Initially, a test group of 30 managers was selected for a system trial. Members of this group provided information on a preliminary form and then commented on the design of the form. The form was revised and reviewed by functional heads and general managers in the operating companies, as well as by personnel managers. Ultimately many kinds of information were incorporated into a computerized personnel inventory that fit the mix of businesses in which Dun & Bradstreet is engaged.

Once a user accesses the personnel inventory, a single computer program will lead her or him through any one or more procedures (e.g., searching employee files, adding new information, generating different types of reports on employees) by asking a series of questions requiring only "yes" or "no" or "choose-one" responses. For example, to use the personnel inventory to identify candidates for promotion to a specific job, the user first must specify the selection criteria to be used (e.g., education, experience, foreign language competency). Then the computer will identify appropriate candidates by name, and, according to instructions from the user, it will generate long or short résumés either on a screen or in hard copy. Multiple selection criteria may be used in the candidate identification process, and they may be changed during the search.[17]

HUMAN RESOURCE FORECASTS

The purpose of human resource forecasting is to estimate labor requirements at some future time period. Such forecasts are of two types: (1) the external and internal supply of labor, and (2) the aggregate external and internal demand for labor. The two types of forecasts should be considered separately because each rests on a different set of assumptions and depends on a different set of variables.[51]

Internal supply forecasts relate to conditions *inside* the organization, such as the age distribution of the workforce, terminations, retirements, and new hires within job classes. Both internal and external demand forecasts, on the other hand, depend primarily on the behavior of some business factor (e.g., student enrollments, projected sales, product volume) to which human resource needs can be related. Unlike internal and external supply forecasts, internal and external demand forecasts are subject to many uncertainties—in domestic or worldwide economic conditions, in technology, and in consumer behavior, to name just a few. In the following sections we will consider several human resource forecasting techniques that have proven to be practical and useful.

Forecasting External Human Resource Supply

Recruiting and hiring new employees is essential for virtually all firms, at least over the long run. Whether this is due to projected expansion of operations or to normal workforce attrition, forays into the labor market are necessary.

Several agencies regularly make projections of external labor market conditions and estimates of the supply of labor to be available in general categories. Included among these agencies are: the Bureau of Labor Statistics of the U.S. Department of Labor, the Engineering Manpower Commission, and the Public Health Service of the Department of Health and Human Services. For new college and university graduates, the Northwestern Endicott-Lindquist Report is one of the most respected barometers of future hiring decisions.

Organizations in both the public and private sectors are finding such projections of the external labor market to be helpful in preventing surpluses or deficits of employees.

Managers in Japan pay especially close attention to such forecasts, because in major metropolitan areas there are approximately 132 job openings for every 100 applicants. It was no surprise, therefore, to find out that in a recent poll of senior HR executives taken in the United States and Japan, managers from both countries gave top priority to executive development and recruiting. However, while a third major concern of the Americans was compensation, for the Japanese it was workforce planning.[23]

Forecasting Internal Human Resource Supply

A reasonable starting point for projecting a firm's future supply of labor is its current supply of labor. In the case of management employees, perhaps the simplest type of internal supply forecast is the *management succession plan*, a concept that has been discussed in the planning literature for over 20 years.[22,34] The process for developing such a plan includes setting a planning horizon, identifying replacement candidates for each key position, assessing current performance and readiness for promotion, identifying career development needs, and integrating the career goals of individuals with company goals. The overall objective, of course, is to assure the availability of competent executive talent in the future or, in some cases, immediately, as when a key executive dies suddenly.[6] The chapter opening vignette described the general approach. Here is how one particular firm does it.

SUCCESSION PLANNING IN THE MINISTRY OF TRANSPORTATION AND COMMUNICATIONS (MTC), PROVINCE OF ONTARIO

■ **COMPANY EXAMPLE**

MTC, one of the leading transportation authorities in North America, is responsible for the management of a highway network comprising approximately 13,000 miles of provincial roads. It also manages the subsidy allocation for an additional 62,500 miles of municipal roads and is involved in the planning for provincial commuter rail and air services. Major operational activities include planning, design, construction, maintenance, and research related to transportation systems and facilities.

The full-time workforce consists of approximately 2600 management and 7700 bargaining-unit employees, although for practical reasons, succession planning has been limited to middle and senior management (about 1300 positions). Succession planning is one of the responsibilities of every manager.

Current and future business plans and the assessed skills and potential of the management workforce provide the main inputs to the planning system. Meaningful forecasts can be done only for large job families. Hence, MTC's operations have been divided into five primary and eight secondary functions, and separate analyses are done for each of these functions. Figure 4-10 illustrates the various data that are used in the forecast to determine potential shortages, surpluses, the numbers of promotable staff blocked from promotion (e.g., because there is no higher-level job to progress to in a particular job family), and the annual training and development effort required to maintain backup strength.

■ Current strength is determined from a personnel inventory maintained by the corporate planning group.

■ Losses are made up of resignations, dismissals, transfers, and retirements. Resignations, dismissals, and transfers are assessed from historical data, modified by current and future trends. Retirement figures are based on a review of individual retirement ranges.

■ Backup is determined from two sources: (1) As part of the annual appraisal process, managers identify those employees who are considered

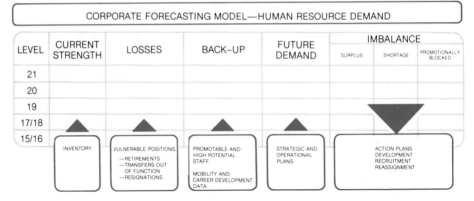

FIGURE 4-10

Corporate human resource demand forecasting model used at the Ontario Ministry of Transportation and Communications. See text for explanations of the data that go into each column.

promotable within the next 1-year planning cycle; and (2) in a separate annual process, managers identify those high-potential individuals who have the ability to progress to two responsibility levels higher—in more than one function—during a 5-year forecast period.

- Future demand is forecast on the basis of current as well as future business plans. These are determined by MTC's strategic policy committee (comprised of the CEO and senior executives) with input from six planning groups.

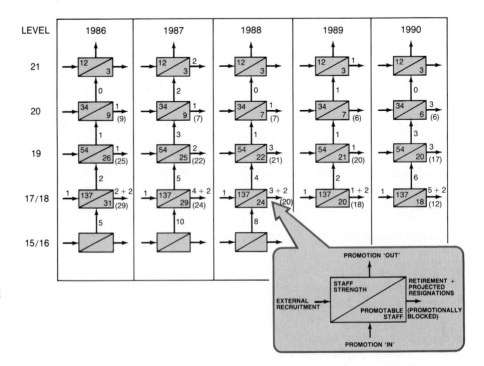

FIGURE 4-11

Management succession forecasting model used at the Ontario Ministry of Transportation and Communications. An explanation of the numbers in each box is contained in the lower right corner of the figure. For example, at job level 17/18 in 1988, staff strength is 120 persons, of whom 24 are promotable. Four persons were promoted "out," 8 were promoted "in," 1 was recruited externally, 3 retired, 2 were projected to resign, and 20 were promotionally blocked.

Finally, the data for management succession planning for each function are manipulated by means of a computerized forecasting model (Figure 4-11). The model was chosen because it is simple to use and because it is flexible enough to be able to analyze situations that vary according to staffing levels, turnover rates, and replacement strategies.[36]

The previous company example illustrated succession planning in a large firm. But what about small firms, such as family-owned businesses? Only about 30 percent of family businesses outlive their founders, usually for lack of planning. Since many founders of small companies started in the post-World War II boom are now retiring, the question of succession is becoming more pressing. Here are some of the ways families are trying to solve the problem:

- 35 percent plan to groom one child from an early age to take over.
- 25 percent plan to let the children compete and choose one or more successors with help from the board of directors.
- 15 percent plan to let the children compete and choose one or more successors without input from a third party.
- 15 percent plan to form an "executive committee" of two or more children.
- 10 percent plan to let the children choose their own leader, or leaders.[7]

Forecasting Human Resource Demand

In contrast to supply forecasting, demand forecasting is beset with multiple uncertainties—changes in technology; consumer attitudes and patterns of buying behavior; local, national, and international economies; number, size, and types of contracts won or lost; and government regulations that might open new markets or close off old ones, just to name a few. Consequently, forecasts of human resource demand are often more subjective than quantitative, although in practice a combination of the two is typically used.

This section presents one subjective approach—the Delphi technique—and one quantitative approach—trend analysis—for forecasting demand. The techniques are basically easy to describe and understand, but applying them may be complex, for they require a variety of data.

The Delphi technique Delphi is a structured approach for reaching a consensus judgment among experts about future developments in any area that might affect a business (e.g., the level of a firm's future demand for labor). Originally developed as a method to facilitate group decision making, it has also been used in human resource forecasting. Experts are chosen on the basis of their knowledge of internal factors that might affect a business (e.g., projected retirements), their knowledge of the general business plans of the organization, or their knowledge of external factors that might affect demand for the firm's product or service and hence its internal demand for labor. Experts may range from first-line supervisors to top-level managers. Sometimes experts internal to the firm are used, but if the required expertise is not available internally, then one or more outside experts may be brought in to contribute their opinions. To estimate the level of future demand for labor, an organization might select as experts, for example, managers from corporate planning, human resources, marketing, production, and sales.

The Delphi technique was developed during the late 1940s at the Rand Corporation's "think tank" in Santa Monica, California. Its objective is to predict future developments in a particular area by integrating the *independent* opinions of experts.[13] Face-to-face group discussion among the experts is avoided since differences in job status among group members may lead some individuals to avoid criticizing others and to compromise on their good ideas. To avoid these problems, an intermediary is used. The intermediary's job is to pool, summarize, and then feed back to the experts the information generated independently by all the other experts during the first round of forecasting. The cycle is then repeated, so that the experts are given the opportunity to revise their forecasts and the reasons behind their revised forecasts. Successive rounds usually lead to a convergence of expert opinion within three to five rounds.

In one application, Delphi did provide an accurate 1-year demand forecast for the number of buyers needed for a retailing firm.[29] To be most useful, the following guidelines should be followed:

- Give the expert enough information to make an informed judgment. That is, give him or her the historical data that have been collected, as well as the results of any relevant statistical analysis that has been conducted, such as staffing patterns and productivity trends.
- Ask the kinds of questions that a unit manager can answer. For example, instead of asking for total staffing requirements, ask by what percentage staffing is likely to increase or only ask about anticipated increases in key employee groups, such as marketing managers or engineers.
- Do not require precision. Allow the experts to round off figures, and give them the opportunity to indicate how sure they are of the forecasted figures.
- Keep the exercise as simple as possible, and especially avoid questions that are not absolutely necessary.
- Be sure that classifications of employees and other definitions are understood in the same way by all experts.
- Enlist top management's and the experts' support for the Delphi process by showing how good forecasts will benefit the organization and small-unit operations and how they will affect profitability and workforce productivity.[20]

Trend Analysis

There are many factors affecting what goes on in any particular business organization. The basic idea behind this method of forecasting human resource demand is to determine which factor of a business most significantly relates to its workforce in terms of size and makeup. Then we measure the past trends of this business factor in relation to the numbers of people employed, and we project from that what the future trend will be and, hence, the future demand in terms of the workforce.

There are six steps in this quantitative method:[53]

1. Find an appropriate business factor that relates to the number of people employed.
2. Plot the historical record of that factor in relation to workforce size.
3. Compute the average output per individual worker per year. This is known as labor productivity.
4. Determine the trend in labor productivity.
5. Make necessary adjustments in the trend, past and future.
6. Project to the target year.

Now let's discuss each of these six factors.

The business factor For a university, the appropriate factor might be student enrollments, for a hospital it might be patient-days, for a retail shoe operation it might be inventory-adjusted sales revenue, and for a steel company it might be tons of steel output. To be useful, the business factor must satisfy at least two requirements. First, *it should relate directly to the essential nature of the business* so that business planning is done in terms of that factor. Thus it makes little sense for the retail shoe operation to project human resource needs against units sold if all other business planning is done in relation to dollar volume of sales and if frequent price changes make conversion from dollars to units difficult.

Second, *changes in the selected factor must be proportional to the number of employees required*. For example, after a $15 million automation of Arrow Company's domestic plants, the shirtmaker boosted worker productivity by 25 percent and was able to make far more dress shirts with far fewer people. Now, for example, one worker controlling two machines can attach plackets (slits in a garment that form a closure) to 95 dozen shirts in 1 hour. Using older machines, it would have taken more than 4½ hours to do the same amount of work.[30] Plackets per hour might therefore be used as the business factor against which to project human resource requirements.

Selecting the proper business factor can be a major problem in some industries, particularly where workforce size is not proportional to product volume. In the airline industry, for example, it takes just as many air traffic controllers and ground personnel to handle airplane landings when the planes are full as when they are almost empty. Moreover, the same organization may produce many products, some of which require high labor input while others do not. Under these circumstances, human resource forecasts for the entire organization may be misleading, and separate forecasts must be made for different product groups or segments of the workforce (e.g., research, production, maintenance).

The historical relationship between the business factor and workforce size
This may be difficult to determine, especially if HRP is new to the firm and if such historical data do not exist or are burdensome to retrieve. A hospital needs to know, for example, that last year it took 1050 nurses to provide care over 1400 patient-days, or approximately three nurses for every four patients per 24-hour day.

Labor productivity This ratio—output per individual worker—is known as *labor productivity*. Figure 4-12 presents hypothetical figures showing the average daily number of patients cared for per three shifts of registered nurses from 1978 to 1990. In this figure, the total number of patient-days per year is multiplied by the labor productivity figure for that year to yield the total number of nurses employed. Thus in calendar year 1990, let's say St. Elsewhere hospital recorded 1920 patient-days × $^3/_6$ (nurse/patient ratio) = 960 nurses employed to care for these patients. To forecast staffing requirements accurately, it is necessary to know the *rate* at which labor productivity and the business factor are changing. These rates of change are critical because projections of the demand for labor for the target year must reflect the labor productivity and the demand for goods or services anticipated at that time.

Determining the trend in labor productivity and adjustments to the trend
To determine the average annual rate of productivity change during the past 5 or, preferably, 10 years, data representing output and the size of the labor force during that period must be collected. With those data we can calculate the average annual productivity change and, along with projected changes in the business factor, use it as a forecast of what the change will be for the forthcoming year(s).

Unless, of course, there are reasons for considering why the change will be different from average for the forthcoming year. That is why we should be especially keen about analyzing the data from the past and evaluating the causes of any past changes deviating from the average annual change in productivity.

In Figure 4-12, for example, note the significant changes both in the business

FIGURE 4-12
Hypothetical human resource demand for registered nurses in a hospital. To determine the number of nurses employed in any given year, multiply column 2, patient-days per year, by column 3, the nurse/patient ratio. In 1978, for example, the hospital recorded 3000 patient-days × 3/15 (nurse/patient ratio) = 600 nurses employed. Assume that these are *actual*, not *projected*, employment levels.

	BUSINESS FACTOR	LABOR PRODUCTIVITY	HUMAN RESOURCE REQUIREMENTS
CALENDAR YEAR	PATIENT-DAYS PER YEAR	NURSE/PATIENT RATIO	NUMBER OF REGISTERED NURSES EMPLOYED
1978	3,000	3/15	600
1982	2,880	3/12	720
1986	2,800	3/10	840
1990	1,920	3/6	960

factor (patient-days per year) and in labor productivity (the nurse/patient ratio). Such changes must be tempered with the judgment of experienced line managers, who interpret the reasons for past changes, anticipate the impact of future changes, and estimate how much both past and future changes will affect forecasts of human resource needs.

Projecting future staffing needs to the target year Once the data have been collected, the projection of staffing needs to the target year is straightforward (Figure 4-13). In part *A* of this figure, actual and projected levels of the business factor (that is, patient-days per year) and actual and projected labor productivity are shown through the year 2002. Just as in Figure 4-12, when labor productivity is multiplied by the number of patient-days projected, the number of registered nurses needed in any given year can be determined. In Figure 4-13*B*, required staffing levels are plotted by calendar year. Notice also how adjustments to the projection (e.g., to account for the slower rate of increase in patient-days, plus the constant nurse/patient ratio anticipated from 1994 through 2002) yield a net figure for human resource demand at that time. In the year 2002, therefore, St. Elsewhere expects 1660 patient-days × ¾ (nurse/patient ratio) = 1245 registered nurses needed at that time.

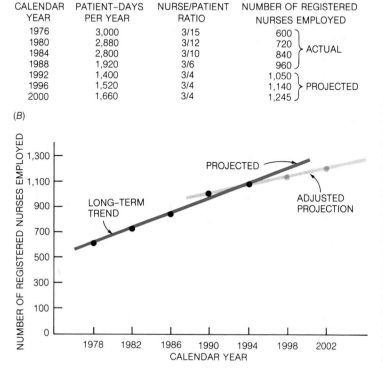

(A)	BUSINESS FACTOR	LABOR PRODUCTIVITY	HUMAN RESOURCE REQUIREMENTS
CALENDAR YEAR	PATIENT–DAYS PER YEAR	NURSE/PATIENT RATIO	NUMBER OF REGISTERED NURSES EMPLOYED
1976	3,000	3/15	600 ⎫
1980	2,880	3/12	720 ⎬ ACTUAL
1984	2,800	3/10	840 ⎪
1988	1,920	3/6	960 ⎭
1992	1,400	3/4	1,050 ⎫
1996	1,520	3/4	1,140 ⎬ PROJECTED
2000	1,660	3/4	1,245 ⎭

FIGURE 4-13

Hypothetical human resource demand forecast for registered nurses in a hospital. To determine the number needed in any given year, multiply patient-days per year (the business factor) by the nurse/patient ratio (labor productivity). These figures are shown in part *A* of the figure. Part *B* shows the number of nurses *actually* employed through 1990 and *projected* to be employed through 2002, based on adjustments to the long-term employment trend.

Finally, a forecast of *net* human resource demand (shortages or surpluses) is determined simply by subtracting the supply forecast from the demand forecast. For example, suppose that in 2002 St. Elsewhere forecasts an internal *supply* of 1100 nurses, but, as Figure 4-13 shows, the *demand* for nurses is projected to be 1245. The net demand for nurses in 2002, therefore, is +145.

How Accurate Is Accurate?

Accuracy in forecasting the demand for labor varies considerably by firm and by industry type (e.g., utilities versus women's fashions): roughly from 2 to 20 percent error.[53] Certainly factors such as the duration of the planning period, the quality of the data on which forecasts are based (e.g., expected changes in the business factor and labor productivity), and the degree of integration of HRP with strategic business planning all affect accuracy. How accurate a labor demand forecast should be depends on the degree of flexibility in staffing the workforce. That is, to the extent that people are geographically mobile, multiskilled, and easily hired, there is no need for precise forecasts.[20]

Matching Forecast Results to Action Plans

Labor demand forecasts affect a firm's programs in many different areas, including recruitment, selection, performance appraisal, training, transfer, and many other types of career enhancement activities. These activities all comprise "action programs." Action programs help organizations adapt to changes in the environment of business. In the past decade or so, one of the most obvious changes in the business environment has been the large influx of women and minorities into the workforce. To adapt to these changes, organizations have provided extensive training programs designed to develop management skills in the women and minorities. Also, they have provided training programs for supervisors and coworkers in human relations skills to deal effectively with the women and minorities.[31,44]

Assuming a firm has a choice, however, is it better to *select* workers who already have developed the skills necessary to perform competently or to select workers who do not have the skills immediately but who can be *trained* to perform competently? This is the same type of "make-or-buy" decision that managers often face in so many other areas of business. Managers have found that it is often more cost effective to buy, rather than to make. This is also true in the context of selection versus training.[37] Put your money and resources into selection. Always strive *first* to develop the most accurate, the most valid selection process that you can, for it will yield higher-ability workers. *Then* apply those action programs that are most appropriate in further increasing the performance of your employees.

With high-ability employees, the productivity gain from a training program in, say, Lotus 1-2-3 might be greater than the gain from the same program with lower-ability employees. Further, even if the training is about equally effective with well-selected, higher-ability employees and poorly selected, lower-ability em-

IMPACT OF JOB ANALYSIS AND HRP ON PRODUCTIVITY, QUALITY OF WORK LIFE, AND THE BOTTOM LINE

Earlier we noted that jobs are dynamic, not static, in their requirements. This is especially true of jobs at the bottom and at the top of today's organizations. Entry-level jobs now demand workers with new and different kinds of skills. Even simple clerical work now requires computer knowledge, bank tellers need more knowledge of financial transactions and sales techniques, and foreign competition means that assembly line workers need more sophisticated understanding of mathematics and computer-aided manufacturing in order to cut costs and improve quality.

Information technology, once the exclusive purview of computer systems managers, must now be an integral part of corporate strategy, requiring extensive training of senior executives and providing more opportunity for the computer literate.[9]

Current information on the behavioral requirements of jobs is critically important if firms are to develop meaningful specifications for selecting, training, or appraising the performance of employees in them, and if employees are to perform their jobs successfully. Human resource planning information is no less important so that firms can institute action plans now to cope with projected HR needs in the future.

What are firms actually doing? A recent survey of 2100 firms by the Hay Group found that HR planning was formal and developed at only 21 percent of the firms. It was undeveloped or rudimentary at another 30 percent. Most firms said that finding and keeping key people is a top priority. However, without solid planning they may miss seeing the need for new talent and the need to develop new ways of selecting and training that talent.

ployees, the required training *time* may be reduced for higher-ability employees. Thus training costs will be reduced, and the *net* effectiveness of training will be greater when applied along with a highly valid personnel selection process. This point becomes even more relevant if one views training as a strategy for building sustained competitive advantage. Firms that *select* high caliber employees, and then commit resources to *develop* them continually, gain a competitive advantage that no other organization can match: a deep reservoir of firm-specific human capital.

CONTROL AND EVALUATION OF HRP SYSTEMS

The purpose of control and evaluation is to guide HRP activities, identifying deviations from the plan and their causes. For this reason, we need yardsticks to measure performance. Qualitative and quantitative objectives can both play useful roles in HRP. Quantitative objectives make the control and evaluation process more objective and measure deviations from desired performance more precisely. Nevertheless, the nature of evaluation and control should always match the degree of development of the rest of the HRP process.[51] In newly instituted HRP systems, for example, evaluation is likely to be more qualitative than quantitative, with little emphasis placed on control. This is because supply and demand forecasts are likely to be based more on "hunches" and subjective opinions than on hard data. Under these circumstances, human resource planners should attempt to assess the following:[51]

- The extent to which they are tuned into human resource problems and opportunities and the extent to which their priorities are sound
- The quality of their working relationships with staff specialists and line managers who supply data and use HRP results (How closely do the human resource planners work with these specialists and line managers on a day-to-day basis?)
- The extent to which decision makers, from line managers who hire employees to top managers who develop long-term business strategy, are making use of HRP forecasts, plans, and recommendations
- The perceived value of HRP among decision makers (Do they view the information provided by human resource planners as useful to them in their own jobs?)[51]

In more established HRP systems where objectives and action plans are both underpinned by measured performance standards, key comparisons might include the following:[18]

- Actual staffing levels against forecast staffing requirements (In Figure 4-13, for example, St. Elsewhere forecast that 1050 registered nurses will be needed in 1994. In 1995, as a basis for evaluating future projections, it is important that the hospital compare the *actual* number employed in 1994, say 1075, to the *forecasted* number.)
- Actual levels of labor productivity against anticipated levels of labor productivity (In Figure 4-13, for example, the hospital anticipated a ¾ nurse/patient ratio in 1994. In 1995 it is important to know whether or not this level actually occurred.)
- Actual personnel flow rates against desired rates
- Action programs implemented against action programs planned (Were there more or fewer? Why?)
- The *actual* results of the action programs implemented against the *expected* results (e.g., improved applicant flows, lower quit rates, improved replacement ratios)
- Labor and action program costs against budgets
- Ratios of action program benefits to action program costs

The advantage of quantitative information is that it highlights potential problem areas and it can provide the basis for constructive discussion of the issues. Let us see how this is done in one company.

CONTROL AND EVALUATION OF HRP AT CORNING, INC.

An in-depth study provided considerable insight into each phase of the HRP process.[19] With regard to control and evaluation, the broad process is as follows: Four human resource development managers are responsible for assembling and analyzing corporate demand and supply of managers and professionals in four functional areas: manufacturing and engineering; sales and marketing; finance, data processing, and planning; and human resources. These managers estimate the number of likely vacancies that will occur in key positions in their functional areas during the forecast year.

These results are used to stimulate discussion and action planning by appropriate line managers. Action planning (e.g., decisions to provide skill training, job rotation) in the four functional areas can be highly complex since solutions often cut across divisional lines and may require sacrifices by various units. Thus a job rotation program may require that a manager spend time in all four functional areas. Although beneficial results have not come easily, successes have been experienced, particularly with plant manager positions. Since HRP was instituted, vacancies at this level have been reduced by roughly 50 percent, and geographic transfers have been curtailed sharply.

Ongoing evaluation and control takes place during the quarterly reviews held with each human resource development manager by the director of management and professional personnel. These reviews follow a standard format. Each human resource development manager reports on 14 areas: staffing levels; equal employment opportunity and affirmative action; key vacancies and candidates; other vacancies and candidate pools; surpluses; losses of employees; transfers in; transfers out; internal movement rates; recruiting; other additions to the workforce; performance problems; organizational issues; and other (e.g., audit completions, career path reviews, policy communications). Within each area, the human resource development manager indicates major variances from forecasts or plans and discusses possible corrective action. The sessions typically produce agreement about action to be taken in the division during the upcoming quarter.

After the review sessions, the human resource development managers carry the quarterly reviews to their divisions. In these meetings, priorities are reexamined by the line managers, and action plans are established as needed. The occasional disagreements that arise between line managers and the staff are usually worked through at the division level. The resolution is carried back to the director of management and professional personnel, who typically accepts the line managers' decisions but who may try to influence them directly.[19]

■ HUMAN RESOURCE MANAGEMENT IN ACTION:
CONCLUSION

SUCCESSION PLANNING—A PRACTICAL AND WORKABLE APPROACH

As the organization grows and evolves, and as individuals develop and increase their qualifications, the HR staff assists top management in bringing these two activities together to fill position openings as they occur. Openings are thus filled by individuals who (1) are responsible for their own career development, and (2) have had no explicit or implicit promises about future opportunities made to them by the organization, whose requirements for managerial skills and capabilities are constantly changing. Hence if each party—the organization and developing individuals—does what is best for itself, the result will be what is best for the organization as a whole.

No system of succession planning is perfect. The primary reason that many systems fail is that they are not flexible enough to adapt to changes in the business environment and organization structure, unexpected events in the lives of managers, and all the other "unpredictables" that typically happen over the course of a corporation's planning time horizon.

The reason this system works is that it has the flexibility necessary to adapt to almost any kind of change, and because it reflects genuine organizational needs and projections.

SUMMARY

We are witnessing vast changes in the very nature of work itself, as well as in the types and numbers of jobs available. To be maximally efficient, therefore, careful attention needs to be paid to a thorough understanding of the behavioral requirements of jobs and to the determination of human resource needs.

An overall written summary of the task requirements for a particular job is called a job description, and an overall written summary of people requirements is called a job specification. Together they comprise a job analysis. This information is useful for a variety of organizational purposes ranging from human resource planning to career counseling.

Some combination of available job analysis methods should be used (job performance, observation, interviews, critical incidents, structured questionnaires), for all have advantages and disadvantages. Key considerations in the choice of methods are the method-purpose fit, cost, practicality, and an overall judgment of the appropriateness of the methods for the situation in question.

Job analysis provides one input to the human resource planning process. Strategic and operational planning provide others. Strategic business planning is the long-range process of setting organizational objectives and deciding on action programs to achieve the objectives. Operational, or tactical, planning deals with

IMPLICATIONS FOR MANAGEMENT PRACTICE

More and more, HR issues are seen as people-related business issues. As a manager, this suggests that you should do the following:

■ Keep a management view, not an HR staff department view, of critical issues and opportunities. Consider a comment by the director of human resources at Merck & Co.:

> Line managers are starting to address the needs of individual and organizational performance—e.g., they know why every job exists in the organization, who the people in these jobs are, and how competent they are; and they know it is important to keep their skills updated. There is a saying at Merck: "Human resources are too important to be left to the HR department." Fully one-third of the performance evaluation of line managers is related to people management. (ref. 40, p. 13)

■ Plan within the context of managing the business strategically.

■ Execute the strategy—doing so requires effective management consensus, communications to educate, and involvement of all parties.[37] This is not a "pie in the sky" recommendation. In a recent survey, only 37 percent of senior managers thought other key managers completely understood new business goals. Only 4 percent thought middle managers totally understood. Not surprisingly, as understanding drops, so does compliance.[24]

the normal, ongoing growth of current operations or with specific problems that temporarily disrupt the pace of normal growth. Annual budgeting decisions provide specific timetables, allocations of resources, and implementation standards. The shorter the planning time frame, the more specific must be the planning details.

Strategic and operational business objectives dictate what human resource objectives must be. So also do internal and external labor markets. Human resource planning (HRP) parallels general business planning. Broadly speaking, HRP is an effort to anticipate future business and environmental demands on an organization and to meet the human resource requirements dictated by those conditions. This general view suggests several interrelated activities that together comprise an integrated HRP system. These include (1) an inventory of personnel currently on hand, (2) forecasts of human resource supply and human resource demand at some future time period, (3) action plans such as training or job transfer to meet forecasted human resource needs, and (4) control and evaluation procedures.

DISCUSSION QUESTIONS

4■1 In your opinion, what are some of the key reasons for the deep changes we are seeing in the way jobs are done?

4∙2 How can job analysis be useful to the operating manager?

4∙3 For purposes of management succession planning, what information would you want in order to evaluate "potential"?

4∙4 What do you see as the key uses of a personnel inventory? What kinds of information do you need to provide these uses?

4∙5 Discuss the pros and cons of alternative safeguards for employee information privacy.

4∙6 In your opinion, is it more cost-effective to "buy" or to "make" competent employees?

4∙7 Why should the output from forecasting models be tempered with the judgment of experienced line managers?

REFERENCES

1. Alfred, T. M. (1967). Checkers or choice in manpower management. *Harvard Business Review*, **45**, 157–167.

2. Alpander, G. C., & Botter, C. H. (1981). An integrated model of strategic human resource planning and utilization. *Human Resource Planning*, **4**, 189–208.

3. Ash, R. A., & Edgell, S. L. (1975). A note on the readability of the Position Analysis Questionnaire (PAQ). *Journal of Applied Psychology*, **60**, 765–766.

4. A work revolution in U.S. industry (1983, May 16). *Business Week*, pp. 100–110.

5. Baron, J. N., Davis-Blake, A., & Bielby, W. T. (1986). The structure of opportunity: How promotion ladders vary within and among organizations. *Administrative Science Quarterly*, **31**, 248–273.

6. Bennett, A. (1988, April 29). Many companies aren't prepared to deal with sudden death of chief executive. *The Wall Street Journal*, p. 25.

7. Brown, B. (1988, Aug. 4). Succession strategies for family firms. *The Wall Street Journal*, p. 23.

8. Cascio, W. F. (1991). *Applied psychology in personnel management* (4th ed.). Englewood Cliffs, NJ: Prentice-Hall.

9. Chira, S. (1989, Oct. 1). In 1990's, what price scarce labor? *The New York Times*, pp. 29F, 33F.

10. Christal, R. E. (1974, January). *The United States Air Force occupational research project.* Occupational Research Division, AFHRL-TR-73-75, Lackland Air Force Base, TX.

11. Conley, P. R., & Sackett, P. R. (1987). Effects of using high- versus low-performing job incumbents as sources of job-analysis information. *Journal of Applied Psychology*, **72**, 434–437.

12. Cook, S. H. (1987). Privacy rights: Whose life is it anyway? *Personnel Administrator*, **32**(4), 58–65.

13. Dalkey, N. (1969). *The Delphi method: An experimental study of group opinion.* Santa Monica, CA: Rand.

14. DiNisi, A. S., Cornelius, E. T., III, & Blencoe, A. G. (1987). Further investigation of common knowledge effects on job analysis ratings. *Journal of Applied Psychology*, **72**, 262–268.

15. Dowell, B. E., & Wexley, K. N. (1978). Development of a work behavior taxonomy for first-line supervisors. *Journal of Applied Psychology*, **63**, 563–572.

16. Driessnack, C. H. (1979, December). Financial impact of effective human resource management. *The Personnel Administrator*, pp. 62–66.

17. Dunn, B. D. (1982, September–October). The skills inventory: A second generation. *Personnel*, pp. 40–44.

18. Dyer, L. (1982). Human resource planning. In K. M. Rowland & G. R. Ferris (eds.), *Personnel management*. Boston: Allyn & Bacon.
19. Dyer, L., Shafer, R. A., & Regan, P. J. (1982). Human resource planning at Corning Glass Works: A field study. *Human Resource Planning*, 5, 115–184.
20. Frantzreb, R. B. (1981). Human resource planning: Forecasting manpower needs. *Personnel Journal*, **60**, 850–857.
21. Friedman, L., & Harvey, R. J. (1986). Can raters with reduced job descriptive information provide accurate Position Analysis Questionnaire (PAQ) ratings? *Personnel Psychology*, **39**, 779–789.
22. House, R. J., & Singh, J. V. (1987). Organizational behavior: Some new directions for I/O psychology. *Annual Review of Psychology*, **38**, 669–718.
23. Labor Letter (1990, May 22). *The Wall Street Journal*, p. A1.
24. Labor Letter (1990, May 1). *The Wall Street Journal*, p. A1.
25. Levine, E. L., Ash, R. A., & Bennett, N. (1980). Exploratory comparative study of four job analysis methods. *Journal of Applied Psychology*, **65**, 524–535.
26. Levine, E. L., Ash, R. A., Hall, H., & Sistrunk, F. (1983). Evaluation of job analysis methods by experienced job analysts. *Academy of Management Journal*, **26**(2), 339–348.
27. Lorange, P., & Vancil, R. F. (1976). How to design a strategic planning system. *Harvard Business Review*, **54**, 75–81.
28. McCormick, E. J., Jeanneret, P. R., & Mecham, R. C. (1972). A study of job characteristics and job dimensions as based on the Position Analysis Questionnaire (PAQ). *Journal of Applied Psychology*, **56**, 347–368.
29. Milkovich, G. T., Annoni, A. J., & Mahoney, T. A. (1972). The use of the Delphi procedure in manpower forecasting. *Management Science*, **19**, 381–388.
30. Mitchell, C. F. (1986, Oct. 14). Coming home: Some firms resume manufacturing in U.S. after foreign fiascoes. *The Wall Street Journal*, pp. 1, 29.
31. Mitchell, C. (1987, Sep. 28). Corporate classes: Firms broaden scope of their education programs. *The Wall Street Journal*, p. 35.
32. Olian J. D., & Rynes, S. L. (1984). Organizational staffing: Integrating practice with strategy. *Industrial Relations*, **23**, 170–183.
33. Page, R. C., & Van De Voort, D. M. (1989). Job analysis and HR planning. In W. F. Cascio (ed.), *Human resource planning, employment, and placement*. Washington, DC: Bureau of National Affairs, pp. 2-34 to 2-72.
34. Perham, J. (1981). Management succession: A hard game to play. *Dun's Review*, **117**, 54–55, 58.
35. Reynolds. L. G., Masters, S. H., & Moser, C. H. (1986). *Labor economics and labor relations* (9th ed.). Englewood Cliffs, NJ: Prentice-Hall.
36. Reypert, L. J. (1981). Succession planning in the Ministry of Transportation and Communications, Province of Ontario. *Human Resource Planning*, **4**, 151–156.
37. Schmidt, F. L., Hunter, J. E., & Pearlman, K. (1982). Assessing the economic impact of personnel programs on workforce productivity. *Personnel Psychology*, **35**, 333–347.
38. Schmitt, N., & Cohen, S. A. (1989). Internal analyses of task ratings by job incumbents. *Journal of Applied Psychology*, **73**, 96–104.
39. Schneider, B., & Konz, A. (1989). Strategic job analysis. *Human Resource Management*, **28**, 51–63.
40. Schuler, R. S., & Walker, J. W. (1990, Summer). Human resources strategy: Focusing on issues and actions. *Organizational Dynamics*, pp. 5–19.
41. Sebastian, P. (1988, Sept. 16). Labor pains. *The Wall Street Journal*, pp. 1, 12.

42. Sharn, L. (1989, Sept. 7). Help wanted: Mechanics for busy airlines. *USA Today*, pp. 1, 2.

43. Snow, C. C. (ed.) (1987). *Strategy, organization design, and human resources management.* Greenwich, CT: JAI Press.

44. Solomon, J. (1989, Nov. 7). Firms grapple with language barriers. *The Wall Street Journal*, pp. B1, B12.

45. Solomon, J. (1989, April 4). As firms' personnel files grow, worker privacy falls. *The Wall Street Journal*, p. B1.

46. Stewman, S. (1986). Demographic models of internal labor markets. *Administrative Science Quarterly*, **31**, 212–247.

47. The man who McDonalized Burger King (1979, Oct. 8). *Business Week*, pp. 132, 136.

48. Tichy, N. M., Fombrum, C. J., & Devanna, M. A. (1982). Strategic human resource management. *Sloan Management Review*, **23**, 47–61.

49. Tornow, W. W., & Pinto, P. R. (1976). The development of a managerial taxonomy: A system for describing, classifying, and evaluating executive positions. *Journal of Applied Psychology*, **61**, 410–418.

50. Ulrich, D. (1986). Human resource planning as a competitive edge. *Human Resource Planning*, **9**(2), 41–50.

51. Walker, J. W. (1980). *Human resource planning.* New York: McGraw-Hill.

52. Wallace, M. J., & Fay, C. H. (1988). *Compensation theory and practice* (2d ed.). Boston: Kent.

53. Wikstrom, W. S. (1971). *Manpower planning: Evolving systems.* New York: The Conference Board.

■ C H A P T E R 5 ■

Recruiting

■ **HUMAN RESOURCE MANAGEMENT IN ACTION**

SMALL BUSINESS FACES A TOUGH TEST: RECRUITMENT IN THE 1990s*

Ronald P. Sandmeyer, a man who patrols the shop floor in a three-piece suit and provides holiday turkeys to all hands, exudes old-school attitudes about how to run a business. But that does not extend to having unusually high employee recruitment standards.

"Don't give us your best and brightest," the 59-year-old head of the Sandmeyer Steel Company tells people who may know someone looking for a job. "Give us the people who are average or mediocre and don't know what they want to do with their lives."

Yet Mr. Sandmeyer has trouble finding workers to meet even his modest standards. His predicament is a measure of how hard it is for many American manufacturers to find workers these days, for reasons that embrace culture, education and demographics.

*From: R. D. Hershey, Jr. As labor pool ebbs, factories fish harder. *The New York Times,* December 22, 1989, pp. D1, D4. Copyright © 1989 by The New York Times Company. Reprinted by permission.

Indeed, what Mr. Sandmeyer calls the people problem is getting worse in many parts of the country, hastening America's decline as a manufacturer and undermining the ability to compete against countries like Japan and Germany, where factory work has . . . higher status and the numbers of skilled workers are larger.

The problem is particularly bad in urban areas like Philadelphia, where the middle class has higher aspirations, the poor have no skills and the television-weaned youth of both groups are shocked to discover that the modern factory is still often noisy, smelly, dirty and uncomfortably hot or cold. . . .

Mr. Sandmeyer calls the people problem his biggest worry in managing his family's stainless-steel company in the northeast corner of the city: "It's held down our growth. We have not been able to gain as much market share as we would have been able to had we had more productive man-hours with capable employees.". . .

With imaginative searching that enlisted the aid of a local priest—and has resulted in 30 percent to 40 percent of its work force being foreign-born—Sandmeyer Steel has largely managed to fill its ranks. It has succeeded despite stiff competition from large employers that typically offer similar pay but more training, more prestige, better fringe benefits and less physical discomfort.

A newly hired employee with no previous work experience is paid $5.50 an hour, Mr. Sandmeyer said. Someone with a year or two of experience and a record of dependability might get $6.50 to $8.50. He said the tight labor situation had bid up the company's wage costs.

"It's hot and dirty; it's heavy manufacturing," Mr. Sandmeyer acknowledged of his plant. Instead of air-conditioning, he said, "we open all the doors and all the windows and when it gets above 90, everybody gets free soda."

Challenges

1. Serious labor shortages do exist in many places, but these are not the only reasons for the recruiting problems experienced by many small businesses. What are some others?

2. As a manager in such a small business, what sources might you use to find new workers?

3. What special advantages does a small business have over a large one? How can you incorporate these into the recruitment process?

QUESTIONS THIS CHAPTER WILL HELP MANAGERS ANSWER

1. What factors are most important to consider in developing a recruitment policy?

2. What kinds of decisions are implied by alternative workforce utilization results?

3. How can recruitment operations be managed most effectively?

4. Under what circumstances does it make sense to retain an executive search firm?

5. Do alternative recruitment sources yield differences in the quality of employees?

6. How can we communicate as realistic a picture as possible of the job and organization to prospective new employees? What kinds of issues are most crucial to them?

7. If I lose my current job in management, what's the most efficient strategy for finding a new one?

As the chapter opening vignette illustrates, recruitment is a form of business competition. Just as corporations compete to develop, manufacture, and market the best product or service, so they must also compete to identify, attract, and hire the most qualified people. Recruitment is a business, and it is big business.[24] Yet each set of organizational circumstances differs, and the range of recruitment needs is broad. A small manufacturer in a well-populated rural area faces recruitment challenges that are far different from those of the high-technology firm operating in global markets. Let's begin our treatment by examining the "big picture" of the employee recruitment and selection process, along with some important legal issues. Then we'll focus specifically on the processes of planning, managing, and evaluating recruitment efforts.

THE EMPLOYEE RECRUITMENT/SELECTION PROCESS

Recruitment begins, as Figure 5-1 indicates, by specifying human resource requirements (numbers, skills mix, levels, time frame), which are the typical result of job analysis and human resource planning activities.

The step following recruitment is *initial screening*, which is basically a rapid, rough "selection" process. Sixty years ago, when line supervisors hired factory workers outside the gates of a plant, they simply looked over the candidates and then pointed to various people. "You, you, and you—the rest of you come back another day." That's an example of initial screening, and it was probably done only on the basis of physical characteristics. The *selection process* following initial screening is more rigorous. For example, physical characteristics alone do not provide many clues about a person's potential for management, or for any other kind of work for that matter. What is needed, of course, are samples of behavior, either through tests and personal interviews or through the testimony of others about a candidate, as with reference checks.

Past the selection stage, we are no longer dealing with job candidates, we are dealing with new employees. Typically the first step in their introduction to company policies, practices, and benefits (technically, this is called "socialization") is an *orientation program*. Orientation may take up several hours or several weeks; it may be formal, informal, or some combination of the two. As we shall see in Chapter 7, orientation has more significant and lasting effects than most people might expect.

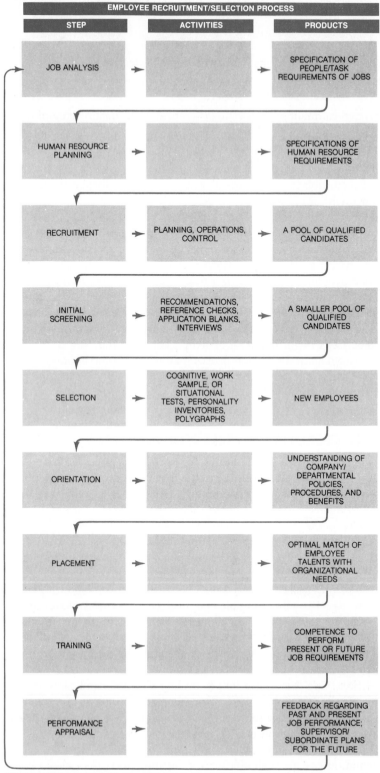

FIGURE 5-1
The employee recruitment/selection process.

Placement occurs after orientation; placement is the assignment of individuals to jobs. In large firms, for example, individuals may be selected initially on the basis of their potential to succeed in general management. After they have been observed and assessed during an intensive management training program, however, the organization is in a much better position to assign them to specific jobs within broader job families, such as marketing, production, or sales. (There are instances in which employees are selected specifically to fill certain positions; these are so-called one-shot selection-placement programs.) The technical expertise and the resources necessary to implement optimal placement programs (select, orient, then place) are found mostly in very large organizations, such as the military.

Once new employees are selected, oriented, and placed, they can then be *trained* to achieve a competent level of job performance. As we shall see in the next chapter, training is big business.

Finally, *performance appraisal* provides feedback to employees regarding their past and present job performance proficiency, and it provides a basis for improving performance in the future.

The first time a new employee's performance is appraised, it is like pushing the button that starts a continuous loop, more precisely a continuous feedback loop comprising the employee's performance, the manager's appraisal of it, and the communication between the two about performance and appraisal.

Of course, all the phases of recruiting and selecting employees are interrelated. But the final test of all phases comes with the appraisal of job performance. There is no point in reporting that, say, 150 possible candidates were recruited and screened, that 90 offers were extended, and that 65 candidates were hired and trained if the first appraisal of their performance indicates that most were inept. You must always remember that when you evaluate the performance of new hires, you are doing so within the context of a system, a network of human resource activities, and you are really appraising recruitment, selection, and training, among other HRM activities.

Developing Recruitment Policies: Legal and Labor Market Issues

As a framework for setting recruitment policies, let us consider four different possible company postures:[33]

1. *Passive nondiscrimination* is a commitment to treat all races and both sexes equally in all decisions about hiring, promotion, and pay. No attempt is made to recruit actively among prospective minority applicants. This posture fails to recognize that discriminatory practices in the past may block prospective applicants from seeking present job opportunities.

2. *Pure affirmative action* is a concerted effort by the organization actively to expand the pool of applicants so that no one is excluded because of past or present discrimination. However, the decision to hire or to promote is based on the best-qualified individual, regardless of race or sex.

3. *Affirmative action with preferential hiring* goes further than pure affirmative action; it systematically favors women and minorities in hiring and promotion decisions. This is a "soft-quota" system.
4. *Hard quotas* represent a mandate to hire or promote specific numbers or proportions of women or minority-group members.

Both private and government employers find hard quotas an unsavory strategy for rectifying the effects of past or present unfair discrimination. Nevertheless, the courts have ordered "temporary" quotas in instances where unfair discrimination has obviously taken place and where no other remedy is feasible.[31] Temporary quotas have bounds placed on them. For example, a judge might order an employer to hire two black employees for every white employee until the number of black employees reaches x percent.

Passive nondiscrimination misses the mark. This became obvious as far back as 1968, when the secretary of labor publicly cited the Allen-Bradley Company of Milwaukee for failure to comply with Executive Order 11246 by not actively recruiting blacks. The company was so well known in Milwaukee as a good place to work that it usually had a long waiting list of friends and relatives of current employees. As a matter of established business practice, the company preferred to hire referrals from current employees; almost no public recruiting was done for entry-level job openings. As a result, because almost all present employees were white, so were almost all referrals.

As noted in Chapter 3's discussion of legal issues in employment, preferential selection is a sticky issue. However, in several landmark cases the Supreme Court established the following principle:[1] *Personnel selection decisions must be made on a case-by-case basis; race or sex can be taken into account as one factor in an applicant's favor, but the overall decision to select or reject must be made on the basis of a combination of factors,* such as entrance test scores and previous performance. That leaves us with pure affirmative action as a recruitment and selection strategy. Indeed, in a free and open competitive labor market, that's the way it ought to be.

Workforce Utilization

Workforce utilization is simply a way of identifying whether or not the composition of the workforce—measured by race and sex—employed in a particular job category in a particular firm is representative of the composition of the entire labor market available to perform that job. To see what considerations this implies, let's consider this situation: There is a town where the workforce comprises 100 workers; half are white, and half are black; among the black workers there are 10 qualified arc welders, and among the whites there are 5 qualified arc welders. Now let's say that the firm in this town needs and has on staff 12 arc welders, 6 white and 6 black. What's going on here? For one thing, all 5 white welders are employed. And where did that sixth white welder come from? He commutes from a town 60 miles away, while 4 local black welders remain unemployed! Now can you begin to see what workforce utilization is all about?

One of the main things that must be considered in workforce utilization is the available labor market, which the courts seem to prefer to refer to as the "relevant labor market." As you might detect from the example, the relevant labor market for a particular job comprises the workers who have the skills needed to perform that job[38] and who are within reasonable commuting distance to that job.

In computing workforce utilization statistics, a table such as Table 5-1 is prepared, where the job group "managers" is examined. (Similar analyses must also be done for eight other categories of employees specified by the EEOC.) This table shows that of 90 managers, 20 are black and 15 are female. However, labor market data indicate that 30 percent and 10 percent of the available labor market for managers are black and female, respectively. Hence, for workforce representation to reach parity with labor market representation, 0.30×90, or 27, of the managers should be black and 0.10×90, or 9, should be female. The recruitment goal, therefore, is to hire 7 more blacks to reach parity with the available labor force. What about the 6 excess female managers? The utilization analysis serves simply as a "red flag," calling attention to recruitment needs. The extra female managers will not be furloughed or fired. However, they may be given additional training, or they may be transferred to other jobs that might provide them with greater breadth of experience, particularly if utilization analyses for those other jobs indicate a need to recruit additional females.

At this point, a logical question is, how large a disparity between the composition of the workforce employed and the composition of the available labor market constitutes a prima facie case of unfair discrimination by the employer? Fortunately the Supreme Court has provided some guidance on this question in its ruling in *Hazelwood v. United States.*[14] To appreciate the Court's ruling, it is necessary to describe the reasoning behind it. In examining disparities between workforce representation and labor force representation, the first step is to compute the difference between the *actual* number of employees in a particular job category (e.g., the 20 black managers in Table 5-1) and the number *expected* if the workforce were truly representative of the labor force (27 black managers). The Court ruled that

■ **TABLE 5·1**
BLACK AND FEMALE UTILIZATION ANALYSIS FOR MANAGERIAL JOBS

Managers employed by the firm			Percent available in relevant labor market		Utilization*		Goal	
Total	Blacks	Females	Blacks	Females	Blacks	Females	Blacks	Females
90	20	15	30	10	−7 (22%)	+6 (17%)	27	9

*Under the "utilization" column, the −7 for blacks means that according to the relevant labor market, the blacks are underrepresented by 7 managers, and the +6 for females means that not only are the females adequately represented, but there are 6 more female managers than needed to meet parity according to the relevant labor market.

if the difference between the actual number and the expected number is so large that the difference would have only 1 chance in 20 of occurring by chance alone, then it is reasonable to conclude that race was a factor in the hiring decisions made. If the odds of the difference occurring by chance alone are greater than 1 in 20 (e.g., 1 in 10), then it is reasonable to conclude that race was not a factor in the hiring decisions. Statistical tests can be used to compute the probability that the differences occurred by chance.

RECRUITMENT—A TWO-WAY PROCESS

Recruitment frequently is treated as if it were a one-way process—something organizations do to search for prospective employees. This approach may be termed a "prospecting" theory of recruitment. In practice, however, prospective employees and managers seek out organizations just as organizations seek them out. This view, termed a "mating" theory of recruitment, appears more realistic. Recruitment success (from the organization's perspective) and job search success (from the candidate's perspective) are both critically dependent on timing. If there is a match between organizational recruitment efforts and a candidate's job search efforts, then conditions are ripe for the two to meet.

In order for organizations and candidates actually to meet, however, three other conditions must be satisfied. There must be a common communication medium (e.g., the organization advertises in a trade journal read by the candidate), the candidate perceives a match between his or her personal characteristics and the organization's stated job requirements, and the candidate must be motivated to apply for the job. Comprehensive recruitment planning efforts must address these issues.

RECRUITMENT PLANNING

Recruitment begins with a clear specification of (1) human resources needed (e.g., through human resource forecasts and workforce utilization analyses) and (2) when they are needed. Implicit in the latter specification is a time frame—the duration between the receipt of a résumé and the time a new hire starts work. This time frame is sometimes referred to as "the recruitment pipeline." The "flow" of events through the pipeline is represented in Table 5-2. The table shows that if an operating manager sends a requisition for a new hire to the Human Resources Department today, it will take almost a month and a half, 43 days on average, before the employee fulfilling that requisition actually starts work. The HR department must make sure that operating and staff managers realize and understand information such as is represented by this pipeline.

One of the ways that operating and staff managers can be sure that their recruitment needs will fit the length of the recruitment pipeline is by examining the segments of the overall workforce by job group (e.g., clerical, sales, production, engineering, or managers). For each of these job groups, the HR department, with the cooperation of operating managers who represent each job group, should examine what has occurred over the past several years in terms of new hires,

■ **TABLE 5·2**
EVENTS AND THEIR DURATION
COMPRISING A HYPOTHETICAL
RECRUITMENT PIPELINE

Average number of days from	
Résumé to invitation	5
Invitation to interview	6
Interview to offer	4
Offer to acceptance	7
Acceptance to report for work	21
Total length of the pipeline	43

promotions, transfers, and turnover. This will help provide an index of what to expect in the coming year, other things remaining equal.

INTERNAL RECRUITMENT

In deciding where, when, and how to implement recruitment activities, initial consideration should be given to a company's current employees, especially for filling jobs above the entry level. If external recruitment efforts are undertaken without considering the desires, capabilities, and potential of present employees (e.g., the six excess female managers shown in Table 5-1), both short- and long-run costs may be incurred. In the short run, morale may degenerate; in the long run, an organization with a reputation for consistent neglect of in-house talent may find it difficult to attract new employees and to retain experienced ones. This is why soundly conceived action plans (that incorporate developmental and training needs for employees and managers) and management succession plans are so important.

One of the thorniest issues confronting internal recruitment is the reluctance of managers to grant permission for their subordinates to be interviewed for potential transfer or promotion. As one reviewer put it, "Most supervisors are about as reluctant to release a current employee as they are to take a cut in pay."[24] To overcome this aversion, promotion-from-within policies must receive strong top-management support, coupled with a company philosophy that permits employees to consider available opportunities within the organization.

Among the channels available for internal recruitment, the most popular ones are succession plans (discussed in Chapter 4), job posting, employee referrals, and temporary worker pools.

Job Posting

Advertising available jobs internally began in the early days of affirmative action, as a means of providing equal opportunity for women and minorities to compete. It served as a method for getting around the "old boy" network, where jobs sometimes were filled more by "who you knew" than by "what you knew." Today it is an established practice in many organizations, especially for filling jobs up to the lower executive level.

Openings are published on bulletin boards or in lists available to all employees. Interested employees must reply within a specified number of days, and they may or may not have to obtain the consent of their immediate supervisors.[9] Some job posting systems apply only to the plant or office in which a job is located, while other companies will relocate employees.

An example of the latter practice occurred when the Gannett Company, Inc., inaugurated its national newspaper *USA Today*. It filled 50 positions at the new office with experienced people from the chain's other 133 newspapers. Employees who worked on the start-up had the option of staying with *USA Today* once it was under way, or of returning to their previous job assignments.

While there are clear advantages to job posting, potential disadvantages arise if employees "game" the system by transferring to new jobs in other company departments or locations that do not require different or additional skills, simply as a way of obtaining grade or salary increases. To avoid this problem, it is critical to establish consistent pay policies across jobs and locations.

Another problem might arise from poor communication. For example, if employees who unsuccessfully apply for open jobs do not receive feedback that might help them to be more competitive in the future, and if they have to find out through the grapevine that someone else got the job they applied for, then a job posting program cannot be successful. The lesson for managers is obvious: Regular communication and follow-up feedback is essential if job posting is to work properly.

Employee Referrals

Referral of job candidates by present employees has been and continues to be a major source of new hires at many levels, including professionals. It is an internal recruitment method, since internal rather than external sources are used to attract candidates. Typically such programs offer a cash or merchandise bonus when a current employee refers a successful candidate to fill a job opening. The logic behind employee referral is that "it takes one to know one." Interestingly, the rate of employee participation seems to remain unaffected by such efforts as higher cash bonuses, cars, or expense-paid trips.[24] This suggests that good employees will not refer potentially undesirable employees even if the rewards are outstanding.

The Apple Bank for Savings in New York City has a typical referral program. Current employees who recruit new workers receive $250 after the new recruits have remained with the bank for 3 months and an additional $250 when the recruit has been employed for 1 year. The employee who recruits the new worker must also remain with the bank to receive the payment. Thus the program incorporates the twin advantage of attracting new employees and retaining old ones. The bank hires about 50 percent of the candidates referred by current employees.[2]

Three factors seem to be instrumental in the prescreening process of referrals:

the morale of present employees, the accuracy of job information, and the closeness of the intermediary friend.[16]

Temporary Worker Pools

Unlike workers supplied from temporary agencies, in-house "temporaries" work directly for the hiring organization and may receive benefits, depending on the number of scheduled hours worked per week. Temporary workers (e.g., in clerical jobs, accounting, word processing) help meet fluctuating labor demands due to such factors as illness, vacations, terminations, or resignations. Companies save on commissions to outside agencies, which may be as high as 50 percent or more of a temporary employee's hourly wages.[24]

In the health-care field, Humana operates an internal pool of 2000 itinerant registered nurses who circulate among the company's 83 hospitals in 19 cities on 13-week assignments. The nurses get a $450 a month housing allowance, even if they stay with their families or friends, and they keep accruing benefits and seniority rather than starting anew each time they take an assignment.[15]

The Travelers Corporation established a pool of temporaries made up of its own retirees. A recent survey showed the growing popularity of this practice. Almost half the firms surveyed used retirees under some contractual arrangement, about 10 percent allowed retirees to share jobs with other employees, and most retirees continued to receive pension and insurance benefits when they came back to work. About 40 percent of the respondents paid market rates for jobs performed by retirees, while 26 percent paid retirees what they had received at the time they retired.[9]

EXTERNAL RECRUITMENT

To meet demands for talent brought about by business growth, a desire for fresh ideas, or to replenish the stock of employees who leave, organizations periodically turn to the outside labor market. In doing so they may employ a variety of recruitment sources. In this section we will describe four of the most popular ones: university relations, executive search firms, employment agencies, and recruitment advertising.

University Relations

What used to be known as "college recruiting" is now considerably broader in many companies. The companies have targeted certain schools that best meet their needs and have broadened the scope of their interactions with them. Such activities may now include, in addition to recruitment, gifts and grants to the institutions, summer employment and consulting projects for faculty, and inviting placement officers to visit company plants and offices.

Mobil is a good example of this trend. The company now deals with only about 50 colleges and universities, instead of the 200 or so on its list a few years ago. It also uses separate teams (comprised of six to eight people from various Mobil units) for each school. Many of the team members are alumni or alumnae of the school they are assigned to, and they help plan the dozen or so campus activities each year, such as providing talent for student organizations, conducting career information days, holding receptions, and sponsoring ceremonies at which recruiters present Mobil Foundation checks to support some campus activity. The recruitment team strategy has already helped to increase the number of graduates hired from targeted schools.[9]

To enhance the yield from campus recruitment efforts, employers should consider the following research-based guidelines:[17]

1. Establish a "presence" on college campuses beyond just the on-campus interviewing period (as Mobil has done).

2. Upgrade the content and specificity of recruiting brochures. Many are far too general in nature. Instead, provide more detailed information about the characteristics of entry-level jobs, especially those that have had a significant positive effect on prior applicants' decisions to join the organization.

3. Devote more time and resources to train on-campus interviewers to answer specific job-related questions of applicants.

4. For those candidates who are invited for on-site company visits, provide itineraries and agendas prior to their arrival. Written materials should answer candidates' questions dealing with travel arrangements, expense reimbursements, and contact personnel.

5. Ensure that the attributes of vacant positions are comparable to those of competitors. This is as true for large as it is for small organizations. Some of the key job attributes that influence the decisions of applicants, according to a Roper poll of 1000 college students, are promotional opportunities, job security, and long-term income potential. They ranked starting salary in sixth place, after "opportunities for creativity or to exercise initiative" and employee benefits packages.[35]

Executive Search Firms

Such firms are retained typically to recruit for senior-level positions that command salaries over $50,000 and total compensation packages worth in excess of $100,000. The reasons for doing so may include a need to maintain confidentiality from an incumbent or a competitor, a lack of local resources to recruit executive-level individuals, or insufficient time. To use an executive search consultant most effectively requires time and commitment from the hiring organization. It must allow the consultant to become a company "insider," to develop knowledge and familiarity with the business, its strategic plans, and key players.[24] Despite its advantages, consider the following facts: Only 55 to 60 percent of all contracts to search for qualified personnel are fulfilled; of those fulfilled, only 40 percent are fulfilled within the promised time estimate. Some 50 percent of the fulfilled searches take two or three times longer than originally estimated.[8] In short, many employers are being sold recruitment services that will never be provided. Employers evaluating a search firm should carefully consider the following indications that the firms can do competent work:[8,23]

- The firm has defined its market position by industries rather than by disciplines or sells itself as a jack-of-all-trades.
- The firm understands how your organization functions within the industries served.
- The firm is performance-oriented and compensates the search salesperson substantially on the basis of assignment completion.
- The firm combines the research and recruiting responsibilities into one function. Doing so allows the researcher-recruiter to make a more comprehensive and knowledgeable presentation to targeted candidates on behalf of the client.
- The firm uses primary research techniques for locating sources. Secondary research techniques in the form of computerized databases, résumé files, and directories will not locate the real performers in any industry or discipline. In fact, only one in 300 unsolicited résumés is likely to be shown to a client. Only one in 3000 may get a job.[21]
- The firm is organized to function as a task force in the search for candidates, particularly where they are being recruited for multiple assignments or when speed of placement is essential.

Compared to other recruitment sources, executive search firms are quite expensive. Total fees may reach 30 to 35 percent of the compensation package of the new hire. Fees are often paid as follows: a retainer amounting to one-third the total fee as soon as the search is commissioned; one-third due 60 days into the assignment; and a final third due upon completion. If an organization hires a candidate on its own prior to the completion of the search, it still must pay all or some portion of the search firm's fee, unless it makes other arrangements.[24]

Employment Agencies

These are some of the most widely available and used outside sources. However, there is great variability in size and quality across agencies. To achieve best results from this channel, cultivate a small number of firms, thoroughly describe the characteristics (e.g., education, training, experience) of candidates needed, the fee structure, and method of resolving disputes.[9]

Agency fees generally vary from 10 percent of the starting salary for clerical and support staff, to 20 to 30 percent of the starting salary for professional, exempt-level hires. Unlike executive search firms, however, employment agencies receive payment only if one of their referrals results in a hire. In addition, most agencies offer prorated funds if a candidate proves unacceptable. For example, an agency might return 90 percent of its fee if a candidate leaves within 30 days, 60 percent if the new hire lasts between 30 and 60 days, and 30 percent if the new hire leaves after 60 to 90 days on the job.[24] Table 5-3 summarizes the differences between executive search firms and employment agencies.

■ **TABLE 5·3**
DIFFERENCES BETWEEN EXECUTIVE SEARCH FIRMS AND EMPLOYMENT AGENCIES

Services	Executive search firms	Employment agencies
Financial arrangements	Fees based on 30 to 35 percent of candidate's salary and time needed to recruit, or a flat rate plus expenses.	Fees based on 20 to 35 percent of candidate's starting salary.
	Retainer fee required; payment due even if opening filled through other sources.	No retainer fee; fee due only if position filled by agency.
	Staff compensation may include salary, bonus, profit-sharing, and incentives for business generation.	Staff compensation usually depends on commissions for placements made.
Case load	Personal consultant handles only three to five cases at once.	Agent works with many open job orders at one time.
	Firms usually handle openings at higher levels of organization.	Agencies typically assigned lower-level vacancies.
Relationship with clients	Firms represent employers only.	Agencies represent employers and job seekers.
	General management involved in decision to retain search firm.	HR department makes decision to use agency.
	Consultant thoroughly researches client organization and position requirements before search.	Agents spend less time on initial research and job specifications. Some assignments handled by phone with no personal contact.
	Firms conduct assignments on an exclusive basis.	Agencies compete with similar companies for placements.
Time commitment	Consultant invests 40 to 50 hours per month on each search.	Limited investment of time on any one client, due to lack of guaranteed payment.
Referral rates and guarantees	Two to four highly qualified candidates recommended to each client.	Large numbers of applicants referred to increase odds of a placement.
	Recruitment and evaluation efforts target broad range of candidates, most of whom are not in job market.	Recruitment focuses mainly on candidates actively seeking new employment.
	Process- and results-oriented.	Placement-oriented.
	Reputable firms offer a professional guarantee and commitment to thorough, ethical practices.	Contingency fee arrangement eliminates any obligation to produce results.
Level of client involvement	Minimal HR and management time involvement required.	Considerable HR time required to screen, interview, and evaluate candidates.

Source: J. S. Lord, (1989). External and internal recruitment. In W. F. Cascio (ed.), *Human resource planning, employment, and placement.* Washington, D.C.: Bureau of National Affairs, 1989, pp. 2-87, 2-88.

FIGURE 5-2
A Burger King franchise in Michigan uses billboards to advertise a benefit designed to help employees earn money for college tuition.

Recruitment Advertising

When this medium is mentioned, most people think of want ads in the local newspaper. But think again. This medium has become just as colorful, lively, and imaginative as consumer advertising. In addition to newspapers, such advertising media include magazines, direct mail, radio and television, and even billboards (see Figure 5-2).

RECRUITMENT AS A LONG-TERM STRATEGY— THE CASE OF BURGER KING

■ **COMPANY EXAMPLE**

A Burger King franchisee in western Michigan made recruitment part of his long-term strategy after experiencing turnover at his restaurants as high as 150 percent in 1 year. He hired a public relations firm to help target two groups of potential employees: working mothers and students. The recruitment program emphasized two things: a free day-care program and an education bonus program. The day-care program helped to increase the employee base by 30 percent within a year after it was started. Currently half the franchisee's employees participate in the day-care program.

The education bonus project allows students to earn $1 for every hour worked, up to $2500 a year, to further their education beyond high school. The same program is also offered to senior citizens—with a twist: They can either use the money themselves or else pass it along as a gift to younger members of their family.

To spread the word about these benefits, the franchisee and the public relations firm distributed posters and brochures to women's centers, high schools, adult education centers, colleges, and other locations where the target audiences of mothers and teenagers were likely to see the message. They also held news conferences and placed stories in newspapers.[2]

Themes in Advertisements

Fads in ads are common. At one time, employers of engineers stressed the recreational attractions of their locations, so many sandy beaches and sunny slopes appeared in recruitment materials. Today, however, the following trends are more evident:[9]

- Widespread use of employees in ads
- Emphasis on intangible benefits, such as room for creativity, alternative development paths, and independence
- Point-of-purchase advertising techniques, including returnable coupons and mini-resumes
- More reliance on entertainment—witty headlines and amusing illustrations that have nothing to do with the job

This is just a brief glimpse into external recruitment sources. Others include career fairs, outplacement firms, former employees, trade shows, co-op and work-study programs, government employment agencies, alumni associations, affirmative action organizations, and free-standing computer-based name banks. With respect to the latter, some, such as Career Placement Registry, are generalized lists of job seekers. Others, such as Bank Executive Network, specialize. Both get used a lot; Career Placement says employers order 1800 resumes a month.[18]

SPECIAL INDUCEMENTS—RELOCATION AID, HELP FOR THE TRAILING SPOUSE, AND SIGN-ON BONUSES

Especially with higher-level jobs, newly recruited managers expect some form of relocation assistance. Such assistance may include disposal of the residence left behind, lease-breaking expenses, temporary living expenses, and moving costs, to name just a few. Such costs add up quickly. The American Management Association estimates that it can cost $50,000 in search and relocation expenses to recruit a general manager earning $80,000 per year. Furthermore, 25 percent of companies surveyed don't set any limit on temporary living expenses, which could boost the hiring cost to $100,000.[22]

Prodded by the emergence of the dual career family, firms are finding that many managers and professionals, men and women alike, are reluctant to relocate unless the spouse will be able to find suitable employment in a new location. One way that recruiters are dealing with this is to trade information informally. Thus, beginning in 1979, employment managers from Armco, National Cash Register, and Mead Corporation began meeting regularly to exchange information about trailing spouses who were seeking employment. By 1987, the group had expanded to include 38 companies. This type of network is not unusual in most metropolitan areas.[9]

Another recruiting inducement, independent of any relocation assistance, is the sign-on bonus. Originally used in the sports world, signing bonuses are now common among executives, professionals (particularly in high-technology firms), and other ranks as well. Sun Life of Canada pays $200 to $1000 to any employee who brings in a new worker. In New York, Personnel Pool, an office-temp firm, offers $50 finder fees.[19] The practice is even more widespread in health care, in the tight labor market for registered nurses. In large cities, nurses are receiving bonuses of $3000 to $4000 for coming aboard, bonuses for staying, bounties for finding recruits, freedom to set their own schedules, and free tuition for advanced courses. Some employers even offer maid service and free housing for those who are willing to shuttle from city to city to relieve the critical demand for medical care.[15]

Summary Findings Regarding Recruitment Sources

Now that we have examined some of the most popular sources for internal and external recruiting, it seems reasonable to ask, "Which sources are most *popular* with employers and job applicants?" Among employers, evidence indicates that:

- Informal contacts are used widely and effectively at all occupational levels
- Use of the public employment service declines as required skills levels increase
- The internal market is a major recruitment source except for entry-level, unskilled, and semiskilled workers
- Larger firms are the most frequent users of walk-ins, write-ins, and the internal market[6]

However, for recruiting minority workers, a study of 20,000 applicants in a major insurance company revealed that female and black applicants consistently used formal recruitment sources (employment agencies, advertising) rather than informal ones (walk-ins, write-ins, employee referrals). Nevertheless, informal sources produced the best-quality applicants for all groups (males, females, blacks, Hispanics, under and over 40 years old), and lead proportionately to more hires.[16]

Factors Affecting Recruitment Needs

A recent survey of 500 companies revealed how factors such as the source of résumés, the type of position, geographic location, and time constraints all can influence recruitment success.[24] With regard to résumés, managers surveyed judged only about 7 percent of incoming résumés to be worth routing to hiring managers. However, those from employment agencies generated more qualified applicants than did general inquiries or advertisements.

The rate of invitations to visit varied markedly (from 8 to 60 percent), depending on the type of position in question. Generally candidates for technical and lower-level positions had the highest invitation rates; the invitation rate fell as the level of position rose. About 40 percent of those interviewed received job offers, with candidates for lower-level positions earning the highest offer rates. Nontechnical positions generated twice as many acceptances (82 percent) as technical positions (41 percent).

With respect to geographical location, positions requiring relocation generated fewer acceptances to interview requests and (not surprisingly) fewer employment offers. A final factor that affects recruitment needs is time. Adequate assessment of recruitment needs begins with accurate staffing analysis and forecasting. However, a large number of unexpected retirements, resignations, or terminations may place unrealistic time demands on recruiters. Although time frames differ from job to job and industry to industry, 3 months from the receipt of a requisition to the new employee's start date is considered an acceptable time period for recruiting a journey-level professional.[24]

Affirmative Action Recruiting

Special measures are called for in affirmative action recruiting: employers should use women and minority-group members (1) in their personnel offices as interviewers; (2) on recruiting trips to high schools, colleges, and job fairs; and (3) in employment opportunity advertisements.[3]

Employers need to establish contacts in the minority community based on credibility between the employer and the contact and credibility between the contact and the minority community. Various community organizations might be contacted, and minority-group leaders should be encouraged to visit the employer and to talk with employees. For example, the current edition of *The Black Resource Guide* lists over 3000 church leaders, political figures, educators, newspapers, radio stations, and national associations.[4] Allow plenty of lead time for the minority-group contacts to notify prospective applicants and for the applicants to apply for available positions.

For companies that use search firms to recruit executives, some offer an additional 5 percent of the first year's salary—in addition to the usual 30 percent fee—if the search consultant can find qualified minorities to fill a position.[20]

Frequent use of the phrase "an equal opportunity employer" is an affirmative action "must."

Recognize two things: (1) that it will take time to establish a credible, workable affirmative action recruitment program and (2) that there is no payoff from passive nondiscrimination.

MANAGING RECRUITMENT OPERATIONS

Administratively, recruitment is one of the easiest activities to foul up—with potentially long-term negative publicity for the firm. The following guidelines can help to avoid such snafus:

- Incoming applications and résumés must be logged in at some central point (they have a way of getting lost in a hurry).
- Activities at important points in the recruitment pipeline must be recorded for each candidate at the same central point. It is truly embarrassing when a candidate appears for a company visit but no one at the company has been notified in advance.
- Acknowledgments and "no interest" letters must be entered against the candidates' central records. Failure to respond to an inquiry or formal application connotes one of two things: incompetence or snobbishness.
- Offers, acceptances, and the terms of employment (e.g., salary) must be recorded and evaluated relative to open personnel requisitions. Drastically different salary offers to the same candidate by managers in different departments also signal confusion.
- Records of individuals who do not receive offers should be kept for a reasonable period of time (e.g., 1 year).

Evaluation and Control of Recruitment Operations

The reason for evaluating past and current recruitment operations is simple: to improve the efficiency of future recruitment efforts. To do this, it is necessary to analyze systematically the performance of the various recruitment sources. The following kinds of information should be considered:

- *Cost of operations*, that is, labor costs of company recruitment personnel, operational costs (e.g., recruiting staff's travel and living expenses, agency fees, advertising expenses, brochures, supplies, and postage), and overhead expenses (e.g., rental of temporary facilities and equipment)
- *Cost per hire, by source*
- *Number and quality of résumés by source*
- *Acceptance/offer ratio*
- *Analysis of postvisit and rejection questionnaires*
- *Salary offered—acceptances versus rejections*

Evidence indicates, unfortunately, that the evaluation of recruitment activities by large organizations is honored more in the breach than in the observance. Few firms link their recruitment practices to posthire effectiveness, and evaluation is more subjective than quantitative.[17] In one study, for example, just over half the firms even bothered to calculate the average cost per hire in their college recruitment operations (over $2100 in 1987 dollars).[32] The cost per hire for inexperienced people making under $30,000 averaged $2593 in 1987. For those making over $100,000 it averaged $44,750.[10] Given the rapid proliferation of human resource information systems, with at least a dozen that provide applicant-tracking features at a cost ranging from $500 to $10,000, there is no excuse for not evaluating this costly activity.[13]

Which recruitment sources are most *effective*? According to a survey of 245 firms, newspaper advertisements are the most effective sources for recruiting office/clerical, production/service, professional/technical, and commissioned sales workers. For recruiting managers, promotion-from-within is most effective, followed by newspaper ads. Walk-ins are the most popular method for recruiting production/service workers.[6]

However, a study of 10 different recruitment sources used by more than 20,000 applicants for the job of insurance agent showed that recruiting source explained 5 percent of the variation in applicant quality, 1 percent of the variation in the survival of new hires, and none of the variation in commissions.[16] If sources do not differ appreciably on these important characteristics, then organizations probably should rely on those that are less costly (e.g., newspaper ads) and produce higher quality applicants (informal sources) than more expensive sources (employment agencies).

A study of the recruitment process from the perspective of applicants examined how applicants regarded the various sources of information (on-campus interviewer-recruiter, friend, job incumbent, professor) about a job opportunity.[12] The researchers investigated whether applicants regarded the information source as credible or not, which sources provided favorable or unfavorable job information, and which sources led to greater acceptances of job offers. The study indicated that the on-campus interviewer-recruiter, the first and often the only representative of a company seen by applicants, was not liked, not trusted, and not perceived as knowing much about the job. The study also indicated that applicants were more inclined to believe unfavorable information than favorable information. Furthermore, applicants were more likely to accept jobs when the source of information about the job was not the interviewer. Later research has shown that job attributes (supervision, job challenge, location, salary, title) are more important to applicants' reactions than are recruitment activities (e.g., demographic characteristics of recruiter, behavior during the interview); in short, the recruitment message predominates over its media.[34]

A conceptual framework that might help explain these findings is that of the "realistic job preview" (RJP).[29] An RJP requires that, in addition to telling applicants about the nice things a job has to offer (e.g., pay, benefits, opportunities for advancement), recruiters must also tell applicants about the unpleasant aspects of the job. For example, "It's hot, dirty, and sometimes you'll have to work on weekends." Research in actual company settings has indicated consistent results.[30] That is, when the unrealistically positive expectations of job applicants are lowered to match the reality of the actual work setting *prior to hire*, job acceptance rates

RECRUITERS AND COMPUTERS

A new computer-based requisition tracking system is giving recruiters at New England Medical Center more time for the professional aspects of their jobs and cutting the time needed for the purely clerical aspects of the operation by about 20 hours per week. The old system was built on three sets of logs. One was kept by the receptionist who took in job requisitions, the second was kept by the secretary who distributed the requisitions to the various recruiters, and the third was kept by the recruiters, who used the logs to keep track of their individual positions.

Every other week, the recruiters brought up to date a *jobs posting list* consisting of over 300 positions. These lists, often with illegible corrections, were given to the secretary for preparing an update. Another weekly report, *number of days to fill positions*, was prepared from the same information. *Offer letters* were typewritten forms with fill-in blanks, done by hand, for information such as name, salary, position, and title.

The new system involves a "master" station and three "slaves" networked together, one for each of the recruiters. The system tracks all position requisitions, logs the resulting hire information, and feeds back the information in various forms. It serves as an *automated log book*, and it produces a series of reports, including the biweekly job postings, open requisition reports, new-hire orientation reports, and other management data. It also produces the offer letters.

The system provides a series of menus backed up with "Help" screens for each one so that people do not need a lot of technical knowledge to use it. With new network software becoming available, management expects the unit to be able to upload the data from this system directly into the mainframe computer, thereby saving another data entry.[11]

may be lower and job performance is unaffected, but job satisfaction and survival are higher for those who receive an RJP. These conclusions have held up in different organizational settings (e.g., manufacturing versus service jobs) and when different RJP techniques are used (e.g., plant tours versus slide presentations versus written descriptions of the work). In fact, RJPs improve retention rates, on average, by 9 percent.[25]

Longitudinal research shows that RJPs should be *balanced* in their orientation. That is, they should be conducted to enhance overly pessimistic expectations and to reduce overly optimistic expectations. Doing so helps to bolster the applicant's perceptions of the organization as caring, trustworthy, and honest.[26] Of course, it is important actually to be honest. Indeed, at least one state court has ruled that a company has an obligation to tell job applicants if the company is on shaky financial ground and plans to cut back. A woman who was offered a job with Security Pacific Information Services, Inc., relocated from New Orleans to Denver. Seven weeks after she started work, the unit she worked for collapsed for lack of business. A jury awarded her $250,000 for actual and punitive damages, and the Colorado Court of Appeals upheld the jury's verdict.[27]

A final recommendation is to develop RJPs even when there is no turnover problem (proactively rather than reactively). They should employ an audiovisual medium and, where possible, show actual job incumbents.[36]

Nevertheless, RJPs are not appropriate for all types of jobs. They seem to work best (1) when few applicants are actually hired (that is, the *selection ratio* is low), (2) when used with *entry-level positions* (since those coming from outside to inside the organization tend to have more inflated expectations than those who make changes internally), and (3) when *unemployment is low* (since job candidates are more likely to have alternative jobs to choose from).[37]

THE OTHER SIDE OF RECRUITMENT—JOB SEARCH

At some time or another, whether voluntarily or otherwise, almost everyone faces the difficult task of finding a job. Much of this chapter has emphasized recruitment from the organization's perspective. But as we noted at the outset, a mating theory of recruitment—in which organizations search for qualified candidates just as candidates search for organizations—is more realistic. How do people find jobs? Research shows that 70 percent land another job through personal contacts, 15 percent through placement agencies, 10 percent through direct mailings of their résumés, and only 5 percent through published job openings.[7]

Consider the following scenario, which has happened all too frequently over the last decade (as a result of mergers, restructurings, and downsizings) and is expected to occur often this decade as economic conditions change.[28] Keep in mind as you read this that while labor markets in general are predicted to be tight throughout the 1990s, there will always be variability in the supply of and demand for labor in specific markets. You are a midlevel executive, well regarded, well paid, and seemingly well established in your chosen field. Then—whammo!—a change in business strategy or a change in economic conditions results in your layoff from the firm you hoped to retire from. What do you do? How do you go about finding another job? According to management consultants and executive recruiters the following are some of the key things *not* to do.[7]

- Don't panic—a search takes time, even for well-qualified middle- and upper-level managers. Seven months to a year is not unusual. Be prepared to wait it out.
- Don't be bitter—bitterness makes it harder to begin to search; it also turns off potential employers.
- Don't kid yourself—do a thorough self-appraisal of your strengths and weaknesses, your likes and dislikes about jobs and organizations. Face up to what has happened, decide if you want to switch fields, figure out where you and your family want to live, and don't delay the search itself for long.
- Don't drift—develop a plan, target companies, and go after them relentlessly. Realize that your job is to find a new job. Cast a wide net; consider industries other than your own.

IMPACT OF RECRUITMENT ON PRODUCTIVITY, QUALITY OF WORK LIFE, AND THE BOTTOM LINE

A close fit between individual strengths and interests and organizational and job characteristics almost guarantees a happy "marriage." On the other hand, since the bottom line of recruitment success lies in the number of stressful placements made, the effects of ineffective recruitment may not appear for years. For this reason alone, a regular system for measuring and evaluating recruitment efforts is essential. Moreover, it's difficult to manage what you can't measure.[17] With the cost of new college hires between $1500 and $6000, it seems more important than ever to assess whether such costs are outweighed by easier and improved selection procedures, better employee retention, lower training needs and costs, or higher levels of productivity.[17] Finding, attracting, and retaining top talent is now and will continue to be an important management challenge with direct impacts on productivity, quality of work life, and the bottom line.

- Don't be lazy—the heart of a good job hunt is research. Use reference books, public filings, and annual reports when drawing up a list of target companies. If negotiations get serious, talk to a range of insiders and knowledgeable outsiders to learn about politics and practices. You don't want to wind up in a worse fix than the one you left.
- Don't be shy *or* overeager—since personal contacts are the most effective means to land a job, pull out all the stops to get the word out that you are available. At the same time, resist the temptation to accept the first job that comes along. Unless it's absolutely right for you, the chances of making a mistake are quite high.
- Don't ignore your family—some executives are embarrassed and don't tell their families what's going on. A better approach, experts say, is to bring the family into the process and deal with them honestly.
- Don't lie—experts are unanimous on this point. Don't lie and don't stretch a point—either in résumés or in interviews. Be willing to address failures as well as strengths. Discuss openly and fully what went wrong at the old job.
- Don't jump the gun on salary—always let the potential employer bring this subject up first, but once it surfaces, thoroughly explore all aspects of your future compensation and benefits package.

Those who have been through the trauma of job loss and the challenge of finding a job often describe the entire process as a wrenching, stressful one. Avoiding the mistakes shown above can ensure that finding a new job need not take any longer than necessary.

IMPLICATIONS FOR MANAGEMENT PRACTICE

Social and demographic trends indicate quite clearly that job hunting has become a seller's market in the 1990s. More and more, employers must consider the needs of employees if they wish to retain them. The following elements should be part of any successful recruitment program:[2]

- ■ Always view recruitment as a long-term strategy.
- ■ Be responsive to employees' needs.
- ■ Develop benefits that genuinely appeal to the employees being hired.
- ■ Promote recruitment benefits to the target audience.
- ■ Audit the recruitment programs in place.

As one expert noted only half facetiously, "Employers are going to market jobs the way you might market a car. . . . 'Come to us. We'll give you what we think you want.' "[15]

■ HUMAN RESOURCE MANAGEMENT IN ACTION:
CONCLUSION

SMALL BUSINESS FACES A TOUGH TEST: RECRUITMENT IN THE 1990s

There are three major impediments to successful small business recruitment in the 1990s, especially for small manufacturing companies. One, there are plenty of candidates for jobs that start at $6.50 an hour, but keeping them is another matter. Some fail drug tests, some are surprised at how hard the work is, and others simply have little notion of what is involved in holding any job. At Steeltin Can, for example, turnover among hourly workers averaged 5.66 percent per month in 1989, or 68 percent annually. Among all manufacturers nationwide, the comparable figures were 0.8 percent per month, and 9.6 percent annually.[5]

Two, small companies have also been hurt by an increasing mismatch between the small-shop orientation of much of the machine-parts industry and the need for sophisticated training that only fairly large companies can afford. And, as noted at the beginning of this vignette, fewer new workers are being trained in vocational schools to replace a generation of experienced workers approaching retirement.

Three, apart from the lack of glamour and limited material benefits, manufacturing also seems to suffer from the widespread perception that it has little future. The number of manufacturing jobs has dropped from 20.3 million (22.4 percent of the nonfarm total) in 1980 to 19.5 million (17.8 percent of the nonfarm total) in 1989. At the same time, however, more efficient operations raised total factory output during the 1980s by 37 percent. At

Sandmeyer Steel, even though the size of the workforce has dropped to 165 from more than 200 in the 1960s, the company is doing triple the business that it did in the 1960s as a result of increasing automation. What's the longer-term view? In the opinion of labor experts, a slow-growing workforce and a "creeping deterioration" in the quality of new hires will limit U.S. economic expansion in the 1990s.[39]

SUMMARY

Recruitment begins with a clear statement of objectives, based on the types of knowledge, skills, abilities, and other characteristics that an organization needs. Objectives are also based on a consideration of the sex and ethnic-group representation of the workforce, relative to that of the surrounding labor force. Finally, a recruitment policy must spell out clearly an organization's intention to evaluate and screen candidates without regard to factors such as race, sex, age, or disability, where these characteristics are unrelated to a person's ability to do a job successfully. The actual process of recruitment begins with a specification of human resource requirements—numbers, skills mix, levels, and the time frame within which such needs must be met.

Recruitment may involve internal, external, or both kinds of labor markets. Internal recruitment often relies on succession plans, job posting, employee referrals, or temporary worker pools. Many external recruitment sources are also available. In this chapter we discussed four such sources: university relations, executive search firms, employment agencies, and recruitment advertising. In managing and controlling recruitment operations, consideration should be given to the cost of operations and to an analysis of the performance of each recruitment source since recruitment success is determined by the number of persons who actually perform their jobs successfully.

DISCUSSION QUESTIONS

5•1 Discuss some of the key considerations involved in selecting an executive search firm.
5•2 What special measures might be necessary for a successful affirmative action recruitment effort?
5•3 Discuss the conditions under which realistic job previews are and are not appropriate.
5•4 How can college recruitment efforts be improved?
5•5 Should internal and external recruitment sources be evaluated differently? If yes, how?
5•6 You have just lost your middle-management job. Outline a procedure to follow in trying to land a new one.

REFERENCES

1. Affirmative action upheld by high court as a remedy for past job discrimination (1986, July 3). *The New York Times*, pp. A1, B9.

2. Amante, L. (1989). Help wanted: Creative recruitment tactics. *Personnel*, 66(10), 32–36.

3. Ash, P. (1974). *Meeting civil rights requirements in your selection programs.* Chicago: International Personnel Management Association, Personnel Report 742.

4. *Black resource guide* (7th ed., 1987). 501 Oneida Place NW, Washington, DC 20011.

5. *Bulletin to Management* (1989, 2d Quarter). Washington, DC: Bureau of National Affairs.

6. Bureau of National Affairs (1988, May). *Recruiting and selection procedures* (PPF Survey 146). Washington, DC: Bureau of National Affairs.

7. Cohn, G. (1985, Nov. 19). Advice on what not to do as the search continues. *The Wall Street Journal*, p. 37.

8. Dee, W. (1983). Evaluating a search firm. *Personnel Administrator*, **28**(3), 41–43, 99–100.

9. Farish, P. (1989). Recruitment sources. In W. F. Cascio (ed.), *Human resource planning, employment, and placement.* Washington, DC: Bureau of National Affairs, pp. 2-103 to 2-134.

10. Farish, P. (ed.) (1987, October). *Recruiting Trends*, p. 1.

11. Farish, P. (ed.) (1987, September). *Recruiting Trends*, p. 1.

12. Fisher, C. D., Ilgen, D. R., & Hoyer, W. D. (1979). Source credibility, information favorability, and job offer acceptance. *Academy of Management Journal*, **22**, 94–103.

13. Frantzreb, R. B. (1987). Microcomputer software: What's new in HRM. *Personnel Administrator*, **32**(7), 67–100.

14. *Hazelwood School District v. U.S.*, 433 U.S. 299 (1977).

15. Kilborn, P. T. (1990, May 6). Nurses get V.I.P. treatment, easing shortage. *The New York Times*, pp. 1, 28.

16. Kirnan, J. P., Farley, J. A., & Geisinger, K. F. (1989). The relationship between recruiting source, applicant quality, and hire performance: An analysis by sex, ethnicity, and age. *Personnel Psychology*, **42**, 293–308.

17. Kolenko, T. A. (1990). College recruiting: Models, myths, and management. In G. R. Ferris, K. M. Rowland, & M. R. Buckley (eds.), *Human resource management: Perspectives and issues* (2d ed.). Boston: Allyn & Bacon, pp. 109–121.

18. Labor Letter (1989, Dec. 5). *The Wall Street Journal*, p. A1.

19. Labor Letter (1989, Apr. 4). *The Wall Street Journal*, p. A1.

20. Labor Letter (1989, Mar. 21). *The Wall Street Journal*, p. A1.

21. Labor Letter (1988, May 10). *The Wall Street Journal*, p. 1.

22. Labor Letter (1986, June 17). *The Wall Street Journal*, p. 1.

23. LoPresto, R. (1986). Ethical recruiting. *Personnel Administrator*, **31**(11), 90–91.

24. Lord, J. S. (1989). External and internal recruitment. In W. F. Cascio (ed.), *Human resource planning, employment, and placement.* Washington, DC: Bureau of National Affairs, pp. 2-73 to 2-102.

25. McEvoy, G. M., & Cascio, W. F. (1985). Strategies for reducing employee turnover. A meta-analysis. *Journal of Applied Psychology*, **70**, 342–353.

26. Meglino, B. M., De Nisi, A. S., Youngblood, S. A., & Williams, K. J. (1988). Effects of realistic job previews: A comparison using an enhancement and a reduction preview. *Journal of Applied Psychology*, **73**, 259–266.

27. Menter, E. (1990, Fall). Company must disclose problems to applicants. Denver: *The Legal Vantage* (Pryor, Garney and Johnson), p. 1.

28. O'Boyle, T. F., & Hymowitz, C. (1990, Oct. 4). White-collar blues: Layoffs this time hit professional ranks with unusual force. *The Wall Street Journal*, pp. A1, A9.

29. Popovich, P., & Wanous, J. P. (1982). The realistic job preview as a persuasive communication. *Academy of Management Review, 7,* 570–578.

30. Premack S. L., & Wanous, J. P. (1985). A meta-analysis of realistic job preview experiments. *Journal of Applied Psychology,* **70,** 706–719.

31. Replying in the affirmative (1987, March 9). *Time,* p. 66.

32. Rynes, S. L., & Boudreau, J. W. (1986). College recruiting in large organizations: Practice, evaluation, and research implications. *Personnel Psychology,* **39,** 729–757.

33. Seligman, D. (1973, March). How "equal opportunity" turned into employment quotas. *Fortune,* pp. 160–168.

34. Taylor, M. S., & Bergmann, T. J. (1987). Organizational recruitment activities and applicants' reactions at different stages of the recruitment process. *Personnel Psychology,* **40,** 261–285.

35. Today's students say money isn't everything (1988, Sept. 7). *The Wall Street Journal,* p. 27.

36. Wanous, J. P. (1989). Installing a realistic job preview: Ten tough choices. *Personnel Psychology,* **42,** 117–134.

37. Wanous, J. P. (1980) *Organizational entry: Recruitment, selection and socialization of newcomers.* Reading, MA: Addison-Wesley.

38. *Wards Cove Packing Co. v. Antonio,* 109 S.Ct. 2115 (1989).

39. Winter, R. E. (1990, Mar. 28). Scarcity of workers is kindling inflation. *The Wall Street Journal,* p. A2.

Staffing

■ **HUMAN RESOURCE MANAGEMENT IN ACTION**

CHOOSING A SUCCESSOR
FOR HARRY THOMPSON*

Harry Thompson's mind drifted back over nearly 30 years to when he had founded Auckland Chemical Co. The fledgling company was less than 2 years old when the young George Bolton had joined it. In those precarious years, when the company was in danger of failing, Bolton chipped in his meager savings to keep it afloat. Bolton's tireless energy in scouting out sales prospects for the firm's products had been a critical factor in Auckland's survival. But with the development of a new enzyme, the company suddenly began to prosper. Now, after large-scale diversification, Thompson was chairman and president of a group with annual sales of $250 million. The company was a success.

Now, facing voluntary retirement, Thompson was increasingly concerned over his successor as chief executive officer. It had long been the unspoken

---

*Adapted from: *The Best of Dilemma & Decision*, compiled by the editors of International Management. London: McGraw-Hill, 1985, pp. 185–187. Copyright © 1985 by Reed Business Publication Group. Reprinted by permission.

assumption that the job would go to Bolton, who was 5 years Thompson's junior. But Thompson had begun to have serious reservations about Bolton's judgment. More and more Bolton tended to delay making decisions, and he seemed unwilling to change with the times. At a recent management meeting, he had fought fiercely against installing antipollution equipment in a new plant. Michael Summers, vice president for industrial products, had carried the day, arguing that he felt such pollution control equipment would become a legal necessity. Indeed, 6 months later such a law was passed.

CHOICE OF TWO BRIGHT MANAGERS

Thompson also feared that the bright young managers in the firm might grow restive under Bolton's indecisive leadership. He was particularly worried about the possibility of losing either Summers or Linda Kemp, vice president for pharmaceuticals. Both were in their early forties. Thompson had privately earmarked them both as chief-executive material. At this point, it was almost impossible to choose between the two.

Summers was the more visibly brilliant of the two. His division had grown faster than any of the others. He had a sharp, analytical mind that struck immediately to the heart of a problem. And he was never afraid to make changes and to adjust to new conditions. But Thompson suspected that sometimes Summers changed things just for the sake of change. The industrial products division was noted for the frequency of its executives' vertical and lateral job moves. In Thompson's view, the booming sales of industrial products had been achieved in spite of, not because of, job rotation that occurred as often as three times a year for some executives.

Kemp, on the other hand, was a far less flamboyant manager, but she had a knack for getting people to work effectively together. Perhaps more importantly, she was content to let others get the credit. For instance, Bolton was Auckland's official representative in negotiations over a joint operation last year. But a director of the other firm involved later told Thompson: "We didn't think Auckland would be able to handle this. After all, you had little experience in this field. It was Kemp who finally persuaded us." The operation had since proven profitable.

However, Kemp sometimes seemed to lack decisiveness. She still occasionally referred decisions on whether to go ahead with a new product to Thompson, who had started his career in the pharmaceuticals division. She also had retained some managers, admittedly in relatively unimportant posts, long after they were not performing satisfactorily.

Before his retirement became imminent, Thompson had coasted along, avoiding the soul-searching experience he now faced. For 5 years he had seen the managerial transition as merely a matter of handing the reins over to Bolton. Thus he would fulfill the unspoken promise, and Bolton would realize his dream of running the company he had helped to build. In the meantime, Thompson pictured either Kemp or Summers coming to the fore as Bolton's obvious successor, and the company would have another 5 years' hard work from both these brilliant executives.

In fact, Thompson now admitted to himself, the choice between the two would be just as difficult 5 years hence. The only difference is that he would be spared the unpleasant task of making the choice.

Now, as his departure was imminent, Thompson felt that perhaps he owed it to the company and to its thousands of employees to act decisively, to ruin a lifelong friendship, and to trigger the departure of one valuable executive in order to continue the firm under strong leadership. If he was right, was Summers or Kemp the person for the top job?

Challenges

1. What are some key factors to consider in making such a selection decision?
2. What should Thompson have done differently?
3. Should Thompson postpone his retirement in order to resolve the succession issue?

QUESTIONS THIS CHAPTER WILL HELP MANAGERS ANSWER

1. In what ways do business strategy and organizational culture affect staffing decisions?
2. What screening and selection methods are available, and which ones are most accurate?
3. Can work sample tests improve staffing decisions?
4. What are some advantages and potential problems to consider in using assessment centers to select managers?

The chapter opening vignette describes the sometimes wrenching process of selecting a top manager. In fact, management selection decisions are some of the most important and most difficult personnel decisions that organizations face. Compounding these difficulties is the constant need to align staffing decisions with business strategy and organizational culture. As we shall see in this chapter, there is a wide variety of tools for initial screening and selection decisions, and much is known about each one. We will examine evidence of the relative effectiveness of the tools, so that decision makers can choose those that best fit their long- and short-range objectives.

ORGANIZATIONAL CONSIDERATIONS IN STAFFING DECISIONS

Business Strategy

Clearly there should be a fit between the intended strategy of an enterprise and the characteristics of the people who are expected to implement it. Unfortunately, very few firms actually link strategy and staffing decisions in a structured, logical way. Nevertheless, we can learn how to effect such a fit by considering a two-dimensional model that relates an organization's strategy during the stages of its development to the style of its managers during each stage.[115]

For strategic reasons, it is important to consider the stage of development of a business because many characteristics of a business—such as its growth rate, product lines, market share, entry opportunity, and technology—change as the organization changes. One possible set of relationships between the development stage and the management selection strategies is shown in Figure 6-1. While a model such as this is useful conceptually, in practice the stages might not be as clearly defined, and there are many exceptions.

Organizations that are just starting out are in the *embryonic* stage. They are characterized by high growth rates, basic product lines, heavy emphasis on product engineering, and little or no customer loyalty.

Organizations in the *high-growth* stage are concerned with two things: fighting for market share and building excellence in their management teams. Product lines are refined and extended, and customer loyalty begins to build.

Mature organizations emphasize the maintenance of market share, cost reductions through economies of scale, more rigid management controls over workers' actions, and the generation of cash to develop new product lines. In contrast to the "freewheeling" style of an embryonic organization, there is much less flexibility and variability in the mature organization.

Finally, an *aging* organization struggles to hold market share in a declining market, and it demands extreme cost control obtained through consistency and centralized procedures. Economic survival becomes the primary motivation.

Different management styles seem to "fit" each of these development stages best. At the embryonic stage there is a need for enterprising managers who can thrive in high-risk environments. These are known as enterpreneurs (Figure 6-1). They are decisive individuals who can respond rapidly to changing conditions.

During the high-growth stage there is still a need for entrepreneurs, but it is also important to select the kinds of managers who can develop stable management systems to preserve the gains achieved during the embryonic stage. We might call these managers "growth directors."

As an organization matures, there is a need to select the kind of manager who does not need lots of variety in her or his work, who can oversee repetitive daily operations, and who can search continually for economies of scale. Individuals who fit best in mature organizations have a "bureaucratic" style of management.

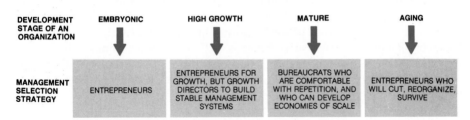

DEVELOPMENT STAGE OF AN ORGANIZATION	EMBRYONIC	HIGH GROWTH	MATURE	AGING
MANAGEMENT SELECTION STRATEGY	ENTREPRENEURS	ENTREPRENEURS FOR GROWTH, BUT GROWTH DIRECTORS TO BUILD STABLE MANAGEMENT SYSTEMS	BUREAUCRATS WHO ARE COMFORTABLE WITH REPETITION, AND WHO CAN DEVELOP ECONOMIES OF SCALE	ENTREPRENEURS WHO WILL CUT, REORGANIZE, SURVIVE

FIGURE 6-1

The relationship between the development stage of an organization and the management selection strategy that best "fits" each stage.

Finally, an aging organization needs "movers and shakers" to reinvigorate it. Strategically it becomes important to select (again) entrepreneurs capable of doing whatever is necessary to ensure the economic survival of the firm. This may involve divesting unprofitable operations, firing unproductive workers, or eliminating practices that are considered extravagant.

Admittedly, these characterizations are coarse, but at least they provide a starting point in the construction of an important link between the development stage of an organization and its staffing strategy. Such strategic concerns may be used to recast job analyses from static descriptions of how jobs *are* done to dynamic prescriptions of how they *should* be done. The prescriptions of how jobs should be done will then guide the selections of the people to do them.

Organizational Culture

A logical extension of the mating theory of recruitment (i.e., concurrent search efforts by organizations and individuals for a match) is the mating theory of selection. That is, just as organizations choose people, people choose jobs and organizations that fit their personalities and career objectives and from which they can satisfy needs that are important to them.[112]

In the context of selection, it is important for an organization to describe the dimensions of its "culture." Culture is the pattern of basic assumptions that a given group has invented, discovered, or developed in learning to adapt to both its external environment and its internal environment. The pattern of assumptions has worked well enough to be considered valid and, therefore, to be taught to new members as the correct way to perceive, think, and feel in relation to those problems. Organizational culture is embedded and transmitted through mechanisms such as the following:

1. Formal statements of organizational philosophy and materials used for recruitment, selection, and socialization of new employees
2. Promotion criteria
3. Stories, legends, and myths about key people and events
4. What leaders pay attention to, measure, and control
5. Implicit and possibly unconscious criteria that leaders use to determine who "fits" key slots in the organization[107,108]

Organizational culture has two implications for staffing decisions. One, cultures vary across organizations; individuals will consider this information if it is available to them in their job search process.[97] Firms such as Mobil Oil, Hershey Food, and Scott Paper Co. make sure that it is.[67,116] Two, other things being equal, individuals who choose jobs and organizations that are consistent with their own values, beliefs, and attitudes are more likely to be productive and satisfied employees.

The Logic of Personnel Selection

If variability in physical and psychological characteristics were not so prevalent, there would be little need for *selection* of people to fill various jobs. Without variability among individuals in abilities, aptitudes, interests, and personality traits, we would expect all job candidates to perform comparably. Research shows clearly that as jobs become more complex, individual differences in output variability also increase.[51] Likewise, if there were 10 job openings available and only 10 qualified candidates, selection again would not be a significant issue since all 10 candidates must be hired. Selection becomes a relevant concern only when there are more qualified candidates than there are positions to be filled, for selection implies choice and choice means exclusion.

Since practical considerations (safety, time, cost) make job tryouts for all candidates infeasible in most selection situations, the relative level of job performance of each candidate must be *predicted* in advance on the basis of available information. As we shall see, some methods for doing this are more accurate than others. However, before considering them, we need to focus on the fundamental technical requirements of all such methods—reliability and validity.

Reliability of Measurement

The goal of any selection program is to identify applicants who score high on measures that purport to assess knowledge, skills, abilities, or other characteristics that are critical for job performance. Yet we always run the risk of making errors in personnel selection decisions. Selection errors are of two types: selecting anyone who should be rejected (erroneous acceptances) and rejecting anyone who should be accepted (erroneous rejections). These kinds of errors can be avoided by using measurement procedures that are reliable and valid.

A measurement is considered to be reliable if it is free of error or if it is consistent under conditions that might introduce error.[55] By *errors* we mean any factors that cause a person's *obtained* score to deviate from his or her *true* score. Examples of errors are *the time period when a measure was taken,* e.g., blood pressure readings taken at 8 A.M. and at 4 P.M. may differ significantly; *the particular sample of items chosen,* for example, form A and form B of a test of mathematical aptitude; or *scorer variance,* that is, different interpretations of the same individual's score on some measure by two raters working independently. As you might suspect, errors are present to some degree in all measurement situations.

By *consistency* we mean the stability or dependability of a person's scores over time. Examples of consistent measurements under conditions that might introduce errors are identical scores on a hearing test administered first on Monday morning and then again on Friday night, or nearly identical scores on a measure of vocational interests administered at the beginning of a student's sophomore year in college and then again at the end of her or his senior year.

In employment settings, people are generally assessed only once. That is, they are given, for example, one test of their knowledge of a job or one application form or one medical exam or one interview. The procedures through which these assessments are made must be standardized in terms of content, administration, and scoring. Standardization will assure that the results of each such assessment will produce the "truest," most accurate picture of each person's abilities.

Those who desire more specific information about how reliability is actually estimated in quantitative terms should consult the technical appendix at the end of this chapter.

Validity of Measurement

Reliability is certainly an important characteristic of any measurement procedure, but it is simply a means to an end, a step along the way to a goal. Unless a measure is reliable, it cannot be valid. This is so because unless a measure produces consistent, dependable, stable scores, we cannot begin to understand what implications high versus low scores have for later job performance and economic returns to the organization. Such understanding is the goal of the validation process. In fact, the various validation strategies all focus on two broad issues: (1) *what* a test or other assessment procedure measures, and (2) *how well* it measures (i.e., the relationship between scores from the procedure and some measure or rating of actual job performance).

Although evidence of validity may be accumulated in many ways, validity always refers to the degree to which the evidence supports *inferences* that are drawn from scores or ratings on a selection procedure. It is the inferences regarding the specific use of a selection procedure that are validated, not the procedure itself.[3] Hence a user must first specify exactly *why* he or she intends to use a particular selection procedure (that is, what inferences are to be drawn from it). Then the user can make an informed judgment about the adequacy of the available evidence of validity in support of that particular selection procedure when used for a particular purpose.

Scientific standards for validation are described in greater detail in *Principles for the Validation and Use of Personnel Selection Procedures,*[98] and legal standards for validation are contained in the *Uniform Guidelines on Employee Selection Procedures.*[121] For those who desire an overview of the various strategies used to validate personnel selection procedures, see the technical appendix at the end of the chapter.

Quantitative evidence of validity is often expressed in terms of a correlation coefficient (that may assume values between -1 and $+1$) between scores on a predictor of later job performance (e.g., a test or an interview) and a criterion that reflects actual job performance (e.g., supervisory ratings, dollar volume of sales). In employment contexts, predictor validities typically vary between about .20 and .50. In the following sections we will consider some of the most commonly used methods for screening and selection decisions, together with validity evidence for each one.

SCREENING AND SELECTION METHODS

Employment Application Forms

Employment application forms are indiscriminate and unrestrictive. That is the way they must be. Thus the screening process does not begin with the application form; it begins after the HR department receives it. As a result, organizations frequently find themselves deluged with applications for employment for only a trickle of jobs to be filled. As an example, consider that a typical public utility company *receives* about 75 applications a day (each of which must be screened), *interviews* about 4 of the 75 applicants, and *selects* maybe 1 of the 4. Considerable staff-hours are required just for screening these applications. Alaska Airlines attempted to cause applicants to screen themselves before applying for 40 jobs as flight attendants. How did they do that? By charging applicants a $10 fee for filing an application for employment. More than 5000 people applied and paid the filing fee![1] Other airlines noticed. Now they too charge each job applicant a $10 "processing fee."[68,70] It is not clear whether such fees discourage any applicants. But at least the companies can recover some of the costs associated with screening the applicants.

An important requirement of all employment application forms is that they ask only for information that is valid and fair with respect to the nature of the job. Recent studies of application blanks used by 200 organizations indicated that, for the most part, the questions required information that was job-related and necessary for the employment decision.[79,85] On the other hand, over 95 percent of the forms included one or more legally indefensible questions. Employment application forms should be reviewed regularly to be sure that the information they require complies with equal employment opportunity guidelines and case law. Here are some guidelines that will suggest what questions should be deleted:[85]

- Any question that might lead to an adverse impact on the employment of women, minorities, the disabled, or people over 40 years old
- Any question that does not appear to be job-related or that does not concern a bona fide occupational qualification
- Any question that could possibly constitute an invasion of privacy

Some organizations have sought to identify statistically significant relationships between responses to questions on application forms and later measures of job performance (e.g., tenure, absenteeism, theft).[9] Such "weighted application blanks" (WABs) are often highly predictive.[49] In one study, for example, 28 objective questions were examined for a random sample of the employment applications representing 243 current and former circulation route managers at a metropolitan daily newspaper.[73] A statistical procedure (multiple regression analysis) was used to identify which people were most likely to stay on the job for more than 1 year (the breakeven point for employee orientation and training costs). Several inter-

VIDEO RÉSUMÉS?

Yes, they're here—but maybe not to stay. With the popularity of videocassette recorders at home and at work, the video résumé may seem like an inevitable development. Candidates can look their best, rehearse answers to questions, and, in general, present themselves in the "best possible light."

These efforts get mixed reviews from employers and recruiters, many of whom consider video résumés to be costly gimmicks that fail to provide as much useful information as an ordinary résumé. Here are some of their objections: Answers are shallow rather than in-depth, the videos take considerable time to review, and they could cause legal problems for employers who reject candidates from protected groups. As the director of human resources for Apple Computer noted: "We get 9000 résumés a month; we don't have time to watch videos when we're going through our screening process."[61] Stay tuned for future developments.

esting findings resulted from the study: (1) questions on the WAB that best predicted time on the job at the beginning of the study did not predict time on the job several years later. Hence, WAB questions need to be rechecked periodically. (2) The statistical analysis showed that those items that "conventional widsom" might suggest or those used by interviewers did not predict employee turnover accurately. (3) An independent check in a new sample of job candidates showed that the WAB was able to identify employees who would stay on the job longer than 1 year in 83 percent of the cases. (4) The length of the time employees stayed on previous jobs was unrelated to their length of stay on their current jobs. (5) The best predictors were "experience as a sales representative," "business school education," and "never previously worked for this company."

Executives balk at spending the time and money on personnel research. Nevertheless, poor hires are expensive. SmithKline Beckman Corporation spends an average of $10,000 to recruit and train each worker.[69] That's $1 million for every 100 workers hired. Those kinds of numbers often tend to cast new light on this neglected area.

Recommendations and Reference Checks

The most common techniques used to screen outside job applicants are recommendations and reference checks.[18] They can provide four kinds of information about a job applicant: (1) education and employment history, (2) character and interpersonal competence, (3) ability to perform the job, and (4) the willingness of the past or current employer to rehire the applicant.

A recommendation or reference check will be meaningful only if the person providing it (1) has had an adequate opportunity to observe the applicant in job-relevant situations, (2) is competent to evaluate the applicant's job performance, (3) can express such an evaluation in a way that is meaningful to the prospective employer, and (4) is completely candid.[83]

Unfortunately, evidence is beginning to show that there is little candor, and thus little value, in written recommendations and referrals, especially those that must, by law, be revealed to applicants if they petition to see them. Specifically, the Family Educational Rights and Privacy Act of 1974 (the Buckley Amendment) gives students the legal right to see all letters of recommendation written about them.

Recent research suggests that if letters of recommendation are to be meaningful, they should contain the following information:[60]

- Degree of writer familiarity with the candidate—time known, and time observed per week.
- Degree of writer familiarity with the job in question. To help the writer make this judgment, the reader should supply to the writer a description of the job in question.
- Reader expectations about how negative information and the letter's confidentiality influence the reader's evaluation of the candidate.
- Specific examples of performance—goals, task difficulty, work environment, and extent of cooperation from coworkers.
- Individuals or groups to whom the candidate is compared.

When seeking information about a candidate from references, consider the following guidelines:[76,103]

- Request job-related information only; put it in written form to prove that your hire or no-hire decision was based on relevant information.
- Obtain from job candidates their written permission to check references prior to doing so.
- Stay away from subjective areas, such as the candidate's *personality*.
- Evaluate the credibility of the source of the reference material. Under most circumstances, an evaluation by a past immediate supervisor will be more credible than an evaluation by a representative of the HR department.
- Wherever possible, use public records to evaluate on-the-job behavior or personal conduct—e.g., court records, bankruptcy, workers' compensation records.
- Remember that the courts have ruled that a reference check of an applicant's prior employment record does not violate his or her civil rights as long as the information provided relates solely to work behavior and to reasons for leaving a previous job.[76,103]

What should you do if you are asked to *provide* reference information? Here are some useful guidelines:[103]

- Obtain written consent from the employee prior to providing reference data.
- Do not blacklist former employees.
- Keep a written record of all released information.
- Make no subjective statements, such as "He's got a bad attitude." Be specific, such as "He was formally disciplined three times last year for fighting at work."
- So long as you know the facts and have records to back you up, you can feel free to challenge an ex-employee's ability or integrity. But official records are not always candid. A file might show that an executive "resigned," but not that the company avoided a scandal by letting him quit instead of firing him for dishonesty. When there is no supporting data, never even whisper about the man's sticky fingers.[53]
- If you are contacted by phone, use a telephone "call back" procedure to verify information provided on a job application by a former employee. Ask the caller to give her or his name, title, company name, and the nature and purpose of the request. Next, obtain the written consent of the employee to release the information. Finally, call back the company by phone. Do not provide any information; only say whether or not the information the caller already has is correct.

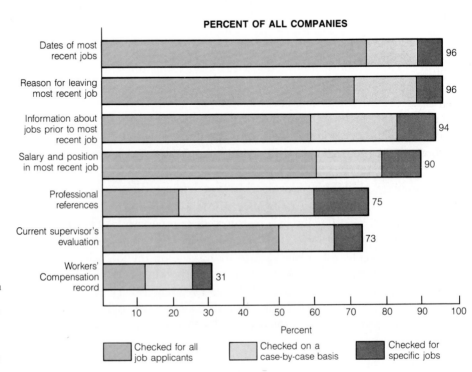

FIGURE 6-2
Employment information most commonly checked. (*Source:* Bureau of National Affairs. *Recruiting and selection procedures.* PPF Survey 146, May 1988. Washington, DC: Bureau of National Affairs, p. 22.)

■ Release only the following general types of information (subject to written consent of the employee): dates of employment, job titles during employment and time in each position, promotions, demotions, attendance record and salary, and reason for termination (no details, just the reason). Sweetening of résumés and previous work history is common.[80] Key aspects of previous history should always be verified.[89] How common? It has been reported that 20 to 25 percent of all résumés and job applications include at least one major fabrication.[76]

What is the current status of reference checking in practice? A 1990 survey found that 81 percent of companies check references before offering a job. Yet 41 percent have written policies against giving out anything other than confirmation of employment. In large measure this is due to a series of well-publicized suits for slander,[102] such as the $25 million in punitive damages received by a former employee of John Hancock Co.[101]

Currently an employer has no legal duty or obligation to provide information to prospective employers. However, if an employer's policy is to disclose reference information, providing false or speculative information could be grounds for a lawsuit. Reference checking is not an infringement on privacy when fair reference checking practices are used. It is a sound evaluative tool that can provide objectivity for employers and fairness for job applicants. Figure 6-2 shows the kinds of employment information checked most often.

THE USE OF TESTS AND INVENTORIES IN SELECTION

Job candidates can be evaluated and selected on the basis of the results of psychological measurements. The term *measurements* is used here in the broad sense, implying tests and inventories. *Tests* are standardized measures of behavior (e.g., math, vocabulary) that have right and wrong answers, and *inventories* are standardized measures of behavior (e.g., interests, attitudes, opinions) that do not have right and wrong answers. Inventories can be falsified to present an image that a candidate *thinks* a prospective employer is looking for. Tests cannot be falsified. In the context of personnel selection, tests are preferable, for obvious reasons. Inventories are probably best used for purposes of placement or development because in those contexts there is less motivation for a job candidate to present an image other than what he or she really is. Nevertheless, as we shall see, inventories have been used (with modest success) in selection. What follows is a brief description of available methods and techniques, together with an assessment of their track records to date.

Drug Testing

Drug screening tests that began in the military and spread to the sports world are now becoming more common in employment. A survey by the American Management Association found 63 percent of firms using drug tests in 1991, compared to 51 percent in 1990.[66]

Critics charge that such screening violates an individual's right to privacy and that frequently the tests are inaccurate.[16,88] Employers counter that the widespread abuse of drugs is reason enough for wider testing. The "man in the street" tends to agree, for in a recent poll, nearly 70 percent of the respondents said they would favor a drug-testing program in their company.[90]

Do the results of such drug tests forecast certain aspects of later job performance? In the largest reported study of its kind, the U.S. Postal Service took urine samples from 5465 job applicants. It never used the results to make hiring decisions and did not tell local managers of the findings. When the data were examined 6 months to a year later, workers who had tested positive prior to employment were absent 41 percent more often and were fired 38 percent more often. There were no differences in turnover between those who tested positive and those who did not. These results held up even after adjustment for factors such as age, sex, and race. As a result, the Postal Service is now implementing preemployment drug testing nationwide.[123]

Is such drug testing legal? In two rulings in 1989, the Supreme Court upheld: (1) the constitutionality of the government regulations that require railroad crews involved in accidents to submit to prompt urinalysis and blood tests and (2) urine tests for U.S. Customs Service employees seeking drug-enforcement posts. The extent to which such rulings will be limited to safety-sensitive positions has yet to be clarified by the court. Nevertheless, an employer has a legal right to ensure that employees perform their jobs competently and that no employee endangers the safety of other workers. So if illegal drug use either on or off the job may reduce job performance and endanger coworkers, the employer has adequate legal grounds for conducting drug tests.

To avoid legal challenge, consider instituting the following common-sense procedures:[4,114,117]

1. Inform all employees and job applicants, in writing, of the company's policy regarding drug use.
2. Include the policy, and the possibility of testing, in all employment contracts.
3. Present the program in a medical and safety context. That is, drug screening will help improve the health of employees and will also help ensure a safer workplace.
4. Check the testing laboratory's experience, its analytical methods, and the way it protects the security and identity of each sample.
5. If drug testing will be used with employees as well as job applicants, tell employees in advance that it will be a routine part of their employment.

Integrity Tests

It is estimated that white-collar crime costs businesses $67 billion per year, and according to a congressional study, crime increases retail prices by 15 percent.[52] With statistics like these, it should come as no surprise that written integrity tests

TWO CONTROVERSIAL SELECTION TECHNIQUES

Handwriting Analysis

Handwriting analysis (graphology) is reportedly used as a hiring tool by 85 percent of all European companies.[74] In Israel, graphology is more widespread than any other personality measurement. Its use is clearly not as widespread in the United States, although sources estimate that over 3000 U.S. firms retain handwriting analysts as personnel consultants. Such firms generally require job applicants to provide a one-page writing sample. Experts then examine it (at a cost of $60 to $500) for 3 to 10 hours. More than 300 personality traits, including enthusiasm, imagination, and ambition are assessed.[38,81,119] Are the analysts' predictions valid? In one study involving the prediction of sales success, 103 writers supplied two samples of their handwriting—one "neutral" in content, the second autobiographical. The data were then analyzed by 20 professional graphologists to predict supervisors' ratings of each salesperson's job performance, each salesperson's *own* ratings of his or her job performance, and sales productivity. The results indicated that the type of script sample did not make any difference. There was some evidence of interrater agreement, but there was no evidence for the validity of the graphologists' predictions.[100] Similar findings have been reported in other well-controlled studies.[12] In short, there is little to recommend the use of handwriting analysis as a predictor of job performance.

Polygraph Examinations

Polygraph (literally, "many pens") examinations are quick and inexpensive ($25 to $50 per person) in comparison to reference checks or background investigations ($100 to $500 and up, depending on the degree of detail required). Professional polygraphers claim their tests are accurate in more than 90 percent of criminal and employment cases *if* interpreted by a competent examiner. Critics claim that the tests are accurate only two-thirds of the time and are far more likely to be unreliable for a subject who is telling the truth.[58,93,106]

Prior to 1988, some 2 million polygraph tests were administered each year, 98 percent in private industry.[96] However, a federal law passed in 1988, the Employee Polygraph Protection Act, severely restricts the use of polygraphs in the employment context (except in the case of firms providing security services and those manufacturing controlled substances). Polygraph examinations of current employees are permitted only under very restricted circumstances. The prohibition is a huge setback for the polygraph industry, which is expected to lose about 85 percent of its $100 million in annual revenues.[38] Indeed, arbitrators had long held that the refusal of an employee to submit to a polygraph exam does not constitute "just cause" for discharge, even when the employee has agreed in advance (e.g., on a job application) to do so on request.[118]

are being used more frequently by employers. However, a question commonly asked is, "Does anybody really admit to criminal activity?" The answer is yes. Among 225,000 job applicants, 6.1 percent admitted involvement in theft investigations in previous employment, 4.4 percent admitted committing a felony crime, 6.4 percent admitted committing minor criminal acts, and 4.5 percent admitted relatively frequent illegal drug use on company premises.[7] Yet the validity of the tests is suspect.[75,104,105] If an employer does decide to use the tests, the best advice is to use the results simply as one additional piece of information, in addition to other screening devices. Do not base an employment decision *solely* on the outcome of an integrity (sometimes called an "honesty") test.

Mental Ability Tests

The major types of mental ability tests used in business today include measures of general intelligence; verbal, nonverbal, and numerical skills; spatial relations ability (the ability to visualize the effects of manipulating or changing the position of objects); motor functions (speed, coordination); mechanical information, reasoning, and comprehension; clerical aptitudes (perceptual speed tests); and inductive reasoning (the ability to draw general conclusions on the basis of specific facts

■ **TABLE 6·1**
AVERAGE VALIDITIES OF ALTERNATIVE PREDICTORS OF JOB PERFORMANCE

Entry-level + training		Current performance used to predict future performance	
Cognitive ability tests	.53	Work-sample tests	.54
Job tryout	.44	Cognitive ability tests	.53
Biographical inventories	.37	Peer ratings	.49
Reference checks	.26	Ratings of the *quality* of performance in past work experience (behavioral consistency ratings)	.49
Experience	.18	Job knowledge tests	.48
Interview	.14	Assessment centers	.43
Ratings of training and experience	.13		
Academic achievement	.11		
Amount of education	.10		
Interest	.10		
Age	−.01		

Source: J. E. Hunter & R. E. Hunter, Validity and utility of alternative predictors of job performance, *Psychological Bulletin*, 96, 1984, 72–98. Copyright 1984 by the American Psychological Association. Reprinted by permission.

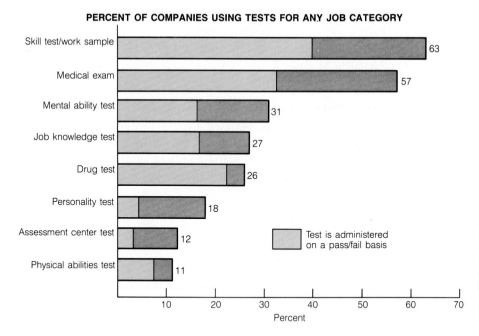

FIGURE 6-3
Most common tests and examinations used for selection. (*Source:* Bureau of National Affairs. *Recruiting and selection procedures.* PPF Survey 146, May 1988. Washington, DC: Bureau of National Affairs, p. 19.)

presented). When job analysis shows that the abilities or aptitudes measured by such tests are important for successful job performance, the tests are among the most valid predictors currently available (see Table 6-1 and Figure 6-3). With respect to the selection of managers, reviews of research conducted between 1919 and 1972 indicated that successful managers were most accurately forecast by tests of their intellectual ability, by their ability to draw conclusions from verbal or numerical information, and by their interests.[36,59,77] Further research has found two other types of mental abilities that are related to successful performance as a manager: fluency with words and spatial relations ability.[40,63,64]

Validity generalization A traditional belief of testing experts is that validity is situation-specific. That is, a test with a demonstrated validity in one setting (e.g., to select bus drivers in St. Louis) might not be valid in another, similar setting (e.g., bus drivers in Atlanta), possibly as a result of differences in specific job tasks, duties, and behaviors. Thus it would seem that the same test used to predict bus driver success in St. Louis and in Atlanta would have to be validated separately in each city.

Recent research has cast serious doubt on this assumption (see refs. 50 and 110 for reviews). In fact, it has been shown that the major reason for the variation in validity coefficients across settings is the size of the samples—they were too small. When the effect of sampling error is removed, the validities observed for similar test-job combinations across settings do not differ significantly. In short, the results of a validity study conducted in one situation can be generalized to other situations as long as it can be shown that jobs in the two situations are similar.

Since thousands of studies have been done on the prediction of job performance, validity generalization allows us to use this database to establish definite values for the average validity of most predictors. The average validities for predictors commonly in use are shown in Table 6-1.

Objective Personality and Interest Inventories

Objective personality and interest inventories provide a clear stimulus, such as statements about preferences for various ways of behaving, and a clear set of responses from which to choose. Here is an example of an objective measure of personality; the examinee's task is to select the alternatives that are most (M) and least (L) descriptive of herself or himself:

Prefers to get up early in the morning	M	L
Does not get enough exercise	M	L
Follows a well-balanced diet	M	L
Does not care for popular music	M	L

Ever since 1944, Sears has used objective personality and interest inventories as part of a larger "executive battery" of measures to predict management success. It has done so very successfully.[13,14] Measures of "general activity" have proven especially accurate, as have measures of conscientiousness and dependability.[10,46] This is consistent with the finding that successful managers prefer immediate rather than delayed action.[86,87]

Projective Measures

Projective measures present an individual with ambiguous stimuli (primarily visual) and allow him or her to respond in an open-ended fashion (Figure 6-4): for example, by telling a story regarding what is happening in the picture. Based on how the individual structures the situation through the story he or she tells, an examiner (usually a clinical psychologist) makes inferences concerning the individual's personality structure.

Basically, the difference between an objective and a projective test is this: In an objective test, the test taker tries to guess what the examiner is thinking. In a projective test, the examiner tries to guess what the test taker is thinking.[54]

Although early research showed projective measures *not* to be accurate predictors of management success,[57] they can provide useful results when the examinee's responses are related to motivations to manage (e.g., achievement motivation, willingness to accept a leadership role).[15,39,82] Moreover, measures of intelligence are unrelated to scores on projective tests. So a combination of both types of instruments can provide a fuller picture of individual "can-do" (intelligence) and "will-do" (motivational) factors than can either one used alone.

FIGURE 6-4

Sample projective stimulus. Candidates are told to look at the picture briefly and then to write the story it suggests. Stories are scored in terms of the key themes expressed.

Measures of Leadership Ability

At first glance, one might suspect that measures of leadership ability are highly predictive of managerial success since they appear to tap directly a critical management job requirement. Scales designed to measure two key aspects of leadership behavior, *consideration* and *initiating structure*, have been developed and used in many situations. Consideration reflects management actions oriented toward developing mutual trust, respect for subordinates' ideas, and consideration of their feelings. Initiating structure, on the other hand, reflects the extent to which an individual defines and structures her or his role and those of her or his subordinates toward task accomplishment.

Unfortunately, questionnaires designed to measure consideration and initiating structure have been inaccurate predictors of success in management.[56,113] This is not to imply that leadership is unimportant in managerial jobs. Rather, it may be that the majority of such jobs are designed to encourage and reward managing (doing things right) rather than leading (doing the right things).

Personal-History Data

Based on the assumption that one of the best predictors of future behavior is past behavior, biographical information has been used widely and successfully in managerial selection. As with any other method, careful, competent research is necessary if "biodata" are to prove genuinely useful as predictors of managerial success. Here is one example of this kind of effort.

During the development of its management selection process, Standard Oil of New Jersey (SONJ) asked prospective managers to complete a background survey of the following areas: home and family, education, vocational planning, finances, hobbies and leisure-time activities, health history, and social relations. SONJ then identified items in the background survey that were related statistically to overall success as a manager. These items comprise a "success index."[72] They can be used legally because the company showed that they were job-related. The success index considers an individual's entire career—the many judgments and decisions that many managers have made about him or her—and not the favorable or unfavorable biases of one or a few supervisors. Successful executives in SONJ tend to show a total life pattern of successful endeavors. They were high performers in college, they actively pursue leadership opportunities, and they see themselves as forceful, dominant, assertive, and confident.

Employment Interviews

Employment interviewing is a difficult mental and social task. Managing a smooth social exchange while instantaneously processing information about a job candidate makes interviewing uniquely difficult among all managerial tasks.[42] Researchers have been studying the employment interview for more than 60 years for two purposes: (1) to determine the reliability (consistency) and validity (accuracy) of the employment decisions based on assessments derived from the interview and (2) to discover the various psychological factors that influence interviewer judgments. Hundreds of research articles on these issues have been published, along with periodic reviews of the "state of the art" of interviewing research and practice.[5,23,41] Until recently, the employment interview was considered an unreliable basis for employment decisions (note that in Table 6-1 the average validity for the interview is only .14). However, research is beginning to indicate that the interview works well when:

1. The interview is limited to information that a prior job analysis indicates is important for successful job performance.
2. Interviewers are trained to evaluate behavior objectively.
3. The interview is conducted along a specific set of guidelines.[6,22,43]

The interview was originally considered a poor basis for employment decisions because interviewers' decisions were influenced by such factors as first impressions, personal feelings about the kinds of characteristics that lead to success on the job, and contrast effects, among other nonobjective factors. *Contrast effects* describe a tendency among interviewers to evaluate a current candidate's interview performance relative to those that immediately preceded it. If a first candidate received a very positive evaluation and a second candidate is just "average," interviewers tend to evaluate the second candidate more negatively than is deserved. The second candidate's performance is "contrasted" to that of the first. Finally, research indicates that when interviewers' evaluations of job candidates are in the form of specific predictions of job behavior rather than in terms of general impressions about each candidate, less distortion between actual and perceived interview behavior is found. Employers are therefore likely to achieve nonbiased hiring decisions if they concentrate on shaping interviewer behavior.[31,91,95]

One way to shape interviewer behavior is to establish a specific system for conducting the employment interview. Here are some things to consider to set up such a system:[22,32]

- Determine the requirements of the job through a job analysis that considers the input of the incumbent along with the inputs of the supervisor and the HR representative.
- To know what to look for in applicants, focus only on those knowledges, skills, abilities, and other characteristics (KSAOs) necessary for the job. Be sure to distinguish between entry-level and full-performance KSAOs.
- Screen résumés and application forms by focusing on (1) key words that match job requirements, (2) quantifiers and qualifiers that show whether applicants have these requirements, and (3) skills that might transfer from previous jobs to the new job.
- Develop interview questions that are strictly based on the job analysis results; use "open-ended" questions (those which cannot be answered with a simple yes or no response); and use questions relevant to the individual's ability to perform, motivation to do a good job, and overall "fit" with the firm. Also consider asking "what would you do if . . . ?" questions. Such questions comprise the "situational" interview, which is based on the assumption that a person's expressed behavioral intentions are related to subsequent behavior. In the situational interview, candidates are asked to describe how they think they would respond in certain job-related situations. Alternatively, they are asked to provide detailed accounts of actual situations. For example, instead of asking, "How would you reprimand an employee," now it's "Give me a specific example of a time you had to reprimand an employee. What action did you take, and what was the result?" Their answers tend to be remarkably consistent with their actual (subsequent) job behavior.[71,122]
- Conduct the interview in a relaxed physical setting. Begin by putting the applicant at ease with simple questions and general information about the organization and the position being filled. Throughout, note all nonverbal cues, such as lack of eye contact and facial expressions, as possible indicators of the candidate's interest in and ability to do the job.

■ To evaluate applicants, develop a form containing a list of KSAOs weighted for overall importance to the job, and evaluate each applicant relative to each KSAO.

A systematic interview developed along these lines will minimize the uncertainty so inherent in decision making that is based predominantly on "gut feeling."

■ **COMPANY EXAMPLE**

ROI FROM STRUCTURED INTERVIEWING AT J. C. PENNEY

For most organizations, return-on-investment (ROI) analyses are an integral part of the decision process of any purchase, marketing strategy, new product development, etc. And, although they commonly are not, ROI analyses should be part of any assessment of human resources programs. The J. C. Penney Company tried to determine ROI from a structured interviewing program and began by developing a standard interview for identifying, evaluating, and selecting employees to fit each of a number of different, specific jobs in the company. Each standard interview was based on an intensive training program that taught interviewers how to evaluate their own behavior as well as that of job candidates.

The first step toward developing a standard interview was an analysis of each job that focused on present as well as anticipated future job-related KSAOs required from the first day on the job. Extensive involvement of upper-level management throughout the design helped to assure continued support and commitment to the program.

The aim of each job analysis was to identify the skills, experience, and personal characteristics that workers needed to perform each job successfully. From those qualifications for each job category, the best methods of screening and selecting applicants were determined. These methods turned out to be structured interviews, work simulations, written tests, or some combination of the three. No matter which screening-selection method was used, they were all called "Certified Interview" programs because the structured interview was at the core of all the programs. Interviewers were trained in intensive 4-day workshops; they were reviewed annually to determine that they were maintaining established company standards in the screening-selection process. Those falling below company standards were required to attend 1-day refresher training sessions.

The actual selection process differs slightly for external and internal candidates. External candidates undergo a screening interview, during which they receive basic information about the company and the job they are applying for, including a Supplemental Information Form detailing exactly what the job entails. The external candidates who survive this screening stage are joined by internal candidates; each is interviewed by at least one certified interviewer. Interviewers record examples of behavior elicited in an interviewing booklet specially designed for each job category. If additional data are required to assess applicants for a particular job, then simulations, written tests, or other selection instruments are administered after the interview by other trained individuals. Hence, candidates may see several different company people during the selection-promotion process. All evaluators then meet to integrate their data and to select the most suitable candidates.

EVALUATING THE SYSTEM

To evaluate the system, J. C. Penney conducted a study of several hundred hired candidates comprising two groups. One group represented candidates selected through traditional methods; the other represented candidates selected through the certified interviewing (C) program. The objective was to compare each group's attrition and performance over a 2½-year period. Except for the fact that more minority-group members had been hired through the CI program than through traditional methods, no other statistically significant difference occurred on any demographic variable at the beginning of the study. The members of both groups had been selected and placed in their positions at approximately the same time and into the same type of company units throughout the United States. Hence all company policies as well as U.S. economy changes impacted on both groups identically. Finally, there were no significant differences found on any of the component test scores between candidates from minority groups and any others.

RESULTS

After 2½ years, the CI group hirees had 45 percent less turnover than hirees in the traditional group. Moreover, minorities hired through the CI program showed 54.4 percent less turnover than minorities hired traditionally. To gauge the program's impact on performance all employees were rated on the same performance appraisal system. Without knowing which employees were hired under which system, supervisors consistently rated the CI employees higher in performance and more readily promotable than those in the traditional group.

To evaluate these results, two types of ROI analyses were done. One focused on the savings generated by CI in terms of turnover percentages. To retain 1000 people in a position after 2 years, the company would have to hire either 1733 through the traditional method or 1304 through the CI program. Hiring 429 fewer individuals through the CI program at an average annual salary of $21,000 yields a savings (in 1990 dollars) of over $9 million *in salary alone*, not counting additional recruiting and training costs.

Another, more comprehensive, ROI analysis was based on a utility analysis of the total personnel system under the traditional and CI approaches.

Utility analysis is basically a method that allows a manager to compare all the costs associated with selecting, training, and paying workers against the dollar benefits resulting from their work. The utility analysis indicated a net payoff for the CI program of over $10 million (in 1990 dollars) over 2½ years.[30]

What do these figures mean? Currently most organizations implement programs with little, if any, means of evaluating their long-range impact. However, it may make more sense simply to get basic comparative measures in place. Any model that shows a reasonable ROI (i.e., any return that covers program costs plus some surplus) may well change the attitude of the organization toward funding human resource programs based on their positive impact on the bottom line.

As the J. C. Penney case illustrates, the first step in developing a program for evaluating and selecting new employees is to do a comprehensive job analysis. The results of that process—the specification of critical job dimensions and employee KSAOs—provide *clues* regarding what types of selection measures to use to assess critical job requirements.

Peer Assessment

In the typical peer assessment procedure, raters are asked to predict how well a peer will do if placed in a leadership or managerial role. Such information can be enlightening, since peers evaluate managerial behavior from a different perspective than do the managers themselves. Actually the term *peer assessment* is a general term denoting three basic methods that members of a well-defined group use in judging each others' performance: *Peer nomination* requires each group member to designate a certain number of group members as highest or lowest on a performance dimension. *Peer rating* requires each group member to rate the performance of every group member. *Peer ranking* requires each group member to rank the performance of all other members from best to worst.

Reviews of over 50 studies found all three methods of peer assessment to be reliable, valid, and free from bias.[111] Peer assessments implicitly require people to consider privileged information about their coworkers. Hence it is essential that peers be thoroughly involved in the planning and design of the peer assessment method to be used.

Work-Sample Tests

Work-sample, or situational tests are standardized measures of behavior whose primary objective is to assess the ability to do rather than the ability to know. They may be *motor*, involving physical manipulation of things (e.g., trade tests for carpenters, plumbers, electricians) or *verbal*, involving problem situations that are primarily language-oriented or people-oriented (e.g., situational tests for supervisory jobs).[8] Since work samples are miniature replicas of actual job requirements, they are difficult to fake, and they are unlikely to lead to charges of discrimination or invasion of privacy. Their use in one study of 263 applicants for city government jobs led to a reduction of turnover from 40 percent to less than 3 percent in the 9 to 26 months following their introduction. The reduction in turnover saved the city over $600,000 in 1990 dollars.[25] Nevertheless, since each candidate must be tested individually, work-sample tests are probably not cost-effective when large numbers of people must be evaluated.

Two types of situational tests are used to evaluate and select managers: *group exercises*, in which participants are placed in a situation where the successful completion of a task requires interaction among the participants, and *individual exercises*, in which participants complete a task independently. The following sections consider three of the most popular situational tests: the leaderless group discussion, the in-basket test, and the business game.

Leaderless group discussion (LGD) The LGD is simple and has been used for decades. A group of participants is given a job-related topic and is asked simply to carry on a discussion about it for a period of time. No one is appointed leader, nor is anyone told where to sit. Instead of using a rectangular table (with a "head" at each end), a circular table is often used so that each position carries equal weight. Observers rate the performance of each participant.

For example, IBM uses an LGD in which each participant is required to make a 5-minute oral presentation of a candidate for promotion and then subsequently defend her or his candidate in a group discussion with five other participants. All roles are well-defined and structured. Seven characteristics are rated, each on a 5-point scale of effectiveness: aggressiveness, persuasiveness or selling ability, oral communications, self-confidence, resistance to stress, energy level, and interpersonal contact.[125]

LGD ratings have forecast managerial performance accurately in virtually all the functional areas of business.[11,120] Previous LGD experience appears to have little effect on present LGD performance, although prior training clearly does.[65,94] Individuals in one study who received a 15-minute briefing on the history, development, rating instruments, and research relative to the LGD were rated significantly higher than untrained individuals. To control for this, all those with prior training in the LGD should be put into the same groups.

In-basket test A situational test designed to simulate important aspects of a position, the in-basket tests an individual working independently. In general, it takes the following form:

> It consists of the letters, memoranda, notes of incoming telephone calls, and other materials which have supposedly collected in the in-basket of an administrative officer. The subject who takes the test is given appropriate background information concerning the school, business, military unit, or whatever institution is involved. He is told that he is the new incumbent of the administrative position and that he is to deal with the

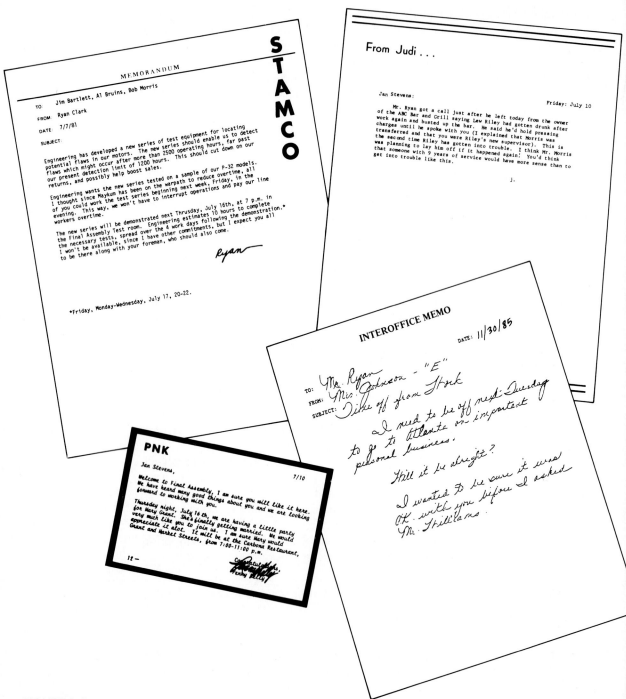

FIGURE 6-5
Sample in-basket items.

DOWNTOWN KEY-WANIS CLUB
Box 8003
Midville, Indiana

December 1, 1985

Mr. Sam Ryan, Superintendent
Midville Youth Development Center
Midville, Indiana

Dear Mr. Ryan:

We would like very much to have you speak at our luncheon meeting on Thursday, January 8th, at 12:30 p.m. at the Midville Hotel. Perhaps you could use the topic "The Extent of the Problem of Drug Abuse and Crime." The programs at our luncheon meetings usually run from 30-45 minutes.

We sincerely hope that you will be able to be with us on the 8th. Please let me know at the address shown above (or at telephone number 822-0136). If your schedule will not permit your accepting this invitation, perhaps one of your staff could present this program.

Yours truly,

Jack Williams

J.W. ("Jack") Williams
Program Chairman

2310 Lakewood Drive
Midville, Indiana
November 24, 1985

Mr. Sam Ryan
Midville Youth and Adult Development Center
Midville, Georgia

Dear Mr. Ryan:

The Youth Fellowship of Greenbriar Church would like to come to the Center and put on a Christmas Party for the people there. We would provide refreshments, presents for everybody, decorations and all the rest.

Would you please let me know if this is possible. If it is, our committee will come out and talk to you about the plans. My phone number is 823-9322.

Sincerely,

Andy Fuller

Cindy Fuller
President, Greenbriar
Youth Fellowship

---

*Bill—
How does this
sound to you?
SR 11/25/85*

*MR. RYAN—
THE LAST TIME WE HAD A
CHURCH GROUP PUT ON A PARTY
OUT HERE WAS BEFORE YOU
CAME. THINGS WERE O.K.
UNTIL THE HOUSEPARENTS
TOOK A COFFEE BREAK. WHILE
THEY WERE GONE, IT GOT
COMPLETELY OUT OF HAND.
WE COULD HAVE
PROBLEMS.
BILL 11/28/85*

MIDVILLE APPLIANCE AND HARDWARE STORE
149 Peabody Street
Midville, Indiana

November 28, 1985

Mr. Sam Ryan
Superintendent
Midville Youth and Adult
Development Center
Midville, Indiana

Dear Mr. Ryan:

As you know, my store is located between your rehabilitation center and Midville Vocational and Technical School. During the past several months we have had several cases of shoplifting from our store, and the police haven't been able to do anything about it. Also, your people have been observed acting funny with a dazed look in their faces, as though they are on drugs.

I initially was a supporter of the rehabilitation center being in this neighborhood. However, I am about to change my mind, and I can assure you that my weight on the zoning commission carries a lot of weight in this community.

I would appreciate hearing from you within the next week. Otherwise, I will be forced to take appropriate measures to insure protection of my store and this community.

Sincerely,

Arch Turkey

Arch Turkey

---

memo   7/3/81   from *Charlie Vernon*

*Bob:
We've had an 80% increase in
rejects this week on our 38B
model and most of them have
been a result of poor armature
wiring. Isn't that Mr. Grady's
operation? This doesn't help our
production indel, you know.*

material in the in-basket. The background information is sufficiently detailed that the subject can reasonably be expected to take action on many of the problems presented by the in-basket documents. The subject is instructed that he is not to play a role, he is not to pretend to be someone else. He is to bring to the new job his own background of knowledge and experience, his own personality, and he is to deal with the problems as though he were really the incumbent of the administrative position. He is not to say what he would do; he is actually to write letters and memoranda, prepare agenda for meetings, make notes and reminders for himself, as though he were actually on the job (ref. 33, p. 1).

Some sample in-basket items are shown in Figure 6-5.

Although the situation is relatively unstructured for the candidate, each candidate faces the same complex set of materials. At the conclusion of the in-basket test, each candidate leaves behind a packet full of notes, memos, letters, etc., that provide a record of his or her behavior. The test is then scored by describing (if the purpose is development) or evaluating (if the purpose is selection for promotion) what the candidate did in terms of such dimensions as self-confidence, organizational and planning abilities, written communications, decision making, risk taking, and administrative abilities. The dimensions to be evaluated are identified through job analysis prior to designing or selecting the exercise. The major advantages of the in-basket, therefore, are its flexibility (it can be designed to fit many different types of situations) and the fact that it permits *direct* observation of individual behavior within the context of a job-relevant, standardized problem situation.

More than two decades of research on the in-basket indicate that it validly forecasts subsequent job behavior and promotion.[17,18,120] Moreover, since performance on the LGD is not strongly related to performance on the in-basket,[120] in combination they are potentially powerful predictors of managerial success.

Business games The business game is a situational test, a living case in which candidates play themselves, not an assigned role, and are evaluated within a group. Like the in-basket, business games are available for a wide variety of executive activities, from marketing to capital asset management. They may be simple (focusing on very specific activities) or complex models of complete organizational systems. They may be computer-based or manually operated, rigidly programmed or flexible.[28,29,37] They will probably be used more frequently for training purposes, given the continued development and availability of personal computers and simulation software—for example, stock market simulations, and battle simulations for the military academies.

■ **COMPANY EXAMPLE**   IBM'S MANUFACTURING PROBLEM

In this exercise, six participants must work together as a group to operate a manufacturing company. They must purchase raw materials, manufacture a product, and sell it back to the market. Included in the exercise are a product forecast and specific prices (that fluctuate during the exercise) for raw materials and completed products. No preassigned roles are given to the participants, but each one is rated in terms of aggressiveness, persuasiveness or selling ability, resistance to stress, energy level, interpersonal contact, administrative ability, and risk taking. In one IBM study, performance on the manufacturing problem accurately forecast changes in position level for 94 middle managers 3 years later.[125] When the in-basket score was added as an additional predictor, the forecast was even more accurate.

Business games have several advantages. One, they compress time; events that might not actually occur for months or years are made to occur in a matter of hours. Two, the games are interesting because of their realism, competitive nature, and the immediacy and objectivity of feedback. And three, such games promote increased understanding of complex interrelationships among organizational units.

Business games also have several drawbacks. One, in the context of training, some participants may become so engrossed in "beating the system" that they fail to grasp the underlying management principles being taught. And two, creative approaches to solving problems presented by the game may be stifled, particularly if the highly innovative manager is penalized financially during the game for her or his unorthodox strategies.[124]

Based on available research, a rough "scorecard" indicating the overall effectiveness of predictors commonly used to assess managerial potential is shown in Table 6-2.

Assessment Centers

The assessment center approach was first used by German military psychologists during World War II to select officers. They felt that paper-and-pencil tests took too narrow a view of human nature; therefore, they chose to observe each candidate's behavior in a complex situation to develop a broader appraisal of his or her reactions. Borrowing from this work and that of the War Office Selection Board of the British Army during the early 1940s, the U.S. Office of Strategic Services used the method to select spies during World War II. Each candidate had to develop a cover story that would hide her or his identity during the assessment. Testing for the ability to maintain cover was crucial, and ingenious situational tests were designed to seduce candidates into breaking cover.[84,92]

After World War II many military psychologists and officers joined private companies, where they started small-scale assessment centers. In 1956, AT&T was the first to use the method as the basis for a large-scale study of managerial progress and career development. As a result of extensive research conducted over 25 years,

■ **TABLE 6-2**

ACCURACY OF VARIOUS PROCEDURES USED TO ASSESS POTENTIAL FOR MANAGEMENT

Procedure	Accuracy
Mental ability tests	5
Objective personality and interest inventories	4
Projective techniques	3
Measures of leadership ability	1
Interviews	2
Personal history data	4
Peer assessment	4
Situational tests (when used in combination, as in an assessment center)	5

Procedures are rated on a 1-to-5 scale, where 1 = poor prediction and 5 = accurate prediction. It is important to stress, however, that no single procedure or combination of procedures is perfectly accurate. Even the most accurate procedures available account for only about 25 percent of the variability in actual job performance among managers. The following rating scheme was therefore used for each procedure, based on the average correlation between scores on the procedure and measures of actual job performance:

Average correlation	Accuracy score
.00 to .10	1
.10 to .20	2
.20 to .30	3
.30 to .40	4
.40 to .50	5

AT&T found that managerial skills and abilities are best measured by the following procedures:[19]

1. *Administrative skills.* Performance on the in-basket test
2. *Interpersonal skills.* LGD, manufacturing problem
3. *Intellectual ability.* Paper-and-pencil ability tests
4. *Stability of performance.* In-basket, LGD, manufacturing problem
5. *Work-oriented motivation.* Projective tests, interviews, simulations
6. *Career orientation.* Projective tests, interviews, personality inventories
7. *Dependency on others.* Projective tests

But assessment centers do more than just *test* people. The assessment center method is a process that evaluates a candidate's potential for management from three sources: (1) multiple assessment techniques, such as situational tests, tests of mental abilities, and interest inventories; (2) standardized methods of making inferences from such techniques, because assessors are trained to distinguish between effective and ineffective behaviors of the candidates; and (3) pooled judgments from multiple assessors to rate each candidate's behavior.

Today assessment centers take many different forms, for they are used in a wide variety of settings and for a variety of purposes. Over 2000 organizations are now using the assessment center method, and more are doing so every year.[34] In addition to evaluating and selecting managers, the method is being used to train and upgrade management skills, to encourage creativity among research and engineering personnel, to resolve interpersonal and interdepartmental conflicts, to assist individuals in career planning, to train managers in performance appraisal, and to provide information for human resource planning and organization design.[34]

The assessment center method offers great flexibility. The specific content and design of a center can be tailored to the characteristics of the job in question. For example, when used for management selection, the assessment center method should be designed to predict how a person would behave in that next-higher-level management job. By relating each candidate's performance on the assessment center exercises to such indicators as the management level subsequently achieved 2 (or more) years later or current salary, researchers have shown that the predictions for each candidate are very accurate. An accurate reading of each candidate's behavior *before* the promotion decision is made can help avoid potentially costly selection errors (erroneous acceptances as well as erroneous rejections).

As a specific example of the flexibility of the assessment center method in using multiple assessment techniques, consider the following six types of exercises used to help select U.S. Army recruiters:[17,99]

- *Structured interview.* Assessors ask a series of questions targeted at the subject's level of achievement motivation, potential for being a "self-starter," and commitment to the Army.
- *Cold calls.* The subject has an opportunity to learn a little about three prospects and must phone each of them for the purpose of getting them to come into the office. Assessor role players have well-defined characters (prospects) to portray.
- *Interviews.* Two of the three cold-call prospects agree to come in for an interview. The subject's job is to follow up on what was learned in the cold-call conversations and to begin promoting Army enlistment to these people. A third walk-in prospect also appears for an interview with the subject.
- *Interview with concerned parent.* The subject is asked to prepare for and conduct an interview with the father of one of the prospects that he or she interviewed previously.
- *Five-minute speech about the Army.* The subject prepares a short talk about an Army career that she or he delivers to the rest of the group and to the assessors.
- *In-basket.* The subject is given an in-basket filled with notes, phone messages, and letters on which he or she must take some action.

A third feature of the assessment center method is assessor training. Assessors are typically line managers two or more levels above the candidates, trained (from 2 days to several weeks depending on the complexity of the center) in interviewing techniques, behavior observation, and in-basket performance. In addition, assessors usually go through the exercises as participants before rating others. This experience, plus the development of a consensus by assessors on effective versus ineffective responses by candidates to the situations presented, enables the assessors to standardize their interpretations of each candidate's behavior. Standardization ensures that each candidate will be assessed fairly, that is, in terms of the same "yardstick."

Instead of professional psychologists, line managers are often used as assessors for several reasons:

1. They are thoroughly familiar with the jobs for which candidates are being assessed.
2. Their involvement in the assessment process contributes to its acceptance by participants as well as by line managers.
3. Participation by line managers is a developmental experience for them and may contribute to the identification of areas where they need improvement themselves.[78]
4. Assessors can be more objective in evaluating candidate performance since they usually do not know the candidates personally.[21]

Despite these potential advantages, cumulative evidence across assessment center studies indicates that professional psychologists provide more valid assessment center ratings than do managers.[34]

With the assessment center method, the judgments of multiple assessors are pooled in rating each candidate's behavior. The advantage of pooling is that no candidate is subject to ratings from only one assessor. Since judgments from more than one source tend to be more reliable and valid, pooling enhances the overall accuracy of the judgments made. Each candidate is usually evaluated by a different assessor on each exercise. Although assessor judgments are made independently, the judgments must be combined into an overall rating on each dimension of interest. A summary report is then prepared and shared with each candidate.

These features of the assessment center method—flexibility of form and content, the use of multiple assessment techniques, standardized methods for interpreting behavior, and pooled assessor judgments—account for the successful track record of this approach over the past three decades. It has consistently demonstrated high validity, with correlations between assessment center performance and later job performance as a manager sometimes reaching the .50s and .60s.[34,47,59] Both minorities and nonminorities, and men and women, acknowledge that the method provides them a fair opportunity to demonstrate what they are capable of doing in a management job.[48]

In terms of its bottom-line impact, two studies have shown that assessment centers *are* cost-effective, even though the per-candidate cost may vary from as little as $50 to over $2000. Using the general utility equation (Equation 6-1 in the Appendix to this chapter, p. 211), both studies have demonstrated that the assessment center method should not be measured against the cost of implementing it, but rather against the cost (in lost sales and declining productivity) of promoting the wrong person into a management job.[26,27] In a first-level management job, the gain in improved job performance as a result of promoting people via the assessment center method is about $2700 per year. However, if the average tenure of first-level managers is, say, 5 years, the gain per person is about $13,500.

Despite its advantages, the method is not without potential problems. These include:[2,35,59,126]

- Adoption of the assessment center method without carefully analyzing the need for it, and without adequate preparations to use it wisely
- Blind acceptance of assessment data without considering other information on candidates, such as past and current performance
- The tendency to rate only general "exercise effectiveness," rather than performance relative to individual behavioral dimensions, as the number of dimensions exceeds the ability of assessors to evaluate each dimension individually.
- Lack of control over the information generated during assessment: for example, "leaking" assessment ratings to operating managers
- Failure to evaluate the utility of the program in terms of dollar benefits relative to costs
- Inadequate feedback to participants

Here is an interesting finding: Ratings of management potential made after a review of personnel files correlated significantly (.46) with assessment ratings, suggesting that assessment to some extent might duplicate a much simpler and less costly process.[45] This conclusion held true for predictions made regarding each candidate's progress in management 1 and 8 years after assessment.[44] However, when the rating of management potential was added to the assessment center prediction, the validity of the two together (.58) was higher than either one alone. What does the assessment center prediction add? Not much if we are simply trying to predict each candidate's rate and level of *advancement*. But if we are trying to predict *performance* in management—that is, to clarify and evaluate the promotion system in an organization—then assessment centers can be of considerable help, even if they serve only to capture the promotion policy of the organization.[44]

Choosing the Right Predictor

Determining the right predictor depends on the following:

- *The nature of the job*
- An estimate of the *validity of the predictor* in terms of the size of the correlation coefficient that summarizes the strength of the relationship between applicants'

INTERNATIONAL APPLICATION:
THE JAPANESE APPROACH TO PERSONNEL SELECTION

Soon after Toyota announced that it would build an auto assembly plant in Kentucky, some 90,000 job applications poured in for the 2700 production jobs and 300 office jobs available. To narrow the field, Toyota uses common tests to an uncommon degree. Even someone applying for the lowest paying job on the shop floor goes through at least 14 hours of testing, administered on Toyota's behalf by state employment offices and Kentucky State University.

Rigorous testing is also standard procedure for the U.S. auto plants of Mazda Motor Corporation, for a joint venture of Isuzu Motors, Ltd., and Fuji Heavy Industries, Ltd., and for Diamond-Star Motors Corporation, a joint venture of Mitsubishi and Chrysler.

Initial tests cover reading and mathematics, manual dexterity, "job fitness," and for skilled trades, technical knowledge. "Job fitness" is actually an attitude measure in which applicants are asked whether they agree or disagree with 100 different statements. Here are two examples: "It's important for workers to work past quitting time to get the job done when necessary"; and "Management will take advantage of employees whenever possible."

Next come workplace simulations. Groups of applicants are assigned such problems as ranking the features of a hypothetical auto according to how well the market would accept them. As the job seekers discuss the options, trained assessors record their observations and later pool their findings in order to assess each candidate. Other problems focus on manufacturing and making repairs—though not of autos, since Toyota is interested in aptitude more than experience.

There are also mock production lines, where applicants assemble tubes or circuit boards. The objective is to identify applicants who can keep to a fast pace, endure tedious repetition, and yet stay alert. The tube-assembly procedure is intentionally flawed, and applicants are asked how they would improve it.

Only 1 applicant in 20 makes it to an interview, which is conducted by a panel representing various Toyota departments. By then, says an HRM staffer, "we're going to know more about these people than perhaps any company has ever known about people." The final steps are a physical examination and a drug test.

For all the testing being done by the Japanese auto makers, there are some who use other methods. Honda, for example, uses few tests at its Marysville, Ohio, plant. Instead it puts every potential hire through three interviews. And Nissan Motor Co., which has been operating in Smyrna, Tennessee, since the early 1980s, prefers to give probable hires at least 40 hours of "preemployment" training—without pay. The training is intended partly as a final check on whether the company and those in training are really right for each other.[62]

scores on the predictor and their corresponding scores on some measure of performance

- *The selection ratio,* or percentage of applicants selected
- *The cost of the predictor*

To the extent that job performance is multidimensional (as indicated in job analysis results), multiple predictors, each focused on critical knowledge, skills, abilities, or other characteristics, might be used. Other things being equal, predictors with the highest estimated validities should be used; they will tend to minimize the number of erroneous acceptances and rejections, and they will tend to maximize workforce productivity. Table 6-1, page 186, summarizes the accumulated validity evidence on a number of potential predictors. The predictors fall into two categories: those that can be used for entry-level hiring into jobs that require subsequent training and those that depend on the use of current job performance or job knowledge to predict future job performance.

It is important to take into account the selection ratio in evaluating the overall usefulness of any predictor, regardless of its validity. On the one hand, low selection ratios mean that more applicants must be evaluated; on the other hand, low selection ratios also mean that only the "cream" of the applicant crop will be selected. Hence predictors with lower validity may be used when the selection ratio is low since we need distinguish only the very best qualified from everyone else.

Finally, the cost of selection is a consideration, but not a major one. Of course, if two predictors are roughly equal in estimated validity, then the less costly procedure should be used. However, the trade-off between cost and validity should almost always be resolved in favor of validity. Go for the more valid procedure, because the major concern is not the cost of the procedure, but rather the cost of a mistake if the wrong candidate is selected or promoted. In management jobs, such mistakes are likely to be particularly costly.[26]

IMPACT OF STAFFING DECISIONS ON PRODUCTIVITY, QUALITY OF WORK LIFE, AND THE BOTTOM LINE

Some companies avoid validating their screening and selection procedures because they think that validation is too costly—and its benefits too elusive. Alternatively, scare tactics ("validate or else lose in court") have not encouraged widespread validation efforts either. However, recent research has shown that separate validity studies are not necessary when similar jobs are performed in different organizations (e.g., clerical jobs, computer programmers). Research has also shown that the dollar gains in productivity associated with the use of valid selection and promotion procedures *far* outweigh the cost of those procedures. Think about that. If people who score high (low) on selection procedures also do well (poorly) on their jobs, then high scores suggest a close "fit" between individual capabilities and organizational needs. Low scores, on the other hand, suggest a poor fit. In both cases, productivity, quality of work life, and the bottom line stand to gain from the use of valid selection procedures. In short, there are strong *positive* inducements for employers to use the most valid procedures available. As these research findings become more widely publicized, we fully expect that employers will do so.

■ **HUMAN RESOURCE MANAGEMENT IN ACTION**
CONCLUSION

CHOOSING A SUCCESSOR
FOR HARRY THOMPSON

Almost at the last moment, with very little information, with much necessary homework not done, Harry Thompson is considering appointing his successor to head a $250 million, highly diversified chemicals company. He is prepared to choose between two of his vice presidents, about both of whom he has serious reservations. He believes that he owes it "to the company and to its thousands of employees to act decisively." He is confusing decisiveness with correctness. He does not recognize that a decisive, actively implemented, wrong decision is the worst possible legacy he can leave behind.

What is wrong with his proposed decision? First, the decision is being made in the absence of any clear, long-range plan for the organization. Where is Auckland Chemical going? What kind of organization will it be 10 years from now? Will it be stressing the development of new products or the broadening of sales and market penetration with the existing ones? How will the organization be structured? The best choice for president will be that person who is best able to promote the company's continued growth. But until the company's long-range objectives have been stated in specific terms, it will be difficult to say who might best accomplish them. In addition, Thompson is considering only the job of the C.E.O. He needs to be considering his entire top operating group.

Once the long-range objectives of the company have been stated in specific terms, it will be possible for Thompson to list the performance criteria and characteristics of the *ideal* candidate for the position. Not that the ideal president will ever be found. But the best real-life candidate will be that person who most nearly resembles the ideal. Without a profile of the ideal president against which to compare, it would be nearly impossible to recognize the best candidate.

Are Summers and Kemp the only possible candidates for the position? Doesn't Thompson owe it to the company to at least look outside for someone closer to the ideal? Of course, an outsider might well disrupt the inside group. In no case, however, would the disruption approach the havoc created by promoting the wrong person.

Stating objectives and developing a behavioral profile of the ideal candidate is just the beginning. Before making his selection, Thompson must examine the specific consequences of giving the job to that particular individual. What will happen as a result of the move? What kind of a top operating team will this make? Will this selection create other problems? If so, what can be done to lessen their impact?

Even after making the selection, Thompson's task is not over. He will have to work with the new president for several months. As the founder of Auckland Chemical, Thompson is carrying a major amount of history, know-how, and procedures in his head. These need to be preserved and transferred to the new boss. Only when all the foregoing steps have been completed can Thompson feel that he has fully discharged his obligation to Auckland Chemical and to its employees.

SUMMARY

In staffing an organization or an organizational unit, it is important to consider its developmental stage—embryonic, high growth, mature, or aging—in order to align staffing decisions with business strategy. It also is important to communicate an organization's culture, since research shows that applicants will consider this information to choose among jobs if it is available to them. In order to use selection techniques meaningfully, however, it is necessary to specify the kinds of knowledge, skills, abilities, and other characteristics necessary for success.

Applicants may be screened through recommendations and reference checks, the information on application forms, or employment interviews. In addition, some firms use written ability or integrity tests, work-sample tests, drug tests, polygraph examinations, or handwriting analysis. In each case, careful attention must be paid to the reliability and validity of the information obtained. *Reliability* refers to the

IMPLICATIONS FOR MANAGEMENT PRACTICE

The research evidence is clear: Valid selection procedures can produce substantial economic gains for organizations. The implication for policymakers also is clear:

- *Select* the highest caliber managers and lower-level employees, for they are most likely to profit from development programs.
- Do not assume that a large investment in training can transform marginally competent performers into innovative and motivated top performers.
- A wide variety of screening and selection procedures is available. It is your responsibility to ask "tough" questions of staff specialists about the reliability, job-relatedness, and validity of each one proposed for use.
- Recognize that no predictor is perfectly valid and therefore that some mistakes in selection (erroneous acceptances or erroneous rejections) are inevitable. By consciously selecting managers and lower-level employees based on their "fit" with demonstrated job requirements, the strategic direction of a business, and organizational culture, mistakes can be minimized and optimum choices can be made.

consistency or stability of scores over time or over different situations that might introduce error into the scores. The process of *validation* is an attempt to learn two things: (1) what a test or other selection procedure measures, and (2) how well it measures. In the context of managerial selection, numerous techniques are available, but the research literature indicates that the most effective ones have been mental ability tests, objective personality and interest inventories, peer assessments, personal-history data, and situational tests. Projective techniques and leadership ability tests have been less effective. The use of situational tests, such as the leaderless group discussion, the in-basket, and the business game, lies at the heart of the assessment center method. Key advantages of the method are its high validity and fair evaluation of each candidate's ability and its flexibility of form and content. Other features include the use of multiple assessment techniques, assessor training, and pooled assessor judgments in rating candidate behavior.

Recent research indicates, at least for ability tests, that a test that accurately forecasts performance on a particular job in one situation will also forecast performance on the same job in other situations. Hence it may not be necessary to conduct a new validity study each time a predictor is used. Recent research has also demonstrated that the dollar benefits to the organization that uses valid selection procedures may be substantial. In choosing the right predictors for a given situation, careful attention must be paid to four factors: the nature of the job, the estimated validity of the predictor(s), the selection ratio, and the cost of the predictor(s). Doing so can pay handsome dividends to organizations and to employees alike.

DISCUSSION QUESTIONS

6•1 How can the accuracy of preemployment interviews be improved?

6•2 Why are reliability and validity key considerations for all assessment methods?

6•3 Discuss the pros and cons of using polygraph examinations in employment decisions.

6•4 How does business strategy affect management selection?

6•5 "At lower levels, managers do basically the same things regardless of functional specialty." Do you agree or disagree with this statement, and why?

6•6 What are some of the special problems that bedevil management selection?

TECHNICAL APPENDIX

The Estimation of Reliability

A quantitative estimate of the reliability of each measure used as a basis for personnel decisions is important for two reasons: (1) If any measure is challenged legally, reliability estimates are important in establishing a defense, and (2) a measurement procedure cannot be any more valid (accurate) than it is reliable (consistent and stable). To estimate reliability, a *coefficient of correlation* (a measure of the degree of relationship between two variables) is computed between two sets of scores obtained independently. As an example, consider the set of scores shown in Table 6-3.

■ **TABLE 6·3**
TWO SETS OF HYPOTHETICAL SCORES FOR THE SAME INDIVIDUALS ON FORM A AND FORM B OF A MATHEMATICAL APTITUDE TEST

Person no.	Form A	Form B
1	75	82
2	85	84
3	72	77
4	96	90
5	65	68
6	81	82
7	93	95
8	59	52
9	67	60
10	87	89

The coefficient of correlation between these sets of scores is .93. It is computed from the following formula:

$$r = \frac{\Sigma \, Z_x Z_y}{N}$$

where r = the correlation coefficient
Σ = sum of
Z_x = the standard score on form A, where $Z = x$, each person's raw score on form A, minus $\bar{x}$, the mean score on form A, divided by the standard deviation of form A scores
Z_y = the standard score on form B
N = the number of persons in the sample (10 in this case)

In Table 6-3, two sets of scores were obtained from two forms of the same test. The resulting correlation coefficient is called a *parallel forms reliability estimate*. By the way, the correlation coefficient for the two sets of scores shown in Table 6-3 is .93, a very strong relationship. (The word "test" is used in the broad sense here to include any physical or psychological measurement instrument, technique, or procedure.) However, the scores in Table 6-3 could just as easily have been obtained from two administrations of the same test at two different times (*test-retest reliability*) or from independent ratings of the same test by two different scorers (*interrater reliability*). Finally, in situations where it is not practical to use any of the preceding procedures and where a test can be administered only once, a procedure known as *split-half reliability* is used. With this procedure, a test is split statistically into two halves (e.g., odd items and even items) after it has been given, thus yielding two scores for each individual. In effect, therefore, two sets of scores (so-called parallel forms) from the same test are created for each individual. Scores on the two "half tests" are then correlated. However, since reliability increases as we sample larger and larger portions of a particular area of knowledge, skill, or ability, and since we have cut the length of the original test in half, the correlation between the two half tests *underestimates* the true reliability of the total test. Fortunately, formulas are available to correct such underestimates.

Validation Strategies

Although a number of procedures are available for evaluating validity, three of the best known strategies are *construct validity*, *content validity*, and *criterion-related validity*. The three differ in terms of the conclusions and inferences that may be drawn, but they are interrelated logically and also in terms of the operations used to measure them.

Evaluation of the *construct validity* of a psychological measurement procedure begins by formulating hypotheses about the characteristics of those with high scores on a particular measurement procedure, in contrast to those with low scores. For example, we might hypothesize that sales managers will score significantly higher on the managerial interests scale of the California Psychological Inventory (CPI) than will pharmacy students (in fact, they do), and that they will also be more decisive and apt to take risks as well. The hypotheses form a tentative theory about the nature of the psychological construct, or trait, that the CPI is believed to be measuring. These hypotheses may then be used to predict how people at different score levels on the CPI will behave on other tests or in other situations during their careers. Construct validation is not accomplished in a single study. It requires that evidence be accumulated from different sources to determine the meaning of the test scores in terms of how people actually behave. It is a logical as well as an empirical process.

The *content validity* of a measurement procedure is also a judgmental, rational process. It requires an answer to the following question: *Is the content of the measurement procedure a fair, representative sample of the content of the job it is supposed to represent?* Such judgments can be made rather easily by job incumbents, supervisors, or other job experts when job-knowledge or work-sample tests are used (e.g., typing tests and tests for electricians, plumbers, and computer programmers). However, content validity becomes less appropriate as the behaviors in question become less observable and more abstract (e.g., the ability to draw conclusions from a written sample of material). In addition, since judgments of content validity are not expressed in quantitative terms, it is difficult to justify *ranking* applicants in terms of predicted job performance, and it is difficult to estimate directly the dollar benefits to the firm from using such a procedure. To overcome these problems, we need a criterion-related validity strategy.

The term *criterion-related validity* calls attention to the fact that the chief concern is with the relationship between predictor [the selection procedure(s) used] and criterion (job performance) scores, not with predictor scores per se. Indeed, the content of the predictor measure is relatively unimportant, for it serves only as a vehicle to predict actual job performance.

There are two strategies of criterion-related validation: *concurrent* and *predictive*. A *concurrent strategy* is used to measure job incumbents. Job performance (criterion) measures for this group are already available; so immediately after a selection measure is administered to this group, a correlation coefficient between predictor scores and criterion scores (over all individuals in the group) can be computed. A procedure identical to that shown in Table 6-3 is used. If the selection measure is valid, then those employees with the highest (or lowest) job performance scores should also score highest (or lowest) on the selection measure. In short, if the selection measure is valid, then there should exist a systematic relationship between scores on that measure and job performance. The higher the test score, the better the job performance (and vice versa).

When *predictive validity* is used, the procedure is identical, except that job candidates are measured. Methods currently used to select employees are used, and the new selection procedure is simply added to the overall process. However, candidates are selected *without using* the results of the new procedure. At a later date (e.g., 6 months to a year) when a meaningful measure of job performance can be developed for each new hire, scores on the new selection procedure can be correlated with job performance scores. At that point, the strength of the predictor-criterion relationship can be assessed in terms of the size of the correlation coefficient.

ESTIMATING THE ECONOMIC BENEFITS OF SELECTION PROGRAMS

If we assume that n workers are hired during a given year and that the average job tenure of those workers is t years, the dollar increase in productivity can be determined from Equation 6-1. Admittedly, this is a "cookbook recipe," but the formula was derived over 40 years ago and is well established in applied psychology (cf. refs. 24 and 109):

$$\Delta U = ntr_{xy} \, SD_y \, \overline{Z}_x \qquad (6\text{-}1)$$

where ΔU = increase in productivity in dollars
      n = number of persons hired
      t = average job tenure in years of those hired
    r_{xy} = the validity coefficient representing the correlation between the predictor and job performance in the applicant population
    SD_y = the standard deviation of job performance in dollars (roughly 40 percent of annual wage)[50]
    $\overline{Z}_x$ = the average predictor score of those selected in the applicant population, expressed in terms of standard scores

When Equation 6-1 was used to estimate the dollar gains in productivity associated with use of the Programmer Aptitude Test (PAT) to select computer programmers for federal government jobs, given that an average of 618 programmers per year are selected, each with an average job tenure of 9.69 years, the payoff per selectee was $64,725 over his or her tenure on the job. This represents a per-year productivity gain of $6679 for each new programmer.[109] Clearly the dollar gains in increased productivity associated with the use of valid selection procedures (the estimated true validity of the PAT is .76) are not trivial. Indeed, in a globally competitive environment, businesses need to take advantage of every possible strategy for improving productivity. The widespread use of valid selection and promotion procedures should be a priority consideration in this effort.

Valid selection and promotion procedures also benefit applicants in several ways. One, a more accurate matching of applicant knowledge, skills, ability, and other characteristics and job requirements helps enhance the likelihood of successful performance. This, in turn, helps workers feel better about their jobs and adjust to changes in their jobs, as they are doing the kinds of things they do best. Moreover, since we know that there is a positive spillover effect between job satisfaction and life satisfaction, the accurate matching of people and jobs will also foster an improved quality of life, not just an improved quality of work life, for all concerned.

REFERENCES

1. Alaska Airlines sets job application handling fee (1983, Jan. 19). *Aviation Daily, p. 1.*
2. Alexander, L. D. (1979). An exploratory study of the utilization of assessment center results. *Academy of Management Journal,* **22,** 157–162.
3. American Psychological Association, American Educational Research Association, & National Council on Measurement in Education (Joint Committee) (1985). *Standards for educational and psychological testing.* Washington, DC: American Psychological Association.
4. Angarola, R. T. (1985). Drug testing in the workplace: Is it legal? *Personnel Administrator,* **30**(9), 79–89.
5. Arvey, R. D. & Campion, J. E. (1982). The employment interview: A summary and review of recent research. *Personnel Psychology,* **35,** 281–322.
6. Arvey, R. D., Miller, H. E., Gould, R., & Burch, P. (1987). Interview validity for selecting sales clerks. *Personnel Psychology,* **40,** 1–12.
7. Ash, P. (1987, March). Honesty test scores, biographical data, and delinquency indicators. Paper presented at the annual meeting of Criminal Justice Sciences, St. Louis, MO.
8. Asher, J. J., & Sciarrino, J. A. (1974). Realistic work sample tests: A review. *Personnel Psychology,* **27,** 519–533.
9. Barge, B. N. (1987, August). Characteristics of biodata items and their relationship to validity. Paper presented at the 95th annual meeting of the American Psychological Association, New York.
10. Barrick, M. R., & Mount, M. K. (1991). The big five personality dimensions and job performance: A meta analysis. *Personnel Psychology,* **44,** 1–26.
11. Bass, B. M. (1954). The leaderless group discussion. *Psychological Bulletin,* **51,** 465–492.

12. Ben-Shakhar, G., Bar-Hillel, M., Bilu, Y., Ben-Abba, E., & Flug, A. (1986). Can graphology predict occupational success? Two empirical studies and some methodological ruminations. *Journal of Applied Psychology*, **71**, 645–653.

13. Bentz, V. J. (1983, August). Executive selection at Sears: An update. Paper presented at the Fourth annual conference on frontiers of industrial psychology. Virginia Polytechnic Institute.

14. Bentz, V. J. (1968). The Sears experience in the investigation, description, and prediction of executive behavior. In J. A. Myers, Jr. (ed.), *Predicting managerial success*. Ann Arbor: Foundation for Research on Human Behavior.

15. Berman, F. E., & Miner, J. B. (1985). Motivation to manage at the top executive level: A test of the hierarchic role motivation theory. *Personnel Psychology*, **38**, 377–391.

16. Bogdanich, W. (1987, Feb. 2). False negative: Medical labs, trusted as largely error-free, are far from infallible. *The Wall Street Journal*, pp. 1, 14.

17. Borman, W. C. (1982). Validity of behavioral assessment for predicting military recruiter performance. *Journal of Applied Psychology*, **67**, 3–9.

18. Brass, G. J., & Oldham, G. R. (1976). Validating an in-basket test using an alternative set of leadership scoring dimensions. *Journal of Applied Psychology*, **61**, 652–657.

19. Bray, D. W. (1973). New data from the management progress study. *Assessment and Development*, **1**, 3.

20. *Bulletin to Management* (1983, May 5). ASPA-BNA survey No. 45: Employee selection procedures. Washington, DC: Bureau of National Affairs.

21. Byham, W. C. (1970). Assessment centers for spotting future managers. *Harvard Business Review*, **48**, 150–160.

22. Campion, M. A., Pursell, E. D., & Brown, B. K. (1988). Structured interviewing: Raising the psychometric properties of the employment interview. *Personnel Psychology*, **41**, 25–42.

23. Cascio, W. F. (1991). *Applied psychology in personnel management* (4th ed.). Englewood Cliffs, NJ: Prentice-Hall.

24. Cascio, W. F. (1991). *Costing human resources: The financial impact of behavior in organizations* (3d ed.). Boston: PWS-Kent.

25. Cascio, W. F., & Phillips, N. (1979). Performance testing: A rose among thorns? *Personnel Psychology*, **32**, 751–766.

26. Cascio, W. F., & Ramos, R. A. (1986). Development and application of a new method for assessing job performance in behavioral/economic terms. *Journal of Applied Psychology*, **71**, 20–28.

27. Cascio, W. F., & Silbey, V. (1979). Utility of the assessment center as a selection device. *Journal of Applied Psychology*, **64**, 107–118.

28. Coppard, L. C. (1976). Gaming simulation and the training process. In R. L. Craig (ed.), *Training and development handbook: A guide to human resource development*. New York: McGraw-Hill.

29. Craft, C. J. (1967). Management games. In R. L. Craig & L. R. Bittel (eds.), *Training and development handbook*. New York: McGraw-Hill.

30. Daum, J. W. (1983, August). Two measures of R.O.I. on intervention—Fact or fantasy? Paper presented at the annual convention of the American Psychological Association, Anaheim, CA.

31. Dipboye, R. L. (1982). Self-fulfilling prophecies in the recruitment-selection interview. *Academy of Management Review*, **7**, 579–586.

32. Felton, B., & Lamb, S. R. (1982). A model for systematic selection interviewing. *Personnel*, **59**(1), 40–49.

33. Fredericksen, N. (1962). Factors in in-basket performance. *Psychological Monographs*, **76**(22, Whole No. 541).

34. Gaugler, B. B., Rosenthal, D. B., Thornton, G. C., III, & Bentson, C. (1987). Meta-analysis of assessment center validity. *Journal of Applied Psychology*, **72**, 493–511.

35. Gaugler, B. B., & Thornton, G. C., III (1989). Number of assessment center dimensions as a determinant of assessor accuracy. *Journal of Applied Psychology*, **74**, 611–618.

36. Ghiselli, E. E. (1973). The validity of aptitude tests in personnel selection. *Personnel Psychology*, **26**, 461–467.

37. Goldstein, I. L. (1986). *Training in organizations: Needs assessment, development, and evaluation* (2d ed.). Monterey, CA: Brooks/Cole.

38. Gorman, C. (1989, Jan. 23). Honestly, can we trust you? *Time*, p. 44.

39. Grant, D. L., Katkovsky, W., & Bray, D. W. (1967). Contribution of projective techniques to assessment of management potential. *Journal of Applied Psychology*, **51**, 226–231.

40. Grimsley, G., & Jarrett, H. F. (1975). The relation of past managerial achievement to test measures obtained in the employment situation: Methodology and results—II. *Personnel Psychology*, **28**, 215–231.

41. Guion, R. M., & Gibson, W. M. (1988). Personnel selection and placement. *Annual Review of Psychology*, **39**, 349–374.

42. Hakel, M. D. (1989). Merit-based selection: Measuring the person for the job. In W. F. Cascio (ed.), *Human resource planning, employment, and placement*. Washington, DC: Bureau of National Affairs, pp. 2-135 to 2-158.

43. Harris, M. M. (1989). Reconsidering the employment interview: A review of recent literature and suggestions for future research, *Personnel Psychology*, **42**, 691–726.

44. Hinrichs, J. R. (1978). An eight-year follow-up of a management assessment center. *Journal of Applied Psychology*, **63**, 596–601.

45. Hinrichs, J. R. (1969). Comparison of "real life" assessments of management potential with situational exercises, paper-and-pencil ability tests, and personality inventories. *Journal of Applied Psychology*, **53**, 425–433.

46. Hough, L. M., Eaton, N. K., Dunnette, M. D., Kamp, J. D., & McCloy, R. A. (1990). Criterion-related validities of personality constructs and the effect of response distortion on those validities. *Journal of Applied Psychology Monograph*, **75**, 581–595.

47. Howard, A. (1974). An assessment of assessment centers. *Academy of Management Journal*, **17**, 115–134.

48. Huck, J. R., & Bray, D. W. (1976). Management assessment center evaluations and subsequent job performance of white and black females. *Personnel Psychology*, **29**, 13–30.

49. Hunter, J. E., & Hunter, R. E. (1984). Validity and utility of alternative predictors of job performance. *Psychological Bulletin*, **96**, 72–98.

50. Hunter, J. E., & Schmidt, F. L. (1983). Quantifying the effects of psychological interventions on employee job performance and work-force productivity. *American Psychologist*, **38**, 473–478.

51. Hunter, J. E., Schmidt, F. L., & Judiesch, M. K. (1990). Individual differences in output variability as a function of job complexity. *Journal of Applied Psychology*, **75**, 28–42.

52. Jacobs, S. L. (1985, March 11). Owners who ignore security make worker dishonesty easy. *The Wall Street Journal*, p. 25.

53. Job references: Handle with care (1987, March 9). *Business Week*, p. 124.

54. Kelly, G. A. (1958). The theory and technique of assessment. *Annual Review of Psychology*, **9**, 323–352.

55. Kerlinger, F. N. (1986). *Foundations of behavioral research* (3d ed.). New York: Holt, Rinehart, and Winston.

56. Kerr, S., & Schriesheim, C. (1974). Consideration, initiating structure, and organizational criteria—An update of Korman's 1966 review. *Personnel Psychology*, **27**, 555–568.

57. Kinslinger, H. J. (1966). Application of projective techniques in personnel psychology since 1940. *Psychological Bulletin*, **66**, 134–150.

58. Kleinmutz, B. (1985, July–August). Lie detectors fail the truth test. *Harvard Business Review*, **63**, 36–42.

59. Klimoski, R., & Brickner, M. (1987). Why do assessment centers work? The puzzle of assessment center validity. *Personnel Psychology*, **40**, 243–260.

60. Knouse, S. B. (1987). An attribution theory approach to the letter of recommendation. *International Journal of Management*, **4**(1), 5–13.

61. Knowlton, J. (1987, June 22). Smile for the camera: Job seekers make more use of video résumés. *The Wall Street Journal*, p. 29.

62. Koenig, R. (1987, Dec. 1). Exacting employer: Toyota takes pains, and time, filling jobs at its Kentucky plant. *The Wall Street Journal*, p. 1, 31.

63. Korman, A. K. (1968). The prediction of managerial performance: A review. *Personnel Psychology*, **21**, 295–322.

64. Kraut, A. I. (1969). Intellectual ability and promotional success among high-level managers. *Personnel Psychology*, **22**, 281–290.

65. Kurecka, P. M., Austin, J. M., Jr., Johnson, W., & Mendoza, J. L. (1982). Full and errant coaching effects on assigned role leaderless group discussion performance. *Personnel Psychology*, **35**, 805–812.

66. Labor Letter (1991, March 19). *The Wall Street Journal*, p. A1.

67. Labor Letter (1990, May 8). *The Wall Street Journal*, p. A1.

68. Labor Letter (1988, Oct. 18). *The Wall Street Journal*, p. 1.

69. Labor Letter (1987, June 30). *The Wall Street Journal*, p. 1.

70. Labor Letter (1986, May 13). *The Wall Street Journal*, p. 1.

71. Latham, G. P., & Saari, L. M. (1984). Do people do what they say? Further studies of the situational interview. *Journal of Applied Psychology*, **69**, 569–573.

72. Laurent, H. (1966). *EIMP applied to the International Petroleum Co.* Technical Report, Standard Oil of New Jersey.

73. Lawrence, D. G., Salsburg, B. L., Dawson, J. G., & Fasman, Z. D. (1982). Design and use of weighted application blanks. *Personnel Administrator*, **27**(3), 47–53, 101.

74. Levy, L. (1979). Handwriting and hiring. *Dun's Review*, **113**, 72–79.

75. Lohman, B. (1986, June 29). "Honesty test" is lying in wait for jobseekers. *Honolulu Star Bulletin*, p. B4.

76. LoPresto, R. L., Mitcham, D. E., & Ripley, D. E. (1986). *Reference checking handbook.* Alexandria, VA: American Society for Personnel Administration.

77. Lord, R. G., DeVader, C. L., & Alliger, G. M. (1986). A meta-analysis of the relationship between personality traits and leadership perceptions: An application of validity generalization procedures. *Journal of Applied Psychology*, **71**, 402–410.

78. Lorenzo, R. V. (1984). Effects of assessorship on managers' proficiency in acquiring, evaluating, and communicating information about people. *Personnel Psychology*, **37**, 617–634.

79. Lowell, R. S., & DeLoach, J. A. (1982). Equal employment opportunity: Are you overlooking the application form? *Personnel*, **59**(4), 49–55.

80. Mansfield, S. (1982, April 5). Job fraud rampant in the U.S. *The Denver Post*, pp. 1c–2c.

81. McCarthy, M. J. (1988, Aug. 25). Handwriting analysis as personnel tool. *The Wall Street Journal*, p. B1.

82. McClelland, D. C., & Boyatzis, R. E. (1982). Leadership motive pattern and long-term success in management. *Journal of Applied Psychology*, **67**, 737–743.

83. McCormick, E. J., & Ilgen, D. R. (1985). *Industrial psychology* (8th ed.). Englewood Cliffs, NJ: Prentice-Hall.

84. McKinnon, D. W. (1975). Assessment centers then and now. *Assessment and Development*, **2**, 8–9.

85. Miller, E. C. (1980). An EEO examination of employment applications. *Personnel Administrator*, **25**(3), 63–69, 81.

86. Mintzberg, H. (1975). The manager's job: Folklore and fact. *Harvard Business Review*, **53**(4), 49–61.

87. Mintzberg, H. (1973). *The nature of managerial work*. New York: Harper & Row.

88. Morgan, J. P. (1989, Aug. 20). Employee drug tests are unreliable and intrusive. *Hospitals*, p. 42.

89. Morris, J. (1982, July 26). Craft can checkmate the "creative" résumé. *The Miami Herald*, p. 16b.

90. Most in survey favor drug tests (1986, Sep. 15). *The Denver Post*, p. 9A.

91. Mullins, T. W. (1982). Interviewer decisions as a function of applicant race, applicant quality, and interviewer prejudice. *Personnel Psychology*, **35**, 163–174.

92. Office of Strategic Services (OSS) Assessment Staff (1948). *Assessment of men*. New York: Rinehart.

93. Patrick, C. J., & Iacono, W. G. (1989). Psychopathy, threat, and polygraph test accuracy. *Journal of Applied Psychology*, **74**, 347–355.

94. Petty, M. M. (1974). A multivariate analysis of the effects of experience and training upon performance in a leaderless group discussion. *Personnel Psychology*, **27**, 271–282.

95. Phillips, A. P., & Dipboye, R. L. (1989). Correlational tests of a prediction from a process model of the interview. *Journal of Applied Psychology*, **74**, 41–52.

96. Polygraph testing hit (1986, October). *Resource*, p. 13.

97. Power, D. J., & Aldag, R. J. (1985). Soelberg's job search and choice model: A clarification, review, and critique. *Academy of Management Review*, **10**, 48–58.

98. Principles for the validation and use of personnel selection procedures (3d ed., 1987). College Park, MD: Society of Industrial-Organizational Psychology.

99. Pulakos, E. D., Borman, W. C., & Hough, L. M. (1988). Test validation for scientific understanding: Two demonstrations of an approach to studying predictor-criterion linkages. *Personnel Psychology*, **41**, 703–716.

100. Rafaeli, A., & Klimoski, R. J. (1983). Predicting sales success through handwriting analysis: An evaluation of the effects of training and handwriting sample content. *Journal of Applied Psychology*, **68**, 212–217.

101. Reference preference: Employers button lips (1990, Jan. 4). *The Wall Street Journal*, p. B1.

102. Revenge of the fired (1987, Feb. 16). *Newsweek*, pp. 46, 47.

103. Rice, J. D. (1978). Privacy legislation: Its effect on pre-employment reference checking. *Personnel Administrator*, **23**, 46–51.

104. Sackett, P. R. (1985). Honesty testing for personnel selection. *Personnel Administrator*, **30**(9), 67–76.

105. Sackett, P. R., Burris, L. R., & Callahan, C. (1989). Integrity testing for personnel selection: An update. *Personnel Psychology*, **42**, 491–529.

106. Saxe, L., Dougherty, D., & Cross, T. (1985). The validity of polygraph testing. *American Psychologist*, **40**, 355–356.

107. Schein, E. H. (1989, Spring). Conversation with Edgar H. Schein. *Organizational Dynamics*, **17**, 60–76.

108. Schein, E. H. (1983, Summer). The role of the founder in creating organization culture. *Organizational Dynamics*, **11**, 13–28.

109. Schmidt, F. L., Hunter, J. E., McKenzie, R., & Muldrow, T. (1979). The impact of valid selection procedures on workforce productivity. *Journal of Applied Psychology*, **64**, 609–626.

110. Schmidt, F. L., Pearlman, K., Hunter, J. E., & Hirsch, H. R. (1985). Forty questions about validity generalization and meta-analysis. *Personnel Psychology*, **38**, 697–798.

111. Schmitt, N., Gooding, R. Z., Noe, R. A., & Kirsch, M. (1984). Meta-analysis of validity studies published between 1964 and 1982 and the investigation of study characteristics. *Personnel Psychology*, **37**, 407–422.

112. Schneider, B. (1987). The people make the place. *Personnel Psychology*, **40**, 437–453.

113. Schriesheim, C., House, R. A., & Kerr, S. (1976). Leader initiating structure: A reconciliation of discrepant research results and some empirical tests. *Organizational Behavior and Human Performance*, **15**, 297–321.

114. Shults, T. F. (1986, June 3). If a company tests for drugs. *The New York Times*, p. A27.

115. Smith, E. C., (1982). Strategic business planning and human resources: Part I. *Personnel Journal*, **61**, 606–610.

116. Solomon, J. (1989, Dec. 4). The new job interview: Show thyself. *The Wall Street Journal*, pp. B1, B2.

117. Stone, D. L., & Kotch, D. A. (1989). Individuals' attitudes toward organizational drug testing policies and practices. *Journal of Applied Psychology*, **74**, 518–521.

118. Susser, P. A. (1986). Update on polygraphs and employment. *Personnel Administrator*, **31**(2), pp. 28, 32.

119. The write stuff (1983, July 4). *Time*, p. 46.

120. Tziner, A., & Dolan, S. (1982). Validity of an assessment center for identifying future female officers in the military. *Journal of Applied Psychology*, **67**, 728–736.

121. Uniform guidelines on employee selection procedures (1978). *Federal Register*, **43**, 38,290–38,315.

122. Weekley, J. A., & Gier, J. A. (1987). Reliability and validity of the situational interview for a sales position. *Journal of Applied Psychology*, **72**, 484–487.

123. Wessel, D. (1989, Sep. 7). Evidence is skimpy that drug testing works, but employers embrace practice. *The Wall Street Journal*, pp. B1, B8.

124. Wexley, K. N., & Latham, G. P. (1981). *Developing and training human resources in organizations*. Glenview, IL: Scott, Foresman.

125. Wollowick, H. B., & McNamara, W. J. (1969). Relationship of the components of an assessment center to management success. *Journal of Applied Psychology*, **53**, 348–352.

126. Zedeck, S., & Cascio, W. F. (1984). Psychological issues in personnel decisions. *Annual Review of Psychology*, **35**, 461–518.

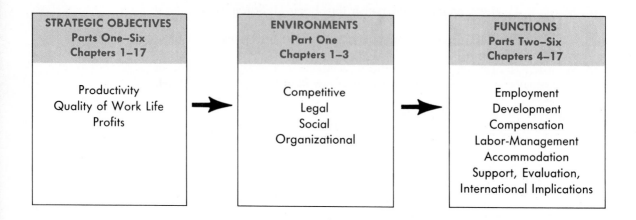

STRATEGIC OBJECTIVES Parts One–Six Chapters 1–17	ENVIRONMENTS Part One Chapters 1–3	FUNCTIONS Parts Two–Six Chapters 4–17
Productivity Quality of Work Life Profits	Competitive Legal Social Organizational	Employment Development Compensation Labor-Management Accommodation Support, Evaluation, International Implications

RELATIONSHIP OF HRM FUNCTIONS TO HRM ACTIVITIES

FUNCTIONS	ACTIVITIES
PART 2 EMPLOYMENT	Job Analysis, Human Resource Planning, Recruiting, Staffing (Chapters 4–6)
PART 3 DEVELOPMENT	Orientation, Training, Performance Appraisal, Managing Careers (Chapters 7–9)
PART 4 COMPENSATION	Pay, Benefits, Incentives (Chapters 10–12)
PART 5 LABOR-MANAGEMENT ACCOMMODATION	Union Representation, Collective Bargaining, Procedural Justice, Ethics (Chapters 13, 14)
PART 6 SUPPORT, EVALUATION, INTERNATIONAL IMPLICATIONS	Job Safety and Health, Costs/Benefits of HRM Activities, International Dimensions of HRM (Chapters 15–17)

PART THREE

Development

Once employees are "on board," their personal growth and development over time become a major concern. Change is a fact of organizational life, and to cope with it effectively, planned programs of employee orientation, development, and career management are essential. These issues are addressed in Chapters 7 through 9. Chapter 7 examines what is known about orienting and training management and nonmanagement employees. Chapter 8 is concerned with performance appraisal—particularly with the design, implementation, and evaluation of appraisal systems. Finally, Chapter 9 considers the many issues involved in managing careers—from the perspective of individuals at different career stages, and from the perspective of organizational staffing decisions. The overall objective of Part Three is to establish a framework for managing the development process of employees as their careers unfold in organizations.

Orienting and Training

■ **HUMAN RESOURCE MANAGEMENT IN ACTION**

LOVE THY CUSTOMER AND KNOW THY FISH
IF YOU WANT TO WORK AT RED LOBSTER*

The scene, at a Red Lobster restaurant that opened recently here, is a cross between a pep rally and a pop quiz. A large room is filled with raucous students learning the basics of their trade—waiting on tables. Their enthusiastic teacher raises his clenched fists over his head, fires off questions, and exhorts his students to answer as loudly as they can:

"What's the first thing we do at the table?"

"SMILE!" booms the class.

"And the second thing?"

"SAY SOMETHING PERSONAL!"

"And the third thing?"

"DESCRIBE THE SPECIAL FEATURES!"

---

*From: D. McGill, Why they smile at Red Lobster. *The New York Times*, April 23, 1989, pp. F1, F6. Copyright © 1989 by The New York Times Company. Reprinted by permission.

"Very good! And what will be our vegetables of the month?"

"BROCCOLI AND CARROTS!" comes the roaring reply.

And so, in a burst of energy, begins a new Red Lobster restaurant, another eating house added to the world's largest—and still rapidly growing—seafood restaurant chain. . . . It now includes 513 restaurants in this country, Canada, and Japan, with sales in North America of $1.13 billion last year.

The hottest feature at Red Lobster . . . is not a menu item—nor even the restaurant's reasonable prices (the average dinner check is around $11), their large selection (more than 100 seafood items on the menu), or the restaurant's clean, tasteful decor.

No, the big ticket item . . . is, simply, good service, as in having your waiter greet you with a smile, ask you a friendly question, and tell you about the vegetables of the day. To insure good service, the restaurant mounts a 4-day training course for servers before each restaurant opens and thereafter requires its staff to attend monthly classes to polish skills and learn new trends in salad presentation, garnishing techniques, and the like.

Trainees are not let off easy. . . . every minute of every session was taken up in classes, trial runs, quizzes, and contests. On the first day the students were given homework (to memorize the entire menu) and the next morning were given a written test on the material (the highest scorer won $100). There was a contest to see who could use the computer the fastest, and another to determine which server was best at describing desserts accurately, temptingly, and entertainingly.

Some of the seminars taught precisely the phrases to be used in such presentations. Judy Limbach, for instance, taught a class on entrée items. She circled a long table covered with every main dish on the menu, which she picked up, one by one, and described in detail.

When she put down the last dish, she walked back to the first one, picked it up, and commenced a surprise quiz. "Now that I've told *you* about the dishes, you can tell *me* about them," she began, smiling dryly at the worried faces that flashed through her class. "Chris, tell me about the popcorn shrimp."

"Popcorn shrimp," said Chris, stammering, blanching, "Oh . . . it's shrimp . . . and it's, ahh, it's popcorn-sized, and . . ."

"It's bite sized, lightly breaded, and golden fried," Judy corrected quickly. "You need to know this. . . . You need to describe it so it sounds really good.". . .

Most crucially, . . . all Red Lobster waiters and waitresses are encouraged, during training, to show a bit of their personality while meeting customers. The old Red Lobster uniform of shirts and slacks has been discarded in favor of a maroon apron, under which servers can wear clothing of their choice. And while stock descriptive phrases are taught in the seminars, the servers are encouraged to improvise their sales pitch.

"We try to remove the spiel and inject the personality," explained Jeff

O'Hara, president of Red Lobster USA. "We're trying to bring it down to an intensely personal experience."

The company is also well known among waiters and waitresses, in most areas where it is found, as a good employer that offers solid benefits, a chance for advancement, and flexible hours. Most of all, it is known as a restaurant where the tipping is good. . . .

Challenges

1. What are the key distinguishing features of this approach to training?
2. How can the company determine whether or not its training is effective?
3. How might Red Lobster's training program contribute to the company's orientation process for new employees? What lessons does it teach?

1. How should new-employee orientation be managed for maximum positive impact?
2. What kind of evidence is necessary to justify investments in training and development programs?
3. What are the key issues that should be addressed in the design, conduct, and evaluation of training programs?

QUESTIONS THIS CHAPTER WILL HELP MANAGERS ANSWER

Change, growth, and sometimes displacement are facts of modern organizational life. The stock market crash of October 19, 1987, vividly illustrated this fact. In the wave of layoffs following the crash, over 18,000 professionals in the financial services industry lost their jobs. As they found new jobs, they found out what all new employees do: It is necessary to "relearn the ropes" in the new job setting. Orientation, the subject of the first part of this chapter, can ease that process considerably, with positive results both for the new employee and for the company. Like orientation, training also helps deal with change—technological and social. Training is big business in the United States, and the second half of this chapter examines some current issues in the design, conduct, and evaluation of training programs.

NEW EMPLOYEE ORIENTATION: AN OVERVIEW

One definition of *orientation* is "familiarization with and adaptation to a situation or environment." Eight out of every 10 organizations in the United States that have more than 50 employees provide orientation.[24] However, the time and effort devoted to its design, conduct, and evaluation are woefully inadequate. In practice, orientation is often just a superficial indoctrination into company philosophy, policies, and rules; sometimes it includes the presentation of an employee handbook and a quick tour of the office or plant. This can be a very costly mistake. Here is why.

In one way, a displaced worker from the factory who is hired into another environment is similar to a new college graduate. Upon starting a new job, both will face a kind of "culture shock." As they are exposed for the first time to a new organizational culture, they find that the new job is not quite what they imagined it to be. In fact, coming to work at a new company is not unlike visiting a foreign country. Either you are told about the local customs or else you learn them on your own by a process of trial and error. An effective orientation program can help lessen the impact of this shock. But there must be more, such as a period of "socialization," or learning to function as a contributing member of the corporate "family."

The cost of hiring, training, and orienting a new person is far higher than most of us realize. In the insurance industry, for example, the 1987 replacement cost for a field examiner was approximately $55,000, and for a competent salesperson it was $72,000.[13] As another example, consider that in 1986 the U.S. Navy estimated that it would lose 550 fighter pilots as a result of attrition. At a cost of $1 million to train one new fighter pilot, that adds up to an annual training cost of over half a billion dollars![49]

Moreover, since the turnover rate among new college hires can be as great as 40 percent during the first 12 months, such costs can be quite painful. In the case of stockbroker trainees, it takes approximately 2 years for the average broker trainee to become fully productive.[6] Yet during this period, depending on the level of wage and how it is determined, the trainee is drawing 100 percent of his or her wage before the organization can recoup its investment.

The experiences during the initial period with an organization can have a major impact on a new employee's career. A new hire stands on the "boundary" of the organization—certainly no longer an outsider, but not yet embraced by those within. There is great stress. The new hire wants to reduce this stress by becoming incorporated into the "interior" as quickly as possible. Consequently, it is during this period that an employee is more receptive to cues from the organizational environment than she or he is ever again likely to be. Such cues to proper behavior may come from a variety of sources; for example:

- Official literature of the organization
- Examples set by senior people
- Formal instructions given by senior people
- Examples given by peers
- Rewards and punishments that flow from his or her efforts
- Responses to her or his ideas
- Degree of challenge in the assignments that he or she receives

Special problems may arise for a new employee whose young life has been spent mainly in an educational setting. As he approaches his first job, the recent graduate may feel motivated entirely through personal creativity. He is information-rich but experience-poor, eager to apply his knowledge to new processes and problems. Unfortunately, there are conditions that may stifle this creative urge. During his undergraduate days, the new employee exercised direct control over his work. But now he faces regular hours, greater restrictions, possibly a less pleasant environment, and a need to work *through* other people—often finding that most of the work is mundane and unchallenging. In short, three typical problems face the new employee:

1. *Problems in entering a group.* The new employee asks herself whether she will (a) be acceptable to the other group members, (b) be liked, and (c) be safe—that is, free from physical or psychological harm. These issues must be resolved before she can feel comfortable and productive in the new situation.

2. *Naive expectations.* Organizations find it much easier to communicate factual information about pay and benefits, vacations, and company policies than they do about employee norms (rules or guides to acceptable behavior), company attitudes, or "what it really takes to get ahead around here." Simple fairness suggests that employees ought to be told about these intangibles. The bonus is that being upfront and honest with job candidates produces positive results. As we saw in Chapter 5, the research on realistic job previews (RJPs) indicates that job acceptance rates will likely be lower for those who receive an RJP, but job survival rates will be higher.

3. *First-job environment.* Does the new environment help or hinder the new employee trying to climb aboard? Can peers be counted on to socialize the new employee to desired job standards? How and why was the first job assignment chosen? Is it clear to the new employee what she or he can expect to get out of it?

The first year with an organization is the critical period during which an employee will or will not learn to become a high performer. The careful matching of company and employee expectations during this period can result in positive job attitudes and high standards, which then can be reinforced in new and more demanding jobs.

PLANNING, PACKAGING, AND EVALUATING AN ORIENTATION PROGRAM*

New employees need specific information in three major areas:

- Company standards, expectations, norms, traditions, and policies
- Social behavior, such as approved conduct, the work climate, and getting to know fellow workers and supervisors
- Technical aspects of the job

---

*Much of the material in this section is drawn from two sources: Lubliner[42] and St. John.[66]

These needs suggest two levels of orientation: company and departmental. There will be some matters of general interest and importance to all new employees, regardless of department, and there will also be matters relevant only to each department. The HR department should have overall responsibility for program planning and follow-up (subject to top-management review and approval), but specific responsibilities of the HR department and the immediate supervisor should be made very clear to avoid duplication or omission of important information.

Approaches to orientation that should be avoided are:[66]

Emphasis on paperwork. The new employee is given a cursory welcome, after completing forms required by the HR department. Then the employee is directed to his or her immediate supervisor. The likely result: The employee does not feel like part of the company.

Sketchy overview of the basics. A quick, superficial orientation, and the new employee is immediately put to work—sink or swim.

Mickey Mouse assignments. The new employee's first tasks are insignificant duties, supposedly intended to teach the job "from the ground up."

Suffocation. Giving too much information too fast is a well-intentioned but disastrous approach, causing the new employee to feel overwhelmed and "suffocated."

We know from other companies' mistakes what works and what does not. For example, at the outset of orientation, each new employee should be given an information kit or packet prepared by the HR department to supplement the verbal and/or audiovisual orientation. Such a kit might include the materials and information shown in Table 7-1.

At the outset of a group orientation session, one or more representatives of top management should talk about company philosophy and expectations—describing exactly what employees can expect from management and vice versa. These statements can also be reinforced and made official policy when included in a prominent place in the employee handbook or orientation kit. Following this, HR department representatives should discuss issues that are of general importance to all departments. These issues might include an overview of the company (its history, traditions, and products and services), a review of key policies and procedures, a summary of employee benefits, an outline of safety and accident-prevention procedures, a discussion of employee-management and union-management relations, and a description of the physical facilities.

Obviously not all these topics will apply in every situation in every organization. The list should be tailored to fit the particular needs of the firm—be it a hospital, a manufacturing facility, a bank, or a service organization. The departmental or job orientation provided by supervisors will likely be even more variable, for it must describe the organization of the department, how it interfaces with other departments, the departmental policies and procedures, and the job duties,

■ **TABLE 7·1**
SAMPLE ITEMS TO BE INCLUDED IN AN EMPLOYEE
ORIENTATION KIT

- A current company organization chart
- A projected company organization chart
- Map of the facility
- Key terms unique to the industry, company, and/or job
- Copy of policy handbook
- Copy of union contract
- Copy of specific job goals and descriptions
- List of company holidays
- List of benefits
- Copies of performance evaluation forms, dates, and procedures
- Copies of other required forms (e.g., supply requisition and expense reimbursement)
- List of on-the-job training opportunities
- Sources of information
- Detailed outline of emergency and accident-prevention procedures
- Sample copy of each important company publication
- Telephone numbers and locations of key personnel and operations
- Copies of insurance plans

Source: W. D. St. John, The complete employee orientation program, *Personnel Journal*, May 1980, p. 375.

standards of performance, and responsibilities, and it must include a tour of the department and introduce the new employees to their coworkers.

Orientation Follow-Up

The worst mistake a company can make is to ignore the new employee after orientation. Almost as bad is an informal open-door policy: "Come see me sometime if you have any questions." Many new employees are simply not assertive enough to seek out the supervisor or HR representative—more than likely they fear looking "dumb." What is needed is formal and systematic orientation follow-up: for example, by the immediate supervisor after the new employee has been on the job 1 day and again after 1 week, and by the HR representative after the new employee has been on the job 1 month. Many of the topics covered during orientation will need to be explained briefly again, once the employee has had the opportunity to experience them firsthand. This is natural and understandable in view of the blizzard of information that needs to be communicated during orientation. In completing the orientation follow-up, a checklist of items covered should be reviewed with each new employee or small group of employees to ensure that all items were in fact covered. The completed checklist should then be signed by the supervisor, the HR representative, and the new employee prior to being filed in the new employee's personnel file.

Evaluation of the Orientation Program

At least once a year, the orientation program should be reviewed to determine if it is meeting its objectives and to suggest future improvements. To improve orientation, candid, comprehensive feedback is needed from everyone involved in the program. This feedback can be provided in several ways: through roundtable discussions with new employees after their first year on the job, through in-depth interviews with randomly selected employees and supervisors, and through questionnaires for mass coverage of all recent hires. Issues such as the following should guide the evaluation of an orientation program:[42]

1. *Is the program appropriate?* Do all the elements—the physical setting, the literature, the means of presentation—convey an accurate impression of the company's character?

2. *Is the program easy to understand?* Since employees representing diverse jobs and backgrounds are often oriented during the same session, do the content and style of the program apply to all of them? Is the written and visual information well organized, not condescending, and easily understood?

3. *Is the program interesting?* Will it capture and hold the new employees' attention? A 1-minute slide presentation with prerecorded narration is often more effective than a 15-minute reading by an HR representative. When interest wavers, listener resistance rises, and minimal information is communicated.

4. *Is the program flexible?* Since much of a good orientation presentation deals with a company's scope of business, is it possible that this segment of orientation might also be used as part of other employee and nonemployee communication? In this way management can get extra mileage out of the dollars invested in the orientation program. Finally, can changes in the program be made easily if the company diversifies or drops an operation?

5. *Is the program personally involving?* Does it stress the importance of people to the company? Many firms have impressive-looking plants, machinery, and facilities. The differences, for the most part, lie with the people who make up the organization. Employees, especially the newly hired, should come away from orientation with a sense that management cares about them, their families, and their communities.

In one study, for example, 18 of 20 Hewlett-Packard executives interviewed spontaneously claimed that the success of their company depends on the company's people-oriented philosophy. It's called "the HP Way." Here is how founder Bill Hewlett describes it:

> I feel that, in general terms, it is the policies and actions that flow from the belief that men and women want to do a good job, a creative job—and that if they are provided

with the proper environment, they will do so. It is the tradition of treating every individual with consideration and respect and recognizing personal achievements. This sounds almost trite, but Dave (co-founder Packard) and I honestly believe in this philosophy. (ref. 54, p. 6F)

6. *Is the program economical?* From a management perspective, is the cost of the entire orientation process reasonable? An effective orientation program including visuals, literature, and collateral material can be written, designed, and produced at less cost than the annual salary paid to one medium-level employee.

NEW EMPLOYEE ORIENTATION AT CORNING, INC.

■ **COMPANY EXAMPLE**

In the early 1980s Corning faced a problem similar to that found in many other firms: New people were getting the red-carpet treatment while being recruited, but once they started work, it was often a different story—a letdown. Often their first day on the job was disorganized and confusing, and sometimes this continued for weeks. One new employee said, "You're planting the seeds of turnover right at the beginning."

It became clear to managers at Corning that a better way was needed to help new employees make the transition to their new company and community. Corning needed a better way to help these new people get off on the right foot—to learn the how-tos, the wheres, and the whys, and to learn about the company's culture and its philosophies. And the company had to ensure the same support for newly hired secretaries in a district office, sales representatives working out of their homes, or engineers in a plant.

THE CORNING ORIENTATION SYSTEM AND HOW IT WORKS

Three features distinguish the Corning approach from others:

1. It is an *orientation* process, not a program.
2. It is based on guided self-learning. New people have responsibility for their own learning.
3. It is long-term (15 to 18 months), and it is in-depth.

The new person learns with help and information from:

- The immediate supervisor, who has guidelines and checklists
- Colleagues, whom the new person interviews before starting regular assignments
- Attendance at nine 2-hour seminars at intervals during the first 6 months
- Answers to questions in a workbook for new employees

Figure 7-1 provides an overview of how the system works.

Material distribution. As soon as possible after a hiring decision is made, orientation material is distributed:

- The new person's supervisor gets a pamphlet entitled *A Guide for Supervisors.*

- The new person gets an orientation plan.

The prearrival period. During this period the supervisor maintains contact with the new person, helps with housing problems, designs the job, and makes a preliminary MBO (management by objectives) list after discussing this with the new person, gets the office ready, notifies the organization that this has been done, and sets the interview schedule.

The first day. On this important day, new employees have breakfast with their supervisors, go through processing in the personnel department, attend a *Corning and You* seminar, have lunch with the seminar leader, read the workbook for new employees, are given a tour of the building, and are introduced to coworkers.

The first week. During this week, the new employee (1) has one-to-one interviews with the supervisor, coworkers, and specialists; (2) learns the how-tos, wheres, and whys connected with the job; (3) answers questions in the workbook; (4) gets settled in the community; and (5) participates with the supervisor in firming up the MBO plan.

The second week. The new person begins regular assignments.

The third and fourth weeks. The new person attends a community seminar and an employee benefits seminar (a spouse or guest may be invited).

The second through the fifth month. During this period, assignments are intensified and new people have biweekly progress reviews with their supervisors, attend six two-hour seminars at intervals (on quality and productivity, technology, performance management and salaried compensation plans, financial and strategic management, employee relations and EEO, and social change), answer workbook questions about each seminar, and review answers with their supervisor.

The sixth month. The new employee completes the workbook questions, reviews the MBO list with the supervisor, participates in a performance review with the supervisor, receives a certification of completion for Phase I orientation, and makes plans for Phase II orientation.

The seventh through the 15th months. This period features Phase II orientation: division orientation, function orientation, education programs, MBO reviews, performance reviews, and salary reviews.

FIGURE 7-1
Timetable of events in the Corning, Inc. orientation system.

OBJECTIVES OF THE PROGRAM

Corning set four objectives, each aimed at improving productivity. The first was to reduce voluntary turnover in the first 3 years of employment by 17 percent. The second was to shorten by 17 percent the time it takes a new person to learn the job. The third was to foster a uniform understanding among employees about the company: its objectives, its principles, its strategies, and what the company expects of its people. The fourth was to build a positive attitude toward the company and its surrounding communities.

MEASURING RESULTS

After 2 years, voluntary turnover among new hires was reduced by 69 percent—far greater than the 17 percent expected after 3 years. Corning also anticipates a major payback on its investment in the orientation system: an 8:1 benefit/cost ratio in the first year and a 14:1 ratio annually thereafter. These computations are shown in Figure 7-2.

A. Benefit Estimate:

A 17 percent decrease in the number of voluntary separations among those with three years or less of service:

$ 852M

A decrease in the time required to learn the job—from six months to five months:

489M

TOTAL $1,341M

B. Cost Estimate:

	First Year Only	Ongoing Annual
Materials and salaries of developers, instructors, administrators	$171M	$95M

C. Benefit/Cost Ratio:

First year: $1,341M : 171M = 8 : 1
Ongoing annual: $1,341M : 95M = 14 : 1

The following formula was used to estimate productivity gains per year.

Improved Retention Rate:

| Number of voluntary separations (3 or less years' service), 1980 | × | 17% expected decrease with orientation | × | $30M investment in new hire | = | Annual productivity gain |

Shorten Learning Curve from Six Months to Five Months:

| One month average base salary × 65% | × | Number of new hires per year | = | Annual productivity gain |

FIGURE 7-2
Calculation of benefits and costs in the Corning, Inc. orientation program. Note: The term *M* denotes thousands.

LESSONS LEARNED

As a result of the 2 years it took to develop the system and Corning's 2 years of experience with it, the company offers the following considerations to guide the process of orienting new employees. They apply to any type of organization, large or small, and to any function or level of job:[45]

1. The impressions formed by new employees within their first 60 to 90 days on a job are lasting.
2. Day 1 is crucial—new employees remember it for years. It must be managed well.
3. New employees are interested in learning about the *total* organization—and how they and their unit fit into the "big picture." This is just as im-

portant as is specific information about the new employee's own job and department.

4. Give new employees major responsibility for their own orientation, through guided self-learning, but with direction and support.
5. Avoid information overload—provide it in reasonable amounts.
6. Recognize that community, social, and family adjustment is a critical aspect of orientation for new employees.
7. Make the immediate supervisor ultimately responsible for the success of the orientation process.
8. Thorough orientation is a "must" for productivity improvement. It is a vital part of the total management system—and therefore the foundation of any effort to improve employee productivity.

In summary, the results of Corning's research are exciting and provocative. They suggest that we should be at least as concerned with preparing the new employee for the social context of his or her job and for coping with the insecurities and frustrations of a new learning situation as with the development of the technical skills necessary for job performance. The question of how best to teach those technical skills is also critically important. The design, conduct, and evaluation of employee training programs is a strategic issue that simply cannot be ignored.

EMPLOYEE TRAINING

What Is Training?

Traditionally, lower-level employees were "trained," while higher-level employees were "developed." This distinction, focusing on the learning of hands-on skills versus interpersonal and decision-making skills, has become too blurry in practice to be useful. Throughout the remainder of this chapter, therefore, the terms *training* and *development* will be used interchangeably.

Training consists of planned programs designed to improve performance at the individual, group, and/or organizational levels. Improved performance, in turn, implies that there have been measurable changes in knowledge, skills, attitudes, and/or social behavior.

Unfortunately, too much emphasis is often placed on the techniques and methods of training to be used and not enough on first defining what the employee should learn in relation to desired job behaviors. Furthermore, very few organizations place much emphasis on assessing the outcomes of training activities. That is, they overlook the need to determine whether the training objectives were met.

Training Trends

As we have seen, both economic and demographic trends suggest radical changes in the composition of the workforce of the 1990s. Other factors that affect the number, types, and requirements of available jobs include automation; continuing worker displacement as a function of mergers, acquisitions, and downsizing; and the shift from manufacturing to service jobs.[12,15]

These issues suggest four reasons why the time and money budgeted for training will increase during the next decade:[23]

1. The number of unskilled and undereducated youth who will be needed for entry-level jobs
2. Increasingly sophisticated technological systems that will impose training and retraining requirements on the existing workforce
3. The need to train currently underutilized groups of minorities, women, and older workers
4. Training needs stimulated by the internationally competitive environments of many organizations

These changes suggest a dual responsibility: The organization is responsible for providing an atmosphere that will support and encourage change, and the individual is responsible for deriving maximum benefit from the learning opportunities provided.

Indeed, as the demands of the second industrial revolution spread, companies are coming to regard training expenses as no less a part of their capital costs than plants and equipment. Total training outlays by U.S. firms are now $30 billion—and rising.[61] At the level of the individual firm, Motorola is exemplary. It budgets about 1 percent of annual sales (2.6 percent of payroll) for training. It even trains workers for its key suppliers, many of them small- to medium-size firms without the resources to train their own people in such advanced specialties as computer-aided design and defect control. Taking into account training expenses, wages, and benefits, the total cost amounts to about $90 million. The results have been dramatic, according to a company spokesperson: "We've documented the savings from the statistical process control methods and problem-solving methods we've trained our people in. We're running a rate of return of about 30 times the dollars invested—which is why we've gotten pretty good support from senior management" (ref. 5, p. 87).

Retraining, too, can pay off. A study by the Work in America Institute found that retraining current workers for new jobs is more cost-effective than firing them and hiring new ones—not to mention the difference that retraining makes to employee morale.[5] And in "downsizing" industries where there are no alternatives to furloughs, unions are working with management to retrain displaced workers. Yet there are serious potential difficulties with retraining efforts, as the following example illustrates.

| ■ **COMPANY** | POTENTIAL PITFALLS IN WORKER RETRAINING |

■ COMPANY EXAMPLE

POTENTIAL PITFALLS IN WORKER RETRAINING

For years, conventional wisdom has held that the best way to deal with workers who lose their jobs when industry shrinks is to teach them to do something else. But in many cases retraining is more talked about than done. A critical problem, one that is almost uniquely American, is the way employers juggle their labor forces, laying people off when business dips and calling them back when it brightens. This practice has been going on for decades in some industries, especially in automobile manufacturing and defense contracting.

Workforce juggling occurs most often in communities where a single employer dominates an economy and pays the highest wages. Consider Whirlpool Corporation, the biggest and highest paying employer in Fort Smith, Arkansas. In 1988 the company employed 5400 people in Fort Smith. But with a series of big cuts in 1989, it chopped the payroll to 1900. Management says it doesn't expect to need 5400 workers again, but it did call back 500 workers in February 1990, and 1500 more through April. Many of those recalled were then let go in September. According to the company, the juggling is unavoidable because the company's business in Fort Smith, the manufacture of refrigerators, is historically seasonal and cyclical.

Whirlpool's struggle for survival plays havoc with a comprehensive community retraining program for 670 workers from the company and its suppliers. According to retraining experts, as long as workers think there is hope for a recall and a Whirlpool wage, they are unlikely to join the program. Many who might have enrolled will choose to take a Whirlpool paycheck instead, even though they are likely to lose it again. While retraining, the workers would collect only unemployment benefits and, if they qualify, an extra $50 a week.

To be sure, there have been some successes in retraining laid-off workers, especially young people who are able to handle major changes in their lives. But for most former workers, retraining is difficult because wages for new jobs can be half and even a third those of the old factory jobs, leaving them little incentive to seek retraining. As one retrainer said, "It almost seems you're playing with workers' lives."[29]

The lesson to be learned from this case is that even well-planned, well-executed training efforts may fail unless companies and communities help workers see training as a long-term investment in their own career success. The ups and downs of Whirlpool's economic fortunes suggest that this will pose an enduring challenge.

CHARACTERISTICS OF EFFECTIVE TRAINING PRACTICE

One survey of corporate training and development practices found that four characteristics seemed to distinguish companies with the most effective training practices.[63]

- Top management is committed to training and development; training is part of the corporate culture. Thus Xerox Corporation invests about $300 million annually, or about 2.5 percent of revenue, on training. This translates to about $2500 per year per employee. It is an ongoing process for all employees, including the chief executive officer.[67] Hewlett-Packard spends about 5 percent of its revenues, or $250 million, to train its 87,000 workers. Marriott Corporation simply says, "Training is part of our culture."[35]
- Training is tied to business strategy and objectives and is linked to bottom-line results. The chapter opening vignette is a clear example of this.
- A comprehensive and systematic approach to training exists; training and retraining are done at all levels on a continuous, ongoing basis.
- There is a commitment to invest the necessary resources, to provide sufficient time and money for training.

While the potential returns from well-conducted training programs are hefty, considerable planning and evaluation are necessary in order to realize these returns. The remainder of this chapter examines some key issues that managers need to consider. Let us begin by considering the broad phases that comprise training systems.

ASSESSING TRAINING NEEDS AND DESIGNING TRAINING PROGRAMS

One way to keep in mind the phases of training is to portray them graphically, in the form of a model that illustrates the interaction among the phases. One such model is shown in Figure 7-3.

The *assessment* (or planning) *phase* serves as a foundation for the entire training effort. As Figure 7-3 shows, both the *training phase* and the *evaluation phase* depend on inputs from assessment. If the assessment phase is not carefully done, then the training program as a whole will have little chance of achieving what it is intended to do.

Assuming that the objectives of the training program are carefully specified, the next task is to design the environment in which to achieve those objectives. This is the purpose of the training phase, "a delicate process that requires a blend of learning principles and media selection, based on the tasks that the trainee is eventually expected to perform" (ref. 22, p. 21).

Finally, if both the assessment phase and the training phase have been done competently, then evaluation should present few problems. Evaluation is a twofold process that involves (1) establishing indicators of success in training, as well as on the job, and (2) determining exactly what job-related changes have occurred as

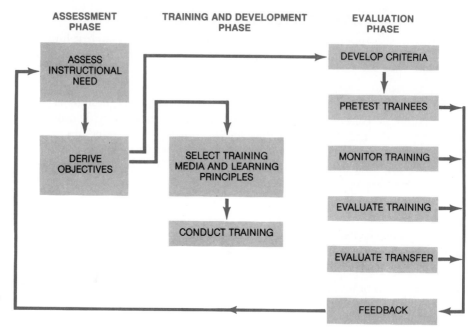

FIGURE 7-3
A general systems model of the training and development process. Note how information developed during the evaluation phase provides feedback, and therefore new input, to the assessment phase. This initiates a new cycle of assessment, training and development, and evaluation.

a result of the training. Evaluation must provide a continuous stream of feedback that can be used to reassess training needs, thereby creating input for the next stage of employee development.

Now that we have a broad overview of the training process, let us consider the elements of Figure 7-3 in greater detail.

Assessing Training Needs

There are three levels of analysis for determining the needs that training can fulfill:[46]

> *Organization analysis* focuses on identifying where within the organization training is needed.
>
> *Operations analysis* attempts to identify the content of training—what an employee must do in order to perform competently.
>
> *Individual analysis* determines how well each employee is performing the tasks that make up his or her job.

Training needs might surface in any one of these three broad areas. But to ask productive questions regarding training needs, an "integrative model" such as shown in Figure 7-4 is needed.

At a general level, training needs must be analyzed against the backdrop of organizational objectives and strategies. Unless this is done, time and money may

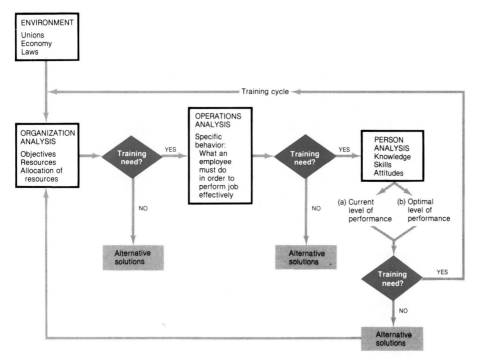

FIGURE 7-4
Training needs assessment model.

well be wasted on training programs that do not advance the cause of the company.[48] People may be trained in skills they already possess (as happened to members of a machinists' union of a major airline not long ago); the training budget may be squandered on "rest and recuperation" sessions, where employees are entertained but learn little in the way of required job skills or job knowledge; or the budget may be spent on glittering hardware that meets the training director's needs but not the organization's.

Analysis of the organization's external environment and internal climate is also essential. Trends in the strategic priorities of a business, judicial decisions, civil rights laws, union activity, productivity, accidents, turnover, absenteeism, and on-the-job employee behavior will provide relevant information at this level. The important question then becomes "Will training produce changes in employee behavior that will contribute to our organization's goals?"

In short, the critical first step is to relate the assessment of training needs to the achievement of organizational goals. If that connection cannot be made, the training is probably unnecessary. However, if a training need is identified at this organizational level, then an operations analysis is the next step.

Operations analysis requires a careful examination of the job to be performed *after* training. It involves: (1) a systematic collection of information that describes exactly *how* jobs are done, so that (2) standards of performance for those jobs can be determined; (3) how tasks are to be performed to meet the standards; and (4) the knowledge, skills, abilities, and other characteristics necessary for effective task performance. Job analyses, performance appraisals, interviews (with jobholders, supervisors, and higher management), and analyses of operating problems (quality control, downtime reports, and customer complaints) all provide important inputs to the analysis of training needs.

Finally there is *individual analysis*. At this level, training needs may be defined in terms of the following general idea: The difference between desired performance and actual performance is the individual's training need. Performance standards, identified in the operations analysis phase, constitute desired performance. Individual performance data, diagnostic ratings of employees by their supervisors, records of performance kept by workers in diary form, attitude surveys, interviews, or tests (job knowledge, work sample, or situational) can provide information on *actual* performance against which each employee can be compared to *desired* job performance standards. A gap between actual and desired performance may be filled by training.

However, assessing the needs for training does not end here. To evaluate the results of training and to assess what training is needed in the future, needs must be analyzed regularly *and* at all three levels.

- At the organizational level, needs must be analyzed by the managers who set the organization's goals.
- At the operations level, needs must be analyzed by the managers who specify how the organization's goals are going to be achieved.
- At the individual level, needs must be analyzed by the managers and workers who do the work to achieve those goals.

■ **COMPANY EXAMPLE**

FROM NEEDS ANALYSIS, TO TRAINING, TO RESULTS!

At Pacific Northwest Bell, installers were uncertain about whether and how much they could charge for work on noncompany equipment and wiring, so they were billing very little. The company, in turn, seeing little revenue generated by the labor hours spent, had stopped marketing the technicians' services.

A team of internal consultants—a company manager, a representative of the International Brotherhood of Electrical Workers, and a representative of the Communications Workers of America—recognized this problem and tried to solve it by involving a cross section of interested parties. The new task force agreed on two goals: to increase revenues and to increase job security.

A subcommittee of two task developers and two technicians developed a training program designed to teach installers *how* and *what* to charge, and also *why* they should keep accurate records: to increase their job security. The committee agreed to measure the revenues generated by time and materials charging so that these revenues could be weighed against labor costs in layoff decisions.

The training consisted of two 6-hour days and was presented by technicians to about 400 installers throughout Washington State and Oregon. In addition to the course, the task force identified the need for a hot line that technicians could call when bidding for a job. The line was set up, and one of the course instructors was promoted to a management position for answering calls.

RESULTS

The results of the training and hot line were phenomenal, as shown by the pattern of revenues from work on noncompany equipment. In January, prior to the training course, the installers had billed $589. In April, when half the workers had completed the training, they billed $21,000 in outside work. By the following February, billings for customized work and charges reached $180,000. Total revenues over the 14-month period were about $1.4 million, or nearly twice the task force's projection of $831,000.

In light of these results, the company now markets the installers' services aggressively. For example, if an installation crew drives by a construction site on their way from another job, they stop and bid on the work. The hot line receives about 50 calls per day from systems technicians, installers, the business office, and customers.

The efforts of the task force increased company revenues, and also the job security of the installers. Demand for their services grew with increased bidding on jobs, and more installers were added, providing union members in other job titles with opportunities for promotions or transfers into this work group. Future layoffs are unlikely, since the savings in labor costs must be weighed against the revenues generated by the installers.[27] Careful assessment of the need for training, coupled with the delivery of a training program that met targeted needs, produced results that startled management, the union, and the installation technicians. Everybody won.

FURTHER ISSUES IN THE DESIGN AND CONDUCT OF TRAINING PROGRAMS

Equal Employment Opportunity

The federal "Uniform Guidelines on Employee Selection Procedures" affect five areas of training:[68] job entry, training program admission, the training process itself, career decisions, and affirmative action plans.

Job entry training may be necessary before a person can be considered for entry to a job: for example, passing a pole-climbing course prior to being considered for a job as a telephone installer or repairer. Legal problems may arise in instances where women or minorities are less likely to pass the training course than white men (that is, "adverse impact" exists) *and* the company has no proof that the training requirements are related to job proficiency. To avoid such difficulties, all trainees must be given an equal chance to complete the training successfully. And, of course, the validity of the training requirements must be demonstrated. The company must be able to show that people with the training perform their jobs better than those without the training.

Another area affected by the guidelines is *admission into the training program*. Legally, Title VII of the 1964 Civil Rights Act prohibits discrimination against individuals on the basis of their race, sex, age, religion, or national origin in admission to apprenticeship or other training programs. When discriminatory practices have been uncovered and brought to court, the courts have made decisions effecting far-reaching changes.[52]

The training process itself may have an adverse impact on women and minorities. For example, physical equipment for training may be designed primarily for men, thereby making it difficult for some women to use because of their generally shorter legs and arm reach. (Redesign of the equipment might eliminate this problem.) The vocabulary level in training manuals may require a reading ability far higher than is necessary to perform the job itself, thus eliminating those with less education. In short, if the training process itself consistently results in inferior performance by women and minorities, the program may have to be redesigned *unless* such inferior training performance is reflected in corresponding inferior job performance.

Career decisions, such as retention in the training program or preferential job assignment, are sometimes made on the basis of measures collected during training. Again, if women and minorities consistently perform poorly in training, the performance measures themselves must be validated to show that performance in training reflects later performance on the job. Sound HRM practice dictates that this be done anyway to assess whether training dollars are being spent well.

Affirmative action plans commonly specify goals for the recruitment, selection, and training of women and minorities. In the biggest consent decree ever, General Motors agreed (with the EEOC) to spend $42.5 million over 6 years to hire, train, and promote more women and minorities. GM agreed to establish companywide hiring goals for women and minorities in eight job categories, including apprentices, supervisors, security officers, and sales managers. The company also agreed to spend over $21 million on training this target group for higher-level positions and to provide an additional $15 million educational package of endowments and scholarships for more than 100,000 employed and laid-off women and minorities and their families.[39] Clearly the legal aspects of training programs should not be underestimated. However, neither should they preoccupy us to the point of not considering other, equally critical, aspects of training design and implementation, such as maximizing trainees' learning.

Trainability

Organizations provide training to those who are most likely to profit from it; individuals prefer to be trained in the things that interest them and in which they can improve. To provide instruction for trainees in areas in which they have no aptitude or interest will not benefit them and will certainly not benefit the organization.

From a cost-benefit perspective, the largest cost component of training is the cost of paying the trainees during the training period. Hence, cost savings are possible if training time can be reduced. Perhaps the easiest way to do this is by identifying and training only those employees who clearly are "trainable." *Trainability* refers to how well a person can acquire the skills, knowledge, and behavior necessary to perform a job, achieving its specified outcome within a given time.[59] It is a combination of an individual's ability and motivation.

Can a person's ability to learn a job be predicted? Recent research suggests that the answer is a cautious yes.[58] For example, one study showed that current methods for assigning enlisted Navy personnel to specific jobs could be improved by using a concept called "miniature training and evaluation testing."[62] Using this approach, a recruit is trained (and then subsequently tested) on a sample of the tasks that he or she will be expected to perform on the job. The approach is based on the premise that a recruit who demonstrates that he or she can learn to perform a *sample* of the tasks of a Navy job will be able to learn and to perform satisfactorily *all* the tasks of that job, given appropriate on-the-job training. In fact, a battery of nine training-evaluation situations derived from a job analysis of typical entry-level tasks for various naval occupations, such as sailor, firefighter, and air crew member, was able to improve substantially the accuracy of prediction of job performance over that obtained with standard written tests. Similar results were obtained for seven "minicourses" designed to select personnel for jobs involving new technologies in the telecommunication industry.[56]

Although "can-do" (ability) factors are necessary, it is important to recognize that "will-do" (motivational) factors also play a vital role in the prediction of trainability. For example, the Navy School for Divers found that a seven-item trainee confidence measure significantly predicted graduation from its 10-week training program in Scuba and Deep Sea Air procedures.[60] Each of the following items is answered on a 6-point scale from "disagree strongly" (score of 1) to "agree strongly" (score of 6):

1. I have a better chance of passing this training than most others do.
2. I volunteered for this training program as soon as I could.
3. The knowledge and experience that I gain in this training may advance my career.
4. Even if I fail, this training will be a valuable experience.
5. I will get more from this training than most people.
6. If I have trouble during training, I will try harder.
7. I am more physically fit for this training than most people.

Trainees most likely to profit from training can be identified reasonably accurately when measures such as these are combined with two other kinds of information: (1) the extent of each potential trainee's job involvement and career planning[50,51] and (2) each employee's choice to select the training in question.[26] Once these trainees have been identified, it becomes important to structure the training environment for maximum learning. Attention to the fundamental principles of learning is essential.

Principles of Learning

To promote efficient learning, long-term retention, and application of the skills or factual information learned in training back to the job situation, training programs should incorporate principles of learning developed over the past century. Which principles should be considered? It depends on whether the trainees are learning skills (e.g., drafting) or factual material (e.g., principles of life insurance).[70]

To be most effective, *skill learning* should include four essential ingredients: (1) goal setting, (2) behavior modeling, (3) practice, and (4) feedback.

However, when the focus is on *learning facts*, the sequence should change only slightly: namely, (1) goal setting, (2) meaningfulness of material, (3) practice, and (4) feedback. Let's consider each of these in greater detail.

Motivating the trainee: goal setting A person who wants to develop herself or himself will do so; a person who wants to be developed rarely is. This statement illustrates the role that motivation plays in training—to learn, you must *want* to learn. And it appears from evidence that the most effective way to raise a trainee's motivation is by setting goals. Goal setting has a proven track record of success in improving employee performance in a variety of settings and cultures.[44,47] On average, goal setting leads to a 10 percent improvement in productivity, and it works best with tasks of low complexity.[71]

Goal theory is founded on the premise that an individual's conscious goals or intentions regulate her or his behavior.[40] Research indicates that once a goal is accepted, difficult but attainable goals result in higher levels of performance than do easy goals or even a generalized goal such as "do your best."[41] These findings have three important implications for motivating trainees:

1. The objectives of the training program should be made clear at the outset. Each objective should describe the desired behavior, the conditions under which it should occur, and the success criteria by which the behavior will be judged.[43] For example:

> In a 4-hour performance test at the end of 1 month of training [conditions], you will be able to reupholster an armchair, a couch, and a hassock, demonstrating the correct procedures at each step in the process [desired behavior]. All steps must be executed in the correct order and must meet standards of fit and trim specified in the textbook [success criteria].

PYGMALION IN ACTION:
MANAGERS GET THE KIND OF PERFORMANCE THEY EXPECT

To test the Pygmalion effect and to examine the impact of instructors' prior expectations about trainees on the instructors' subsequent style of leadership toward the trainees, a field experiment was conducted at a military training base.[13] A total of 105 trainees in a 15-week combat command course were matched on aptitude and assigned randomly to one of three experimental groups. Each group corresponded to a particular level of expectation that was communicated to the instructors: high, average, or no prespecified level of expectation (due to insufficient information). Four days before the trainees arrived at the base, and prior to any acquaintance between instructors and trainees, the instructors were assembled and given a score (known as command potential, or CP) for each trainee that represented the trainee's potential to command others. The instructors were told that the CP score was developed on the basis of psychological test scores, data from a previous course on leadership, and ratings by previous commanders. The instructors were also told that course grades predict CP in 95 percent of the cases. The instructors were then given a list of the trainees assigned to them, along with their CPs, and asked to copy each trainee's CP into his or her personal record. The instructors were also requested to learn their trainees' names and their CPs before the beginning of the course.

The Pygmalion hypothesis that the instructor's prior expectation influences the trainee's performance was confirmed. Trainees of whom instructors expected better performance scored significantly higher on objective achievement tests, exhibited more positive attitudes, and were perceived as better leaders. In fact, the prior expectations of the instructors explained 73 percent of the variability in the trainees' performance, 66 percent in their attitudes, and 28 percent in leadership. The lesson to be learned from these results is unmistakable: Trainers (and managers) get the kind of performance they expect.

2. Goals should be challenging and difficult enough that the trainees can derive personal satisfaction from achieving them, but not so difficult that they are perceived as impossible to reach.

3. The ultimate goal of "finishing the program" should be supplemented with subgoals during training, such as trainer evaluations, work-sample tests, and periodic quizzes. As each hurdle is cleared successfully, trainee confidence about attaining the ultimate goal increases.

While goal setting clearly affects the trainees' motivation, so also do the *expectations* of the trainer. In fact, expectations have a way of becoming self-fulfilling prophecies so that the higher the expectations, the better the trainees perform. Conversely, the lower the expectations, the worse the trainees perform. This phenomenon of the self-fulfilling prophecy is known as the *Pygmalion effect*. Legend has it that Pygmalion, a king of Cyprus, sculpted an ivory statue of a maiden named Galatea. Pygmalion fell in love with the statue, and, at his prayer, Aphrodite, the goddess of love and beauty, gave it life. Pygmalion's fondest wish, his expectation, came true.

Behavior modeling Much of what we learn is acquired by observing others. We will imitate other peoples' actions when they lead to desirable outcomes for those involved (e.g., promotions, increased sales, or more accurate tennis serves). The models' actions serve as a cue as to what constitutes appropriate behavior.[2] A *model* is someone who is seen as competent, powerful, and friendly and has high status within an organization. We try to identify with this model because her or his behavior is seen as desirable and appropriate. Modeling tends to increase when the model is rewarded for behavior and when the rewards (e.g., influence, pay) are things the imitator would like to have. In the context of training (or coaching or teaching), we attempt to maximize the trainees' identification with a model. For us to do this well, research suggests that we do the following:

1. The model should be similar to the observer in age, sex, and race. If the observer sees little similarity between himself or herself and the model, it is unlikely that he or she will imitate the model's behaviors.
2. Portray the behaviors to be modeled clearly and in detail. To focus the trainees' attention on specific behaviors to imitate, provide them with a list of key behaviors to attend to when observing the model, and allow them to express the behaviors in language that is most comfortable for them. For example, when one group of supervisors was being taught how to "coach" employees, the supervisors received a list of the following key behaviors:[28] (1) focus on the problem, not on the person; (2) ask for the employees' suggestions, and get their ideas on how to solve the problem; (3) listen openly; (4) agree on the steps that each of you will take to solve the problem; and (5) plan a specific follow-up date.
3. Rank the behaviors to be modeled in a sequence from least to most difficult; be sure the trainees observe lots of repetitions of the behaviors being modeled.
4. Finally, have the behaviors portrayed by several models, not just one.[21,38]

Research continues to demonstrate the effectiveness of behavior modeling over other approaches to training.[20] To a large extent, this is because behavior modeling overcomes one of the shortcomings of earlier approaches to training: telling instead of showing. For example, trainees used to be told to be "good communicators"— a behavior that most people agree is useful and that most trainees were already familiar with prior to the program—but the trainees were never shown *how* to be good communicators. Behavior modeling teaches a desired behavior effectively by:

> providing the trainee with numerous, vivid, detailed displays (on film, videotape, or live) of a manager-actor (the model) performing the specific behaviors and skills we wish the viewer to learn (i.e., modeling); giving the trainee considerable guidance in and opportunity and encouragement for behaviorally rehearsing or practicing the behaviors he/she has seen the model perform (i.e., role playing); [and] providing him/her with positive

feedback, approval, or reward as the role playing enactments increasingly approximate the behavior of the model (i.e., social reinforcement). . . . (ref. 21, p. 37)

Meaningfulness of the material Factual material is learned more easily and remembered better when it is meaningful.[46] *Meaningfulness* refers to material that is rich in associations for the trainees and is therefore easily understood by them. To structure material to maximize its meaningfulness:

1. Provide trainees with an overview of the material to be presented during the training. Seeing the overall picture helps trainees understand how each unit of the program fits together and how it contributes to the overall training objectives.[70]
2. Present the material by using examples, terms, and concepts that are familiar to the trainees in order to clarify and reinforce key learning points. Such a strategy is *essential* when training the hard-core unemployed.[25]
3. Complex intellectual skills are invariably comprised of simpler skills, and it is necessary to master these simpler skills before the complex skills can be learned.[18] This is true whether one is learning accounting, computer programming, or x-ray technology.

Thus the basic principles of training design consist of (a) identifying the component tasks of a final performance, (b) ensuring that each of these component tasks is fully achieved, and (c) arranging the total learning situation in a sequence that will ensure a logical connection from one component to another.[19]

Practice (makes perfect) For anyone learning a new skill or acquiring factual knowledge, there must be the opportunity to practice what is being learned. Practice has three aspects: active practice, overlearning, and the length of the practice session. Let's consider each of these.

Active practice During the early stages of learning, the trainer should be available to oversee directly the trainee's practice; if the trainee begins to "get off the track," the inappropriate behaviors can be corrected immediately, before they become ingrained in the trainee's behavior. This is why low instructor-trainee (or teacher-pupil) ratios are so desirable. It also explains why so many people opt for private lessons when trying to learn or master a sport such as tennis, golf, skiing, or horseback riding. Particularly during skills learning, it is simply not enough for a trainee to verbalize (or to read out of an instruction book) what she or he is expected to do. Only active practice provides the internal cues that regulate motor performance. As practice continues over time, inefficient motions are discarded and internal cues associated with smooth, precise performance are retained. To develop a deeper appreciation of these principles, watch almost any professional athlete performing his or her specialty. Then you will see why "practice makes perfect."

Overlearning When trainees are given the opportunity to practice far beyond the point where the task has been performed correctly several times, the task becomes "second nature" and is said to be "overlearned." For some tasks, over-learning is critical. This is true of any task that must be performed infrequently and under great stress: for example, attempting to kick a winning field goal with only seconds left in a football game. It is less important in types of work where an individual practices his or her skills on a daily basis (e.g., auto mechanics, electronics technicians, assemblers). Overlearning has several advantages:

- It increases the length of time that the training material will be retained.
- It makes the learning more "reflexive" so that tasks become "automatic" with continued practice.
- The quality of performance is more likely to be retained during periods of emergency or added stress.
- It facilitates the transfer of training to the job situation.

Length of the practice session Consider these two situations: (1) You have only 1 week to memorize the lines of a play, and (2) you have only 1 week to learn how to pole-vault. In both cases you have only 12 hours available to practice. What practice schedule will produce the greatest improvement? Should you practice 2 hours a day for 6 days, should you practice for 6 hours each of the final 2 days before the deadline, or should you adopt some other schedule? The two extremes represent *distributed* practice (which implies rest intervals between sessions) and *massed* practice (in which the practice sessions are crowded together). Although there are exceptions, most of the research evidence on this question indicates that for the same amount of practice, learning is better when practice is distributed rather than massed.[22] Here are two reasons why:

- Continuous practice is fatiguing, so that individuals cannot show all that they have learned. Their performance is therefore lower than it would be if they were rested.
- During a practice session, people usually learn both the correct performance and also some irrelevant performances that interfere with it. But the irrelevant performances are likely to be less well practiced and so may be forgotten more rapidly between practice sessions. Performance should therefore improve if there are rest intervals between practice sessions.

One exception to this rule is when difficult material, such as hard puzzles or other "thought" problems, must be learned. There seems to be an advantage in staying with the problem for a few massed practice sessions at first, rather than spending a day or more between sessions.

Feedback *Feedback* is a form of information about one's attempts to improve. Feedback is essential for learning and for trainee motivation.[36] The emphasis should be on *when* and *how* the trainee has done something correctly: for example, "You did a good job on that report you turned in yesterday—it was brief and to the heart of the issues." Feedback promotes learning and motivation in three ways:

1. It provides direct information to trainees about the correctness of their responses, thereby allowing them to make adjustments in their subsequent behavior.
2. When somebody who cares about your success is paying close attention to you, be it trainer, coach, or teacher, it makes the learning process more interesting and hence maximizes your willingness to learn.
3. Feedback leads to the setting of specific goals for maintaining performance.[14,44]

It is also important to emphasize that feedback affects group, as well as individual, performance.[55] For example, application of performance-based feedback in a small fast-food store over a 1-year period led to a 15 percent decrease in food costs and to a 193 percent increase in profits.[17]

To have the greatest impact, feedback should be provided as soon as possible after the trainee's behavior. It need not be instantaneous, but there should be no confusion regarding exactly what the trainee did and the trainer's reaction to it. Feedback need not always be positive either.

To be acquired, modified, and sustained, behavior must be rewarded, or reinforced.[37,64] The principle of reinforcement also states that punishment leads only to a temporary suppression of behavior and is a relatively ineffective influence on learning. Reward says to the learner, "Good, repeat what you have done." Punishment says, "Stop it, you made the wrong response." Mild punishment may serve as a warning for the learner that he or she is getting off the track, but unless the learner is told immediately what he or she needs to do to get back on the track (corrective feedback), punishment can be intensely frustrating.

Both rewards and mild punishment can and should be used in a training situation, but keep in mind that the most powerful rewards are likely to be those provided by the trainee's immediate supervisor. In fact, if the supervisor does not reinforce what is learned in training, then the training will be transferred ineffectively to the job, if at all.

Individual Differences

Individual differences are glaringly obvious in the training environment. Some trainees are fast learners, some are slow learners, some begin at higher initial states than others, some are capable of higher terminal states than others, and some improve very little despite continued practice. These variations in learning patterns are the result of differences in ability and motivation among trainees. Trainers need to be flexible enough to modify their training strategies to accommodate these differences (e.g., through optional additional practice sessions or more detailed explanations and demonstrations). However, research on human learning

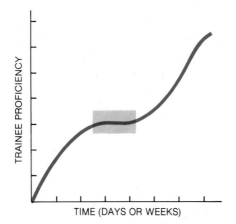

FIGURE 7-5
A typical S-shaped learning curve with a plateau.

TRAINEE PROFICIENCY

TIME (DAYS OR WEEKS)

indicates that there are remarkable similarities in the overall learning pattern of trainees: It follows the S-shaped pattern shown in Figure 7-5.[16]

During the early practice trials, rapid improvement occurs (in common parlance this is sometimes called beginner's luck). Eventually, however, there is a period of no improvement in the learning curve, described as a *plateau* because it has been preceded by improvement and will be followed by improvement. There are several possible reasons for the plateau: There may be a temporary decrease in motivation related to discouragement with the decreasing gains in the typical learning curve; the trainee may be in the process of integrating different skills (e.g., moving from a letter habit to a word habit in learning to type); or the trainee may need a different method of instruction. In any case, it is important to recognize that this leveling process is normal; to maintain motivation and continued improvement, it is essential that trainees be given continued support and encouragement at this time.

Transfer of Training

Transfer refers to the extent to which knowledge, skills, abilities, or other characteristics learned in training can be applied on the job. Transfer may be *positive* (i.e., it enhances job performance), *negative* (i.e., it hampers job performance), or *neutral*. Long-term training or retraining probably includes segments that contain all three of these conditions. Training that results in negative transfer is costly in two ways—the cost of the training (which proved to be useless) and the cost of hampered performance.

Here's how one company facilitates positive transfer from learning to doing.

■ **COMPANY EXAMPLE**

TRW'S STRATEGIC MANAGEMENT SEMINAR

At TRW, *systems learning* helps focus attention on the important concept of "transfer of training."[42] All training activities are designed with a built-in compatibility between what managers are expected to learn and what they are expected to do on their jobs. Here is an example.

Following instruction in the concepts of competitive strategy, a three-phase strategic management seminar was presented to natural business teams within TRW: for example, a division vice president and his or her staff. In phase I, each team receives two things: (1) more instruction in the concepts of competitive strategy and (2) a detailed assignment. The teams must apply the concepts to their business and develop an action strategy. Each team must plan a maximum of six actions that it will take over the next 18 months, and it must designate responsibility to particular team members for each action. The teams then "go home" to work on their strategies for about 8 weeks.

Phase II of the seminar is called the "midterm review." A seminar faculty member visits each team to review its progress on the assignment and provides detailed feedback on how well the team is applying the concepts. Sometimes major changes are made at this point as teams recognize, for example, that their competitive analysis is not thorough enough.

Over the following 8 weeks, Phase III of the program, each team prepares its final strategic presentation—to be delivered in the presence of two or three other teams. After each team presents its strategy, the audience provides constructive comments and criticisms. Next, the audience votes on whether to accept or reject the strategy, indicating on their ballots what they like and dislike about the strategy. The votes and comments are collected and offered to the presenting team, along with comments and concerns from the faculty member. What's happening here? A powerful peer review process.

To encourage a tight "fit" between training and application, some changes in TRW's organizational practices were necessary—such as changing the process of developing strategic plans, modifying the compensation system so that long-term success is rewarded, and changing the performance appraisal process to emphasize long-term thinking, planning, and action. However, the biggest change of all was senior management's willingness to encourage the kind of risk taking required to implement some of the strategies. This is the essence of systems learning.

TRW's approach to "systems learning" suggests that transfer of training (that is, the adoption of concepts and practices learned in training to practice on the job) will be greatest when the following steps are taken:

1. Define the content of the program(s) in terms of the strategic needs of the organization. Failure to do this will result in training that will have no impact on organizational outcomes.
2. Identify and assign individuals to training based on careful selection standards.

To do this, survey employee interests, obtain input from immediate supervisors, and review career development plans and performance appraisals. Always ask, "Does this person really need the training?"

3. Ensure that classroom content is directly relevant to the work setting (i.e., that the training is content valid). Specific behaviors, activities, and goals that are required on the job should be reflected in the content of the training.

4. Ensure the practical application of the training to the work setting by means of systematic follow-up. Close the training program with an "application plan" session that reiterates the most important and relevant learning points, reduces them to specific goals, reduces the goals to specific activities, identifies appropriate coworkers to assess progress toward the goals, and establishes a time frame for self-monitoring. At the end of the self-monitoring period, a "coach" (perhaps the original trainer) then meets with each participant to review progress and use of the applications plan. The ultimate objective is to ensure that participants have a reason for using what they have learned and actually adopt the new behaviors in the work setting.[2]

Team Training

Up to this point, we have been discussing training and development as an individual enterprise. Yet today there is an increasing emphasis on *team* performance. Management teams, research teams, and temporary task forces are common features of many organizations. *A team is a group of individuals who are working together toward a common goal.* It is this common goal that really defines a team, and if team members have opposite or conflicting goals, the efficiency of the total unit is likely to suffer. For example, consider the effects on a basketball team when one of the players *always* tries to score, regardless of the team's situation.

Research has revealed two broad principles regarding the composition of teams. One, the overall performance of a team strongly depends on the individual expertise of its members.[4] Thus individual training and development is still important. But individual training is only a partial solution, for interactions among team members must also be addressed. This interaction is what makes team training unique—it always uses some form of simulation or real-life practice, and it always focuses on the interaction of team members, equipment, and work procedures.[3]

Two, managers of effective work groups tend to monitor the performance of their team members regularly, and they provide frequent feedback to them.[32] In fact, as much as 35 percent of the variability in team performance can be explained by the frequency of use of monitors and consequences. Incorporating these findings into the training of team members and their managers should lead to better overall team performance.

Selecting Training Methods

New training methods appear every year. While some are well-founded in learning theory or models of behavior change (e.g., behavior modeling), others result more from technological than from theoretical developments (e.g., videotape, computer-based business games).

Training methods can be classified in three ways: information presentation, simulation methods, or on-the-job training.[9]

Information presentation techniques include lectures, conference methods, correspondence courses, motion pictures, reading lists, closed-circuit TV and video-tapes, behavior modeling and systematic observation, programmed instruction, computer-assisted instruction, sensitivity training, and organization development—systematic, long-range programs of organizational improvement.

Simulation methods include the case method, role playing, programmed group exercises, the in-basket technique, and business games.

On-the-job training methods include orientation training, apprenticeships, on-the-job training, near-the-job training (using identical equipment but away from the job itself), job rotation, committee assignments (or junior executive boards), understudy assignments, on-the-job coaching, and performance appraisal.

In the context of developing interpersonal skills, training methods are typically chosen to achieve one or more of three objectives:

- To promote self-insight and environmental awareness—that is, an understanding of how one's actions affect others and how one is viewed by others. For example, at Parfums Stern, staffers act out customer-salesperson roles to better understand customers' emotions. Wendy's International videotapes disabled customers; in one video a blind person asks that change be counted out loud. Meridian Bancorp has workers walk with seeds in their shoes to simulate older customers' corns and callouses.[33]
- To improve the ability of managers and lower-level employees to make decisions and to solve job-related problems in a constructive fashion.
- To maximize the desire to perform well.

To choose the training method (or combination of methods) that best fits a given situation, *what is to be taught* must first be defined carefully. That is the purpose of the needs assessment phase. *Only then* can the method be chosen that best fits these requirements. To be useful, the chosen method should meet the minimal conditions needed for effective learning to take place; that is, the training method should:

- Motivate the trainee to improve his or her performance.
- Clearly illustrate desired skills.
- Provide for active participation by the trainee.
- Provide an opportunity to practice.
- Provide timely feedback on the trainee's performance.
- Provide some means for reinforcement while the trainee learns.

- Be structured from simple to complex tasks.
- Be adaptable to specific problems.
- Encourage positive transfer from the training to the job.

■ **COMPANY EXAMPLE**

VIDEO IS A POPULAR TEACHER AT SMALL FIRMS

One of the most popular instruction methods, especially at small firms, is video. It helps solve a perennial headache: how to find affordable training. While small businesses may need employee training desperately, they often can't afford to hire trainers or to send staff members to expensive outside courses. Video is about 75 percent cheaper than bringing in an outside consultant.[57]

Many small business managers, forced to master dozens of different skills, find that video instruction can also make their lives easier. Thus when one manager bought a new computer database management program for his business, he faced a 200-page manual that explained how the new program worked. Instead of reading the manual, he bought a 1-hour video instruction tape that showed how to use the program. He figures that 1 hour with the tape saved 8 to 10 hours of reading.[57]

But tapes still have drawbacks. Because the market is smaller for a tape, say, on the proper way to display lettuce than for a blockbuster movie, the programs aren't cheap. Training tapes commonly sell for about $800 each and include discussion guides. Beyond that, there is the question of the relative effectiveness of video (interactive or not) versus alternatives, such as simulation or on-the-job training methods. Controlled research that evaluates the outcomes of the various methods is essential in order to select the most cost-effective techniques.

Basic Skills Training

Considerable emphasis today is being placed on training (or retraining) in basic skills, as applied to the performance of individual jobs. Thus among major employers, 22 percent offer basic training in reading, 41 percent in writing, and 31 percent in arithmetic.[34] Since managers are confronting this issue more and more often, it seems appropriate to outline a proven method for delivering such training. It's known as Job Instruction Training (JIT), and it was developed by the War Manpower Commission to train large numbers of new recruits during World War II.[69] It includes four steps that incorporate the principles of learning that we have discussed thus far.

Step 1: prepare the learner The purpose of this step is to motivate the learner. It requires the trainer to analyze the job in question into its major components, to prepare an instruction plan that proceeds from simple to more advanced material in a logical fashion, and to put the learner at ease—to build feelings of self-efficacy and self-confidence.

Step 2: present instruction (following the plan developed in step 1) The purpose of this step is to promote understanding on the part of the learner. To do this, show, tell, and demonstrate. Instruct clearly and completely, one point at a time. Don't overwhelm the learner. Rather, question patiently and carefully to check progress.

Step 3: application or tryout The purpose of this step is to foster active participation by the learner. Have him or her instruct the supervisor in how the job is done. Let the learner do the job, but ask questions and correct errors. Provide positive as well as negative feedback, and provide opportunities for practice. Finally, review and retrain until you are satisfied with the level of performance.

Step 4: follow-up The purpose of this step is to apply what was learned. Let learners perform on their own. Check them frequently at first, encouraging questions. Tell them where to go for help. Gradually taper off progress checks. Recognize good performance.

Although the specific manner in which the JIT is implemented may differ slightly, depending on the objectives of the training (e.g., learning manual versus interpersonal skills), its principles of instruction are timeless. If followed diligently, the JIT will help people to learn efficiently and effectively.

EVALUATING TRAINING PROGRAMS

Training must be evaluated by systematically documenting the outcomes of the training in terms of how trainees actually behave back on their jobs and the relevance of the trainees' behavior to the objectives of the organization.[65] To assess the utility or value of training, we seek answers to four questions:

1. Did change occur?
2. Is the change due to training?
3. Is the change positively related to the achievement of organizational goals?
4. Will similar changes occur with new participants in the same training program?[22]

In evaluating training programs, we measure change in terms of four categories:[30]

Reaction. How do the participants feel about the training program?
Learning. To what extent have the trainees learned what was taught?
Behavior. What on-the-job changes in behavior have occurred because of attendance at the training program?

Results: To what extent have cost-related behavioral outcomes (e.g., productivity or quality improvements, turnover or accident reductions) resulted from the training?[31]

Since measures of reaction and learning are concerned with outcomes of the training program per se, they are referred to as *internal criteria*. Measures of behavior and results indicate the impact of training on the job environment; they are referred to as *external criteria*.

Measures of reaction typically focus on participants' feelings about the subject and the speaker, suggested improvements in the program, and the extent to which the training will help them do their jobs better. Trainee learning can be assessed by giving a paper-and-pencil test (especially when factual information has been presented) or through performance testing following skill training.

Assessing changes in on-the-job behavior is more difficult than measuring reaction or learning because factors other than the training program may also effect improved performance (e.g., lengthened job experience, outside economic events, and changes in supervision or performance incentives). To rule out these rival hypotheses, it is essential to design a plan for evaluation that includes *before* and *after* measurement of the trained group's performance relative to that of one or more untrained control groups. However, the post-training appraisal of performance should not be done sooner than 3 months (or more) following the training so that the trainees have an opportunity to put into practice what they have learned.

Finally, the impact of training on organizational results is the most significant but most difficult measure to make. *Measures of results are the bottom line of training success.* Exciting developments in this area have come from recent research showing how the general utility equation (Equation 6-1 in Chapter 6) can be modified to reflect the dollar value of improved job performance resulting from training.[10,11] Utility formulas are now available for evaluating the dollar value of a single training program compared to a control group, a training program readministered periodically (e.g., annually), and a comparison among two or more different training programs.

■ **COMPANY EXAMPLE**

EVALUATING THE BUSINESS IMPACT OF MANAGEMENT TRAINING AT CIGNA CORPORATION

CIGNA (the insurance company) set out to demonstrate the impact on productivity and performance of a 7-day training program in basic management skills.[53] The evaluations were based on repeated measures of work-unit performance both *before* and *after* training. Some specific features of the program were:

Productivity was a central focus of the program.

As part of their training, the participants were taught how to create productivity measures.

The participants were taught how to use productivity data as performance feedback and as support for performance goal setting.

The participants wrote a productivity action plan as part of the training, and they agreed to bring back measurable results to a follow-up session.

Individualized productivity measures were put in place as part of the action plan. These plans were tailored to measure results in specific, objective terms.

The results of the training in basic management skills were evaluated, of necessity, in individual work units. Let us consider one such unit—that of a premium collections manager. Collecting premiums on time is important in the insurance business, because late premiums represent lost investment opportunities. Through survey feedback from her subordinates, the manager of this unit found that her problems (only 75 percent of the premiums were collected on time) stemmed from poor human resource management skills, coupled with a failure to set clear performance goals.

After being trained, this manager dramatically altered many of her management behaviors. One year later her unit was collecting 96 percent of the premiums on time. This improvement yielded extra investment income of $150,000 per year. What was the return on the fully loaded cost of training her? The training costs included the costs of facilities, program development amortized over 25 programs, trainer preparation time, general administration, corporate overhead, and the salaries plus benefits of the participants over the 7-day program. These came to $1600 per participant. It looks like the returns generated by the collections manager as a result of the action plan ($150,000) relative to the training's cost ($1600) were phenomenal. But were *all* these gains due to her training? Probably not.

What would have happened had training not occurred? Extrapolating from the rate of improvement prior to training, the researchers concluded that the collections rate would have been up to about 84 percent, from 75 percent. The additional 12-point improvement that was provided—in part— by the program (which generated about $85,000 in extra investment income) represents the upper bound of the effects of the training program. (Other economic factors, such as lower unemployment, may also have contributed to the gain). Nevertheless, it represents about a 50-to-1 return on the dollars invested.

■ HUMAN RESOURCE MANAGEMENT IN ACTION
CONCLUSION

LOVE THY CUSTOMER AND KNOW THY FISH
IF YOU WANT TO WORK AT RED LOBSTER

Like every detail in a Red Lobster restaurant, the particulars of the service are the result of Red Lobster's careful scrutiny of surveys that tell them exactly what their consumers want. The surveys are conducted both by outside polling agencies and by Red Lobster itself, which runs several regular surveys. One is a bimonthly polling, in different restaurants, of 34,600 people on the quality of their "dining experience." Another is a monthly mailing to 40,000 consumers that rates Red Lobster against 15 competitors. Still other surveys help determine the success of new products and other special projects.

In response to such data and observations, Red Lobster executives have concluded that service, in today's world, provides the ultimate competitive edge. Says the executive vice president in charge of restaurant operations: "What it all boils down to is your experience with the server. I have a dry cleaner where I have my shirts done, and they don't exactly do my shirts the way I think they ought to. But I like them, personally, and that's why I have my shirts done there. It's the people, almost every time."

SUMMARY

Clearly, a new employee's initial experience with a firm can have a major effect on his or her later career. To maximize the impact of orientation, it is important to recognize that new employees need specific information in three major areas: (1) *company standards, traditions, and policies*; (2) *social behavior*, and (3) *technical aspects of the job*. This suggests two levels of orientation: company, conducted by an HR representative, and departmental, conducted by the immediate supervisor. To ensure proper quality control plus continual improvement, an *orientation follow-up* is essential (e.g., after 1 week by the supervisor and after 1 month by an HR representative).

The pace of change in our society is forcing both employed and displaced workers continually to acquire new knowledge and skills. In most organizations, therefore, lifelong training is essential. To be maximally effective, training programs should follow a three-phase sequence: *needs assessment, implementation*, and *evaluation. What is to be learned* must first be defined clearly before a particular method or technique is chosen. To define what is to be learned, a continuous cycle of organization analysis, operations analysis, and analysis of the training needs of employees is necessary.

Training needs must then be related to the achievement of broader organizational goals and be consistent with management's perceptions of strategy and tactics.

IMPACT OF TRAINING AND DEVELOPMENT ON PRODUCTIVITY, QUALITY OF WORK LIFE, AND THE BOTTOM LINE

Recently, quantitative procedures were used to accumulate results across 70 studies that had the following characteristics: (1) Each study involved managers, (2) each evaluated the effectiveness of one or more training programs, and (3) each included at least one control or comparison group. Results indicated that management training and development efforts are, in general, moderately effective. In terms of objective measures of training results over all content areas, training improved job performance by almost 20 percent, although there was considerable variability around this estimate.[7] This is reassuring. Given the pace of change in modern society and technology, retraining is imperative to enable individuals to compete for available jobs (and therefore to maintain their standards of living) and to enable organizations to compete in the marketplace. Continual investment in training and learning is therefore essential, as it has such a direct impact on the productivity of organizations and on the quality of work life of those who work in them.

Beyond these fundamental concerns, issues of equal employment opportunity, trainability, and principles of learning—goal setting, behavior modeling, meaningfulness of material, practice, feedback, and transfer of training—are essential considerations in the design of any training program. The choice of a particular

IMPLICATIONS FOR MANAGEMENT PRACTICE

One of the greatest fears of managers and lower-level employees is obsolescence. Perhaps the Paul Principle expresses this phenomenon most aptly: *Over time, people become uneducated, and therefore incompetent, to perform at a level they once performed at adequately.*[1] Training is an important antidote to obsolescence, but it is important to be realistic about what training can and cannot accomplish.

1. Training cannot solve all kinds of performance problems. In some cases, transfer, job redesign, changes in selection or reward systems, or discipline may be more appropriate.
2. Since productivity (the value of outputs per unit of labor) is a characteristic of a system, such as a firm or an industry, and not of an individual, changes in individual performance are only one possible cause of changes in productivity.[8]
3. As a manager, three key questions to ask with regard to training are these: "Do we have an actual or potential performance problem for which training is the answer?"; "Have we defined what is to be learned and what the content of training should be *before* we choose a particular training method or technique?"; and "What kind of evaluation procedure will we use to determine if the benefits of the training outweigh its costs?"

technique should be guided by the degree to which it fits identified needs and incorporates the learning principles.

In evaluating training programs, we measure change in terms of four categories: *reaction, learning, behavior*, and *results*. Measures of the impact of training on organizational results are the bottom line of training success. Fortunately, advances in utility analysis now make evaluations possible in terms of dollar benefits and dollar costs.

DISCUSSION QUESTIONS

7•1 Why is orientation so often overlooked by organizations?

7•2 Think back to your first day on the latest job you have held. What could have been done to hasten your socialization to the organization and your adjustment to the job?

7•3 Considering the example of Whirlpool Corporation, what strategies can you suggest for reducing the problem of "juggling" workers and for providing retraining incentives for displaced ones?

7•4 Training has been described by some as intensely "faddish." As an advisor to management, describe how the firm can avoid succumbing to training fads.

7•5 How does goal setting affect trainee learning and motivation?

7•6 Outline an evaluation procedure for a training program designed to teach sales principles and strategies.

REFERENCES

1. Armer, P. (1970). The individual: His privacy, self-image, and obsolescence. *Proceedings of the meeting of the panel on science and technology, 11th "Science and Astronautics."* Washington, DC: USGPO.

2. Bandura, A. (1986). *Social foundations of thought and action: A social cognitive theory.* Englewood Cliffs, NJ: Prentice-Hall.

3. Bass, B. M. (1980). Team productivity and individual member competence. *Small Group Behavior*, **11**, 431–504.

4. Bottger, P. C., & Yetton, P. W. (1987). Improving group performance by training in individual problem solving. *Journal of Applied Psychology*, **72**, 651–657.

5. Brody, M. (1987, June 8). Helping workers to work smarter. *Fortune*, pp. 86–88.

6. Brownlee, D. (1983, June). Personal communication.

7. Burke, M. J., & Day, R. R. (1986). A cumulative study of the effectiveness of managerial training. *Journal of Applied Psychology*, **71**, 232–245.

8. Campbell, J. P. (1988). Training design for performance improvement. In J. P. Campbell & R. J. Campbell (eds.), *Productivity in organizations*. San Francisco: Jossey-Bass, pp. 177–215.

9. Campbell, J. P., Dunnette, M. D., Lawler, E. E., & Weick, K. E. (1970). *Managerial behavior, performance, and effectiveness*. New York: McGraw-Hill.

10. Cascio, W. F. (1991). *Costing human resources: The financial impact of behavior in organizations* (3d ed.). Boston: PWS-Kent.

11. Cascio, W. F. (1989). Using utility analysis to assess training outcomes. In I. L. Goldstein (ed.), *Training and development in organizations*. San Francisco: Jossey-Bass, pp. 63–88.

12. Cascio, W. F., & Zammuto, R. F. (1989). Societal trends and staffing policies. In W. F. Cascio (ed.), *Human resource planning, employment, and placement.* Washington, DC: Bureau of National Affairs, pp. 2-1 to 2-33.

13. Eden, D., & Shani, A. B. (1982). Pygmalion goes to boot camp: Expectancy, leadership, and trainee performance. *Journal of Applied Psychology*, **67**, 194–199.

14. Erez, M. (1977). Feedback: A necessary condition for the goal-setting–performance relationship. *Journal of Applied Psychology*, **62**, 624–627.

15. Fiske, E. B. (1989, Sep. 25). Impending U.S. jobs "disaster": Work force unqualified to work. *The New York Times*, pp. A1, B6.

16. Fleishman, E. A., & Mumford, M. D. (1989). Individual attributes and training performance. In I. L. Goldstein (ed.), *Training and development in organizations.* San Francisco: Jossey-Bass, pp. 183–255.

17. Florin-Thuma, B. C., & Boudreau, J. W. (1987). Performance feedback utility in a small organization: Effects on organizational outcomes and managerial decision processes. *Personnel Psychology*, **40**, 693–713.

18. Gagné R. M. (1977). *The conditions of learning.* New York: Holt, Rinehart, & Winston.

19. Gagné, R. M. (1962). Military training and the principles of learning. *American Psychologist*, **18**, 93–91.

20. Gist, M., Rosen, B., & Schwoerer, C. (1988). The influence of training method and trainee age on the acquisition of computer skills. *Personnel Psychology*, **40**, 255–265.

21. Goldstein, A. P., & Sorcher, M. (1974). *Changing supervisor behavior.* New York: Pergamon Press.

22. Goldstein, I. L. (1986). *Training in organizations: Needs assessment, development, and evaluation* (2d ed.). Monterey, CA: Brooks/Cole.

23. Goldstein, I. L., & Gilliam, P. (1990). Training system issues in the year 2000. *American Psychologist*, **45**, 134–143.

24. Gordon, J. (1986). Training magazine's industry report, 1986. *Training*, **23**(10), 26–66.

25. Gray, I., & Borecki, T. B. (1970). Training programs for the hard-core: What the trainer has to learn. *Personnel*, **47**, 23–29.

26. Hicks, W. D., & Klimoski, R. J. (1987). Entry into training programs and its effects on training outcomes: A field experiment. *Academy of Management Journal*, **30**, 542–552.

27. Hilton, M. (1987). Union and management: A strong case for cooperation. *Training and Development Journal*, **41**(1), 54–55.

28. Hogan, P. M., Hakel, M. D., & Decker, P. J. (1986). Effects of trainee-generated versus trainer-provided rule codes on generalization in behavior-modeling training. *Journal of Applied Psychology*, **71**, 469–473.

29. Kilborn, P. T. (1990, Feb. 5). Costly pitfalls in worker retraining. *The New York Times*, p. A14.

30. Kirkpatrick, D. L. (1983). Four steps to measuring training effectiveness. *Personnel Administrator*, **28**(11), 19–25.

31. Kirkpatrick, D. L. (1977). Evaluating training programs: Evidence vs. proof. *Training and Development Journal*, **31**, 9–12.

32. Komaki, J. L., Desselles, J. L., & Bowman, E. D. (1989). Definitely not a breeze: Extending an operant model of supervision to teams. *Journal of Applied Psychology*, **74**, 522–529.

33. Labor Letter (1990, May 8). *The Wall Street Journal*, p. A1.

34. Labor Letter (1990, Feb. 20). *The Wall Street Journal*, p. A1.

35. Labor Letter (1988, Nov. 22). *The Wall Street Journal*, p. A1.

36. Latham, G. P. (1989). Behavioral approaches to the training and learning process. In I. L. Goldstein (ed.), *Training and development in organizations.* San Francisco: Jossey-Bass, pp. 256–295.

37. Latham, G. P., & Frayne, C. A. (1989). Self-management training for increasing job attendance: A follow-up and a replication. *Journal of Applied Psychology,* **74,** 411–416.

38. Latham, G. P., & Saari, L. M. (1979). The application of social learning theory to training supervisors through behavior modeling. *Journal of Applied Psychology,* **64,** 239–246.

39. Lienert, P. (1983, Oct. 19). Discrimination settlement will cost GM $42.5 million. *The Denver Post,* p. 3A.

40. Locke, E. A. (1968). Toward a theory of task motivation and incentives. *Organizational Behavior and Human Performance,* **3,** 157–189.

41. Locke, E. A., Latham, G. P., & Erez, M. (1988). The determinants of goal commitment. *Academy of Management Review,* **13,** 23–39.

42. Lubliner, M. (1978, April). Employee orientation. *Personnel Journal,* pp. 207–208.

43. Mager, R. F. (1962). *Preparing instructional objectives.* Palo Alto, CA: Fearon.

44. Matsui, T., Kakuyama, T., & Onglatco, M. L. U. (1987). Effects of goals and feedback on performance in groups. *Journal of Applied Psychology,* **72,** 407–415.

45. McGarrell, E. J., Jr. (1984). An orientation system that builds productivity. *Personnel Administrator,* **29**(10), 75–85.

46. McGehee, W., & Thayer, P. W. (1961). *Training in business and industry.* New York: Wiley.

47. Mento, A. J., Steel, R. P., & Karren, R. J. (1987). A meta-analytic study of the effects of goal setting on performance: 1966–1984. *Organizational Behavior and Human Decision Processes,* **39,** 52–83.

48. Moore, M. L., & Dutton, P. (1978). Training needs analysis: Review and critique. *Academy of Management Review,* **3,** 532–454.

49. Navy worried about growing jet losses (1986, March 23). *Honolulu Star Bulletin,* pp. A1, A4.

50. Noe, R. A. (1986). Trainees' attributes and attitudes: Neglected influences on training effectiveness. *Academy of Management Review,* **11,** 736–749.

51. Noe, R. A., & Schmitt, N. (1986). The influence of trainee attitudes on training effectiveness: Test of a model. *Personnel Psychology,* **39,** 497–523.

52. Norton, E. H. (1987, May 13). Step by step, the court helps affirmative action. *The New York Times,* p. A27.

53. Paquet, B., Kasl, E., Weinstein, L., & Waite, W. (1987). The bottom line. *Training and Development Journal,* **41**(6), 27–33.

54. Peters, T. J., & Waterman, R. H., Jr. (1983, Apr. 28). In search of excellence. *The Denver Post,* p. 6F.

55. Pritchard, R. D., Jones, S. D., Roth, P. L., Steubing, K. K., & Ekeberg, S. E. (1988). Effects of group feedback, goal setting, and incentives on organizational productivity. *Journal of Applied Psychology,* **73,** 337–358.

56. Reilly, R. R., & Israelski, E. W. (1988). Development and validation of minicourses in the telecommunication industry. *Journal of Applied Psychology,* **73,** 721–726.

57. Ricklefs, R. (1988, Dec. 6). Video is popular teacher at small firms. *The Wall Street Journal,* p. B2.

58. Robertson, I. T., & Downs, S. (1989). Work-sample tests of trainability: A meta-analysis. *Journal of Applied Psychology,* **74,** 402–410.

59. Robertson, I. T., & Downs, S. (1979). Learning and the prediction of performance: Development of trainability testing in the United Kingdom. *Journal of Applied Psychology*, **64**, 42–50.

60. Ryman, D. H., & Biersner, R. J. (1975). Attitudes predictive of diving training success. *Personnel Psychology*, **28**, 181–188.

61. *Serving the new corporation* (1986). Alexandria, VA: American Society for Training and Development.

62. Siegel, A. I. (1983). The miniature job training and evaluation approach: Additional findings. *Personnel Psychology*, **36**, 41–56.

63. Sirota, Alper, & Pfau, Inc. (1989). *Report to respondents: Survey of views toward corporate education and training practices.* New York: Sirota, Alper, & Pfau, Inc.

64. Skinner, B. F. (1969). *Contingencies of reinforcement: A theoretical analysis.* East Norwalk, CT: Appleton-Century-Crofts.

65. Snyder, R. A., Raben, C. S., & Farr, J. L. (1980). A model for the systematic evaluation of human resource development programs. *Academy of Management Review*, **5**, 431–444.

66. St. John, W. D. (1980, May). The complete employee orientation program. *Personnel Journal*, pp. 373–378.

67. Training is "competitive weapon" in global markets, Xerox chief says. (1990, Summer). *BNAC Communicator*, p. 20.

68. Uniform guidelines on employee selection procedures (1978). *Federal Register*, **43**, 38,290–38,315.

69. War Manpower Commission. (1945). *The training within industry report.* Washington, DC: U.S. Government Printing Office.

70. Wexley, K. N., & Latham, G. P. (1991). *Developing and training human resources in organizations*, 2d ed. Glenview, IL: Scott, Foresman.

71. Wood, R. E., Mento, A. J., & Locke, E. A. (1987). Task complexity as a moderator of goal effects: A meta-analysis. *Journal of Applied Psychology*, **72**, 416–425.

Appraising Employee Performance

■ HUMAN RESOURCE MANAGEMENT IN ACTION

A PERFORMANCE MANAGEMENT SYSTEM FOR CORNING, INC.*

The Performance Management System at Corning was designed explicitly to deal with two major conflicts in performance appraisal: (1) employee development versus administrative decisions, and (2) measurement precision versus organization development. The first conflict occurs when supervisors use the appraisal system for employee development while their employees' promotions, salary increases, or other personnel actions are tied closely to it. The second conflict occurs when reliability and validity considerations are overemphasized to the exclusion of similar efforts that focus on the *implementation* of the appraisal system. What happens is that managers may overtly reject it because of a lack of understanding of the technique or because of its lack of practical utility. The Corning system attempts to manage these conflicts constructively.

---

*Adapted from: M. Beer, et al., A performance management system: Research, design, introduction, and evaluation, *Personnel Psychology*, **31**, 1978, 505–535.

Until the mid-1960s there was no formal performance appraisal system at Corning, Inc. The primary method of appraisal was to talk directly to other managers who knew the person rather than to search out performance-related information from the Human Resource Department. In other words, informal exchanges on the telephone or in a bar determined the fate of many careers. Discontent with such a system led to the Performance Management System project.

Corning has a tradition of transferring salaried employees across functions and divisions as part of their management development. Thus an important requirement for the appraisal system was to cover a broad range of performance dimensions and provide performance information relevant for decisions about cross-functional and cross-divisional transfers or promotions. The objective, therefore, was to develop a system that would be sound from a measurement perspective but that would also provide a *common language* for describing the performance of professional and managerial employees.

The system that was finally developed over several years of research has three basic components: Management by objectives (MBO) focuses on tasks, or *what* gets done; performance development and review focuses on methods, or *how* the job gets done; finally, salary and placement review focuses on administrative decision making.

MANAGEMENT BY OBJECTIVES

Like many other companies, Corning originally adopted the MBO approach because it was the "thing to do," although the program was never pushed systematically throughout the corporation. Yet MBO, which is based on setting goals and tracking progress toward them, is popular for several reasons. One, it directs the supervisor's attention exclusively toward task results and away from making judgments about the personal attributes of subordinates. Two, since managers in general have a rather low level of analytical skill regarding individual behavior, they are far more comfortable and skillful in analyzing numbers and tasks.[41] Three, some managers are so results-oriented that they feel they do not have time for any of that "personal stuff." In sum, MBO is acceptable to managers because it makes the performance review process, the feedback of performance results, a little less threatening and less emotionally difficult for them. However, MBO was also used because of research showing that the goal-setting process itself is motivating and because MBO seems to enhance the quality of supervisor-subordinate relationships.

PERFORMANCE DEVELOPMENT AND REVIEW

Unfortunately, the strength of MBO is also its weakness. Although it enhances accountability and responsibility by focusing attention on what needs to be done and on quantifiable measures of accomplishment, it is not especially useful when it comes to improving subordinates' ability to perform effectively. This is so because MBO does not provide diagnostic information about why an individual is *not* performing. Further, it cannot be used exclusively in making personnel decisions because, although a person may be successful in his or her current job, the next-level job may require behaviors and skills that the current job does not demand. Unless the performance appraisal system allows management to determine whether he or she has these attributes, mistakes in promotion decisions are inevitable.

The performance development and review system that emerged was geared mainly to helping supervisors develop their subordinates. It is based on ratings by supervisors of their subordinates on a 76-item questionnaire that taps 19 key areas of behavior. These are:

Openness to influence	Constructive initiative
Priority setting	Work accomplishment
Thoroughness and accuracy	Credibility
Organizational perspective	Formal communications
Collaboration	Decisiveness
Subordinate participation	Flexibility
Support for company	Team building
Unit improvement	Control
Unit's productivity	Supportiveness
Conflict resolution	

Results from the questionnaires are helpful to managers in two ways. One, they force managers to observe the actual performance of their subordinates. Two, they help managers analyze the performance of their subordinates through the "performance profile." This profile is a computer-generated pictorial display of subordinates' strengths and shortcomings as deviations from a centerline that represents the subordinate's *own* mean. The scores are meaningless for comparing individuals to each other, but they are very useful for promoting individual development. Since every profile includes strengths as well as shortcomings, about the only way managers can avoid talking to a subordinate about his or her shortcomings is to "lose" the profile! The combination of MBO and performance development and review thus provides a complete performance appraisal process.

SALARY AND PLACEMENT REVIEW

The results of MBO and performance development and review are intended to flow into salary and placement decisions. Although there is no prescribed way to do this, a form used for these recommendations is included in the total Performance Management System package. The manager is asked to note the subordinate's overall performance and potential after she or he has conducted a performance development and review session and has consolidated her or his impressions in this session and in MBO sessions conducted throughout the previous year. These ratings are reviewed by the manager's supervisor and forwarded to the Human Resource Department. Salary decisions and career discussions with subordinates are expected to reflect the ratings and be consistent with them. In theory, this discussion should be conducted at a time different from the MBO or performance development and review discussions because its emphasis on evaluation would not mix well with the emphasis on development of MBO and performance development and review. In actual practice, however, subordinates are told about their performance and potential ratings immediately following the performance development and review session. As we shall see, this has led to some predictable problems.

IMPLEMENTATION OF THE PERFORMANCE MANAGEMENT SYSTEM

Introducing the system was as important a task as *developing* it. To be effective, the Peformance Management System had to be accepted and used properly. To encourage this, managers attended a 2-day educational program that described the performance development and review system, the rationale for the different components, and the process of splitting MBO, performance development and review, and salary review into three separate interviews with a subordinate. Lecture, discussion, and experience-based training techniques were used in the program.

Considerable time was spent training managers in appraisal feedback interviews. Because the objective of performance development and review was employee development, managers were trained to conduct effective interviews. Certainly the elaborate research that led to the performance development and review rating system would be wasted if managers failed to conduct competent, constructive interviews with their subordinates! To develop such skills, films of effective and ineffective interviews (role-played by Corning managers) were developed for critique and discussion. In addition, participants were asked to role-play a development interview using a performance development and review profile. Finally, they were asked to complete the 76-item questionnaire on one of their subordinates, they were given a profile of the results, and they were asked to prepare for an actual performance development and review session.

There were some other important aspects of the introduction of the performance management system. First, since Corning has a divisional structure and the divisions are fairly heterogeneous, each division was approached separately about the introduction of the system. A division is a homogeneous product group with profit responsibility, headed by a vice president and general manager who has reporting to him or her a staff of functional managers. There are eight divisions within the company. The 2-day educational program was held in the most receptive division first. Education started at the top and ultimately included all salaried employees. As a result of an enthusiastic response to the Performance Management System by the top managers in the division, the system was introduced to the rest of the company, division by division.

As new divisions introduced the system and showed enthusiasm, support grew across the company. In addition, an important strategy for gaining acceptance was to include *both* superior and subordinate managers in the same educational sessions. This made it very clear to everyone involved that they were expected to use this program together, especially the development interview. It communicated to the manager that she or he was expected to behave in accordance with program guidelines, even if this was not consistent with her or his current style of operation. Such a strategy helped both the manager and the subordinate understand the system, and it seemed to encourage participation and enthusiasm. Finally, the presence of both manager and subordinate in the same session made it possible for a subordinate to raise questions later if the Performance Management System was not applied properly. How has the system actually worked in practice? We will find out at the end of the chapter.

Challenges

1. Do you agree or disagree with the three-pronged approach of the Performance Management System? Why?
2. Almost any approach to human resource management has advantages as well as disadvantages associated with it. What do you see as the pros and cons of the Performance Management System?

QUESTIONS THIS CHAPTER WILL HELP MANAGERS ANSWER

1. What steps can I, as a manager, take to make the performance appraisal process more relevant and acceptable to those who will be affected by it?
2. How can we best fit our approach to performance appraisal with the strategic direction of our department and business?
3. Should managers and nonmanagers be appraised from multiple perspectives— for example, by those above, by those below, by coequals, and by customers?
4. What strategy should we use to train raters at all levels in the mechanics of doing appraisal and in the art of giving feedback?

The chapter opening vignette reveals just how complex performance management can be, for it includes both developmental (feedback) and administrative (pay, promotions) issues, and it includes technical aspects (design of an appraisal system) and interpersonal aspects (appraisal interviews). This chapter's objective is to present a balanced view of the appraisal process, considering both its technical and its interpersonal aspects. Let's begin by examining the nature of the performance appraisal process.

PERFORMANCE APPRAISAL: A COMPLEX AND OFTEN MISUNDERSTOOD PROCESS

As the Corning system indicates, performance appraisal has many facets. It is an exercise in observation and judgment, it is a feedback process, and it is an organizational intervention. It is a measurement process as well as an intensely emotional process. Above all, it is an inexact, human process. While it is fairly easy to prescribe how the process *should* work, descriptions of how it *actually* works in practice are rather discouraging.

Two independent surveys involving over 9000 employees found that fewer than 50 percent of American workers think their bosses provide regular performance feedback or help solve interpersonal problems. Seventy percent believed that review sessions had not given them a clear picture of what was expected of them on the job or of where they could advance in the company. Only half said that their bosses helped them set job objectives, and only one in five said that reviews were followed up during the ensuing year.[34,40] Some managers give short shrift to appraisals—and their subordinates know it.

This chapter examines some of the reaons for common problems in the appraisal process and considers how the application of research findings in the area of performance appraisal can improve the process. Let us begin by defining our terms:

- *Performance* refers to an employee's accomplishment of assigned tasks.
- *Performance appraisal* is the systematic description of the job-relevant strengths and weaknesses of an individual or group.
- *Appraisal period* is the length of time during which an employee's job performance is observed in order to make a formal report of it.
- *Performance management* is the total process of observing an employee's performance in relation to job requirements over a period of time (i.e., clarifying expectations, setting goals, providing on-the-job coaching, storing and recalling information about performance) and then of making an appraisal of it. Information gained from the process may be fed back via an appraisal interview to determine the relevance of individual and work-group performance to organizational purposes, to improve the effectiveness of the unit, and to improve the work performance of employees.[46]

Before addressing some common problems in performance appraisal, let us first consider the major organizational purposes served by appraisal systems. In general, appraisal serves a twofold purpose: (1) to improve the work performance of employees by helping them realize and use their full potential in carrying out their firms' missions, and (2) to provide information to employees and managers for use in making work-related decisions. More specifically, appraisals serve the following purposes:

1. Appraisals support personnel decisions to promote outstanding performers; to weed out marginal or low performers; to train, transfer, or discipline others; and to justify merit increases (or no increases). In short, appraisal serves as a key input for administering a formal organizational reward and punishment system.[24]

2. Appraisals are used as criteria in test validation. That is, test results are correlated with appraisal results to evaluate the hypothesis that test scores predict job performance.[17] However, if appraisals are not done carefully, or if considerations other than performance influence appraisal results, then the appraisals cannot be used legitimately for any purpose.

3. Appraisals provide feedback to employees and thereby serve as vehicles for personal and career development.

4. Once the development needs of employees are identified, appraisals can help establish objectives for training programs.

5. As a result of the proper specifications of performance levels, appraisals can help diagnose organizational problems. They do so by identifying training needs and the knowledge, abilities, skills, and other characteristics to consider in hiring, and they also provide a basis for distinguishing between effective and ineffective performers. Appraisal therefore represents the beginning of a process, rather than an end product.[36] These ideas are shown graphically in Figure 8-1.

The Organizational and Human Contexts of Performance Appraisal

Having seen the multiple purposes for which appraisal systems can be used to manage human resources wisely, let us now consider some enlightening findings from actual practice:

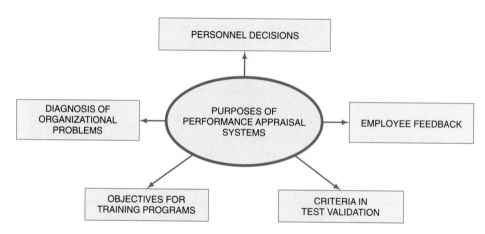

FIGURE 8-1
Purposes of performance appraisal systems.

1. Surveys show that up to 93 percent of performance appraisal programs ask the immediate supervisor to take the *sole* responsibility for doing the appraisal.[25]

2. A typical manager has limited contact with his or her employees. Studies indicate that managers spend only 5 to 10 percent of their workweek with any one subordinate. These contacts are in a limited range of settings, such as formal meetings.[25] Managers therefore have access only to a small (and perhaps unrepresentative) sample of their subordinates' work.

3. Accuracy in appraisal is less important to managers than motivating and rewarding their subordinates. Many managers will not allow excessively accurate ratings to cause problems for themselves, and they attempt to use the appraisal process to their own advantage.[48]

4. Standards and ratings tend to vary widely and, often, unfairly. Some raters are tough, others are lenient. Some departments have highly competent people, others have less competent people. Consequently, employees subject to less competition or to lenient ratings can receive higher appraisals than do equally competent or superior associates.

5. Personal values and bias can replace organizational standards. Thus unfairly low ratings may be given to valued subordinates so that they will not be promoted out of the rater's department, or outright bias may lead to favored treatment for some employees.

6. Sometimes the validity of performance appraisals is reduced by the resistance of supervisors to making them. Rather than confront their less effective subordinates with negative ratings, negative feedback in appraisal interviews, and below-average salary increases, some supervisors take the easy way out and give average or above-average ratings to inferior performers. Alternatively, a supervisor might award average ratings to inferior performers in a misguided attempt to "encourage them to do better." The result is that the average ratings reinforce inferior performance.

7. Some supervisors complain that performance appraisal is pointless paperwork. This author's surveys of over 1000 supervisors in a county hospital over a 3-year period indicated that fewer than 20 percent could cite *any* use of appraisals in human resource management. Is their "pointless paperwork" reaction really a surprise?

8. Performance appraisals interfere with more constructive supervisor-subordinate coaching relationships. Appraisal interviews tend to emphasize the superior position of the supervisor by placing her or him in the role of judge, thus countering her or his equally important roles of teacher and coach. In organizations that are attempting to promote supervisor-subordinate participation in decisions, such situations can be downright destructive. Both IDS Financial Services and Corning (see the chapter opening vignette) handle this problem by separating discussions aimed at employee development (performance development and review and MBO) from those aimed at administrative decisions (salary and placement review).[39]

The appraisal interview can be as stressful for the boss as it is for the subordinate.

It is easy to understand how the foregoing list could engender a sense of hopelessness in any manager or organization thinking about appraisal. However, despite their shortcomings, appraisals continue to be used widely, especially as a basis for tying pay to performance.[23] To attempt to avoid these shortcomings by doing away with appraisals is no solution, for whenever people interact in organized settings, appraisals will be made—formally or informally. The real challenge, then, is to identify appraisal techniques and practices that (1) are most likely to achieve a particular objective and (2) are least vulnerable to the obstacles listed above. Let us begin by considering some of the fundamental requirements that determine whether a performance appraisal system will succeed or fail.

Requirements of Effective Appraisal Systems

Legally and scientifically, the key requirements of any appraisal system are relevance, sensitivity, and reliability. In the context of ongoing operations, the key requirements are acceptability and practicality.[18] Let's consider each of these.

Relevance This implies that there are (1) clear links between the performance standards for a particular job and an organization's goals and (2) clear links between the critical job elements identified through a job analysis and the dimensions to be rated on an appraisal form. In short, relevance is determined by answering the question "What really makes the difference between success and failure on a particular job?"

Performance standards translate job requirements into *levels* of acceptable or unacceptable employee behavior. They play a critical role in the job analysis–performance appraisal linkage, as Figure 8-2 indicates. More will be said about performance standards later in this chapter.

Relevance also implies the periodic maintenance and updating of job analyses, of performance standards, and of appraisal systems. Should the system be challenged in court, relevance will be a fundamental consideration in the arguments presented by both sides.

Sensitivity This implies that a performance appraisal system is capable of distinguishing effective from ineffective performers. If it is not, and the best employees are rated no differently from the worst employees, then the appraisal system cannot be used for any administrative purpose, it certainly will not help employees to develop, and it will undermine the motivation of supervisors ("pointless paperwork") and of subordinates.

A major concern here is the purpose of the rating. One study found that raters process identical sets of performance appraisal information differently, depending on whether a merit pay raise, a recommendation for further development, or the retention of a probationary employee is involved.[68] These results highlight the conflict between appraisals made for administrative purposes and those made for employee development. Appraisal systems designed for administrative purposes demand performance information about differences *between* individuals, while systems designed to promote employee growth demand information about differences *within* individuals. The two different types of information are not interchangeable in terms of purposes, and that is why performance management systems designed to meet both purposes (such as the Corning system) are more complex and costly. In practice, only one type of information is usually collected, and it is used for some administrative purpose.[37] As we have seen, performance appraisal need not be a zero-sum game, but unfortunately it usually is.

Reliability A third requirement of sound appraisal systems is reliability. In this context it refers to consistency of judgment. For any given employee, appraisals

JOB ANALYSIS		PERFORMANCE STANDARDS		PERFORMANCE APPRAISAL
DESCRIBES WORK AND PERSONAL REQUIREMENTS OF A PARTICULAR JOB	→	TRANSLATE JOB REQUIREMENTS INTO LEVELS OF ACCEPTABLE/ UNACCEPTABLE PERFORMANCE	→	DESCRIBES THE JOB-RELEVANT STRENGTHS AND WEAKNESSES OF EACH INDIVIDUAL

FIGURE 8-2
Relationship of performance standards to job analysis and performance appraisal.

made by raters working independently of one another should agree closely. But raters with different perspectives (e.g., supervisors, peers, subordinates) may see the same individual's job performance very differently.[11] To provide reliable data, each rater must have an adequate opportunity to observe what the employee has done and the conditions under which he or she has done it; otherwise, unreliability may be confused with unfamiliarity.

Note that throughout this discusson there has been no mention of the validity or accuracy of appraisal judgments. This is because we really do not know what "truth" is in performance appraisal. However, by making appraisal systems relevant, sensitive, and reliable—by satisfying the scientific and legal requirements for workable appraisal systems—we assume that the resulting judgments are valid as well.

Acceptability In practice, acceptability is the most important requirement of all, for it is true that human resource programs must have the support of those who will use them, or else human ingenuity will be used to thwart them. Unfortunately, many organizations have not put much effort into garnering the front-end support and participation of those who will use the appraisal system. Thus only 62 percent of respondents in an American Productivity & Quality Center survey said that their bosses evaluate them fairly.[39]

Ultimately it is management's responsibility to define as clearly as possible the type and level of job behavior desired of employees. While this might seem obvious, consider three kinds of behavior that managers might exhibit:

1. Managers may not know what they want, and they may find it extremely painful even to discuss the issue.
2. Managers might fear that when employees find out what they want, the employees may not like it.
3. Some managers feel that they lose flexibility by stating their objectives in advance. "If I tell them what I want, then they will do only those things." This is management and appraisal by reaction: "I'll see what they do and then tell them whether I like it or not."

Clearly these attitudes run counter to research findings in performance appraisal. Under these circumstances we are playing power games with people and undermining the credibility and acceptability of the entire appraisal system. How much simpler it is to enlist the active support and cooperation of subordinates by making explicit exactly what aspects of job performance they will be evaluated on! Instead of promoting secrecy, we should be promoting more openness in human resource management, so that we can say, "This is what you must be able to do in order to perform competently." Only then can we expect to find the kind of acceptability and commitment that is so sorely needed in performance appraisal.

Practicality This implies that appraisal instruments are easy for managers and employees to understand and to use. The importance of this was brought home forcefully to me in the course of mediating a conflict between a county's Metropolitan Transit Authority (MTA) and its human resource (HR) unit. Here's what happened:

Practical performance appraisal for bus drivers. The conflict developed over the HR unit's *imposition* of a new appraisal system on all county departments regardless of each department's need for the new system. MTA had developed an appraisal system jointly with its union 5 years earlier, and it was working fine. In brief, each MTA supervisor (high school–educated) was responsible for about 30 subordinates (a total of 890 bus drivers who were also high school–educated or less). The "old" appraisal system was based on a checklist of infractions (e.g., reporting late for work, being charged with a preventable traffic accident), each of which carried a specified number of points. Appraisals were done quarterly, with each driver assigned 100 points at the beginning of each quarter. A driver's quarterly appraisal was simply the number of points remaining after all penalty points had been deducted during the quarter. Her or his annual appraisal (used as a basis for decisions regarding merit pay, promotions, and special assignments) was simply the average of the four quarterly ratings. Both supervisors and subordinates liked the old system because it was understandable and practical and also because it had been shown to be workable over a 5-year period.

The new appraisal system required MTA supervisors to write quarterly narrative reports on each of their 30-odd subordinates. The HR unit had made no effort to determine the ratio of supervisors to subordinates in the various departments. Not surprisingly, therefore, objections to the new system surfaced almost immediately. MTA supervisors had neither the time nor the inclination to write quarterly narratives on each of their subordinates. The new system was highly impractical. Furthermore, the old appraisal system was working fine and was endorsed by MTA management, employees, and their union. MTA managers therefore refused to adopt the new system. To dramatize their point, they developed a single, long, detailed narrative on an outstanding bus driver. Then they made 890 copies of the narrative (one for each driver), placed a different driver's name at the top of each "appraisal," and sent the 2-foot-high stack of "appraisals" to the HR unit. MTA made its point. After considerable haggling by both sides, the HR unit backed down and allowed MTA to continue to use its old (but acceptable and eminently practical) appraisal system.

In a broader context, we are concerned with developing decision systems. From this perspective, *relevance, sensitivity,* and *reliability* are simply technical components of a performance appraisal system designed to make decisions about employees. As we have seen, just as much attention needs to be paid to ensuring the *acceptability* and *practicality* of appraisal systems. These are the five basic requirements of performance appraisal systems, and none of them can be ignored. However, since some degree of error is inevitable in all personnel decisions, the crucial question to be answered in regard to each appraisal system is whether its use results in less human, social, and organizational cost than is currently paid for these errors. Answers to that question can result only in a wiser, fuller utilization of our human resources.

LEGAL ISSUES IN PERFORMANCE APPRAISAL

There is a rich body of case law on performance appraisal, and three reviews of it reached similar conclusions.[3,19,27] To avoid legal difficulties, consider taking the following steps:

1. Conduct a job analysis to determine the characteristics necessary for successful job performance.
2. Incorporate these characteristics into a rating instrument. This may be done by tying rating instruments to specific job behaviors (e.g., BARS, see page 281), but the courts routinely accept less sophisticated approaches, such as simple graphic rating scales. Regardless of the method used, provide written standards to all raters.
3. Train supervisors to use the rating instrument properly, including how to apply performance standards when making judgments. The uniform application of standards is very important. The vast majority of cases *lost* by organizations involved evidence that subjective standards were applied unevenly to minority and nonminority employees.

    As we saw earlier, performance appraisal results are used in the selection process to establish the validity of selection instruments. Steps 1, 2, and 3 are identical in that process.

4. Formal appeal mechanisms, coupled with higher-level review of appraisals, are desirable.
5. Document the appraisals and the reason for any termination decisions. This information may prove decisive in court. Credibility is enhanced with documented appraisal ratings that describe instances of poor performance.
6. Provide some form of performance counseling or corrective guidance to assist poor performers.

Here is a good example of step 6. In *Stone vs. Xerox* the organization had a fairly elaborate procedure for assisting poor performers.[60] Stone was employed as a sales representative and in less than 6 months had been given several written reprimands concerning customer complaints about his selling methods and failure to develop adequate written selling proposals. As a result, he was placed on a 1-month performance improvement program designed to correct these deficiencies. This program was extended 30 days at Stone's request. When his performance still did not improve, he was placed on probation and told that failure to improve substantially would result in termination. Stone's performance continued to be substandard, and he was discharged at the end of the probationary period. When he sued Xerox, he lost.

Certainly, the type of evidence required to defend performance ratings is linked to the *purposes* for which the ratings are made. For example, if appraisal of past performance is to be used as a predictor of future performance (i.e., promotions), evidence must be presented to show (1) that the ratings of past performance are, in fact, valid, and (2) that the ratings of past performance are statistically related to *future* performance in another job.[63] At the very least, this latter step should include job analysis results indicating the extent to which requirements of the lower- and higher-level jobs overlap. Finally, to assess adverse impact, organizations should keep accurate records of who is eligible for and interested in promotion. These two factors, *eligibility* and *interest*, define the "applicant group."

In summary, it is not difficult to offer prescriptions for scientifically sound, court-proof appraisal systems, but as we have seen, implementing them requires diligent attention by organizations, plus a commitment to make them work. In developing a performance appraisal system, the most basic requirement is to determine what you want the system to accomplish. This requires a strategy, a strategy for the management of performance.

The Strategic Dimension of Performance Appraisal

In the study of work motivation, a fairly well-established principle is that people will do things that bring them rewards. So a basic issue for managers is, "What kind of behavior do I want to encourage in my subordinates?" If employees are rewarded for generating short-term results, they will generate short-term results. If they are rewarded (e.g., through progressively higher commissions or bonuses) for generating repeat business or for reaching quality standards over long periods of time, then they will do those things.

At a basic level, therefore, managers could emphasize short- or long-term objectives in the appraisal process. Short-term objectives emphasize such things as bottom-line results for the current quarter. Long-term objectives emphasize such things as increasing market share and securing repeat business from customers. To be most useful, however, the strategic management of performance must be linked to the strategies an organization (or strategic business unit) uses to gain competitive advantage—for example, innovation, quality enhancement, or cost control.[5]

Some appraisal systems that are popular in America, such as management by objectives (MBO), are less popular in other parts of the world, such as Japan and France. MBO focuses primarily on results, rather than on how the results were accomplished. Typically it has a short-term focus, although this need not always be the case.

In Japan, greater emphasis is placed on the psychological and behavioral sides of performance appraisal than on objective outcomes. Thus an employee will be rated in terms of the effort he or she puts into a job, on integrity, loyalty, and cooperative spirit, and on how well he or she serves the customer. Short-term results tend to be much less important than long-term personal development, the establishment and maintenance of long-term relationships with customers (that is, behaviors), and increasing market share.[20,56]

Once managers decide what they want the appraisal system to accomplish, the next step is to develop specific standards of performance against which to evaluate employees. Let's consider how this is done.

DEVELOPING PERFORMANCE STANDARDS

Common sense dictates that fair performance appraisal requires a standard against which to compare employee performance. The clearer the performance standard is, the more accurate the appraisal can be. Thus the first step in effectively managing employee or work-group performance is to review existing standards, and to develop new ones if needed. Unfortunately, many supervisors simply *assume* that employees and work groups know what they are supposed to do on their jobs. Nothing could be further from the truth. At a recent Business Roundtable breakfast, a human resources executive from an insurance company described a study in which his company learned from field interviews with employees that as many as two-thirds could not describe clearly the requirements of their jobs and the performance standards on which they were evaluated!

Performance standards should contain two basic kinds of information for the benefit both of employee and of supervisor: *what* is to be done and *how well* it is to be done. The identification of job tasks, duties, and critical elements (see Chapter 4) describes *what* is to be done. This is crucial, for sound human resource management dictates that the content of the appraisal should reflect the nontrivial content of the job; such information provides content-related evidence of the validity of the appraisal system. Performance standards focus on *how well* the tasks are to be done. To be most useful, each standard should be stated clearly enough so that manager and subordinate or work group know what is expected and whether it has been met. Standards should be written to describe *fully satisfactory* performance for critical as well as noncritical tasks.[16]

Since job tasks and performance standards are interrelated, it is common practice to develop them at the same time. Whatever method of job analysis is used should take into account both quantitative and qualitative aspects of performance.[46] Further, each standard should refer to a specific aspect of the job. Examples are:

Quantitative	Qualitative
Number of forms processed	Accuracy, quality of work
Amount of time used	Ability to coordinate (e.g., staff, activities)
Number of errors	Ability to analyze (e.g., data, machine malfunctions)
Number of pages typed	Ability to evaluate (e.g., customer complaints, market research)

■ **TABLE 8·1**
PERFORMANCE STANDARDS FOR AN ELECTRIC METER READER

Critical (C) or noncritical (NC) tasks	Performance standard (fully satisfactory)
Records readings from residential and commercial meters (C)	Two legibility errors per 480 character entries; one transposition error per 400 meters read as shown by computer and manual checks
Inspects meters for damage or tap-ins (C)	Reports 80 percent of damaged meters found on routes as confirmed by spot checks made by service inspectors
Indicates extremes in usage (NC)	Indicates extremely high or low readings 90 percent of the time as shown by spot computer checks
Complies with safety standards (C)	Complies with safety standards 100 percent of the time
Interacts with customers (C)	No more than two customer complaints per month

Almost all jobs involve both aspects of performance but in varying proportions, depending on the nature of the job. Obviously, it is easier to measure performance against standards that can be described in quantitative terms. However, managerial jobs have an added component. That is, in addition to results that reflect the manager's own performance, other results reflect the performance of the organizational unit for which the manager is responsible. For managerial jobs, therefore, initial performance standards still should be determined by job analysis, even though they may be modified later (as a result of joint agreement by manager and subordinate or work group) to incorporate goals to be achieved. Goals that meet minimum standards are documented in quantitative terms, if possible; for example, a specified kind and amount of work will be done within a certain time limit. Doing so allows managers to assess progress toward goals even before any formal appraisal takes place. An example of a set of performance standards for an electric meter reader is shown in Table 8-1.

Often the first question managers ask is, "What's the best method of performance appraisal, which technique should I use?" As in so many other areas of HR management, there is no simple answer. The following section considers some alternative methods, along with their strengths and weaknesses. Since readers of this book are more likely to be *users* of appraisal systems than *developers* of them, the following will focus most on describing and illustrating them. For more detailed information, consult the References at the end of the chapter.

ALTERNATIVE METHODS OF APPRAISING EMPLOYEE PERFORMANCE

Many regard rating methods or formats as *the* central issue in performance appraisal; this is not the case.[9,31] Broader issues must also be considered—such as *trust* in the appraisal system; the *attitudes* of managers and employees; the *purpose*, *frequency*, and *source* of appraisal data; and rater *training*. Viewed in this light, rating formats play only a supporting role in the overall appraisal process.

Many rating formats focus on employee behaviors, either by comparing the performance of employees to each other (so-called "relative rating systems") or by evaluating each employe in terms of performance standards without reference to others (so-called "absolute rating systems"). Other rating formats place primary emphasis on what an employee produces (so-called "results-oriented systems"); dollar volume of sales, number of units produced, and number of interceptions during a football season are examples. Rating formats that use this results-oriented approach are management by objectives (MBO) and work planning and review.

Evidence indicates that ratings are not strongly related to results.[32] Why? Ratings depend heavily on the mental processes of the rater. Because these processes are complex, there may be judgment errors in the ratings. Conversely, results depend heavily on environmental conditions that may be outside the control of the individual worker, such as the availability of supplies or the contributions of others. Thus most measures of results are highly deficient as *overall* measures of performance. With these considerations in mind, let's examine the behavior- and results-oriented systems more fully.

Behavior-Oriented Rating Methods

Narrative essay The simplest type of absolute rating system is the narrative essay, in which a rater describes, in writing, an employee's strengths, weaknesses, and potential, together with suggestions for improvement. This approach assumes that a candid statement from a rater who is knowledgeable about an employee's performance is just as valid as more formal and more complicated rating methods. The MTA bus driver case presented earlier illustrated this approach.

If essays are done well, they can provide detailed feedback to subordinates regarding their performance. On the other hand, comparisons across individuals, groups, or departments are almost impossible since different essays touch on different aspects of each subordinate's performance. This makes it difficult to use essay information for personnel decisions since subordinates are not compared objectively and ranked relative to each other. Methods that compare employees to each other are more useful for this purpose.

Ranking *Simple ranking* requires only that a rater order all employees from highest to lowest, from "best" employee to "worst" employee. *Alternation ranking* requires that a rater initially list all employees on a sheet of paper. From this list he or she first chooses the best employee (No. 1), then the worst employee (No. n), then the second best (No. 2), then the second worst (No. $n-1$), and so forth, alternating from the top to the bottom of the list until all employees have been ranked.

Paired comparisons This is a more systematic method for comparing employees to each other. Here each employee is compared with every other employee, usually in terms of an overall category such as "present value to the organization." The rater's task is simply to choose the "better" of each pair, and each employee's rank is determined by counting the number of times she or he was rated superior. However, since these comparisons are made on an overall basis (that is, "Who is better?") and not in terms of specific job behaviors or outcomes, they may be subject to legal challenge.[19] On the other hand, methods that compare employees to each other are useful for generating initial rankings for purposes of salary administration.

Forced distribution This is another method for comparing employees to each other. As the name "forced distribution" implies, the overall distribution of ratings is forced into a normal, or bell-shaped, curve under the assumption that a relatively small portion of employees is truly outstanding, a relatively small portion is unsatisfactory, and everybody else falls in between. Figure 8-3 illustrates this method, assuming that five rating categories are used.

Forced distribution does eliminate clustering almost all employees at the top of the distribution (rater *leniency*), at the bottom of the distribution (rater *severity*), or in the middle (*central tendency*). However, it can foster a great deal of employee resentment if an entire group of employees *as a group* is either superior or substandard. It is most useful when a large number of employees must be rated and there is more than one rater.

Behavioral checklist Here the rater is provided with a series of statements that describe job-related behavior. His or her task is simply to "check" which of the statements, or the extent to which each statement, describes the employee. In this approach raters are not so much evaluators as reporters or describers of job behavior. And descriptive ratings are likely to be more reliable than evaluative (good-bad) ratings.[59] In one such method, the Likert method of *summated ratings*, a declarative statement (e.g., "She or he follows up on customer complaints") is followed by several response categories, such as "always," "very often," "fairly often," "occasionally," and "never." The rater checks the response category that he or she thinks best describes the employee. Each category is weighted, for example, from 5 ("always") to 1 ("never") if the statement describes desirable behavior. An overall numerical rating (or score) for each employee is then derived by *summing* the weights of the responses that were checked for each item. A por-

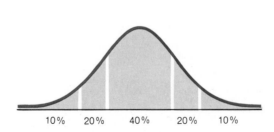

FIGURE 8-3

Example of a forced distribution. Forty percent of the ratees must be rated "average," 20 percent "above average," 20 percent "below average," 10 percent "outstanding," and 10 percent "unsatisfactory."

tion of a summated rating scale for appraising teacher performance is shown in Figure 8-4.

Critical incidents These are brief anecdotal reports by supervisors of things employees did that were particularly effective or ineffective in accomplishing parts of their jobs. They focus on behaviors, not traits. For example, a store manager in a retail computer store observed Mr. Wang, the word processing salesperson, do the following:

> Mr. Wang encouraged the customer to try our new word processing package by having the customer sit down at the computer and write a letter. The finished product was full of typographical and spelling errors, each of which was highlighted for the customer when Mr. Wang applied a "spelling checker" to the written material. As a result, Mr. Wang sold the customer the word processing program plus a typing tutor and a spelling checker program.

These little anecdotes force attention on the ways that situations determine job behavior and also on ways of doing the job successfully that may be unique to the person described. Hence they can provide the basis for training programs. Critical incidents also lend themselves nicely to appraisal interviews because supervisors can focus on actual job behaviors rather than on vaguely defined traits. Performance, not personality, is judged.

Like other rating methods, critical incidents also have their drawbacks. One, supervisors may find that recording incidents for their subordinates on a daily or even a weekly basis in burdensome. Two, the *rater* sets the standards by which subordinates are judged; yet motivation is likely to be enhanced if *subordinates* have some say in setting the standards by which they will be judged. And three, in their narrative form, incidents do not permit comparisons across individuals or departments. To overcome this problem, graphic rating scales may be used.

Graphic rating scale This is probably the most widely used rating method.[44] A portion of one such scale is shown in Figure 8-5.

Many different forms of graphic rating scales exist. In terms of the amount of structure provided, the scales differ in three ways:

FIGURE 8-4
A portion of a summated rating scale. The rater simply checks the response category that best describes the teacher's behavior. Response categories vary in scale value from 5 points (Strongly Agree) to 1 point (Strongly Disagree). A total score is computed by summing the points associated with each item.

	STRONGLY AGREE	AGREE	NEUTRAL	DISAGREE	STRONGLY DISAGREE
THE TEACHER WAS WELL PREPARED.					
THE TEACHER USED UNDERSTANDABLE LANGUAGE.					
THE TEACHER MADE ME THINK.					
THE TEACHER'S FEEDBACK ON STUDENTS' WORK AIDED LEARNING.					
THE TEACHER KNEW HIS OR HER FIELD WELL.					

RATING FACTORS	LEVEL OF PERFORMANCE				
	UNSATISFACTORY	CONDITIONAL	SATISFACTORY	ABOVE SATISFACTORY	OUTSTANDING
ATTENDANCE					
APPEARANCE					
DEPENDABILITY					
QUALITY OF WORK					
QUANTITY OF WORK					
RELATIONSHIP WITH PEOPLE					
JOB KNOWLEDGE					

FIGURE 8-5

A portion of a graphic rating scale.

1. The degree to which the meaning of the response categories is defined (in Figure 8-5, what does "conditional" mean?)
2. The degree to which the individual who is interpreting the ratings (e.g., a higher-level reviewing official) can tell clearly what response was intended
3. The degree to which the performance dimensions are defined for the rater (in Figure 8-5, for example, what does "dependability" mean?)

Graphic rating scales may not yield the depth of essays or critical incidents, but they are less time-consuming to develop and administer, the results can be expressed in quantitative terms, more than one performance dimension is considered, and since the scales are standardized, comparisons across employees can be made. Graphic rating scales have come under frequent attack, but when compared to more sophisticated forced-choice scales, the graphic scales have proven just as reliable and valid and they are more acceptable to raters.[17]

Behaviorally anchored rating scales (BARS) These are a variation of the simple graphic rating scale. Their major advantage is that they define the dimensions to be rated in behavioral terms and use critical incidents to describe various levels of performance. BARS therefore provide a common frame of reference for raters. An example of the job knowledge portion of a BARS for police patrol officers is shown in Figure 8-6. BARS require considerable effort to develop,[10] yet there is little research evidence to support the superiority of BARS over other types of rating systems.[19,36] Nevertheless, the participative process required to develop them provides information that is useful for other organizational purposes, such as communicating clearly to employees exactly what "good performance" means in the context of their jobs.

Results-Oriented Rating Methods

Management by objectives (MBO) This is a well-known process of managing that relies on goal setting to establish objectives for the organization as a whole, for each department, for each manager within each department, and for each

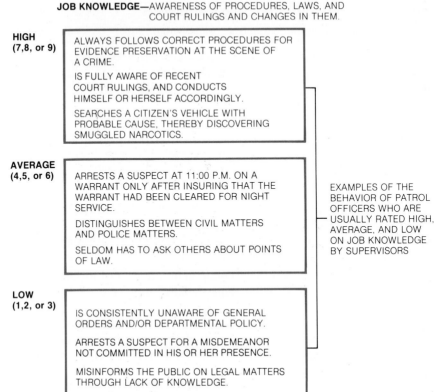

JOB KNOWLEDGE—AWARENESS OF PROCEDURES, LAWS, AND COURT RULINGS AND CHANGES IN THEM.

HIGH (7,8, or 9)

ALWAYS FOLLOWS CORRECT PROCEDURES FOR EVIDENCE PRESERVATION AT THE SCENE OF A CRIME.

IS FULLY AWARE OF RECENT COURT RULINGS, AND CONDUCTS HIMSELF OR HERSELF ACCORDINGLY.

SEARCHES A CITIZEN'S VEHICLE WITH PROBABLE CAUSE, THEREBY DISCOVERING SMUGGLED NARCOTICS.

AVERAGE (4,5, or 6)

ARRESTS A SUSPECT AT 11:00 P.M. ON A WARRANT ONLY AFTER INSURING THAT THE WARRANT HAD BEEN CLEARED FOR NIGHT SERVICE.

DISTINGUISHES BETWEEN CIVIL MATTERS AND POLICE MATTERS.

SELDOM HAS TO ASK OTHERS ABOUT POINTS OF LAW.

EXAMPLES OF THE BEHAVIOR OF PATROL OFFICERS WHO ARE USUALLY RATED HIGH, AVERAGE, AND LOW ON JOB KNOWLEDGE BY SUPERVISORS

LOW (1,2, or 3)

IS CONSISTENTLY UNAWARE OF GENERAL ORDERS AND/OR DEPARTMENTAL POLICY.

ARRESTS A SUSPECT FOR A MISDEMEANOR NOT COMMITTED IN HIS OR HER PRESENCE.

MISINFORMS THE PUBLIC ON LEGAL MATTERS THROUGH LACK OF KNOWLEDGE.

FIGURE 8-6
A behaviorally anchored rating scale to assess the job knowledge of police patrol officers.

employee. MBO is not a measure of employee behavior; rather, it is a measure of each employee's contribution to the success of the organization.[15]

In theory, objectives are established by having the key people affected do three things: (1) meet to *agree on the major objectives* for a given period of time (e.g., 1 year, 6 months, or quarterly); (2) *develop plans* for how and when the objectives will be accomplished; and (3) *agree on the "yardsticks"* for determining whether the objectives have been met. Progress reviews are held regularly until the end of the period for which the objectives were established. At that time, those who established objectives at each level in the organization meet to evaluate the results and to agree on the objectives for the next period.[49]

To some, MBO is a complete system of planning and control and a complete philosophy of management.[1,55] In theory, MBO promotes success in each employee because, as each employee succeeds, so do that employee's manager, the department, and the organization. But this is true *only* to the extent that individual, departmental, and organizational goals are compatible.[4] Very few applications of MBO have actually adopted a formal "cascading process" to ensure such a linkage. An effective MBO system takes from 3 to 5 years to implement, and since relatively few firms are willing to make that kind of commitment, it is not surprising that MBO systems often fail.[38]

Work planning and review This is similar to MBO; however, it places greater emphasis on the periodic review of work plans by the supervisor and the subordinate in order to identify goals attained, problems encountered, and the need for training.[52] This was the approach used by Corning, Inc., as described in the chapter opening vignette. Work planning and review is based primarily on each supevisor's judgment about whether a goal has or has not been attained, while MBO relies more on objective, countable evidence. In practice, the two approaches are often indistinguishable. For example, as Table 8-1 illustrates, performance standards are often written with specific percentages to indicate different levels of effectiveness. Even though the standards might be incorporated into an MBO system, if the percentages can be derived *only* on the basis of judgment, then the supposedly

■ **TABLE 8·2**
A SNAPSHOT OF THE ADVANTAGES AND DISADVANTAGES OF ALTERNATIVE APPRAISAL METHODS

Behavior-oriented methods

Narrative essay—Good for individual feedback and development, but difficult to make comparisons across employees.

Ranking and paired comparisons—Good for making comparisons across employees, but provides little basis for individual feedback and development.

Forced distribution—Forces raters to make distinctions among employees, but may be unfair and inaccurate if a group of employees, *as a group*, is either very effective or ineffective.

Behavioral checklist—Easy to use, provides a direct link between job analysis and performance appraisal, can be numerically scored, and facilitates comparisons across employees. However, the meaning of response categories may be interpreted differently by different raters.

Critical incidents—Focuses directly on job behaviors, emphasizes what employees did that was effective or ineffective, but can be very time-consuming to develop.

Graphic rating scales (including BARS)—Easy to use, very helpful for providing feedback for individual development, and facilitate comparisons across employees. BARS very time-consuming to develop, but dimensions and scale points defined clearly. Graphic rating scales often do not define dimensions or scale points clearly.

Results-oriented systems

Management-by-objectives—Focuses on results, and on identifying each employee's contribution to the success of the unit or organization. However, MBO is generally short-term oriented, provides few insights into employee behavior, and does not facilitate comparisons across employees.

Work planning and review—In contrast to MBO, it emphasizes process over outcomes. Requires frequent supervisor-subordinate review of work plans. Time consuming to implement properly, and does not facilitate comparisons across employees.

results-oriented MBO method quickly becomes a more process-oriented work planning and review system. Table 8-2 presents a summary of the appraisal methods we have just discussed.

When Should Each Technique Be Used?

You have just read about a number of alternative appraisal formats, each with its own advantages and disadvantages. At this point you are probably asking yourself, "What's the bottom line? I know that no method is perfect, but what should I do?" First, remember that the rating format is not as important as the relevance and acceptability of the rating system. Second, here is some advice based on systematic comparisons among the various methods.

An extensive review of the research literature that relates the various rating methods to indicators of performance appraisal effectiveness found no clear "winner."[9] However, the researchers were able to provide several "if . . . then" propositions and general statements based on their study. Among these are:

- If employees must be compared across raters for important employment decisions (e.g., promotion, merit pay), then MBO and work planning and review should not be used. They are not based on a standardized rating scheme for all employees.
- If a BARS is used, then diary keeping should also be made a part of the process. This will improve the accuracy of the ratings, and it also will help supervisors distinguish between effective and ineffective employees.
- If objective performance data are available, then MBO is the best strategy to use. Research indicates that work planning and review is not as effective as MBO under these circumstances.
- In general, the best methods of appraisal are the most dificult to use and maintain: BARS and MBO. Recognize, however, that no rating method is foolproof.
- Methods that focus on describing, rather than evaluating, behavior (e.g., BARS, summated rating scales) produce results that are the most interpretable across raters.
- No rating method has been an unqualified success when used as a basis for merit pay or promotional decisions.
- When certain statistical corrections are made, the correlations between scores on alternative rating formats are very high. Hence all the formats measure essentially the same thing.

Which techniques are most popular? A recent survey of 324 organizations in southern California found that among larger organizations 51 percent use rating scales of some sort, 23 percent use essays, 17 percent use MBO, and 9 percent use all other forms of appraisal systems, which included behavioral checklists, forced choice, and rankings.[47]

WHO SHOULD EVALUATE PERFORMANCE?

The most fundamental requirement for any rater is that he or she has an adequate opportunity to observe the ratee's job performance over a reasonable period of time (e.g., 6 months). This suggests several possible raters.

The immediate supervisor If appraisal is done at all, it will probably be done by this person. She or he is probably most familiar with the individual's performance and, in most jobs, has had the best opportunity to observe actual job performance. Furthermore, the immediate supervisor is probably best able to relate the individual's performance to departmental and organizational objectives. Since she or he also is responsible for reward (and punishment) decisions, it is not surprising that feedback from supervisors is more highly related to performance than that from any other source.[6]

Peers In some jobs, such as outside sales, law enforcement, and teaching, the immediate supervisor may observe a subordinate's actual job performance only rarely (and indirectly, through written reports). Sometimes objective indicators, such as number of units sold, can provide useful performance-related information, but in other circumstances the judgment of peers is even better. Peers can provide a perspective on performance that is different from that of immediate supervisors. Thus a police officer's partner is in a far better position to rate day-to-day performance than is a desk-bound sergeant or lieutenant. However, to reduce potential friendship bias while simultaneously increasing the feedback value of the information provided, it is important to specify exactly what the peers are to evaluate[50]—for example, "The quality of her help on technical problems."

Another approach is to require input from a number of colleagues. Thus at Harley-Davidson, salaried workers have five colleagues critique their work.[39] Even when done well, however, peer assessments are probably best considered as only part of a performance appraisal system that includes input from all sources that have unique information or perspectives to offer concerning the job performance of an individual or a work group.

Subordinates Appraisal by subordinates can be a useful input to the immediate supervisor's development. Subordinates know firsthand the extent to which the supervisor *actually* delegates, how well he or she communicates, the type of leadership style he or she is most comfortable with, and the extent to which he or she plans and organizes. Appraisal by subordinates is used regularly by universities (students rate faculty) and by some large firms where managers have many subordinates. In the small firm or in situations where managers have few subordinates, however, it is easy to identify who said what. Thus considerable trust and openness are necessary before subordinate appraisals can pay off. Like peer assessments, they provide only one piece of the appraisal puzzle.

Self-appraisal There are several arguments to recommend wider use of self-appraisals. The opportunity to participate in the performance appraisal process, particularly if appraisal is combined with goal setting, improves the ratee's motivation and reduces her or his defensiveness during the appraisal interview.[14] On the other hand, self-appraisals tend to be more lenient, less variable, and more biased and to show less agreement with the judgments of others.[29,57] Since employees tend to give themselves higher marks than their supervisors do, self-appraisals are probably more appropriate for counseling and development than for personnel decisions.

Clients served In some situations the "consumers" of an individual's or organization's services can provide a unique perspective on job performance. Examples abound: subscribers to a cable television service, bank customers, clients of a brokerage house, and citizens of a local police or fire-protection district. Although the clients' objectives cannot be expected to correspond completely with the organization's objectives, the information that clients provide can provide useful input for personnel decisions, such as regarding promotion, transfer, and need for training. It can also be used to assess the impact of training or as a basis for self-development. At General Electric, for example, the customers of senior managers are interviewed formally and regularly as part of the managers' appraisal process. Their evaluations are important in appraisal, but at the same time they also build commitment, because customers are giving time and information to help GE.[62]

Computers As noted earlier, employees spend a lot of time unsupervised by their bosses. Now technology has made continuous supervision possible—and very real to millions of workers. What sort of technology? Computer software that monitors employee performance.

In summary, several different sources of appraisal information can be used, although they are more useful for some purposes than for others. The various sources and their uses are shown in Table 8-3.

One of the primary sources of information about issues relevant to appraisal is the *attitudes* of those who will be affected by the system. A survey of employees in one federal agency indicated a strong preference for appraisal by immediate supervisors and, to a lesser extent, by the people for whom they provided service. The majority of respondents favored more than one rater, and some felt that peers and subordinates were potentially valid sources of information.[8] Another important consideration is the timing and frequency of performance appraisal.

■ **TABLE 8·3**
SOURCES AND USES OF APPRAISAL DATA

Use	Source				
	Supervisor	Peers	Subordinates	Self	Clients
Personnel decisions	X	X			X
Self-development	X	X	X	X	X
Personnel research	X	X	X		X

USING COMPUTERS TO MONITOR JOB PERFORMANCE

To proponents, it is a great new application of technology to improve productivity. To critics, it represents the ultimate intrusion of Big Brother in the workplace. For several million workers today, being monitored on the job by a computer is a fact of life.[12]

Computers measure quantifiable tasks performed by secretaries, factory and postal workers, and grocery and airline clerks. For example, several airlines regularly monitor the time that reservation agents spend on each call. Until now, lower-level jobs have been affected most directly by computer monitoring. But as software becomes more sophisticated, even engineers, accountants, and doctors are expected to face electronic scrutiny.

Critics feel that overzealous employers will get carried away with information gathering and overstep the boundary between work performance and privacy. Moreover, being watched every second can be stressful, thereby stifling worker creativity, initiative, and morale.

Not everyone views monitoring as a modern-day version of *Modern Times,* the Charlie Chaplin movie where the hapless hero was tyrannized by automation. At the Third National Bank of Nashville, for example, encoding clerks can earn up to 25 percent more than their base pay if their output is high—and they like that system.

To be sure, monitoring itself is neither good nor bad; how managers use it determines its acceptance in the workplace. Practices such as giving employees access to data collected on them and establishing procedures for challenging erroneous records can alleviate the fears of employees.[22] At American Express, for example, monitored employees are given feedback about their performance every 2 weeks.

Managers who impose monitoring standards *without* asking employees what is reasonable may be surprised at the responses of employees. Tactics can include VDT operators who pound the space bar or hold down the underlining bar while chatting, and telephone operators who hang up on customers with complicated problems. The lesson, perhaps, is that even the most sophisticated technology can be thwarted by human beings who feel they are being pushed beyond acceptable limits.[12]

WHEN AND HOW OFTEN SHOULD APPRAISAL BE DONE?

Traditionally, formal appraisal is done once, or at best twice, a year. Research has indicated that once or twice a year is far too infrequent.[52] Unless he or she keeps a diary, considerable difficulties face a rater who is asked to remember what several employees did over the previous 6 or 12 months. This is why firms such as Western Digital, Southern California Gas, and Fluor add frequent, informal "progress" reviews between the annual ones.[39]

Research indicates that if a rater is asked to assess an employee's performance over a 6- to 12-month period, biased ratings may result, especially if information has been stored in the rater's memory according to irrelevant, oversimplistic, or otherwise faulty categories.[53] Unfortunately, faulty categorization seems to be the rule more often than the exception.

For example, consider the impact of prior expectations on ratings.[33] Supervisors of tellers at a large West Coast bank provided predictions about the future job performance of their new tellers. Six months later they rated the job performance of each teller. The result? Inconsistencies between prior expectations and later performance clearly affected the judgments of the raters. Thus when a teller's actual performance disappointed *or* exceeded a supervisor's prior expectations about that performance, ratings were lower than warranted by actual performance. The lesson to be learned is that it is unwise to assume that raters are faulty, but motivationally neutral, observers of on-the-job behavior.

In the survey of federal employees noted earlier, a majority of the employees were dissatisfied with the use of performance data collected once or twice a year for any important personnel decision. A common recommendation was to do appraisals upon the completion of projects or upon the achievement of important milestones in large-scale projects.[8] Such an approach has merit because the appraisals are likely to provide more accurate inputs to personnel decisions, and they have the additional advantage of sending clear messages to employees about where they stand. There should be no "surprises" in appraisals, and one way to ensure this is to do them frequently.

APPRAISAL ERRORS AND RATER TRAINING STRATEGIES

The use of ratings assumes that the human observer is reasonably objective and accurate. As we have seen, raters' memories are quite fallible, and raters subscribe to their own sets of expectations about people, expectations that may or may not be valid. These biases produce rating errors, or deviations betwen the "true" rating an employee deserves and the actual rating assigned.[33] Some of the most common types of rating errors have been discussed previously; these are leniency, severity, and central tendency. Three other types are halo, contrast, and recency errors.

1. *Halo error* is perhaps the most pervasive error in performance appraisal.[28] Raters who commit this error assigned their ratings on the basis of global (good or bad) impressions of ratees. An employee is rated either high or low on *many* aspects of job performance because the rater knows (or thinks she or he knows) that the employee is high or low on some *specific* aspect. Some examples are: If an employee is intelligent, he or she must also be honest; if a female employee is pretty, she must also be talented; the best worker will also be the best trainer of others.

2. *Contrast errors* result when several employees are compared to each other rather than to an objective standard of performance. If, say, the first two workers are unsatisfactory, while the third is average, the third worker may well be rated outstanding because in contrast to the first two, her or his "average" level of job performance is magnified. Likewise, "average" performance could be unfairly

downgraded if the first few workers are outstanding. In both cases, the "average" worker receives a biased rating.

3. *Recency error* results when supervisors assign ratings on the basis of the employee's most recent performance. It is most likely to occur when appraisals are done only after long periods. Here is how one manager described the dilemma of the recency error: "Many of us have trouble rating for the entire year. If one of my people has a stellar three months prior to the review . . . [I] don't want to do anything that impedes that person's momentum and progress" (ref. 48, p. 188). Of course, if the subordinate's performance peaks 3 months prior to appraisal *every year*, then that suggests a different problem!

Traditionally, rater training has focused on teaching raters to eliminate errors. Unfortunately, such programs usually have only short-term effects. Worse yet, training raters to reduce *errors* may actually reduce the *accuracy* of the ratings![54,58] What can be done?

First, emphasis should be placed on training raters to observe behavior more accurately, rather than on showing them "how to" or "how not to" rate. Such an appraisal might proceed as follows:[45]

1. Participants view a videotape of an employee performing his or her job.
2. Participants evaluate the employee on the videotape using rating scales provided.
3. Each participant's ratings are placed on a flip chart.
4. Differences between ratings and reasons for the differences are argued by participants in a discussion led by the trainer.
5. Raters reach a consensus regarding performance standards and relative levels of effective or ineffective behavior.
6. The videotape is shown again.
7. Ratings are reassigned, this time on the basis of specific examples of behavior as recorded by each rater.
8. Ratings are evaluated relative to the earlier consensus judgments of participants.
9. Specific feedback is provided to each participant.

Second, a recent review of 24 studies on rater training found that, in general, the more actively involved the raters become in the training process, the better the outcome.[58] Third, before raters are asked to observe and evaluate the performance of others, they should be encouraged to discuss the performance dimensions on which they will be rating, and they should be given the opportunity to practice rating a sample of job performance. Finally, they should be provided with "true" (or expert) ratings to which they can compare their own ratings.

In short, application of the basic principles of learning is the key to improving the meaningfulness and usefulness of the performance appraisal process.

INTERNATIONAL APPLICATION: THE IMPACT OF NATIONAL CULTURE ON ORGANIZATIONAL PERFORMANCE APPRAISALS

Western expatriate managers are often surprised to learn that their management practices have unintended consequences when applied in non-Western cultures. To illustrate such differences, consider the results of a study of Taiwanese and U.S. business students that examined preferences for various performance appraisal practices.[51]

Compared to Americans, Taiwanese students indicated the following:

- Less support for performance appraisal as practiced in Western cultures
- More focus on group rather than individual performance
- Greater willingness to consider non-performance factors (e.g., off-the-job behaviors, age) as criteria in appraisal
- Less willingness to attribute performance levels to the skills and efforts of particular individuals
- A preference for less open and direct relations between supervisor and subordinate
- An expectation of closer supervisory styles

These results suggest that U.S. managers will need to modify the performance appraisal process that is familiar to them when working with Taiwanese subordinates in order to make it more consistent with Taiwanese values and culture. Such a process recognizes the importance of groups as well as individuals in the organization and honors the criteria of cooperation, loyalty, and attitudes toward superiors, as well as individual goal accomplishment.

SECRETS OF EFFECTIVE APPRAISAL INTERVIEWS

The use of appraisal interviews, at least in terms of company policies on the subject, is widespread. A survey of over 300 companies found that 89 percent require that appraisal results be discussed with employees.[47] As is well known, however, the existence of a policy is no guarantee that it will be implemented. Thus employees reported the following general reactions to appraisal interviews:[21]

- Employees were less certain about where they stood *after* the interview than before it.
- Employees evaluated supervisors less favorably after the interview than before it.
- Few constructive actions or significant improvements resulted from appraisal interviews.

■ Given today's more participative management approaches, the authoritarian tone so common in performance appraisal (PA) interviews is out of date.

These are discouraging findings. The practices they suggest certainly run counter to those espoused in the research literature. Consider just two examples. First, with regard to feedback, we know that feedback is most effective when it is given immediately following the behavior in question.[63] How effective can feedback be if it is given only once a year during an appraisal interview? Second, for over two decades we have known that when managers use a problem-solving approach, subordinates express stronger motivation to improve performance than when other approaches are used.[66] Yet evidence indicates that most organizations still use a "tell-and-sell" approach in which a manager completes an appraisal independently, shows it to the subordinate, justifies the rating, discusses what must be done to improve performance, and then asks for the subordinate's reaction.[65] Are the negative reactions of subordinates really that surprising?

If organizations are really serious about fostering improved job performance as a result of appraisal interviews, then the kinds of activities shown in Table 8-4 are essential *before*, *during*, and *after* appraisals. Let's briefly examine each of these important activities.

■ **TABLE 8-4**
SUPERVISORY ACTIVITIES BEFORE, DURING, AND AFTER APPRAISAL

Before
Communicate frequently with subordinates about their performance.
Get training in performance appraisal interviewing.
Plan to use a problem-solving approach rather than "tell-and-sell."
Encourage subordinates to prepare for PA interviews.

During
Encourage subordinate participation.
Judge performance, not personality and mannerisms.
Be specific.
Be an active listener.
Set mutually agreeable goals for future improvements.
Avoid destructive criticism.

After
Communicate frequently with subordinates about their performance.
Periodically assess progress toward goals.
Make organizational rewards contingent on performance.

Frequent communication Research on the appraisal interview at General Electric indicated clearly that once-a-year performance appraisals are of questionable value and that coaching should be a day-to-day activity[52]—particularly for poor performers or with new employees.[21] Feedback has maximum impact when it is given as close as possible to the action. If a subordinate behaves effectively (ineffectively), tell him or her immediately. Don't file incidents away so that they can be discussed in 6 to 9 months.

Recent research strongly supports this view. Thus one study found that communication of the appraisal in an interview is most effective when the subordinate already has relatively accurate perceptions of her or his performance *before* the session.[35]

Training in appraisal interviewing As we noted earlier, increased emphasis should be placed on training raters to observe behavior more accurately and fairly than on providing specific illustrations of "how to" or "how not to" rate. Training managers to provide evaluative information and to give feedback should focus on managerial characteristics that are difficult to rate and on characteristics that people think are easy to rate but which generally result in disagreements. Such factors include risk taking and development of subordinates.[67] *Use a problem-solving, rather than a "tell-and-sell," approach*, as noted earlier.

Encourage subordinate preparation Research conducted in a large midwestern hospital indicated that subordinates who spent more time prior to appraisal interviews analyzing their job responsibilities and duties, the problems being encountered on the job, and the quality of their performance were more likely to be satisfied with the appraisal process, more likely to be motivated to improve their performance, and more likely actually to improve.[13]

Encourage participation A perception of ownership, a feeling by the subordinate that his or her ideas are genuinely welcomed by the manager, is related strongly to subordinates' satisfaction with the appraisal interview. Participation encourages the belief that the interview was a constructive activity, that some current job problems were cleared up, and that future goals were set.[30,65]

Judge performance, not personality In addition to the potential legal liability of dwelling on personality rather than on job performance, supervisors are far less likely to change a subordinate's personality than they are his or her job performance. Maintain the problem-solving, job-related focus established earlier, for evidence indicates that supervisory support enhances employees' motivation to improve.[26]

Be specific, and be an active listener By being candid and specific, the supervisor offers very clear feedback to the subordinate concerning past actions. She or he also demonstrates knowledge of the subordinate's level of performance and job duties. By being an active listener, the supervisor demonstrates genuine interest

IMPACT OF PERFORMANCE APPRAISAL ON PRODUCTIVITY, QUALITY OF WORK LIFE, AND THE BOTTOM LINE

Performance appraisal is fundamentally a *feedback* process. And research indicates that feedback may result in increases in performance varying from 10 to 30 percent.[43] That is a fairly inexpensive way to improve productivity; but, to work effectively, feedback programs require sustained commitment. The challenge for managers, then, is to provide feedback regularly to all their employees.

The cost of failure to provide such feedback may result in the loss of key professional employees, the continued poor performance of employees who are not meeting performance standards, and a loss of commitment by *all* employees. In sum, the myth that employees know how they are doing without adequate feedback from management can be an expensive fantasy.[64]

in the subordinate's ideas. Active listening requires that you do the following things well: (1) Take the time to listen—hold all phone calls and do not allow interruptions; (2) communicate verbally and nonverbally (e.g., by maintaining eye contact) that you genuinely want to help; (3) as the subordinate begins to tell his or her side of the story, do not interrupt and do not argue; (4) watch for verbal as well as nonverbal cues regarding the subordinate's agreement or disagreement with your message; and (5) summarize what was said and what was agreed to. Specific feedback and active listening are essential to subordinates' perceptions of the fairness and accuracy of appraisals.[42]

Avoid destructive criticism Destructive criticism is general in nature, frequently delivered in a biting, sarcastic tone, and often attributes poor performance to internal causes (e.g., lack of motivation or ability). It leads to three predictable consequences: (1) It produces negative feelings among recipients and can initiate or intensify conflict, (2) it reduces the preference of individuals for handling future disagreements with the giver of the feedback in a conciliatory manner (e.g., compromise, collaboration), and (3) it has negative effects on self-set goals and on feelings of self-confidence.[2] Needless to say, this is one type of communication to avoid.

Set mutually agreeable goals How does goal setting work to improve performance? Studies demonstrate that goals direct attention to the specific performance in question, that they mobilize effort to accomplish higher levels of performance, and that they foster persistence for higher levels of performance.[61] The practical implications of this work are clear: set specific, challenging goals, for this clarifies for the subordinate precisely what is expected and leads to high levels of performance. We cannot change the past, but appraisal interviews that include goal setting and feedback can affect future job performance.

Continue to communicate, and assess progress toward goals regularly Periodic tracking of progress toward goals (e.g., through work planning and review) has three advantages: (1) It helps keep behavior on target, (2) it provides a better understanding of the reasons behind a given level of performance, and (3) it enhances the subordinate's commitment to perform effectively.

Make organizational rewards contingent on performance Research results are clear-cut on this point. If subordinates see a link between appraisal results and personnel decisions regarding issues like merit pay and promotion, they are more likely to *prepare* for appraisal interviews, to *participate* actively in them, and to be *satisfied* with the overall performance appraisal system.[13] Furthermore, managers who base employment decisions on the results of appraisals are likely to overcome their subordinates' negative perceptions of the appraisal process.

■ HUMAN RESOURCE MANAGEMENT IN ACTION
CONCLUSION

A PERFORMANCE MANAGEMENT SYSTEM FOR CORNING, INC.

Five years after the implementation of the Performance Management System, it was still being used, with some minor changes.[7] Four conclusions seem warranted now:

1. The MBO portion of the system needs strengthening through the training of managers. Apparently MBO is not used consistently throughout the organization. This is not surprising in view of the emphasis on performance development and review (PD&R) in the initial introduction of the Performance Management System.

2. PD&R is the strongest and most widely used and accepted portion of the system. Managers perceive it to be very helpful in conducting employee development interviews because the behavioral statements serve as an agenda and as a tool that aids communication. The following steps were taken in the last 2 years to achieve these results:
   a. Corporate policy now requires all managers of salaried employees to conduct a PD&R *prior* to submitting any recommendations regarding salary actions.
   b. Just as human resource specialists talk with supervisors about the performance of their subordinates, they also ask subordinates about the PD&R interview. Constructive comments about the interview are communicated to the manager, and help is provided where necessary. This amounts to continuous feedback about PD&R.
   c. The computer-generated profile of each employee's strengths and weaknesses has been made optional. A common procedure now used is to have subordinates rate themselves on the behavioral statements

prior to the PD&R interviews. During the interview itself, the supervisor and subordinate go through each behavioral statement, compare ratings, and discuss discrepancies.

3. Plans are being made to link PD&R more closely with career planning by developing lists of behaviors particularly important for various jobs. In this way, the review of each employee's strengths and weaknesses will be more meaningful because it can be assessed in relation to potential success in a different job and in relation to decisions about career directions.

4. Top management is using the system, but there seems to be some doubt within top management about the applicability of PD&R's behavioral statements to their level of management. Their acceptance of the system will probably determine its long-term fate.

Flexibility in design and implementation is the most consistent theme underlying the success of the Performance Management System. At a number of junctures changes were made based on information about problems. The deemphasis of the computer-generated employee profile is a good example, as is the recognition of the need for strengthening MBO. This is a useful way to introduce innovations within organizations.

SUMMARY

Performance appraisal is the systematic description of the job-relevant strengths and weaknesses of an individual or group. It serves two major purposes in or-

IMPLICATIONS FOR MANAGEMENT PRACTICE

Throughout this chapter we have emphasized the difficulty of implementing and managing performance appraisal systems. Yet studies show repeatedly that while employees and managers are dissatisfied with the appraisal process, efforts by managers to improve it are seldom rewarded.[40] So a basic issue for every manager is, "What's in it for me?" If organizations are serious about improving the appraisal process, then top management must consider the following policy changes:

1. Make "quality of performance appraisal feedback to subordinates" and "development of subordinates" integral parts of every manager's job description.

2. Tie rewards to effective performance in these areas.

3. Recognize that performance appraisal is a dialogue involving people and data; both political and interpersonal issues are involved. No appraisal method is perfect, but as the Corning vignette illustrates, with management commitment and employee "buy-in," performance management can be a very useful and powerful tool.

ganizations: (1) to improve the job performance of employees and (2) to provide information to employees and managers for use in making decisions. In practice, many PA systems fail because they do not satisfy one or more of the following requirements: relevance, sensitivity, reliability, acceptability, and practicality. The failure is frequently accompanied by legal challenge to the system based on its adverse impact against a protected group.

Many of the problems of performance appraisal can be alleviated through participative development of performance standards that specify, for each job, *what* needs to be done and *how well* it is being done. Appraisals are usually done by immediate supervisors, although other individuals may also have unique perspectives or information to offer. These include peers, subordinates, the clients served, and the employees themselves.

Performance appraisal is done once or twice a year in most organizations, but research indicates that this is far too infrequent. It should be done upon the *completion* of projects or upon the achievement of important milestones. The rating method used depends on the purpose for which the appraisal is intended. Thus comparisons among employees are most appropriate for generating rankings for salary administration purposes, while MBO, work planning and review, and narrative essays are least appropriate for this purpose. For purposes of employee development, critical incidents or behaviorally anchored rating scales are most appropriate. Finally, rating methods that focus on *describing* rather than *evaluating* behavior (e.g., BARS, behavioral checklists) are the most interpretable across raters.

Rater judgments are subject to various types of biases: leniency, severity, central tendency, and halo, contrast, and recency errors. To improve the reliability and validity of ratings, however, emphasis must be placed on training raters to observe behavior more accurately rather than on showing them "how to" or "how not to" rate. To improve the value of appraisal interviews, systematic training for supervisors is essential.

DISCUSSION QUESTIONS

8▪1 How do you recognize an effective performance appraisal system?

8▪2 What are the major human issues involved in appraisal?

8▪3 The chief counsel for a large corporation comes to you for advice. She wants to know under what circumstances the firm's appraisal system is legally most vulnerable. How would you advise her?

8▪4 Working in small groups, develop a set of performance standards for a supermarket checker.

8▪5 Discuss alternative strategies for controlling rater leniency.

8▪6 How can we overcome employee defensiveness in performance appraisal interviews?

8▪7 Can discussions of employee job performance be separated from salary considerations? If so, how?

REFERENCES

1. Albrecht, K. (1978). *Successful management by objectives: An action manual.* Englewood Cliffs, NJ: Prentice-Hall.
2. Baron, R. A. (1988). Negative effects of destructive criticism: Impact on conflict, self-efficacy, and task performance. *Journal of Applied Psychology,* **73**, 199–207.
3. Barrett, G. V., & Kernan, M. C. (1987). Performance appraisal and terminations: A review of court decisions since *Brito v. Zia* with implications for personnel practices. *Personnel Psychology,* **40**, 489–503.
4. Barton, R. F. (1981). An MCDM approach for resolving goal conflict in MBO. *Academy of Management Review,* **6**, 231–241.
5. Beatty, R. W. (1989). Competitive human resource advantage through the strategic management of performance. *Human Resource Planning,* **12**, 179–194.
6. Becker, T. E., & Klimoski, R. J. (1989). A field study of the relationship between the organizational feedback environment and performance. *Personnel Psychology,* **42**, 353–358.
7. Beer, M. et al. (1978). A performance management system: Research design, introduction, and evaluation. *Personnel Psychology,* **31**, 505–535.
8. Bernardin, H. J. (1986). A performance appraisal system. In R. A. Berk (ed.), *Performance assessment.* Baltimore: Johns Hopkins University Press, pp. 277–304.
9. Bernardin, H. J., & Beatty, R. W. (1984). *Performance appraisal: Assessing human behavior at work.* Boston: PWS-Kent.
10. Bernardin, H. J., & Smith, P. C. (1981). A clarification of some issues regarding the development and use of behaviorally anchored rating scales. *Journal of Applied Psychology,* **66**, 458–463.
11. Borman, W. C. (1974). The rating of individuals in organizations: An alternate approach. *Organizational Behavior and Human Performance,* **12**, 105–124.
12. Brophy, B. (1986, Sep. 29). New technology, high anxiety. *U.S. News & World Report,* pp. 54, 55.
13. Burke, R. S., Weitzel, W. & Weir, T. (1978). Characteristics of effective employee performance review and development interviews: Replication and extension. *Personnel Psychology,* **31**, 903–919.
14. Campbell, D. J., & Lee, C. (1988). Self-appraisal in performance evaluation: Development versus evaluation. *Academy of Management Review,* **13**, 302–314.
15. Campbell, J. P., Dunnette, M. D., Lawler, E. E., & Weick, K. E. (1970). *Managerial behavior, performance, and effectiveness.* New York: McGraw-Hill.
16. Carlyle, J. J., & Ellison, T. F. (1984). Developing performance standards. Appendix B. In H. J. Bernardin and R. W. Beatty, *Performance appraisal: Assessing human behavior at work.* Boston: PWS-Kent.
17. Cascio, W. F. (1991). *Applied psychology in personnel management* (4th ed.). Englewood Cliffs, NJ: Prentice-Hall.
18. Cascio, W. F. (1982). Scientific, legal, and operational imperatives of workable performance appraisal systems. *Public Personnel Management,* **11**, 367–375.
19. Cascio, W. F., & Bernardin, H. J. (1981). Implications of performance appraisal litigation for personnel decisions. *Personnel Psychology,* **34**, 211–226.
20. Cascio, W. F., & Serapio, M. G., Jr. (1991, Winter). Human resource systems in an international alliance: The undoing of a done deal? *Organizational Dynamics,* 63–74.
21. Cederblom, D. (1982). The performance appraisal interview: A review, implications, and suggestions. *Academy of Management Review,* **7**, 219–227.

22. Chalykoff J., & Kochan, T. A. (1989). Computer-aided monitoring: Its influence on employee job satisfaction and turnover. *Personnel Psychology*, **42**, 807–834.

23. Cleveland, J. N., Murphy, K. R., & Williams, R. E. (1989). Multiple uses of performance appraisal: Prevalence and correlates. *Journal of Applied Psychology*, **74**, 130–135.

24. Cummings, L. L. (1973). A field experimental study of the effects of two performance appraisal systems. *Personnel Psychology*, **6**, 489–502.

25. DeVries, D. L., Morrison, A. M., Shullman, S. L., & Gerlach, M. L. (1981). *Performance appraisal on the line*. New York: Wiley.

26. Dorfman, P. W., Stephan, W. G., & Loveland, J. (1986). Performance appraisal behaviors: Supervisor perceptions and subordinate reactions. *Personnel Psychology*, **39**, 579–597.

27. Feild, H. S., & Holley, W. H. (1982). The relationship of performance appraisal system characteristics to verdicts in selected employment discrimination cases. *Academy of Management Journal*, **25**, 392–406.

28. Feldman, J. (1986). A note on the statistical correction of halo error. *Journal of Applied Psychology*, **71**, 173–176.

29. Fox, S., & Dinur, Y. (1988). Validity of self-assessment: A field evaluation. *Personnel Psychology*, **41**, 581–592.

30. Greller, M. M. (1978). The nature of subordinate participation in the appraisal interview. *Academy of Management Journal*, **22**, 646–658.

31. Guion, R. M. (1986). Personnel evaluation. In R. A. Berk (ed.), *Performance assessment*. Baltimore: Johns Hopkins University Press, pp. 345–360.

32. Heneman, R. L. (1986). The relationship between supervisory ratings and results-oriented measures of performance: A meta-analysis. *Personnel Psychology*, **39**, 811–826.

33. Hogan, E. A. (1987). Effects of prior expectations on performance ratings: A longitudinal study. *Academy of Management Journal*, **30**, 354–368.

34. Hymowitz, C. (1985, Jan. 17). Bosses: Don't be nasty (and other tips for reviewing a worker's performance). *Wall Street Journal*, p. 28.

35. Ilgen, D. R., Mitchell, T. R., & Frederickson, J. W. (1981). Poor performers: Supervisors' and subordinates' responses. *Organizational Behavior and Human Performance*, **27**, 386–410.

36. Jacobs, R., Kafry, D., & Zedeck, S. (1980). Expectations of behaviorally anchored rating scales. *Personnel Psychology*, **33**, 595–640.

37. Kavanagh, M. J. (1982). Evaluating performance. In K. M. Rowland & G. R. Ferris (eds.), *Personnel management*. Boston: Allyn & Bacon, pp. 187–226.

38. Kondrasuk, J. N. (1981). Studies in MBO effectiveness. *Academy of Management Review*, **6**, 419–430.

39. Labor Letter (1990, Oct. 16). *The Wall Street Journal*, p. A1.

40. Labor Letter (1987, Dec. 22). *The Wall Street Journal*, p. 1.

41. Labor letter (1984, Aug. 28). *The Wall Street Journal*, p. 1.

42. Landy, F. J., Barnes-Farrell, J., & Cleveland, J. N. (1980). Perceived fairness and accuracy of performance evaluation: A follow-up. *Journal of Applied Psychology*, **65**, 355–356.

43. Landy, F. J., Farr, J. L., & Jacobs, R. R. (1982). Utility concepts in performance measurement. *Organizational Behavior and Human Performance*, **30**, 15–40.

44. Landy, F. J., & Rastegary, H. (1988). Criteria for selection. In M. Smith & I. Robertson (eds.), *Advances in personnel selection and assessment*. New York: Wiley.

45. Latham, G. P., Wexley, K. N., & Pursell, E. D. (1975). Training managers to minimize rating errors in the observation of behavior. *Journal of Applied Psychology*, **60**, 550–555.
46. Levinson, P. (1979). *A guide for improving performance appraisal*. Washington, DC: Office of Personnel Management, USGPO, Stock No. 006-000-01121-7.
47. Locher, A. H., & Teel, K. S. (1988, September). Appraisal trends. *Personnel Journal*, pp. 139–145.
48. Longenecker, C. O., Sims, H. P., Jr., & Gioia, D. A. (1987). Behind the mask: The politics of employee appraisal. *Academy of Management Executive*, **1**, 183–193.
49. McConkie, M. L. (1979). A clarification of the goal-setting and appraisal process in MBO. *Academy of Management Review*, **4**, 29–40.
50. McEvoy, G. M., & Buller, P. F. (1987). User acceptance of peer appraisals in an industrial setting. *Personnel Psychology*, **40**, 785–787.
51. McEvoy, G. M., & Cascio, W. F. (1990). The United States and Taiwan: Two different cultures look at performance appraisal. *Research in Personnel and Human Resources Management*. Supplement 2, pp. 201–219.
52. Meyer, H. H., Kay, E., & French, J. R. P. (1965). Split roles in performance appraisal. *Harvard Business Review*, **43**, 123–129.
53. Mount, M. K., & Thompson, D. E. (1987). Cognitive categorization and quality of performance ratings. *Journal of Applied Psychology*, **72**, 240–246.
54. Murphy, K. R., & Balzer, W. K. (1989). Rater errors and rating accuracy. *Journal of Applied Psychology*, **74**, 619–624.
55. Odiorne, G. S. (1965). *Management by objectives: A system of managerial leadership*. Belmont, CA: Fearon.
56. Schneider, S. C. (1988). National versus corporate culture: Implications for human resource management. *Human Resource Management*, **27**, 231–246.
57. Shore, L. M., & Thornton, G. C., III. (1986). Effects of gender on self- and supervisory ratings. *Academy of Management Journal*, **29**, 115–129.
58. Smith, D. E. (1986). Training programs for performance appraisal: A review. *Academy of Management Review*, **11**, 22–40.
59. Stockford, L., & Bissell, H. W. (1949). Factors involved in establishing a merit rating scale. *Personnel*, **26**, 94–116.
60. *Stone v. Xerox* (1982). 685 F. 2d 1387 (11th Cir.).
61. Tubbs, M. E. (1986). Goal setting: A meta-analytic examination of the empirical evidence. *Journal of Applied Psychology*, **71**, 474–483.
62. Ulrich, D. (1989, summer). Tie the corporate knot: Gaining complete customer commitment. *Sloan Management Review*, **10**(4), 19–27.
63. *United States v. City of Chicago* (1978). 573 F. 2d 416 (7th Cir.).
64. Walther, F., & Taylor, S. (1983). An active feedback program can spark performance. *Personnel Administrator*, **28**(6), 107–111, 147–149.
65. Wexley, K. N. (1986). Appraisal interview. In R. A. Berk (ed.), *Performance assessment*. Baltimore: Johns Hopkins University Press, pp. 167–185.
66. Wexley, K. N., Singh, V. P., & Yukl, G. A. (1973). Subordinate participation in three types of appraisal interviews. *Journal of Applied Psychology*, **58**, 54–57.
67. Wohlers, A. J., & London, M. (1989). Ratings of managerial characteristics: Evaluation, difficulty, co-worker agreement, and self-awareness. *Personnel Psychology*, **42**, 235–261.
68. Zedeck, S., & Cascio, W. F. (1982). Performance appraisal decisions as a function of rater training and purpose of the appraisal. *Journal of Applied Psychology*, **67**, 752–758.

Managing Careers

CORPORATE CAREER MANAGEMENT COMES OF AGE*

In the past several years companies have begun to take a more active, systematic approach to the career development of their employees. This new approach is based on an underlying assumption that would have been considered heresy 10 or 20 years ago—that each employee is responsible for his or her own career development.

In the past, many companies assumed responsibility for the career pathing and growth of their employees. The company determined to what position, and at what speed, people would advance. That approach worked reasonably well in the corporate climate of the 1950s and 1960s. However, the corporate disruptions of the recent past have rendered this approach to employee career development largely unworkable. Acquisitions, divestitures, rapid growth, and downsizing have left many companies unable to deliver on the implicit career promises made to their employees. Organi-

*Adapted from: *Human Resource Consulting Group, Inc. Newsletter,* January, 1987, pp. 1, 2.

zations find themselves in the painful position of having to renege on career mobility opportunities their employees had come to expect. In extreme cases, employees who expected career growth no longer even had jobs!

Increasingly, corporations have come to realize that they cannot win if they take total responsibility for the career development of their employees. The old strategy of controlling the career growth of employees from "hire" to "retire" does not work anymore. In today's turbulent times, companies have found that they cannot even continue to provide jobs for them. No matter what happens, employees often blame top management or "the company" for their own suboptimal career growth.

One company changed its approach to career growth as a result of pressure from its professional workforce. Employees felt suffocated by 20+ years of management determining people's career progress for them. Task teams worked with top management to develop career self-management training for employees, and career counseling skills for managers. As a result, increases in employee productivity, enhanced morale, and decreased turnover of key employees has more than justified the new approach to employee career management.

CHARACTERISTICS OF THE NEW APPROACH

A key feature of the new career management concept is that the company and the employee are *partners* in career development. Employees are responsible for knowing what their skills and capabilities are, what assistance they need from their employers, asking for that assistance, and preparing themselves to assume new responsibilities.

Although primary and final responsibility for career development rests with each employee, the company has complementary responsibilities. The company is responsible for communicating to employees where it wants to go and how it plans to get there (the corporate strategy), providing employees with as much information about the business as possible, and responding to the career initiatives of employees with candid, complete information. One of the most important contributions a company can make to each employee's development is to provide him or her with *honest* performance feedback about current job performance.

This approach to career management can be summed up as follows: Assign employees the responsibility for managing their own careers, then provide the support they need to do it. This support takes different forms in different companies, but usually contains several core components.

Challenges

1. Should employees be responsible for their own career development?
2. Is the new approach to corporate career management likely to be a passing fad, or is it here to stay?

3. What kinds of support mechanisms are necessary to make career self-management work?

QUESTIONS THIS
CHAPTER WILL
HELP MANAGERS
ANSWER

1. What strategies might be used to help employees "self-manage" their careers?
2. What can supervisors do to improve their management of dual-career couples?
3. What steps can managers take to do a better job of responding to the special needs of workers in their early, mid-, and late career stages?
4. How can layoffs be handled in the most humane way?

As the chapter opening vignette demonstrates, corporate career management has come a long way in the last several decades. This chapter presents a number of topics that have sparked this reevaluation. We will consider the impact of mergers, acquisitions, and downsizing on corporate loyalty, the impact of dual-career couples on the career management process, and the major issues that workers and managers must deal with during the early, middle, and late career stages of the adult life cycle. Finally we will examine alternative patterns of career change: promotions, demotions, lateral transfers, relocations, layoffs, and retirements. Career management has many facets, both for the individual and for the organization. The chapter opening vignette emphasized that in the new concept of career management the company and the employee are partners in career development. This theme is emphasized throughout the chapter. Let's begin by attempting to define what is meant by the word "career."

TOWARD A DEFINITION OF "CAREER"

In everyday parlance, the word "career" is used in a number of different ways. People speak of "pursuing a career"; "career planning" workshops are common; colleges and universities hold "career days," during which they publicize jobs in different fields and assist individuals through "career counseling." A person may be characterized as a "career" woman or man who shops in a store that specializes in "career clothing." Likewise, a person may be characterized as a "career military officer." We may overhear a person say, "That movie 'made' his career" (i.e., it enhanced his reputation), or in a derogatory tone, after a subordinate has insulted the CEO, "She can kiss her career goodbye" (i.e., she has tarnished her reputation). Finally, an angry supervisor may remark to her dawdling subordinate, "Watney, are you going to make a career out of changing that light bulb?"

As these examples illustrate, the word "career" can be viewed from a number of different perspectives. From one perspective *a career is a sequence of positions occupied by a person during the course of a lifetime.* This is the *objective* career. From another perspective, though, *a career consists of the changes in values, attitudes, and motivation that occur as a person grows older.*[35] This is the *subjective* career. Both of these perspectives, objective and subjective, focus on the individual. Both assume that people have some degree of control over their destinies, that they can manipulate opportunities in order to maximize the success and satisfaction derived from their careers.[33] They assume further that HR activities should recognize career stages and assist employees with the development tasks they face at each stage. Career planning is important because *the consequences of career success or failure are linked closely with each individual's self-concept, identity, and satisfaction with career and life.*

Not surprisingly, therefore, career development and planning have become "big business" in organizations over the past few years. Here are some reasons why:[73]

1. Rising concerns for quality of work life and for personal life planning
2. Equal employment opportunity legislation and affirmative action pressures
3. Rising educational levels and occupational aspirations, coupled with
4. Slow economic growth and reduced advancement opportunities

CAREER MANAGEMENT BY ORGANIZATIONS

A career is not something that should be left to each employee; instead, it should be *managed* by the organization to ensure efficient allocation of human and capital resources.[5,60] But what is the meaning of "career success"?

Toward a Definition of "Career Success"

Workers in the United States want more from their jobs than money; they want to be able to afford a "decent lifestyle." Loyalty to owner, manager, or organization, in many cases, is temporary. Many high-tech workers, with the help of executive search firms, move all over the country. Some industries have developed work styles that stand in stark contrast to traditional work styles. The tradition-oriented "organization man" of the 1950s had a clear definition of success and a stable model for achieving it. However, the "system-oriented" employees of the 1980s and 1990s have enjoyed sufficient material security to explore alternative models of career success, and they are confronted with a variety of possibilities. As a consequence, organizations are finding today's employees harder to manage. But they are also finding them to be highly motivated and committed to tasks that they value.[20,91]

In practical terms, what does all this mean for the concept of development and success in the work career? Is it occupational success? Job satisfaction? Growth and development of skills? Successful movement through various life stages? Traditionally, career development and success have been defined in terms of *occupational advancement*, which is clear and easy to measure. However, demographers have some unarguable and disturbing news: For people born between 1945 and 1964, the 1990s will be a decade of scarce promotions, frustrated expectations, and job hopping.

Two main forces are behind this trend. Responding to tougher global competition and the threat of being taken over, companies thinned out management ranks to become more efficient and profitable during the 1980s. That means less hierarchy and fewer rungs on the corporate ladder. At the same time, the large number of baby boomers (those born between 1945 and 1964), including record numbers of business school graduates, have come of age and are competing for the remaining rungs.[43] The result? Human resource management problems that organizations have never faced before. The impact on employees will be more stress, more burnout, and more psychological withdrawal. Alternative means of satisfying employees' career aspirations will be needed. Ultimately career success may be defined by each organization in terms of the career programs it creates.[35] The following section examines career management from the individual's perspective; by way of background to this, let's consider adult life-cycle stages.

Adult Life-Cycle Stages

For years, researchers have attempted to identify the major developmental tasks that employees face during their working lives and to organize these tasks into broader career stages (such as early, mid-, and late career). Although a number of models have been proposed, very little research has tested their accuracy. Moreover, there is little, if any, agreement about whether career stages are linked to age or not. Most theorists give age ranges for each stage, but these vary widely. Consequently, it may make more sense to think in terms of career stages linked to time. This would allow a "career clock" to begin at different points for different individuals, based on their backgrounds and experiences.[60]

Such an approach allows for differences in the number of distinct stages through which individuals may pass, the overlapping tasks and issues that they may face at each stage, and the role of transition periods between stages.[73] The lesson for managers is that all models of adult life-cycle stages should be viewed as broad guidelines rather than as exact representations of reality.

CAREER MANAGEMENT: INDIVIDUALS FOCUSING ON THEMSELVES

In thinking about career management, it is important to emphasize the increasingly *temporary* relationships between individuals and organizations. If, as a consequence, organizations are less powerful in providing traditional career guidance, then ultimate responsibility for career development reverts to the individual. Unfortunately, few individuals are technically prepared (and willing) to handle this assignment. This is not surprising, for very few college programs address specifically the problems of managing one's own career. However, as long as it remains difficult for organizations to match the career expectations of their employees (a following section shows actual corporate examples of this), one option for employees will be to switch organizations. Guidelines for doing this fall into the following three major categories.[79]

MERGERS, ACQUISITIONS, RESTRUCTURINGS, AND THE DEMISE OF CORPORATE LOYALTY

Thousands of mergers and acquisitions, among both large and small companies, took place during the 1980s. After most of the buyouts, the merged company eliminates staff duplications and unprofitable divisions.[75] Restructuring, including downsizing, often leads to similar effects—diminished loyalty from employees.[48] In the wave of takeovers, mergers, downsizings, and layoffs, thousands of workers have discovered that years of service mean little to a struggling management or to a new corporate parent. This leads to a rise in stress and to a decrease in satisfaction, commitment, intentions to stay, and perceptions of an organization's trustworthiness, honesty, and caring about its employees.[77]

Companies counter that today's competitive business environment makes it difficult to protect workers. Indeed, some companies see the *overly* loyal employee as a detriment: someone who shuns risk, blindly follows corporate policies, and refrains from expressing himself or herself. Understandably, organizations are streamlining in order to become more competitive by cutting labor costs and to become more flexible in their response to the demands of the marketplace. But the rising disaffection of workers at all levels has profound implications for employers.

It may manifest itself in relatively minor matters, such as an employee's refusal to relocate. Or it may result in an employee's departure, now estimated to cost as much as $65,000 in the case of a middle manager.[65] Such defections are spreading to companies that once had ironclad loyalty. Since the breakup of the Bell System, annual turnover at AT&T has more than tripled, to 13 percent. When Du Pont Company offered a generous early retirement plan to its 113,000 domestic employees, the chemical giant was overwhelmed: 11,200 elected to leave, about twice as many as the company had expected. Among high-tech workers, many are more loyal to their technology than to their employers. In California's Silicon Valley, for example, employee turnover at 231 electronics companies averages 27 percent, more than 5 times the departure rate for all U.S. manufacturing.[65] The result? Average job tenure fell from 12 years in 1981 to 9 in 1988. Soon managers will hold 7 to 10 jobs in a lifetime, up from 3 to 4 in the 1970s.[27] As one observer noted, "People used to be able to count on the organization and its stability. But the myth that institutions will take care of us has been shattered" (ref. 65, p. 29).

Select a Field of Employment and an Employer

1. You cannot manage your career unless you have a macro, long-range objective. The first step, therefore, is to think in terms of where you ultimately want to be, recognizing, of course, that your career goals will change over time.

2. View every potential employer and position in terms of your long-range career goal. That is, how well does this job serve to position me in terms of my ultimate objective?

For example, if you aspire to reach senior management by the year 2000, consider the extent to which your current job helps you develop a global orientation, develop public speaking skills, practice the "bring out the best in people" leadership style, and learn to manage cultural diversity. These are now, and will continue to be, key requirements for such senior positions.[1]

3. Accept short-term trade-offs for long-term benefits. Some low-paying jobs can provide extremely valuable training opportunities or career contacts.

4. Consider carefully whether to accept highly specialized jobs or isolated job assignments that might restrict or impede your career development.

Know Where You Are

1. Always be aware of opportunities available to you in your current position—e.g., training programs that might further your career development.

2. Carefully and honestly assess your current performance. How do you see yourself, and how do you think higher management sees your performance?

3. Try to recognize when you and your organization have outlived your utility for one another. This is not an admission of failure but rather an honest reflection of the fact that there is little more the organization can do for you, and, in turn, that your contribution to the organization has reached a point of diminishing returns.

Here are five important symptoms: You're not excited by what you are doing, advancement is blocked, your organization is poorly managed and is losing market share, you feel that you are not adequately rewarded for your work, or you are not fulfilling your dreams.[69]

Plan Your Exit

1. Try to leave at *your* convenience, not the organization's. To do this you must do two things well: (a) know when it is time to leave (as before) and (b) be aware of career opportunities that fit into your long-range career plan.

2. Leave your current organization on good terms and not under questionable circumstances.

3. Don't leave your current job until you've landed another one, for it's easier to find a new job when you're currently employed. Like bank loans, jobs often go to people who don't seem to need them.[69]

Up to this point it may sound like managing your career is all one-sided. This is not true; the organization should be a proactive force in this process. To do so, organizations must think and plan in terms of shorter employment relationships. This can be done, as it often is in professional sports, through fixed-term employment contracts, with options for renegotiation and extension.

A second strategy for organizations is to invest adequate time and energy in job design and equipment. Given that mobility among workers is expected to increase, careful attention to these elements will make it easier to make replacements fully productive as soon as possible. How does the self-management of careers work in practice? If Hewlett-Packard's experience is any indication, we can expect to see more of it in the future.

HELPING EMPLOYEES SELF-MANAGE
THEIR CAREERS AT HEWLETT-PACKARD

A 3-month course in personal career management was developed at Hewlett-Packard's Colorado Springs Division based on two methods: self-assessment and subsequent application of findings to the workplace to chart a career path for each employee.[89]

The idea of self-assessment as the first step toward career planning is certainly not new. Self-help books have flooded the market for years. However, books alone lack a critical ingredient for success: *the emotional support of a group setting* where momentum and motivation can be shared and maintained. Make no mistake about it, self-assessment can be a grueling process.

Hewlett-Packard uses six devices to generate data for self-assessment (based on earlier work for a second-year Harvard MBA course in career development). These include:

- *A written self-interview.* Participants are given 11 questions about themselves, they are asked to provide facts about their lives (people, places, events), and they are asked to discuss the future and the transitions they have made. This autobiographical sketch provides core data for the subsequent analysis.
- *Strong-Campbell Interest Inventory.* Participants complete this 325-item instrument to determine their preferences about occupations, academic subjects, types of people, and so forth. An interest profile is developed for each individual by comparing her or his responses to those of successful people in a wide range of occupations.
- *Allport-Vernon-Lindzey Study of Values.* Each participant makes 45 choices among competing values in order to measure the relative strength of theoretical, economic, aesthetic, social, political, and religious values.
- *24-hour diaries.* Participants log their activities during one workday and also during one nonworkday. This information is used to confirm, or occasionally to contradict, information from the other sources.
- *Interviews with two "significant others."* Each participant asks a friend, spouse, relative, coworker, or someone else of importance questions about himself or herself. The two interviews are tape-recorded.
- *Lifestyle representations.* Participants depict their lifestyles using words, photos, drawings, or whatever else they choose.

A key ingredient in this program is its emphasis on an *inductive* approach. That is, the program begins by generating new data about each participant, rather than by starting with generalizations and deducing from them more specific information about each person. The process proceeds from the specific to the general (inductive), rather than from the general to the specific (deductive). Participants slowly recognize generalizations or themes within the large amounts of information they have produced. They come to tentative conclusions about these themes, first in each device individually and then in all the workshop's instruments as a whole, by analyzing the data they have collected.[89]

Following the self-assessment, department managers interview subordinates to learn about their career objectives. They record these objectives and describe the people and positions currently in their departments. This information is then available for senior management to use in devising an overall human resource plan, defining skills required, and including a timetable. When data on the company's future needs are matched against each employee's career objectives, department managers can help employees chart a career course in the company (e.g., through training or additional job experience). Career development objectives for each employee are incorporated into performance objectives for future performance appraisals. The department head monitors the employee's career progress as part of the review process, and she or he is responsible for offering all possible support.

RESULTS OF THE CAREER SELF-MANAGEMENT PROGRAM

Senior managers at Hewlett-Packard found that after the workshops they had far more flexibility in moving employees than previously. The company was able either to give employees reasons to stay where they were, to develop a new path for them in the company, or to help them move out. Significantly, the Colorado Springs Division's overall turnover rate was unchanged in the year following the workshops. At an estimated $40,000 replacement cost for a departing middle manager, this was a welcome finding.

Within 6 months after the course, 37 percent of the participants had advanced to new jobs within the company, while 40 percent planned moves within the following 6 months. Of those who advanced, 74 percent credited the program for playing a significant part in their job change. The workshops also helped the company meet its affirmative action targets since the sessions were open to all employees who expressed an interest in career development.

Perhaps the most persuasive reason for helping employees manage their own careers is the need to remain competitive. Although it might seem like a contradiction, such efforts can enhance a company's stability by developing more purposeful, self-assured employees. As noted earlier, today's employees are more difficult to manage. Companies that recognize the need to provide employees with satisfying opportunities will have the decided advantage of a loyal and industrious workforce.

One of the most challenging career management problems that organizations face today is that of the dual-career couple. Let's examine this issue in detail.

Dual-Career Couples: Problems and Opportunities

Dual-career couples face the problems of managing work and family responsibilities. Furthermore, it appears that there may be an interaction effect that compounds the problems and stresses of each separate career.[33] This implies that, by itself, career planning and development may be meaningless unless an employee's role as a family member also is considered, particularly when this role conflicts with work activities.[58] What can be done?

Research indicates that if dual-career couples are to manage their family responsibilities successfully, they must be flexible; they must be mutually committed to both careers; they must adopt coping mechanisms (e.g., separating work and nonwork roles clearly, accepting all role demands as given and finding ways to meet them); and they must develop the competencies to manage their careers through career information and planning, goal setting, and problem solving.[36,78]

From an organizational perspective, successful management of the dual-career couple requires (1) flexible work schedules, (2) special counseling, (3) training for supervisors in career counseling skills, and (4) the establishment of support structures for transfers and relocations. What have organizations actually done?

As part of a package deal, many companies provide assistance to the "trailing" spouse in finding a suitable job consistent with the spouse's career plans. Unisys pays up to $500 for résumé writing and job hunting help for a trailing spouse. U.S. West offers as much as $2500, including insuring against home-sale losses. Cigna will cover a month's pay at the spouse's former salary, while he or she seeks a new job.[51]

Alternatively, companies that have eliminated the nepotism taboo might hire the trailing spouse themselves. This may be a strategy for attracting and retaining top talent, particularly in technical occupations, which more women are entering. Thus a national survey done for General Electric found that 50 percent of all female technologists were married to technologists. However, another reason for the elimination of no-spouse rules is that they have come under attack in the courts on the grounds that they amount to illegal discrimination on the basis of gender. Women are usually the ones who are forced to leave a company or are not hired in the first place.[53] The hiring of couples seems to work best at large concerns, where more jobs are available and it is easier physically to separate spouses from each other in different offices or buildings. This makes it easier to conform to most firms' policies on this issue: *An employee cannot be placed under the direct or indirect supervision of a spouse.* The advantages of hiring both spouses are:

- It helps lure prospective employees to remote communities where suitable jobs for a spouse might be hard to find.
- It cuts recruiting and relocation costs.

■ It encourages executives already on board to accept transfers.

■ It makes employees less susceptible to offers from rival firms.

However, like any other HR policy, the advantages of spouse hiring need to be weighed against the following disadvantages:[18,26]

■ There is considerable risk that disciplining or firing one spouse will cause the other to leave as well.

■ Outplacement assistance for one spouse as a result of a layoff may in reality become outplacement assistance for both spouses, if the other voluntarily quits.

■ Couples employed by the same firm may encounter tremendous strains when one of them encounters problems at work. The partner cannot just say, "This is between you and your boss; I don't want to get into the middle of it."

■ Couples worry that in matters of promotion, transfer, and compensation they will be seen by the company as a team, instead of as individuals.

Although many organizations have been very progressive in the management of dual-career couples, there are also several things that organizations have *not* done. Few firms provide training for supervisors on how to deal with employees who are partners in dual-career couples. Such training is important, for research indicates that when a wife works, the husband often develops lower levels of job and life satisfaction.[81] Wives' employment boosts the mental health of wives but often depresses the mental health of husbands. Why? Some husbands may not yet be ready to abandon the "good provider" role: that is, the traditional role of being sufficiently resourceful as a provider for one's family that one's wife does not *have* to enter the labor force.

In addition to supervisory training, relatively few firms provide job sharing or child care. With regard to child care, demand for the service has never been greater. However, only 2 percent of U.S. workplaces with 10 or more employees (25,000 businesses) have employer-sponsored child-care centers.[44] Among companies with 100 or more employees, only 10 percent offer any child-care or parenting assistance.[3] Here are some reasons why employer-supported child care will continue to grow:

■ Dual-career couples now comprise a preponderance of the workforce.[68]

■ There has been a significant rise in the number of single parents, over half of whom use child-care facilities.

■ More and more, career-oriented women are arranging their lives to include motherhood *and* professional goals.

For firms considering child care, here are three options:[29]

1. Set up a clearinghouse for information about child care available in the local community.

2. Refer employees to existing day-care facilities in the community at a reduced rate. The rate can be reduced by negotiating with one or more local providers, by paying a company subsidy of 10 to 50 percent to the providers, or by giving the employees vouchers that reimburse any local center 100 percent of the child-care expenses.

3. The employer may provide a child-care center on or near the worksite.

To assess the quality of child care provided, parents should actually see the facility to be used. Safety, nutritious food, child curriculum and activities, parent involvement, and space and equipment are key areas to probe.[2]

Employers who presently provide some form of child-care assistance report the following *advantages*:

- Tax savings (the Economic Recovery Tax Act of 1981 allows employers to deduct the cost of child-care benefits, both for on-site and for referral subsidies)
- Reduced turnover
- Improved morale and employer–employee relations
- Effective recruitment tool
- Positive community image

However, there are also *disadvantages* to providing child care. These include:[2]

- The equity of benefits (not all employees can take advantage of employer-assisted child care)
- The company expense of voucher and vendor plans.
- The substantial expense of the on-site option.
- Considerable liability exposure for employers providing on-site child care. The latter disadvantage is probably more myth than reality. Thus one study found that estimates of liability insurance by companies that do not have child-care centers were 6 times higher than the actual amounts. Such costs average about 1 to 3 percent of a center's operating budget. According to the general liability manager of Allstate Insurance Co.: "Businesses are not exposed to any more loss than they have in normal operations."[44]
- Lack of evidence in well-controlled studies that child care increases employee productivity or reduces absenteeism or lateness.[31,61]

Indeed, the lesson from two recent studies is clear: Don't expect that a day-care center or a flexible schedule will keep women managers from leaving corporations. They may be quite willing to throw corporate loyalty to the wind if they aren't getting adequate opportunities for career growth and job satisfaction.[87]

Managing dual-career couples, from an individual as well as from an organizational perspective, is difficult. But if current conditions are any indication of long-term trends, then we can be quite sure of one thing: This "problem" is not going to go away.

CAREER MANAGEMENT: ORGANIZATIONS FOCUSING ON INDIVIDUALS

In this section we will examine current organizational practices used to manage workers at various stages of their careers. Let's begin by considering organizational entry.

Organizational Entry

Once a person has entered the workforce, the next stage is to enter a specific organization, to settle down, and to begin establishing a career there. *Entry* refers to the process of "moving inside," or becoming more involved in a particular organization.[76] To do this well, a process known as socialization is essential. *Socialization* refers to the mutual adaptation of the new employee and the new employer to one another. Learning organizational policies, norms, traditions, and values is an important part of the process. Getting to know one's peers, supervisor, and subordinates is, too. Over time, organizations adapt to new employees—e.g., the younger generation, the older employee, the hard-core unemployed. Since most turnover occurs *early* in a person's tenure with an organization, programs that accelerate socialization will tend also to reduce early turnover (i.e., at entry) and therefore reduce a company's overall turnover rate.

Two of the most effective methods for doing this are realistic job previews (see Chapter 5) and new-employee orientation (see Chapter 7). A third is "mentoring." A mentor is a teacher, an advisor, a sponsor, and a confidante.[13,42] He or she should be bright and well-seasoned enough to understand the dynamics of power and politics in the organization and also be willing to share this knowledge with a new hire. Organizations should actively promote mentor relationships and provide sufficient time for the mentor and the new hire to meet on a regularly scheduled basis, at least initially. The mentor's role is to teach the new hire "the ropes," to provide candid feedback on how he or she is being perceived by others, and to serve as a confidential "sounding board" for dealing with work-related problems. If successful, mentor relationships can help reduce the inflated expectations that newcomers often have about organizations, can relieve the stress experienced by all new hires, and, best of all, can improve the newcomer's chances for survival in the organization.

Unfortunately, women and blacks often find themselves excluded from mentoring relationships. Part of the difficulty is that mentoring is frequently based on friendship, admiration, and nurturing developed outside a 9-to-5 schedule. As one minority recruitment firm noted, "Whites usually don't see blacks at the beach, sailing, or on weekends, because they lead separate lives away from the job."[22] Moreover, some men hesitate to take on female protégés because of the sexual innuendoes that often accompany such relationships.

This may be changing, as firms like Bank of America try to overcome the barriers by assigning mentors to three or four promising young executives for a year at a time. While such company intervention may turn out to be fruitless, just being picked as a mentor, according to one 35-year-old female branch bank manager, boosted her self-esteem. This is a central goal of any mentoring effort.

Early Career: The Impact of the First Job

Many studies of early careers focus on the first jobs to which new employees were assigned. The positive impact of initial job challenge upon later career success and retention has been found many times in a wide variety of settings. Among engineers, challenging early work assignments were related to strong initial performance as well as to the maintenance of competence and performance throughout the engineer's career.[64] In other words, challenging initial job assignments are an antidote to career obsolescence.

The characteristics of the first supervisor are also critical. He or she must be personally secure, unthreatened by the new subordinate's training, ambition, and energy, and able to communicate company norms and values.[76] Beyond that, the supervisor ideally should be able to play the roles of coach, feedback provider, trainer, role model, and protector in an accepting, esteem-building manner.[33]

One other variable affects the likelihood of obtaining a high-level job later in one's career: *initial aspirations*.[74] Employees should be encouraged to "aim high" because, in general, higher aspirations lead to higher performance. Parents, teachers, employers, and friends should therefore avoid discouraging so-called impractical aspirations.

IMPACT OF THE FIRST JOB ON LATER CAREER SUCCESS

■ **COMPANY EXAMPLE**

For over 20 years researchers generally accepted the view that unless an individual has a challenging first job and receives quick, early promotions, the entire career will suffer. This is a "tournament" model of upward mobility. It assumes that everyone has an equal chance in the early contests but that the losers are not eligible for later contests, at least not those of the major tournament. An alternative model is called "signaling" theory. It suggests three cues ("signals") that those responsible for promotion may use: (1) prior history of promotions (a signal of ability), (2) functional-area background, and (3) number of different jobs held.

A recent study examined the patterns of early upward mobility for 180 employees of an oil company over an 11-year period.[25] The company's very detailed job classification systems and actual salary grades served as measures of career attainment. The results generally did not support the tournament model of career mobility, because the losers—those passed over in the early periods—were later able to move up quickly. Rather, the results were more analogous to a horse race: position out of the gate had relatively little effect in comparison to position entering the home stretch.

Different mobility patterns for administration and technical personnel helped to explain why the pattern of the early years did not always persist. Those who started early in administrative positions began to move up early, but also plateaued early. A technical background meant a longer wait before upward movement, followed by relatively rapid promotion. The number of different positions held also predicted higher attainment.

In summary, one's past position, functional background, and number of different jobs all seem to act as signals to those making decisions about promotions. All were related strongly to career attainment. Together they accounted for over 60 percent of the variability in promotions.

Managing Men and Women in Midcareer

The theory that a crisis occurs in the lives of U.S. workers between the ages of 35 and 50 is well supported by research. The crisis is variously known as "middlescence," "middle-age crisis," and "midlife transition." The following issues may arise at this stage:[8]

- Awareness of advancing age and awareness of death
- Awareness of bodily changes related to aging
- Knowing how many career goals have been or will be attained
- Search for new life goals
- Marked change in family relationships
- Change in work relationships (one is now more of a "coach" than a novice or "rookie")
- Growing sense of obsolescence at work (as Satchel Paige once said, "Never look back; someone may be gaining on you")
- Feeling of decreased job mobility and increased concern for job security[9]

One's career is a major consideration during this period. If a person has been in the same job for 10 years or more (sometimes less), he or she must face the facts of corporate politics, changing job requirements, possibilities of promotion, demotion, or job loss altogether.[8] The fact of the matter is, promotions will slow down markedly over the next decade as middle-level managers are put into "holding patterns."

While career success traditionally has been defined in terms of upward mobility, in the 1990s more and more leading corporations are encouraging employees to step off the fast track, and convincing them that they can find rewards and happiness in lateral mobility. In lectures and newsletters, the companies are trying to convince employees that "plateauing" is a fact of life, not a measure of personal failure, and that success depends on lateral integration of the business. At stake is the industrial competitiveness of companies that otherwise risk losing valued workers after spending years training them.

Companies that are moving this way are still a minority, but they include such giants as Monsanto, Motorola, BellSouth, General Electric (GE), and Pacific Gas and Electric. As a senior vice president at GE noted: "You lose the thrill of moving up . . . [but] the trade-off is more of a voice in your work."[43]

Others note that while there are fewer middle managers at medium and large companies as a result of reducing layers of managers during the corporate restructurings of the 1980s, their jobs are more important. Middle managers now focus less on supervision and more on decision making.[27] However, for those who simply cannot accept lateral mobility, there is still hope. Throughout the 1990s, according to the Bureau of Labor Statistics, many firms will face shortages of managers with leadership and technical knowledge (such as engineers with MBA degrees), and those with expertise in human resource management and computer matters.[47]

What can a middle-aged man or woman do? The rapid growth of technology and the accelerating development of new knowledge require that a person in midlife make some sort of *change* for her or his own survival. A 30-year-old might make the statement, "I can afford to change jobs or careers a couple of more times before I have to settle down." But a 50-year-old faces the possibility that there is only one chance left for change, and now may be the time to take it.[8]

Not everyone who goes through this period in life is destined to experience problems, but everyone does go through the transition, and some are better equipped to cope than are others. Why is this so? And how can we cope? Although midcareer might sound as though it is all "gloom and doom," one bright spot is the knowledge that *having realistic expectations about impending crises and transitions can actually ease the stress and pain.*[34] Life planning and career planning exercises are available that encourage employees to face up to feelings of restlessness and insecurity, to reexamine their values and life goals, and to set new ones or to recommit themselves to old ones.

One strategy is to *train midcareer employees to develop younger employees* (i.e., to serve as coaches or mentors). Both parties can win under such an arrangement. The midcareer employee keeps himself or herself fresh, energetic, and up to date, while the younger employee learns to see the "big picture" and to profit from the experience of the older employee. An important psychological need at midcareer is to build something lasting, something that will be a permanent contribution to one's organization or profession.[10] The development of a future generation of leaders could be a significant, lasting, and highly satisfying contribution.[34]

Another strategy for coping with midcareer problems is to *deal with or prevent obsolescence*. To deal with the problem, some firms send their employees to seminars, workshops, university courses, and other forms of "retooling." But a better solution is to prevent obsolescence from occurring in the first place. Research with engineers indicated that this can be done through challenging initial jobs; periodic changes in assignments, projects, or jobs; work climates that contain frequent, relevant communications; rewards that are tied closely to performance; and participative styles of leadership.[64] Furthermore, three personal characteristics tend to be associated with low obsolescence: high intellectual ability, high self-motivation, and personal flexibility (lack of rigidity).

■ **COMPANY**   STRAGEGIES FOR COPING
EXAMPLE   WITH "PLATEAUED" WORKERS

In Chicago, Continental Bank is encouraging employees to move across departmental lines on a horizontal basis since vertical promotions are less frequent. Someone from auditing might switch to commercial training; someone from systems research and development might move into international development. The inflexible HRM policies of the past are rapidly fading to accommodate present and future problems. Another strategy used by Continental Bank is to create dual technical/management ladders. New "technical executive" positions are equal to management jobs in title and dollars. For example, the bank has created senior lending positions and positions for accounting and systems specialists that are equivalent to senior managerial posts in those departments.

An alternative way to placate people who do not move up is to pay them more for jobs well done. For years, companies that rely heavily for growth on creative people—scientists, engineers, writers, artists—have provided incentives for them to stay on. Companies are now offering such incentives to a broader spectrum. For example, at Monsanto, favored scientists can now climb a universitylike track of associate fellow, fellow, senior fellow, to distinguished fellow. The company has 130 fellows, and they earn from $65,000 a year to well over $100,000.[43]

At General Electric, "plateaued" employees (either organizationally, through a lack of available promotions, or personally, through lack of ability or desire[23]) are sometimes assigned to task forces or study teams. These employees have not been promoted in a technical sense, but at least they have gotten a new assignment, a fresh perspective, and a change in their daily work.

Finally, Prudential Life Insurance Company rotates managers to improve their performance. Rockwell International uses task forces, where possible, to "recharge" managers so they do not feel a loss of self-worth if they do not move up as fast as they think they should.[45]

■

Actually there may be a bright side to all of this. Because of increased competition for fewer jobs, the *quality* of middle managers should increase. Those unwilling to wait for promotions in large corporations may become entrepreneurs and start their own businesses. Others may simply accept the status quo, readjust their life and career goals, and attempt to satisfy their needs for achievement, recognition, and personal growth off the job. Research at AT&T supports this proposition. By the time managers were interviewed after 20 years on the job, most had long ago given up their early dreams, and many could not even remember how high they had aspired in the first place. At least on the surface, most had accepted their career plateaus and adjusted to them. Midlife was indeed a crisis to some of the managers, but not to the majority.[39]

It is possible to move through the middle years of life without reevaluation of one's goals and life. But it is probably healthier to develop a new or revised "game plan" during this period.

Managing the Older Worker

"Work is life" is a phrase that philosophers throughout the ages have emphasized. Today, advances in health and medicine make it possible for the average male to live for more than 72 years and for the average female to live for more than 79 years.[4] Longevity has increased by 27 years in this century! The result: an army of healthy, over-65, unemployed adults. Legally, the elimination of mandatory retirement at *any* age has made this issue even more significant. As managers, what can we expect in terms of demographic trends?

Post–World War II baby boomers (those born between 1946 and 1964) are passing into middle life. The Census Bureau predicts that the number of new workers aged 18 to 24 will drop by 16 percent over the next 20 years. Meanwhile, by the year 2010 all the people born during the baby-boom years will be age 45 and older; those born in 1946 will be 64. In the year 2020, the oldest "baby boomers" will be 75 and the youngest will be 56.[15] Figure 9-1 graphically illustrates these trends. In short, the baby boom of the postwar period will become the "rocking-chair boom" of the twenty-first century.

Myths versus facts about older workers Age stereotypes are an unfortunate impediment to the continued growth and development of workers over the age of 55. Here are some common myths about age along with the true facts:

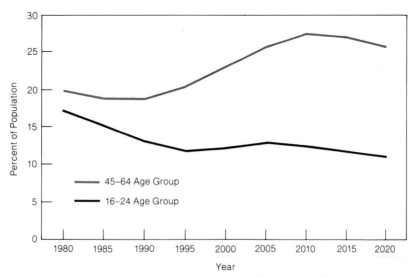

FIGURE 9-1
Population distribution by age group, ages 16–24 and 45–65. (*Source:* U.S. Bureau of the Census, "Estimates of the Population of the United States, by Age, Sex, and Race: 1980 to 1983," *Current Population Reports*, Series P-25, No. 949, May 1984; U.S. Bureau of the Census, "Projections of the Population of the United States, by Age, Sex, and Race: 1983 to 2080," *Current Population Reports*, Series P-25, No. 952, May 1984.)

Myth.   Older workers are less productive than younger workers.

Fact.   Cumulative research evidence on almost 39,000 individuals indicates that in both professional and nonprofessional jobs, age and job performance are generally unrelated. However, insufficient evidence is available on the performance of workers over 70 to draw reliable conclusions about this group.[59] Speed of recall and mental performance slow with age, but essential skills remain intact.[66]

Myth.   It costs more to prepare older workers for a job.

Fact.   Studies show that mental abilities, such as verbal, numerical, and reasoning skills, remain stable into the seventies.

Myth.   Older workers are absent more often because of age-related infirmities and above-average rates of illness.

Fact.   The average number of workdays lost to all acute conditions (e.g., flu, injuries, colds) for persons aged 18 to 44 was 3.3 days per year, while for persons aged 45 and above the average was 2.6 days per year.[15] Fully half of all people now aged 75 to 84 are free from health problems which require special care or which curb their activities.[66]

Myth.   Older workers have an unacceptably high rate of accidents on the job.

Fact.   According to a study by the Department of Health and Human Services, persons aged 55 and over had only 9.7 percent of all workplace injuries, even though they comprised 13.6 percent of the workforce at the time of the study.[15] One might argue that this is because older workers have more experience on a job. But regardless of length of experience, the *younger* the employee, the higher the accident rate (see Chapter 15).

Myth.   Older workers do not get along well with other employees.

Fact.   Owners of small and large businesses alike agree that older employees bring stability and relate well. Indeed, the over-55 worker's sense of responsibility and consistent job performance provide a positive role model for younger workers.

Myth.   The cost of employee benefits outweighs any other possible benefits from hiring older workers.

Fact.   True, when older people get sick, the illness is often chronic and requires repeated doctor's visits and hospitalization. However, the costs of health care for an older worker are lower than those for a younger, married worker with several children.[15]

Myth.   Older people are inflexible about the type of work they will perform.

Fact. A study of job candidates by Right Associates, placement counselors, found that 55 percent of those under age 50, but 63 percent of those age 50 to 59 and 78 percent of those over 60 changed industries. Many older workers saw difficulties in being rehired by their old industries.

Myth. Older people do not function well if constantly interrupted.

Fact. Neither do younger people.

Implications of the aging workforce for HRM Certainly *all* older workers are not model employees, just as *all* older workers do not fit traditional stereotypes. What are the implications of this growing group of able-bodied individuals for human resource management?

We know what the future labor market will look like in general terms: Both the demand for and the supply of older workers will continue to expand. To capitalize on these trends, one approach is to recruit workers from those individuals who would otherwise retire. *Make the job more attractive than retirement, and keep the employee who would otherwise need replacing.*[17] As the following example illustrates, some companies are doing exactly this.

UNRETIREES

■ **COMPANY PRACTICES**

Travelers Corporation is one of a growing number of companies that are finding their own retirees a valuable source of experienced, dependable, and motivated help. The retirees meet seasonal or sporadic employment needs for the company, and the company gets a tax break. In 1980, Travelers invited all of its 5000 retirees to enroll in its Retirees Job Bank in Hartford, Connecticut. By 1990, over 750 did. They fill a variety of jobs, including typists, data-entry operators, systems analysts, underwriters, and accountants. Working a maximum of 40 hours per month, retirees are paid at the midpoint of the salary range for their job classifications. If they work more than half a standard workweek, they risk losing pension benefits. Nevertheless, retirees generally like the program, for it keeps them in better physical, mental, and financial shape than full-time retirement.[14,80]

With an impending labor shortage as baby boomers age, other companies are also seeking workers who once would have been considered "over the hill." McDonald's prints applications for "McMasters" on its tray liners. Days Inns of America holds Senior Power job fairs. One such effort attracted 634 companies and 5000 older people in 26 states. The Polaroid Corporation offers gradual retirement for those who want to continue working part time.[62] According to Chicago's Harris Trust and Savings Bank, which has been rehiring its retirees since the 1940s, the savings from its program come to $3 to $5 per hour, compared with the fees of temporary help agencies.

A second approach is to *survey the needs of older workers and, where feasible, adjust HRM practices and policies to accommodate these needs*:

1. Keep records on why employees retire and on why they continue to work.[11]
2. Implement flexible work patterns and options. For example, older workers might work on Mondays and Fridays and on days before and after holidays, when so many other employees fail to show up.
3. Where possible, redesign jobs to match the physical capabilities of the aging worker.
4. At a broader level, develop career paths that consider the physical capabilities of workers at various stages of their careers.[15]
5. Provide opportunities for retraining in technical and managerial skills. Particularly with older workers, it is important to provide a nonthreatening training environment that does not emphasize speed and does not expose the older learner to unfavorable comparisons with younger learners. Verbal assurances, ample time, and privacy are key ingredients for successfully training older workers.[4]
6. Examine the suitability of performance appraisal systems as bases for employment decisions affecting older workers. To avoid age discrimination suits, be able to provide documented evidence of ineffective job performance.
7. Despite the encouraging findings presented earlier, in the section "Myths versus Facts about Older Workers," research has indicated no overall improvement in attitudes toward older workers over a 30-year period.[12]

For their part, older workers say their biggest problem is discrimination by would-be employers who underestimate their skills. They say they must convince supervisors and coworkers, not to mention some customers, that they're not stubborn, persnickety, or feeble.[38] To change this trend, workers and managers alike need to know the facts about older workers, so that they do not continue to espouse myths.

Career Management and Equal Employment Opportunity

Pressures from government funding agencies, courts, social action groups, and top management have been of great benefit in *attracting* and *selecting* women and minorities. This might be termed "Phase I" of EEO.[83] It is important to add, however, that the "buck doesn't stop here." *Employee development activities*, so-called Phase II of EEO, are essential. The Xerox Corporation's Prosper program is a good example of Phase II activity.[6] The program has two objectives: (1) to increase the white manager's awareness of propensities to discriminate unfairly on the job and (2) to facilitate the continued movement and growth of women and minorities through the corporation.

Corning, Inc., has a similar program, with two broad goals: (1) to develop a better mix of women and blacks in the company's management and professional ranks and (2) to make a virtue of the mix. Corning wants a salad, not a puree—

In many fields, older workers are especially valuable because they have a lifetime of experience to draw from.

blacks who are proud to be black, and women who are proud to be mothers and engineers. To accomplish its goals, the company is making extraordinary efforts in recruitment and retention and is trying to make its small community an attractive place for women and minorities to relocate.[42] Equal employment opportunity is not a program or a fad; it is a commitment to fairness that permeates all hierarchical levels and all company relationships. As is implicit throughout this chapter, it also permeates career management programs.

CAREER MANAGEMENT: ORGANIZATIONS FOCUSING ON THEIR OWN MAINTENANCE AND GROWTH

Ultimately it is top management's responsibility to develop and implement a cost-effective career planning program. The program must fit the nature of the business, its competitive employment practices, and the current (or desired) organizational structure. This process is complex because organizational career management combines areas that previously have been regarded as individual issues: performance appraisal, development, transfer, and promotion. Before coaching and counseling take place, however, it is important to identify characteristic career paths that employees tend to follow.

Career paths represent logical and possible sequences of positions that could be held, based on an analysis of what people actually do in an organization.[88] Career paths should:

- Represent real progression possibilities, whether lateral or upward, without implied "normal" rates of progress or forced specialization in a technical area.
- Be tentative and responsive to changes in job content, work priorities, organizational patterns, and management needs.
- Be flexible, taking into consideration the compensating qualities of a particular employee, managers, subordinates, or others who influence the way that work is performed.
- Specify the skills, knowledge, and other attributes required to perform effectively at each position along the paths and specify how they can be acquired. (If specifications are limited to educational credentials, age, and experience, some capable performers may be excluded from career opportunities.)

Data derived from HRM research are needed to define career paths in this manner. Worker-oriented job analyses (see Chapter 4) that can be expressed in quantitative terms are well-suited for this task since they focus directly on the behavioral requirements of each job. Clusters or families of jobs requiring similar patterns of behavior can then be identified.

Once this is done, the next task is to identify career paths within and among the job families and to integrate the overall network of these paths as a single career system. The process is shown graphically in Figure 9-2.

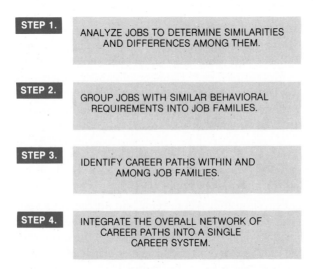

FIGURE 9-2
Development of a career system, comprised of individual career paths.

Federal guidelines on employee selection require a job-related basis for all employment decisions. Career paths based on job analyses of employee behaviors provide a documented, defensible basis for organizational career management and a strong reference point for individual career planning and development activities.[56,88]

In practice, organizational career management systems sometimes fail for the following reasons: (1) Employees believe that supervisors do not care about their career development; (2) neither the employee nor the organization is fully aware of his or her needs and organizational constraints; and (3) career plans are developed without regard for the support systems necessary to fulfill the plans.[73] The following section gives examples of several companies that avoided these pitfalls.

Internal Staffing Decisions: Patterns of Career Change

From the organization's point of view, there are four broad types of internal moves: up, down, over, and out (Figure 9-3). These moves correspond to promotions (up), demotions (down), transfers and relocations (over), and layoffs, retirements, and resignations (out). Technically, dismissals also fall into the last category, but we will consider them in the context of disciplinary actions and labor relations. Briefly, let's consider each of these patterns of movement.

Promotions Promoted employees usually assume greater responsibility and authority in return for higher pay, benefits, and privileges. Psychologically, promotions help satisfy needs for security, belonging, and personal growth. Promotions are important organizational decisions that should receive the same careful attention as any other personnel selection decision. They are more likely to be successful to the extent that:

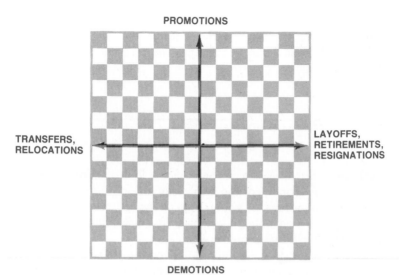

FIGURE 9-3

As in chess, people can make a variety of internal moves in an organization.

1. An extensive search for candidates is conducted.
2. Standardized, clearly understandable information is available on all candidates.
3. The actual decision process involves affected parties in the final choice.[82]

A major reason for including affected parties in the final choice is that the organization must continue to live with those who are bypassed for promotion. This situation is very different from that of the applicant who is rejected during the hiring process. To minimize defensive behavior, it is critical that the procedures used for promotion decisions (e.g., assessment centers plus performance appraisals) be acceptable, valid, and fair to the unsuccessful candidates.

In unionized situations, the collective bargaining contract will determine the relative importance given to seniority and ability in promotion decisions. Management tends to emphasize ability, while unions favor seniority. Although practices vary considerably from firm to firm, a compromise is usually reached through which promotions are determined by a formula, such as promoting the employee with the greatest seniority *if* ability and experience are equal. However, if one candidate is clearly a superior performer relative to others, many contracts will permit promotion on this basis regardless of seniority.

A further issue concerns promotion from within versus outside the organization. Many firms, such as Delta Airlines, have strict promotion-from-within policies. However, there are situations in which high-level jobs or newly created jobs require talents that are just not available in-house. Under these circumstances, even the most rigid promotion-from-within policy must yield to a search for outside candidates.

A relatively recent phenomenon is *refusal* of promotions, particularly in dual-career families where a promotion for one spouse may pose problems for the other.[51] Refusal causes two kinds of organizational problems. First, the company has invested time and money in the career development of an employee for a position that is refused. Second, those who refuse promotions can become deadwood, blocking the career paths of lower-level employees who would normally rise behind them. To avert this problem, firms need to make a variety of career paths available.

■ **COMPANY EXAMPLE**
PROMOTIONS TO PARTNER
AT GOLDMAN SACHS & CO.

Goldman, Sachs & Co. is one of the last of Wall Street's major private partnerships. Each year the firm picks a small number of new partners from among its hundreds of young executives. Winners are set for life, and they typically retire as multimillionaires after only a decade or so. But it's getting harder to decide who gets the prize.

Exactly what goes on behind the scenes of the 2-month-long competition is a closely held secret. Current partners describe it, of course, as a rigorous but fair process in which politics are unimportant. The process certainly is rigorous. It starts with a winnowing down of the worldwide workforce of 6600 to a list of 50 to 60 serious candidates. Each potential new partner must then be nominated by a current partner.

What do partners look for? In addition to keen business judgment and a proven track record of success, partners look for team players and "culture carriers." Such people fit Goldman's conservative style and its customer-oriented tradition that dates back to the 1860s, when Marcus Goldman began hawking commercial paper on the streets of New York.

Partners, who are expected to back their nominees' causes throughout the process, then file mountains of endorsement letters. For the next several weeks, an eight-member management committee reviews these materials and checks out the nominees. Members of the committee who are not in a candidate's division grill department heads and other partners about the candidate's qualifications, and then report back. Candidates themselves are never interviewed. In fact, they're not even supposed to know that they are candidates. But of course they do.

After a dizzying round of management-committee summit meetings, a final "town meeting" of all current partners is held, at which the management committee presents its final list for discussion and debate—even though it's pretty clear that the committee's list is final. Following the "town meeting" the partners announce the list of newly minted millionaires. In 1990, Goldman added 32 members to its exclusive club, which now numbers 148.[72]

Demotions Employee demotions usually involve a cut in pay, status, privilege, or opportunity. They occur infrequently since they tend to be accompanied by problems of employee apathy, depression, and inefficiency that can undermine the morale of a work group. For these reasons, many managers prefer to discharge or to move employees laterally rather than demote them. In either case, careful planning, documentation, and concern for the employee should precede such moves.[30,71]

Aside from disciplinary actions, demotions may result from staff reductions, from the inability of an employee to handle the requirements of a higher-level job, from health problems, or from changing interests. In many cases, demotion is mutually satisfactory to the organization and to the affected employee.

Transfers and relocations Who is most likely to be transferred? A survey by Atlas Van Lines found that salesmen 31 to 40 years old earning $30,000 to $50,000 a year are most likely to be transferred by their companies. And they are apt to be moved every 3 to 5 years. Female workers are much less likely to be transferred. At two-thirds of the responding companies, less than 5 percent of the transferees were women.[46]

With respect to relocations, senior management is facing growing resistance from employees. The effect of a move on a family can be profound. *For the employee,* relocation often means increased prestige and income. However, the costs of moving and the complications resulting from upsetting routines, loss of friends, and changing schools and jobs are borne by *the family.* Uprooted families often suffer from loss of credentials as well. They do not enjoy the built-in status that awaits the employee at the new job; they must start from scratch. Wives may become more dependent on their husbands for social contacts (or vice versa, depending on who is transferred).[40]

There is one bright side to all this, however. Research has shown that transfers produce little short-term impact on the mental or physical health of children.[49]

Indeed, a growing number of all transfers now involve a trailing spouse who is male.[21,32] Transferred employees who are promoted estimate that it will take them a full 9 months to get up to speed in their new posts. Lateral transfers take an average of 7.8 months. However, the actual time taken to reach competency varies with (1) the degree of similarity between the old and new jobs and (2) the amount of support from peers and superiors at the new job.[70] In sum, personal adjustments—not problems with housing—are the biggest obstacles to relocation.[21] To minimize these disruptions, some companies have developed frequency standards whereby no manager can be relocated more than once in 2 years or three times in 10 years. Another firm has set up one-stop rotational programs at its larger facilities to replace what used to be four stints of 6 months each at different plants over a 2-year training period.

The financial implications of relocation are another major consideration. In 1970 most relocation programs consisted of a few cost categories: house-hunting trips, the shipment of household goods, temporary living expenses at the new location, and often 1 month's salary bonus to cover other incidentals. In the 1990s typical relocation expenses and services included all those offered in 1970 plus ongoing living-cost differentials; mortgage interest differentials; home disposal and home-finding expenses; expenses to help defray losses on home sales; real estate commissions; home purchase expenses; home maintenance, repair, and refurbishing costs; equity loans; and, for renters, lease-breaking expenses. Spouse employment assistance programs are also offered by some firms (about 25 percent)[21] and, for employees on temporary assignments, home property management expenses. In fact, financing a relocation program in 1990, at a total cost of about $50,000, was more than 6 times more costly than in 1968, at a total cost of $7500.[50,84]

Organizations are well aware of these social and financial problems and in many cases they are responding by providing improved support systems. Despite the problems, transfers and relocations are expected to continue. For example, every one of the 10 "best-managed" companies identified in a *Dun's Review* survey said that more moves are in store once an employee demonstrates competence in one managerial position. Annually over 15 percent of the managers at all levels are likely to transfer or relocate. This represents about 250,000 families.[16]

Layoffs, retirements, and resignations These all involve employees moving *out* of the organization.

Layoffs. How safe is my job? For many people, that is *the* issue of the 1990s. It's becoming clear that corporate cutbacks were not an oddity of the 1980s but rather are likely to persist through the new decade.[9] To avoid legal problems, consider doing the following:[37]

- Conduct regular performance reviews of employees, using objective, standardized measures of performance.
- Provide clear, business-related reasons for any dismissal, backed by written documentation when possible.
- Seek legal waivers from older workers who agree to leave under an early retirement plan. Note that under the Older Workers Benefit Protection Act, which took effect in 1990, employees have 45 days to consider such waivers, and 7 days to revoke them.
- Follow any written company guidelines for termination, or be prepared to show in court why they are not binding in the particular instance.
- Don't make oral promises of job security to employees who might later be laid off.

Involuntary layoffs are never pleasant, and management policies must consider the impacts on those who leave, on those who stay, on the local community, and on the company. For workers laid off, efforts should be directed toward a rapid, successful, and orderly career transition. How long does it take on average to find a new job? While it depends a great deal on the amount of effort put into the job search, a rough rule of thumb for managers is 1 month for every $10,000 in salary.[41,86] Outplacement programs that help laid-off employees deal with the psychological stages of career transition (anger, grief, depression, family stress), assess individual strengths and weaknesses, and develop support networks should be emphasized.[55,85]

Termination is a traumatic experience. Egos are shattered, and employees may become bitter and angry. Family problems may also occur because of the added emotional and financial strain.[24] For those who remain, it is important that they retain the highest level of loyalty, trust, teamwork, motivation, and productivity possible. This doesn't just happen—and unless there is a good deal of face-to-face, candid, open communication between senior management and "survivors," it probably won't. Within the community, layoff policies should consider the company's reputation and image, in addition to the impact of the layoff on the local economy and social services agencies. Although layoffs are intended to *reduce* costs, some costs may in fact *increase*. These include:

Direct costs	Indirect costs
Severance pay, pay in lieu of notice	Recruiting and employment cost of new hires
Accrued vacation and sick pay	Training and retraining
Supplemental unemployment benefits	Increase in unemployment tax rate
Outplacement	Potential charges of unfair discrimination
Pension and benefit payoffs	Low morale among remaining employees
Administrative processing costs	Heightened insecurity and reduced productivity

What are the options? One approach is to initiate a program of *job sharing* to perform the reduced workload. While no one is laid off, everyone's workweek and pay are reduced. This helps the company to reduce labor costs. In an area experiencing high unemployment, it may be better to have all employees share the "misery" rather than to lay off selected ones. Some of the benefits of job sharing are:

- Twice as much talent and creativity is available.
- Benefits continue.
- Overtime is reduced.
- Workers retain a career orientation and the potential for upward mobility.
- It eliminates the need for training a temporary employee, for example, when one employee is sick or is on vacation, because the other can take over.[67]

Job sharing is not without its drawbacks:

- There is a lack of job continuity.
- Supervision is inconsistent.
- Accountability is not centered in one person.
- Expenses increase because many benefits are a function of the employee, not the amount of pay.[28]
- When workers are represented by a union, seniority is bypassed, and senior workers may resist sharing jobs.[63]

However, when Motorola reviewed job sharing at its facilities in Arizona, it found that avoiding layoffs saved an average of $1868 per employee—and $975,000 in total.[54]

Retirements.   For selected employees, *early retirement* is a possible alternative to being laid off. Early retirement programs take many forms, but typically they involve partial pay stretched over several years along with extended benefits. Early retirement programs are intended to provide incentives to terminate; they are not

IMPACT OF CAREER MANAGEMENT ON PRODUCTIVITY, QUALITY OF WORK LIFE, AND THE BOTTOM LINE

From first-job effects through midcareer transition to preretirement counseling, career management has a direct bearing on productivity, quality of work life, and the bottom line. It is precisely because organizations are sensitive to these concerns that career management activities have become as popular as they are. The saying "Organizations have many jobs, but individuals have only one career" is as true today as it ever was. While organizations find themselves in worldwide competition, most individuals are striving for achievement, recognition, personal growth, and "the good life." Unless careers are managed effectively by both individuals and organizations, neither can achieve their goals.

intended to replace regular retirement benefits. Any losses in pension resulting from early retirement are usually offset with attractive incentive payments.

For example, in 1988, IBM offered workers at its Boca Raton, Florida, plant a voluntary severance program that included up to 2-years' pay, with benefits, plus a $25,000 bonus. In 1990, Digital Equipment offered thousands of workers voluntary severance packages of between 40 weeks and 2 years of pay, plus benefits.

Yet some voluntary severance and early retirement programs backfire. IBM lost skilled, senior-level employees in past cutbacks. To overcome that problem, the firm targeted subsequent programs to specific groups of employees, such as those in manufacturing and in some administrative jobs.[90] The keys to success are *to identify, before the incentives are offered, exactly which jobs are targeted for attrition and to understand the needs of the employees targeted to leave.*

Since mandatory retirement at a specified age can no longer be required legally, most employees will choose their own times to retire. More of them are choosing to retire earlier than age 65. In 1948, for example, 50 percent of males and 9 percent of females continued to work past the age of 65. By 1988, those numbers had dropped to 16 percent and 7 percent, respectively.[4]

Research indicates that both personal and situational factors affect retirement decisions. Personally, individuals with Type A behavior patterns (hard-driving, aggressive, impatient) are less likely to prefer to retire, while those with obsolete job skills, chronic health problems, and sufficient financial resources are more likely to retire. Situationally, employees are more likely to retire to the extent that they have reached their occupational goals, that their jobs have undesirable characteristics, that home life is seen as preferable to work life, and that there are attractive alternative (leisure) activities.[7]

While retirement is certainly attractive to some, many retirees are returning to the workforce in the United States, as they have long done in Japan. As a matter of tradition, Japanese workers usually retire from their jobs before age 60, but they do not quit working. They lose seniority, their normal salary, their usual authority, but not their chance to work. Often they are rehired by the same company, but in a less demanding position. In retiring so early, Japanese workers have a better chance to adapt to their new jobs and thus not drop entirely out of the workforce. It should come as no surprise, then, that Japan has a higher proportion of men over age 65 in the labor force than any other industrialized country.[19]

Things are changing in the United States, too. Retirees are the fastest growing part of the temporary workforce. Many are bored with retirement, have high energy levels, and can maintain flexible schedules.[52] At a broader level, nearly 2 million nonworking Americans 50 to 64 years old are ready and able to work. Of these, more than 1.1 million would be highly qualified and motivated since they have reasonable wage expectations, would accept difficult working conditions, and have interest in available jobs: managerial, computer, sales, home day care, and teacher's aide.[57]

Resignations.   Resignation, or voluntary worker turnover, has been increasing steadily over the past 15 years, particularly among white-collar and professional workers.[79] Employees who resign should avoid "burning bridges" behind them, leaving anger and resentment in their wake; instead, they should leave gracefully and responsibly, stressing the value of company experience.[14]

■ HUMAN RESOURCE MANAGEMENT IN ACTION
CONCLUSION

CORPORATE CAREER MANAGEMENT COMES OF AGE

Programs of corporate career management often include one or more of the following support mechanisms.

Self-assessment   The goal of self-assessment is to help employees focus on appropriate career goals. Training typically takes the form of workshops designed to help employees walk themselves through the difficult and sometimes emotional self-assessment process. It is a process of identifying and calibrating one's professional aptitudes and capabilities and of identifying improvements that will enhance one's career growth. As we saw in the Hewlett-Packard example, that company has pioneered in offering self-assessment training to its employees at all levels.

Career planning   Workshop training is also used to teach employees how to plan their career growth once they have determined where they want to go. They learn skills for career self-management as well as how to "read" the corporate environment and to become "savvy" about how to get ahead in their own companies. General Electric and Citibank have been leaders in raising this kind of awareness in their employees.

Supervisory training Employees frequently turn first to their immediate supervisors for help with career management. At Sikorsky Aircraft, for example, supervisors are taught how to provide relevant information and to question the logic of each employee's career plans, but *not* to give specific career advice. Giving advice relieves the employee of responsibility for managing his or her own career.

Succession planning Simply designating replacements for key managers and executives is no guarantee that those replacements will be ready when needed. Enlightened companies are adopting an approach to succession planning that is consistent with the concept of career self-management. They develop their employees broadly, to prepare them for any of several positions that may become available. As business needs change, broadly developed people can be moved into positions that are critical to the success of the business.

The practice of making career self-management part of the corporate culture has spread rapidly over the past several years. Companies are using this approach to build a significant competitive advantage. Given today's turbulent, sometimes convulsive corporate environments, plus workers who seek greater control over their own destinies, it may be the only approach that can succeed over the long term.

SUMMARY

A career is a sequence of positions occupied by a person during the course of a lifetime. Career planning is important because the consequences of career success or failure are closely linked with an individual's self-concept and identity, as well as with career and life satisfaction. This chapter has addressed career management

IMPLICATIONS FOR MANAGEMENT PRACTICE

To profit from current workforce trends, consider taking the following steps:

1. Develop explicit policies to attract and retain dual-career couples.
2. Plan for more effective use of "plateaued" workers and also those who are in midcareer transitions.
3. Educate other managers and workers in the facts about older workers; where possible, hire them for full-time or part-time work.
4. Commit to Phase II of equal employment opportunity—to broadening career opportunities for women and members of protected groups.

from three perspectives. The first was that of *individuals focusing on themselves*: self-management of one's own career, establishment of career objectives, and dual-career couples. The second perspective was that of *organizations focusing on individuals*: that is, managing individuals during early career (organizational entry, impact of the first job); midcareer, including strategies for coping with midlife transitions and "plateaued" workers; and late career (age 50 and over) stages. We considered the implications of each of these stages for human resource management, both in large- and in small-business settings and also in the context of equal employment opportunity. Finally, a third perspective was that of *organizations focusing on their own maintenance and growth*. This requires the development of organizational career management systems based on career paths defined in terms of employee behaviors. It involves the management of patterns of career movement up, down, over, and out.

DISCUSSION QUESTIONS

9▪1 Why is the design of one's first permanent job so important?

9▪2 What practical steps can be taken to minimize midcareer crises?

9▪3 What strategies can you suggest for avoiding the problems associated with older workers clogging the career paths of younger workers?

9▪4 Discuss the special problems faced by dual-career couples.

9▪5 You have just learned that you are being transferred to another location. Your supervisor asks what the company can do to smooth the process. What would you tell her?

9▪6 What kinds of problems are associated with managing older and younger workers?

REFERENCES

1. Aburdene, P. (1990, September). How to think like a CEO for the 1990s. *Working Woman*, pp. 134–137.

2. Adolph, B., & Rose, K. (1985). *The employer's guide to child care*. New York: Praeger.

3. Allen, R. E. (1989, Nov. 6). It pays to invest in tomorrow's work force. *The Wall Street Journal*, p. A16.

4. American Association of Retired Persons (1990). *The aging work force*. Washington, DC: American Association of Retired Persons.

5. Anderson, J. C., Milkovich, G. T., & Tsui, A. (1981). A model of intra-organizational mobility. *Academy of Management Review*, **6**, 529–538.

6. Bass, B. M., Cascio, W. F., McPherson, J. W., & Tragash, H. J. (1976). Prosper—Training and research for increasing management awareness of affirmative action in race relations. *Academy of Management Journal*, **19**, 353–369.

7. Beehr, T. A. (1986). The process of retirement: A review and recommendations for future investigation. *Personnel Psychology*, **39**, 31–55.

8. Bell, J. E. (1982, August). Mid-life transition in career men. *AMA Management Digest*, pp. 8–10.

9. Bennett, A. (1990, Sept. 11). A white-collar guide to job security. *The Wall Street Journal*, pp. B1, B12.

10. Bennett, A. (1990, Sept. 11). Layoff victims tell of trials and fulfillment. *The Wall Street Journal*, pp. B1, B12.

11. Beutell, N. J. (1983). Managing the older worker. *Personnel Administrator*, **28**(8), 31–38, 64.

12. Bird, C. P., & Fisher, T. D. (1986). Thirty years later: Attitudes toward the employment of older workers. *Journal of Applied Psychology*, **71**, 315–317.

13. Brewster, L. S. (1990, Spring). Attracting a mentor. In *Managing your career*. Supplement to *The Wall Street Journal*, pp. 16–17.

14. Brooks, A. (1985, Dec. 2). Quitting a job gracefully. *The New York Times*, p. B12.

15. Bureau of National Affairs (1987). Older Americans in the workforce: Challenges and solutions. *Labor Relations Week*, **1**(27), 1–237.

16. Collie, H. C. (1986). Corporate relocation: Changing with the times. *Personnel Administrator*, **31**(4), 101–106.

17. Copperman, L. F., & Keast, F. D. (1981, Summer). Older workers: A challenge for today and tomorrow. *Human Resource Management*, pp. 13–18.

18. Couples at same firm—An idea catches on (1983, Sep. 12). *U. S. News and World Report*, p. 71.

19. Davis, K. (1988, Oct. 18). Our idle retirees drag down the economy. *The New York Times*, p. A31.

20. Deutschman, A. (1990, Aug. 27). What 25-year-olds want. *Fortune*, pp. 42–50.

21. Driessnack, C. H. (1987). Spouse relocation: A moving experience. *Personnel Administrator*, **32**(8), 94–102.

22. Feinstein, S. (1987, Nov. 10). Women and minority workers in business find a mentor can be a rare commodity. *The Wall Street Journal*, p. 39.

23. Ference, T. P., Stoner, J. A., & Warren, E. K. (1977). Managing the career plateau. *Academy of Management Review*, **2**, 602–612.

24. Foderaro, L. W. (1990, Sep. 24). Jobless executives get solace and aid in support groups. *The New York Times*, pp. A1, B2.

25. Forbes, J. B. (1987). Early intraorganizational mobility: Patterns and influences. *Academy of Management Journal*, **30**, 110–125.

26. Ford, R., & McLaughlin, F. (1986). Nepotism: Boon or bane? *Personnel Administrator*, **31**(11), 78–86.

27. Fowler, E. M. (1989, Feb. 21). A good side to unwanted job changes. *The New York Times*, p. 1H.

28. Frease, M., & Zawacki, R. A. (1979). Job sharing: An answer to productivity problems. *Personnel Administrator*, **24**(10), 35–38.

29. Friedman, D. E. (1985). *Corporate financial assistance for child care*. New York: Conference Board.

30. Geyelin, M. (1989, Sep. 7). Fired managers winning more lawsuits. *The Wall Street Journal*, p. B1.

31. Goff, S. J., Mount, M. K., & Jamison, R. L. (1990). Employer supported child care, work/family conflict, and absenteeism: A field study. *Personnel Psychology*, **43**, 793–810.

32. Gould, C. (1987, Feb. 22). A helping hand for the "trailing spouse." *The New York Times*, p. 11.

33. Greenhaus, J. H. (1987). *Career management*. Chicago: Dryden.

34. Hall, D. T. (1976). *Careers in organizations*. Pacific Palisades, CA: Goodyear.

35. Hall, D. T. , & Richter, J. (1990). Career gridlock: Baby boomers hit the wall. *The Academy of Management Executive*, **4**(3), 7–22.

36. Hall, F. S., & Hall, D. T. (1979). *The two-career couple*. Reading, MA: Addison-Wesley.

37. Hayes, A. S. (1990, Nov. 2). Layoffs take careful planning to avoid losing the suits that are apt to follow. *The Wall Street Journal*, pp. B1, B10.

38. Hirsch, J. S. (1990, Feb. 26). Older workers chafe under younger managers. *The Wall Street Journal*, pp. B1, B6.
39. Howard, A., & Bray, D. W. (1982, March 21). AT&T: The hopes of middle managers. *The New York Times*, p. 1F.
40. Hunsaker, J. S. (1983). Work and family life must be integrated. *Personnel Administrator*, **28**, 87–91.
41. Hymowitz, C., & Schellhardt, T. D. (1986, Oct. 20). After the ax. *The Wall Street Journal*, p. 27.
42. Kilborn, P. T. (1990, Oct. 4). A company recasts itself to erase bias on the job. *The New York Times*, pp. A1, D21.
43. Kilborn, P. T. (1990, Feb. 27). Companies that temper ambition. *The New York Times*, pp. D1, D6.
44. Kleiman, C. (1990, March 19). Report dispels child-care liability myth. *Denver Post*, p. 4C.
45. Labor Letter (1991, Feb. 19). *The Wall Street Journal*, p. A1.
46. Labor Letter (1990, May 1). *The Wall Street Journal*, p. A1.
47. Labor Letter (1990, Jan. 23). *The Wall Street Journal*, p. A1.
48. Labor Letter (1990, Jan. 16). *The Wall Street Journal*, p. A1.
49. Labor Letter (1989, Nov. 17). *The Wall Street Journal*, p. A1.
50. Labor Letter (1989, Oct. 10). *The Wall Street Journal*, p. A1.
51. Labor Letter (1989, April 11). *The Wall Street Journal*, p. A1.
52. Labor Letter (1989, March 7). *The Wall Street Journal*, p. A1.
53. Labor Letter (1987, Sep. 8). *The Wall Street Journal*, p. A1.
54. Labor Letter (1986, April 1). *The Wall Street Journal*, p. A1.
55. Latack, J. C., & Dozier, J. B. (1986). After the ax falls: Job loss as a career transition. *Academy of Management Review*, **11**, 375–392.
56. Ledvinka, J. (1975). Technical implications of equal employment law for manpower planning. *Personnel Psychology*, **28**, 299–323.
57. Lewin, T. (1990, Jan. 28). For work force, 2 million who'd quit retirement. *The New York Times*, p. 18.
58. London, M., & Stumpf, S. A. (1982). *Managing careers*. Reading, MA: Addison-Wesley.
59. McEvoy, G. M., & Cascio, W. F. (1989). Cumulative evidence of the relationship between employee age and job performance. *Journal of Applied Psychology*, **74**, 11–20.
60. Milkovich, G. T., & Anderson, J. C. (1982). Career planning and development systems. In K. M. Rowland & G. R. Ferris (eds), *Personnel management*. Boston: Allyn & Bacon, pp. 364–389.
61. Miller, T. I. (1984). The effects of employer-sponsored child care on employee absenteeism, turnover, productivity, recruitment, or job satisfaction: What is claimed and what is known. *Personnel Psychology*, **37**, 277–289.
62. More retirees choose to work (1989, Sep. 7). *The New York Times*, p. C13.
63. Noble, K. B. (1988, March 15). Union experiment provokes a fight. *The New York Times*, pp. A1, B20.
64. Northrup, H. R., & Malin, M. E. (1986). *Personnel policies for engineers and scientists*. Philadelphia: Industrial Research Unit, The Wharton School, University of Pennsylvania.
65. O'Boyle, T. (1985, July 11). Loyalty ebbs at many companies as employees grow disillusioned. *The Wall Street Journal*, p. 29.
66. Older—but coming on strong (1988, Feb. 22). *Time*, pp. 76–79.
67. Owen-Cooper, T. (1990, Oct. 1). Job sharing slowly gaining in appeal. *Denver Post*, pp. 1C, 5C.

68. Pappas, V. J. (1990, Spring). The new job market. In *Managing your career*. Supplement to *The Wall Street Journal*, pp. 4–7.

69. Petras, K., & Petras, R. (1989). *The only job book you'll ever need*. New York: Simon & Schuster.

70. Pinder, C. C., & Schroeder, K. G. (1987). Time to proficiency following job transfers. *Academy of Management Journal*, **30**, 336–353.

71. Ploscowe, S. A., & Goldstein, M. M. (1987, March). Trouble on the firing line. *Nation's Business*, pp. 36, 37.

72. Power, W., & Siconolfi, M. (1990, Oct. 19). Who will be rich? How Goldman Sachs chooses new partners: With a lot of angst. *The Wall Street Journal*, pp. A1, A8.

73. Quaintance, M. K. (1989). Internal placement and career management. In W. F. Cascio (ed.), *Human resource planning, employment, and placement*. Washington, DC: Bureau of National Affairs, pp. 2-200 to 2-235.

74. Raelin, J. A. (1983). First-job effects on career development. *Personnel Administrator*, **28**(8), 71–76, 92.

75. Rebuilding to survive (1987, Feb. 16). *Time*, pp. 44–48.

76. Schein, E. H. (1978). *Career dynamics: Matching individual and organizational needs*. Reading, MA: Addison-Wesley.

77. Schweiger, D. M., & Denisi, A. S. (1991). Communication with employees following a merger: A longitudinal field experiment. *Academy of Management Journal*, **34**, 110–135.

78. Sekaran, U. (1986). *Dual career families*. San Francisco: Jossey-Bass.

79. Sikula, A. F., & McKenna, J. F. (1983). Individuals must take charge of career development. *Personnel Administrator*, **28**(10), 89–97.

80. Solomon, J., & Fuchsberg, G. (1990, Jan. 26). Great number of older Americans seem ready to work. *The Wall Street Journal*, p. B1.

81. Staines, G. L., Pottick, K. J., & Fudge, D. A. (1986). Wives' employment and husbands' attitudes toward work and life. *Journal of Applied Psychology*, **71**, 118–128.

82. Stumpf, S. A., & London, M. (1981). Management promotions: Individual and organizational factors influencing the decision process. *Academy of Management Review*, **6**, 539–549.

83. Super, D. E., & Hall, D. T. (1978). Career development: Exploration and planning. *Annual Review of Psychology*, **29**, 333–372.

84. Swasy, A. (1990, Aug. 21). Housing slump boosts relocation costs. *The Wall Street Journal*, p. B1.

85. Sweet, D. H. (1989). Outplacement. In W. F. Cascio (ed.), *Human resource planning, employment, and placement*. Washington, DC: Bureau of National Affairs, pp. 2-236 to 2-261.

86. The higher the pay the longer the job hunt (1989, Dec. 15). *The Wall Street Journal*, p. B1.

87. Trost, C. (1990, May 2). Women managers quit not for family but to advance their corporate climb. *The Wall Street Journal*, pp. B1, B8.

88. Walker, J. W. (1980). *Human resource planning*. New York: McGraw-Hill.

89. Wilhelm, W. R. (1983). Helping workers to self-manage their careers. *Personnel Administrator*, **28**(8), 83–89.

90. Wilke, J. R. (1990, April 13). Firms oust "no layoff" tradition. *The Wall Street Journal*, pp. B1, B2.

91. Yuppies look beyond corporate, cash success (1989, Jan. 15). *Denver Post*, p. 4H.

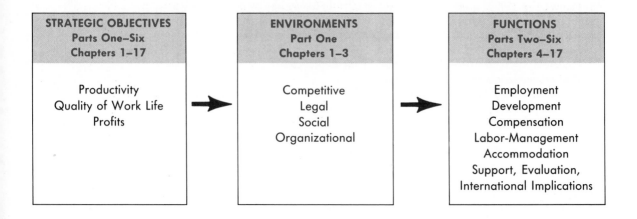

STRATEGIC OBJECTIVES Parts One–Six Chapters 1–17	ENVIRONMENTS Part One Chapters 1–3	FUNCTIONS Parts Two–Six Chapters 4–17
Productivity Quality of Work Life Profits	Competitive Legal Social Organizational	Employment Development Compensation Labor-Management Accommodation Support, Evaluation, International Implications

RELATIONSHIP OF HRM FUNCTIONS TO HRM ACTIVITIES

FUNCTIONS	ACTIVITIES
PART 2 EMPLOYMENT	Job Analysis, Human Resource Planning, Recruiting, Staffing (Chapters 4–6)
PART 3 DEVELOPMENT	Orientation, Training, Performance Appraisal, Managing Careers (Chapters 7–9)
PART 4 COMPENSATION	Pay, Benefits, Incentives (Chapters 10–12)
PART 5 LABOR-MANAGEMENT ACCOMMODATION	Union Representation, Collective Bargaining, Procedural Justice, Ethics (Chapters 13, 14)
PART 6 SUPPORT, EVALUATION, INTERNATIONAL IMPLICATIONS	Job Safety and Health, Costs/Benefits of HRM Activities, International Dimensions of HRM (Chapters 15–17)

PART FOUR

Compensation

C ompensation, which includes direct cash payments, indirect
payments in the form of employee benefits, and incentives to
motivate employees to strive for higher levels of productivity,
is a critical component of the employment relationship. Compensation is affected by forces as diverse as labor market factors, collective bargaining, government legislation, and top management's philosophy regarding pay and benefits. This is a dynamic area, and Chapters 10, 11, and 12 present the latest developments in compensation theory and examples of company practices. Chapter 10 is a nontechnical introduction to the subject of pay systems. Chapter 11 focuses on employee benefits, and Chapter 12 considers alternative strategies for motivating employees to improve their performance and productivity. You will find that the material in all three chapters has direct implications for sound management practice.

Pay Systems

THE TRUST GAP*

Among chief executive officers, three of today's most popular buzzwords are "employee involvement" and "empowerment" of employees. CEOs say, "We're a team; we're all in this together." But employees look at the difference between their pay and the CEO's. They see top management's perks—oak dining rooms and heated garages versus cafeterias for lower-level workers and parking spaces a half mile from the plant. And they wonder, "Is this togetherness?" As the disparity in pay widens (see Figure 10-1), the wonder grows. Hourly workers and supervisors indeed agree that "we're all in this together," but what we're in turns out to be a frame of mind that mistrusts senior management's intentions, doubts its competence, and resents its self-congratulatory pay.

Study after study, involving hundreds of companies and thousands of workers, has found evidence of a trust gap—and it is widening. Indeed, the attitudes of middle managers and professionals toward the workplace are

---

*Adapted from: A. Farnham, The trust gap, *Fortune*, December 4, 1989, pp. 56–78.

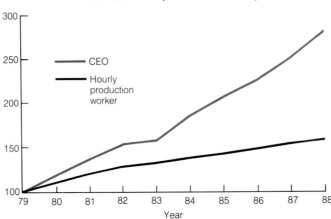

COMPENSATION (INDEX: 1979 = 100)

FIGURE 10-1
Change in average
CEO pay relative to the
change in average pay
of hourly production
workers, 1979 to 1988,
where 1979 index =
100. (*Source:* A. Farn-
ham, The trust gap,
Fortune, December 4,
1989, p. 56.)

becoming more like those of hourly workers, historically the most disaffected group.

Opinion Research Corp. of Chicago found clear evidence of a trust gap when it surveyed 100,000 middle managers, professionals, supervisors, salespeople, and technical, clerical, and hourly workers of Fortune 500 companies. With the exception of the sales group, employees believed top management now was less willing to listen to their problems than 5 years earlier. The groups also felt top management now accorded them less respect. Said one observer, "Organizations audit their financial resources regularly but fail to take the temperature of their own employees." Such employers are flying blindly. Concluded another, the "open doors" of many corporations are only "slightly ajar."

To be sure, much of the trust gap can be traced to inconsistencies between what management says and what it does—between saying "People are our most important asset" and in the next breath ordering layoffs, or between sloganeering about quality while continuing to evaluate workers by how many pieces they push out the back door.

The result is a world in which top management thinks it's sending crucial messages, but employees never hear a word. Thus another recent survey found that 82 percent of Fortune 500 executives believe their corporate strategy is understood by everyone who needs to know. Unfortunately, less than a third of employees in the same companies say management provides clear goals and direction.

Confidence in top management's competence is collapsing. The days when top management could say, "Trust us; this is for your own good" are over. Employees have seen that if the company embarks on a new strategic tack and it doesn't work, employees lose their jobs, not management.

While competence may be hard to judge, pay is known, and to the penny. The rate of increase in top management's pay split from workers in 1979 and has rocketed upward ever since (see Figure 10-1). CEOs who make 100 times the average hourly worker's pay are no longer rare. European and Japanese CEOs, who seldom earn more than 15 times the employee average, look on in amazement. Said one observer, "The gap is widening beyond what the guy at the bottom can even understand. . . . There's very little common ground left in terms of the experience of the average worker and the CEO" (ref. 10, pp. 58, 62).

While most U.S. workers are willing to accept substantial differentials in pay between corporate highs and lows, and acknowledge that the highs should receive their just rewards, more and more of the lows—and the middles—are asking, "Just how just is just?"

Challenges

1. To many people, a deep-seated sense of unfairness lies at the heart of the trust gap. What are some of the ways that perceptions of unfairness might develop?
2. What are some of the predictable consequences of a trust gap?

---

1. How can we tie compensation strategy to general business strategy?
2. What economic and legal factors should be considered in establishing pay levels for different jobs?
3. What is the best way to develop pay systems that are understandable, workable, and acceptable to employees at all levels?

QUESTIONS THIS CHAPTER WILL HELP MANAGERS ANSWER

The chapter opening vignette illustrates important changes in current thinking about pay: Levels of pay will always be evaluated by employees in terms of "fairness," and unless pay systems are acceptable to those affected by them, they will breed mistrust and lack of commitment. Pay policies are critically important, for they affect every single employee, from the janitor to the CEO. This chapter explores four major questions: (1) What economic and legal factors determine pay levels within a firm? (2) How do firms tie compensation strategy to general business strategy? (3) How do firms develop systematic pay structures that reflect different levels of pay for different jobs? (4) What key policy issues in pay planning and administration must managers address? These "challenges" are shown graphically in Figure 10-2.

As an educated consumer or manager, it is important that you become knowledgeable about these important issues. This chapter will help you develop that knowledge base.

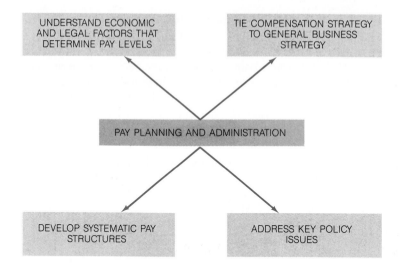

FIGURE 10-2
Four key challenges in planning and administering a pay system.

CHANGING PHILOSOPHIES REGARDING PAY SYSTEMS

In 1970, experts made predictions concerning the future of pay systems. The economy of the 1970s was expected to be strong, and median incomes were expected to rise substantially: They did. Inflation was expected to drop from the abnormally high rate of 4 percent: It did not. The makeup of the workforce (male-female) was expected to remain fairly constant: It did not. The population over the age of 65 was expected to approach 23 million: It did. The average workweek was expected to move to 35 hours (or fewer) per week. By 1990 it did. It fell to 34.3 hours because of increased part-time work by women. These economic and population trends are still with us. They will help shape what occurs in the 1990s and beyond, as they did in the 1980s and 1970s. And they are relevant to a number of factors that will determine the future of pay systems.[24]

One example of this is the continuing move away from policies of "salary entitlement," where *inflation*, not *performance*, was the driving force. Pay for performance suffered during this time. With budgets for salary increases eroded by inflationary pressures, high performers were awarded raises only slightly larger than those of average performers. Such a policy leads to predictable effects: *reduced motivation to perform well*. In the current atmosphere of cost containment, however, we are seeing three major changes in company philosophies concerning pay and benefits:

1. Increased willingness to reduce the size of the workforce and to restrict pay to control the costs of wages, salaries, and benefits.

2. Less concern with pay position relative to competitors, and more concern with what the company can afford.

3. Implementation of programs to encourage and reward performance. In fact, a recent study revealed that this is one of the most critical compensation issues facing large companies today.[5]

We will consider each of these changes, as with other material in this and the following chapter, from the perspective of the line manager, not from that of the technical compensation specialist.

Cost Containment Actions

Until the early 1980s, employees were accustomed to hefty annual pay increases and an ever richer banquet of benefits. Now many chief executives are preparing for a future that they think will be characterized by lowered business expectations, tougher competition, government ineptitude in economics, and a need for greater productivity. To cope with these changes, they are attempting to contain staff sizes, payrolls, and the costs of benefits. Some of the cutbacks are only temporary, such as pay freezes, postponements of raises, and suspensions of cost-of-living allowances. Other changes are meant to be permanent: firing executives or offering them early retirement; asking employees to work longer hours, to take fewer days off, and to shorten their vacations; reducing the coverage of medical plans or asking employees to pay part of the costs; trimming expense accounts with bans on first-class travel and restrictions on phone calls and entertainment.[27]

If such a strategy is to work, however, CEOs will first need to demonstrate to employees at all levels, by means of tangible actions, that they are serious about closing the "trust gap" (see chapter opening vignette).

Given that wage and salary payments comprise about 60 percent of all costs of nonfinancial corporations, employers have an obvious interest in controlling them.[26] One example of this is overtime.

CONTROLLING OVERTIME AMONG
NEW YORK CITY EMPLOYEES

■ **COMPANY
EXAMPLE**

Led by a supervising electrician in the Department of Corrections who was paid more than the mayor, New York City employees made $426 million in overtime in 1989, a 28.5 percent increase over the 1988 amount, and the ninth consecutive increase in overtime spending. The electrician, a 29-year veteran employee, earned over $84,000 for working 1926 hours of overtime in 1989, at a rate of $43.65 an overtime hour. With a base pay of about $52,000 per year, his total income exceeded $136,000—topping the mayor's annual salary of $130,000.

In response the mayor noted: "Overtime is not an inherently dirty word. Some overtime spending is a necessary part of the city's response to short-term emergency situations or special events."[6] But he added that unnecessary overtime drains funds. Then he ordered city agency heads to control overtime. The order prohibits city employees from receiving overtime pay in excess of 5 percent of their base salaries without prior approval from their agency heads and only for special reasons.[6]

In good times managers did not have to get rid of poor performers. Bad times made that unpleasant task harder to avoid. Certainly any serious effort to cut management costs must focus on the payroll. This is because an executive costs a company roughly *double* his or her annual salary. Here's why. Benefits cost an average of almost 40 percent of base pay. Office, secretarial, and travel expenses make up the rest. Hence, getting rid of a $75,000-a-year executive and not replacing him or her saves about $150,000 per year.

Paying What the Company Can Afford

To cover its labor costs and other expenses, a company must earn sufficient revenues through the sales of its products or services. It follows, then, that an employer's ability to pay is constrained by its ability to compete. The nature of the product or service market affects a firm's external competitiveness and the pay level it sets.[29]

Key factors in the product or service markets are the degree of competition among producers (e.g., fast-food outlets) and the level of demand for the products or services (e.g., the number of customers in a given area). Both of these affect the ability of a firm to change the prices of its products or services. If an employer cannot change prices without suffering a loss of revenues due to decreased sales, then the employer's ability to raise the level of pay is constrained. If the employer does pay more, it has two options: try to pass the increased costs on to consumers, or hold prices fixed and allocate a greater portion of revenues to cover labor costs.[29]

As is well known, the U.S. steel industry struggled with a host of problems in the 1980s. These ranged from the lofty, uncompetitive wages of unionized employees, to the antiquated state of many mills and fabricating plants, to the relentless pressure of foreign competitors who themselves were burdened with bulging capacity and weak domestic markets. Because of excessively generous wage settlements throughout the 1970s, steelworker employment costs in 1980 averaged $17.46 an hour, versus $9.63 for their Japanese counterparts. Said the chairman of USX: "Our labor costs alone put us out of the ball game."[14] As a result, U.S. steel was not competitive in world markets. While it is true that labor is only one part of overall production costs, unless the cost per unit produced is lower than the competition's (by reducing costs other than labor), then high labor costs will render a company uncompetitive.

To avoid annihilation, U.S. steel companies poured $9 billion into upgrading their mills between 1982 and 1989. At the same time, a massive downsizing effort resulted in 60 percent of the industry's 428,000 workers losing their jobs. Those who remained gave generous pay concessions, such that in 1989 steelworkers earned $22.63 an hour ($15.48 in 1980 dollars)—versus $18.52 in Japan. The result? U.S. steel companies are much better positioned to compete in world markets in the 1990s. In fact, after years of decline, employment levels are expected to rise slowly as the industry rebounds.[14]

Programs That Encourage and Reward Performance

Firms are continuing to relocate to areas where organized labor is weak and pay rates are low. They are developing pay plans that channel more dollars into incentive awards and fewer into fixed salary. They are trying to get rid of automatic cost-of-living raises, and they are passing over more employees for raises so that they can award top performers meaningful pay increases. These programs all have a profit and productivity orientation and a commitment to share success with employees who produce.

On the other hand, employees will not *automatically* accept this orientation toward improved performance, for, in a sense, firms are "changing the rules" of the compensation game. The key to a genuine pay-for-performance system is for management to promote this kind of understanding in everything it says and does: *Better performance will increase productivity, and outstanding performers will see a share of that benefit in their paychecks.*[3] Chapter 12 will discuss more fully the pay-for-performance theme and how it can be put into effect.

COMPONENTS AND OBJECTIVES OF ORGANIZATIONAL REWARD SYSTEMS

At a broad level, an organizational reward system includes anything an employee values and desires that an employer is able and willing to offer in exchange for employee contributions. More specifically, the reward system includes both compensation and noncompensation rewards. Compensation rewards include direct financial payments plus indirect payments in the form of employee benefits (see Chapter 11). Noncompensation rewards include everything in a work environment that enhances a worker's sense of self-respect and esteem by others (e.g., work environments that are physically, socially, and mentally healthy; training to improve job skills; and status symbols to enhance individual perceptions of self-worth).

Rewards bridge the gap between organizational objectives and individual expectations and aspirations. To be effective, organizational reward systems should provide four things: (1) a sufficient *level* of rewards to fulfill basic needs, (2) equity with the external labor market, (3) equity within the organization, and (4) treatment of each member of the organization in terms of his or her individual needs.[22,23] More broadly, pay systems are designed to attract, retain, and motivate employees. Indeed, much of the design of compensation systems involves working out tradeoffs among more or less seriously conflicting objectives.[12]

INTERNATIONAL APPLICATION: TYING PAY TO PERFORMANCE IN THE UNITED STATES AND JAPAN

In an effort to hold down labor costs, thousands of U.S. companies are changing the way they increase workers' pay. Instead of the traditional annual increase, millions of workers in industries as diverse as supermarkets and aircraft manufacturing are receiving cash bonuses. For most workers, the plans mean less money. The bonuses take many names: "profit sharing" at Abbott Laboratories and Hewlett-Packard, "gain sharing" at Mack Trucks and Dana Corporation, and "lump-sum payments" at Boeing. All have two elements in common: (1) They can vary with the company's fortunes, and (2) they are not permanent. Because the bonuses are not folded into base pay, there is no compounding effect over time. This means that both wages and benefits rise more slowly. The result: a flattening of wages nationally.[45]

Today, 40 percent of all workers covered by major union agreements have bonus provisions in their contracts. How have unions reacted? In the view of the AFL-CIO, "Where there is justification for belt-tightening, then profit sharing is not an unreasonable means of passing on earnings when times improve" (ref. 45, p. D3).

In summary, "flexible pay"—tied mostly to profitability and promising better job security, but not guaranteeing it—is at the heart of the evolving bonus system. Employees are being asked to share the risks of the new global marketplace. How large must the rewards be? MIT economist Martin Weitzman estimates that over the long run the proper bonus level is 20 to 25 percent of total compensation, because it would give workers a pay increase equal to the rate of inflation plus productivity gains. But in the United States most bonus payments have been averaging about 10 percent of a worker's base pay annually. Conversely, the Japanese currently pay many workers a bonus system that represents about 25 percent of base pay. No other industrial nation bases pay on a bonus system.

Have such plans generated greater productivity in the U.S. manufacturing sector in recent years? Maybe, but an equally plausible explanation is that the gains were due to automation, to company efforts to give workers more of a say in how they do their jobs, and to the fear of workers that if they did not improve their productivity, their plants would become uncompetitive and would be closed.[45] In short, the jury is still out on the productivity impact of bonus systems as well as on their effect on worker motivation and organizational commitment.

Perhaps the most important objective of any pay system is fairness or equity. Equity can be assessed on at least three dimensions:

- *Internal equity* (i.e., in terms of the relative worth of individual jobs to an organization, are pay rates fair?),
- *External equity* (i.e., are the wages paid by an organization "fair" in terms of competitive market rates outside the organization?)
- *Individual equity* (i.e., is each individual's pay "fair" relative to other individuals doing the same or similar jobs?)

Several theories for determining equitable payment for work have been proposed.[29,41] They have three points in common. One, each assumes that employees perceive a fair return for what they contribute to their jobs, Two, all include the concept of *social comparison*, whereby employees determine what their equitable return should be after comparing their inputs (skills, education, effort, etc.) and outcomes (pay, promotion, job status, etc.) with those of their coworkers (comparison persons). Third, the theories assume that employees who perceive themselves to be in an inequitable situation will seek to reduce that inequity. They may do so by mentally distorting inputs or outcomes, by directly altering inputs or outcomes, or by leaving the organization. Reviews of both laboratory and field tests of equity theory are quite consistent: Individuals tend to follow the equity norm and to use it as a basis for distributing rewards. They report inequitable conditions as distressing, although there may be individual differences in the relative sensitivity to equity.[17]

A final objective is balance—the optimal combination of direct and indirect compensation, of financial and nonfinancial rewards. Perhaps the major issue is the extent to which benefit dollars as contrasted with wage and salary dollars contribute to employee motivation and to competitive realities.[12] Another aspect of balance concerns the relative size of pay differentials among different segments of the work-force. If pay systems are to accomplish the objectives set for them, then ultimately they must be perceived as adequate and equitable. For example, there should be a balance in relationships between supervisors and the highest-paid subordinates reporting to them. According to the public accounting firm Coopers & Lybrand, among companies judged to be well managed, this differential is generally 15 percent.[20] As the chapter opening vignette illustrated, ratios of 100:1 between highest- and lowest-paid employees are generally regarded as out of balance.

STRATEGIC INTEGRATION OF COMPENSATION PLANS AND BUSINESS PLANS

Unfortunately, the rationale for many compensation programs is "Two-thirds of our competitors do it" or "That's corporate policy." Compensation plans need to be tied to the strategic mission of an organization and should take their direction from that strategic mission. They must support general business strategy.[15] From a managerial perspective, therefore, the most fundamental decision is: "What do you want your pay system to accomplish?"

This approach to managing compensation and business strategies dictates that actual levels of compensation should *not* strictly be a matter of what is being paid in the marketplace. Instead, compensation levels derive from an assessment of what *must* be paid to attract and retain the right people, what the organization can *afford*, and what will be *required* to meet the strategic goals of the organization. Table 10-1 illustrates how different compensation strategies can be applied in firms that differ (a) in their business strategies and (b) in their market positions and maturity.

■ **TABLE 10·1**
LINKING COMPENSATION STRATEGY TO BUSINESS STRATEGY

Business strategy	Market position and maturity	Compensation strategy	Blend of compensation
Invest to grow	Merging or growing rapidly	Stimulate entrepreneurialism	High cash with above-average incentives for individual performance Modest benefits
Manage earnings— protect markets	Normal growth to maturity	Reward management skills	Average cash with moderate incentives on individual, unit, or corporate performance Standard benefits
Harvest earnings— reinvest elsewhere	No real growth or decline	Stress cost control	Below-average cash with small incentive tied to cost control Standard benefits

Source: Adapted from R. J. Greene & R. G. Roberts, Strategic integration of compensation and benefits, *Personnel Administrator*, **28**(5), 1983, 82. Copyright, 1983. Reprinted with permission from *HRMagazine* (formerly *Personnel Administrator*) published by the Society for Human Resource Management, Alexandria, VA.

In firms that are growing rapidly, business strategy tends to be focused on one objective: Invest to grow. To be consistent with this business strategy, compensation strategy should stimulate an enterprising, entrepreneurial style of management (see Chapter 4). To do this, the firm should emphasize high cash payments with above-average incentives ("high risk, high reward"). In "mature" firms (see Chapter 4), business strategy is oriented primarily toward managing earnings and protecting markets. Compensation strategy should therefore reward management skills, and, to do this, there should be a blend of average cash payments, moderate incentives, and standard benefits. In the "aging" firm (see Chapter 4), the most appropriate strategy is to harvest earnings and reinvest them elsewhere. Compensation strategy emphasizes the control of costs. To implement such a strategy, standard benefits are combined with below-average cash, and modest incentives are tied directly to the control of costs.

Compensation consultants say that currently only about 20 percent of firms tailor their compensation plans to different stages of development, but that's up from 5 percent in the late 1980s.[9]

Compensation Strategies for Special Situations

Many companies now recognize that their pay policies must change in order to cope with special situations, such as restructurings linked to takeover attempts, or massive divestitures. Restructurings linked to takeover attempts are among the most common triggers for special pay plans. Consider the case of Owens-Corning Fiberglas Corporation.

After the company took on huge debt to ward off a hostile takeover bid from the Wickes Companies, the main objective was to persuade managers to stay with the company and return it to stability. So it installed an all-stock bonus plan for 150 top people that would not pay out for 7 years. The payout was not tied to specific goals, but managers knew that the stock price wouldn't move until they got debt down and profits up.

The scheme paid off: The management team stayed, Owens-Corning is ahead of schedule on paying its debt, and its stock, which was at $12 when the plan was instituted, traded in the low $20s in mid-1990.

Different plans are needed to retain managers during divestitures. In 1987 the Penn Central Corporation spun off Sprague Technologies, its electronics components subsidiary. To persuade a handful of executives to go with Sprague, Penn Central offered a "retention transition bonus." If they stayed with Sprague for a year, their Penn Central Stock options, which would normally expire 90 days after an employee's departure, would stay in effect, and they would receive an extra year's salary and bonus. The executives went with Sprague, and are still with the company.

Now things have changed at Sprague again. It is liquidating one of its divisions, and it has put in a one-shot bonus plan for the division's three key people, payable after the liquidation is over—and their jobs have been eliminated.

Top managers are generally the beneficiaries of special-situation pay plans. However, some companies (especially those in pharmaceuticals and consumer products) are starting to extend bonus plans to researchers, package designers, and other midlevel people involved in product development. The plans, which usually involve cash bonuses, pay in stages—when a product is developed, when it is introduced, and when it achieves a specified market share. After that, the profits the product generates all count toward the general bonus pool.[9] A summary of such plans for these and other special situations is presented in Figure 10-3.

TEMPORARY PAY PLANS TO SUIT THE SITUATION

SITUATION	TYPICAL PAY PLAN	EXAMPLE
High debt, as in a leveraged buyout	Cash bonuses or equity based on cash flow, cost cutting	RJR Nabisco, Inc.
Closed plant; liquidated division	Cash bonus payable at end of shut-down operation	Sprague Technologies, Inc.
Start-up division; introduction of new product	Stock or cash awarded first for meeting development deadlines, then for market-share growth	Williams Telecommunications
Divestiture	Stock or cash payable to managers who stay on a year after divestiture	The Penn Central Corporation

FIGURE 10-3
Pay plans for special situations. (*Source:* C. H. Deutch, Revising pay packages, again, *The New York Times,* February 25, 1990, p. F29.) Copyright © 1990 by The New York Times Company. Reprinted by permission.)

DETERMINANTS OF PAY STRUCTURE AND LEVEL

In simplest terms, marginal revenue product theory in labor economics holds that the value of a person's labor is what someone is willing to pay for it.[29] In practice, a number of factors *interact* to determine wage levels. Some of the most influential of these are labor market conditions, legislation, collective bargaining, management attitudes, and an organization's ability to pay. Let us examine each of these.

Labor Market Conditions

As noted in Chapter 4, "tight" versus "loose" labor markets have a major impact on wage structures and levels. Thus if the demand for certain skills is high while the supply is low (a "tight" market), there tends to be an *increase* in the price paid for these skills. Conversely, if the supply of labor is plentiful, relative to the demand for it, wages tend to *decrease*. As an example, consider the following starting salaries for 1990 college graduates with Bachelor's degrees:[28]

Area	Average starting salary
Engineering, Petroleum	$35,202
Chemistry	27,494
Computer Science	29,804
Mathematics, Statistics	27,032
Accounting	26,391
Business Administration	23,529
Foreign Languages	23,607
Marketing	23,543
Journalism	19,488

To a considerable extent, these differences in starting salaries reflect different labor market conditions in the various fields. Another impact of labor market supply and demand factors can be seen in the wages paid by companies in different geographic locations. Virtually all large companies and, as of 1991, even the federal government use some kind of geographic adjustment. For example, an employee earning an annual salary of $43,000 in Seattle could expect to receive the following salary by geographic area, adjusted to 1990 dollars:[28]

Anchorage	$48,588	Memphis	$37,491
Fresno, CA	43,200	Richmond, VA	42,802
Los Angeles	49,301	San Diego	51,441
Syracuse, NY	37,966	Indianapolis	39,671
Philadelphia	50,411	Houston	40,741

Another labor market phenomenon that causes substantial differences in pay rates, even among people who work in the same field and are of similar age and education, is the payment of wage premiums by employers to attract the best talent available. This is known as the "efficiency wage hypothesis" in labor economics, and it has received considerable support among economic researchers.[34]

A final factor that can affect the supply of labor and hence tighten the market is the relative *hazard* level of the work. Consider the following example.

"JUMPERS" WHO MAKE 12 HOURS' PAY FOR 10 MINUTES' WORK

■ COMPANY EXAMPLE

The catch—and there has to be one—is the job site. Every year the nuclear industry recruits hundreds of "jumpers" who fix the aging innards of the nation's nuclear generating stations. The atmosphere is so radioactive that jumpers can stay only about 10 minutes before, in industry parlance, they "burn out." As compensation for their 10 minutes' work, they receive 12 hours' pay. Typically, jumpers are people with few skills or job prospects elsewhere. They crawl into the power plants unsupported by any labor union, health insurance plan, or job security.[47] Repairs often have to do with corrosion or leakage of water pipes, a process that can be slowed but not stopped completely.

What are the risks? The Nuclear Regulatory Commission estimates that if each of 10,000 workers is exposed to 5000 millirems (roughly 250 chest x-rays) over the course of a year, three to eight of them will eventually die of cancer as a result of the exposure. If they are exposed to that level for 30 years, 5 percent of them will die of cancer.

The system pleases jumpers because it makes for lots of jobs. Said one, "Last year I think I got over 4000 millirems. I like to work till I get my limit. If you don't reach your limit, you're wasting your time"(ref. 47, p. 19).

Jumpers have a particular incentive to absorb the maximum radiation permitted on a given job. They get a bonus of several hundred dollars each time they "burn out" on an assignment. Between jobs they complete a battery of medical records, security checks, and psychological evaluations. "They don't want someone nutty in the reactor, messing things up," said one jumper. "You have to be a little weird to do this job. You just can't be *too* weird" (ref. 47, p. 19).

Highly hazardous work pays well; but then again it has to, in order to attract workers who are willing to take the risks. The forces discussed thus far affect pay levels to a considerable extent. So also does government legislation.

Legislation

As in other areas, legislation related to pay plays a vital role in determining internal organization practices. Although all the relevant laws cannot be analyzed here, a summary of the coverage, major provisions, and federal agencies charged with administering four major federal wage-hour laws is presented in Table 10-2. Wage-hour laws set limits on minimum wages to be paid and maximum hours to be worked.

■ **TABLE 10·2**
FOUR MAJOR FEDERAL WAGE-HOUR LAWS

	Scope of coverage	Major provisions	Administrative agency
Fair Labor Standards Act (FLSA) of 1938 (as amended)	Employers involved in interstate commerce with two or more employees and annual revenues greater than $500,000. Exemption from overtime provisions for managers, supervisors, executives, outside salespersons, and professional workers.	Minimum wage of $4.25 per hour for covered employees (as of April 1991); time and one-half pay for over 40 hours per week; restrictions by occupation or industry on the employment of persons under 18; prohibits wage differentials based exclusively on sex—equal pay for equal work. No extra pay required for weekends, vacations, holidays, or severance.	Wage and Hour Division of the Employment Standards Administration, U.S. Department of Labor
Davis-Bacon Act (1931)	Federal contractors involved in the construction or repair of federal buildings and public works, with a contract value over $2000.	Employees on the project must be paid prevailing community wage rates for the type of employment used. Overtime at time and one-half for more than 40 hours per week. Three-year blacklisting of contractors who violate this act.	Comptroller General and Wage and Hour Division
Walsh-Healy Act (1936)	Federal contractors manufacturing or supplying materials, articles, or equipment to the federal government, with a value exceeding $10,000 annually.	Same as Davis-Bacon. Under the Defense Authorization Act of 1986, overtime is required only for hours worked in excess of 40 per week, not 8 per day, as previously.[26]	Same as FLSA
McNamara-O'Hara Service Contract Act (1965)	Federal contractors who provide services to the federal government with a value in excess of $2500.	Same as Davis-Bacon.	Same as Davis-Bacon

Of the four laws shown in Table 10-2, the Fair Labor Standards Act (FLSA) affects almost every organization in the United States. It is the source of the terms "exempt employees" (exempt from the overtime provisions of the law) and "non-exempt employees." It established the first national minimum wage (25 cents an hour) in 1938; subsequent changes in the minimum wage and in national policy on equal pay for equal work for both sexes (the Equal Pay Act of 1963) were passed as amendments to this law.

There are many loopholes in FLSA minimum-wage coverage.[32] Certain occupations, including casual babysitters and most farm workers, are excluded, as well as employees of small businesses and firms not engaged in interstate commerce. State minimum-wage laws are intended to cover these workers. At the same time, if a state's minimum is higher than the federal minimum, then the state minimum applies.

In the 1980s, the minimum wage really lived up to its name. From 1981, when it was raised to $3.35 an hour, to 1990, when it jumped to $3.80 an hour, inflation had eroded its purchasing power by more than 27 percent. Even in 1991, when the minimum reached $4.25 an hour, that was still less than 50 percent of the average hourly wage paid in the United States. How many people earn the minimum wage? Only about 4 million of the nation's 60 million hourly workers. About 40 percent of them are teenagers.[21]

An important feature of the FLSA is its provision regarding the employment of young workers. On school days, 14-year-olds and 15-year-olds are allowed to work no more than 3 hours, or 18 hours during the 5-day school week. On weekend days, 14-year-olds and 15-year-olds are allowed to work 8 hours. They may also work 40-hour weeks during the summer and during school vacations, but they may not work outside the hours of 7 A.M. to 7 P.M. (or 9 P.M. June 1 to Labor Day). Both federal and state laws allow 16-year-olds and 17-year-olds to work any hours but forbid them from hazardous occupations, such as driving or working with power-driven meat slicers.

According to the Department of Labor, the number of child-labor violations has doubled since 1982 as worker shortages in some areas impelled employers to hire more workers of high school age. Most offenders allow teenagers to work too many hours on school days or allow students to use dangerous equipment.[7,39]

The remaining three laws shown in Table 10-2 apply only to organizations that do business with the federal government in the form of construction or by supplying goods and services.

Collective Bargaining

Another major influence on wages in unionized *as well as* nonunionized firms is collective bargaining. Nonunionized firms are affected by collective bargaining agreements made elsewhere since they must compete with unionized firms for the services and loyalties of workers. Collective bargaining affects two key factors: (1) the *level* of wages and (2) the *behavior of workers* in relevant labor markets. In an open, competitive market, workers tend to gravitate toward higher-paying jobs.

To the extent that nonunionized firms fail to match the wages of unionized firms, they may have difficulty attracting and keeping workers. Furthermore, benefits negotiated under union agreements have had the effect of increasing the "package" of benefits in firms that have attempted to avoid unionization. In addition to wages and benefits, collective bargaining is also used to negotiate procedures for administering pay, procedures for resolving grievances regarding compensation decisions, and methods used to determine the relative worth of jobs.[30]

Managerial Attitudes and an Organization's Ability to Pay

These factors have a major impact on wage structures and levels. It was noted earlier how the labor costs of U.S. steelworkers had to be reduced in order to compete in global markets. This is an important principle. Regardless of an organization's espoused competitive position on wages, its ability to pay will ultimately be a key factor that limits actual wages.

This is not to downplay the role of management philosophy and attitudes on pay. On the contrary, management's desire to maintain or to improve morale, to attract high-caliber employees, to reduce turnover, and to improve employees' standards of living also affect wages, as does the relative importance of a given position to a firm.[33] A safety engineer is more important to a chemical company than to a bank. Wage structures tend to vary across firms to the extent that managers view any given position as more or less critical to their firms. Despite the appearance of scientific precision, compensation administration will always reflect management judgment to a considerable degree. Ultimately top management renders judgments regarding the overall competitive pay position of the firm (above-market, at-the-market, or below-market rates), factors to be considered in determining job worth, and the relative weight to be given seniority and performance in pay decisions. They are key determinants of the structure and level of wages.

AN OVERVIEW OF PAY SYSTEM MECHANICS

The procedures described below for developing pay systems help those involved in the development process to apply their judgments in a systematic manner. Hallmarks of success in compensation management, as in other areas, are understandability, workability, and acceptability. Our broad objective in developing pay systems is to assign a monetary value to each job in the organization (a base rate) and an orderly procedure for increasing the base rate (e.g., based on merit, seniority, or some combination of the two). To develop such a system, we need four basic tools:

1. Updated job descriptions
2. A job evaluation plan
3. Pay surveys
4. A pay structure

Job descriptions were considered in Chapter 4. In the context of pay system design, they serve two purposes:

1. They identify important characteristics of each job so that the relative worth of jobs can be determined.
2. From them we can identify, define, and weight *compensable factors* (common characteristics of all jobs that an organization is willing to pay for, such as skill, effort, responsibility, and working conditions). Once job descriptions have been developed, the next step is to evaluate the jobs.

■ TABLE 10·3a
QUANTITATIVE JOB EVALUATION METHODS

Approach	Methodology	Advantages	Disadvantages
Point factor	Select compensable factors. Define the degrees within each factor on a numerical scale. Weight the compensable factors. Analyze and describe the jobs in terms of the compensable factors. Determine which degree definition for each factor best fits the job. Assign points for each factor based on the evaluation. Arrange a job-worth hierarchy based on the total points for each job.	Reliable Relatively objective Easy to evaluate new or revised jobs	Expensive to develop or purchase Difficult to control evaluator bias[1,31]
Factor comparison	Select compensable factors. Analyze and describe the jobs in terms of the compensable factors. Vertically rank the jobs on each factor. Weight each factor in terms of its relative importance to the organization. Calculate the total points for each job. Develop a job-worth hierarchy based on total points.	Relatively reliable Scales are easy to use Compensable factors tailored to organization Easy to communicate	No degree definitions Difficult to evaluate new or revised job
Job component	In the job component approach, one or more independent variables are related to a "dependent" variable in a statistical equation. Choose a dependent variable and independent variables that are considered important in predicting and explaining pay relationships. Enter the data using a statistical software package. The resulting statistical model can be used for auditing current systems or for assigning pay rates in a new system.	Objective Comprehensive Statistically accurate Management-oriented	Expensive to develop or purchase Time-consuming Complex Difficult to communicate to employees

A number of job evaluation methods have been developed since the 1920s, and many, if not most, of them are still used. They all have the same final objective, and they all yield similar results.[13] The objective of all the methods is to rank jobs in terms of their relative worth to the organization so that an equitable rate of pay can be determined for each job. A brief description of some common approaches to job evaluation, along with their relative advantages and disadvantages, is presented in Tables 10-3a and 10-3b.

Job evaluation is used widely, but not universally, among firms. One reason is that several policy issues must be resolved first. These include:[16]

- Does management perceive meaningful differences among jobs?
- Can meaningful criteria for distinguishing among jobs be identified and operationalized?
- Will job evaluation result in meaningful distinctions in the eyes of employees?
- Are jobs stable, and will they remain stable in the future?

■ **TABLE 10·3b**
NONQUANTITATIVE, "WHOLE-JOB" JOB CONTENT METHODS

Approach	Methodology	Advantages	Disadvantages
Ranking	Identify the most "important" job in the job set. Identify the next most important job. Continue this process until all jobs are arranged in a hierarchy.	Simple to administer Inexpensive Quickly implemented Little training required	No specific standards No detail or documentation May be superficial Incumbent may unduly influence evaluation
Classification	Create job grades with generic definitions at each grade level. Compare the job descriptions with the grade descriptions. Assign each job to the grade most closely matching the level of work performed.	Simple to administer Inexpensive Quickly implemented Little training required	Jobs may be forced into classes they do not fit Descriptions can be rigged to fit a class
Slotting	Use the existing hierarchy. Compare the new or revised job with the jobs already assigned to existing job grades. Assign the job to the grade containing other jobs that appear similar in overall worth.	Simple to administer Inexpensive Quickly implemented Little training required	Cannot be used as stand-alone method because it is based on a preexisting structure No specific standards

Nonquantitative, whole-job evaluation methods require *each* evaluator individually (1) to determine which compensable factors he or she will use to compare the jobs, (2) to "weight" the compensable factors, and (3) to define and apply factors to jobs. These may produce inconsistent ratings across evaluators.

- Is job evaluation consistent with the organization's goals and strategies? For example, if the goal is to assure maximum flexibility among job assignments, then a knowledge- or skill-based pay system may be most appropriate.

Under such a system, workers are not paid on the basis of the job they currently are doing, but rather on the basis of the number of jobs they are *capable* of doing. For example, at Volvo's Uddevalla, Sweden, plant, workers assemble entire cars in teams of 8 to 10 persons. After 6 months of classroom and on-the-job training, a new employee can assemble about one-third of a new car. Through its company-funded training programs, Volvo encourages employees to continue to learn how to assemble different components of a car, and it rewards them for doing so. In such a "learning environment," the more workers learn, the more they earn.

Although firms such as General Foods, General Motors, Procter and Gamble, and Anheuser-Busch have been experimenting with knowledge-based pay,[44] the point-factor method remains the most popular approach. As an illustration (see page 358), let's consider a point-factor method developed and used by Hay and Associates.

Linking Internal Pay Relationships to Market Data

Once point totals have been derived, the next task is to translate them into a pay structure. A key component in this process is to identify and to survey pay rates in relevant labor markets. This can often be a complex problem since employers must pay attention not only to *labor* markets but also to *product* markets.[35] Pay practices must be designed not only to attract and retain employees but also to ensure that labor costs (as part of the overall costs of production) do not become excessive in relation to those of competing employers.

The definition of relevant labor markets requires two key decisions: which jobs to survey and which markets are relevant for each job. Jobs selected for a survey generally are characterized by stable tasks and stable job specifications (e.g., computer programmers, purchasing managers). Jobs with these characteristics are known as "key" jobs. Other jobs that are characterized by high turnover or that are difficult to fill also should be included.

As we noted earlier, the definition of relevant labor markets should consider geographical boundaries (e.g., local, regional, national, or international) as well as product-market competitors. Such an approach might begin with product-market competitors as the initial market, followed by adjustments downward (e.g., from national to regional markets) on the basis of geographical considerations.

Once target populations and relevant markets have been identified, the next task is to obtain survey data. Surveys are available from a variety of sources, including the federal government (Bureau of Labor Statistics), associations of employers, trade and professional associations, users of a given job evaluation system (e.g., clients of the Hay Group), or from compensation consulting firms.

Managers should be aware of two potential problems with pay survey data.[11] The most serious is the assurance of an accurate job match. If only a "thumbnail

ILLUSTRATION: A BRIEF LOOK
AT THE HAY JOB EVALUATION SYSTEM

At the outset it is important to note two principles: (1) A job evaluation study often becomes an exercise in semantics—trying to express in words perceptible differences in jobs; and (2) jobs have to be explained in response to probing questions about what they require. Usually both tasks are accomplished by a committee comprised of employees who are familiar with company jobs, with guidance from an outside consultant.

The process of job evaluation is an enormously time-consuming, complex, and often frustrating task that is subject to all the political pressures and biases so "natural" among committee members who represent different functional areas. To establish the relationship among jobs in terms of relative worth to the firm, the job evaluation committee uses a systematic procedure that compares one job with another.

Experience has shown that this is easier to do if the committee compares *aspects* of jobs (that is, compensable factors) that are common to all jobs, to various degrees, rather than *whole* jobs. In the Hay system, three compensable factors are analyzed. They are *know-how*, *problem solving*, and *accountability*. Each is defined on a guide chart. An example of the Hay guide chart for the know-how factor is shown in Figure 10-4.

Each guide chart is composed of a point scale, similar to the one shown in Figure 10-4, in which adjacent terms differ by approximately 15 percent. The guide charts themselves reveal what is meant by "know-how," "problem solving," and "accountability." Each of these compensable factors is broken down in terms of more specific "building blocks." For example, know-how (see Figure 10-4) has three components:

1. Scientific disciplines, specialized techniques, and practical procedures

2. Managerial know-how

3. Human relations skills

Within component, 1, A, B, C, and D are the degrees of trained skills where know-how is characterized by education plus work experience. The specialized technical and professional skills built on subjects not included in a secondary education are represented by E, F, G, and H.

Management know-how (component 2) deals exclusively with the management process independent of scientific disciplines (component 1) and human relations skills (component 3). The intersection of ratings on components 1, 2, and 3 falls into one of three "slots." Jobs in slot I primarily consist of specialized "on-the-spot" execution; coordination of people or activities is minimal. Jobs in slot II involve coordination and integration of activities (as distinct from merely supervising them). Jobs in slot III emphasize total departmental operations or administration of a strategic corporate function (e.g., the job "director of computer operations").

Human relations (component 3) has three degrees:

1. *Basic.* Ordinary courtesy is sufficient.
2. *Important.* Handling people in situations where repercussions are anticipated but are not critical considerations in the overall content of the position.
3. *Critical.* Motivating others to do something is a critical requirement of the job, and the job cannot be done without such emphasis on human relations skills.

Working with job descriptions and the three guide charts, the task of the evaluation committee is to develop a point "profile" of each job on each compensable factor. The total number of points for each job is determined by adding the points assigned to each of the three factors. Note that points are assigned to jobs *independently* of market wage rates.

To provide a structure for evaluating all the jobs in an organization, the committee begins with a group of jobs called "benchmarks." Benchmark jobs:

- Are well established, with clear job contents
- Represent each functional area and vary from low to high job content
- Represent a large number of in-house jobs

Job evaluation committee members make their judgments independently, through secret voting. Differences among members are resolved subsequently in an open discussion. Each member's task is to arrive at a point total for each job on each factor. In the case of know-how, for example, the total is found in the slot that represents the intersection of ratings on components 1, 2, and 3. As an illustration, let's consider the job of "administrative clerk." Here is what compensation specialists call a "thumbnail sketch" (i.e., an abbreviated job description) of the job:

Performs a variety of clerical tasks such as payroll, accounts receivable, accounts payable, or other specialized clerical work requiring knowledge of policies and procedures and a moderate degree of independent judgment.

In terms of Figure 10-4, the job evaluation committee might decide that the job of administrative clerk rates a C-I-1 on the compensable factor know-how. That is, the level of scientific disciplines is a C (vocational), the level of managerial know-how is a I, and the level of human relations skill involved also merits a 1. Note that within each cell there are three different point totals to choose from. This is done to allow the committee some flexibility in arriving at a point total. In the C-I-1 cell, let's assume that the committee assigned a total of 87 points to know-how.

As judgments accumulate within a slot, the slot assumes a pattern into which new jobs can reliably be fit. The pattern itself is established through the consensus of the committee members. Once set, it should not be tampered with as long as the jobs themselves do not change.

GUIDE  CHART

KNOW-HOW

© HAY ASSOCIATES 1984

● ● ● Human Relations Skills ⟶

DEFINITION: Know-How is the sum total of every kind of skill, however acquired, needed for acceptable job performance. Know-How has three dimensions — the requirements for:

● Practical procedures, specialized techniques, and scientific disciplines.

● ● Know-How of integrating and harmonizing the diversified functions involved in managerial situations occurring in operating, supporting, and administrative fields. This Know-How may be exercised consultatively (about management) as well as executively, and involves in some combination the areas of organizing, planning, executing, controlling and evaluating.

● ● ● Active, practicing, person-to-person skills in the area of human relationships.

MEASURING KNOW - HOW: Know-How has both scope (variety) and depth (thoroughness). Thus, a job may require some knowledge about a lot of things, or a lot of knowledge about a few things. The total Know-How is the combination of scope and depth. This concept makes practical the comparison and weighing of the total Know-How content of different jobs in terms of: "HOW MUCH KNOWLEDGE ABOUT HOW MANY THINGS."

PRACTICAL PROCEDURES

A. BASIC

Basic work routines plus work indoctrination.

B. ELEMENTARY VOCATIONAL

Familiarization in uninvolved, standardized work routines and/or use of simple equipment and machines.

C. VOCATIONAL

Procedural or systematic proficiency, which may involve a facility in the use of specialized equipment.

D. ADVANCED VOCATIONAL

Some specialized (generally nontechnical) skill(s), however acquired, giving additional breadth or depth to a generally single functional element.

SPECIALIZED TECHNIQUES

E. BASIC TECHNICAL - SPECIALIZED

Sufficiency in a technique which requires a grasp either of involved practices and precedents; or scientific theory and principles; or both.

F. SEASONED TECHNICAL - SPECIALIZED

Proficiency, gained through wide exposure or experiences in a specialized or technical field, in a technique which combines a broad grasp either of involved practices and precedents or of scientific theory and principles; or both.

G. TECHNICAL - SPECIALIZED MASTERY

Determinative mastery of techniques, practices and theories gained through wide seasoning and/or special development.

SCIENTIFIC DISCIPLINES

H. PROFESSIONAL MASTERY

Exceptional and unique mastery in scientific or other learned disciplines.

● ● ● H U M A N   R E L A T I O N S   S K I L L S

1. **BASIC:** Ordinary courtesy and effectiveness in dealing with others through normal contacts, and request for or providing information.

2. **IMPORTANT:** Understanding, influencing and/or serving people are important considerations in performing the job, causing action or understanding in others.

3. **CRITICAL:** Alternative or combined skills in understanding, selecting, developing and motivating people are important in the highest degree.

FIGURE 10-4

Illustrative industrial Hay guide chart for the compensable factor "know-how."

●●BREADTH OF MANAGEMENT KNOW-HOW																
I. NONE OR MINIMAL			II. RELATED			III. DIVERSE			IV. BROAD			V. TOTAL				
Performance or supervision of an activity (or activities) highly specific as to objective and content, with appropriate awareness of related activities.			Operational or conceptual integration or coordination of activities which are relatively homogeneous in nature and objective.			Operational or conceptual integration or coordination of activities which are diverse in nature and objectives, in an important management area.			Integration of major functions in an operating complex, or Company-wide coordination of a strategic function which significantly affects corporate planning or operations.							
1	2	3	1	2	3	1	2	3	1	2	3	1	2	3	
50	57	66	66	76	87	87	100	115	115	132	152	152	175	200	
57	66	76	76	87	100	100	115	132	132	152	175	175	200	230	A
66	76	87	87	100	115	115	132	152	152	175	200	200	230	264	
66	76	87	87	100	115	115	132	152	152	175	200	200	230	264	
76	87	100	100	115	132	132	152	175	175	200	230	230	264	304	B
87	100	115	115	132	152	152	175	200	200	230	264	264	304	350	
87	100	115	115	132	152	152	175	200	200	230	264	264	304	350	
100	115	132	132	152	175	175	200	230	230	264	304	304	350	400	C
115	132	152	152	175	200	200	230	264	264	304	350	350	400	460	
115	132	152	152	175	200	200	230	264	264	304	350	350	400	460	
132	152	175	175	200	230	230	264	304	304	350	400	400	460	528	D
152	175	200	200	230	264	264	304	350	350	400	460	460	528	608	
152	175	200	200	230	264	264	304	350	350	400	460	460	528	608	
175	200	230	230	264	304	304	350	400	400	460	528	528	608	700	E
200	230	264	264	304	350	350	400	460	460	528	608	608	700	800	
200	230	264	264	304	350	350	400	460	460	528	608	608	700	800	
230	264	304	304	350	400	400	460	528	528	608	700	700	800	920	F
264	304	350	350	400	460	460	528	608	608	700	800	800	920	1056	
264	304	350	350	400	460	460	528	608	608	700	800	800	920	1056	
304	350	400	400	460	528	528	608	700	700	800	920	920	1056	1216	G
350	400	460	460	528	608	608	700	800	800	920	1056	1056	1216	1400	
350	400	460	460	528	608	608	700	800	800	920	1056	1056	1216	1400	
400	460	528	528	608	700	700	800	920	920	1056	1216	1216	1400	1600	H
460	528	608	608	700	800	800	920	1056	1056	1216	1400	1400	1600	1840	

sketch" is used to characterize a job, there is always the possibility of legitimate misunderstanding among survey respondents. To deal with this, some surveys ask respondents if their salary data for a job are direct matches, or somewhat higher or lower than those described (and therefore worthy of more or less pay).

A second problem has resulted from the explosion of "at risk" forms of pay, some of which is based on individual performance and some on the profitability of an organization. Base pay is becoming a smaller part of the total compensation package for a broad range of employees. This makes it unclear what incumbents in a job actually make and can make survey results difficult to interpret. For example, how does one compare salary figures that include only base pay or direct cash payouts with "at-risk" pay that may take the form of a lump-sum bonus, additional time off with pay, or payment into an employee stock ownership plan?

Despite these potential problems, all indications are that pay surveys will continue to be used widely. Fortunately, commercial software packages now available allow analysts to play "What if?" scenarios, estimating the impact of various pay policies, market movements, and organizational changes on total salary costs. The

FIGURE 10-5

Chart relating hourly wage rates to the total points assigned to each job. Three trend lines are shown: minimum, midpoint, and maximum, as well as 11 pay grades. Within each pay grade there is a 30 percent spread from minimum to maximum and a 50 percent overlap from one pay grade to the next.

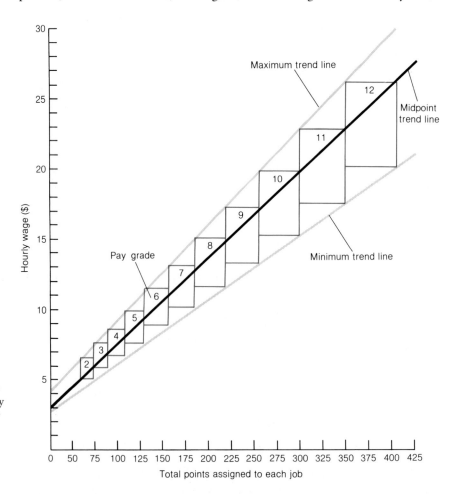

end result is often a chart, as in Figure 10-5, that relates current wage rates to the total points assigned each job. For each point total, a trend line is fitted to indicate the *average* relationship between points assigned to the benchmark jobs and the hourly wages paid for those jobs. Once a midpoint trend line is fitted, two others are also drawn: (1) a trend line that represents the *minimum* rate of pay for each point total and (2) a trend line that represents the *maximum* rate of pay for each point total.[46]

The final step in attaching dollar values to jobs using the point method is to establish *pay grades*, or ranges, characterized by a point spread from minimum to maximum for each grade. Starting wages are given by the trend line that represents the *minimum* rate of pay for each pay grade, while the highest wages that can be earned within a grade are given by the trend line that represents the *maximum* rate of pay. The pay structure is described numerically in Table 10-4.

For purposes of our "administrative clerk" example, let's assume that the job evaluation committee arrived at a total allocation of 142 points across all three compensable factors. The job therefore falls into pay grade 6. Starting pay is $8.75 per hour, with a maximum pay rate of $11.37 per hour.

The actual development of a pay structure is a complex process, but there are certain rules of thumb to follow:

- Jobs of the same general value should be clustered into the same pay grade.
- Jobs that clearly differ in value should be in different pay grades.
- There should be a smooth progression of point groupings.
- The new system should fit realistically into the existing allocation of pay within a company.

■ **TABLE 10·4**
ILLUSTRATIVE PAY STRUCTURE SHOWING PAY GRADES, THE SPREAD OF POINTS WITHIN GRADES, THE MIDPOINT OF EACH PAY GRADE, AND THE MINIMUM AND MAXIMUM RATES OF PAY PER GRADE

Grade	Point spread	Midpoint	Minimum rate of pay	Maximum rate of pay
2	62–75	68	$ 5.00	$ 6.50
3	76–91	83	5.75	7.47
4	92–110	101	6.61	8.60
5	111–132	121	7.60	9.89
6	133–157	145	8.75	11.37
7	158–186	172	10.06	13.07
8	187–219	203	11.57	15.03
9	220–257	238	13.30	17.29
10	258–300	279	15.30	19.88
11	301–350	325	17.59	22.87
12	351–407	379	20.23	26.30

ANNUAL COMPENSATION PLANNING WORKSHEET

ORG. UNIT _____

MGR. OR SUPV. _____

| EMPLOYEE NAME | JOB TITLE | LAST SALARY ADJUSTMENT | | | | CURRENT SALARY | RANGE MINIMUM | RANGE MIDPOINT | RANGE MAXIMUM | PERFORMANCE APPRAISAL | FORECAST SALARY ADJUSTMENT (If Any) | | | | |
		Amt.	%	Date	Type*						Amt.	%	Date	New Salary	Inter-val

*Code for "Type"
1—Promotion
2—Merit

PREPARED BY _____

FIGURE 10-6
Annual compensation
planning worksheet.

- The pay grades should conform reasonably well to pay patterns in the relevant labor markets.[38]

Once such a pay structure is in place, the determination of each individual's pay becomes a more systematic and orderly procedure. A compensation planning worksheet, such as that shown in Figure 10-6, can be very useful to managers confronted with these weighty decisions.

POLICY ISSUES IN PAY PLANNING AND ADMINISTRATION

Comparable Worth

When women dominate an occupational field (such as nursing or secretarial work), the rate of pay for jobs in that field tends to be lower than the pay that men receive when they are the dominant incumbents (e.g., construction, skilled trades). Is the market biased against jobs held mostly by women? Should jobs dominated by women and jobs dominated by men be paid equally if they are of "comparable" worth to an employer? Answering this question involves the knotty problem of how to make valid and accurate comparisons of the relative worth of unlike jobs. The key difference between the Equal Pay Act and comparable worth is this: The act requires equal pay for men and women who do work that is *substantially equal*. Comparable worth would require equal pay for work of *equal value* to an employer (e.g., librarian and electrician).

Job evaluation schemes are typically used to assess "worth" to an employer. Jobs with roughly equal point totals are considered to be of "comparable worth." While it is reassuring to note that research on alternative job evaluation methods has found them generally to be reliable, to yield comparable results, and to be free of systematic bias for or against jobs dominated by one sex,[8] pay levels of jobs can influence judgments of job content.[36] This means that biased market pay structures could work backward through the job evaluation process to produce relatively deflated evaluations for jobs held predominately by women without the need for any direct bias based on sex.

Should managers develop pay systems to ensure comparable worth? Some states have enacted "comparable worth" laws that affect public employees (e.g., Minnesota), and in Canada's Ontario Province, all large private as well as public employers are covered by such a law.[19] But wait. Is it possible that the goals of comparable worth can be achieved through normal labor market processes?

Consider that in recent years women have made dramatic inroads in jobs traditionally held by men. Moreover, as women deserted such low-paying jobs as secretary and nurse, the demand for such jobs held steady or increased, and pay rates climbed.[43] These are healthy trends that are likely to continue as long as aggressive enforcement of Title VII to ensure equal job opportunities for women is combined with vigorous enforcement of the Equal Pay Act. The appropriate response is to remove the barriers, not to undermine market forces that affect labor supply and demand.

Pay Secrecy

The extent to which information on pay is public or private is a basic issue that needs to be addressed by management. Legally, the U.S. courts have generally supported companies in their view that salary information, like a product formula or a marketing strategy, is confidential and the property of management. An employee who ferrets out and releases such data can be discharged for "willful misconduct."[40]

On the other hand, consider that pay secrecy is becoming an increasingly difficult policy to maintain, particularly as companies look to strengthen the link between pay and performance. For example, research with bank managers found that when pay systems are open, managers tend to award higher pay raises to subordinates on whom they depend heavily. Apparently they do so because they need the subordinates' cooperation, and subordinates can check on pay allocations.[2]

Openness versus secrecy is not an either/or phenomenon. Rather, it is a matter of degree. For example, organizations may choose to disclose one or more of the following: (1) the work- and business-related rationale on which the system is based, (2) pay ranges, (3) pay increase schedules, and (4) the availability of pay-related data from the compensation department.[29]

In general, open pay systems tend to work best under the following circumstances: Individual or team performance can be measured objectively, performance measures can be developed for all the important aspects of a job, and effort and performance are related closely over a relatively short time span.

The Effect of Inflation

All organizations must make some allowances for inflation in their salary programs. Given an inflation rate of 8 percent, for example, the firm that fails to increase its salary ranges at all over a 2-year period will be 16 percent behind its competitors. Needless to say, it becomes difficult to recruit new employees under these circumstances, and it becomes difficult to motivate present employees to remain or to produce.

How do firms cope? Automatic pay raises for nonunion employees have almost disappeared at most major concerns. Companies are tying pay more to performance. For example, at Commercial Metals Co. of Dallas, cost-of-living adjustments will not be resumed even if inflation zooms. The company found that its employees—*including average performers*—prefer to be paid on the basis of their performance. However, other firms that have adopted this approach, such as Armco and B.F. Goodrich, note that the switch from automatic to merit increases does not necessarily lower labor costs.[25]

Pay Compression

Pay compression is related to the general problem of inflation. It exists in many forms, including: (1) higher starting salaries for new hires, thereby leading long-term employees to see only a slight difference between their current pay and that of new hires; (2) hourly pay increases for unionized employees that exceed those of salaried and nonunion employees; (3) recruitment of new college graduates for management or professional jobs at salaries above those of current job holders; and (4) excessive overtime payments to some employees, or payment of different overtime rates (e.g., time and one-half for some and double time for others). However, first-line supervisors, unlike middle managers, may actually *benefit* from pay inflation among non-management employees since companies generally maintain a differential between the pay of supervisors and the pay of their highest-paid subordinates. As we noted earlier, these differentials average 15 percent.[18,20]

One solution to the problem of pay compression is to institute *equity adjustments*; that is, increases in pay are given to employees to maintain differences in job worth between their jobs and those of others. Some companies provide for equity adjustments through a constantly changing pay scale. Thus Aluminum Company of America (ALCOA) surveys its competitors' pay every 3 months and adjusts its pay rates accordingly. ALCOA strives to maintain at least a 20 percent differential between employees and their supervisors.[4]

Another approach is to grant benefits that increase gradually to more senior employees. Thus, although the difference between the *direct pay* of this group and that of their shorter-service coworkers may be slim, senior employees have a distinct advantage when the *entire* compensation package is considered.

Overtime as a cause of compression can be dealt with in two ways. First, it can be *rotated* among employees so that all share overtime equally. However, in situations where this kind of arrangement is not feasible, firms might consider establishing an overtime pay policy for management employees; for example, a supervisor may be paid an overtime rate after he or she works a minimum number of overtime hours. Such a practice does not violate the Fair Labor Standards Act, for under the law overtime pay is not *required* for exempt jobs, although it may be adopted voluntarily. Finally, a recent survey indicated that one of the most favored solutions by companies is to provide aids to upward mobility, such as training and rapid advancement; strategies of this type keep the pay structure intact while helping individuals to move within it.[18]

Pay compression is certainly a difficult problem—but not so difficult that it cannot be managed. Indeed it *must* be managed if companies are to achieve their goal of providing pay that is perceived as fair.[4]

Pay Raises

Coping with inflation is the biggest hurdle to overcome in a merit-pay plan. On the other hand, *the only measure of a raise is how much it exceeds the increase in the cost of living*: 12.4 percent inflation in 1980 more than wiped out the average raise. However, the average 6 percent raise that employees received in 1989 provided a *real* increase since inflation was only about 4 percent.[37]

The simplest and most effective method for dealing with inflation in a merit-pay system is to increase salary ranges.[37] By raising salary ranges (e.g., based on a survey of average increases in starting salaries for the coming year) without giving general increases, a firm can maintain competitive hiring rates and at the same time maintain the merit concept surrounding salary increases. Since a raise in minimum pay for each salary range creates an employee group that falls below the new minimum, it is necessary to raise these employees to the new minimum. Such adjustments technically violate the merit philosophy, but the advantages gained by keeping employees in the salary range and at a rate that is sufficient to retain them clearly outweigh the disadvantages.[37]

The size of the merit increase for a given level of performance should *decrease* as the employee moves farther up the salary range. *Merit guide charts* provide a means for doing this. Guide charts identify (1) an employee's current performance rating and (2) his or her location in a pay grade. The intersection of these two

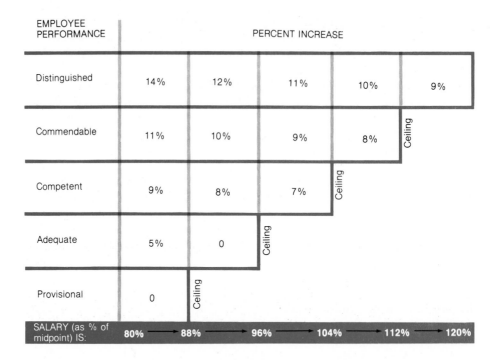

FIGURE 10-7
Example of a merit
guide chart.

dimensions identifies a percentage of pay increase based on the performance level
and location of the employee in the pay grade. Figure 10-7 shows an example of
such a chart. The rationale for the merit guide chart approach is that a person at
the top of the range is already making more than the "going rate" for that job.
Hence she or he should have to demonstrate *more* than satisfactory performance
in order to continue moving farther above the going rate.

A final aspect of the program is to give increases more than once a year (e.g.,
every 6 months). By getting a raise every 6 months, employees tend to feel that
they are keeping up with inflation. The organization also benefits since the increases will cost less. This is so because rather than giving the entire increase for
a full year, employees receive half the increase for 6 months and the rest for the
other 6 months. For example, if an employee making $15,000 per year gets a 15
percent increase, that increase will cost the employer $2250 for the year. If, instead,
the employee gets two 7.5 percent increases, the total cost for the year is only
$1167.[37] Despite this fact, the vast majority of companies continue to award annual
raises, either on an employee's anniversary date or on a common review date for
all employees.[42] The proposal just outlined will not solve all the compensation
problems caused by inflation, but it is important to remember that *it is not an
organization's responsibility to pay wages that keep pace with inflation.* The responsibility
is merely to pay wages that are competitive. What this merit compensation system
will do is to allow most employees to stay close until the economy settles down.

IMPACT OF PAY SYSTEMS ON PRODUCTIVITY, QUALITY OF WORK LIFE, AND THE BOTTOM LINE

High salary levels alone do not ensure a productive and motivated workforce. This is evident in the auto industry where wages are among the highest in the country—yet quality problems and high absenteeism persist. A critical factor, then, is not *how much* a company pays its workers but, more important, *how the pay system is designed, communicated, and managed.* As we have seen repeatedly throughout this chapter, excessively high labor costs, coupled with benefits offered *only* because "everybody else is doing it," adversely affect productivity, work quality, and the bottom line. Although management's desire to improve the standard of living of all company employees is understandable, excessively high labor costs can bankrupt a company. This is especially likely if, to cover its labor costs, the company cannot price its products competitively. If that happens, productivity and profits both suffer directly, and the quality of work life suffers indirectly. A systematic pay structure helps ensure that each employee is paid equitably and competitively. Current data from a wage survey must then be used to maintain the company's relative position on pay. When sensible compensation policies are established using the principles discussed in this chapter, everybody wins, the company, the employees, and their families as well.

■ HUMAN RESOURCE MANAGEMENT IN ACTION
CONCLUSION

THE TRUST GAP

What steps can companies take to sew corporate top and bottom back together? Here are seven suggestions. One, start with the obvious. Tie the financial interests of high- and low-level workers closer together by making exposure to risk and to reward more equitable. Thus when NUCOR, a steel company in Charlotte, North Carolina, went through tough times, President Ken Iverson took a 60 percent cut in pay. Said a compensation consultant, "How often do you see that? . . . It makes a real difference if employees see that their CEO is willing to take it in the shorts along with them" (ref. 10, p. 66).

Two, consider instituting profit-sharing, a Scanlon plan, gain sharing (see Chapter 12), or some other program that lets employees profit from their efforts. Make sure, however, that incentive pay is linked to performance over which the beneficiaries have control.

Three, rethink perquisites. Now that perks come under taxable income, they just don't have the same appeal to executives as they used to. Yet they still have at least the same downside with the rank and file.

Four, look at the office layout with an eye toward equity. In Sweden, for example, same-size offices are the norm. When an American visitor asked his Swedish corporate hosts how they could give the same amount of space to a secretary as to an engineer they said, "How can we hire a secretary and expect her to be committed to our company, when, by the size of the office we give her, we tell her she's a second-class citizen?" (ref. 10, p. 66).

Five, make sure your door is really open. If that means meeting with employees at unorthodox times, such as when their shifts end, then do it. Not a single one of the CEOs interviewed by *Fortune* could recall employees ever abusing an open-door policy. The lesson is clear for managers at all levels: Employees don't walk through your door unless they have to.

Six, if you don't survey employee attitudes now, start. What you find can help identify problems before they become crises. Share findings, and be sure employees know how subsequent decisions may be related to them. Don't worry about raising expectations too high. As one executive commented, "Employees by and large are reasonable people. They understand you can't do everything they want. As long as they know their views are being considered and they get some feedback from you to that effect, you will be meeting their expectations" (ref. 10, p. 70).

Seven, explain things—personally. While one study found that 97 percent of CEOs believe that communicating with employees has a positive impact on job satisfaction, and 79 percent think it benefits the bottom line, only 22 percent do it weekly or more often.

There is no doubt that these seven steps can help close the trust gap that exists in so many U.S. organizations today. On the other hand, virtually all experts cite one important qualification: It is suicidal to start down this road unless you are absolutely sincere.

SUMMARY

Contemporary pay systems (outside the entertainment and professional sports fields) are characterized by cost containment, pay and benefit levels commensurate with what a company can afford, and programs that encourage and reward performance.

Generally speaking, pay systems are designed to attract, retain, and motivate employees, to achieve internal, external, and individual equity, and to maintain a balance in relationships between direct and indirect forms of compensation, and between the pay rates of supervisory and nonsupervisory employees. Pay systems need to be tied to the strategic mission of an organization, and they should take their direction from that strategic mission. However, actual wage levels depend on labor market conditions, legislation, collective bargaining, management attitudes, and an organization's ability to pay. Our broad objective in developing pay systems is to assign a monetary value to each job in the organization (a base rate) and an orderly procedure for increasing the base rate. To develop such a system,

IMPLICATIONS FOR MANAGEMENT PRACTICE

Remember: The *amount* of pay that employees receive affects only their decisions about whether to stay or leave. How hard they work, and the productivity resulting from their efforts, is determined by *the way in which pay is administered*. To maximize the productivity gain from pay systems, be sure that the design of the system is consistent with the objectives of the business you are in. Objectives, in turn, are related to the stage of development of the business (e.g., start-up versus mature enterprise), as well as to any special situations, such as restructuring or downsizing. Beyond that, remember that people respond to the world as they perceive it, not as it exists. Internal, external, and individual equity are crucial considerations in all pay systems.

we need four basic tools: job analyses and job descriptions, a job evaluation plan, pay surveys, and a pay structure.

Finally, we examined the following pay policy issues: whether pay systems should be designed to achieve comparable worth, pay secrecy versus openness, the effect of inflation on pay systems, pay compression, and pay raises.

DISCUSSION QUESTIONS

10▪1 What steps can a company take to integrate its compensation system with its general business strategy?

10▪2 Discuss the pitfalls to be avoided in analyzing pay survey results. (*Hint*: See ref. 35.)

10▪3 How do the pay practices of unionized firms affect those of nonunionized firms?

10▪4 How do management's attitudes and philosophy affect pay systems?

10▪5 What can companies do to ensure internal, external, and individual equity for all employees?

10▪6 Discuss the advantages and disadvantages of pay-for-knowledge systems.

REFERENCES

1. Arvey, R. D. (1986). Sex bias in job evaluation procedures. *Personnel Psychology*, **39**, 315–335.

2. Bartol, K. M., & Martin, D. C. (1988). Influences on managerial pay allocations: A dependency perspective. *Personnel Psychology*, **41**, 361–378.

3. Bates, M. W. (1983, March). A look at cash compensation. *Personnel Journal*, pp. 198–200.

4. Bergmann, T. J., Hills, F. S., & Priefert, L. (1983, Second Quarter). Pay compression: Causes, results, and possible solutions. *Compensation Review*, **6**, 17–26.

5. Bennett, A. (1990, April 18). Pay for performance. *The Wall Street Journal Supplement: Executive Pay*, pp. R7, R8.

6. Buder, L. (1990, May 6). With overtime, electrician out-earns mayor. *The New York Times*, p. 39.

7. Burger King faces charges it violated child labor laws. (1990, March 10). *The New York Times*, p. 8.
8. Cascio, W. F. (1991). *Applied psychology in personnel management* (4th ed.). Englewood Cliffs, NJ: Prentice-Hall.
9. Deutch, C. H. (1990, Feb. 25). Revising pay packages, again. *The New York Times*, p. F29.
10. Farnham, A. (1989, Dec. 4). The trust gap. *Fortune*, pp. 56–78.
11. Fay, C. H. (1989). External pay relationships. In L. R. Gomez-Mejia (ed.), *Compensation and benefits*. Washington, DC: Bureau of National Affairs, pp. 3-70 to 3-100.
12. Foulkes, F. K., & Livernash, E. R. (1989). *Human resources management: Cases and text* (2d ed.). Englewood Cliffs, NJ: Prentice-Hall.
13. Gomez, L. R., Page, R. C., & Tornow, W. W. (1982). A comparison of the practical utility of traditional, statistical, and hybrid job evaluation approaches. *Academy of Management Journal*, **25**, 790–809.
14. Gorman, C. (1989, Feb. 13). Big steel is red hot again. *Time*, p. 61.
15. Greene, R. J., & Roberts, R. G. (1983). Strategic integration of compensation and benefits. *Personnel Administrator*, **28**(5), 79–82.
16. Hills, F. S. (1989). Internal pay relationships. In L. R. Gomez-Mejia (ed.), *Compensation and benefits*. Washington, DC: Bureau of National Affairs, pp. 3-29 to 3-69.
17. Huseman, R. C., Hatfield, J. D., & Miles, E. W. (1987). A new perspective on equity theory: The equity sensitivity construct. *Academy of Management Review*, **12**, 222–234.
18. Kanter, R. M. (1987, March–April). The attack on pay. *Harvard Business Review*, pp. 60–67.
19. Kovach, K. A., & Millspaugh, P. E. (1990). Comparable worth: Canada legislates pay equity. *The Academy of Management Executive*, **4**(2), 92–101.
20. Labor Letter (1990, Oct. 2). *The Wall Street Journal*, p. A1.
21. Lacayo, R. (1989, Nov. 13). A pay hike for the poor. *Time*, p. 36.
22. Lawler, E. E., III (1989). Pay for performance: A strategic analysis. In L. R. Gomez-Mejia (ed.), *Compensation and benefits*. Washington, DC: Bureau of National Affairs, pp. 3-136 to 3-181.
23. Lawler, E. E., III (1977). Reward systems. In J. R. Hackman & J. L. Suttle, *Improving life at work: Behavioral science approaches to organizational change*. Santa Monica, CA: Goodyear.
24. Look back in wonder: Hits and misses in predictions for 1990 (1990, May). *Money*, p. 22.
25. Lublin, J. (1984, March 13). Labor letter. *The Wall Street Journal*, p. 1.
26. Mahoney, T. A. (1989). Employment compensation planning and strategy. In L. R. Gomez-Mejia (ed.), *Compensation and benefits*. Washington, DC: Bureau of National Affairs, pp. 3-1 to 3-28.
27. Main, J. (1982, Sep. 20). Hard times catch up with executives. *Fortune*, pp. 50–54.
28. Managing your career (1991, Spring). *The Wall Street Journal Supplement*, pp. 40, 41.
29. Milkovich, G. T., & Newman, J. M. (1990). *Compensation* (2d ed.). Homewood, IL: BPI-Irwin.
30. Mills, D. Q. (1989). *Labor-management relations* (4th ed.). New York: McGraw-Hill.
31. Mount, M. K., & Ellis, R. A. (1987). Investigation of bias in job evaluation ratings of comparable worth study participants. *Personnel Psychology*, **40**, 85–96.
32. Ormiston, K. A. (1988, May 10). States know best what labor's worth. *The Wall Street Journal*, p. 38.

33. Pfeffer, J., & Davis-Blake, A. (1987). Understanding organizational wage structures: A resource dependence approach. *Academy of Management Journal*, **30**, 437–455.

34. Raff, D. M., & Summers, L. H. (1987, October). Did Henry Ford pay efficiency wages? *Journal of Labor Economics*, **5**(4) (Part 2, Supplement), S57–S87.

35. Rynes, S. L., & Milkovich, G. T. (1986). Wage surveys: Dispelling some myths about the "market wage." *Personnel Psychology*, **39**, 71–90.

36. Rynes, S. L., Weber, C. L., & Milkovich, G. T. (1989). Effects of market survey rates, job evaluation, and job gender on pay. *Journal of Applied Psychology*, **74**, 114–123.

37. Schwartz, J. D. (1982, February). Maintaining merit compensation in a high-inflation economy. *Personnel Journal*, pp. 147–152.

38. Sibson, R. E. (1967). *Wages and salaries: A handbook for line managers* (rev. ed.). New York: American Management Association.

39. Sleeth, P. (1990, March 25). New child-labor laws to tax strapped system. *Denver Post*, pp. 1G, 7G.

40. Solomon, J. (1990, April 18). Hush money. *The Wall Street Journal Supplement*, pp. R22–R24.

41. Sweeney, P. D., McFarlin, D. B., & Inderrieden, E. J. (1990). Using relative deprivation theory to explain satisfaction with income and pay level: A multistudy examination. *Academy of Management Journal*, **33**, 423–436.

42. Time for a raise? (1986, July 31). *The Wall Street Journal*, p. 25.

43. Tolchin, M. (1989, March 26). Hospitals' drive for more nurses brings pay rise. *The New York Times*, p. 18.

44. Tosi, H., & Tosi, L. (1987). What managers need to know about knowledge-based pay. In D. A. Balkin & L. R. Gomez-Mejia (eds.), *New perspectives on compensation*. Englewood Cliffs, NJ: Prentice-Hall, pp. 43–48.

45. Uchitelle, L. (1987, June 26). Bonuses replace wage raises and workers are the losers. *The New York Times*, pp. A1, D3.

46. Wallace, M. J., Jr., & Fay, C. H. (1988). *Compensation theory and practice* (2d ed.). Boston: PWS-Kent.

47. Williams, M. (1983, Oct. 12). Ten minutes' work for 12 hours' pay? What's the catch? *The Wall Street Journal*, pp. 1, 19.

Indirect Compensation: Employee Benefit Plans

■ **HUMAN RESOURCE MANAGEMENT IN ACTION**

THE FUTURE LOOK OF EMPLOYEE BENEFITS*

It's Wednesday, September 4, 2008, and another day at the office. You drop off your daughter, 12 years old, and your father-in-law, 80, at the first-floor family care center. In your office, you look over yesterday's mail (you aren't working Tuesdays this summer) and find a message from the company's school services: They've received the tuition bill for your son's freshman year in college and have paid it. You write a memo to your boss, outlining your plan for a 3-month unpaid sabbatical to work with homeless children.

The traditional definition of employee benefits is familiar to most workers. Designed to meet the needs of the majority, benefits are the extras that employers provide to make life outside of work more manageable and secure. To most companies, they are no longer "fringe" benefits. They are the first line of defense against the contingencies of life: sickness, disability, old age, and death.

---

*Adapted from: J. Solomon, The future look of employee benefits, *The Wall Street Journal*, September 7, 1988, p. 27. Reprinted by permission of *The Wall Street Journal*, © 1988 Dow Jones & Company, Inc. All rights reserved worldwide.

But this basic concept, itself only a few decades old, is changing. As the male breadwinner is replaced by a host of demographic variables, more companies are finding that benefits cannot be reduced to a simple, common package. To attract the most talented workers, they are beginning to offer a wider range of benefits—letting employees pick those that are most important to them. Moreover, these new benefits often revolve around life inside the office, instead of just outside extras.

How far will these changes go? According to benefits consultants and corporate executives, most agree that over the next 20 years today's core benefits—life, health and disability coverage, vacation, and pension—will remain, although they probably will be restructured. Companies will take steps to halt, or at least to slow, the rapid rise in how much they pay, by adopting "defined contribution" benefit plans, for example. Such plans increase a company's contribution to employee benefits by a fixed dollar amount each year. As a result, employees will often end up paying a bigger share.

Many benefits that are just now appearing, such as child and elder care, may be standard in 20 years. Indeed, demographic changes in the workforce are likely to spawn new benefits, many of which seem as far-fetched now as today's benefits did a couple of decades ago. In the conclusion to this case, we'll look at some specific predictions.

Challenges

1. Do you think that companies should provide a broader menu of "exotic" benefits (e.g., veterinary care, dietary counseling) or improve the menu of "core" benefits (e.g., health care, insurance, pensions)? Why?
2. How might one's preference for various benefits change as one grows older, or as one's family situation changes?

---

1. What strategic considerations should guide the design of benefits programs?
2. What steps should be taken to control the rapid escalation of health care costs?
3. Should we offer a uniform "package" of benefits, or a flexible plan that allows employees to choose these benefits that are most meaningful to them, up to a certain dollar amount?
4. In view of the considerable sums of money that are spent each year on employee benefits, what is the best way to communicate this information to employees?

QUESTIONS THIS CHAPTER WILL HELP MANAGERS ANSWER

Benefits currently account for almost 40 percent of the total compensation costs for each employee. Yesterday's "fringes" have become today's (expected) benefits and services. Here are some reasons why benefits have grown:[24,71]

- The imposition of wage ceilings during World War II forced organizations to offer more benefits in place of wage increases to attract, retain, and motivate employees.
- The interest by unions in bargaining over benefits has grown, particularly since wages have risen to the point where they now satisfy basic employee needs. Once granted, benefits are unlikely to be withdrawn.
- Internal Revenue Service Code treatment of benefits makes them preferable to wages. Even after the Tax Reform Act of 1986, many benefits remain nontaxable to the employee and are deductible by the employer. With other benefits, taxes are deferred. Hence employees' disposable income increases since they are receiving benefits and services that otherwise they would have to purchase with after-tax dollars.
- Granting benefits (in a nonunionized firm) or bargaining over them (in a unionized firm) confers an aura of social responsibility on employers; they are "taking care" of their employees.

STRATEGIC CONSIDERATIONS IN THE DESIGN OF BENEFITS PROGRAMS

As is the case with compensation systems in general, managers need to think carefully about what they wish to accomplish by means of their benefits programs. At a cost of about $11,000 for every employee on the payroll,[68] benefits represent substantial annual expenditures. In order to leverage the impact of these expenditures with employees, managers should be prepared to answer questions such as the following:

- Is the type and level of our benefits coverage consistent with our long-term strategic business plans?
- Given the characteristics of our workforce, are we meeting the needs of our employees?
- What legal requirements must we satisfy in the benefits we offer?
- Are our benefits competitive in cost, structure, and value to employees and their dependents?
- Is our benefits package consistent with key objectives of our total compensation strategy, namely, adequacy, equity, cost control, and balance?

In the following sections, we will discuss each of these.

Long-Term Strategic Business Plans

Such plans outline the basic directions in which an organization wishes to move in the next 3 to 5 years. One strategic issue that should influence the design of benefits is the stage of development of an organization. For example, a start-up venture probably will offer low base pay and benefits but high incentives; a mature firm with well-established products and substantial market share will probably offer much more generous pay and benefits, combined with moderate incentives.

Other strategic considerations include the projected rate of employment growth, downsizing, geographic redeployment, acquisitions, centralization or decentralization, and expected changes in profitability.[46] Each of these conditions suggests a change in the optimum "mix" of benefits in order to be most consistent with an organization's business plans.

Characteristics of the Workforce

Young employees who are just starting out are likely to be more concerned with direct pay (e.g., for a house purchase) than with a generous pension program. Older workers may desire the reverse. Unionized workers may prefer a uniform benefits package, while single parents, older workers, or disabled workers may place heavy emphasis on flexible work schedules. Employers that hire large numbers of temporary or part-time workers may offer entirely different benefits to these groups. In 1989, for example, only 16.5 percent of firms gave part-time employees all the health, retirement, and vacation benefits that full-timers received.[68]

Legal Requirements

The government plays a central role in the design of any benefits package. While controlling the cost of benefits is a major concern of employers, the social and economic welfare of citizens is the major concern of government.[45] As examples of such concern, consider the four income-maintenance laws shown in Table 11-1.

Income-maintenance laws were enacted to provide employees and their families with income security in case of death, disability, unemployment, or retirement.

At a broad level, government tax policy has had, and will continue to have, a major impact on the design of benefits programs. Two principles have had the greatest impact on benefits.[45] One is the *doctrine of constructive receipt*, which holds that an individual must pay taxes on benefits that have monetary value when the individual receives them. The other principle is the *antidiscrimination rule*, which holds that employers can obtain tax advantages only for those benefits that do not discriminate in favor of highly compensated employees. According to the Tax Reform Act of 1986, a highly compensated employee is one who owns at least 5 percent of company stock or partnership rights, is a company officer earning more than $45,000 a year, or who earns more than $50,000 a year *and* has income in the top 20 percent of the workforce. These dollar amounts are adjusted periodically.

These two tax-policy principles define the conditions for the preferential tax treatment of benefits. Together they hold that if benefits discriminate in favor of highly paid or "key" employees, then the employer and the employee receiving those benefits may have to pay taxes on the benefits when they are received.

■ **TABLE 11·1**

FOUR MAJOR INCOME-MAINTENANCE LAWS

Law	Scope of coverage	Funding	Benefits	Administrative agency
Social Security Act (1935)	Full coverage for retirees, dependent survivors, and disabled persons insured by 40 quarters of payroll taxes on their past earnings or earnings of heads of households. Federal government employees hired prior to January 1, 1984, and railroad workers are excluded.	For 1991, payroll tax of 7.65% for employees and 7.15% for employers on the first $53,400 in earnings. Self-employed persons pay 13.02% of this wage base. Of the 7.65%, 6.2% is allocated for retirement, survivors, and disability insurance, and 1.45% for Medicare. The Revenue Reconciliation Act of 1990 extended the 1.45% Medicare payroll tax to wages up to $125,000 from $51,300.	Full *retirement payments* after age 65, or at reduced rates after 62, to worker and spouse. Size of pension depends on past earnings. *Survivor benefits* for the family of a deceased worker or retiree. At age 65 a widow or widower receives the full age-65 pension granted to the deceased. A widow or widower of any age with dependent children under 16, and each unmarried child under 18, receives a 75% benefit check. *Disability benefits* to totally disabled workers, after a 5-month waiting period, as well as to their spouses and children. *Health insurance* for persons over 65 (Medicare). All benefits are adjusted upward whenever the consumer price index (CPI) increases more than 3% in a calendar year and trust funds are at a specified level.	Social Security Administration

■ **TABLE 11·1**
FOUR MAJOR INCOME-MAINTENANCE LAWS (*Cont.*)

Law	Scope of coverage	Funding	Benefits	Administrative agency
			Otherwise, the adjustment is based on the lower of the CPI increase or the increase in average national wages (1983 amendments).	
Federal Unemployment Tax Act (1935)	All employees except some state and local government workers, domestic and farm workers, railroad workers, and some nonprofit employees.	Payroll tax of at least 3.4% of first $7000 of earnings paid by employer. (Employees also taxed in Alaska, Alabama, and New Jersey.) States may raise both the percentage and base earnings taxed through legislation. Employer contributions may be reduced if state experience ratings for them are low.	Benefits average roughly 50% of average weekly earnings and are available for up to 26 weeks. Those eligible for benefits have been employed for some specified minimum period and have lost their jobs through no fault of their own. Most states exclude strikers. During periods of high unemployment, benefits may be extended for up to 52 weeks.	U.S. Bureau of Employment Security, U.S. Training and Employment Service, and the several state employment security commissions
Workers' compensation (state laws)	Generally, employees of nonagricultural, private-sector firms are entitled to benefits for work-related accidents and illnesses leading to temporary or permanent disabilities.	One of the following options, depending on state law: self-insurance, insurance through a private carrier, or payroll-based payments to a state insurance system. Premiums depend on the riskiness of the occupation and the experience rating of the insured.	Benefits average about two-thirds of an employee's weekly wage and continue for the term of the disability. Supplemental payments are made for medical care and rehabilitative services. In case of a fatal accident, survivor benefits are payable.	Various state commissions

(continues)

■ **TABLE 11·1**
FOUR MAJOR INCOME-MAINTENANCE LAWS (*Cont.*)

Law	Scope of coverage	Funding	Benefits	Administrative agency
Employee Retirement Income Security Act (ERISA) (1974)	Private-sector employees over age 21 enrolled in noncontributory (i.e., 100% employer-paid) retirement plans who have 1 year's service.	Employer contributions.	The 1986 Tax Reform Act authorizes several formulas to provide vesting of retirement benefits after a certain length of service (5–7 years). Once an employee is "vested," receipt of the pension is not contingent on future service. Authorizes tax-free transfer of vested benefits to another employer or to an individual retirement account ("portability") if a vested employee changes jobs and if the present employer agrees. Employers must fund plans on an actuarially sound basis. Pension trustees ("fiduciaries") must make prudent investments. Employers may insure vested benefits through the federal Pension Benefit Guaranty Corporation.	Department of Labor, Internal Revenue Service, Pension Benefit Guaranty Corporation

Social Security, which accounts for $1 of every $5 spent by the federal government, has had, and will continue to have, an effect on the growth, development, and design of employee benefits. National health policy increasingly is shifting costs to the private sector and emphasizing cost containment; such pressures will intensify. Finally, national policy on unfair discrimination, particularly through the Equal Pay Act, Title VII, and the Age Discrimination in Employment Act, has caused firms to reexamine their benefit policies.

The Competitiveness of the Benefits Offered

The issue of benefits program competitiveness is much more complicated than that of salary competitiveness.[46] In the case of salary, both employees and management focus on the same item: direct pay. However, in determining the competitiveness of benefits, senior management tends to focus mainly on cost, while employees are more interested in value. The two may conflict. Thus employees' perceptions of the value of their benefits as competitive may lead to excessive costs, in the view of top management. On the other hand, achieving cost competitiveness provides no assurance that employees will perceive the benefits program as valuable to them.

To deal with these potential problems, some firms are offering flexible or cafeteria-style benefits programs, which effectively separate the cost of benefit programs from their form.[46] However, for benefits offerings to have the greatest impact, it is essential to identify first the wants and needs of employees. Then with the help of financial, tax, and insurance specialists, management can collect and analyze cost data on a variety of alternative benefits that might simultaneously contain costs and provide genuine value to employees.

Total Compensation Strategy

The broad objective of the design of compensation programs (that is, direct as well as indirect compensation) is to integrate salary and benefits in a package that will encourage the achievement of an organization's goals. For example, while a generous pension plan may help retain employees, it probably does little to motivate them to perform on a day-to-day basis. This is because the length of time between performance and the reward is too great. On the other hand, a generous severance package offered to targeted segments of the employee population may facilitate an organization's objective of downsizing to a specified staffing level. In all cases, considerations of adequacy, equity, cost control, and balance should guide decision making in the context of a total compensation strategy.

With these considerations in mind, let us now examine some key components of the benefits package.

COMPONENTS OF THE BENEFITS PACKAGE

There are many ways to classify benefits, but we will follow the classification scheme used by the U.S. Chamber of Commerce. According to this system, benefits fall into three categories: security and health, payments for time not worked, and employee services. Within each of these categories there is a bewildering array

■ **TABLE 11·2**

EMPLOYER BENEFIT PAYMENTS AS A PERCENTAGE OF PAYROLL

Type of program	1955	1965	1975	1988
Legally required payments	3.6	4.9	8.0	8.9
Welfare and retirement plans	8.2	9.6	13.7	15.2
Paid time off	8.5	10.2	13.7	12.9
Total	20.3	24.7	35.4	37.0

Source: *Employee Benefits, 1988.* Washington, DC: U.S. Chamber of Commerce, 1989.

of options. The following discussions consider only the most popular options and cover only those which have not been mentioned previously.

Table 11-2 illustrates changes in the costs of employer payments for benefits as a percentage of payroll from 1955 to 1988. As the saying goes, "You've come a long way, baby."

Security and Health Benefits

The following are included in the security and health category:

Life insurance
Workers' compensation
Disability insurance
Hospitalization, surgical, and maternity coverage
Health maintenance organizations (HMOs)
Other medical coverage
Sick leave
Pension plans
Social Security
Unemployment insurance
Supplemental unemployment insurance
Severance pay

Insurance is the basic building block of almost all benefits packages, for it protects employees against income loss caused by death, accident, or ill health. Most organizations provide *group* coverage for their employees. The plans may be contributory (in which employees share in the cost of the premiums) or noncontributory.

It used to be that when a worker switched jobs, he or she lost health insurance coverage. The worker had to "go naked" for months until coverage began at a new employer. No longer. Under the Consolidated Omnibus Budget Reconciliation Act (COBRA) of 1986, companies with at least 20 employees must make medical coverage available at group insurance rates for as long as 18 months after the employee leaves—whether the worker left voluntarily, retired, or was dismissed. The law also provides that, following a worker's death or divorce, the employee's family has the right to buy group-rate health insurance for as long as 3 years. Employers who do not comply can be sued and denied corporate tax deductions related to health benefits.[53]

However, since some corporate medical plans do not cover preexisting conditions, some employees found that when they changed jobs (and health plans), their benefits were sharply reduced. To alleviate that problem, the 1989 budget act allows workers who encounter existing-condition clauses to retain medical coverage at their former jobs for selected periods of time, even if they join the health plan at their new company. Companies are allowed to charge former employees a bit more to retain coverage, but their costs are still likely to go up, since workers apt to take advantage of the law are those with serious medical problems.[12]

With this in mind, let us consider the major forms of security and health benefits commonly provided to employees.

Group life insurance This type of insurance is usually yearly renewable term insurance; that is, each employee is insured 1 year at a time. Actual amounts of coverage vary, but one rule of thumb is to have it equal roughly 2 years' income. This amount provides a reasonable financial cushion to the surviving spouse during the difficult transition to a different way of life. Thus a manager making $40,000 per year may have a group term-life policy with a face value of $80,000 or $100,000. To discourage turnover, almost all companies cancel this benefit if an employee terminates.

Life insurance has been heavily affected by flexible benefits programs. Typically such programs provide a core of basic life coverage (e.g., $25,000) and then permit employees to choose greater coverage (e.g., in increments of $10,000 to $25,000) as part of their optional package.[49] Keep in mind, however, that the Omnibus Budget Reconciliation Act of 1987 imposed Social Security taxes on the cost of group term-life insurance carried by an employer for an employee.[14]

Workers' compensation These payments vary by state, as pointed out in Table 11-1. Disability benefits, which have been extended to cover stress and occupational disease, tend to be highest in states where organized labor is strong.[41] A state's industrial structure also plays a big part in setting disability insurance rates. Thus serious injuries are more common and costly among Oregon loggers and Michigan machinists than among assembly line workers in a Texas semiconductor plant. Sometimes the costs can get out of hand. In Maine, for example (which changed its disability law in 1983), employment in the Bass shoe division of Chesebrough-Pond's Inc. rose 40 percent from 1978 to 1983. However, during the same period workers' compensation premiums went from $150,000 to $3.6

million, a 2300 percent increase.[8] Trends such as these have prompted high-cost states, such as Minnesota, Florida, Michigan, and Maine, to lower workers' compensation premiums so that they can continue to attract and retain businesses in their states.

Currently all 50 states have a workers' compensation law. While specific terms and levels of coverage vary by state, all state laws share the following features:[47]

■ All job-related injuries and illnesses are covered.

■ Coverage is provided regardless of who caused the injury or illness (i.e., regardless of who was "at fault").

■ Payments are usually made through an insurance program financed by employer-paid premiums.

■ A worker's loss is usually not covered fully by the insurance program. Most cash payments are at least two-thirds of the worker's weekly wage, but together with disability benefits from Social Security, the payments cannot exceed 80 percent of the worker's weekly wage.

Workers' compensation programs protect employees, dependents, and survivors against income loss resulting from total disability, partial disability, or death, medical expenses, and rehabilitation expenses.

Disability insurance Such coverage provides a supplemental one-time payment when death is accidental, and it provides a range of benefits when employees are disabled—that is, when they can't perform the "main functions" of their occupations.[62] Long-term disability (LTD) plans cover employees who are disabled 6 months or longer, usually at 50 to 75 percent of their base pay, until they begin receiving pension benefits. Fewer than 50 percent of medium and large businesses provide such coverage, but as one expert noted: "Long-term disability is more important than life insurance. The person is still alive and may have no income at all without such coverage."[65]

Typically, employees are delighted to have their companies pay their insurance premiums. Think again. If the company pays the premium and the day comes when an employee needs to collect benefits, the benefits are taxable to the employee as ordinary income. If the employee paid the premiums, the benefit would be tax-free.[52]

As an example, assume that an employee paid his own premiums (a total of about $1250) from age 40 to 50, then became disabled and remained that way to age 65. His policy would pay him $2000 a month, or $24,000 a year. If he had to pay tax on the money at 28 percent, his monthly insurance check would drop from $2000 to $1440. Over the course of 15 years, taxes would consume $100,800 of the $360,000 he got.

LTD costs are extremely high. Based on seven case studies, *direct* nonmedical disability costs (hidden plus visible costs), given as a percentage of annual salary, for an executive earning $40,000 per year were as follows:[13]

Hidden direct costs	
Predisability productivity loss (prior 5 years)	28%
Postdisability productivity loss (until a replacement becomes fully productive)	39
Replacement cost	30
Retraining cost	32
Visible direct costs	
Salary continuance until disability pay	48
Disability payments (percent of salary to age 65)	62
Increased pension payments	15
Increased life insurance	11

An executive earning $40,000 per year at age 40 who did not previously qualify for pension benefits will cost her or his employer, on average, over $848,000, excluding medical costs until retirement age. If payment is not required as a lump sum, the net present value of the payments reduces the liability to $511,000.[13] This expenditure is still very large for *one*, possibly preventable, medical event.

Hospitalization, surgical, and maternity coverage These are essential benefits for most working Americans. Self-insurance is out of the question since the costs incurred by one serious, prolonged illness could easily wipe out a lifetime of savings and assets and place a family in debt for years to come. Major medical coverage (economic insulation against catastrophic illness) has grown in popularity, partly in response to runaway medical costs. In 1990, for example 12.2 percent of the U.S. gross national product (the total value of retail prices of all goods and services produced in 1990) was spent on medical care, compared with only 5.4 percent in 1960.[4,25] That is over $1800 for every man, woman, and child in the United States!

U.S. health costs are the highest in the world, and they have been rising at more than triple the rate of inflation over the past 3 years.[4] By contrast, Japan's equal 6.7 percent of GNP. As a result, both management and labor in the United States worry that a gap that large makes U.S. companies less competitive. At the level of the individual firm, Chrysler Corp. estimates that health costs add $700 to the price of each of its cars, $300 to $500 more per car than foreign competitors pay for health.[4] Why?

Analysts point to five key reasons:[9]

1. *Cost shifting.* This refers to the transfer of responsibility for paying medical bills, principally from the government to the private sector. As a result, private insurance plans pay more as Medicare, Medicaid, and managed care plans pay less, and the ranks of the uninsured grow. Because of Medicare's diagnosis-related grouping (DRG), which caps payment in 467 diagnostic categories, the dollar value of cost shifting is staggering. For example, the Colorado Hospital Association

found that 36.4 percent of an average $7438 hospital bill in the state—a full $2710—reflected the impact of cost shifting.[20]

2. *Recovering past losses.* Health insurers are making up for past mistakes: underestimating costs, underpricing, and trying to buy market share through unrealistically low discounts.

3. *Increasing costs for physicians.* Inflation and higher expenses associated with running physicians' practices each account for 30 percent of the increase. The rest comes from the growth in physicians' income (15 percent), higher use of services (15 percent), and demographic trends (10 percent).

4. *Increasing hospital costs.* Higher labor costs and inflation each account for 40 percent of the increase. More demand, new technology, and a changing mix of hospital employees each represent another 5 percent, with the final 5 percent attributable to miscellaneous reasons.

5. *Fragmentation in health plans.* As health plans have multiplied, they have failed to gain enough market share to wield real clout with physicians, hospitals, and others.

SMALL BUSINESS AND HEALTH-CARE INSURANCE

Of the 36 million Americans who had no health insurance in 1990, about two-thirds were employees of small businesses.[20] It's not that small business owners don't care about their employees. Rather, health insurers refuse to insure employees in at least 40 industries, based on the nature of the work, the rate of claims, or the administrative costs.[16] Here are some examples:

Hazardous work: mines, quarries, lumberyards, logging, sanitation businesses, munitions plants, pest-control services, and charter and unscheduled airlines

Low-paying or seasonal work: hotels, motels, restaurants, car washes, laundries, service stations, convenience stores, golf clubs, ski resorts, entertainment and arts groups

Higher rate of claims: doctors, dentists, nurses, chiropractors, and other medical workers

Higher administrative costs: small cities and towns, government-financed non-profit organizations

The insurance exclusions are felt most by groups of fewer than 50 employees, whose combined premiums frequently do not meet the cost of a single expensive illness. To deal with this crisis, the Small Business Service Bureau arranges coverage for pooled groups of its members with nonprofit Blue Cross and Blue Shield plans and health maintenance organizations that have fewer barriers to membership.[16]

As a result of widespread publicity of this problem, "cost containment" has become a watchword in the boardroom as well as in the health-care industry itself.

Here are some measures that firms have taken to gain tighter management control over the cost of health care:

1. Raise deductibles and copayments by employees. Such steps are a belated adjustment for inflation. Plans with $50 deductibles were established in the 1950s, when that sum paid for 2 days in the hospital; now it does not cover room-only costs for a 4-hour stay in an outpatient clinic. Furthermore, copayments by employees may encourage more responsible use of the health-care system. Employees are clearly bearing more of the economic load.

For example, between 1989 and 1990, Georgia-Pacific Corp. raised its deductibles 50 percent—to $300 a year for individuals and $600 a year for families.[34] A 1989 survey found that only 34 percent of firms pay all hospital room-and-board charges incurred by employees or their dependents. In 1979, 69 percent did.[27]

2. Induce employees voluntarily to choose reduced medical coverage through flexible benefit plans (more on this shortly).

3. Remove the irrational incentives in plans that favor hospitalization over less costly outpatient care. For example, Sperry Corp. pays 100 percent for home health care but less if an employee checks into a hospital.[44]

4. Require a second surgical opinion prior to elective surgery. At Chrysler and at J. C. Penney, for example, if the employee fails to get a second opinion, the company will not pay the entire bill. One study of such programs estimates they could save $2.63 for every dollar spent on second opinions.

5. If employees must go to the hospital, set some rules. Refuse to let them enter on the weekend if treatment is not scheduled until Monday. Have large hospital bills audited (this could cut expenses by as much as 8 percent). Require preadmission certification, that is, doctor's clearance for the treatment desired for the employee before he or she enters the hospital. If additional treatment or tests are given, companies refuse to pay bills unless doctors can confirm that a deviation from the original plan was necessary.[57]

The latter strategy has been termed "managed care," and it is being offered by large insurers such as Cigna Corp. One of its clients is Allied-Signal Corp. and its 86,500 employees and their dependents. Managed care relies on a "gatekeeper" system of cost controls. The gatekeeper is a primary-care physician who monitors the medical history and care of each employee and his or her family. The doctor orders testing, makes referrals to specialists, and recommends hospitalization, surgery, or outpatient care, as appropriate. To make this approach pay off, Cigna must deliver high-quality medical care and still keep a tight lid on medical expenses. Yet Allied-Signal embraced the plan. Why? It's health-care bill escalated 39 percent in the year before it adopted managed care.[19]

HMOs

A final proposed cost containment approach is the health maintenance organization (HMO). An *HMO* is an organized system of health care that assures the delivery of services to employees who enroll voluntarily under a prepayment plan. The emphasis is on preventive medicine, that is, maintaining the health of each employee. Legally, HMOs are authorized under the HMO Act of 1973 (as amended in 1976 and 1978). Major features of the law are: (1) invalidation of state laws prohibiting HMOs, (2) a program of federal loans and grants for HMO development, (3) management and service criteria that an HMO must meet for federal qualification, and (4) the "dual choice" provision, whereby employers that have 25 or more employees and that are covered by minimum-wage requirements must offer the HMO option if the area has a federally qualified HMO.[23]

The objective of HMOs is to control health-care costs by keeping people *out* of the hospital. Deere & Co., the agricultural equipment manufacturer, used to pay for a staggering 1400 hospital days each year for every 1000 workers. Then in 1980 Deere took the lead in helping local doctors to establish an HMO, and annual hospitalization has since dropped to 500 days per thousand workers. Yet there are drawbacks. Plan members give up the freedom to choose their doctors, and for companies with scattered employment sites, the location of the HMO may be inconvenient. As of 1990, there were about 600 HMOs nationwide, enrolling almost 35 million people.[30,64]

Yet HMOs have not contained the rise in health care costs as effectively as many had hoped.[64] Despite sharp increases in premiums during the late 1980s, HMO premiums still did not rise as fast as conventional health insurance plans, which reimburse employees for most of the cost of care by the provider of their choice. Their relatively low out-of-pocket costs still make them popular among employees, particularly on the west coast, where enrollments run as high as 60 percent or more of some employee groups.

Nevertheless, employer dissatisfaction runs deep. In a recent survey of almost 2000 employers offering HMOs, only 28 percent believed that their rates fairly reflected services delivered. In response, HMOs have adopted two strategies. One, many are offering "open-ended" options that permit members to be partly repaid for care received outside the HMO's network of providers. Two, others are modifying premiums to reflect the medical track record of different employee groups. This is a departure from the HMO principle of lowering costs by spreading risks uniformly over a large group.[64]

To overcome some employees' complaints about the lack of freedom to choose their doctors in an HMO, some firms have contracted with organizations of health-care professionals (including physicians, dentists, and hospitals), so-called preferred provider organizations (PPOs), to deliver health-care services at reduced rates and with close utilization review. In return, the PPO is guaranteed a certain volume of patients.[75] As many as 300 PPOs now exist, with heavy concentrations in Florida and Washington, DC.[18,23]

Other Medical Coverage

Medical coverage for areas such as dental care, vision care, drug abuse, alcoholism, and mental illness is growing rapidly. For example, the Bureau of Labor Statistics found these percentages of medium and large firms offering benefits: 40 percent offered vision care, 71 percent offered dental care, and 99 percent offered mental health care.[69]

Sick-Leave Programs

These programs provide short-term insurance to workers against loss of wages due to short-term illness. However, in many firms such well-intended programs have often *added* to labor costs because of abuse by employees and because of the widespread perception that sick leave is a right and that if it is not used, it will be lost ("use it or lose it"). To overcome the negative effects of sick-pay programs, one firm instituted a "well-pay program" that rewards employees for *not* being absent or sick.[22] Over a 1-year period, the firm barely broke even after paying out well-pay bonuses.

Pensions

A *pension* is a sum of money paid at regular intervals to an employee (or to his or her dependents) who has retired from a company and is eligible to receive such benefits. Before World War II, private pensions were rare. However, two developments in the late 1940s stimulated their growth: (1) clarification of the tax treatment of employer contributions and (2) the 1948 Inland Steel case, in which the National Labor Relations Board ruled that pensions were subject to compulsory collective bargaining.[74]

There were no standards and little regulation, which led to abuses in funding many pension plans and to the denial of pension benefits to employees who had worked many years. Perhaps the most notorious example of this occurred in 1963 when Studebaker closed its South Bend, Indiana, car factory and stopped payments to the seriously underfunded plan that covered the workers. Only those already retired or on the verge of retirement received the pension benefits they expected. Others got only a fraction—or nothing.[11]

Incidents like these led to the passage of the Employee Retirement Income Security Act (ERISA, see Table 11-1) in 1974. Despite increased regulation, ERISA has generally been beneficial. In 1970, 30 percent of couples aged 65 to 69 received a private pension. By 2004, 88 percent will.[74]

Today, 91 percent of full-time workers at companies with more than 100 employees enjoy pension coverage. Yet only 26 percent of workers at mostly rural companies with 60 or fewer employees are covered.[36,38] In total, 870,000 pension, profit-sharing, and savings plans cover 76 million participants and retirees.[70] They paid retirees $220 billion in 1988, half again as much as the $148 billion that Social Security paid out.[33]

Money set aside by employers to cover pension obligations has become the nation's largest source of capital.[73] Pension funds hold 26 percent of the equity and 15 percent of the taxable bonds in the U.S. economy, comprising a total of $2.5 trillion.[29] That's roughly $8000 for every man, woman, and child in the United States! This is an enormous force in the nation's (and the world's) capital markets.

Pension fund managers tend to invest for the long term, and big corporate pension funds (95 percent of pension fund assets are covered by 5 percent of the plans) have less than 1 percent of their assets invested in leveraged buyouts, or high-risk, high-yield junk bonds.[73]

In general, the financial health of most private pension plans is good. However, to ensure that covered workers will receive their accrued benefits even if their companies fail, ERISA created the Pension Benefit Guaranty Corporation (PBGC). This agency acts as an insurance company, collecting annual premiums from companies with defined benefit plans that spell out specific payments upon retirement. A company can still walk away from its obligation to pay pension benefits to employees entitled to receive them, but it must then hand over up to 30 percent of its net worth to the PBGC for distribution to the affected employees.

Since 1974, the PBGC has taken over 1476 pension plans of companies that went out of business or could not finance their retirement plans. Payouts increased from $36 million in 1979 to $300 million in 1989.[70] To shore up the PBGC, Congress tripled the employer insurance premium to $8.50 per worker in 1986.[5] While that step might seem extreme, consider that the PBGC insures the pensions of one out of every three U.S. workers. It is important that as retirees, most workers end up getting nearly all that is promised to them—and they do.

How pension plans work Contributions to pension funds are typically managed by trustees or outside financial institutions, frequently insurance companies. As an incentive for employers to begin and maintain such plans, the government defers taxes on the pension contributions and their earnings. Retirees pay taxes on the money as they receive it.

Traditionally, most big corporate plans have been *defined-benefit plans*—under which an employer promises to pay a retiree a stated pension, often expressed as a percentage of preretirement pay. Currently, 80 percent of all pension participants are covered by these plans.[49] The most common formula is 1.5 percent of average salary over the last 5 years prior to retirement ("final average pay") times the number of years employed. In determining final average pay, the company may use base pay alone or base pay plus bonuses and other compensation. Standard Oil of Ohio uses the former method, Standard Oil of California, the latter.[55] Examples of annual pension as a function of years of service and final average pay are shown in Figure 11-1. When combined with Social Security benefits, that percentage is often about 50 percent of final average pay. The company then pays into the fund each year whatever is needed to cover expected benefit payments.

A second type of pension plan, popular as a support to an existing defined-benefit plan, is called a *defined-contribution plan*. Examples include stock bonuses, savings plans, profit sharing, and various kinds of employee stock-ownership plans. Defined-contribution plans fix a rate for employer *contributions* to the fund. Future *benefits* depend on how fast the fund grows. Such plans therefore favor young, short-service employees (because they contribute for many years). Defined-benefit plans favor older, long-service workers.

Defined-contribution plans have great appeal for employers because the company will never owe more than what was contributed. However, since the amount

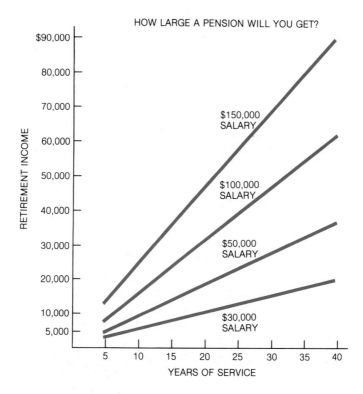

FIGURE 11-1
Relationship of annual retirement benefits to years of service and final average salary.

of benefits received depends on the investment performance of the monies contributed, employees cannot be sure of the size of their retirement checks. In fact, regardless of whether a plan is a defined-benefit or defined-contribution plan, employees will not know what the *purchasing power* of their pension checks will be, because the inflation rate is variable.

What appears to be evolving is a system that will make employees (instead of employers) more responsible for how much money they have for retirement. Individual Retirement Accounts (IRAs) are a good example of this. Created by the Economic Recovery Tax Act of 1981, IRAs allow individuals to contribute up to $2000 per year. The Tax Reform Act of 1986 eliminated the tax deduction for contributions to IRAs for those employees who (1) are active participants in a qualified retirement plan at work and (2) have an adjusted gross income of $50,000 or more on a joint return or $35,000 on a single return. However, the *interest* on all IRA contributions continues to compound tax-free until it is withdrawn.

The ideal pension plan is one that is adjusted (indexed) each year to maintain the purchasing power of the dollar according to changes in the cost of living. *ERISA does not require indexing.* Although Social Security benefits have been indexed to changes in the consumer price index since 1975, only about 3 percent of private pension plans have some form of indexation, and even that amount is limited.[31] For example, Aetna and Grumman both use the consumer price index as a basis for adjusting pension payments, but they limit the maximum yearly increase to 3 percent. Pension managers strongly resist indexation for two reasons: (1) The amount of money paid out will increase for those already retired, and (2) larger reserves have to be set aside to fund future increases on a sound basis. Tying pensions to inflation could add 1 to 2 percent of payroll to an employer's retiree costs, atop the 4 to 7 percent of payroll that companies now set aside.[40]

Unisex pensions Nathalie Norris, an employee of the state of Arizona, paid $199 per month into an annuity retirement plan offered by the state—the amount deducted from the paychecks of both male and female state employees earning the same salary. But Norris discovered that upon retirement she would get $34 per month *less* than male employees. This figure was based on actuarial tables showing that women, on average, live longer than men. Norris sued the state, and in a 1983 Supreme Court ruling, she won. The Court ruled that federal laws prohibiting sex discrimination in employment also bar employee-sponsored retirement plans that pay men higher benefits than women. Starting August 1, 1983, all contributions to such plans must be used to finance a system of *equal* payments to employees of both sexes. However, the Court denied retroactive relief to women, which could have cost insurance companies as much as $1.2 billion annually.[1] As a result of this ruling, many insurance companies have developed "merged-gender mortality tables" that show the combined number of persons living, the combined number of persons dying, and the merged-gender mortality rate for each age. The effect on benefits depends on the income option(s) elected at the time retirement income begins. For men aged 65, this could mean a monthly income decrease of up to 8 percent, while for women aged 65, it could mean a monthly income increase of up to 8 percent.[67]

Pension reforms that benefit women These reforms were incorporated into the Retirement Equity Act of 1984. Corporate pension plans must now include younger workers and permit longer breaks in service. Women typically start work at younger ages than do men, and they are more likely to stop working for several years in order to have and care for children. However, since the new rules apply to both sexes, men also will accrue larger benefits. There are five major changes under the act:[54]

1. As of January 1, 1985, pension plans must include all employees 21 or older (down from 25). This will extend pension coverage to an additional 600,000 women and to 500,000 men.
2. Employers must use 18 rather than 22 as the starting age for counting years of service. Typically employees need 10 years of service to be fully "vested," or entitled to receive their pensions regardless of any future service. Thus a worker hired at age 19 can join a plan at 21 and can be fully vested by age 29.
3. Employees may have breaks in services of as long as 5 years before losing credit for prior years of work. In addition, a year of maternity or paternity leave cannot be considered a break in service.

4. Pension benefits may now be considered a joint asset in divorce settlements. State courts can award part of an individual's pension to the ex-spouse.

5. Employers must provide survivor benefits to spouses of fully vested employees who die before reaching the minimum retirement age.

Social Security

Provisions for this program were outlined in Table 11-1. Social Security is an income-maintenance program, not a pension program. It is the nation's best defense against poverty for the elderly, and it has worked well. Without it, according to one study, the poverty rate among the elderly would have jumped from 12.4 to 47.6 percent.[50] Although this national program of old-age, survivors', disability, and health insurance was strengthened considerably by the 1983 amendments to the law, many people are convinced that they could have invested their payroll taxes (which, as Figure 11-2 shows, doubled between 1982 and 1990) more wisely than the government has. Are they right? The Social Security Administration calculated what an individual, ignoring Medicare and some other insurance features, would have to spend at age 65 just to finance a monthly annuity similar to the one that she or he will get from Social Security.

A single male who retired at age 65 in 1980 would have had to invest $64,000 *immediately* at an interest rate exceeding inflation by 2.5 percent to generate an income stream of approximately $125,000—the amount he will get from Social Security if he lives another 14.3 years (average male life expectancy). This is a ratio of about $6 in benefits for every $1 paid in taxes. By any standard, that is a pretty good return on investment. Most individuals could not have done better by investing on their own.

However, future beneficiaries will receive, in general, relatively smaller benefits in relation to their payroll taxes. Nevertheless, your own benefits will probably be higher than you expect. In fact, you are likely to get more in today's dollars than someone retiring now does. For example, suppose you are planning to retire in

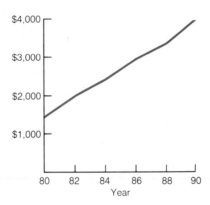

MAXIMUM SOCIAL SECURITY TAX

FIGURE 11-2
Maximum Social Security payroll taxes paid by individuals between 1980 and 1990.

INTERNATIONAL APPLICATION: SOCIAL SECURITY IN OTHER COUNTRIES

Many countries outside the United States have adopted pension programs that combine Social Security with private retirement accounts. In Britain, for example, workers can opt out of part of the state pension system by applying up to 44 percent of their social security tax to their own private individual investment accounts. Japan, Finland, Sweden, France, and Switzerland have similar programs. In these countries, the social security component of the pension system remains on a pay-as-you-go basis in which current tax receipts are used to pay for both current benefits and other government programs.

Singapore uses a payroll tax to fund retirement, but it works like a private pension system. The revenues are invested in individually owned accounts and, unlike U.S. Social Security taxes, are tax-deductible and not subject to income taxes.

Employees can withdraw money from their retirement funds to purchase housing, and, as a result, 80 percent of Singapore's citizens own their own residences. If an employee is dissatisfied with the return earned by the public fund, he or she can transfer the account to investments in the Singapore stock market or other approved vehicles. The asset balance in a Singaporean's retirement fund passes to his or her beneficiaries upon death. Among the countries that have systems similar to Singapore's are India, Kenya, Malaysia, Zambia, and Indonesia.[58]

2025, at age 65. In 1990 dollars, the maximum age-65 payout in that year is projected to be $17,829 a year, compared with $11,700 today.[63]

The Congressional Budget Office projects that the system will be solvent through the year 2030. At that time, however, given the large number of retirements by baby boomers, Social Security tax outlays will exceed tax revenues. To meet such long-term funding needs, the system will have to be reformed again.

Actually, one element of reform is already in place, thanks to the 1983 Social Security amendments. The normal retirement age will increase from 65 in two stages. It will rise to 66 at the rate of 2 months a year for those turning 62 between 2000 and 2005, and to 67 for those turning 62 between 2017 and 2022. Actually, the idea of retiring at age 65 is increasingly archaic. If 65 was the proper retirement age in the United States in 1940, then today, based on rising life expectancy, it should be 73.[21]

Unemployment Insurance

Although 97 percent of the workforce is covered by federal and state unemployment insurance laws, each worker must meet eligibility requirements in order to receive benefits. That is, an unemployed worker must: (1) be able and available to work and be actively seeking work; (2) not have refused suitable employment; (3)

not be unemployed because of a labor dispute (except in Rhode Island and New York); (4) not have left a job voluntarily; (5) not have been terminated for gross misconduct; and (6) have been employed previously in a covered industry or occupation, earning a designated minimum amount for a specific minimum amount of time. Many claims are disallowed for failure to satisfy one or more of these requirements.

Every unemployed worker's benefits are "charged" against one or more companies. The more money paid out on behalf of a firm, the higher is the unemployment insurance rate for that firm.

The tax in most states amounts to 6.2 percent of the first $7000 earned by each worker. The state receives 5.4 percent of this 6.2 percent and the remainder goes to the federal government. However, the tax rate may fall to 0 percent in some states for employers who have had no recent claims by former employees, and it may rise to 10 percent for organizations with large numbers of layoffs. Nationwide, the average cost fell throughout the 1980s, to an average of $224 per worker in 1989.[35]

This decline was due partly to the generally buoyant economy that saw fewer people filing claims. However, it also was due to a growing sensitivity by state governments that high unemployment insurance taxes can be a black eye on a state's business climate. In 1987, for example, unemployment taxes per worker varied from a high of $680 in Alaska to a low of $112 in New Hampshire.[15] Benefit levels generally have kept up with inflation. They average about 35 percent of what workers were earning at their last jobs.[59]

Supplemental Unemployment Insurance

This type of insurance is common in the auto, steel, rubber, flat glass, and farm equipment industries. Employers contribute to a special fund for this purpose. Initially, the primary purpose of such plans was to replace employees' pay during seasonal layoffs, but the provisions also apply in the case of permanent layoffs. Such plans, when combined with unemployment compensation, usually replace nearly all after-tax base wages for 6 months, with extensions under certain conditions. Only 8 percent of employees are covered by supplemental unemployment insurance plans, but most others are protected by some form of severance pay. Both types of arrangements are covered by ERISA, and this point has been affirmed by the Supreme Court.[47]

Severance Pay

Such pay is not legally required, and, because of unemployment compensation, many firms do not offer it. However, some provide severance payments to employees when they leave instead of giving them advance notice of their dismissal. Length of service, organization level, and the cause of the termination are key factors that affect the size of severance agreements. Most lower-level employees receive 1 week of pay for each year that they work for a company.[60] Executives earning $50,000 to $150,000 a year can expect 8 months' pay, and for those making $150,000 to $200,000, the average is 11 months' pay.[39] Chief executive officers with management contracts may receive 2 to 3 years of salary in the event of a takeover.[42] How is severance handled in other countries? In Japan, ousted chief executives receive an average of 2.5 times their annual compensation. They get at least 2 years' pay in the Netherlands, Belgium, and Germany.[37]

Payments for Time Not Worked

Included in this category are such benefits as the following:

Vacations	Personal excused absences
Holidays	Grievances and negotiations
Reporting time	Sabbatical leaves

■ **COMPANY EXAMPLE**

PAID PUBLIC-SERVICE LEAVES AT XEROX

Some employees work with the disabled, others do alcohol and drug counseling, and still others do preretirement counseling. All are Xerox employees on 1-year leaves with full pay. Social commitment is a driving force behind the Xerox program, begun in 1971, but it is not the only rationale for the leaves. Public-service leaves boost the morale and skills of employees, according to those responsible for the program, and they make Xerox a more desirable place to work. Former leave takers say their careers were not affected by the leaves, and many feel that their careers were advanced. Nevertheless, the program also has its problems. Of 131 leave takers surveyed, 40 percent reported major or moderate reentry difficulties on returning to work. More than one-third have quit, regarding their Xerox work as "not very rewarding or extremely unrewarding," in contrast with their high opinion of volunteer work. Many reported that their Xerox bosses acted as if they had been let down because the employees had left. Despite these problems, Xerox aims to continue the program, at a direct cost of about $500,000 per year. Employees want such a program, and society needs them.[66]

Employee Services

A broad group of benefits falls into the employee services category. Employees qualify for them purely by virtue of their membership in the organization, and not because of merit. Some examples are:

Tuition aid	Thrift and short-term savings plans
Credit unions	Stock purchase plans

Auto insurance	Fitness and wellness programs
Food service	Moving and transfer allowances
Company car	Transportation and parking
Career clothing	Merchandise purchasing
Legal services	Christmas bonuses
Counseling	Service and seniority awards
Child adoption	Umbrella liability coverage
Child care	Social activities
Elder care	Referral awards
Gift matching	Purchase of used equipment
Charter flights	

At many companies these benefits go begging, sometimes as a result of employees' lack of knowledge that they exist, and sometimes as a result of cultural norms. Consider paternity leave as an example. Very few men ever take advantage of it. Why? Largely because of fear of adverse consequences to their careers. As one manager noted, "No CEO would ever speak out against family leave. It's subtle, unspoken, never in print—it's just the way the game is played. If you're in an environment where the nature of the business is chaotic, you just can't afford to be gone if you want to be a player" (ref. 2, p. B1).

Special Benefits for Executives

Top executives are sometimes privy to three special perquisites. The first of these is the *golden parachute*, an employment contract provision that guarantees (typically) one to six top executives a cash severance equal to several years' salary if they are fired without cause after a takeover or if their status or responsibilities are downgraded by the new management. The Tax Reform Act of 1986 preserved golden parachute provisions for closely held firms; but for others, any payment to an executive that exceeds 3 times the annual salary and is made in connection with a change in control of a business becomes nondeductible to the paying corporation. On top of that, the recipient must pay an additional 20 percent tax on the payment.[51] In 1987 the directors of UAL, Inc., the holding company for United Airlines, took action consistent with the new law. Fearing a change in control of UAL, they made 37 executives eligible for severance payments of 1 to 3 times their base salaries until 1992, or retirement, if that is earlier.[26] Among major companies, nearly one in three provides golden parachutes to top executives who lose their jobs in hostile takeovers. But only one in 60 covers shop-floor employees.[32]

A second special benefit for top executives is the *supplemental retirement benefit plan*. Such plans are particularly desirable because of changes wrought by the Tax Reform Act of 1986. That law drastically cut guaranteed retirement benefits under qualified (by the IRS) pension plans. Such benefits are typically figured as a percentage of the retiring executive's average salary in the final 3 to 5 years, multiplied by years of service. But as of 1987, companies cannot consider annual salary that exceeds $120,000 in those years.[6] Supplemental retirement agreements are sometimes negotiated to make up for this shortfall in the pensions of highly paid executives. Of course, the agreements are not insured by the government, and they could become worthless should the company go bankrupt.

The *"key executive" life insurance policy* is a third special benefit. The company pays the premiums, and, when the executive retires, he or she gets the cash value of the policy, including appreciation, in a lump sum. If he or she dies before retiring, the company gets back what it has contributed in premiums, and the spouse receives the remainder of the settlement. Leveraged whole-life insurance programs purchased by companies to fund these benefits have become less attractive as a result of the Tax Reform Act of 1986, because the interest on premium loans over $50,000 per executive is no longer deductible. Such benefits will probably continue to be offered, but companies will need to find different methods to fund them.[48]

BENEFITS ADMINISTRATION

Benefits and Equal Employment Opportunity

Equal employment opportunity requirements also affect the administration of benefits. Consider as examples health-care coverage and pensions. Effective in 1987, an amendment to the Age Discrimination in Employment Act eliminates mandatory retirement at any age. It also requires employers to continue the same group health insurance coverage offered to younger employees to employees over the age of 70. Medicare payments are limited to what Medicare would have paid for in the absence of a group health plan and to the actual charge for the services. This is another example of government "cost shifting" to the private sector.

The Older Workers Benefit Protection Act of 1990 restored age discrimination protection to employee benefits, a notion that had been scrapped by a 1989 Supreme Court decision. However, early retirement offers are now legal if they are granted at least 45 days prior to the decision, and, if they are accepted, employees are given 7 days to revoke them. Employers also were granted some flexibility in plant closings, to offset retiree health benefits or pension sweeteners against severance pay. That is, an employer is entitled to deny severance pay if an employee is eligible for retiree health benefits.

With regard to pensions, the IRS considers a plan *discriminatory* unless the employer's contribution for the benefit of lower-paid employees covered by the plan is comparable to contributions for the benefit of higher-paid employees. An example of this is a salary reduction plan [known as 401(k)] authorized by the Tax Equity and Fiscal Responsibility Act. The plan permits significant savings out of pretax compensation, produces higher take-home pay, and results in lower Social Security taxes. The catch: *The plan has to be available to everyone in any company that implements it.* Although the Tax Reform Act of 1986 capped employee contributions at $7000 per year, indexed to changes in the cost of living, two-thirds of eligible employees—the same as prior to the act—are salting away part of their earnings in such plans as this.[43] Currently, 86 percent of employers with 401(k) plans give employees between 50 cents and $1 for every dollar they contribute.[61] Together, the tax deferral and matching features can add up to produce handsome results: A worker making the 1990 maximum contribution of $7979 with a 50 percent employer match and earning an annual 9 percent return would take just under 25 years to reach $1 million.

Costing Benefits

Despite the high cost of benefits, many employees take them for granted. A major reason for this is that employers have failed to do in-depth cost analyses of their benefit programs and thus have not communicated the value of their benefit programs to employees. Four approaches are used widely to express the costs of employee benefits and services. Although each has value individually, a combination of all four often enhances their impact on employees. The four methods are:[47]

- *Annual cost of benefits for all employees.* Valuable for developing budgets and for describing the total cost of the benefits program
- *Cost per employee per year.* Calculated by dividing the total cost of each benefit program by the number of employees participating in it
- *Percentage of payroll.* Total annual cost divided by total annual payroll (this figure is valuable in comparing benefits costs across organizations)
- *Cents per hour.* Calculated by dividing the total annual cost of benefits by the total number of hours worked by all employees during the year

A company example of actual benefits costs (the name of the firm is fictitious) is presented in Table 11-3. All four methods of costing benefits have been incorporated into the table. Can you find an example of each?

Cafeteria, or Flexible, Benefits

As noted earlier in the chapter, the theory underlying this approach to benefits is simple: Instead of all workers at a company getting the same benefits, each worker can pick and choose among alternative options "cafeteria style." Thus the elderly bachelor might pass up maternity coverage for additional pension contributions. The mother whose children are covered under her husband's health insurance may choose legal and auto insurance instead. The typical plan works like this:

Workers are offered a package of benefits that includes "basic" and "optional" items. Basics might include modest medical coverage, life insurance equal to a year's salary, vacation time based on length of service, and some retirement pay. But then employees can use "flexible credits" to choose among such additional benefits as full medical coverage, dental and eye care, more vacation time, additional disability income, and higher company payments to the retirement fund.

■ **TABLE 11·3**
EMPLOYEE BENEFITS: THE FORGOTTEN EXTRAS

Listed below are the benefits for the average full-time employee (annual salary $24,000).

Benefit	Who pays	SUN's annual cost	Percentage of base earnings	What you receive
Health, dental, and life insurance	SUN and You	$1922.40	8.01	Comprehensive health and dental plus life insurance equivalent to 1 times your annual salary
Holidays	SUN	1200.00	5.00	13 paid holidays
Annual leave (vacation)	SUN	924.00	3.85	10 days vacation per year (additional days starting with sixth year of service)
Sick days	SUN	1106.40	4.61	12 days annually
Company retirement	SUN	2623.20	10.93	Vested after 5 years of service
Social security	SUN and You	1608.00	6.70	Retirement and disability benefits
Workers' compensation and unemployment insurance	SUN	240.00	1.00	Compensation if injured on duty and if eligible; income while seeking employment
Total		$9624.00, or $4.63 per hour	40.10	

The dollar amount and percentages will differ slightly depending upon your salary. If your annual salary is less than $24,000, the percentage of your base pay will be greater. If your salary is greater than $24,000, the percentage will be less but the dollar amount will be greater.
Benefit costs to SUN, Inc., on behalf of our 5480 employees represent over $52,700,000 per year.

Nationwide, about 22 percent of firms have flexible benefit plans.[7] They were devised largely in response to the rise in the number of two-income families. When working spouses both have conventional plans, their basic benefits, such as health and life insurance, tend to overlap. Couples rarely can use both plans fully. But if at least one spouse is covered by a "flex" plan, the family can add benefits, such as child care, prepaid legal fees, and dental coverage, that otherwise they might have to buy on their own.

There are advantages for employers as well. Under conventional plans, employers risked alienating employees if they cut benefits, regardless of increases in the costs of coverage. Flexible plans allow them to pass some of the increases onto workers more easily. Instead of providing employees a set package of benefits, the employer says, "Based on your $27,000 annual salary, I promise you $5500 to spend any way you want." If health-care costs soar, the employee—not the employer—decides whether to pay more or to take less coverage.

This is what has happened at PepsiCo ever since "flex" was introduced in 1980. But company surveys show that fully 80 percent of the participants are satisfied with the plan.[56] Besides, there's help for employees even under these circumstances if they work for firms that sponsor "flexible spending accounts" (about 50 percent

IMPACT OF BENEFITS ON PRODUCTIVITY, QUALITY OF WORK LIFE, AND THE BOTTOM LINE

Generally speaking, employee benefits do not enhance productivity. Their major impact is on attraction and retention, and on improving the quality of life for employees and their dependents. Today there is widespread recognition among employers and employees that benefits are an important component of total compensation.[46] As long as employees perceive that their total compensation is equitable and that their benefit options are priced fairly, then benefit programs can achieve the strategic objectives set for them. The challenge for executives will be to maintain control over the costs of benefits, while providing genuine value to employees in the benefits offered. If they can do this, then everybody wins.

of all large firms in 1990). Employees can save for expenses such as additional health insurance or day care with pre-tax dollars, up to a specified amount. As a result, it's a win-win situation for both employer and employee.[10]

Two other potential obstacles have now been removed. One, the Tax Reform Act of 1986 has removed any doubt about the legality of flexible benefits plans. Two, personal-computer software programs have slashed the cost and the administrative complexity of flexible benefits plans. As a result, such plans are now being designed for companies with as few as 20 employees.[17]

Despite these potential advantages, two disadvantages, neither insurmountable, remain. One, insurers fear that employees' adverse selection of benefits will drive up costs (e.g., the only employees who choose dental insurance coverage are those with bad teeth). But this fear has been eased by new methods of pooling small-business risks and by better ways of predicting (and thus pricing) the benefits that employees will choose.[17] Two, major communications efforts are needed to help employees understand their benefits fully. Since employees have more choices, they often experience anxiety about making the "right" choices. In addition, they need benefits information on a continuing basis to ensure that their choices continue to support their changing needs.[3] Careful attention to communication can enhance recruitment efforts, help cut turnover, and make employees more aware of their total package of benefits.

Communicating the Benefits

Try to make a list of good reasons why any company should not make a deliberate effort to market its benefits package effectively. It will be a short list. Generally speaking, there are four broad objectives in communicating benefits:[47]

1. To make employees *aware* of them. This can be done by reminding them of their coverages periodically and of how to apply for benefits when needed.
2. To help employees *understand* the benefits information they receive in order to take full advantage of the plans.

3. To make employees confident that they can *trust* the information they receive.

4. To convince present and future employees of the *worth* of the benefits package.

Traditionally employers concentrated their communications about benefits at the start of employment and assumed that that was sufficient in relation to future events. Today the emphasis is on *event-centered* communications—that is, on providing to employees "the benefits information you need, when you need it."[47] This is done by providing information (1) as new benefits become available and (2) at important milestones (e.g., illness or disability, retirement, death—information to survivors, or termination of employment).

Today, we are in what might be called the "third generation of employee benefits communication." Printed materials provided by insurance companies comprised the first generation. The booklets were written from the insurer's viewpoint, not from the reader's. Their technical language provided little real communication.

The second generation started when companies began to provide personalized, computer-generated statements of the dollar value of benefits to employees—in plain English (see Table 11-3). Today, with the rapid proliferation of office automation, we are in the third generation of benefits communication. Micro-computers, telephone hotlines, and interactive videos have added a new dimension to this process.[28] Here are some innovative applications:

- A food-processing corporation installed computers at work locations. Now employees can obtain quick answers to "coverage" situations.
- Computer-aided design methods are being used to show how all elements of a benefits program combine to produce an image consistent with a company's culture. This is typically a series of unrelated shapes that, when combined, produce the image of, say, an airplane (for an airline), a company's major product (e.g., a car), or a company symbol (e.g., a pyramid).
- Aetna has developed a microcomputer system that captures and records employee benefit choices, producing personalized confirmation letters.

Initiating communictions technology can be time-consuming and expensive. But so is a benefits plan that no one understands or appreciates.[72]

■ HUMAN RESOURCE MANAGEMENT IN ACTION
CONCLUSION

THE FUTURE LOOK OF EMPLOYEE BENEFITS

Experts in the field of employee benefits see seven changes that are likely to emerge over the next 20 years. They include the following:

Leave In about 10 years, some companies may offer 1 to 2 months of paid leave for dependent care, followed by unpaid leaves of 6 months, with jobs guaranteed on return. A driving force behind such a change will be the growing problem of "elder care."

Education and training   Hoping to ease employees' worries about college tuition, and to keep them from shopping around for higher-paying jobs, companies are likely to offer low-cost education loans, and, later, outright payments, as benefit-plan options. Moreover, the unemployment compensation system may be transformed. Money will be set aside not only for unemployment insurance, as is done now, but also for unemployment training, so that anyone out of work would draw weekly supplements for schooling in new skills.

Career planning   As part of a broader definition of benefits, many corporations will help employees plan careers that adjust to their changing lives. People will be able to move up, down, over, or even out (temporarily) and still be a part of the corporation. Thus managers may meet with employees once a year in an effort to find out what the employee can handle over the coming months. Can the employee travel a lot? Work extra hours? Work full time? Companies will have to identify the time commitment each job requires — and then try to match jobs with people's needs and wants.

Housing   Colgate-Palmolive Co. in New York, already helps salaried employees buy or refinance a primary residence. Employees receive a mortgage through the same financial company that handles Colgate's employee-relocation program. Colgate picks up the loan-origination fee, or part of it, depending on the size of the mortgage. Other companies may offer their employees variable-rate loans, pegged slightly below market rates. Employees would lose the rate advantage, however, if they leave the company.

Late retirement   As baby boomers age, and as shortages of workers and skills increase, companies will be bending over backward to keep their older employees. The result — "platinum handcuffs" consisting of company-paid vacation trips, shorter hours, and bonus plans that reward employees for staying on past a certain age or period of service. Similarly, companies could pay a progressively larger percentage of health insurance costs for retirees who quit working at 60, 65, or 70 than for those quitting at 55.

Flextime   At almost all companies, executives and consultants say, hours will be more flexible. Part-time workers will share jobs, and most employees will be able to work at least part of the time at home. Said one executive: "The good Lord didn't say, 'Thou shalt work 40 hours a week, 9 to 5, with an hour for lunch' ".*

---

*From J. Solomon, The future look of employee benefits, *The Wall Street Journal*, September 7, 1988, p. 27. Reprinted by permission of *The Wall Street Journal*, © 1988 Dow Jones & Company, Inc. All rights reserved worldwide.

Vacation   Ben & Jerry's Homemade Inc., a Waterbury, Vermont, ice-cream maker, is considering a "flexbanking" system. Under such a plan, all benefits would be assigned credits in a common currency, like Monopoly money. Each employee could spend the credits as he or she wants, with some restrictions. For example, employees could "buy" extra vacation time if they want it.

Ben & Jerry's, however, has one benefit that can't be banked—and is unlikely to be a staple at other firms in the future. Each employee is allowed to take home three pints of ice cream a day.

SUMMARY

Managers need to think carefully about what they wish to accomplish by means of their benefits programs. At a cost of about $11,000 for every employee, and about 37 percent of total payroll costs, benefits represent substantial annual expenditures. Factors such as the following are important strategic considerations in the design of benefits programs: the long-term plans of a business, its stage of development, its projected rate of growth or downsizing, characteristics of the workforce, legal requirements, the competitiveness of the overall benefits "package," and its total compensation strategy.

There are three major benefit components: security and health, payments for time not worked, and employee services. Despite the high cost of benefits, many employees take them for granted. A major reason for this is that employers have not done in-depth cost analyses or communicated the value of their benefits programs. This is a multimillion-dollar oversight. Certainly the counseling that must accompany the implementation of a flexible benefits program, or at least a personalized statement of annual benefits, can do much to alleviate this problem.

IMPLICATIONS FOR MANAGEMENT PRACTICE

As you think about the design and implementation of employee benefit plans, consider three practical issues:

1. What are you trying to accomplish by means of the benefits package? Ensure that the benefits offered are consistent with the strategic objectives of the unit or organization as a whole.
2. Take the time to learn about alternative benefit arrangements. Said one General Electric executive: "We know more about what goes into the cost of a 75-cent box of screws we use on the factory floor than we know about what goes into the cost of health care" (ref. 53, p. 96).
3. Develop an effective strategy for communicating benefits regularly to all employees.

DISCUSSION QUESTIONS

11•1 Do you agree or disagree with the statement "Disability insurance is more important than life insurance." Why or why not?

11•2 Should employees have more or less control over how their company-sponsored retirement funds are invested?

11•3 Discuss the impact of benefits on employee motivation.

11•4 What can firms do to control health-care costs?

11•5 Discuss the pros and cons of flexible benefits.

REFERENCES

1. A bow to unisex pensions (1983, July 18). *Newsweek*, p. 66.

2. Alexander, S. (1990, Aug. 24). Fears for careers curb paternity leaves. *The Wall Street Journal*, pp. B1, B4.

3. Anthony, R. J. (1986). A communication program model for flexible benefits. *Personnel Administrator*, **31**(6), 65–76.

4. Bacon, K. H. (1989, Nov. 11). Business and labor reach a consensus on need to overhaul health-care system. *The Wall Street Journal*, p. A14. See also Stout, H. (1991, April 23). U.S. spending on health care keeps growing. *The Wall Street Journal*, p. B4.

5. Beazley, J. E. (1987, May 21). Agency in crisis. *The Wall Street Journal*, pp. 1, 12.

6. Bettner, J. (1986, Oct. 28). Executive dreams: What benefits to request under the new tax law. *The Wall Street Journal*, p. 35.

7. Cafeteria benefit plans, flex-time, and child care assistance help ease burdens of dual career couples (1989, November/December). *Investment Vision*, p. 24.

8. Carlsen, E. (1983, Oct. 11). States' widely varying laws on disability costs irk firms. *The Wall Street Journal*, p. 35.

9. Coddington, D. C., Keen, D. J., Moore, K. D., & Clarke, R. L. (1990). *The crisis in health care*. San Francisco: Jossey-Bass.

10. Cohen, L. (1990, Oct. 1). Special account eases workers' medical burden. *Denver Post*, p. 3C.

11. Colvin, G. (1982, Oct. 4). How sick companies are endangering the pension system. *Fortune*, pp. 72–78.

12. Coverage continues when the job doesn't (1990, March 21). *The Wall Street Journal*, p. B1.

13. Edwards, M. R. (1981). Permanent disability: What does it cost? *Human Resource Planning*, **4**, 209–220.

14. Financing and managing public employee benefit plans in the 1990s (1988, October). *Government Finance Review*, pp. 32, 33.

15. Firms' unemployment taxes fell in most states this year (1987, Dec. 29). *The Wall Street Journal*, p. 17.

16. Freudenheim, M. (1990, Feb. 5). Health insurers, to reduce losses, black-list dozens of occupations. *The New York Times*, pp. A1, D5.

17. Galante, S. P. (1986, July 21). Employers acquiring a taste for providing benefit "menus." *The Wall Street Journal*, p. 17.

18. Gannes, S. (1987, April 13). Strong medicine for health bills. *Fortune*, pp. 70–74.

19. Garcia, B. E. (1989, Feb. 16). Cigna's "managed" health care is all-or-nothing game. *The Wall Street Journal*, p. A6.

20. Graham, J. (1990, Oct. 1). Spiraling costs anger employers in Colo., U. S. *Denver Post*, p. 3C.

21. Hardy, D. R. (1989, Aug. 21). Social Security's insecure future. *The Wall Street Journal*, p. A24.

22. Harvey, B. H., Schultze, J. A., & Rogers, J. F. (1983). Rewarding employees for not using sick leave. *Personnel Administrator*, **28**(5), 55–59.

23. Hayes, M. (1986). The crisis in health care costs. *Personnel Administrator*, **31**(7), 56–62, 126, 130.

24. Henderson, R. I. (1989). *Compensation management* (5th ed.). Englewood Cliffs, NJ: Prentice-Hall.

25. James, F. E. (1987, Sep. 29). Medical expenses resist control and keep going one way: Higher. *The Wall Street Journal*, p. 29.

26. Kilman, S., & Valente, J. (1987, April 21). UAL officials get "golden parachute" employment pacts. *The Wall Street Journal*, p. 2.

27. Kramon, G. (1989, Feb. 21). Business and health. *The New York Times*, p. C2.

28. Labor letter (1991, Jan. 8). *The Wall Street Journal*, p. A1.

29. Labor letter (1990, May 15). *The Wall Street Journal*, p. A1.

30. Labor letter (1990, May 8). *The Wall Street Journal*, p. A1.

31. Labor letter (1990, April 3). *The Wall Street Journal*, p. A1.

32. Labor letter (1990, Feb. 20). *The Wall Street Journal*, p. A1.

33. Labor letter (1990, Jan. 16). *The Wall Street Journal*, p. A1.

34. Labor letter (1989, Nov. 28). *The Wall Street Journal*, p. A1.

35. Labor letter (1989, March 21). *The Wall Street Journal*, p. A1.

36. Labor letter (1988, Nov. 22). *The Wall Street Journal*, p. A1.

37. Labor letter (1988, Nov. 8). *The Wall Street Journal*, p. A1.

38. Labor letter (1988, Sep. 13). *The Wall Street Journal*, p. A1.

39. Labor letter (1988, Jan. 19). *The Wall Street Journal*, p. A1.

40. Labor letter (1987, Nov. 10). *The Wall Street Journal*, p. 1.

41. Labor letter (1987, Sep. 22). *The Wall Street Journal*, p. 1.

42. Labor letter (1987, Sep. 8). *The Wall Street Journal*, p. 1.

43. Labor letter (1987, May 15). *The Wall Street Journal*, p. 1.

44. Labor letter (1984, Sep. 18). *The Wall Street Journal*, p. 1.

45. Ledvinka, J., & Scarpello, V. G. (1991). *Federal regulation of personnel and human resource management*. Boston: PWS-Kent.

46. McCaffery, R. M. (1989). Employee benefits and services. In L. R. Gomez-Mejia (ed.), *Compensation and benefits*. Washington, DC: Bureau of National Affairs, pp. 3-101 to 3-135.

47. McCaffery, R. M. (1988). *Employee benefit programs: A total compensation perspective*. Boston: PWS-Kent.

48. McMillan, J. D. (1986). Tax reform: What it means (part one). *Personnel Administrator*, **31**(12), 95–100.

49. Milkovich, G. T., & Newman, J. M. (1990). *Compensation* (3d ed.). Homewood, IL: BPI-Irwin.

50. *Older Americans in the workforce: Challenges and solutions* (1987). Washington, DC: Bureau of National Affairs.

51. Padwe, G. W. (1987, March). How golden are your parachutes? *Nation's Business*, p. 62.

52. Pay your own disability premium (1989, December). *Money*, p. 175.

53. Peers, A. (1987, June 29). Firms now must offer health insurance to some ex-workers— but at what price? *The Wall Street Journal*, p. 29.

54. Pension reform has something for everyone (1984, Aug. 27). *U. S. News & World Report*, p. 67.

55. Personal affairs (1982, Nov. 22). *Forbes*, pp. 230–233.

56. Reibstein, L. (1986, Sep. 16). To each according to his needs: Flexible benefits plans gain favor. *The Wall Street Journal*, p. 33.

57. Richman, L. S. (1983, May 2). Health benefits come under the knife. *Fortune*, pp. 95–110.

58. Roberts, P. C. (1990, Feb. 1). Let workers own their own retirement funds . . . that's how it's done in other countries. *The Wall Street Journal*, p. A21.

59. Rosenbaum, D. E. (1990, Dec. 2). Unemployment insurance aiding fewer workers. *The New York Times*, pp. 1, 38.

60. Schultz, E. E. (1990, Oct. 17). A financial survival guide for the newly unemployed. *The Wall Street Journal*, pp. C1, C17.

61. Schultz, E. E. (1990, April 27). Taking full control of retirement funds. *The Wall Street Journal*, pp. C1, C21.

62. Schultz, E. E. (1990, April 17). Disability Coverage? Well, I have some. . . . *The Wall Street Journal*, pp. C1, C23.

63. Schurenberg, E. (1990, August). Finally, the good news about Social Security. *Money*, pp. 91–94.

64. Shellenbarger, S. (1990, Feb. 27). As HMO premiums soar, employers sour on the plans and check out alternatives. *The Wall Street Journal*, pp. B1, B9.

65. Slater, K. (1986, May 23). Medical and disability plans: How to tell if a firm's employee benefits measure up. *The Wall Street Journal*, p. 21.

66. Tannenbaum, J. A. (1981, May 6). Paid public service leaves buoy workers, but return to old jobs can be wrenching. *The Wall Street Journal*, p. 29.

67. The *Norris* decision and merged-gender annuity rates (1983, August). TIAA-CREF, Notice to Annuity Owners.

68. U.S. Chamber of Commerce (1989). *Employee benefits.* Washington, DC: U.S. Chamber of Commerce.

69. U.S. Department of Labor (1987, June). *Employee benefits in medium and large firms.* Washington, DC: USGPO, Bulletin 2281.

70. Wallace, A. C. (1989, Aug. 5). Pension experts aren't worried. *The New York Times*, pp. 31, 32.

71. Wallace, M. J., Jr., & Fay, C. H. (1988). *Compensation theory and practice.* (2d ed.) Boston: PWS-Kent.

72. Watters, D. A. (1986). New technologies for benefits communication. *Personnel Administrator*, **31**(11), 110–114.

73. White, J. A. (1990, March 20). Pension funds try to retire idea that they are villains. *The Wall Street Journal*, pp. C1, C8.

74. Widder, P. (1982, May 31). Individuals gain more control over their pensions. *Denver Post*, pp. 1C, 8C.

75. Winslow, R. (1989, Sep. 12). Health costs. *The Wall Street Journal*, p. B1.

Motivational Strategies for Improving Performance and Productivity

■ **HUMAN RESOURCE MANAGEMENT IN ACTION**

THE 100 CLUB: A MILLION-DOLLAR INCENTIVE PLAN*

In 1981 the 325 employees who manufactured paper egg cartons at a Diamond International plant in Palmer, Massachusetts, faced an uncertain future. Styrofoam containers were creating stiff competition, the recession was affecting profits adversely, and workers were worried about being laid off. Labor-management relations were strained at best. Over 65 percent of the plant's workforce felt that management did not treat them with respect, 56 percent approached their work pessimistically, and 79 percent thought they were not being rewarded for a job well done.

Then the director of human resources of the Diamond plant devised a system of productivity incentives called the "100 Club." It is disarmingly simple. Employees are allocated points in recognition of above-average performance. Any employee who works a full year without having an industrial accident is awarded 20 points; 100 percent attendance is worth 25

---

*Adapted from: Hot 100, *Time*, July 4, 1983, p. 46.

points. Every year on February 2 (the anniversary of the program's launching date), points are tallied and a record is sent to the individual's home. Upon reaching 100 points, the worker gets a light-blue nylon jacket emblazoned with the company logo and a patch signifying membership in the "100 Club." Every one of the plant's employees has now earned a jacket.

Those who accumulate more than 100 points can receive additional gifts. With 500 points, employees can choose from such items as a blender, cooking accessories, a wall clock, or a cribbage board. Diamond's management is quick to point out that none of the prizes is beyond the purchasing power of the workers; the real value is this: *It's a sign of appreciation from the company.* "For too long, the people who have gotten the majority of attention have been those who cause problems," says Diamond's director of human resources. "[Our] program's primary focus is the recognition of good employees."

Challenges

1. Do you think recognition alone is enough to motivate employees, or does it always have to be tied to pay?
2. How might Diamond's recognition program affect error rates, grievances, and time lost due to absences?
3. Can such a program be sustained over time? If so, how?

1. As a manager, what issues should I consider in choosing one or more strategies to motivate my subordinates?
2. What specific steps should I take to implement my chosen strategy?
3. What costs and benefits might I anticipate from implementing individual, group, or organizationwide incentives?
4. In implementing a merit-pay system, what key traps must I avoid in order to make the system work as planned?

QUESTIONS THIS CHAPTER WILL HELP MANAGERS ANSWER

The chapter opening vignette raises an issue that is compelling to many managers—how can we gain and sustain employee motivation for high quality and high productivity? The constant interplay between theory and practice is shown throughout this chapter. Let us begin by reviewing and integrating theories of applied motivation, suggesting a unified motivational framework for management practice, and then illustrating this framework with a company example.

ALTERNATIVE STRATEGIES FOR BUILDING EMPLOYEE TRUST AND PRODUCTIVITY

As pointed out in Chapter 1, there has been a decline in the rate of increase of U.S. industrial productivity relative to that of other industrialized nations. A number of reasons have been suggested for this decline, and among these reasons are changes in the motivation and work ethic of the U.S. worker. Critics point to the declining role of work in U.S. life coupled with rising demands for more leisure.

However, many management policies and practices are at least partly to blame for employees' attitudes. Many firms proudly point to their productivity increases and claim that the increases are due to employees' working smarter, not harder. But in many other firms, managements fail to reward employees for working either harder or smarter.

Many powerful tools lie within management's control, but the tools have to be applied consistently and within the framework of an overall *strategy* for performance improvement. Such a strategy must coordinate the various elements of human resource management into a unified program whose focus is to enhance employees' motivation to work; too often, managers have sacrificed *equitable* treatment for *equality* of treatment.[55] To see how such a strategy might be applied in practice, let's examine three popular categories of motivation theories.

Motivation Theories

A close look at all theories of human motivation reveals a common driving principle: *People do what they are rewarded for doing.*[11] In general, the theories can be classified as need theories, reinforcement theories, expectancy theories, and goal-setting theories.

Need theories These suggest that individuals have certain physical and psychological needs that they attempt to satisfy. *Motivation* is a force that results from an individual's desire to satisfy these needs (e.g., hunger, thirst, social approval). Conversely, a satisfied need is not a motivator. Thus, while a hungry man might well be susceptible to a "Big Mac Attack," after several Big Macs that same individual might find the prospect of yet another to be distinctly uninviting. The most popular need theories are:

- Maslow's hierarchy of needs, ranging from physiological needs to safety, belonging, esteem, and self-actualization needs.[53]
- Herzberg's two-factor theory, whereby the satisfaction of needs has one of two effects: It either causes employees to be *satisfied* with their jobs or it prevents employees from being *dissatisfied* with their jobs.[32]
- McClelland's classification of needs according to their intended effects: that is, they satisfy employee needs for achievement, affiliation, or power.[54]

Reinforcement theories Also known as incentive theories or operant conditioning, reinforcement theories are based on a fundamental principle of learning—the Law of Effect.[69] Its statement is simple: *Behavior that is rewarded tends to be repeated; behavior that is not rewarded tends not to be repeated.* If management rewards behaviors such as high-quality work, high productivity, timely reports, or creative suggestions, these behaviors are likely to increase. However, the converse is also true:

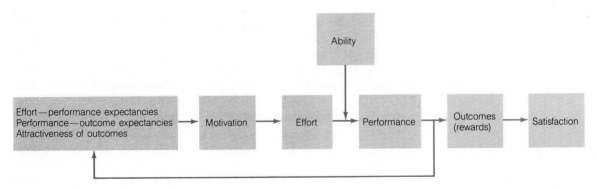

FIGURE 12-1

The expectancy theory of work motivation. [*Source*: E. E. Lawler, III (1989). Pay for performance: A strategic analysis. In L. R. Gomez-Mejia (ed.), *Compensation and benefits*. Washington, DC: Bureau of National Affairs, p. 3-141.]

Managers should not expect sustained, high performance from employees if they consistently ignore employees' performance and contributions.

Expectancy theories While reinforcement theories focus on the *objective relationship* between performance and rewards, expectancy theories emphasize the *perceived relationships*—what does the person expect?

Expectancy concepts form the basis for a general model of behavior in organizational settings, as shown in Figure 12-1.* Working from left to right in the model, motivation serves as the force leading to a level of effort by an individual. By itself, however, effort is insufficient to generate performance. Performance is a combination of effort and ability, that is, an individual's skills, training, information, and talents.

Performance, in turn, leads to certain outcomes (rewards). Outcomes (positive or negative) may result either from the environment (e.g., supervisors, coworkers, or the organization's reward system) or from performance of a task itself (e.g., feelings of accomplishment, personal worth, or achievement). Sometimes people perform but do not receive rewards. However, as the performance-reward process occurs again and again, actual events provide further information to support a person's beliefs (expectancies), and beliefs affect future motivation. This influence appears in Figure 12-1 by the line connecting the performance-outcome link with expectancies.

The model also suggests that satisfaction is best characterized as a result of performance rather than as a cause of it. However, satisfaction can increase people's motivation by strengthening their beliefs about the consequences of performance. It can also decrease the importance of outcomes (as with Big Macs, a satisfied need is not a motivator) and, as a result, lower motivation for performances linked to whatever reward has become less important.

Don't be deceived by the simplicity of the model or lulled into believing that all a manager must do to motivate employees is to relate pay and other valued

---

*Much of this section is drawn from the excellent summary presented by Lawler (1989).

rewards to obtainable levels of performance. Such a link is insufficient on its own, and it is also difficult to establish.

For employees to believe that a pay-for-performance relationship exists, an organization must establish a visible connection between performance and rewards, and it must generate trust and credibility among its workforce. The belief that performance will lead to rewards is a prediction about what will happen in the future. For individuals to make this kind of prediction, they have to trust the system that is promising them rewards. If this occurs, and if they see clear linkages between rewards and their behavior, then they will be motivated to perform well.

Goal-setting theories As discussed in Chapters 2 and 7, goal setting is one of the most well-accepted motivational strategies in organizational science. There are three related reasons why it affects performance. One, it has a *directive* effect—that is, it focuses activity in one particular direction. Two, given that a goal is accepted, people tend to exert *effort* in proportion to the difficulty of the goal. Three, difficult goals lead to more *persistence* (i.e., directed effort over time) than easy goals. These three dimensions—direction (choice), effort, and persistence—are central to the motivational process.[76]

Rewards That Motivate Behavior

Managers have long known that individual rewards—such as piece-rate payments, sales commissions, and performance bonuses that tie individual rewards to individual performance—can be effective motivators if they "fit" the type of work performed. They are obviously inappropriate for assembly line jobs, where work is paced automatically, or for team jobs, where outcomes do not depend on the efforts of any single individual.

Nevertheless, research indicates that when incentives geared to reward *individuals* do fit the situation, performance increases an average of 30 percent, while incentives geared to reward *groups* increase performance an average of 18 percent.[50] However, as noted in Chapter 11, the total compensation package that each employee receives includes indirect as well as direct financial payments. Benefits, cafeteria privileges, and company-subsidized tuition are examples of indirect payments, or "system rewards," that employees receive for being members of the system.[36] They have little impact on the day-to-day performance of employees, but they do tie people to the system. They tend to reduce turnover and to increase loyalty to the company. As you can see, there are a number of alternative strategies available for building employee trust and productivity. However, at this point you are probably also asking yourself, "How do I proceed, and when should I use each strategy?"

Integration and Application of Motivation Theories

The intent here is to develop meaningful prescriptions for managers to follow in motivating subordinates, based on the above brief review of motivation theories and types of rewards. Broadly speaking, managers need to focus on three key areas

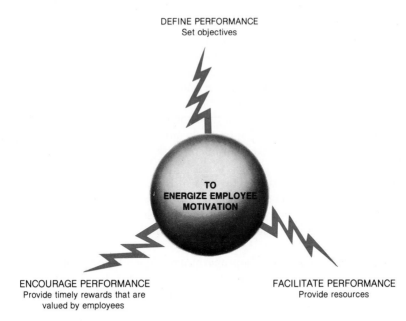

FIGURE 12-2
Steps that managers can take to motivate employees to improve their performance.

of responsibility in order to coordinate and integrate human resource policy:[55]

1. Performance definition
2. Performance facilitation
3. Performance encouragement

These key areas are shown graphically in Figure 12-2.

Performance definition This is a description of what is expected of employees, plus the continuous orientation of employees toward effective job performance. The discussions of job analysis and performance standards in Chapters 4 and 8, respectively, are clearly relevant here. Performance description includes three elements: goals, measures, and assessment.

As we have seen, *goal setting* is an effective performance improvement strategy. It enhances accountability and clarifies the direction of employee effort. At Hewlett-Packard, for example, the president commented, "The corporate goals [concerning profit, customers, fields of interest, growth, people, management, and citizenship] provide the basic framework for the management-by-objectives system, which gives individual managers a lot of freedom to be entrepreneurial and innovative. They are a kind of glue—the basic philosophy, the basic sense of direction, sort of a value set—that draws everyone together" (ref. 61, p. 55).

The mere presence of goals, however, is not sufficient. Management must also be able to operationalize and therefore *measure* the accomplishment of goals. This is where performance standards play a vital role, for they specify what "fully suc cessful" performance means. Goals such as "make the company successful" are too vague to be useful.

The third aspect of performance definition is *assessment*. Regular assessment of progress toward goals encourages a continuing orientation toward job performance. If management takes the time to identify measurable goals but then fails to do assessment, it is asking for trouble. This is so because if there is no assessment of performance on these goals, then the goals cannot motivate employees to improve their performance.[55] The goals only send negative messages to employees regarding management's commitment to the goals.

Performance facilitation This area of responsibility involves the elimination of roadblocks to performance. Like performance definition, it also has three aspects: removing performance obstacles, providing the means and adequate resources for performance, and carefully selecting personnel.

Removing obstacles. Improperly maintained equipment, delays in receiving supplies, poor physical design of work spaces, and inefficient work methods are obstacles to performance that management must eliminate in order to create highly supportive task environments. Otherwise, motivation will decline as employees become convinced that management does not really care about getting the job done.

Adequate resources. A similar problem can arise when management fails to provide adequate financial, material, or human resources to get a job done right. Such a strategy is self-defeating and excessively costly in the long run, for employees begin to doubt whether their assigned tasks *can* be done well.

Careful selection of employees. This is essential to employee motivation to perform. Poor staffing procedures ("placing round pegs in square holes") guarantee reduced motivation by placing employees in jobs that either demand too little of them or require more of them than they are qualified to do. Such a strategy results in overstaffing, excessive labor costs, and reduced productivity.

Performance encouragement This is the last key area of management responsibility in a coordinated approach to motivating employee performance. It has five aspects:

- Value of rewards
- Amount of rewards
- Timing of rewards
- Likelihood of rewards
- Equity or fairness of rewards

The *value and amount of the rewards* relate to the choice of rewards to be used. Management must offer rewards to employees (e.g., job redesign, flexible benefits systems, alternative work schedules) that employees personally value. Then a sufficient *amount* of reward must be offered to motivate the employee to put forth effort to receive it. How much is enough?

When one manager was asked how much of a raise he gave his top performer, he replied proudly, "Why I gave him 8 percent." When asked what his worst performer got, the manager responded, "7 percent, but the difference really was based on merit."[55] Certainly the belief that a 1 percent differential is sufficient to reward high performance is wishful thinking.

The *timing and likelihood of rewards* relate to the link between performance and outcomes. Whether the rewards are in the form of raises, incentive pay, promotions, or recognition for a job well done, timing and likelihood are fundamental to an effective reward system. If there is an *excessive delay* between effective performance and the receipt of rewards, the rewards lose their potential to motivate subsequent high performance.

Equity or fairness can also encourage or discourage effective performance. Fairness is related to, but is not the same thing as, pay satisfaction. Satisfaction depends on the *amount* of reward received and on how much is still desired. Satisfaction is comprised of four aspects: the level of pay and benefits, the extent to which workers perceive their earnings as fair or deserved, comparisons with other people's pay, and noneconomic satisfactions, such as intrinsic satisfaction with the content of one's work.[6] Pay satisfaction certainly includes perceptions of fairness or unfairness, but the concepts of fairness and unfairness are distinctly different:

1. Equity or fairness depends on a comparison between the rewards one receives and one's contributions to the organization, relative to some comparison standard. Such a standard might be:

Others. A comparison with other people either within or outside the organization

Self. A comparison with one's own rewards and contributions at a different time and/or with one's evolving views of self-worth

Systems. A comparison with what the organization has promised

These comparison standards are used in varying degrees, depending on the availability of information and on the relevance of the standard to the individual.[4,35,46] Fairness is also related to the employees' understanding of their company's pay system. Those who say that they understand the system also tend to perceive it as fair.[59]

2. The practices most likely to produce feelings of unfairness are *adjustments* in pay. However, organizations with carefully designed policies need only ensure that actions match intentions. It probably makes much less difference to employees' perceptions of pay fairness what these policies are than seeing that they are followed consistently. But organizations that say one thing and do another find that pay injustice is one of their most important products.[4]

Thus, while pay satisfaction is important, from the organization's standpoint it is even more important that every employee consider her or his pay to be fair, with some room for improvement. The point is that employees should be encouraged to improve their salaries, presumably by improving their performance. In formulating future human resource policies, therefore, management must:[55]

- Quit relying on employee *indebtedness* to encourage performance and instead consider what the organization *owes* to good performers.
- Consider the *context* of performance and productivity problems.
- Determine whether or not current human resource management policies and practices really do motivate employees to perform their jobs better.

Now, in an extended company example, let's see how these ideas were implemented in practice.

■ COMPANY EXAMPLE

INCREASING PERFORMANCE AND PRODUCTIVITY AT NORTH AMERICAN TOOL & DIE, INC. (NATD)*

This example is recounted in the words of the president and chief executive officer of NATD, a computer components contract manufacturer in San Leandro, California. His is an old-fashioned philosophy, the belief that *people* make the difference between success and failure.

"My partner and I set three objectives when we bought NATD in June 1978: (1) to expand the company while raising profits, (2) to share whatever wealth was created, and (3) to create an atmosphere that would allow everyone to feel satisfaction and even to have fun on the job. The only way to do this, we decided, was to create an atmosphere of complete trust between us (the owners) and *all* our employees. However, when you say you want such an atmosphere you truly have to believe in it. Then you have to work at improving relations every day in every situation. Otherwise, your employees will sense the hypocrisy and all will be for naught."

GOAL 1: GROWTH AND PROFITS

"We bought a job shop with a reputation for acceptable but not outstanding quality. The only way our quality would improve is if our employees improved it—every day, on every job, on every part. Ours is a highly technical business. We produce hundreds of different parts with a tolerance of 0.019 of an inch. That's about one-fourth the thickness of a human hair. NATD manufactures each of those different parts by the thousands each year. Thus

---

*Adapted from: T. H. Melohn, How to build employee trust and productivity, *Harvard Business Review*, January–February 1983, pp. 56–59.

the company's well-being depends entirely on employees caring a great deal about their performance.

"To encourage this feeling, we spread the gospel of quality and repeatedly recognize employee efforts to eliminate all rejects. Each month, there's a plantwide meeting—on company time—with a threefold purpose. First, we recognize one employee (no supervisors allowed) who has done a super job of producing good quality during that month. A check for $50 is just a token of what we give. Of much greater import is the 'Super Person of the Month' plaque. The employee's name is engraved on the plaque, and it is prominently and permanently displayed in the plant. Second, each employee is given a silver dollar for every year of service if his or her employment anniversary occurs during the month of the meeting. Finally, we share with our 'family' where we've been, where we are, and where we're going—in percentages when appropriate. In that way, each employee knows firsthand what's going on at his or her company."

GOAL 2: SHARING THE WEALTH

"We share ownership primarily through our employee stock ownership plan. We give each employee shares of NATD stock each year, according to three simple selection criteria. The employee must be at least 24 years old, work at least 1000 hours a year, and be on the payroll at year end. In our judgment, our people have earned the right to be given company stock without any cash outlay of their own. It's not a warrant, a reduced-price purchase plan, matching dollars, or an option. It's free.

"By the way, my partner and I waived our right to participate in this program. We wanted the number of shares allotted for our employees to be that much larger, that much more meaningful. The shares we grant annually are newly issued—we do not realize any gain by selling our own. NATD's employee stock ownership program has also been instrumental in lowering our rejection rates from customers and improving our productivity and delivery time.

"We also try to stress equitable compensation as a motivational tool. We hold compensation reviews twice annually. This is not a rubber-stamp operation. Each employee has a one-on-one performance review with his or her boss. Each is told, 'Here's where you're doing well, and here's where you need to improve, and here's what the company can do to help.'

"Finally, we use cash bonuses to reward innovative employees. In recent months several employees have taken action to help the company and win cash. In one instance, a young employee decided on his own to develop a means to rivet a very difficult part and also to automate the entire process. In another, a department foreman who saw that our labor cost for an important job was too high devised a new method of doing ten operations at one time. He challenged his young associate to 'top this' and soon found the entire production step completely automated! Our labor costs were reduced 80 percent."

GOAL 3: SATISFACTION AND FUN

"With our strong belief in the importance of our employees, we pay careful attention to the selection process. We hire a certain kind of person—one who cares about himself, his family, and his company. The person must be honest, willing to speak up, and curious, be it as a sweeper, machine operator, plant foreman, or office manager. That's why I interview each prospective employee myself. My purpose is to determine if the candidate will fit into the NATD family. Perhaps that concept seems old-fashioned, but to us it's pivotal. This process of lengthy evaluation and interviewing is a lot of work, but the results are well worth it.

"Let's face it, the traditional adversary role between management and employees is not productive. In encouraging employee satisfaction at NATD, we follow the tenet that our employees deserve the same treatment we expect from them. They want to know about their future compensation, their potential career paths, how they are contributing, and what they can do to grow. To keep people involved and caring, we work at giving out *real* compliments—not just the perfunctory 'Good job, Smith'—but statements of sincere appreciation for each person's special efforts and accomplishments.

"Compliments don't cost a company anything. We all need them and even crave them. Recognition—both personal and professional—is a major motivating factor. At least two or three times a week we go through the plant chatting with each employee and complimenting those who've worked well. Employees care deeply about their work. If you can tap this well of concern and mesh it with the goals of your corporation, the results will truly stun you.

"To summarize the last three years at NATD, our sales have gone from $1.8 million to over $6 million, our pretax earnings have increased well over 600 percent, our stock appreciated 36 percent in 1980 and again in 1981, our customer reject rate has declined from 5 percent to 0.3 percent, our productivity has doubled, our turnover rate has dropped from 27 percent to 6 percent, and we've all had a good time."

EFFECTIVE IMPLEMENTATION

"My job as CEO is to outline the company's objectives and the strategies to attain these goals. To achieve them, we place heavy emphasis on true delegation of responsibility.

"We believe that our managers really want to manage, but we realize that certain conditions must be met before they can become effective managers. First, we work *with* managers to be sure the goals are clear and in fact attainable. Second, we give our employees the tools to reach the goals. Third, we let our managers alone and allow them flexibility. The last thing any manager needs is a second-guessing or a preemptive superior.

"Each supervisor is responsible for on-time production with no rejects and at maximum efficiency. How the supervisor does it is totally up to him or her. We then make sure our managers and employees get credit for their successful accomplishments—from us, from their peers, and in their pay-checks.

"Incidentally, we attach no blame to failure. If we have given a job 'our best shot,' there's no problem. If our people are inhibited by the fear of failure, they won't dare to try. If we don't try the unexplored and the untested, then our growth rate and profitability will suffer. And that's no fun."

OVERALL SUMMARY AND INTEGRATION

NATD has applied a logic and a framework to its management practice that has resulted in a coordinated human resource management policy. Such a policy clearly has impacted all three of the general themes of this book: productivity, quality of work life, and the bottom line. It also dovetails nicely with the motivation guidelines suggested earlier:

- *Performance definition.* NATD has established goals, measures, and assessments.
- *Performance facilitation.* NATD has removed obstacles to effective per-formance, it has provided the resources that its employees need to per-form their jobs well, and it has emphasized careful personnel selection.
- *Performance encouragement.* NATD has provided rewards that employ-ees value (recognition, stock ownership, cash bonuses) in sufficient *amount* to encourage future performance, with a *high likelihood* of ac-tually receiving the rewards, with appropriate *timing* (twice a year com-pensation reviews), and with a genuine concern for employees' percep-tions of *fair* treatment.

Performance definition, facilitation, and encouragement "set the stage" for employees to become motivated. Then managers must choose among a range of specific motivational strategies. One of the most popular of these, in recent years, has been job design.

JOB DESIGN

Information, rewards, knowledge, and power are central issues for all organiza-tions. How they are positioned in an organization determines its core management style. When they are concentrated at the top, traditional control-oriented man-agement exists. When they are moved downward, some form of participative man-agement or employee involvement is being practiced.[49] In light of the need for innovation and productivity improvement in our globally interdependent econ-omy, more and more firms are trying to institute some form of high-involvement strategy.

Before examining some current company practices, let's first consider these two fundamental questions:

1. Is there a demonstrable *need* to redesign jobs? Will some other approach to change (e.g., training, selection, performance feedback, financial incentives) or no change at all be appropriate?
2. Is it *feasible* to redesign jobs, given the present structure of the jobs, the technological constraints, and the characteristics of the people who do them?

To begin with, maybe job design is not the problem at all. Managers need to be wary of jumping on the behavioral science bandwagon and adopting a technique simply because "everybody else is doing it." Without hard diagnostic data, implementation of any new change will be premature and may spell only failure in the long run.

If it begins to appear that job redesign is needed, there may be larger things to consider first. It just may not be feasible to implement job redesign, given current organizational constraints. Care needs to be taken, for example, in assessing current technology and the cost of proposed modifications (Volvo built a brand-new plant in Uddevalla, Sweden, before its job redesign ideas could be implemented).

A second consideration is the values and beliefs of key participants. For example, employee involvement requires that managers believe in the capabilities, sense of responsibility, and commitment of people throughout the organization. They need to believe not only that people are a key organizational resource but that people can and will behave responsibly if given the opportunity.[49]

A final consideration is the present organization of work. Is it done by individuals, groups, or some other arrangement? (In this section we will focus on an approach to work redesign for individuals, and in the next section we will focus on group-work redesign.)

Designing Jobs for Individuals

The dominant approach to job design for individuals over the last decade has been the job characteristics theory of Hackman and Oldham.[27,28] The model representing this theory is shown graphically in Figure 12-3.

As you can see from the diagram, according to the theory, four positive *personal and work outcomes*—high internal work motivation, high-quality work performance, high work satisfaction, and low absenteeism and turnover—result when an employee works in an environment of three *critical psychological states*—which are experienced meaningfulness of the work, experienced responsibility for work outcomes, and knowledge of the actual results of work activities. All three of the psychological states must be present for the positive outcomes to be realized.

As the illustration depicts, the three critical psychological states evolve from a job's having five *core dimensions*—skill variety (doing different things at work that require a variety of one's skills), task identity (the opportunity to do a whole piece of work), task significance (the degree to which the job has a substantial impact

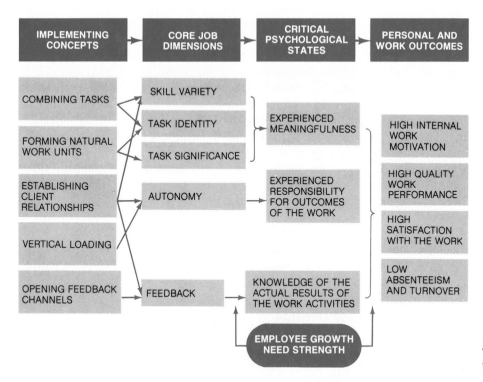

FIGURE 12-3
The full job characteristics model.

on the lives or work of other people), autonomy (the opportunity to decide on one's own how to do the work), and feedback (the extent to which managers, coworkers, or the job itself provide information about how well a job is done).

The theory also states that only people who strongly value and desire personal feelings of accomplishment and growth and who are satisfied with the organization's internal environment (pay, security, supervisors, and coworkers) will respond positively to a job that is highly characterized by these five core dimensions.

The strategy for "stimulating" the five core job dimensions to produce an environment of the three critical psychological states is referred to as *"implementing concepts."* As Figure 12-3 shows, these are: (1) combining tasks—if possible, to form larger modules of work; (2) forming natural work units—identifying basic work items and grouping them into natural categories; (3) establishing client relationships—that is, by identifying who the client is, establishing the most direct contact possible, and specifying criteria by which the client can judge the quality of the product or service she or he receives; (4) vertical loading—closing the gap between planning, doing, and controlling the work; and (5) opening feedback channels— by establishing client relationships, placing quality control close to the worker, and providing summaries of performance to the worker.

This overall job characteristics theory was applied to a data entry operation at the Travelers Insurance Co.[29] Diagnosing the operation revealed that all five core dimensions were deficient. An experiment was then designed in which the jobs of one group of employees were enriched using all five of the implementing concepts, while a geographically separate control group, similar in size and demographics, was monitored for comparison. After 1 year, the results between the two groups were considerably different. In comparison to the control group, the experimental group showed significant improvements in work quantity and employee attitudes, and decreases in error rates, absenteeism, and controls. The role of the supervisor likewise changed from merely supervising employees closely and dealing with crises to developing feedback systems and developing work modules—that is, instead of merely supervising, the supervisor became a manager. In current (1990) dollars, Travelers estimated that the job redesign efforts would save the company about $225,000 *each year*.

Research has generally supported the validity of the job characteristics model.[16,17,22] However, the actual success of any job design effort is likely to depend not only on changes in job content but also on the context in which those changes are implemented. Characteristics of the reward system (will salaries increase as job responsibility increases?) and management policy (does it support worker participation?) cannot be ignored.

Designing Jobs for Groups

In terms of efficiency and practicality, some jobs can be done only by a group. Consider a surgical team in a hospital operating room. Anesthesiologist, surgeon(s), nurse(s), and technicians (those who sterilize and pass instruments) must work interdependently. So also must workers building a ship or a plane, for the sheer weight of the parts and complexity of the task require many heads, hands, and muscles. Knowledge workers also work in teams. For example, the evaluation of a grant or a contract proposal often requires that a group of individuals, each with special expertise, pool their evaluations of various parts of the proposal in order to reach a decision on funding. In fact, more organizations in industrialized countries have implemented work designs with autonomous work groups than have implemented job characteristics approaches oriented to individuals.[75]

Our focus in this section is *not* on loose aggregations of people with only casual working relationships or on groups that do not have the authority to decide how the members will work together. It *is* on self-managing work groups.[26] Such groups are defined by three characteristics:[27]

1. They are *real*, meaning that they are intact, identifiable social systems, even if small or temporary.
2. They are *work* groups that have to do a specified piece of work that results in a product, service, or decision whose acceptability is measurable.
3. They are *self-managing* groups whose members have the authority to manage their own task and interpersonal processes as they carry out their work.

Groups with these characteristics are sometimes called "autonomous work groups" or "self-managed work teams," though we also consider temporary task forces, decision-making committees, and many kinds of management teams in this category. All are parts of a broader sociotechnical system.

Are autonomous work groups worth the substantial time and effort, the break with custom and tradition, required to make them work? A rigorous, 3-year evaluation of a nonunion British company that produces confectionery for home and export markets yielded some surprising answers.[75] The autonomous work group design produced a strong and sustained effect on employees' satisfaction with the work itself, and a more temporary effect on their satisfaction with the work environment, including pay, but it had no effect on work motivation or job performance. The approach also produced clear economic benefits. With responsibility for decision making delegated to the shop floor, the need for supervision declines, indirect labor costs decrease, and productivity benefits expand.

SELF-MANAGED WORK TEAMS AT GM'S SATURN PLANT

■ COMPANY EXAMPLE

Is this an American auto plant or a factory from another planet? It certainly is different. Situated 35 miles south of Nashville, in the small town of Spring Hill, Tennessee, the Saturn plant and its 3000 team members represent a profound change in the ways that GM manages its people. For General Motors, which invested 8 years and $3.5 billion to launch Saturn, the venture has a specific competitive goal: to build small cars as well as the Japanese—and then some.

Saturn is a medium-tech plant. At its core, however, is one of the most radical labor-management agreements ever developed in the United States, one that involves the United Auto Workers in every aspect of the business—including sharing the executive suite. Beyond sharing power at the top, however, the agreement established 165 work teams, which have been given more power than assembly line workers anywhere else in GM or at any Japanese plant. For example, teams at Saturn do the following:

■ Interview and approve new hires for their teams (average size: 10 workers).

■ Take responsibility for managing their own areas. When workers see a problem, they can pull a blue handle and shut down the entire line.

■ Assume budget responsibility. For example, one team in Saturn's final-assembly area voted to reject some proposed pneumatic car-assembly equipment and went to another supplier to buy electronic gear that its members believed to be safer.

The workers not only gain a more direct voice in shop-floor operations (as is true in Japan), but also take over managerial duties, such as work and vacation scheduling, ordering materials, and hiring new members. This is how U.S. practices diverge from those used in Japan. Indeed, such diver-

Brainstorming: At Saturn, factory employees are organized into teams of about 10 members, who share decisions on everything from hiring coworkers to buying equipment for the plant.

gence is essential to avoid imposing a foreign work culture on U.S. workplaces.

To be sure, many of Saturn's ideas were borrowed from around the world by the Group of 99, a team of Saturn workers who traveled 2 million miles in 1984 to visit some 160 pioneering enterprises, including Hewlett-Packard, McDonald's, Volvo, Kawasaki, and Nissan. Their main conclusions: that most successful companies provide employees with a sense of ownership, have few and flexible guidelines, and impose virtually no job-defining shop rules.

From that blueprint grew the most radical feature of Saturn's philosophy: the provision for consensus decision making. All teams must be committed to decisions affecting them before those changes are put into place—from choosing an advertising agency to selecting an outside supplier. Says the plant's director of human resources: "That means a lot of yelling sometimes, and everything takes a lot longer, but once they come out of that meeting room, they're 100 percent committed" (ref. 25, p. 77).

Saturn's workers were recruited from U.A.W. locals in 38 states and carefully screened. By accepting a job at Saturn, they gave up their rights ever to work for any other GM division. Instead of hourly pay, they work for a salary (average: $34,000), 20 percent of which is at risk. Whether they get that 20 percent depends on a complex formula that measures car quality, worker productivity, and company profits.

Perhaps the most important lesson from this example is that U.S. companies are now discovering what the Japanese learned long ago: that people—not technology alone or marketing ploys—are the keys to success in global competition. Indeed, U.S. workers can be just as productive as Japanese workers. This has been demonstrated conclusively by the success of Honda, Toyota, and Nissan using U.S. labor in U.S. plants. Rather than some mystical Asian work ethic, Japan's advantages boil down to teamwork, efficient use of resources, and a tireless effort to improve quality.[25,34,70]

Role of the Manager of a Self-Managed Work Team

"A self-managed work team's manager!" That may seem like an oxymoron, which you may not remember from English 101 means "a combination of contradictory words" (for example, "jumbo shrimp"). However, a self-managed work team needs a manager, but one whose tasks and responsibilities are different from those of a manager in the traditional sense. For example, the manager of a self-managed work team is not responsible for initiating, organizing, and directing work processes. The group is. Rather, the kinds of things managers *should* be doing for self-managed work teams include: (1) monitoring the basic design of the group and broader organizational events that might affect the group, making alterations as needed for effective group performance; and (2) consulting with the group so that it becomes increasingly capable of managing its own affairs in the social, technical, and economic arenas.[27]

Unfortunately, most first- and second-line managers currently do not have the power that is needed to adjust how a group is set up or to make changes in its working environment (e.g., revising compensation arrangements or task design). Nor is it delegated to them when they become managers of self-managed work teams. Furthermore, most managers may not be skilled or practiced in interpersonal consulting; a manager without these skills who tries to "help the group over the rough spots" may appear to the group to be "meddling" rather than helping. Managers who experience this feel that their status has been reduced and the meaningfulness of their work eroded.

What can be done to alleviate these kinds of problems for first-line managers? First, it is essential that higher management pay special attention to the *role* and to the *person* of the first-line manager when work is designed for teams.[27] Particularly, the managerial role must ensure the power to do what needs to be done to help the work groups develop into effective teams that fit well with their organizational environment. This includes selecting, training, and supporting the first-line managers so that they can gain the skills they will need in their roles as managers of self-managed groups.

Modifying Work Schedules

Restructuring work schedules is not a job design strategy; it does not change the way jobs are done. Nevertheless, we mention it here for two reasons. One, the positive effects on productivity of the condensed workweek and flexible working hours have been touted widely. Two, since the rigid rules regarding individual work hours are altered, these approaches can at least be considered *secondary job design strategies.*

Let us briefly consider the evidence for and against the condensed workweek and flexible hours, and also consider a new phenomenon: telecommuting.

Condensed workweek Under this arrangement, employees can work 40 hours in fewer than 5 days. Typically this is done by having employees work four 10-hour days per week (known as 4/40). Some firms simply do not do business on the fifth day. More commonly, however, organizations stagger work schedules so that they can remain in operation during all normal business days.[12] Advocates of the condensed workweek stress the potential dollar savings from fewer weekly start-ups and lower absenteeism and tardiness. The expected benefits to employees are less commuting time, more leisure time, and heightened job satisfaction. Critics note, however, that employees generally experience more fatigue due to the longer workday (possibly posing a safety risk), and some employees complain that longer workdays infringe on their evening activities. Organizations with condensed work-weeks may have scheduling problems when interacting with firms that maintain the standard 8-hour day, 5-day week; they may also have to pay overtime to nonmanagerial employees who work more than 8 hours in a given day.

Flexible working hours With the condensed workweek, the employee gains no control over when he or she will work. In contrast, flexible working hours, or a flextime schedule, gives such control to an employee. Typically the organization defines a core time (e.g., 10 A.M. to 3 P.M.), during which all employees are expected to work, and then allows a range of time before and after this core period from which employees can decide their own arrival and quitting times. For example, Equifax, Inc., allows workers who enter numbers into data banks to put in their 7.5 hours anytime between 7:30 A.M. and 9:30 P.M. US West permits its workers to set any schedule they want—if their supervisors agree.[45]

Obviously flextime (first adopted in Europe) provides a real opportunity to reconcile personal and organizational demands that may conflict. While there are numerous documented examples of reduced absenteeism and turnover and increased performance from flextime,[12,44] there are costs as well. Utility expenses may go up since the firm is operating more hours per day. More sophisticated management control systems may be necessary to ensure that employees are indeed working their full shifts each day.

Two field experiments on the impact of condensing the work week to 4/40, and introducing flexible work schedules, revealed some surprising results.[13] In both cases, the changes affected job performance only to the extent that the changed schedule met organizational needs and constraints, such as improved service to customers. Moreover, it was possible to anticipate worker reactions to the alternative schedules *before* their introduction. Before being placed on the 4/40 or flexible schedules, workers told the researchers (through pretest assessments) the ways they believed that they would and would not react to the changed schedules; after 3 to 6 months of experience with the new schedules, these were the reactions that actually emerged. These results suggest that active employee input during the design and implementation of alternative work schedules may provide accurate predictions of the likely impact of the schedules on employees and their organizations.

Telecommuting For over 15 million Americans, the daily commute to the office is done without leaving home. Inexpensive personal computers, modems, photocopiers, and facsimile machines allow a much broader range of corporate employees to work out of their homes. For slightly more than half of these workers there are children in the house or in the office for at least part of the work day.[10,41] These workers are called "telecommuters." Both low- and high-skill workers are involved, although telecommuting is not for everyone. Research indicates that only 15 percent of U.S. workers react favorably to working alone or independently. "Mix-and-match" programs that let workers and managers prearrange a schedule of days spent at home and in the office are the most common and most popular telecommuting arrangements.[58]

To date, telecommuting remains an anomaly for corporate America. Just one major U.S. company—Pacific Telesis Group's Pacific Bell unit—has a large-scale formal program that allows salaried employees to telecommute full time. Many other firms have tried telecommuting on a small scale, only to abandon it after managers complained that they could not supervise—much less get to know—employees they could not see. For example, a Johnson & Johnson manager described the following scene at a meeting: "Half the people are in the office, while the other half are just voices coming out of a little box on the desk. . . . The phone works OK, but it's just not as effective in terms of getting people to feel like a team."[1]

Company Practices with New Work Design Approaches

Two basic changes are taking place in work design: (1) changes that leave the existing organization of work intact but make it more efficient, such as combining duties and eliminating superfluous jobs, and (2) changes in the work system itself, such as instituting teamwork where formerly there was none. Here are some examples of both kinds of changes in the design of work and the results.[2]

Changes External to the Work System

1. Continental Illinois National Bank and Trust redesigned its check-processing (assembly) line by developing a modular arrangement processed through a computer terminal (Figure 12-4). Instead of working only on one task, as in the

BEFORE—THE TOTAL CHECK-PROCESSING TASK WAS FRAGMENTED, ASSEMBLY-LINE STYLE

STEP 1	STEP 2	STEP 3	STEP 4	STEP 5
RECORD DEPOSITS	ENTER TOTALS ON SUMMARY SHEET	MAIL CONFIRMATIONS TO CUSTOMERS	SORT CHECKS TO PROCESSING POINTS (e.g., TRUST DEPT., COMMERCIAL BOOKKEEPING)	DELIVER CHECKS TO PROCESSING POINTS

AVERAGE NUMBER OF CHECKS PROCESSED PER HOUR: 35

AFTER—TASKS WERE COMBINED AND WORK IS DONE THROUGH COMPUTER TERMINALS

EACH EMPLOYEE USES A COMPUTER TERMINAL TO:

1. PROCESS CHECKS ARRIVING BY MAIL

2. DEPOSIT THEM IN CUSTOMERS' ACCOUNTS

3. KEEP A RUNNING TOTAL OF THE DEPOSITS

4. ELECTRONICALLY SORT AND DELIVER CHECKS TO PROCESSING POINTS

5. MAIL CONFIRMATIONS TO CUSTOMERS

AVERAGE NUMBER OF CHECKS PROCESSED PER HOUR: 50

FIGURE 12-4
Sample check-processing tasks before and after the tasks were combined for processing by computer.

old assembly line approach, each worker now uses a computer terminal to process checks that arrive in the mail and to deposit them in customers' accounts. The same worker can also telephone customers with current information on their accounts and can mail data to them. Under the automated system, each employee processes an average of 50 checks per hour, a 43 percent increase in productivity over the old approach.

2. In manufacturing plants, skilled craftspeople are often the most resistant to work-rule changes, partly because they are the highest-paid factory workers and consider themselves an elite group. But at Goodyear's largest tire plant, in Gadsden, Alabama, the 420 craftspeople agreed to work outside their crafts up to 25 percent of the time. This type of work arrangement can mean large savings. Such cross-utilization at a Chrysler plant in New Castle, Indiana, reduced costs by 30 percent, resulting in savings of over $3 million in current dollars.

3. Boston's transit system has reduced its workforce by 10 percent, or 700 employees, since the state legislature passed the Management Rights Act in 1980,

giving the transit system the right to redesign jobs regardless of union objections. Management now farms out the cleaning of buses and subway cars; staffs each train with an operator and just one doorman, instead of two doormen; and has hired 300 part-time bus drivers to fill in during peak traffic periods. Despite much confrontation with workers over the changes, savings of $50 million were realized in the first 18 months of the program.

Changes within the Work System Itself

Some companies are now trying to combine jobs that were fragmented years ago. Increasingly they are moving to flexible systems that emphasize teamwork and worker participation in shopfloor decision making. While Japan and Germany have used the team-assembly concept for years, it was rare in the United States and confined to a few nonunion companies. Today, however, even unionized firms are giving teamwork a try. Here are two examples, the first in a nonunion firm, the second in a unionized one:

1. Hewlett-Packard (HP) eliminated the moving conveyor belt for assembling small products in the 1950s, feeling that it was "disrespectful" of the employees to set their production pace. HP formalized the team concept in the 1960s, and now most of its 50 product divisions, each with 500 to 2000 people, are using teams.

2. General Motors' (GM) Packard Electric Division, which produces components for GM cars and other products, may well be the leader in applying the work-team concept in a unionized setting. With the cooperation of Local 717 of the International Union of Electrical Workers, it now has some 2000 employees at four Warren, Ohio, area plants involved in work teams. Says the director of Warren assembly operations, "Productivity has improved substantially because people believe in what they're doing. They care for each other, they're interested in job security and cost reduction, and they work smarter." Adds the shop chairperson of Local 717, "It's the wave of the future. We should look at our people not only as dues-paying members, but we should use their minds and expand their horizons" (ref. 2, p. 110).

PAY FOR PERFORMANCE

Over the past decade, pay-for-performance plans have boomed in popularity. Between 70 and 80 percent of U.S. companies regard pay for performance as an important compensation objective and offer some form of performance incentive.[74]

Although pay for performance is often treated as a single approach, in fact it is many different approaches. Since the different approaches have different consequences, they need special treatment.[48] One way to classify them is according to the level of performance targeted—individual, group, or the total organization. Within these broad categories, literally hundreds of different approaches for relating pay to performance exist. In this chapter we will consider the three categories described above, beginning with merit pay for individuals and special incentives for executives. First, however, let's consider some fundamental requirements of *all* incentive programs.

REQUIREMENTS OF EFFECTIVE INCENTIVE SYSTEMS

At the outset it is important to distinguish merit systems from incentive systems. Both are designed to motivate employees to improve their job performance. Most commonly, merit systems are applied to exempt employees in the form of permanent increases to their base pay. The goal is to tie pay increases to each employee's level of job performance. Incentives (e.g., sales commissions, profit sharing) are one-time supplements to base pay. They are also awarded on the basis of job performance, and they are applied to broader segments of the labor force, including nonexempt and unionized employees.

Properly designed incentive programs work because they are based on two well-accepted psychological principles: (1) Increased motivation improves performance, and (2) recognition is a major factor in motivation.[64] Unfortunately, however, many incentive programs are improperly designed, and they do not work. They violate one or more of the following rules (shown graphically in Figure 12-5):

Be simple. The rules of the system should be brief, clear, and understandable.

Be specific. It is not sufficient to say, "Produce more," or "Stop accidents." Employees need to know precisely what they are expected to do.

Be attainable. Every employee should have a reasonable chance to gain something.

Be measurable. Measurable objectives are the foundation on which incentive plans are built. Program dollars will be wasted (and program evaluation hampered) if specific accomplishments cannot be related to dollars spent.

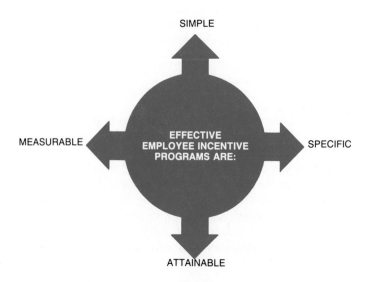

FIGURE 12-5
Requirements of effective incentive programs.

MERIT PAY SYSTEMS

In some ways it is easier to assemble a list of reasons why merit pay *won't* work[74] than to describe the conditions under which it *will*. Often merit-pay systems fail for one or more of the following reasons:

1. *The incentive value of the reward offered is too low.* A person earning $2000 per month who gets a 5 percent merit increase subsequently earns $2100 per month. The "stakes," after taxes, are nominal.[43]

2. *The link between performance and rewards is weak.* If performance is measured annually on a one-dimensional scale, then employees will remain unclear about just what is being rewarded. In addition, the timing of a merit-pay award may have little or no relevance to the performance of desirable behaviors.[65]

3. *Supervisors often resist performance appraisal.* Few supervisors are trained in the art of giving feedback accurately, comfortably, and with a minimum likelihood of creating other problems. (See Chapter 8.) As a result, many are afraid to make distinctions among workers—and they do not. For example, some 2.1 million middle-level employees of the federal government work under a pay system that has a merit component. To be eligible, employees must be rated "fully successful" or better. A full 99.5 percent of them are. The result? The "merit-pay" system has become a de facto seniority system.[74]

4. *Union contracts influence pay-for-performance decisions within and between organizations.* Multiyear contracts (some with cost-of-living provisions) create pressures on pay at other levels and for nonunion employees. Failure to match union wages over a 3- or 4-year period (especially during periods of high inflation) invites dissension and turnover.

5. *The "annuity" problem.* As past "merit payments" are incorporated into an individual's base salary, the payments form an annuity (a sum of money received at regular intervals) and allow formerly productive individuals to slack off for several years and still earn high pay. The annuity feature also leads to another problem: topping out. After a long period in a job, individuals often reach the top of the pay range for their jobs. As a result, pay no longer serves as a motivator because it cannot increase as a result of performance.[48]

These reasons for the failure of merit-pay systems are shown graphically in Figure 12-6.

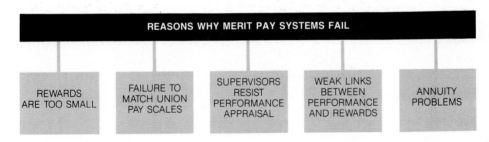

FIGURE 12-6
Why merit-pay systems fail.

Barriers Can Be Overcome

IBM increased labor productivity in the manufacturing of typewriters by nearly 200 percent over a 10-year period. At least half of this increase in productivity was due to two practices:

1. Pay employees for productivity, and only for productivity.
2. Promote employees for productivity, and only for productivity.[73]

Furthermore, research on the effect of merit-pay practices on performance in white-collar jobs indicates that all merit reward systems are not equal.[40] *Those that tie performance more closely to rewards are likely to generate higher levels of performance,* particularly after a year or two. In addition, *merit systems that incorporate a wide range of possible increases tend to generate higher levels of job performance after 1 year.* Some typical ranges used in successful merit systems are: Digital Equipment, 0 to 30 percent; Xerox, 0 to 13 percent; and Westinghouse, 0 to 19 percent.

GUIDELINES FOR EFFECTIVE MERIT-PAY SYSTEMS

Those affected by the merit-pay system must support it if it is to work as designed. This is in addition to the requirements for incentive programs shown in Figure 12-5. From the very inception of a merit-pay system, it is important that employees feel a sense of "ownership" of the system. To do this, consider implementing a merit-pay system on a step-by-step basis (for example, over a 2-year period), coupled with continued review and revision. Here are five steps to follow:

1. *Establish high standards of performance.* Low expectations tend to be self-fulfilling prophecies. In the world of sports, successful coaches such as Landry, Wooden, and Shula have demanded excellence. Excellence rarely results from expectations of mediocrity.
2. *Develop accurate performance appraisal systems.* Focus on job-specific, results-oriented criteria. Consider using multiple raters and appraisal formats that focus on the behavior of employees.
3. *Train supervisors in the mechanics of performance appraisal and in the art of giving feedback to subordinates.* Ineffective performance must be managed constructively.
4. *Tie rewards closely to performance.* Use semiannual performance appraisals to reward or to deny merit increases.
5. *Use a wide range of increases.* Make pay increases meaningful.

FIGURE 12-7
Guidelines for effective merit-pay systems.

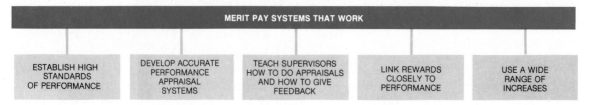

MERIT PAY SYSTEMS THAT WORK				
ESTABLISH HIGH STANDARDS OF PERFORMANCE	DEVELOP ACCURATE PERFORMANCE APPRAISAL SYSTEMS	TEACH SUPERVISORS HOW TO DO APPRAISALS AND HOW TO GIVE FEEDBACK	LINK REWARDS CLOSELY TO PERFORMANCE	USE A WIDE RANGE OF INCREASES

Merit-pay systems can work, but diligent application of these guidelines is essential if they are to work effectively. The guidelines are depicted in Figure 12-7.

Merit Pay in the Context of Overall Compensation

Within this framework, managers need to consider the following issues along with merit pay per se.

- Consult union contract provisions (if appropriate) concerning *who* must be involved in the design and implementation of merit-pay systems and grievance procedures.
- Do a thorough job analysis to capture the work behaviors and work outcomes used to appraise performance. Share these with job incumbents and reach consensus on job requirements before proceeding further.
- Establish a pay range for each class of jobs.
- The midpoint of a pay range (see Figure 10-5) is the basis for comparing employees in terms of their pay levels. It represents a proper rate of pay for an experienced worker performing satisfactorily.
- Inexperienced, newly hired employees are normally paid at the minimum of the range. However, market adjustments (based on labor supply and demand) may result in a starting rate above the minimum for certain jobs. Experienced people entering a job class are normally paid a rate consistent with their experience (e.g., at the midpoint of the pay range).
- Satisfactory performers may progress from their starting rates to the midpoints of their rate ranges on the basis of merit.
- Above-average performers may progress by above-average increments to the midpoint of the pay range (50th percentile) or even to a level midway between the midpoint and the maximum (75th percentile). Ordinarily no more than 30 percent of employees in a job category are in this group (Figure 12-8).
- Superior performers may progress to the maximum of the pay range. Ordinarily no more than 20 percent of employees in a job class will fall between the 75th percentile and the maximum (Figure 12-8).

Once installed, merit-pay systems must be audited periodically to ensure that they are achieving the goals for which they were designed.[33] Questions like the following should be addressed:

- What is the percentage range of pay increases within high, average, and low performance levels?
- What is the increase *by supervisor* within each performance category? Is the same level of performance rewarded similarly across supervisors?
- What is the relationship between merit increases and turnover? Are leavers predominantly from the lower end of the performance scale?

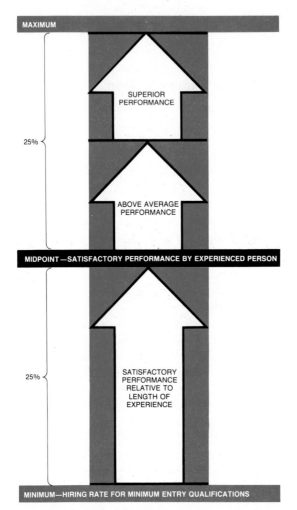

FIGURE 12-8
Performance-based movements within rate ranges characterized by a 25 percent spread from minimum to midpoint and a 25 percent spread from midpoint to maximum.

Merit pay represents a significant cost outlay as well as a powerful motivational tool. It pays to check periodically whether it is working as designed.

INCENTIVES FOR EXECUTIVES

Companies with a history of outperforming their rivals, regardless of industry or economic climate, have two common characteristics: (1) a long-term, strategic view of their executives and (2) stability in their executive groups.[56] It makes sense, therefore, to develop integrated plans for total executive compensation so that rewards are based on achieving the company's long-term strategic goals. This may require a rebalancing of the elements of executive reward systems (Figure 12-9): base salary, annual (short-term) incentives, long-term incentives, regular employee benefits, and special benefits for executives (perquisites).

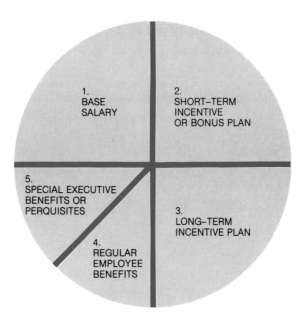

FIGURE 12-9
Elements of executive
reward systems.

Regardless of the exact form of rebalancing, base salaries will continue to be the center point of executive compensation.[8] This is because they generally serve as an index for benefit values. Objectives for short- and long-term incentives frequently are defined as a percentage of base salary. However, incentives are likely to become more long- than short-term-oriented. Here's why:

1. Annual, or short-term, incentive plans encourage the efficient use of existing assets. They are usually based on indicators of corporate performance, such as net income, total dividends paid, or some specific return on investment (i.e., net profit divided by net assets). Most such bonuses are paid immediately in cash, with CEOs receiving an average of 48 percent of their base pay, senior management 35 percent, and middle management 22 percent.[9]

2. Long-term plans encourage the development of new processes, plants, and products that open new markets and restore old ones. Hence long-term performance encompasses qualitative progress as well as quantitative accomplishments. Long-term incentive plans are designed to reward strategic gains rather than short-term contributions to profits. They are as common in owner-controlled firms (at least 5 percent of outstanding stock is held by an individual or organization not involved in the actual management of a company) as they are in management-controlled firms (no individual or organization controls more than 5 percent of the stock).[18] This is the kind of view that we should be encouraging among executives, for it relates consistently to company success.

Let's examine this topic in more detail.

Objectives of Long-Term Incentives

There are a number of possible long-term incentive plans, but it becomes possible to choose one or more only after the strategic objectives of the program have been identified. Long-term incentives then allow a firm to execute its strategy. In general, two strategic objectives are to:

1. Motivate executives to maximize the future growth and profitability of the company.
2. Retain outstanding executives, and attract executives from the outside labor market.

Specific objectives of alternative long-term incentive plans might include the following.

1. Minimize the potential impact of the plan on earnings.
2. Provide favorable tax treatment for the company.
3. Minimize potential negative cash flow and dilution on earnings.
4. Minimize the cash outlay required by executives.
5. Provide executives with a means of accumulating capital at comparatively favorable tax rates.
6. Dissociate executives' rewards from dependence on the stock market (especially since the stock market crash of October 19, 1987).[19,62]

Since some of these objectives are incompatible with others, it is important (1) first to select objectives that are most relevant to the organization's overall compensation strategy and (2) then to decide which long-term incentive plan can best meet or fulfill the objectives. There is a long menu to choose from, and some of the most popular forms are described below.

Forms of Long-Term Incentives

In general, long-term incentive plans fall into two broad categories. The first applies to firms that have decided *not* to dissociate executives' rewards from dependence on the stock market; that is, executive gain is tied to the growth in stock prices. Examples of incentives in this category are stock options, stock appreciation rights (SARs), and restricted stock. The second category ties the gain to predefined levels of company performance; examples include offering the executive performance units or performance shares.[19]

Long-term incentive plans in both categories are described in Table 12-1, and Figure 12-10 shows how these long-term incentives relate to one another in terms of what an executive can hope to gain from them.

■ **TABLE 12·1**
A GLOSSARY OF LONG-TERM INCENTIVE PLANS

Plan	Description
Incentive stock option (ISO)	Executive receives right to purchase stock at stipulated price over specific period of time, in conformance with Internal Revenue Code.
Nonqualified stock option (NQSO)	Similar to incentive stock option, but without conformance with Internal Revenue Code.
Stock appreciation rights (SARs)	Company grants executive the right to appreciation in underlying stock over time.
Phantom stock plans	Executive receives units analogous to company shares and, at some point in the future, receives the value of the stock appreciation plus dividends.
Restricted stock awards	Executive receives outright grant of shares free or with discount, but is restricted from transferring stock until certain conditions are met; if conditions are not met, stock is forfeited.
Performance unit plan	Executive earns specially valued units at no cost, based on achievement of predetermined performance targets.
Performance share plan	Executive receives shares of stock, based on achievement of predetermined performance targets.
Formula value stock plan	Executive earns rights to special class of stock (not publicly traded) that is valued according to a formula, such as book value.

Source: A glossary of long-term incentive plans, *The Wall Street Journal,* Apr. 10, 1987, p. 29. Reprinted by permission of *The Wall Street Journal,* © Dow Jones & Company, Inc., 1987. All rights reserved worldwide.

Impact of the Tax Reform Act of 1986 on Incentives for Executives

This act has had a major impact on executive benefits, principally on long-term incentives and on retirement benefits. Since the impact on retirement benefits was discussed in Chapter 11, the focus here will be on long-term incentives.

Diversification of incentives is more important than ever. Since no one knows how the tax law will ultimately affect markets and corporate balance sheets, ideally executives should receive compensation from several sources. Such a combination might include restricted stock, unfettered performance shares, and stock options. Since more than 90 percent of the largest U.S. companies offer some type of stock option to their executives, let's consider them in detail.[5]

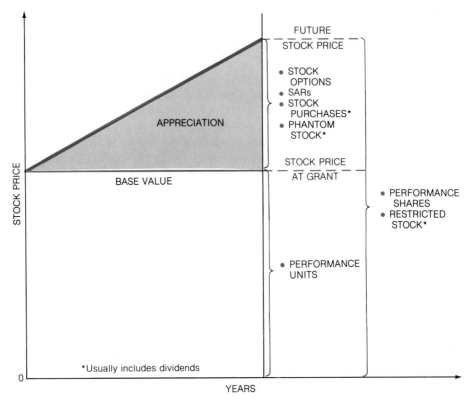

FIGURE 12-10
Potential gains to executives from alternative long-term incentives. (Reprinted, by permission of the publisher, from "Long-term Incentives for Management, Part I: An Overview," by F. W. Cook, from *Compensation Review*, second quarter, p. 18, © 1980 American Management Association, New York. All rights reserved.)

There are two kinds of stock options: incentive options and nonqualified options. Only the former are affected by the Tax Reform Act of 1986. Here's how. In the past, executives could exercise an incentive option and—after holding the stock for 1 year—have the difference between the option and sale price taxed at low capital gains rates. As of 1988, however, capital gains are taxed like ordinary income, and so this break has disappeared. However, such options still retain an important advantage: They are not taxed when exercised, only when sold, assuming that the shares have appreciated in value. Nonqualified options are taxed twice: when the options are exercised and when the shares are sold.[7] When the options are exercised, executives pay taxes on the "bargain element," the difference between the exercise price and the stock's current trading price. *However, that same amount is a tax deduction that an employer gets when the options are exercised.* Employers stand to reap millions of dollars in tax savings, therefore, if they can persuade executives to give up the special tax status of their ISOs.[8] As an executive, what can you do?

The best way to receive nonqualified options under the new tax law is through a tandem plan that includes a cash offset for the taxes that are due when the option is exercised. Typically linked to company profitability goals, such plans often let executives accumulate performance units equal to the amount of taxes on the options they are granted.[7]

Stock appreciation rights (SARs) are also less attractive now, but for a different reason. SARs were embraced in the 1970s, but the bull market of the 1980s and the takeover craze have made them less attractive to companies. The problem is that gains in the value of the SARs must be charged against company earnings quarter by quarter because SARs can be exercised at any time and must be honored, usually in cash. For a company granting SARs, the better its stock performs, the bigger the drain on earnings. For example, suppose an executive gets 10,000 shares at $50 per share, a normal award for a big company. If the stock price increases to $100 per share, the executive has a profit of $500,000. In a typical big company, she or he will be one of about 40 SAR holders. So the company has a charge to earnings of $20 million. Because companies tend to award SARs every year, the cumulative effect on earnings can be staggering.[60]

To counter these effects, dozens of large companies (such as Walt Disney, Westinghouse, and United Technologies) are devising ingenious ways to lessen and even avoid the drain on earnings. These include interest-free loans to executives to exercise their stock options, "tax-offset bonuses" to compensate for taxes due, allowing executives to pay for options with company stock they already own, and substituting restricted stock for SARs. With restricted stock the company takes a known charge to earnings at the time of the grant and none thereafter.

Experts in executive compensation expect the current trend toward using long-term performance incentives to continue. However, plans that measure success only in terms of gains in stock prices have been criticized for not rewarding individual or corporate performance. As a result, some employers are now tying incentive awards to *unit* as well as to companywide performance. The following company examples show how two firms approach this issue differently.

LONG-TERM PERFORMANCE INCENTIVES AT CHAMPION INTERNATIONAL

■ **COMPANY EXAMPLE**

Champion measures its managers by comparing the growth in earnings per share of Champion stock with that of 15 competitors in the forest products industry. It is an all-or-nothing program. If Champion International beats the industry average, 12 senior executives receive an award equal to one-fourth of their total regular bonuses over a 4-year term. If growth in earnings per share falls below the average, they get nothing.

Champion feels that basing long-term executive incentive compensation on how well the company does against its competitors helps reduce one of the main criticisms of performance plans: that external factors such as inflation, interest rates, and general economic activity are often more crucial to a company's prosperity than are the best efforts of its executives. These kinds of external factors affect all firms in an industry to the same extent.

■ COMPANY
EXAMPLE

COMBINING INCENTIVES AT HONEYWELL

Honeywell awards incentive pay to 70 of its division managers, based equally on the performance of their units and of the corporation. The managers receive stock for meeting certain return-on-investment goals for their units over a 3-year period. Says the director of corporate compensation: "We're sending two messages: One is you are a key player and you are responsible for total corporate results. But we also want you to be concerned about improving your own operating units. . . . If you want incentive pay to change [managerial] behavior, a manager has got to believe he has some control over what's being measured."[63]

The plan also reflects Honeywell's diverse and decentralized structure. Its units sell everything from computers to alarm systems, and decision making is pushed down to the various units. Combining corporate and unit incentives makes sense in light of the diverse nature of Honeywell's business. This is a good example of how one company ties its long-term incentives to its long-term business strategy.

Other companies have tried to refine such policies even further, using different measurements to correspond to the unit's strategy. The idea is that executives of a new, risky unit should be judged on, say, building market share, while executives of a stable, mature unit should be judged on generating cash or on cutting costs.[63] Given the number of mergers and acquisitions that took place through the 1980s, these kinds of arrangements are likely to be even more popular in the future.

INCENTIVES FOR LOWER-LEVEL EMPLOYEES

As noted earlier in this chapter, a common practice is to supplement employees' pay with increments related to performance. These are known variously as "incentives," "bonuses," "commissions," or "piecework plans." All are offered as rewards for improvements in job performance.

Most of these plans have a "baseline," or normal, work standard; performance above this standard is rewarded. The baseline should be high enough so that employees are not given extra rewards for what is really just a normal day's work. On the other hand, the baseline should not be so high that it is impossible to earn additional pay.

It is more difficult to specify work standards in some jobs than in others. At the level of top management, for instance, what constitutes a "normal" day's output? To overcome this, top managers are provided with targets, such as:

■ Growth in earnings per share of company stock.
■ Penetration of new markets or the introduction of successful new products.

- Success of diversification or integration programs.
- When set realistically, targets are designed to motivate high performance and to provide a measure of executive worth.

As one moves down the organizational hierarchy, however, jobs can be defined more clearly and shorter-run goals and targets are established.

Setting Workload Standards

All incentive systems depend on workload standards. The standards provide a relatively objective definition of the job, they give employees targets to shoot for, and they make it easier for supervisors to assign work equitably. Once the workload standards are set, employees have an opportunity to earn more than their base salaries, often as much as 20 to 25 percent more. In short, they have an incentive to work harder *and* smarter.

In setting workload standards for production work, the ideal job (ideal only in terms of ability to measure performance, not in terms of improving work motivation or job satisfaction) should (1) be highly repetitive, (2) have a short job cycle, and (3) produce a clear, measurable output. However, before explicit workload standards can be set, management must do the following:

- Describe the job by means of job analysis.
- Decide *how* the job is to be done (motion study).
- Decide *how fast* the job should be done (time study).

The standards themselves will vary, of course, according to the *type* of product or service (e.g., a hospital, a factory, or a cable television company); the *method of service delivery;* the degree to which service can be *quantified;* and *organizational needs,* including legal and social pressures. In fact, the many different forms of incentive plans for lower-level employees really differ only along two dimensions:

1. How the premium rates are determined
2. How the extra payments are made

Increasingly, companies are dangling incentive compensation down to lower-level managers and key workers, such as engineers, investment officials, and others who especially aid the company. For example, John Hancock Mutual Life Insurance Co. rewards lower managers with up to 10 percent of their salaries for "extraordinary work." Shawmut Co. has a similar plan for its bank lenders, giving as much as 25 percent of base pay. And Hewlett-Packard gives 200 to 300 special stock options a year to employees who show extra accomplishment.

Indeed, a 1990 survey of 644 companies found that fully half offer variable-pay programs to salaried and hourly employees below executive ranks.[42] Among com-

panies that provide incentive awards, these are the most popular: lump-sum individual awards (65 percent), productivity bonuses (17 percent), team performance
awards (15 percent), and cash profit sharing (15 percent).[20] Among companies that
give team performance awards, American Greetings Corp. even bases its cost-of-
living increases on merit, and bonuses are based on each unit's results. Pacific Gas
& Electric has a similar team award program for 8000 management-level workers.[47]

While many firms offer incentives, about one in three is dissatisfied with them.
Possibly that's because some firms implement incentive programs only because the
competition does it, and not for strategic reasons. What are some reasons for
implementing incentives? Among firms whose incentive plans "work," they say
they implemented them to motivate workers, to keep them focused on specific
goals, and to share organizational successes.[42]

Incentive systems are certainly sound from a motivational standpoint. Rewards
are tied directly to (i.e., made contingent upon) performance, and reinforcement
(via the measurement of performance) is immediate. Yet incentive plans often
generate conflict. *Work groups* may impose ceilings on output for the following
reasons:

1. Employees may fear that if they earn too much, management will cut premium
   rates and/or increase workload standards.
2. As a result of excess inventory and production, employees will work themselves
   out of a job.
3. Unlimited incentives threaten status hierarchies within work groups. That is,
   older workers (higher status) may not be able to match the pace of their younger
   colleagues. So to protect their social position, work groups establish ceilings,
   or "bogeys," of what is safe or proper output.

Union Attitudes

A unionized employer may establish an incentive system, but it is subject to negotiation through collective bargaining. Unions may also wish to participate in
the day-to-day management of the incentive system, and management ought to
consider that demand seriously. As noted earlier, employees often fear that management will manipulate the system to the disadvantage of employees. Joint participation helps reassure employees that the plan is fair.

Union attitudes toward incentives vary with the type of incentive offered.
Unions tend to oppose individual piece-rate systems because they pit worker
against worker, and they can create unfavorable intergroup conflict. However,
unions tend to support organizationwide systems, such as profit sharing, because
of the extra earnings they provide to their members. Thus in 1988 each of Ford's
156,500 eligible U.S. salaried and hourly employees received an average of $3700,
or 11 percent of their base pay, as a result of the company's profit-sharing plan.[67]

INDIVIDUAL INCENTIVES AT LINCOLN ELECTRIC

From its earliest years, 90-year-old Lincoln Electric Company of Cleveland, Ohio, has charted a unique path in worker-management relations, featuring high wages, guaranteed employment, few supervisors, a lucrative bonus incentive system, and piecework compensation. The company is the world's largest maker of arc-welding equipment; it has 2650 U.S. employees, sales and distribution offices in Canada, France, and Australia, and no unions. Among the innovative management practices that set Lincoln apart are these:

- Guaranteed employment for all full-time workers with more than 2 years' service, and no mandatory retirement. No worker has been laid off for more than 40 years.
- High wages, including a substantial annual bonus (roughly 50 percent of base pay) based on the company's profits. Wages at Lincoln are roughly equivalent to wages for similar work elsewhere in the Cleveland area, but the bonuses the company pays make its compensation substantially higher. Lincoln has never had a strike and has not missed a bonus payment since the system was instituted in 1934. Individual bonuses are set by a formula that judges workers on four points: ideas and cooperation, output, ability to work without supervision, and work quality.
- Piecework—more than half of Lincoln's workers are paid according to what they produce, rather than an hourly or weekly wage. If a worker is sick, he or she does not get paid.
- Promotion is almost exclusively from within, according to merit, not seniority.
- Few supervisors, with a supervisor-to-worker ratio of 1 to 100, far lower than in much of the industry.
- No break periods, and mandatory overtime. Workers must work overtime, if ordered, during peak production periods and must agree to job transfers to meet production schedules or to maintain the company's guaranteed employment program.

While the company insists on individual initiative—and pays according to individual effort—it works diligently to foster the notion of teamwork. And it did so long before the Japanese became known for emphasizing such concepts. If a worker is overly competitive with fellow employees, the worker is rated poorly in terms of cooperation and team play on his or her semiannual rating reports. Thus that worker's bonus will be smaller. Says one company official: "This is not an easy style to manage; it takes a lot of time and a willingness to work with people."[68]

GROUP INCENTIVES

To provide broader motivation than is furnished by incentive plans geared to individual employees, several other approaches have been tried. Their aim is two-fold: to increase productivity and to improve morale by giving employees a feeling of participation in and identification with the company. Group incentives comprise one of these.

Group incentives provide an opportunity for each group member to receive a bonus based on the output of the group as a whole. Groups may be as small as 4 to 7 employees, or as large as 35 to 40 employees. *Group incentives are most appropriate when jobs are highly interrelated.* In fact, highly interrelated jobs are the wave of the future, and in many cases, the wave of the present. In the past, relatively few firms used group incentives. In the future, they will need to be more creative in using group performance appraisal and group incentives. Here's an example of one firm's efforts to do so. At the Saturn plant described earlier, incentives are geared to team performance with respect to car quality. If a team produces fewer defects than the targeted amount, its members receive 100 percent of their salaries. If they perform even better, they are eligible for a bonus.[25]

Group incentives have the following advantages:

1. They make it possible to reward workers who provide essential services to line workers (so-called indirect labor), yet who are paid only their regular base pay. These employees do things like transport supplies and materials, maintain equipment, or inspect work output.
2. They encourage cooperation, not competition, among workers.

On the other hand, group incentives also have their disadvantages, which are as follows:

1. Fear that management will cut rates if employees produce too much.
2. Competition between groups.
3. Inability of workers to see their individual contributions to the output of the group. If they do not see the link between their individual effort and increased rewards, they will not be motivated to produce more.

To overcome some of the first two disadvantages of group incentives, many firms have introduced organizationwide incentives.

ORGANIZATIONWIDE INCENTIVES

In this our final section, we consider three broad classes of organizationwide incentives: profit sharing, gain sharing, and employee stock ownership plans. As we shall see, each is different in its objectives and implementation.

Profit Sharing

In the United States, profit sharing is the most common method that companies use to provide retirement income for their employees. Firms use it for any one or more of the following reasons: to provide a group incentive for increased productivity, to institute a flexible reward structure that reflects a company's actual economic position, to enhance employees' security and identification with the company, to attract and retain workers more easily, and/or to educate individuals about the factors that underlie business success and the capitalistic system.[15,67]

Employees receive a bonus that is normally based on some percentage (e.g., 10 to 30 percent) of the company's profits beyond some minimum level. Profit shares may be paid directly to employees at the end of the fiscal year (as is done by about 40 percent of all plans), but more often they are *deferred*; that is, they are placed in a managed stock and bond fund or a guaranteed investment contract with an insurance company. Increasingly, however, both small and large businesses are offering employees more alternatives with their profit sharing and savings accounts. In fact, one survey of 812 employers found that 68 percent made more than one investment option available to employees.[21]

A most ambitious profit sharing program was started by Du Pont in 1988 for nearly all of its 20,000 managers and employees in the fibers business in the United States. Under the plan, employees can earn up to 12 percent of their base pay if the business exceeds its profit goals, but they also can lose part of their original increase if the profit goals aren't met.[31] In late 1990, when it appeared that workers would lose as much as 4 percent of their base pay as a result of poor sales in the fibers unit, discontent among workers was so high that Du Pont canceled the plan.[39] Although there were many reasons for the plan's failure, two of the most telling were: (1) employees felt powerless to influence profits; and (2) employee resentment over loopholes for high-level managers in the fibers unit, who were still able to benefit from Du Pont's companywide bonus program. That program is geared to the company's total profits, not just to the profits of the fibers unit.

This case illustrates the two-sided nature of profit sharing. On the one hand, compensation costs become more variable, since a company pays only if it makes a profit. On the other hand, from the employee's perspective, benefits and pensions are insecure. Certainly the success of profit sharing plans depends on the company's overall human resource management policy and on the state of labor-management relations. This is even more true of gain-sharing plans.

Gain Sharing

Gain sharing is a formal reward system that has existed in a variety of forms for over 50 years. Sometimes known as the Scanlon plan, the Rucker plan, or Improshare, gain sharing is the generic term, and its definition is comprised of three elements:[24]

1. A philosophy of cooperation
2. An involvement system
3. A financial bonus

The philosophy of cooperation refers to an organizational climate characterized by high levels of trust, two-way communication, participation, and harmonious industrial relations. The involvement system refers to the structure and process for improving organizational productivity. Typically it is a broadly based suggestion system implemented by an employee-staffed committee structure that usually reaches all areas of the organization. Sometimes this structure involves work teams, sometimes quality circles, but usually it is simply an employee-based suggestion system. The employees involved develop and implement ideas related to productivity. The third component, the financial bonus, is determined by a calculation that measures the difference between expected and actual costs during a bonus period.

The three components mutually reinforce each other.[24] High levels of cooperation lead to information sharing, which in turn leads to employee involvement, which leads to new behaviors, such as offering suggestions to improve organizational productivity. This increase in productivity then results in a financial bonus (based on the amount of the productivity increase), which rewards and reinforces the philosophy of cooperation.

It is important to distinguish gain sharing from profit sharing. The two approaches differ in three important ways:[30]

1. Gain sharing is based on a measure of productivity. Profit sharing is based on a global profitability measure.
2. Gain sharing, productivity measurement, and bonus payments are frequent events, distributed monthly or quarterly, in contrast to the annual measures and rewards of profit sharing plans.
3. Gain-sharing plans are current distribution plans, in contrast to most profit sharing plans, which have deferred payments. Hence gain-sharing plans are true incentive plans, rather than employee benefits. As such, they are more directly related to individual behavior, and therefore can motivate worker productivity.

When gain-sharing plans such as the Scanlon plan work, they work well. For example, consider a 17-year evaluation of such a plan in a manufacturing operation, DeSoto, Inc., of Garland, Texas. The bonus formula, which measures labor productivity, revealed that average bonuses ranged from 2.5 percent to over 22 percent, with an overall average of 9.6 percent. Moreover, over the 17-year period of the study, output (as measured by gallons of paint) increased by 78 percent.[23] Nevertheless, in the 50 years since the plan's inception, it has been abandoned by firms about as often as it has been retained. Here are some reasons why:

1. Generally it does not work well in piecework operations.

2. Some firms are uncomfortable about bringing unions into business planning.
3. Some managers feel that they may be giving up their prerogatives.[57,71]

Neither the size of a company nor the type of technology it employs seems to be related to Scanlon plan success.[78] However, employee participation, positive managerial attitudes, the number of years a company has had a Scanlon plan, favorable and realistic employee attitudes, and involvement by a high-level executive are strongly related to the success of a Scanlon plan.[78] To develop an organizationwide incentive plan that has a chance to survive, let alone succeed, careful and in-depth planning must precede implementation. It is true of all incentive plans, though, that *none will work well except in a climate of trustworthy labor-management relations and sound human resource management practices.*

Employee Stock Ownership Plans (ESOPs)

ESOPs have become popular in both large and small companies in the United States, as they have in Western Europe, Yugoslavia, and China.[3] More than 10,000 U.S. firms now share ownership with more than 10 million employees. In at least 1000 companies, employees own the majority of the stock. Employee ownership can be found in every industry, in every size firm, and in every part of the country.[73,77]

Generally ESOPs are established for any of the following reasons:

- As a means for tax-favored and company-financed transfer of ownership from a departing owner to a firm's employees. This is often done in small firms with closely held stock.[14]
- As a way of borrowing money relatively inexpensively. A firm borrows money from a bank using its stock as collateral, places the stock in an employee stock ownership trust, and, as the loan is repaid, it distributes the stock at no cost to employees. Companies can deduct the principal as well as interest on the amount borrowed, and lenders pay taxes on only 50 percent of their income from ESOP loans.[3]
- To fulfill a philosophical belief in employee ownership. For example, at Avis, employees bought the company for $1.75 billion as a way to provide stability and to end 10 tumultuous years in which the company had five corporate owners.[72]
- As an additional employee benefit.

Do ESOPs improve employee motivation and satisfaction? Longitudinal research spanning 45 case studies found that stock ownership alone does not make employees work harder or enjoy their day-to-day work more.[37,38,66] It also does not promote an increase in perceived employee influence in company decisions or status on the job. Nevertheless, certain features do affect employee motivation, satisfaction, and commitment through stock ownership.

IMPACT OF INCENTIVES ON PRODUCTIVITY, QUALITY OF WORK LIFE, AND THE BOTTOM LINE

In this area, perhaps more than any other, there is a closer relationship between effective human resource management practice and the three major themes of this book: productivity, quality of work life, and profits. When employees can see a clear link between an increase in their efforts and an increase in rewards that they personally value, they are motivated to perform "above and beyond the call of duty." Increased motivation to perform well leads to increased productivity. And increased productivity should be rewarded in the form of incentives that can be earned on *top* of base pay. When work has high incentive value to employees, their quality of work life improves significantly. Actually employees benefit in two ways: (1) from the rewards they receive and (2) from the intrinsic satisfaction that results from a job well done. Organizations also benefit because rewards are granted *only* for increases in productivity, and increases in productivity mean improved bottom-line performance. In short, if the deep well of employee motivation can be tapped through an imaginative incentive plan (such as the "100 Club"), everybody wins.

1. ESOP satisfaction tends to be highest in companies where (a) the company makes relatively large annual contributions to the plan; (b) management is committed to employee ownership; and (c) there are extensive company communications about the ESOP.

2. Employees tend to be most satisfied with stock ownership when the company established its ESOP for employee-centered reasons (management was committed to employee ownership) rather than for strategic or financial reasons (e.g., as an antitakeover device or to gain tax savings).

3. Satisfaction breeds satisfaction. That is, the same individual-level and ESOP characteristics that lead to ESOP satisfaction also lead (somewhat less strongly) to organizational commitment.

How does employee stock ownership affect economic performance? *If the above three conditions are met*, employee-owned firms have been shown to be 150 percent as profitable, to have twice the productivity growth, and to generate three times more new jobs than their competitors. High-tech companies that share ownership widely grow 2 to 4 times as fast as those that do not. Publicly held companies that are at least 10 percent employee-owned outperform 62 to 75 percent of their competitors, depending on the measure used.[66]

While such data do not prove that employee stock ownership causes success (it may be that successful firms are more likely to make employees part owners), they do suggest that if implemented properly, such plans can improve employee attitudes *and* economic productivity. Nevertheless, ESOPs are not risk-free to employees. ESOPs are not insured, and if a company goes bankrupt, its stock may be worthless to employees.[77]

IMPLICATIONS FOR MANAGEMENT PRACTICE

In thinking about how managers motivate their subordinates, expect to see three trends continue:

1. The movement to performance-based pay plans, in which workers put more of their pay "at risk" in return for potentially higher rewards.
2. The movement toward the use of teamwide or organizationwide incentive plans at all levels.
3. Use of a wide range of pay increases, in an effort to make distinctions in performance as meaningful as possible.

■ HUMAN RESOURCE MANAGEMENT IN ACTION
CONCLUSION

THE 100 CLUB: A MILLION-DOLLAR INCENTIVE PLAN

By 1983, productivity at the Diamond International plant was up 16.5 percent, and quality-related errors were down 40 percent. Worker grievances decreased 72 percent, and lost time due to industrial accidents decreased 43.7 percent. The turnaround meant more than $1 million in gross financial benefits for Diamond's parent company.

Remember how negative employee attitudes were in 1981 when the program began? When the survey was repeated in 1983, 86 percent of the employees said that management considered them important or very important, 81 percent felt that their work was recognized, and 79 percent reported that their work and the products of their work were of much greater concern to them.

Not surprisingly, labor relations also improved. Even though employees were due a 58-cent-per-hour wage hike in July 1983, they agreed to forgo it because of concerns about competition. Labor leaders credited the 100 Club with keeping the company afloat and fostering a new atmosphere of cooperation with management. As the director of human resources noted, "I'm a little tired of all those Japanese success stories. What we've done here shows that you can have American success stories as well." As a sign of that success, the 100 Club has been phased in at Diamond's three other fiber-product plants in Mississippi, California, and New York.

SUMMARY

To enhance employees' motivation to work, the various elements of human resource management must be coordinated into a unified program. To do this, managers need to focus on three key areas of responsibility: (1) *performance definition* (describing what is expected of employees, plus the continuous orientation of employees toward effective job performance); (2) *performance facilitation* (eliminating roadblocks to performance, providing adequate resources, and careful personnel selection); and (3) *performance encouragement* (providing a sufficient amount of highly valued rewards in a fair, timely manner).

The most effective incentive programs are simple, specific, attainable, and measurable. One of the most popular is merit pay, and merit pay works best when the following guidelines are followed: (1) establish high standards of performance; (2) develop appraisal systems that focus on job-specific, results-oriented criteria; (3) train supervisors in the mechanics of performance appraisal and in the art of giving constructive feedback; (4) tie rewards closely to performance; and (5) provide a wide range of possible pay increases.

Long-term incentives for executives fall into two broad categories: those that tie executive gain to stock price growth and those that relate gains to predefined levels of company performance. The Tax Reform Act of 1986 has had a major impact on such incentives, and on retirement benefits. Finally, we discussed a wide variety of individual, group, and organizationwide incentive plans (e.g., profit sharing, gain sharing, and employee stock ownership plans) in terms of their impact on employee motivation and economic outcomes.

DISCUSSION QUESTIONS

12•1 What can managers do to motivate subordinates?
12•2 Critique the approach to managing people used by North American Tool and Die.
12•3 How has the Tax Reform Act of 1986 affected executive incentives?
12•4 How can union concerns be accommodated in the design and implementation of a gain-sharing plan?
12•5 If you were implementing an employee stock ownership plan, what key factors would you consider?

REFERENCES

1. Ansberry, C. (1987, April 20). When employees work at home, management problems often arise. *The Wall Street Journal*, p. 25.
2. A work revolution in U.S. industry (1983, May 16). *Business Week*, pp. 100–110.
3. Becker, G. S. (1989, Oct. 23). ESOPs aren't the magic key to anything. *Business Week*, p. 20.
4. Belcher, D. W. (1979, Second Quarter). Pay equity or pay fairness? *Compensation Review*, **2**, 31–37.
5. Bennett, A. (1987, April 10). Firms trim annual pay increases and focus on long term. *The Wall Street Journal*, p. 29.

6. Berkowitz, L., Fraser, C., Treasure, F. P., & Cochran, S. (1987). Pay equity, job gratifications, and comparisons in pay satisfaction. *Journal of Applied Psychology*, **72**, 544–551.

7. Bettner, J. (1986, Oct. 28). Executive dreams: What benefits to request under the new tax law. *The Wall Street Journal*, p. 35.

8. Bettner, J. (1987, July 28). Executives get bonus for swap in stock options. *The Wall Street Journal*, p. 25.

9. Bigger bonuses (1987, Sep. 17). *Wall Street Journal*, p. 37.

10. Brainstorming (1990, Feb. 1). *Boardroom Reports*, p. 15.

11. Cherrington, D. J., & Wixom, B. J., Jr. (1983). Recognition is still a top motivator. *Personnel Administrator*, **28**(5), 87–91.

12. Cohen, A. R., & Gadon, H. (1978). *Alternative work schedules: Integrating individual and organizational needs*. Reading, MA: Addison-Wesley.

13. Dunham, R. B., Pierce, J. L., & Castaneda, M. B. (1987). Alternative work schedules: Two field quasi-experiments. *Personnel Psychology*, **40**, 215–242.

14. ESOPs offer way to sell stakes in small firms (1988, May 3). *The Wall Street Journal*, p. 33.

15. Florkowski, G. W. (1987). The organizational impact of profit sharing. *Academy of Management Review*, **12**, 622–636.

16. Fried, Y., & Ferris, G. R. (1987). The validity of the Job Characteristics Model: A review and meta-analysis. *Personnel Psychology*, **40**, 287–322.

17. Gerhart, B. (1987). How important are dispositional factors as determinants of job satisfaction? Implications for job design and other personnel programs. *Journal of Applied Psychology*, **72**, 366–373.

18. Gomez-Mejia, L. R., Tosi, H., & Hinkin, T. (1987). Managerial control, performance, and executive compensation. *Academy of Management Journal*, **30**, 51–70.

19. Gomez-Mejia, L. R., & Welbourne, T. M. (1989). Strategic design of executive compensation programs. In L. R. Gomez-Mejia (ed.), *Compensation and benefits*. Washington, DC: Bureau of National Affairs, pp. 3-216 to 3-269.

20. Good job (1986, Oct. 24). *The Wall Street Journal*, p. 27.

21. Gottschalk, E. C. (1987, April 16). Self-control: Firms let workers manage own profit-sharing funds. *The Wall Street Journal*, p. 27.

22. Graen, G. B., Scandura, T. A., & Graen, M. R. (1986). A field experimental test of the moderating effects of growth need strength on productivity. *Journal of Applied Psychology*, **71**, 484–491.

23. Graham-Moore, B. (1990). Seventeen years of experience with the Scanlon plan: DeSoto revisited. In B. Graham-Moore & T. L. Ross (eds.), *Gainsharing*. Washington, DC: Bureau of National Affairs, pp. 139–173.

24. Graham-Moore, B., & Ross, T. L. (1990). Understanding gainsharing. In B. Graham-Moore & T. L. Ross (eds.), *Gainsharing*. Washington, DC: Bureau of National Affairs, pp. 3–18.

25. Gwynne, S. C. (1990, Oct. 29). The right stuff. *Time*, pp. 74–84.

26. Hackman, J. R. (1978). The design of self-managing work groups. In B. King, S. Streufert, and F. E. Fiedler (eds.), *Managerial control and organizational democracy*. Washington, DC: Winston and Sons.

27. Hackman, J. R. , & Oldham, G. R. (1980). *Work redesign*. Reading, MA: Addison-Wesley.

28. Hackman, J. R., & Oldham, G. R. (1976). Motivation through the design of work: Test of a theory. *Organizational Behavior and Human Performance*, **16**, 250–279.

29. Hackman, J. R., Oldham, G. R., Janson, R., & Purdy, K. A. (1975, Summer). A new strategy for job enrichment. *California Management Review*, pp. 57–71.

30. Hammer, T. H. (1988). New developments in profit sharing, gainsharing, and employee ownership. In J. P. Campbell & R. J. Campbell (eds.), *Productivity in organizations*. San Francisco: Jossey-Bass, pp. 328–366.

31. Hays, L. (1988, Dec. 5). All eyes on Du Pont's incentive-pay plan. *The Wall Street Journal*, p. B1.

32. Herzberg, F. (1966). *Work and the nature of man*. New York: Mentor Executive Library.

33. Hills, F. S., Madigan, R. M., Scott, K. D., & Markham, S. E. (1987). Tracking the merit of merit pay. *Personnel Administrator*, **32**(3), 50–57.

34. Hoerr, J. (1989, July 10). The payoff from teamwork. *Business Week*, pp. 56–62.

35. Huseman, R. C., Hatfield, J. D., & Miles, E. W. (1987). A new perspective on equity theory: The equity sensitivity construct. *Academy of Management Review*, **12**, 222–234.

36. Katz, D., & Kahn, R. L. (1978). *The social psychology of organizations* (2d ed.). New York: Wiley.

37. Klein, K. J. (1987). Employee stock ownership and employee attitudes: A test of three models. *Journal of Applied Psychology*, **72**, 319–332.

38. Klein, K. J., & Hall, R. J. (1988). Correlates of employee satisfaction with stock ownership: Who likes an ESOP most? *Journal of Applied Psychology*, **73**, 630–638.

39. Koenig, R. (1990, Oct. 25). Du Pont plan linking pay to fibers profit unravels. *The Wall Street Journal*, pp. B1, B5.

40. Kopelman, R. E., & Reinharth, L. (1982, Fourth Quarter). Research results; The effect of merit-pay practices on white-collar performance. *Compensation Review*, **5**, 30–40.

41. Kutner, L. (1988, Dec. 8). Working at home, or, the midday career change. *The New York Times*, p. C8.

42. Labor letter (1990, June 11). *The Wall Street Journal*, p. A1.

43. Labor letter (1990, Feb. 20). *The Wall Street Journal*, p. A1.

44. Labor letter (1989, Dec. 12). *The Wall Street Journal*, p. A1.

45. Labor letter (1988, Nov. 8). *The Wall Street Journal*, p. A1.

46. Labor letter (1987, July 7). *The Wall Street Journal*, p. 1.

47. Labor letter (1987, March 31). *The Wall Street Journal*, p. 1.

48. Lawler, E. E., III (1989). Pay for performance: A strategic analysis. In L. R. Gomez-Mejia (ed.), *Compensation and benefits*. Washington, DC: Bureau of National Affairs, pp. 3-136 to 3-181.

49. Lawler, E. E., III (1988). Choosing an involvement strategy. *Academy of Management Executive*, **2**, 197–204.

50. Locke, E. A., Shaw, K. N., Saari, L. M., & Latham, G. P. (1981). Goal-setting and task performance: 1969–1980. *Psychological Bulletin*, **90**, 125–152.

51. Lublin, J. (1984, March 13). Labor letter. *The Wall Street Journal*, p. 1.

52. Mannheim, B., & Angel, O. (1986). Pay systems and work-role centrality of industrial workers. *Personnel Psychology*, **39**, 359–377.

53. Maslow, A. H. (1954). *Motivation and personality*. New York: Harper.

54. McClelland, D. C. (1961). *The achieving society*. New York: Van Nostrand Reinhold.

55. McFillen, J., & Podsakoff, P. M. (1983). A coordinated approach to motivation can increase productivity. *Personnel Administrator*, **29**(7), 45–53.

56. Meyer, P. (1983). Executive compensation must promote long-term commitment. *Personnel Administrator*, **28**(5), 37–42.

57. Moore, B., & Ross, T. (1978). *The Scanlon way to improved productivity*. New York: Wiley.

58. Needle, D. (1986, May 19). Telecommuting: Off to a slow start. *InfoWorld*, pp. 43–46.
59. Perceptions of pay (1986, July 7). *The Wall Street Journal*, p. 13.
60. Perham, J. (1987, July). Stock incentive backlash. *Business Month*, pp. 28–29.
61. Perry, N. J. (1984, Jan. 9). America's most admired corporations. *Fortune*, pp. 50–62.
62. Redling, E. T. (1982, March–April). The 1981 Tax Act: Boon to managerial compensation. *Personnel*, pp. 52–59.
63. Reibstein, L. (1987, April 10). More employers link incentives to unit results. *The Wall Street Journal*, p. 29.
64. Robbins, C. B. (1983). Design effective incentive plans. *Personnel Administrator*, **28**(5), 8–10.
65. Rollins, T. (1987, June). Pay for performance. The pros and cons. *Personnel Journal*, pp. 104–107.
66. Rosen, C., Klein, K. J., & Young, K. M. (1986). When employees share the profits. *Psychology Today*, **20**, 30–36.
67. Schroeder, M. (1988, Nov. 7). Watching the bottom line instead of the clock. *Business Week*, pp. 134, 136.
68. Serrin, W. (1984, Jan. 15). The way that works at Lincoln. *The New York Times*, p. D1.
69. Skinner, B. F. (1957). *Science and human behavior*. East Norwalk, CT: Appleton-Century-Crofts.
70. Taylor, A., III (1990, Nov. 19). Why Toyota keeps getting better and better and better. *Fortune*, pp. 66–79.
71. Tyler, L. S., & Fisher, B. (1983). The Scanlon concept: A philosophy as much as a system. *Personnel Administrator*, **29**(7), 33–37.
72. Ungeheuer, F. (1989, Feb. 6). They own the place. *Time*, pp. 50, 51.
73. Vough, C. F. (1979). *Productivity: A practical program for improving efficiency*. New York: AMACOM.
74. Waldman, S., & Roberts, B. (1988, Nov. 14). Grading "merit pay." *Newsweek*, pp. 45, 46.
75. Wall, T. D., Kemp, N. J., Jackson, P. R., & Clegg, C. W. (1986). Outcomes of autonomous workgroups: A long-term field experiment. *Academy of Management Journal*, **29**, 280–304.
76. Wexley, K. N., & Latham, G. P. (1991). *Developing and training human resources in organizations* (2d ed.). Glenview, IL: Scott, Foresman.
77. White, J. A. (1991, Jan. 25). As ESOPs become victims of '90s bankruptcies, workers are watching their nest eggs vanish. *The Wall Street Journal*, pp. C1, C16.
78. White, J. K. (1979). The Scanlon plan: Causes and consequences of success. *Academy of Management Journal*, **22**, 292–312.

■ A CONCEPTUAL VIEW OF HUMAN RESOURCE MANAGEMENT ■
STRATEGIC OBJECTIVES, ENVIRONMENTS, FUNCTIONS

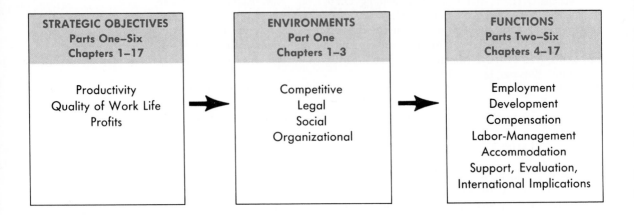

RELATIONSHIP OF HRM FUNCTIONS TO HRM ACTIVITIES

FUNCTIONS	ACTIVITIES
PART 2 EMPLOYMENT	Job Analysis, Human Resource Planning, Recruiting, Staffing (Chapters 4–6)
PART 3 DEVELOPMENT	Orientation, Training, Performance Appraisal, Managing Careers (Chapters 7–9)
PART 4 COMPENSATION	Pay, Benefits, Incentives (Chapters 10–12)
PART 5 LABOR-MANAGEMENT ACCOMMODATION	Union Representation, Collective Bargaining, Procedural Justice, Ethics (Chapters 13, 14)
PART 6 SUPPORT, EVALUATION, INTERNATIONAL IMPLICATIONS	Job Safety and Health, Costs/Benefits of HRM Activities, International Dimensions of HRM (Chapters 15–17)

Labor-Management Accommodation

.**H**armonious working relations between labor and management are critical to organizations. Traditionally both parties have assumed a win-lose, adversarial posture toward each other. This must change if U.S. firms are to remain competitive in the international marketplace. Part Five is entitled "Labor-Management Accommodation" to emphasize a general theme: To achieve long-term success, labor and management must learn to *accommodate* one another's needs, rather than *repudiate* them. By doing so, management and labor can achieve two goals at once: increase productivity and improve the quality of work life. In the current climate of wants and needs, there is no other alternative.

The focus of Chapter 13 is on union representation and collective bargaining. Chapter 14 focuses on procedural justice, ethics, and concerns for privacy in employee relations. These are some of the most dominant issues in this field in the 1990s. As is true of all chapters in this book, Chapters 13 and 14 are oriented toward the development of sound human resource management practices by line managers.

Union Representation and Collective Bargaining

IMPROVEMENT OF QWL THROUGH POSITIVE UNION-MANAGEMENT RELATIONS*

Union and management groups provide perhaps the most vivid example of win-lose conflict. Even though they depend on one another to achieve their objectives, their relationship is frequently characterized by bitterness, hostility, and mutual antagonism, rather than by cooperation. Like true enemies, either may be willing to place itself in peril to deprive the other of a victory. Legally, each group is equally powerful in terms of influencing outcomes, and therefore neither can impose its will unilaterally on the other.

This case describes a situation at the Hillside plant, a large, modern facility. It illustrates typical union-management relations—plagued by conflict and punctuated by strikes and threats of strikes. Win-lose attitudes of mutual suspicion and distrust extended to every phase of union-management

---

*Adapted from: R. R. Blake & J. S. Mouton, Developing a positive union-management relationship, *Personnel Administrator*, **28**(6), 1983, 23–32, 140. Copyright, 1983. Reprinted with permission from HRMagazine (formerly Personnel Administrator) published by the Society for Human Resource Management, Alexandria, VA.

relations. With the expiration of the current contract only 5 months away, unless union-management relations became more cooperative, a strike seemed inevitable.

Against this backdrop of mutual antagonism, the corporate employee relations manager proposed a 3-day union-management development seminar. Both parties were skeptical that anything positive might result, but both agreed reluctantly to take part in the effort. Two behavioral science consultants (Drs. Blake and Mouton) agreed to serve as facilitators for the seminar. A total of six members of management (plant manager, personnel manager, assistant personnel manager, manufacturing superintendent, maintenance supervisor, and corporate director of employee relations) and six union officials (president, vice president, three stewards, and the international union representative) attended the seminar.

THE SEMINAR BEGINS

In a general session with each group convened around a separate table across from the other, one of the consultants posed the question. "What would a sound relationship between the union and the company be like?" The participants spontaneously nominated cooperation, mutual trust, and recognition. With this general tone, the question "What is the actual union-management relationship?" was quickly answered with "no trust" and "total lack of cooperation."

ELEMENTS OF AN IDEAL RELATIONSHIP

In a separate session away from the union, members of the management group began with the recurrent theme that "the union wants to run the plant by eroding management's prerogatives." Their fear was that agreement with the union to any union demand would signal management weaknesses and lead to pressure by the union to give even more. The group continued by questioning the motives of the union president. They knew that he wielded considerable power over the membership. If the president wanted a management proposal accepted, he would present it in a straightforward, positive way. If he wanted it rejected, he would twist the proposal to emphasize its negative implications.

After this initial period of "ventilation," the consultant encouraged the management group to concentrate on its original objective: to identify the elements of an ideal relationship. Ultimately, the group developed the following list of elements of an ideal relationship:

- Mutual trust and respect for one another
- Honesty in dealings with one another
- Effective communication within and between the two groups

- Problem solving in order to resolve real issues between the parties
- Good supervision in terms of work and contract administration
- Timely resolution of grievances
- Consistency in contract interpretation

The union's list (also developed in a separate session) closely paralleled management's, but the union felt, as did management, that the likelihood of achieving the desired relationship was very slight. The union wanted:

- *Trust.* Standing behind your work
- *Openness.* Speaking freely without fear of reprisal
- *Communication.* Listening to both sides with an open mind
- *Problem solving.* Living by the spirit of the contract in day-to-day dealings
- *Consistency.* Applying the contract uniformly in every section of the plant

GROUP PRESENTATIONS

When members of the two groups reconvened to share their ideal elements and to determine the possibility of getting agreement on a sound model, time was provided for seeking additional information or clarification. The consultants invited the groups to question one another, but there was little interchange. Each side was preoccupied with the details of recent conflict and with perceived injustices and was anxious to move into descriptions of actual conditions. The ideal seemed so remote from actual experience that neither could view it as realistic. In short, both the union and management were anxious to get to the heart of the problem: describing what the other group had done to create the deeply disturbed current situation.

MANAGEMENT'S VIEW OF THE ACTUAL RELATIONSHIP

Again meeting in separate session, members of the management group assembled an 11-item list of actual conditions, but their major theme revolved around the exercise of power and authority. From management's perspective, the union intended to usurp authority and responsibility that rightfully belonged to the company. This explained the distrust and disrespect, poor communication, and severely reduced ability to solve problems jointly that prevailed at the Hillside plant. It also caused management to be as tough as possible in interpreting the contract.

THE UNION VIEW

Predictably, the union held opposite opinions. It sought only what it had earned through contract bargaining; the union did not want to run the plant, but it certainly wanted people in the plant to be treated with dignity and

respect. As the people's voice and their elected representatives, union officers expected a degree of consideration—not contempt. In their joint meeting at the conclusion of the first day's session, each group made a brief
presentation of its actual model. The groups were stunned, particularly management, and no further discussion seemed appropriate. The first scheduled
activity for the next day was separate meetings to discuss the content and
implications of the other group's descriptions of the actual relationship.

THE MANAGERS' DISCUSSION

Management's discussion of the union's description of actual conditions centered on the union's contention of "hopelessness." The plant manager had
warned of a possible strike, but it was apparent that management had been
blind to the depth of the union's despair at achieving a turnaround prior to
the expiration of the contract. In an effort to evaluate the implications of
these circumstances, management concluded that (1) the union president
had the backing of the employees and (2) he had the power to call a strike
even though the union meetings routinely had poor attendance. The management group ended its discussion on the sobering note that a strike was
a realistic possibility. They committed themselves to asking open-ended and
honest questions in a search for genuine understanding and avoidance of
further polarization.

THE UNION'S DISCUSSION

The union's discussion of management's description of actual conditions was
"more of the same old stuff." Their feeling was that management was deaf
and blind to union efforts to deal with management constructively.

THE JOINT DISCUSSION

In the joint discussion of actual conditions, the union was astonished to learn
that management saw their joint relationship as a game of win or lose. In
fact, the union vice president felt that during the past 6 to 8 months management had tried to bypass the union and to go directly to the employees.

Overtime was an example. Employees had been told that many situations
were emergencies and that the company therefore needed them to work
overtime. It was only when employees would *not* work overtime that management came to the union. Members of the management group responded
that they were responsible for getting the work out and needed people to
do it. Nevertheless, the union was firm on the matter: Management had no
credibility and no right to expect respect from people who were dehuman-
ized and depersonalized in every possible way.

As the session continued, the beginnings of a reversal in the attitude of
the management group became evident. Group members became less intent

on defending their own positions and more interested in obtaining genuine understanding of the union perspective. They raised a series of questions about each of the union's points.

What past and current actions led the union to conclude that management was concerned only with production? The managers admitted that they were not perfect, but they also stressed that they were not responsible for every problem in the plant. They pointed out that they had inherited a number of problems, and they expressed the need to have the union's help to solve them.

The union group explained that its feeling of hopelessness was based on the constraints of the present system. Once they were locked into a contract, their only relief was the grievance procedure. They felt hopeless because management forced them to resolve grievances through arbitration by a third party. Since arbitration incurred expenses for their members, the union could not afford to pursue every grievance.

Other issues raised by the union included concrete examples of inconsistent enforcement of rules, of unwarranted suspensions, and of "unnecessary" grievances. After this exchange, there were no further questions between the two groups. Each returned to its own separate session for further deliberation on the issues.

Challenges

1. How might the approach used at the Hillside plant contribute to an improvement in quality of work life?
2. Based on the information presented, how did management contribute to the problems? How did the union contribute?
3. Do you see any possibility for long-term resolution of the problems facing the Hillside plant? Why?

QUESTIONS THIS CHAPTER WILL HELP MANAGERS ANSWER

1. How have changes in product and service markets affected the way labor and management relate to each other?
2. How should management respond to a union organizing campaign?
3. To what extent should labor-management cooperative efforts be encouraged?
4. What kinds of dispute resolution mechanisms should be established in order to guarantee due process for all employees?

WHY EMPLOYEES JOIN UNIONS

Study after study has found consistently that unions form as a result of frustration by employees over their inability to gain important rewards.[1] More specifically, there seem to be two main factors underlying employees' interest in unions.[5] The first of these is *dissatisfaction with working conditions and a perception by employees that they cannot change those conditions.*

One study of over 87,000 salaried clerical, sales, and technical employees representing 250 units of a national retailing firm found that attitude measures taken 3 to 15 months *prior* to any organizing activity predicted the level of *later* organizing. Consistent with the maxim that "the best union organizer is the boss," this study found that the best predictors of the severity of unionization activity were items dealing with the supervision the workers receive.[24]

Another study of over 1200 employees who voted in 31 union representation elections supported these findings. Correlations between job satisfaction and votes for or against union representation are shown in Table 13-1.

Dissatisfaction with wages, job security, fringe benefits, treatment by supervisors, and chances for promotion was significantly related to a vote *for* union representation. However, dissatisfaction with the *kind* of work being done did not correlate strongly with a vote for union representation. Hence, *employee interest in unionization was triggered by working conditions, not by the work itself.*

The second factor that seems to underlie employee interest in unionization is *the degree to which employees accept the concept of collective action and whether they believe unionization will yield positive rather than negative outcomes for them.* Thus, in the study shown in Table 13-1, dissatisfied employees tended *not* to vote for unioni-

■ **TABLE 13·1**

CORRELATIONS BETWEEN JOB SATISFACTION AND VOTES FOR OR AGAINST UNION REPRESENTATION

Item	Correlation with vote*
1. Are you satisfied with your wages?	− .40
2. Do supervisors in this company play favorites?	− .34
3. Are you satisfied with the type of work you are doing?	− .14
4. Does your supervisor show appreciation when you do a good job?	− .30
5. Are you satisfied with your fringe benefits?	− .31
6. Do you think there is a good chance for you to get promoted in this company?	− .30
7. Are you satisfied with your job security at this company?	− .42
8. Taking everything into consideration, are you satisfied with this company as a place to work?	− .36

*The negative correlations indicate that satisfied employees tended to vote against union representation.
Source: Adapted from: J. M. Brett, Why employees want unions. Reprinted, by permission of the publisher, from *Organizational Dynamics*, **8**(4), Spring 1980, p. 51, © 1980 American Management Association, New York. All rights reserved.

zation if they believed the union was unlikely to improve the working conditions that dissatisfied them.[5] Recent research supports the finding that beliefs about the effects of a union at a person's *own workplace* are critical determinants of voting intentions.[12] In addition, employees who hold a negative image of labor unions (i.e., those who feel that unions have too much political influence, abuse their power by calling strikes, cause high prices, misuse union dues and pension funds, and have leaders who promote their own self-interests) tend to vote *against* union representation.[33] In fact, knowing an employee's opinion on these issues allowed researchers to predict with 79 percent accuracy how he or she would vote on the issue of union representation.[5]

On the other hand, it is pure folly to assume that pro-union attitudes are based simply on expected economic gains; much deeper values are at stake.[3] As one author noted:

> If one talks to any worker long enough, and candidly enough, one discovers that his loyalty to the union is not simply economic. One may even be able to show him that, on a strictly cost-benefit analysis, measuring income lost from strikes, and jobs lost as a result of contract terms, the cumulative economic benefits are delusions. It won't matter. In the end, he will tell you, the union is the only institution that insures and protects his "dignity" as a worker, that prevents him from losing his personal identity, and from being transformed into an infinitesimal unit in one huge and abstract "factor of production." (ref. 38, p. 28)

This conclusion that deeper values than money are at stake was illustrated in the 11-year battle to organize workers at the J. P. Stevens plant in North Carolina. The organizing drive was much publicized—the award-winning movie *Norma Rae* was based on it—and the settlement was heralded widely as a historic breakthrough in a decades-old attempt to organize southern industry. Even though the wages at the unionized Stevens plants are not substantially higher now than at the company's nonunionized plants or than the wages at other nonunion textile plants in the south, the wage level was never the biggest issue. The union contract has meant expanded benefits, a seniority system to protect workers when jobs are lost and to provide opportunities when jobs open, and a grievance procedure with access to binding arbitration. For the company, the settlement allowed it to put its past squabbles with the workers behind and to concentrate on battling foreign textile imports. Among union members, however, worker after worker echoes the same sentiment: The collective bargaining agreement has meant that they are treated with new dignity on the job.[59]

Understanding Trade Unionism

Whatever trade unions may or may not be, they are not pro-socialist institutions. Indeed, one of the most striking facts of the twentieth century is that trade unions do not fit comfortably *either* into a socialist (left) or a capitalist (right) political ideology. What we call "militancy" is as characteristic of an American union (e.g., the Teamsters) whose leadership may endorse Republican candidates as it is of a British union (e.g., the coal miners) whose leadership is openly socialist.

Nor does it matter whether the industries in which unions operate are nationalized or privately owned, public or private sector. The ways unions behave (as distinct from what their leaders say) are pretty much the same in either case. *Trade unions seem to be engaged in a peculiar kind of class struggle that is immune to conventional political preferences.*[38]

At a general level, the goal of unions is to increase their membership through improvement of economic and other conditions of employment. Increased membership and economic improvement are not independent of one another, as a study by the National Bureau of Economic Research shows. The study encompassed *all* manufacturing industries and indicated that union wages rise about 10 percentage points, on average, as the proportion of union members in an industry rises to 80 percent from 20 percent. One reason for the increase in wages is that unions in highly organized industries need not worry so much about losing jobs to nonunion companies when they demand higher wages. The bottom line is that *high unionization in an industry tends to increase the pay gap between union and nonunion workers.*[65]

UNION MEMBERSHIP IN THE UNITED STATES

During the 1980s, U.S. union membership dropped off dramatically. Between 1980 and 1989, 2 million union jobs in manufacturing were lost, largely due to plant closings and layoffs. Many of those jobs are gone for good.[40] Overall, the percentage of workers who do not belong to unions has risen steadily from 71.6 percent in 1965 to 83.6 percent in 1990.[68] Yet these overall figures may mask underlying trends. One of every four union members is a woman now, and while total union membership dropped during the 1980s, the number of female union members increased substantially.[69] The women tend to work in *service industries* represented by such unions as: the Retail Clerks; the Service Employees International Union; the American Federation of State, County, and Municipal Employees; and the United Federation of Teachers.

Several economic and demographic forces favor a resurgence of unions. Corporate cost cutting has rattled many workers; a recent survey showed them to be more receptive to unions than at any time since 1979. In addition, labor shortages in certain markets have emboldened workers who no longer fear losing their jobs. And both women and minority-group members, who are expected to continue entering the work force at a high rate, tend to favor unions.[15,34] However, these same workers are also sympathetic to business. Many came of age during the oil shocks of the mid-1970s, the back-to-back recessions that followed, and then the trade wars. This has led them to appreciate the importance of business in creating jobs and has made them want unions that cooperate with management rather than confront it.[23]

What complicates organizing efforts is that many in this new generation are white-collar workers—in fields as diverse as insurance and electronics.[21] Their goals and desires are different from those of labor's traditional blue-collar stalwarts, who seemed to want little more than high wages and steady work. And because so many young workers are highly mobile (workers under 35 stay on a job a median of 2.5 years, compared to 12 years for those over 45), they might not be willing to support a 6-month unionization drive that might culminate in a strike to win a first contract.[23] Finally, many young workers are taking jobs in the rapidly growing service sector—banking, computer programming, financial services—jobs that unions traditionally have not penetrated.[40]

Although only 16.4 percent of nonfarm workers in the United States belong to unions, unions are a powerful social, political, and organizational force. In the unionized firm, managers must deal with the union rather than directly with employees on many issues. Indeed, the "rules of the game" regarding wages, hours, and conditions of employment are described in a collective bargaining agreement (or contract) between management and labor. As we saw in the Hillside case, adversarial "us" and "them" feelings are frequently an unfortunate by-product of this process.

Economic and working conditions in unionized firms directly affect those in nonunionized firms, as managers strive to provide competitive working conditions for their employees. Yet the nature of the internal and external environments of most U.S. firms changed during the 1980s as never before. This has led to fundamental changes in labor-management relations. In our next section we will consider some of these changes.

THE CHANGING NATURE OF INDUSTRIAL RELATIONS IN THE UNITED STATES

In today's world, firms face more competitive pressures than ever before. That competition arises from abroad (e.g., Toyota, Nissan, Hyundai, Sanyo, Pohang, and third-world steelmakers), from domestic, nonunion operators (e.g., Nucor in steel), and from nonregulated new entities (e.g., dozens of new telecommunications companies). The result? The management of human resource cost and productivity moves back toward the center of business concerns.[18,58]

These competitive pressures have forced business to develop the ability to shift rapidly, to cut costs, to innovate, to enter new markets, and to devise a flexible labor force strategy. As managers seek to make the most cost-effective use of their human resources, the old "rules of the labor-management game" are changing.

Traditionally, the power of unions to set industrywide wage levels and to relate these in "patterns" was based on the market power of strong domestic producers, or industries sheltered by regulation. As employers lost their market power in the 1970s and 1980s, union wage dominance shrank and fragmented. One union segment had to compete with another and with nonunion labor both in the United States and abroad. Management's objective was (and is) to get labor costs per unit of output to a point below that of the competition at the product-line level. Out of this approach has come wage-level differences and, with it, the breakdown of pattern bargaining.[18] As a result, even under union bargaining pressures, wages are now far more responsive to economic conditions at the industry and firm levels, and even at the product-line level, than they traditionally have been.[18]

Related to wage-level flexibility is employment-level flexibility. By contracting out work more freely, using subcontracts for business services, and using more part-time and temporary workers, management is trying to make employment levels more fluid and adjustable, to make labor costs even more variable, and to gain power for rapid downsizing and cost cutting. This approach, which may well characterize the 1990s, has been termed "Kanban employment," using the Japanese term for just-in-time delivery and no stockpiling or inventorying of resources.[18]

The labor relations system that evolved during the 1940s and lasted until the early 1980s was institutionalized around the market power of the firm and around those unions that had come to represent large proportions, if not nearly all, of an industry's domestic workforce. The driving force for change in the late 1980s and early 1990s has been business conditions in the firm. Those conditions have changed for good—and so must the U.S. industrial relations system if it is to survive. In order to put that system into better perspective, let us examine the approach taken in other countries. Keep in mind, however, that direct comparisons are difficult. The next section shows why.

DIFFICULTIES IN COMPARING INDUSTRIAL RELATIONS SYSTEMS

It is difficult to compare industrial relations systems across national boundaries for at least three reasons:[13]

1. The same concept may be interpreted differently in different industrial relations contexts. For example, consider the concept of collective bargaining. In the United States it is understood to mean negotiations between a labor union local and management. In Sweden and Germany, however, the term refers to negotiation between an employers' organization and a trade union at the industry level.

2. The objectives of the bargaining process may differ in different countries. For example, European unions view collective bargaining as a form of class struggle, but in the United States collective bargaining is viewed mainly in economic terms.

3. No industrial relations system can be understood without an appreciation of its historical origin. Such historical differences may be due to managerial strategies for labor relations in large companies, ideological divisions within the trade union movement, the influence of religious organizations on the development of trade unions, methods of union regulation by governments, or the mode of technology and industrial organization at critical stages of union development.[55]

To illustrate such differences in industrial relations systems, we will present a brief overview of the Japanese system.

The Japanese Industrial Relations Systems*

Although the Trade Union Act was passed in December 1945, the basic framework of the industrial relations system was established in 1956 after the economic boom of the Korean War. Workers in the private sector were guaranteed three basic rights: to organize labor unions, to bargain collectively, and to take industrial action to insist on their interests.

Forms of trade unions Most Japanese unions in the private sector are enterprise unions. This concept, based on the idea of *groupism*, has its roots in the lifestyle and social values of farmers and fishers. Workers moving from rural areas to large cities expected (correctly) that their idea of groupism would be maintained even in the context of manufacturing operations.

Union membership is limited to regular employees of a single company regardless of whether they are blue-collar or white-collar employees. Subcontractors and temporary workers are not eligible for membership, but supervisors of blue-collar workers and subsection heads of white-collar workers may be union members if the company-level collective bargaining agreement permits. Top executives and middle managers are often former members of their company's labor union, because they usually have worked their way up through the ranks.

An enterprise union usually joins one of four so-called national centers of labor unions. These centers play an important role in developing policies of their member labor unions, in coordinating interests of the member unions, and in influencing government economic and industrial relations policies. They also play a leading role in directing the Spring Labor Offensive, which usually determines the main direction of collective bargaining at each company.

The Spring Labor Offensive (Shunto-hoshiki) was established in 1956 to overcome the weakness of enterprise unionism. About 80 percent of all labor negotiations take place at the beginning of the spring, especially in March, April, and May. This time was chosen because April is the beginning of the accounting term and the month when new school graduates come into companies. One of the main reasons why employers accept the coordinated wage settlement is that they can avoid severe competition among themselves on wages and other benefits under the guidance of their trade association.

Employers' organizations Of the four main employers' associations, Keidanren (Japan Federations of Economic Organization) is the most influential with respect to labor relations issues. It includes 54 trade associations and all the regional employers' associations. Its main function is to coordinate employers' opinions on economic policies and labor problems and to present these to the public and to the government.

---

*Much of the material in this section has been adapted from: K. Okubayashi, The Japanese industrial relations system, *Journal of General Management*, **14**, 1989, 67–88.

The structure of collective bargaining For the most part, as we have noted, collective bargaining is based on negotiations between an enterprise union and its employer. Contents of the collective agreement include clauses dealing with topics such as wages, annual wage increases, benefits, working hours, and criteria for dismissal. It also includes sections dealing with issues such as union membership as a condition of continued employment, time-card stamping at the beginning and end of work, and the conduct of union activities during working hours. Finally, the agreement includes sections dealing with joint consultation and grievance resolution procedures.

The joint consultation system This system, in addition to collective bargaining, plays a very important role in promoting industrial democracy in Japanese industrial relations. About 71 percent of companies with more than 1000 employees have adopted such a system. Employee representatives at each level of a company (shop floor, factory, and the company as a whole) meet monthly with their counterparts in management to exchange information about the company's policies, production schedule, and changes of practices on the shop floor. At these meetings, management often shares confidential information concerning production plans, financial conditions, staffing plans, and the introduction of new technology, for example. Union representatives can express their opinion of this information and provide counterproposals to management. Differences between the two groups are handled in one of two ways: management subsequently may modify its proposal, or else execution of the original proposal is suspended for a cooling off period. These mechanisms help avoid severe conflicts or strikes.

In practice, employee representatives are union officials. Therefore rigid differentiation between collective bargaining and the joint consultation system is very difficult in the sense that both work effectively to promote communication between management and employees.

The idea of participative management is supported by labor unions, employers, and workers themselves. However, the main forms of participation in Japanese industrial systems are collective bargaining, the joint consultation system, suggestion systems, and small group activities such as quality circles. Employee representation on boards of directors, or participation in high-level strategic business decisions, as is the case in Germany, is not practiced in Japan.

Worker participation at industrial and national levels The activities of enterprise unions extend beyond their companies to include joint consultation between representatives of confederations of labor unions and corresponding associations of employers. Such systems exist in mining, textiles, iron and steel, electric power, machinery and metal fabrication, shipbuilding, automobiles, chemical, plastics, and oil industries, for example. Representatives exchange opinions on general industrial policies, business trends, and main strategies of the Spring Labor Offensive, as well as employment security within their own industries, safety, work hours, and minimum wages. These meetings do not have the authority to conclude industrywide collective agreements concerning industrial policies, but they are very effective mechanisms for the exchange of perceptions about industrial situations. This facilitates consensus between enterprise unions and employers.

In summary, the Japanese industrial relations system is comprised of the following framework: enterprise unions that work with company managements to conclude collective bargaining agreements during the Spring Labor Offensive, and to promote industrial democracy through the joint consultation system, as well as union-management discussions at the industrial and national levels.

As we noted earlier, examination of another country's industrial relations system, such as that of Japan, helps to put the U.S. system into better perspective. The remainder of this chapter will examine that system in greater detail.

Fundamental Features of the U.S. Industrial Relations System

Six distinctive features of the U.S. system, compared to those in other countries, include the following:[14]

1. *Exclusive representation*—one and only one union in a given job territory, selected by majority vote. This is in contrast to continental Europe, where affiliations by religious and ideological attachment exist in the same job territory.

2. *Collective agreements* that embody a sharp distinction between *negotiation of and interpretation of an agreement*. Most agreements are of fixed duration, often 2 or 3 years, and they result from legitimate, overt conflict that is confined to a negotiations period. They incorporate no-strike (by employees) and no-lockout (by employer) provisions during the term of the agreement, and the interpretation of the agreement by private arbitrators or umpires. In contrast, the British system features open-ended and nonenforceable agreements.

3. *Decentralized collective bargaining*, largely due to the size of the United States, the diversity of its economic activity, and the historic role of product markets in shaping the contours of collective bargaining. By contrast, in Sweden the government establishes wage rates, and in Australia, most wages are set by arbitration councils.[16]

4. *Relatively high union dues and large union staffs* to negotiate and administer private, decentralized agreements, including grievance arbitration to organize against massive employer opposition and to lobby before legislative and administrative tribunals.

5. *Opposition by both large and small employers to union organization*, compared to other countries, has been modified in its forms only slightly by 50 years of legislation.

6. *The role of government* in the U.S. industrial relations system has been relatively passive in dispute resolution, and highly legalistic in both administrative procedures and in the courts. As regulation has expanded over health and safety, pension benefits, and equal employment opportunity, the litigious quality of relations has grown in many relationships.

THE UNIONIZATION PROCESS

Legal Basis

The Wagner or National Labor Relations Act of 1935 affirmed the right of all employees to engage in union activities, to organize, and to bargain collectively without interference or coercion from management. It also created the National Labor Relations Board to supervise representation elections and to investigate charges of unfair labor practices by management. The Taft-Hartley Act of 1947 reaffirmed these rights and, in addition, specified unfair labor practices *both* for management and for unions. These are shown in Table 13-2. The act was later amended (by the Landrum-Griffin Act of 1959) to add the *secondary boycott* as an unfair labor practice. A secondary boycott occurs when a union appeals to firms or other unions to stop doing business with an employer who sells or handles a struck product.

A so-called free-speech clause in the act specifies that management has the right to express its opinion about unions or unionism to employees, provided that it

■ **TABLE 13-2**

UNFAIR LABOR PRACTICES FOR MANAGEMENT AND UNIONS UNDER THE TAFT-HARTLEY ACT OF 1947

Management

1. Interference with, coercion of, or restraint of employees in their right to organize
2. Domination of, interference with, or illegal assistance of a labor organization
3. Discrimination in employment because of union activities
4. Discrimination because the employee has filed charges or given testimony under the act
5. Refusal to bargain in good faith
6. "Hot cargo" agreements: refusals to handle another employer's products because of that employer's relationship with the union

Union

1. Restraint or coercion of employees who do not want to participate in union activities
2. Any attempt to influence an employer to discriminate against an employee
3. Refusal to bargain in good faith
4. Excessive, discriminatory membership fees
5. Make-work or featherbedding provisions in labor contracts that require employers to pay for services that are not performed
6. Use of pickets to force an organization to bargain with a union, when the organization already has a lawfully recognized union
7. "Hot cargo" agreements: that is, refusals to handle, use, sell, transport, or otherwise deal in another employer's products[9]

does not threaten or promise favors to employees to obtain antiunion actions. The Taft-Hartley Act covers most private-sector employers and nonmanagerial employees, except railroad and airline employees (they are covered under the Railway Labor Act of 1926). Federal government employees are covered by the Civil Service Reform Act of 1978. That act affirmed their right to organize and to bargain collectively over working conditions, established unfair labor practices both for management and unions, established the Federal Labor Relations Authority to administer the act, authorized the Federal Services Impasse Panel to take whatever action is necessary to resolve impasses in collective bargaining, and prohibited strikes in the public sector.

The Organizing Drive

There are three ways to kick off an organizing campaign: (1) Employees themselves may begin it, (2) employees may request that a union begin one for them, or (3) in some instances, national and international unions contact employees in organizations that have been *targeted* for organizing. In all three cases, employees are asked to sign *authorization cards* that designate the union as the employees' exclusive representative in bargaining with management.

Well-defined rules govern organizing activities:

1. Employee organizers may solicit fellow employees to sign authorization cards on company premises but not during working time.
2. Outside organizers cannot solicit on premises *if* a company has an existing policy of prohibiting all forms of solicitation and if that policy has been enforced consistently.[50]
3. Management representatives can express their views about unions through speeches to employees on company premises. However, they are legally prohibited from interfering with an employee's freedom of choice concerning union membership.

The organizing drive usually continues until the union obtains signed authorization cards from 30 percent of the employees. At that point it can petition the National Labor Relations Board (NLRB) for a representation election. If the union secures authorization cards from more than 50 percent of the employees, however, it may ask management *directly* for the right to exclusive representation. Usually the employer refuses, and then the union petitions the NLRB to conduct an election.

The Bargaining Unit

When the petition for election is received, the NLRB conducts a hearing to determine the appropriate (collective) bargaining unit; that is, *the group of employees eligible to vote in the representation election.* Sometimes labor and management agree jointly on the appropriate bargaining unit. When they do not, then the NLRB must determine the unit. The NLRB is guided in its decision, especially if there is no previous history of bargaining between the parties, by a concept called "community of interest." That is, the NLRB will define a unit that reflects the shared interests of the employees involved. Such elements include: similar wages, hours, and working conditions; the physical proximity of employees to each other; common supervision; the amount of interchange of employees within the proposed unit; and the degree of integration of the employer's production process or operation.[31] Under the Taft-Hartley Act, however, professional employees cannot be forced into a bargaining unit with nonprofessionals without their majority consent.

The *size* of the bargaining unit is critical both for the union and for the employer because it is strongly related to the outcome of the representation election. The larger the bargaining unit, the more difficult it is for the union to win. In fact, if a bargaining unit contains several hundred employees, it is almost invulnerable.[30]

The Election Campaign

Emotions on both sides run high during a representation election campaign. However, management typically is unaware that a union campaign is underway until most or all of the cards have been signed. At that point, management has some tactical advantages over the union. It can use company time and premises to stress the positive aspects of the current situation, and it can emphasize the costs of unionization and the loss of individual freedom that may result from collective representation. Supervisors may hold informal meetings to emphasize these anti-union themes. However, certain practices by management are prohibited by law, such as:

1. Physical interference, threats, or violent behavior toward union organizers
2. Interference with employees involved with the organizing drive
3. Discipline or discharge of employees for pro-union activities
4. Promises to provide or withhold future benefits depending on the outcome of the representation election

Unions are also prohibited from unfair labor practices (see Table 13-2), such as coercing or threatening employees if they fail to join the union. In addition, the union can picket the employer *only* if (1) the employer is not presently unionized, (2) the petition for election has been filed with the NLRB in the past 30 days, and (3) a representation election has not been held during the previous year. Unions tend to emphasize two themes during organizing campaigns:

- The union's ability to help employees satisfy their economic and personal needs
- The union's ability to improve working conditions

The campaign tactics of management and the union are monitored by the NLRB. If the NLRB finds that either party engaged in unfair labor practices during the campaign, the election results may be invalidated and a new election conducted. However, a federal appeals court has ruled that the NLRB cannot *force* a company to bargain with a union that is not recognized by a majority of the workers, even if the company has made "outrageous" attempts to thwart unionization.[74] Earlier court rulings did allow the NLRB automatically to certify the union as the sole representative of the bargaining unit if evidence showed that management had interfered directly with the representation election process. This ruling may therefore indicate a change in sentiment toward labor by the courts.

The Representation Election and Certification

If management and the union jointly agree on the size and composition of the bargaining unit, then a representation election occurs shortly thereafter. However, if management does not agree, then a long delay may ensue. Since such delays often erode rank-and-file union support, they work to management's advantage.[56] Not surprisingly, therefore, few organizations agree with unions on the size and composition of the bargaining unit. In 1983, for example, the NLRB had a backlog of 1336 cases that resulted in delays of up to 2 years before representation elections could be held. This situation led one union representative to describe such tactics by management as the "ultimate antiunion weapon."[45]

When a date for the representation election is finally established, the NLRB conducts a *secret ballot* election. If the union receives a majority of the ballots *cast* (not a majority of votes from members of the bargaining unit), then the union becomes certified as the exclusive bargaining representative of all employees in the unit. Once a representation election is held, regardless of the outcome, no further elections can be held in that bargaining unit for *1 year*. The entire process is shown graphically in Figure 13-1.

The records of elections won and lost by unions and management have changed drastically from the 1950s to the 1980s. In the 1950s, unions won over 70 percent of representation elections. By the late 1980s, that figure had slipped to 45 percent.[44]

The Decertification of a Union

If a representation election results in union certification, the first thing many employers want to know is when and how they can *decertify* the union. Under NLRB rules, an incumbent union can be decertified if a majority of employees within the bargaining unit vote to rescind the union's status as their collective bargaining agent in another representation election conducted by the NLRB.[62]

Since decertification is most likely to occur the first year or so after certification, unions will often insist on multiyear contracts to insulate themselves against decertification. Once the terms and duration of the labor contract are agreed to by both parties, the employer is obligated to recognize the union and to follow the provisions of the contract for the stipulated contract period. The American Federation of Labor and Congress of Industrial Organizations (AFL-CIO), a 14-

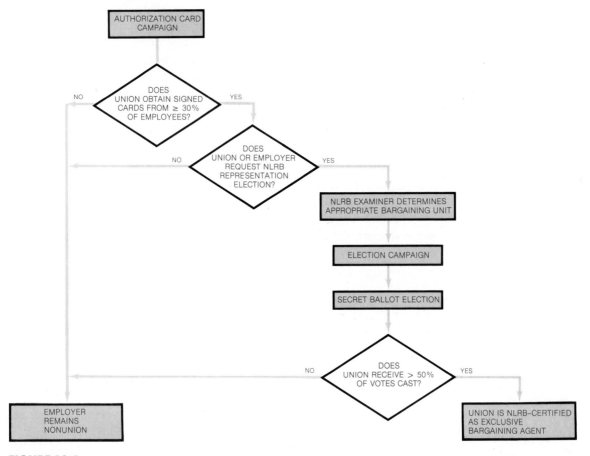

FIGURE 13-1

Steps involved and decisions to be made in a union organizing campaign.

million member federation of local, national, and international unions in the United States, estimates that even after winning a certification election, unions are unable to sign contracts a third of the time. For example, after the Service Employees International Union won a 1981 election at the Hyatt Regency Hotel in New Orleans, it took the union 5 years to negotiate its first contract. By then, most of the original workers had left the hotel, and the union was decertified within 7 months.[36]

A petition for decertification must be supported by evidence that at least 30 percent of employees in the bargaining unit *want* a decertification election. NLRB cases indicate that two or more of the following types of evidence are necessary:

- Employees have verbally repudiated the union.
- There is a marked decline in the number of employees who subscribe to union dues checkoff, and hence a minority of employees remain on checkoff.
- A majority of employees did not support the union during a strike.

- The union has become less and less active as a representative of employees.
- There was substantial turnover among employees subsequent to certification.
- The union has admitted a lack of majority support.

As with certification elections, once a decertification election is held, a full year must elapse before another representation election can take place.

Once a union is legally certified as the exclusive bargaining agent for workers, the next task is to negotiate a contract that is mutually acceptable to management and labor. In our next section we examine this process in more detail.

COLLECTIVE BARGAINING: CORNERSTONE OF AMERICAN LABOR RELATIONS

Origins of Negotiation in America

The first American strike occurred in the late eighteenth century (the Philadelphia cordwainers), and many other "turnouts" followed during the first half of the nineteenth century. These disputes were neither preceded by nor settled by negotiation. *Negotiation* is a two-party transaction whereby both parties intend to resolve a conflict.[25] Employers unilaterally established a scale of wages. If the wages were unacceptable, journeymen drew up a higher scale, sometimes inserting it into a Bible on which each swore that he or she would not work for less. The scale was presented to the employer, and if he or she did not agree, the workers "turned out" and stayed out until one side or the other caved in. There was no counterproposal, no discussion, no negotiation.

Horace Greeley, who was simultaneously a union sympathizer and an employer, found a better way. In 1850 he told a workers' mass meeting in Tammany Hall, "I do not agree that the journeymen should dictate a scale, but they should get the employers to agree to some scale." A few years later Greeley proposed that workers come to negotiations with statistics and arguments supporting the fairness of their cause. He set the United States on the course known to the twentieth century as collective bargaining.[72]

The Art of Negotiation

What constitutes a "good" settlement? To be sure, the best outcome of negotiations occurs when both parties win. Sometimes negotiations fall short of this ideal. A really bad bargain is when both lose, yet this is a risk that is inherent in the process. Despite its limitations, abuses, and hazards, negotiation has become an indispensable process in free societies in general and in the American labor movement in particular. The fact is that negotiation is the most effective device thus far invented for realizing common interests while compromising conflicting interests.[72] Any practice that threatens the process of collective bargaining will be resisted vigorously by organized labor.

In general, there are two postures that the parties involved in bargaining might assume: win-lose and win-win. In win-lose, or distributive, bargaining, the goals of the parties initially are irreconcilable—or at least they appear that way. Central to the conflict is the belief that there is a limited, controlled amount of key resources available—a "fixed pie" situation. Both parties may want to be the winner; both may want more than half of what is available.[42]

In contrast, in win-win, or integrative, bargaining, the goals of the parties are not mutually exclusive. If one side pursues its goals, this does not prohibit the other side from achieving its own goals. One party's gain is not necessarily at the other party's expense. The fundamental structure of an integrative bargaining situation is that it is possible for both sides to achieve their objectives.[70] While the conflict initially may appear to be win-lose to the parties, discussion and mutual exploration usually will suggest win-win alternatives.

How do skilled negotiators actually behave? In one study skilled negotiators were defined in terms of three criteria: (1) they were rated as effective by both sides, (2) they had a "track record" of significant success, and (3) they had a low incidence of "implementation" failures. Of the 48 skilled negotiators studied, 17 were union representatives, 12 were management representatives, 10 were contract negotiators, and 9 were classified as "other." The behavior of this group was then compared to that of an "average" group over 102 negotiating sessions. The following areas were assessed:[49]

- *Planning time.* No significant difference between the groups.
- *Exploration of options.* Skilled negotiators considered a wider range of outcomes or options for action (5.1 per issue) than average ones (2.6 per issue).
- *Common ground.* Skilled negotiators gave over 3 times as much attention to finding common ground areas as did average negotiators.
- *Long-term versus short-term orientation.* The skilled group made twice as many comments of a long-term nature as did the average group.
- *Setting limits.* The average negotiators tended to plan their objectives around a fixed point (e.g., "We aim to settle at 81"). Skilled negotiators were much more likely to plan in terms of upper and lower limits—to think in terms of ranges.
- *Sequence and issue planning.* Average negotiators tended to link issues in sequence (A then B then C then D), whereas skilled negotiators tended to view issues as independent and not linked by sequence. The advantage: *flexibility*.

Face-to-Face Negotiating Behavior

- *Irritators.* Certain words and phrases that are commonly used during negotiations have negligible value in persuading the other party, but do cause irritation. One of the most prevalent is "generous offer," used by a negotiator to describe his or her own proposal. Average negotiators used irritators more than 4 times more often than did skilled negotiators.
- *Counter proposals.* During bargaining, one party frequently puts forward a proposal and the other party immediately counters. Skilled negotiators make

immediate counter proposals significantly less frequently than do average negotiators.

■ *Argument dilution.* If one party has five reasons for doing something, is this more persuasive than having only one reason? Apparently not. Skilled negotiators used an average of 1.8 reasons; average negotiators used 3.0.

■ *Reviewing the negotiation.* Over two-thirds of the skilled negotiators claimed they *always* set aside some time after a negotiation to review it and to consider what they had learned. In contrast, just under half of average negotiators made the same claim.

What's the bottom line in all this? If you want to become a win-win negotiator, these are the behaviors to imitate or avoid.

Preparation for Negotiations

Like any other competitive activity, physical or mental, the outcome of collective bargaining is influenced significantly by the preparation that precedes actual negotiations. What's worse, mistakes made during union-management negotiations are not easily corrected. Although there is no single "best" set of prebargaining activities or an optimum lead time to conduct them, the model shown in Figure 13-2 may provide a useful guide for planning.

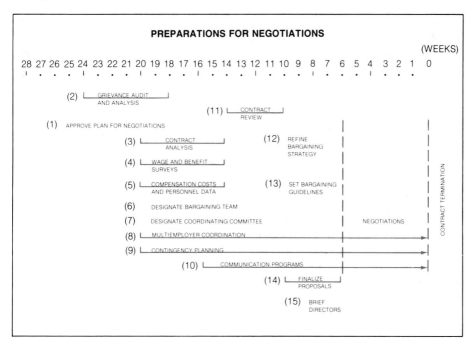

FIGURE 13-2

Activities and lead times involved in preparation for negotiations.

In a general sense, planning for subsequent negotiations begins when the previous round of bargaining ends. However, as Figure 13-2 indicates, the formal process begins about 6 months (roughly 24 weeks) prior to the expiration of the current labor agreement. It includes the following 15 activities:[47]

1. *Approve the plan for negotiation* with top management, identifying management's objectives, intermediate and long-term plans, significant changes in the production mix, major technological innovations, and so forth.

2. *Conduct an audit and analysis of grievances* under the existing contract to provide such information as the number of grievances by section of the contract, interpretations of contract provisions through grievance settlements and arbitration awards, and weaknesses in contract language or provisions. One such analysis is shown in Table 13-3.

3. *Contract analysis* includes a section-by-section comparison with other benchmark collective bargaining agreements. This is particularly important if the agreements tend to establish patterns in an industry. In addition, a review of union demands during prior negotiations may help identify areas of mounting interest.

■ **TABLE 13·3**
ANALYSIS OF 2 YEARS OF GRIEVANCES IN ONE COMPANY

Type of grievance	Total
Temporary layoff benefits	98
Transfer clause	64
Supervisor working	60
Noncontractual and local agreement	32
Discharge and discipline	27
Discrimination for union activities	26
Overtime pay	20
Overtime equalization	13
Call-out pay	11
Safety and welfare (safety shoes)	9
Contractor doing bargaining-unit work	9
Pension, supplemental unemployment benefits, and insurance	7
New job rate	6
Daily upgrade	5
Holiday pay	4
Schedule change	3
Report pay	3
Timeliness of grievance	2
Seniority	1
Total grievances during contract	400

4. *Wage and benefit surveys of competitors*, both union and nonunion, are essential. Data on changes in the cost of living should be included, along with an assessment of the structure and operation of employee benefits. These data should be interpreted with respect to the current and projected composition of the workforce: for example, by age and sex.

5. *Compensation costs and personnel data* should be presented in a form that allows management to determine changes in costs. For example:

- Demographic profile of the workforce by sex, age, race, seniority group, shift, and job classification.

- Wage payments and premiums: current rates, overtime premiums, shift differential payments, report-in and call-in payments. In recent years employers in aerospace, steel, auto, telephone, and other industries have been trying to substitute annual (or "lump-sum") bonus checks for raises, as a way of controlling labor costs. In companies such as Boeing, workers have been receiving them since 1983, and they have become a way of life.[67] Figure 13-3 illustrates the effect of bonuses versus raises over a 6-year period.

- Benefit payments: pay for sickness, vacations, holidays, and civic duties, and premiums for pensions, medical, and disability insurance coverage. (An example of one such calculation, costing out a holiday, is shown in Figure 13-4.)

- The costs of benefits that are required by law: unemployment insurance, workers' compensation, Social Security.

Since 1983, Boeing Company employees have received bonuses totaling 31% of their gross pay instead of wage increases. For a full-time worker making $12 an hour, these bonuses totaled about $7,740; if the annual bonuses had been wage increases instead, the employee's additional income would have been about $25,940. Shown are annual earnings in thousands.

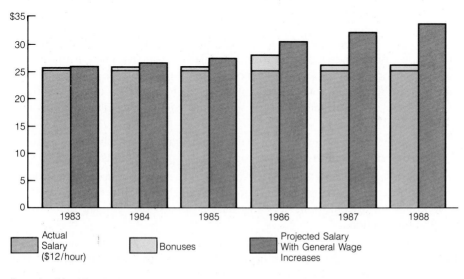

Source: Association of Machinists and Aerospace Workers

FIGURE 13-3

Bonuses versus raises: the trade-off. (*Source:* L. Uchitelle, Boeing's fight over bonuses. *The New York Times*, October 12, 1989, p. D1. Copyright © 1989 by The New York Times Company. Reprinted by permission.)

Average holiday workforce per plant:

  8 first shift, 3 second shift, 3 third shift = 14 workers on, 106 off

    14 workers × 13 plants × 8 hr × $22.00* = $32,032

    106 nonworkers × 13 plants × 8 hr × $11 = $121,264

Total hours worked per year by workforce:

  120 workers/plant × 13 plants × 2080 annual hours/worker = 3,244,800 hr/work year

Cost for holiday workers:

  $$\frac{\$32,032}{3,244,800} = .010 \text{ cent}$$

Cost for nonworkers who are paid:

  $$\frac{\$121,264}{3,244,800} = .037 \text{ cent}$$

Total cost of each holiday:

  .010 + .037 = .047 cent/hr

—————

*Normal $11/hr × double time.

FIGURE 13-4
Costing out a holiday.

- Data on worker performance, including absenteeism, layoffs, promotions, transfers, paid time for union activities, and leaves of absence. (For more detailed information on labor contract costing, see ref. 8.)

6. *Designate a bargaining team* on the basis of technical knowledge, experience, and personality. Include members from line management (not the CEO), human resources-labor relations staff, and finance-accounting (to provide expertise in cost analysis). Unfortunately, evidence indicates that financial officers do *not* negotiate, evaluate, or even participate in major wage and benefit agreements.[20] This is a costly mistake.

7. *Designate coordinating committee* to develop bargaining guidelines for approval by top management and to monitor progress during negotiations.

8. *Provide multiemployer coordination* (as appropriate). This may range from a simple information exchange among loosely connected employers to close coordination among organizations (e.g., regional hospitals) that bargain individually with the same union.

9. *Contingency planning* is essential, for the possibility of a bargaining impasse that may lead to a strike is always present. In the event of a strike, here are the items that one company is prepared to deal with:

Benefits (strikers)	Customer service
Notification of company attorneys	Plant contacts
Continuation of operations	Media communication
Staffing (continuation of production)	Security
Notification responsibilities	Photographic record
General picket report	Strike incident report
Poststrike instructions	Reinstatement of strikers
Treatment of nonstrikers	Vendors
Strike preparation (sales, production)	

10. *Communication programs* designed to facilitate two-way communication between the bargaining team and supervisors help bring supervisors' interests into the planning process. During negotiations, informed supervisors can be an effective means of communication to nonsupervisory personnel.

11. *Contract review*, by the coordinating committee, based on all the data assembled thus far, results in an assessment of contract provisions. Particular attention should be paid to:

- Identification of important differences among contract provisions, workplace practices, and human resource policies.
- Identification of contract provisions to be revised, added, or eliminated. (Examples of ambiguous contract language that can lead to different interpretations are shown in Table 13-4. We might consider these "words to grieve by.")

12. *Refine the bargaining strategy*, once the preparatory activities are completed. The strategy established at the beginning of the planning process should be modified to reflect such factors as union demands and strategy, management's objec-

■ **TABLE 13·4**
WORDS TO GRIEVE BY

Ability	Fully	Possible
Absolutely	Habitually	Practical
Adequate	High degree	Properly
Almost	Immediately	Qualification
Capacity	Minimal	Reasonable
Completely	Minimum	Regular
Day	Necessary	Substantially equal
Equal	Normal	Sufficient number
Forthwith	Periodic	With all dispatch
Frequent		

tives, experience with multiemployer coordination, and the likelihood of a work stoppage.

13. *Set bargaining guidelines* for top management's approval. Ensure that the chief negotiator has the authority to reach a settlement within the guidelines. A procedure should also be established to modify the guidelines as needed once negotiations are underway.

14. *Finalize proposals* in writing, along with acceptable variations, to provide flexibility. Recheck the data bank for accuracy, comprehensiveness, and ease of access. Assure that notices required by contract or by labor law have been issued and acknowledged. Compile bargaining aids (e.g., a bargaining book, data reference sheets, and work sheets), and finalize arrangements for note taking and record keeping.

15. *Brief directors*, as necessary, on the planning process, guidelines, and bargaining strategy. Establish a procedure for additional briefings during negotiations and reinforce the principle that governing board members should stay out of the bargaining process.

■ **TABLE 13·5**
MAJOR SECTIONS OF A TYPICAL COLLECTIVE BARGAINING AGREEMENT

Unchallenged representation	Protection of employees
Employee rights	Continuous hours of work
Management rights	Recall pay
No strikes	Distribution of overtime
Compensation	Out-of-title work
Travel	No discrimination
Health insurance	Benefits guaranteed
Attendance and leave	Job classifications
Workers' compensation leave with pay	Promotional examinations
Payroll	Employee assistance program
Employee development and training	Employee orientation
Safety and health maintenance	Performance rating procedures
Layoff procedures	Day-care centers
Joint labor-management committees	Discipline
Seniority	Grievance and arbitration procedures
Posting and bidding for job vacancies	Resignation
Employee benefit fund	Job abandonment
Workweek and workday	Duration of agreement

Successful bargaining results in an agreement that is mutually acceptable to labor and management. Table 13-5 shows some of the major sections of a typical agreement.

Unfortunately, contract negotiations sometimes fail because the parties are not able to reach a timely and mutually acceptable settlement of the issues—economic, noneconomic, or a combination of both. When this happens, the union may strike, management may shut down operations (a lockout), or both parties may appeal for third-party involvement. Let's examine these processes in detail.

BARGAINING IMPASSES: STRIKES, LOCKOUTS, OR THIRD-PARTY INVOLVEMENT?

In every labor negotiation there exists the possibility of a strike. The right of employees to strike in support of their bargainable demands is protected by the Landrum-Griffin Act. However, there is no *unqualified* right to strike. A work stoppage by employees must be the result of a lawful labor dispute and not in violation of an existing agreement between management and the union. Strikers engaged in activities protected by law may not be discharged, but they may be replaced during the strike. Strikers engaged in activities that are not protected by law need not be rehired after the strike.[2]

Types of Strikes

As you might suspect by now, there are several different types of strikes. Let's consider the major types:

Unfair-labor-practice strikes These are caused or prolonged by unfair labor practices of the employer. Employees engaged in this type of strike are afforded the highest degree of protection under the act, and under most circumstances they are entitled to reinstatement once the strike ends. Management must exercise great caution in handling unfair-labor-practice strikes because the National Labor Relations Board will become involved and company liability can be substantial.

An economic strike This is an action by the union of withdrawing its labor in support of bargaining demands, including those for recognition or organization. Economic strikers have limited rights to reinstatement.

Unprotected strikes All remaining types of work stopages, both lawful and unlawful, are included. These include sit-down strikes, strikes in violation of federal laws (e.g., the prohibition of strikes by employees of the federal government), slowdowns, wildcat strikes, and partial walkouts. Participants in unprotected strikes may be discharged by their employers.

■ TABLE 13·6
RULES OF CONDUCT DURING A STRIKE

- ■ People working in or having any business with the organization have a right to pass freely in and out.
- ■ Pickets must not block a door, passageway, driveway, crosswalk, or other entrance or exit.
- ■ Profanity on streets and sidewalks may be a violation of state law or local ordinances.
- ■ Company officials, with the assistance of local law enforcement agents, should make every effort to permit individuals and vehicles to move in and out of the facility in a normal manner.
- ■ Union officials or pickets have a right to talk to people going in or out. Intimidation, threats, and coercion are not permitted, either by verbal remarks or by physical action.
- ■ The use of sound trucks may be regulated by state law or local ordinance with respect to noise level, location, and permit requirements.
- ■ If acts of violence or trespassing occur on the premises, officials should file complaints or seek injunctions. If you are the object of violence, sign a warrant for the arrest of the person(s) causing the violence.
- ■ Fighting, assault, battery, violence, threats, or intimidation are not permissible under the law. The carrying of knives, firearms, clubs, or other dangerous weapons may be prohibited by state law or local ordinance.

Sympathy strikes These are refusals by employees of one bargaining unit to cross a picket line of a different bargaining unit (e.g., when more than one union is functioning at an employer's plant). Although the National Labor Relations Board and the courts have recognized the right of the sympathy striker to stand in the shoes of the primary striker, the facts of any particular situation will ultimately determine the legal status of a sympathy strike.[2]

During a strike, certain rules of conduct apply to *both* parties; these are summarized in Table 13-6. In addition, certain special rules apply to management; *do not*:

- ■ Offer extra rewards to nonstrikers or attempt to withhold the "extras" from strikers once the strike has ended and some or all strikers are reinstated.
- ■ Threaten nonstrikers or strikers.
- ■ Promise benefits to strikers in an attempt to end the strike or to undermine the union.
- ■ Threaten employees with discharge for taking part in a lawful strike.
- ■ Discharge nonstrikers who refuse to take over a striker's job.

MORE FIRMS KEEP OPERATING IN SPITE OF STRIKES

To an increasing number of companies, "strike" is no longer a frightening word, for they are prepared to continue operating right through a labor walkout. Highly automated firms like American Telephone & Telegraph Company have been operating through strikes for years, but in today's economic climate, where many labor-intensive firms such as Magic Chef, Inc., and Whirlpool Corporation truly believe that their survival depends on not giving in to union demands, such a strategy is revolutionary. Although union officials criticize these management tactics, such actions are producing a flourishing business for security firms. The security firms provide companies with armored cars, vans, and guards to protect nonstriking workers during labor disputes. For example, one security firm helped Dannon Company, the yogurt maker, maintain operations at several New York area plants during a series of strikes by members of the Teamsters union. The security firm provided about 100 guards to escort company trucks. The guards do not carry weapons, but they are armed with cameras. When strikers know that they will be photographed, there tends to be a lot less violence. The cost for the 14-week security service: over $1 million.[22]

Labor's ultimate weapon, the strike, is mostly failing. Automation, recent court decisions, growing antiunion sentiment, and a pool of unemployed workers willing to break a strike make it easier for employers to defeat a walkout.[34] As a result, the number of strikes and lockouts decreased steadily throughout the 1980s. Today, only about 0.02 percent of all work days in the United States are lost due to industrial conflict.[7] Thus when 100 workers at Ludington News Company, a magazine and book distributor, went on strike, 500 people mobbed the plant. They taunted picketers with the chant, "We want your job," as they shoved and grabbed for job applications. The specter of losing jobs forced the union back to the bargaining table.[37]

Proposed alternatives to strikes, including corporate campaigns and in-plant slowdowns, have had mixed success. During a slowdown, while workers adhere to the minimums of their job requirements, they continue to get paid, thereby frustrating management, but such a "work-to-rule" strategy could backfire in the long run; if productivity suffers a prolonged decline and companies fail to meet production schedules, competitors will move in quickly. Then everybody loses. Companies are fighting back by retaliating in kind, firing activist employees and in some cases locking out the entire workforce. A recent NLRB decision that permits companies to replace locked-out workers with temporary employees has strengthened management's hand.[35]

Management's antiunion tactics have been quite successful, but this does not absolve management of the responsibility to treat workers with dignity and respect, to avoid arrogance, and to recognize that it is hard to give up gains that were so difficult to earn in the first place.

■

The Increasingly Bitter Nature of Strikes

Although the number of strikes dropped dramatically during the 1980s, their intensity and general "nastiness" has escalated significantly. Unfair labor practices both by management and labor seem more and more common. For example, when Local 376 of the UAW engaged in a legal strike against the Colt Firearms Co., a judge ruled that the company engaged in dozens of unfair labor practices. It changed working conditions, failed to bargain in good faith, offered to settle separately with employees who quit the union, and rejected the union's offer to have strikers return to work under terms of their old contract. Although the company kept its plants operating by using replacement workers and about 200 union members who crossed the picket lines, a judge ordered that 800 strikers be reinstated in their old jobs.[10]

When the United Mine Workers struck Pittston Co., the company hired replacements and cut off the miners' health-care benefits. Over the course of a bitter 9-month strike, the company was forced to spend about $20 million in security, and the union accumulated $65 million in court fines related to picket-line violence and other violations of court injunctions.[63] By any stretch of the imagination, could this be considered "win-win" negotiating? A similar pattern of violence ensued in the 1990 strikes at Greyhound, Inc., and the *New York Daily News*. When workers see their jobs being lost to replacement workers, violence—including sniper fire, smashed windshields, and threats against substitute workers—often follows. At the *Daily News* strike, the paper itself became a weapon in the war, as one headline pleaded, "Call Off the Thugs."[28,29]

A 1990 Supreme Court decision in *NLRB v. Curtin Matheson Scientific, Inc.*, may undermine a common management strategy. The decision upheld the board's policy that a company cannot oust a striking union by hiring replacement workers and asserting that the new employees don't support the union. Such a policy had been an effective weapon for management because a company is not required to recognize a union that is not supported by a majority of its employees. In short, employers can't eliminate unions simply by replacing the union workers.[73]

What remains unclear is the extent to which the bitterness of strikes will be reduced. In many ways, broader forces are at work, as both companies and their workers are caught in the maw of an economic vise, the jaws of which represent domestic and international competition.

Lockouts

When a collective bargaining agreement has expired and an employer's purpose is to put economic pressure on a union to settle a contract on terms favorable to the employer, it is legal for an employer to lock out its employees.[48] It also is legal for a company to replace the locked-out workers with temporary replacements in order to continue operating during the lockout. However, the use of *permanent* replacements (without first consulting the union) is not permissible, according to the National Labor Relations Board, because such action would completely destroy the bargaining unit and represent an unlawful withdrawal of recognition of a duly designated union.[48] Thus when BASF Corp. ended a 5.5-year lockout of the Oil, Chemical, and Atomic Workers union from its sprawling chemical complex in Geismar, Louisiana, in late 1989, the two parties agreed to a 3-year contract. The settlement affected 110 workers, who were reinstated in their old jobs. However, at the time of the lockout in 1984, the union represented 370 workers at the 1200-employee plant.[4]

Third-Party Involvement

A bargaining impasse occurs when the parties are unable to move further toward settlement. In an effort to resolve the impasse, a neutral third party may become involved. In most private-sector negotiations, the parties have to agree *voluntarily* before any third-party involvement can be imposed on them. Because employees in the public sector are prohibited by law from striking, the use of third parties is more prevalent there.[17]

Three general types of third-party involvement are common: mediation, fact finding, and interest arbitration. Each becomes progressively more constraining on the freedom of the parties.

Mediation Mediation is a process by which a neutral third party attempts to help the parties in dispute to reach a settlement of the issues that divide them. It ordinarily does not involve the neutral third party acting as a judge, deciding the resolution of the dispute (a process referred to as "arbitration").[48] Rather, mediation involves persuasion, opening communications, allowing readjustment and reassessment of bargaining stances, and making procedural suggestions (e.g., scheduling, conducting, and controlling meetings; establishing or extending deadlines).

There is no set time when a mediator will go in and attempt to resolve a dispute. By law the Federal Mediation and Conciliation Service must be notified 30 days prior to the expiration of all labor contracts. But some unions, such as the United Auto Workers, traditionally refuse mediation, and so many others manage to settle by themselves that the agency estimates that it is involved in only 8000 to 9000 of the country's 100,000 yearly labor negotiations. However, their public-sector caseload has been growing sharply.[46]

Mediators have two restrictions on their power: (1) They are involved by invitation only, and (2) their advice lacks even so much as the umpire's option of throwing someone out of the game. Some will do almost anything to get a settlement.

When 55,000 aerospace workers struck Boeing Corp., Douglas Hammond, the federal mediator, actually stepped outside his usual role as a neutral middleman and devised the agreement that resolved the strike. There was tremendous pressure to do *something*. In the Seattle area, personal income had slid $30 million a week during the strike, the White House cited the stoppage as a factor in lower retail sales and industrial production indicators, and calls from the secretary of labor and the Pentagon were becoming routine. Even the U.S. trade deficit was affected because of Boeing's role as a leading exporter.

Had the effort backfired, Mr. Hammond's standing would have been compromised, and negotiations thrown back to square one. Why did he succeed? According to the president of Machinists District 751: "In the negotiating room, Doug Hammond didn't duck. He took a bold stand and I admire him." Added Boeing's top negotiator: "He seems to know the timing, when to separate us and when to get us face-to-face. I trust him, and that's the bottom line" (ref. 71, p. B11).

Fact finding Fact finding is a dispute resolution mechanism that is commonly used in the public sector at the state and local government levels. Disputes over the terms of collective bargaining agreements are more common at these levels since such bargaining ordinarily includes subjects such as pay and benefits that are excluded from bargaining with the federal government.

In a fact-finding procedure, each party submits whatever information it believes is relevant to a resolution of the dispute. A neutral fact finder then makes a study of the evidence and prepares a report on the facts. This procedure is often useful where the parties disagree over the truthfulness of the information each is using.[48]

Actually, the term "fact finding" is a misnomer. This is because fact finders often proceed, with statutory authority, to render a public recommendation of a reasonable settlement. In this respect, fact finding is similar to mediation. However, neither fact finding nor mediation necessarily results in a contract between management and labor. Consequently, the parties often resort to arbitration of a dispute, either as a matter of law (compulsory arbitration) or by mutual agreement between union and management (interest arbitration).

Interest arbitration Like fact finding, interest arbitration is used primarily in the public sector. However, arbitration differs considerably from mediation and fact finding. As one author noted: "While mediation assists the parties to reach their own settlement, arbitration hears the positions of both and decides on binding settlement terms. While fact finding would recommend a settlement, arbitration dictates it" (ref. 17, p. 323).

Interest arbitration is controversial for at least two reasons. One, imposition of interest arbitration eliminates the need for the parties to settle on their own because if they reach an impasse, settlement by an outsider is certain. Two, many municipal employers apparently feel that arbitrators have been too generous in the awards made to public employee unions. As a result, some states now specify the factors arbitrators must consider in making awards. Some of these, such as comparable wage rates, are items favored by unions; others, such as productivity and the ability of the employer to pay, are items favored by management.[48]

When the Strike Is Over

The period of time immediately after a strike is critical, since an organization's problems are not over when the strike is settled. There is the problem of conflict between strikers and their replacements (if replacements were hired) and the accommodation of strikers to the workplace. After an economic strike is settled, the method of reinstatement is best protected by a written *memorandum of agreement* with the union that outlines the intended procedure. A key point of consideration in any strike aftermath is misconduct by some strikers. To refuse reinstatement for such strikers following an economic strike, management must be able to present evidence (e.g., photographs) to prove the misconduct.

The most important human aspect at the end of the strike is the restoration of harmonious working relations as soon as possible so that full operations can be resumed. A letter or a speech to employees welcoming them back to work can help this process along, as can meetings with supervisors indicating that no resentment or ill will is to be shown toward returning strikers. In practice, this may be difficult to do. However, keep this in mind:

Nothing is gained by allowing vindictiveness of any type in any echelon of management.

The burden of maintaining healthy industrial relations now lies with the organization.

There is always another negotiation ahead and rancor has no place at any bargaining table. (ref. 2, p. 22)

TRENDS IN COLLECTIVE BARGAINING

A 5-year study of the financial economics of basic industries in the United States—steel, meat packing, railroads, and trucking—concluded that management and labor have bargained their way into an economic corner. They have set wages and benefits at levels far beyond the ability of many companies to pay. Had the escalation not occurred, many mature industries would not suffer as they now do, and they would have access to the capital necessary to modernize. In the words of the study's author:

I believe that bargaining decisions that have resulted in a rising standard of living and economic health for employees—and that have satisfied the short-term concerns of managers—have also destroyed the economic structures of many mature industries. In labor contracts, managers have bargained away their competitiveness on the assumption that if every domestic company faced the same wage structure, none would suffer a competitive disadvantage. The consumer would pay for the consequences—not labor, management, or the shareholders. But the consumer has not paid. (ref. 20, p. 131)

Whether companies are responding to domestic or international competition, of one thing we can be certain: Over the long term, changes in the makeup of the U.S. labor movement seem inevitable. As John R. Opel, former president of IBM, has noted, "Everybody knows that you're in a world market. You better be prepared to compete as a world-class competitor."[26]

Changes in the Economic Environment

While the impact of foreign competition on U.S. firms is well known, three other changes have also affected the course of collective bargaining in recent years: nonunion domestic competition, deregulation, and recession. New domestic competitors that began and managed to remain unorganized have produced low-cost market competition, which, in turn, has put downward pressure on union wage rates. This has occurred even in industries that are virtually free from foreign competition, such as meatpacking.[7]

The deregulation of many product markets created two key challenges to existing union relationships. One, it made market entry very much easier, as in over-the-road trucking, airlines, and telecommunications. Two, under regulation, management had little incentive to cut labor costs, because high labor costs could be passed on to consumers; conversely, labor-cost savings could not be used to gain a competitive advantage in the product market. Under deregulation, however, even major airlines (which are almost entirely organized) found that low costs translated into low fares and a competitive advantage. As a result, all carriers need to match the lowest costs of their competitors by matching their labor contracts.[7]

Finally, the severity of the recession in the early 1980s put added pressure on firms to reduce labor costs in order to survive. To management, concessions represented a ready means to improve cash flow. To unions, layoffs decimated their ranks, with the United Auto Workers and the United Steelworkers losing about half their memberships. In many unions, therefore, the focus of bargaining shifted to emphasize job security to reduce the risk of job loss.

High-Priority Issues for Management and Labor in the 1990s

Given the changes noted above, management's top priority is to control the growth of labor costs. To do so, companies are pushing for greater cost sharing of health-care expenses, weakening of cost-of-living clauses, greater links between pay and corporate performance, and more emphasis on lump-sum bonuses that don't step up the wage base. They are also trying to increase flexibility by securing changes in restrictive work rules. Frequently such changes lead to reductions in the numbers of employees needed to staff ongoing operations.

Unions, on the other hand, are seeking to phase out two-tier wage schemes (which set lower pay for new employees), to resist cuts in health-care benefits, and to gain improved job security (maintenance of employment at the same firm) and "employment security" for their members. In the latter approach, a company that is laying off a worker would train him or her for another job and try to place that worker at another job.[27]

Recent Bargaining Outcomes

In general terms, median first-year wage raises increased to 3.4 percent on 1089 labor contracts in 1989, from 2.7 percent in 1988. Wage freezes, lump-sum bonuses, and two-tier wage scales (only 6 percent of all agreements) showed up less often, but agreements explicitly covering child care tripled to 41.[39,64]

As for specific agreements, consider the contracts (that run until 1993) between 450,000 UAW workers and GM, Chrysler, and Ford. The companies won changes in work rules that provide greater flexibility to move workers from job to job as conditions dictate, but they failed to gain any immediate reduction in health-care costs. Workers won a 3 percent base wage increase in the first year and 3 percent lump-sum payments in the second and third years of the contract, as well as increases for current and future retirees. Finally, the contracts provide income guarantees for workers laid off from factories shut down for more than 36 weeks during the 3-year period of the contract because of slumping sales.[66]

As another example, consider the agreement between Uniroyal Goodrich Tire Co. and the United Rubber Workers at the company's 71-year-old Eau Claire, Wisconsin, plant. The union agreed to a 63-cent-an-hour reduction in pay, one less vacation week, three fewer annual holidays, no cost-of-living increases, and extensive work-rule changes. Why did the union make such concessions? Uniroyal promised to guarantee the jobs of the workers during the life of the contract.[27]

Labor-Management Cooperation

Make no mistake about it: The recent popularity of cooperation stems largely from the sweeping changes in the economic environment that have occurred over the last decade. Another reason is new technology—factory automation, robotics, and more modern production systems. Cooperation offers a pragmatic approach to problems that threaten the survival of companies, the job and income security of their employees, and the institutional future of their unions.[58]

Despite the economic imperatives, however, there is considerable resistance to joint cooperative efforts. Here are four major obstacles: managers who will not accept the legitimacy of a union, union officials who are ideologically opposed to cooperating with management, internal union politics that impede cooperation with an employer, and fears of employees and union officials that their suggestions may lead to the elimination of their jobs.[53]

A final obstacle is lack of trust—on both sides. Consider the auto industry, where each side has good reason to be wary of the other. At GM's big luxury car assembly plant in Lake Orion, Michigan, more than 120 people work in joint labor-management programs, but the plant has one of the worst labor relations records in the company. In fact, worker opposition forced plant management to abandon an effort to get employees to operate in teams to improve efficiency and quality. Neither is the company without sin, however. In 1987 GM included a plant-closing moratorium in its contract with the UAW. But by calling closedowns "indefinite idlings" instead of "closings," GM has closed four car plants and plans to close three truck plants by 1992. In all, GM has eliminated 1 in 10 of its UAW jobs since 1987.[52]

When cooperation works, however, it works well and often reduces the adversarial confrontations that characterize U.S. labor relations. Consider NUMMI, the joint venture between Toyota and General Motors in Fremont, California. As a result of union-management cooperation, the plant currently has fewer than 30 grievances a year, with an absenteeism rate of less than 6 percent and an unscheduled absenteeism rate of only 1 percent.[6,61]

Labor-management co-operation can work if management is willing to share information with workers and if both sides trust each other.

Institutionalizing cooperative relationships is no easy task. However, successful efforts have been characterized by features such as the following:[11,58]

- The reason for the cooperative effort remains strong.
- Benefits derived from the cooperation are distributed equitably.
- The union is perceived as instrumental in attaining program benefits.
- The cooperative effort does not infringe on traditional collective bargaining issues.
- The program does not threaten management prerogatives.
- Management has refrained from subcontracting out bargaining unit work.
- The program does not overlap the grievance procedure.
- Union leaders are not viewed as being co-opted.
- The cooperative effort is protected from the use of bargaining tactics and maneuvers.
- Union leaders continue to pursue member goals on traditional economic issues.

Current Tactics of Management and Labor

Both sides are becoming quite sophisticated in their attempts to win the minds, hearts, and votes of workers during organizing campaigns and also in response to industrial action. For example, when the UAW tried to organize Nissan's car and truck assembly plant in Smyrna, Tennessee, top Nissan officials made no public statements in the contentious organizing campaign. Instead, Nissan made antiunion employees available to journalists to explain their feelings. The company also relied on frequent and forceful antiunion broadcasts on the plant's closed-circuit television network.[41] Workers rejected the union by a 2:1 margin.

Management also is adopting aggressive antiunion tactics in response to strikes, hiring replacement workers and using lockouts. Thus when 9000 mechanics, baggage handlers, and other members of the International Association of Machinists and Aerospace Workers struck Eastern Airlines in 1989, the company declared bankruptcy. Five years previously the same approach was used by the same management team to break the unions and to reorganize Continental Airlines. In the interim, however, Congress revised the bankruptcy laws to make it impossible for a company unilaterally to abrogate its union contracts. Under current law, the company must prove economic necessity and negotiate with its unions first.[9]

In response to these tactics, unions have taken several specific actions. For example, some unions simply avoid the NLRB through so-called top-down organizing. They organize workers by pressuring companies and sometimes by embarrassing them through picketing and public appeals. In 1986, for example, 87 percent of the United Food and Commercial Workers' 82,000 new members were involved in elections that circumvented the NLRB.

The organizing tactics of unions are becoming more sophisticated as well. Unions such as the Clothing and Textile Workers are using surveys before undertaking expensive organizing campaigns. Unions such as the Airline Pilots Association and the Steelworkers are hiring investment bankers for projects ranging from examining an employer's balance sheet to buying a company, as United Airlines' pilots tried to do.[60] Finally, unions are lobbying hard for pro-labor legislation; for example, legislation that would outlaw "double-breasting," in which unionized construction firms legally transfer work to nonunion subsidiaries.[34] As these few examples demonstrate, it will be a long time before organized labor's obituary is written.

Unions are also trying to broaden their base. Thus only about 11 percent of the 1.3 million members of the Teamsters union actually drive trucks. The remainder includes workers as diverse as pilots, zookeepers, and Disney World's Mickey Mouse.

Another tactic is the *corporate campaign*. This is a system under which pressure is placed not only on the employer but also on stockholders, on boards of directors, on financial institutions that deal with a company, on customers, and on legislators to pressure the company either to recognize unions or to agree to union demands. Thus unions are attempting to achieve their ends by applying secondary pressure—pressure on others to induce them to compel the company management to agree to union demands.[54] Have unions been successful? A recent study of 10 corporate campaigns concluded that union-sponsored boycotts and attempts to influence companies through bankers, investors, and Wall Street have not been very effective—yet. But unions have succeeded in pressuring companies through a variety

IMPACT OF UNION REPRESENTATION ON PRODUCTIVITY, QUALITY OF WORK LIFE, AND THE BOTTOM LINE

Is there a link between unionization and organizational performance? Unionization of a workforce often increases control over wage levels by giving monopoly power to the union as the single seller of labor to an enterprise. It also creates a "voice" mechanism for employees by establishing negotiated grievance procedures and the right to bargain collectively.[19]

Economic studies generally show that the existence of a grievance process that acts as a check or balance on management's authority can enhance productivity. One explanation for this is that higher productivity results from lower turnover, which in turn enhances employees' knowledge of the jobs they perform.[32]

If unions actually do raise productivity, then why do managements oppose them with such vigor? The answer lies in the impact unions have on corporate profits. A number of studies support the argument that while unions may increase productivity, the wage increases associated with unionization exceed productivity gains.[32,43]

of other groups—religious professionals, community and consumer activists, and politicians.[54] The lesson? Corporations may choose to ignore this new tactic, but they do so at their peril.[51] As one analyst noted: "[Unions] have learned to trade wage concessions for stock in their companies, for seats on the board, and for ownership control."[57]

■ HUMAN RESOURCE MANAGEMENT IN ACTION
CONCLUSION

IMPROVEMENT OF QWL THROUGH POSITIVE UNION-MANAGEMENT RELATIONS

One of the members of the management group began the discussion by suggesting that the parties examine what kind of relationship they wanted and what they might do to shift away from win-lose. The plant manager asked what the union would do if management tried to change, and the union said it felt safer with win-lose.

At this point the consultant intervened to suggest that the parties were not using confrontation in a problem-solving way. It appeared as though management had been trying to resolve the conflict with the union in an arbitrary manner and via suppression. She pointed out that management seems to have discovered that "hard" does not work. People become angry, frustrated, and negatively motivated. But "soft" does not work either—the union does not respect it.

The plant manager responded that they wanted to do what was best; the "ideal" relationship that had seemed so remote before now seemed indispensable. He asked the others if they were willing to invest the time and effort necessary to achieve this kind of relationship. The employee relations director assured them that they had corporate support. They were convinced that they had no other option. So they listed five summary statements of their current thoughts and feelings and presented them to the union the next day:

1. We recognize that we have a deep win-lose orientation toward the union.
2. We want to change!
3. Barriers to overcome: Convince the union that we want to change; convince ourselves that we have the patience, skill, and convictions to change.
4. We are responsible to bring the rest of management on board.
5. We recognize the risk, but we want to resist the temptation of reverting to win-lose when things get tough.

As a suggestion for action, management recorded: "Identify concrete problems that require cooperation to solve, and develop strategies for solution of them with the union."

Members of the union group saw management's self-description as a giant step forward from its previous attitudes. They recognized that it must have been hard to initiate such drastic change, and they could not indicate strongly enough how pleased they were with that kind of shift. Members of the union group emphasized their sincere attempt to cooperate in any way in order to be able to assist in the change. Both parties realized that they would not be saying the same thing all the time, but the key was to remember the basic lessons of the seminar. This positive attitude on the part of both groups led to a desire to deal with specific details and to develop a list of outstanding issues between them that could be worked out jointly in the near future.

Five and a half years have elapsed since the seminar. Immediately after the seminar, 10 task forces were appointed to grapple with and solve problems. Each task force brought proposed solutions to the plant manager. He considered their recommendations and either approved them, modified them, or provided a full explanation for why he could not adopt them. This put the union and management on a sound basis and has led to continuing improvements at Hillside. At the time of the seminar, Hillside was eleventh in economic performance of 11 plants owned by the company. Today, Hillside is first.

SUMMARY

At a general level, the goal of unions is to improve economic and other conditions of employment. Although they have been successful over the years in achieving these goals, more recently they have been confronted with challenges that have led to some loss of membership.

IMPLICATIONS FOR MANAGEMENT PRACTICE

Given current conditions in the economic environment, a distributive (win-lose) orientation toward labor is simply inefficient. Rather, view your employees as a potential source of competitive advantage. Treat them with dignity and respect, and they will respond in kind. As for the labor movement itself, it too needs to adjust.

Employees join unions for two reasons: (1) dissatisfaction with working conditions and a belief that employees cannot change them and (2) belief that collective action will yield positive outcomes. The National Labor Relations Board, created by the Wagner Act, supervises union organizing campaigns and representation elections. If the union wins, it becomes the *sole* bargaining agent for employees.

Collective bargaining is the cornerstone of the U.S. labor movement. Anything that threatens its continued viability will be resisted vigorously by organized labor. Both sides typically prepare about 6 months in advance for the next round of negotiations. Such preparation involves an analysis of grievances, current wage and benefits costs, and the costs of proposed settlements. Unfortunately, bargaining sometimes reaches an impasse, at which point the parties may resort to a strike (workers) or a lockout (management). Alternatively, the parties may request third-party intervention in the form of mediation, fact finding, or interest arbitration. In the public sector, such intervention is usually required.

Current trends in industrial relations, such as labor-management cooperation, and new tactics used by management and labor are being fueled by changes in the economic climate. These include foreign competition, domestic nonunion competition, changes in technology, and deregulation. In view of these changes, accommodation of labor and management to each other's needs (win-win bargaining) is more appropriate than the old adversarial win-lose approach.

DISCUSSION QUESTIONS

13•1 Are the roles of labor and management inherently adversarial?

13•2 Discuss the rights and obligations of unions and management during a union organizing drive.

13•3 What are the major advantages and disadvantages of two-tier wage contracts?

13•4 Discuss key differences in the behavior of successful versus average negotiators.

13•5 Contrast the Japanese system of industrial relations to that of the United States.

13•6 Compare and contrast mediation, fact finding, and interest arbitration.

REFERENCES

1. Allen, R. E., & Keaveny, T. J. (1988). *Contemporary labor relations* (2d ed.). Reading, MA: Addison-Wesley, 1988.

2. American Society for Personnel Administration (1983). *Strike preparation manual* (rev. ed.). Berea, OH: ASPA.

3. Ayres, B. D., Jr. (1989, April 27). Coal miners' strike hits feelings that go deep. *The New York Times*, p. A16.

4. BASF is poised to end 5.5-year U.S. lockout (1989, Dec. 18). *International Herald Tribune*, p. 7.

5. Brett, J. M. (1980). Why employees want unions. *Organizational Dynamics*, **8**(4), 47–59.

6. Brown, C., & Reich, M. (1989). When does union-management cooperation work? A look at NUMMI and GM-Van Nuys. *California Management Review*, **31**, 26–41.

7. Capelli, P. (1990). Collective bargaining. In J. A. Fossum (ed.), *Employee and labor relations*. Washington, DC: Bureau of National Affairs, pp. 4-180 to 4-217.

8. Cascio, W. F. (1991). *Costing human resources: The financial impact of behavior in organizations* (3d ed.). Boston: PWS-Kent.

9. Castro, J. (1989, March 20). Eastern goes bust. *Time*, pp. 52, 53.

10. Colt told to rehire 800 strikers; back pay is to be in millions (1989, Sep. 13). *The New York Times*, p. B3.

11. Cooke, W. N. (1990). Factors influencing the effect of joint union-management programs on employee-supervisor relations. *Industrial and Labor Relations Review*, **43**, 587–603.

12. Deshpande, S. P., & Fiorito, J. (1989). Specific and general beliefs in union voting models. *Academy of Management Journal*, **32**, 883–897.

13. Dowling, P. J., & Schuler, R. S. (1990). *International dimensions of human resource management*. Boston: PWS-Kent.

14. Dunlop, J. T. (1988, May). Have the 1980's changed U.S. industrial relations? *Monthly Labor Review*, pp. 29–34.

15. Foegen, J. H. (1989). Labor unions: Don't count them out yet! *Academy of Management Executive*, **3**(1), 67–70.

16. Fossum, J. A. (1990). Employee and labor relations in an evolving environment. In J. A. Fossum (ed.), *Employee and labor relations*. Washington, DC: Bureau of National Affairs, pp. 4-1 to 4-22.

17. Fossum, J. A. (1989). *Labor relations: Development, structure, process* (4th ed.). Homewood, IL: BPI-Irwin.

18. Freedman, A. (1988, May). How the 1980's have changed industrial relations. *Monthly Labor Review*, pp. 35–38.

19. Freeman, R. B., & Medoff, J. (1984). *What do unions do?* New York: Basic Books.

20. Fruhan, W. E., Jr. (1985). Management, labor, and the golden goose. *Harvard Business Review*, **63**(5), 131–141.

21. Gifford, C. (1986). *Directory of U.S. labor organizations: 1986–87 edition*. Washington, DC: Bureau of National Affairs.

22. Greenberger, D. (1983, Oct. 11). Striking back. *The Wall Street Journal*, pp. 1, 18.

23. Greenhouse, S. (1985, Sep. 1). Reshaping labor to woo the young. *The New York Times*, pp. 1F, 6F.

24. Hamner, W. C., & Smith, F. J. (1978). Work attitudes as predictors of unionization activity. *Journal of Applied Psychology*, **63**, 415–421.

25. Hunsaker, J. S., Hunsaker, P. L., & Chase, N. (1981). Guidelines for productive negotiating relationships. *Personnel Administrator*, **26**(3), 37–40, 88.

26. Jacobsen, S. (1984, March 20). Business sees tougher labor stance. *Rocky Mountain News*, p. 1F.

27. Karr, A. R. (1988, June 29). Striking out. *The Wall Street Journal*, pp. 1, 17.

28. Kifner, J. (1990, Nov. 4). Daily News strike becomes a battle for advertisers. *The New York Times*, pp. 1, 38.

29. Kilborn, P. T. (1990, April 9). Money isn't everything in Greyhound strike. *The New York Times*, pp. A1, A12.

30. Kilgour, J. G. (1983, March–April). Union organizing activity among white-collar employees. *Personnel*, pp. 18–27.

31. Kilgour, J. G. (1978, April). Before the union knocks. *Personnel Journal*, pp. 186–192, 212, 213.

32. Kleiner, M. M. (1990). The role of industrial relations in industrial performance. In J. A. Fossum (ed.), *Employee and labor relations*. Washington, DC: Bureau of National Affairs, pp. 4-23 to 4-43.

33. Kochan, T. A. (1979). How American workers view labor unions. *Monthly Labor Review*, **103**(4), 23–31.

34. Kotlowitz, A. (1987, Aug. 28). Labor's turn. *The Wall Street Journal*, pp. 1, 14.

35. Kotlowitz, A. (1987, May 22). Labor's shift: Finding strikes harder to win, more unions turn to slowdowns. *The Wall Street Journal*, pp. 1, 7.

36. Kotlowitz, A. (1987, April 1). Grievous work. *The Wall Street Journal*, pp. 1, 12.

37. Kotlowitz, A. (1986, Oct. 13). Labor's ultimate weapon, the strike, is mostly failing. *The Wall Street Journal*, p. 6.

38. Kristol, I. (1978, Oct. 23). Understanding trade unionism. *The Wall Street Journal*, p. 27.

39. Labor letter (1990, Jan. 23). *The Wall Street Journal*, p. A1.

40. Leib, J. (1989, May 14). Unions face tough battle for members. *Denver Post*, pp. 1G, 12G.

41. Levin, D. P. (1989, July 28). Nissan workers in Tennessee spurn union's bid. *The New York Times*, pp. A1, A6.

42. Lewicki, R. J., & Litterer, J. A. (1985). *Negotiation*. Homewood, IL: Irwin.

43. Linneman, P. D., Wachter, M. L., & Carter, W. H. (1990). Evaluating the evidence on union employment and wages. *Industrial and Labor Relations Review*, **44**(1), 34–53.

44. Lipset, S. M. (1986, Dec. 18). Why do Canada's unions prosper? *The Wall Street Journal*, p. 24.

45. Lublin, J. S. (1983, Nov. 3). NLRB record backlog is said to hamper union drives, prove costly to some firms. *The Wall Street Journal*, p. 10.

46. Merry, R. W. (1979, Jan. 30). Federal mediators find their public-sector caseload growing sharply. *The Wall Street Journal*, p. 1.

47. Miller, R. L. (1978, January). Preparations for negotiations. *Personnel Journal*, pp. 36–39, 44.

48. Mills, D. Q. (1989). *Labor-management relations* (4th ed.). New York: McGraw-Hill.

49. Moran, R. T. (1987). *Getting your yen's worth: How to negotiate with Japan, Inc.* Houston: Gulf.

50. *NLRB v. Babcock & Wilcox* (1956). 105 U.S. 351.

51. Novack, J. (1987, July 13). Publish and be damned. *Forbes*, pp. 380–381.

52. Patterson, G. A. (1990, Aug. 29). Credibility gap. *The Wall Street Journal*, pp. A1, A10.

53. Pennsylvania task force says cooperation critical for labor, management in "new era" (1988, Feb. 26). *Daily Labor Report*, pp. A6, A7.

54. Perry, C. R. (1987). *Union corporate campaigns*. Philadelphia: Industrial Research Unit, Study 66, The Wharton School, University of Pennsylvania.

55. Poole, M. (1986). *Industrial relations: Origins and patterns of national diversity*. London: Routledge & Kegan Paul.

56. Prosten, W. (1979). The rise in NLRB election delays: Measuring business's new resistance. *Monthly Labor Review*, **103**(2), 39–41.

57. Salpukas, A. (1989, Sep. 3). Labor as management: Airline unions grow bold. *The New York Times*, p. 28.

58. Schuster, M. (1990). Union-management cooperation. In J. A. Fossum (ed.), *Employee and labor relations*. Washington, DC: Bureau of National Affairs, pp. 4-44–4-81.

59. Serrin, W. (1985, Dec. 5). Union at Stevens, yes; upheaval, no. *The New York Times*, p. A18.

60. Smith, R., & Valente, J. (1989, Sep. 18). Strange bedfellows. *The Wall Street Journal*, pp. A1, A8.

61. Speakers at labor law forum stress cooperation. (1988, Feb. 29). *Daily Labor Report*, p. A1.

62. Swann, J. P., Jr. (1983). The decertification of a union. *Personnel Administrator*, **28**(1), 47–51.

63. Swasy, A., & Karr, A. R. (1990, Jan. 2). Pittston, UMW tentatively set labor accord. *The Wall Street Journal*, p. A3.

64. Tomsho, R. (1990, Apr. 20). Employers and unions feeling pressure to eliminate two-tier labor contracts. *The Wall Street Journal*, pp. B1, B5.

65. Troubles of U.S. labor unions eased in 1986 (1987, Feb. 15). *The New York Times*, p. 31.

66. UAW OKs Chrysler pact, last of big 3 (1990, Nov. 20). *Denver Post*, p. B2.

67. Uchitelle, L. (1989, Oct. 12). Boeing's fight over bonuses. *The New York Times*, pp. D1, D6.

68. Union membership drops to 16.4% of employees (1990, Feb. 12). *The Wall Street Journal*, p. A1.

69. U.S. union membership shrank again in 1987 (1988, Jan. 25). *Daily Labor Report*, DLR No. 15, p. A1. Also, Union membership down, wages up (1988, Jan. 23). *Philadelphia Inquirer*, p. 5A.

70. Walton, R. E., & McKersie, R. B. (1965). *A behavioral theory of labor negotiations*. New York: McGraw-Hill.

71. Wartzman, R. (1989, Nov. 21). Seizing initiative pays off for Boeing strike mediator. *The Wall Street Journal*, pp. B1, B11.

72. Ways, M. (1979, Jan. 15). The virtues, limits, and dangers of negotiation. *Fortune*, pp. 86–90.

73. Wermiel, S. (1990, Apr. 18). Supreme Court upholds policy barring tactic used to oust a striking union. *The Wall Street Journal*, p. A3.

74. Wermiel, S. (1983, Nov. 16). NLRB can't force companies to bargain with minority unions, U.S. court rules. *The Wall Street Journal*, p. 12.

CHAPTER 14

Procedural Justice and Ethics in Employee Relations

■ HUMAN RESOURCE MANAGEMENT IN ACTION

A RADICAL EXPERIMENT AT GE: HOURLY WORKERS CONTROL A GRIEVANCE REVIEW PANEL*

"Are you crazy?" people in General Electric and in other industrial relations organizations ask when they first hear about the new Grievance Review Panel at GE's Appliance Park-East in Columbia, Maryland. They wonder how and why this nonunion facility—one of the largest in the GE chain— allows a rotating panel of three hourly employees to decide the fate of grievances. Yes, it is true that hourly employees, with a 3-to-2 majority over management, can control the results of most grievances submitted by their peers at the facility.

Why did GE undertake such a radical experiment? To answer this question, it is necessary to consider the previous decade of employee relations at the plant. As the second-largest nonunion plant in GE, located in the highly unionized Baltimore area, the plant had been a constant target of union organizers throughout the 1970s.

---

*Adapted from: R. T. Boisseau & H. Caras, A radical experiment cuts deep into the attractiveness of unions, *Personnel Administrator*, **28**(10), 1983, 76–79. Copyright, 1983. Reprinted with permission from HRMagazine (formerly Personnel Administrator) published by the Society for Human Resource Management, Alexandria, VA.

The production and quality of electric ranges and microwave ovens, as well as sound human relations programs, were severely hampered by extensive time devoted to union campaigns. During the first 8 years of the plant's operations, there were nine campaigns leading to six representation elections. GE's winning majorities were consistently under 60 percent.

More important, each election divided employees into pro- and antiunion camps, causing major morale problems from which it took months to recover. Finally management decided that the best way to put an end to the constant union battles was to make Columbia the best possible place to work.

BACKGROUND ON GRIEVANCES

For years, the Columbia plant had used a formal, written grievance procedure that allowed employees to go immediately to higher levels of management with their grievances. Even though the company had a success rate of over 40 percent (considerably higher than at most union plants), each year there was a steady decline in the use of the formal process. To some extent the decline was due to improved supervision and more consistent application of policies, but some of it also resulted from employees' lack of faith in the process. Many employees admitted honestly that they had a low regard for GE's procedure.

Management brainstormed many different ideas but finally settled on the one recommended by the plant manager at Columbia. At the time, he was the final decision maker in the grievance review process. The plant manager recommended the use of a panel of hourly employees to help him make the best possible decisions. This was the framework:

- Each of five panelists has an equal vote.
- The two management panelists can be outvoted by the three hourly members of the grievance review panel.
- Review-panel decisions are final and binding.

SKEPTICAL RESPONSES

The idea was presented to groups of managers, to first-line supervisors, and to employees. Their responses were all about the same—positive about the concept but skeptical that GE was really serious. Even more skepticism came from human resource managers at local companies and other GE plants: "How can you let yourselves be outnumbered and still maintain your right to run the business?" they invariably asked.

To that question management had a standard response: "If we have a major issue that truly divides the management and hourly members of the panel—and if we cannot convince one of the hourly people that we are right—then we must be wrong."

To explain the new concept to employees and to solicit volunteer panelists, GE scheduled an after-work review of the new procedure. Employees came and listened on their own time. They contributed to the development of the concept, and unofficially they endorsed the plan. Thirty-nine of them volunteered to join an 8-hour program to train panelists. The training was held during off-duty hours, and it emphasized the legal and ethical elements of grievance handling, problem-solving techniques, and effective listening skills. It ended with a role play of an actual grievance.

The response from the panelists was overwhelming. Even some of the most skeptical among them had a totally different perception by the end of the sessions. All were geared up and ready for the first grievance.

ADDITIONAL PUBLICITY

To explain the process further, a special edition of the *GE News*—with full details and comments from a panel of employees who had prior knowledge of the project—announced the grievance-panel idea. Second, the Management Hotline, a 60-second daily telephone commentary on items of interest in the business, encouraged people to take the training. Third, the *GE News* covered the first panel case at the plant. Fourth, a slide-tape program, developed for use at employee roundtable meetings with their supervisors, provided testimonials of how people felt after they had taken the panel training. The panel was then ready to receive its first grievant.

Challenges

1. Discuss two advantages and two disadvantages of the GE grievance review panel.
2. What else needs to be done to improve the overall industrial relations system at the GE plant?
3. The grievance review process at the GE plant is important for what it is and for what it symbolizes. We know what it is and how it works, but what does it symbolize and what does it say about management's assumptions about workers?

QUESTIONS THIS CHAPTER WILL HELP MANAGERS ANSWER

1. How can I ensure procedural justice in the resolution of conflicts between employees and managers?
2. How can I administer discipline without at the same time engendering resentment toward me or the company?
3. How do I fire people legally and humanely?
4. What should be the components of a fair information practice policy?

The chapter opening vignette illustrates another facet of labor-management accommodation: control of a grievance review panel by hourly workers rather than by management. It is another attempt to enhance the productivity and QWL of employees, although (as the case points out) it evolved only after constant union organizing campaigns. Indeed, the broad theme of this chapter is "justice on the job." We will consider alternative methods for resolving disputes, such as grievance (in union and nonunion settings) and arbitration procedures. We also examine discipline and termination in the employment context. Finally, we will examine the growing concern for employee privacy in these four areas: fair information practice in the computer age, the assessment of job applicants and employees, employee searches, and whistle-blowing. Let us begin by defining some important terms.

Some Definitions

In this chapter we are concerned with three broad issues in the context of employee relations: (1) procedural justice, (2) due process, and (3) ethical decisions about behavior.

Employee relations includes all the practices that implement the philosophy and policy of an organization with respect to employment.[23]

Justice refers to the maintenance or administration of what is just, especially by the impartial adjustment of conflicting claims or the assignment of merited rewards or punishments.[75]

Procedural justice focuses on the fairness of the procedures used to make decisions. Procedures are fair to the extent that they are consistent across persons and over time, free from bias, based on accurate information, correctable, and based on prevailing moral and ethical standards.[28]

Due process in legal proceedings provides individuals with rights such as the following: prior notice of prohibited conduct; timely procedures adhered to at each step of the procedure; notice of the charges or issues prior to a hearing; impartial judges or hearing officers; representation by counsel; opportunity to confront and to cross-examine adverse witnesses and evidence, as well as to present proof in one's own defense; notice of decision; and protection from retaliation for using a complaint procedure in a legitimate manner. These are constitutional due process rights. They protect individual rights with respect to state, municipal, or federal government processes. However, they do not normally apply to work situations. Hence, employee rights to due process are based either on a collective bargaining agreement, on legislative protections, or on procedures provided unilaterally by an employer.[77]

Ethical decisions about behavior concern one's conformity to moral standards or to the standards of conduct of a given profession or group.[65] Ethical decisions about behavior take account not only of one's own interests but also equally of the interests of those affected by the decision.[11,55]

PROCEDURAL JUSTICE IN ACTION

Union Security Clauses

Section 14b of the Taft-Hartley Act enables states to enact "right-to-work" laws that prohibit compulsory union membership (after a probationary period) as a condition of continued employment. Table 14-1 indicates that most types of such union security provisions are illegal in the 21 states that have passed right-to-work laws.

Agency shop agreements appear in about 12 percent of all collective bargaining contracts.[52] May the "service charge" for representation be used to pay for activities such as lobbying for pro-labor legislation, organizing efforts, and political activities *in addition to* collective bargaining? Nonunion-member employees of American Telephone & Telegraph Co. sued the Communications Workers of America (CWA) over this issue. The Supreme Court ruled that a union may be violating the rights of nonmembers who are required to pay agency fees for union representation if it uses those fees for political and other activities not directly related to collective bargaining. How much money goes to activities other than collective bargaining? At the trial court level, a federal judge ordered the CWA to rebate 79 percent of the agency fees it had collected one year, because the union could only prove that 21 percent of its collections were devoted to collective bargaining.[57]

■ TABLE 14·1

FORMS OF UNION SECURITY AND THEIR LEGAL STATUS IN RIGHT-TO-WORK STATES

	Legal	Illegal
Closed shop Individual must join the union that represents employees in order to be considered for employment.		X
Union shop As a condition of continued employment, an individual must join the union that represents employees after a probationary period (typically a minimum of 30 days).		X
Preferential shop Union members are given preference in hiring.		X
Agency shop Employees need not join the union that represents them, but, in lieu of dues, they must pay a service charge for representation.		X
Maintenance of membership Employee must remain a member of the union once he or she joins.		X
Checkoff Employee may request that union dues be deducted from his or her pay and be sent directly to the union.	X	

Effect of Mergers and Acquisitions on Employees:
New Company versus "Old" Union

It is no longer unusual to see bankruptcy used as a sword against unions instead of as a shield against creditors. What happens to an old union when a new company buys a failed business? The Supreme Court was asked to decide this issue in *Fall River Dyeing and Finishing Corp. v. National Labor Relations Board* (1987).[20] The Court's ruling has broad implications for corporate acquisitions.

The dispute began when an unprofitable Massachusetts textile company called Sterlingwale was closed and liquidated by the family that had owned it for more than 30 years. A customer and a former executive of Sterlingwale opened a slimmed-down version of the old business after a 7-month hiatus and renamed it the Fall River Dyeing and Finishing Corp.

The new company did not buy all the assets of Sterlingwale, such as its trade name, goodwill, or customer lists. Nor did it assume any of its liabilities. Within 6 months, however, 51 of the 105 people working at Fall River were former employees of the defunct company. After its first month of operation, Fall River's owners heard from the union that had represented Sterlingwale workers for nearly three decades. The union asked the company to negotiate a collective bargaining agreement. Management refused to talk, claiming that the local no longer represented the employees. The union charged that management violated the National Relations Act by refusing to bargain.

A divided NLRB, and later a divided U.S. Court of Appeals, held that Fall River's management had to recognize the union. The court reasoned that the union had satisfied the NLRB standards for showing that Fall River was a "successor" to Sterlingwale.

A pro-management decision by the Supreme Court would encourage acquisitions, since a new corporation would not be encumbered with any agreements that had been made by the liquidated company. Unions would be forced to start from scratch in organizing the workplace, and this would undermine the stability of collective bargaining agreements.[9]

In determining whether one company is a successor to another, the NLRB uses the following criteria:

- Has there been a substantial continuity of the same business operations?
- Does the new employer use the same plant?
- Does the alleged successor have the same or substantially the same workforce?
- Do the same jobs exist under the same working conditions?
- Does the new owner employ the same supervisors?
- Does the new employer use the same machinery, equipment, and methods of production?
- Does the new employer manufacture the same product or offer the same services?

In a 6-3 decision, the Supreme Court ruled that Fall River had a duty to bargain with the old union. It was a successor to Sterlingwale and had demonstrated a substantial continuity with the old company. An analysis of this and related cases revealed the following guiding principles in the context of a merger or an acquisition:[22]

1. A new employer, even if it is found to be a "successor," is not legally required to *adopt* its predecessor's collective bargaining agreement, although it may do so voluntarily.
2. A new employer need not hire its predecessor's employees and need not arbitrate its duty to do so.
3. A new employer may unilaterally alter the terms and conditions of employment in the unit or restructure the workplace, even in the face of unexpired collective bargaining contracts, as long as it does not adopt the unexpired contracts and alters the terms and conditions of employment *before* hiring new employees.
4. If the majority of a new employer's workforce is comprised of previously represented employees, and if the new employer does not make structural changes that alter the basic nature of the business, the new employer will be bound to bargain with the predecessor's union.

Administration of the Collective Bargaining Agreement

To many union and management officials, the real test of effective labor relations comes *after* the agreement is signed, that is, in its day-to-day administration. At that point, the major concern of the union is to obtain in practice the employee rights that management has granted on paper. The major concern of management is to establish its right to manage the business and to keep operations running.[52]

Occasionally during the life of a contract, disputes arise about the interpretation of the collective bargaining agreement, potential violations of federal or state law, violations of past practices or company rules, or violations of management's responsibility (e.g., to provide safe and healthy working conditions). In each instance, an aggrieved party may file a grievance. A grievance is an alleged violation of the rights of workers on the job.[52] A formal process known as a *grievance procedure* is then invoked to help the parties resolve the dispute.

Grievance Procedures in the Unionized Firm

In addition to providing a formal mechanism for resolving disputes, the grievance procedure defines and narrows the nature of the complaint. Thus each grievance must be expressed in writing. The written grievance identifies the grievant, when the incident leading to the grievance occurred (it could, of course be ongoing), and where the incident happened. The written statement also indicates why the complaint is considered a grievance and what the grievant thinks should be done about the matter.[52] A typical grievance procedure in a unionized firm works as shown in Figure 14-1. As the figure indicates, unresolved grievances proceed progressively to higher and higher levels of management and union representation and culminate in voluntary, binding arbitration. Specific time limits for management's decision and the union's approval are normally imposed at each step. For example, 3 days for each party at step 1, 5 days for each party at steps 2 and 3, and 10 days for each party at step 4.

It also is important to note that many unions have a policy that up to step 3 of the procedure the grievance "belongs" to the employee. That is, the union will process a grievance through step 2 (and in some cases through step 3) at the grievant's request. However, if the grievance is not settled and reaches step 3, then it becomes the union's grievance. At that point, the union will decide whether or not the grievance has merit and whether additional time and financial resources of the union should be spent in carrying it forward. Indeed, many local unions let the membership formally vote to decide whether to take a grievance to arbitration.[52] They do this for good reason: The grievance process is expensive.

Costing a grievance One study found that to process 500 grievances (the actual number filed in a single West Coast union local over a 1-year period), a total of 4580 work hours were required, or an average of 9.1 hours per grievance. Assume that the average total compensation (wages plus benefits) for the grievant, union, and management representatives is $65 per hour, or more than $590 per grievance. This translates into an annual cost of almost $300,000 to resolve 500 grievances. However, this figure is conservative, for it reflects only the *direct* time used for formal meetings on grievances. It does not include such other factors as preparation time, informal meetings, clerical time, and administrative overhead for management and the union.[14] In complex grievance cases that proceed all the way to arbitration (step 6 in Figure 14-1), the cost to the company or union may exceed $5000 per grievance.[40,41]

FIGURE 14-1

Example of a formal grievance procedure in a unionized firm.

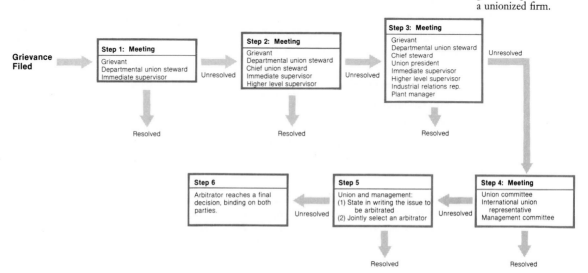

Common grievances and their resolution For the West Coast local just mentioned, the percentage of grievances filed by category is shown in Table 14-2. The majority of grievances were filed over disciplinary issues: the introductory disciplinary memorandum, suspensions, and termination. Seniority, the basis of many individual work rights for union employees, is grieved frequently. Beyond that, no single category accounts for a large proportion of the grievances filed.

Of the grievances that were submitted to arbitration in 1983, unions lost more than half, according to a random sample of 1789 cases by the American Arbitration Association. Unions won in 29 percent of the cases, and in about 18 percent of the cases the union and the company won partial victories.[45] However, the majority of grievances filed are resolved without resorting to arbitration. Of these, *unions* tend to win more grievances related to such issues as the denial of sick benefits, termination, transfer, suspension, and disciplinary memoranda. Ordinarily the burden of proof in a grievance proceeding is on the union. Since fewer issues of

■ **TABLE 14·2**
PERCENTAGE OF GRIEVANCES FILED BY CATEGORY

Grievance category	Percentage
Suspension	20.8
Seniority	10.4
Miscellaneous	8.6
Transfer	7.4
Termination	6.6
Disciplinary memoranda	6.6
Scheduling	6.4
Vacation	5.8
Grievance process	4.4
Management performing production work	4.0
Safety	3.4
Discrimination	3.4
Performance evaluations	3.0
Union representation	2.0
Sick benefits denial	2.0
Pay (differentials, travel, etc.)	1.8
Excused and complimentary time	1.6
Work out of classification	1.2
Training	0.6

Source: D. R. Dalton & W. D. Todor, Win, lose, draw: The grievance process in practice, *Personnel Administrator,* **26**(3), 1981, 27. Copyright, 1981. Reprinted with permission from HRMagazine (formerly Personnel Administrator) published by the Society for Human Resource Management, Alexandria, VA.

interpretation are involved in the areas that unions usually win, this pattern of grievance resolution is not surprising.[14]

In summary, there are two key advantages to the grievance procedure. One, it ensures that the complaints and problems of workers can be heard, rather than simply allowed to fester. Two, grievance procedures provide formal mechanisms to ensure due process and procedural justice for all parties.

On the other hand, the process is not completely objective in that factors other than merit sometimes determine the outcome of a grievance. Some of these factors include the cost of granting a grievance and the perceived need for management to placate disgruntled workers or to settle large numbers of grievances in order to expedite the negotiation process.[50] In addition, personal factors such as the gender of the grievant (sometimes men and sometimes women are more likely to prevail), the gender composition of the supervisor–union steward dyad that hears cases, or the grievant's work history (good performance, long tenure, few disciplinary incidents) also serve to determine the outcomes of grievance procedures.[13,15,38]

What is the role of the line manager in all this? Know and understand the collective bargaining contract, as well as federal and state labor laws. Above all, whether you agree or disagree with the terms of the contract, it is legally binding on both labor and management. Respect its provisions, and manage according to the letter as well as the spirit of the contract.

Arbitration

Arbitration is used by management and labor to settle disputes arising out of and during the term of a labor contract. It appears in about 90 percent of all private sector contracts and in about 75 percent of all public sector contracts.[67] As Figure 14-1 indicates, compulsory, binding arbitration is the final stage of the grievance process. It is also used as an alternative to a work stoppage, and it is used to ensure labor peace for the duration of a labor contract. Arbitrators may be chosen from a list of qualified people supplied by the American Arbitration Association or the Federal Mediation and Conciliation Service.

Arbitration hearings are quasi-judicial proceedings. Prehearing briefs may be filed by both parties, along with lists of witnesses to be called. Witnesses are cross-examined, and documentary evidence may be introduced. However, *arbitrators are not bound by the formal rules of evidence*, as they would be in a court of law.

Following the hearing, the parties may each submit briefs to reiterate their positions, evidence supporting them, and proposed decisions. The arbitrator then considers the evidence, the contract clause in dispute, and the powers granted the arbitrator under the labor agreement, and finally issues a decision. In rare instances where a losing party refuses to honor the arbitrator's decision, the decision can be enforced by taking that party to federal court.[31]

Generally an arbitration award cannot be appealed in court simply because one party believes that the arbitrator made a mistake in interpreting an agreement. This was recently affirmed by a full federal appeals court in California. A mechanic had been fired for not tightening lug bolts on the wheels of a Mercedes-Benz properly. An arbitrator ruled that a 120-day suspension was enough discipline, as had been urged by the man's Machinists Union local. Following extensive precedent, the court ruled that arbitrator awards are extensions of labor contracts, and court deference is the rule.[44]

Grievance Procedures in Nonunion Companies: Corporate Due Process

Grievance arbitration has generally worked well, and this is why many companies have extended it as an option to their nonunion employees. For example, Federal Express Corporation's "guaranteed fair-treatment process" lets employees appeal problems to a peer review board chosen by the worker involved and management. The board rules for employees about half the time. Bosses cannot appeal decisions, but employees can, to a panel of top executives. Frederick Smith and James Barksdale, chief executive and chief operating officer, respectively, sit in on the appeals board almost every Tuesday to decide cases.[19] TWA employees take disputes to a panel comprised of an arbitrator, a representative from the human resources staff, and another employee. One reason for the growing popularity of these programs is that they tend to reduce lawsuits. At Aetna Life & Casualty Co., for example, only one of the almost 300 complaints handled by Aetna's program has gone to litigation.[73]

Figure 14-2 illustrates how such a procedure works in one company. This procedure emphasizes the supervisor as a key figure in the resolution of grievances. As a second step, the employee is encouraged to see the department head, a human resources department representative, or any other member of management. Alternatively, the employee may proceed directly to the roundtable, a body of employee and management representatives who meet biweekly to resolve grievances. Management immediately answers those questions that it can and researches those requiring an in-depth review. The minutes of roundtable meetings, plus the answers to the questions presented, are posted conspicuously on bulletin boards in work areas.[17]

To work effectively, a nonunion grievance procedure should meet three requirements:

1. All employees must know about the procedure and exactly how it operates.
2. They must believe that there will be no reprisals taken against them for using it.
3. Management must respond quickly and thoroughly to all grievances.[17]

Corporate due process is one of the fastest developing trends in industry. In the coming decade, a majority of people-oriented firms are likely to adopt it. But how does one begin? Here are four key steps:[19]

1. *Make sure your HR department has lots of expertise in dispute resolution.* It must be able to handle most of the complaints that cannot be resolved by managers and

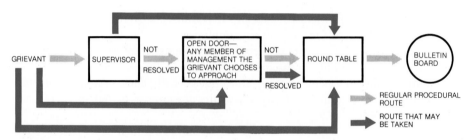

FIGURE 14-2

Example of a nonunion grievance procedure. This diagram indicates the possible routes a grievant may take to resolve a complaint. The regular procedural route is designed to resolve the grievance at the lowest possible level—the supervisor. However, if the grievant feels uncomfortable approaching the supervisor, the grievance may be presented directly to any level of management via the open-door policy or via the roundtable. [*Source:* Reprinted from D. A. Drost & F. P. O'Brien, Are there grievances against your non-union grievance procedure? *Personnel Administrator,* **28**(1), 1983, 37. Copyright, 1983. Reprinted with permission from HRMagazine (formerly Personnel Administrator) published by the Society for Human Resource Management, Alexandria, VA.]

their subordinates; otherwise the "company court" will be inundated with cases. Studies show that up to 20 percent of a workforce goes to HR specialists with complaints of unfair treatment. But at companies such as Polaroid and Citicorp, for example, problem review boards may hear only 12 to 20 cases a year, because of the skill of the HR department in dispute resolution.

2. *Train all managers and supervisors in your company's due process approach.* They simply must know company HR policy because it is the "law" governing company courts and adjudicators. Coach them in how to handle complaints, so that they can resolve problems immediately. And if subordinates take their complaints to the company court, teach your managers to accept reversals as a fact of business life, for in a good due process system, they are bound to occur. Three separate studies reported reversal rates that ranged from 20 to 40 percent.[19,59,64]

3. *Decide whether you want a panel system or a single adjudicator.* Panel systems, such as the one described in the chapter opening vignette, enjoy high credibility and, for the panelists, mutual support. About 100 companies, including Control Data, Digital Equipment, and Borg-Warner, now use peer review panels (the roundtable in Figure 14-2) to resolve disputes over firings, promotions, and disciplinary actions. A panel typically consists of three peers and two management representatives. Most companies do not permit grievants to have outside representation; instead, they provide a human resource staff member if help is needed in preparing the case. The panel's decisions are binding on both sides.

An adjudicator system, in which a single investigator acts first as a fact finder and then changes hats and arbitrates the facts, has the advantages of speed, flexibility, and maximum privacy. International Business Machines and Bank of America both use the single-adjudicator approach.

4. *Make your due process system visible.* At a minimum, the system should be described in the employee handbook and publicized by HR specialists. SmithKline

Beecham goes even further. Periodically it features its grievance procedure on closed-circuit television for all company employees.

The trend toward corporate due process represents an effort by companies to broaden employees' rights in disciplinary matters. Companies also say that such procedures build an open, trusting atmosphere, help deter union organizing, and stem the rising number of costly lawsuits claiming wrongful discharge and discrimination.

Discipline

Make no mistake about it: Most employees want to conduct themselves in a manner acceptable to the company and to their fellow employees. Occasionally problems of absenteeism, poor work performance, or rule violations arise. When informal conversations or coaching sessions fail to resolve these problems, formal disciplinary action is called for.

Employee discipline is the final area of contract administration that we shall consider. Typically the "management rights" clause of the collective bargaining agreement retains for management the authority to impose *reasonable* rules for workplace conduct and to discipline employees for *just cause*. As developed in thousands of arbitration cases over the past 60 years, the concept of just cause requires an employer not only to produce persuasive evidence of an employee's culpability or negligence, but also to provide the employee a fair hearing and to impose a penalty appropriate for the proven offense.[77] Unions rarely object to employee discipline, *provided that* (1) it is applied consistently, (2) the rules are publicized clearly, and (3) the rules are considered reasonable.

Discipline is indispensable to management control. Ideally it should serve as a corrective mechanism to prevent serious harm to the organization.[6] Unfortunately, some managers go to great lengths to avoid using discipline. To some extent this is understandable, for discipline is one of the hardest HR actions to face. Managers may avoid imposing discipline because of (1) ignorance of organizational rules, (2) fear of formal grievances, or (3) fear of losing the friendship of employees. Yet failure to administer discipline can result in implied acceptance or approval of the offense. Thereafter, problems may become more frequent or severe, and discipline becomes that much more difficult to administer.[58]

As an alternative, some companies are experimenting with a technique called "positive discipline." On its face, it sounds a lot like traditional discipline dressed up in euphemisms. It works as follows: Employees who commit offenses first get an oral "reminder" rather than a "reprimand." Then comes a written reminder, followed by a paid day off—called a "decision-making leave day" (a suspension in traditional parlance). After a pensive day off, the employee must agree in writing (or orally at some union shops) that he or she will behave responsibly for the next year. The paid day off is a one-shot chance at reform. The process is documented, and, if the employee does not change, termination follows.

How has positive discipline worked? At Tampa Electric, which has used it for 8 years, more employees have improved their job performance than have left the company. Says one power station manager: "Before, we punished employees and treated them worse and worse and expected them to act better. I don't ever recall suspending someone who came back ready to change."[5] These arguments for not imposing punishment are persuasive. But evidence also indicates that discipline (that is, punishment) may be beneficial.[60] Consider that:

- Discipline may alert the marginal employee to his or her low performance and result in a change in behavior.
- Discipline may signal other employees regarding expected levels of performance and standards of behavior.
- If the discipline is perceived as legitimate by other employees, it may increase motivation, morale, and performance.

In fact, a statistical reanalysis of the original Hawthorne experiments concluded that managerial discipline was the major factor in increased rates of output.[24] A subsequent study supports these conclusions.[60] Department managers in a retail store chain who used informal warnings, formal warnings, and dismissals more frequently than their peers had higher departmental performance ratings (in terms of annual cost and sales data and ratings by higher-level managers). This relationship held even when length of service was taken into account. More frequent use of sanctions was associated with improved performance. Why is this so?

First, the performance ratings used reflected *departmental* performance, not *individual* performance. Supervisors must deal with the behavior of individuals in a *social* context, not with the isolated behavior of a single person. Hence, generalizations based on reinforcement theory (a theory of individual behavior) may not hold true when applied in a social context.

A more powerful explanation for these results may lie in social learning theory.[3] *Individuals in groups look to others to learn appropriate behaviors and attitudes.* They learn them by modeling the behavior of others, by adopting standard operating procedures, and by following group norms. Individuals whose attitudes or behaviors violate these norms may cause problems. Tolerance of such behavior by the supervisor may *threaten* the group by causing feelings of uncertainty and unfairness. On the other hand, management actions that are seen as maintaining legitimate group standards may instill feelings of fairness and result in improved performance. Failure to invoke sanctions may lead to a loss of management control and unproductive employee behavior. Finally, do not underestimate the *symbolic* value of disciplinary actions, especially since punitive behavior tends to make a lasting impression on employees.[12,62]

Progressive discipline Many firms, both unionized and nonunionized, follow a procedure of progressive discipline that proceeds from an oral warning to a written warning to a suspension to dismissal. However, to administer discipline without at the same time engendering resentment by the disciplined employee, managers should follow what Douglas McGregor called the "Red Hot Stove Rule." Discipline should be:

Immediate. Just like touching a hot stove, where feedback is immediate, there should be no misunderstanding about why discipline was imposed. People are disciplined not because of who they are (personality) but because of what they did (behavior).

With warning. Small children know that if they touch a hot stove, they will be burned. Likewise, employees must know very clearly what the consequences will be of undesirable work behavior. They must be given adequate warning.

Consistent. Every time a person touches a red hot stove, she gets burned. Likewise, if discipline is to be perceived as fair, it must be administered consistently, given similar circumstances surrounding the undesirable behavior. Consistency *among* individual managers across the organization is essential, but evidence indicates that line managers tend to be less concerned with consistency than with satisfying immediate needs within their work units.[39]

Impersonal. A hot stove is blind to who touches it. So also, managers cannot play favorites by disciplining subordinates they do not like while allowing the same behavior to go unpunished for those they do like.

Documenting performance-related incidents Documentation is a fact of organizational life for most managers. While such paperwork is never pleasant, it should conform to the following guidelines:

- Describe what led up to the incident—the problem and the setting. Is this a first offense or part of a pattern?
- Describe what actually happened, and be specific: i.e., include names, dates, times, witnesses, and other pertinent facts.
- Describe what must be done to correct the situation.
- State the consequences of further violations.

Conclude the warning by obtaining the employee's signature that he or she has read and understands the warning. A sample written warning is shown in Figure 14-3. Note how it includes each of the ingredients just described.

The disciplinary interview Generally such interviews are held for one of two reasons: (1) over issues of *workplace conduct*, such as attendance or punctuality, or (2) over issues of *job performance*, such as low productivity.[60] They tend to be very legalistic. As an example, consider the following scenario:

You are a first-line supervisor at a nonunion facility. You suspect that one of your subordinates, Susan Fox, has been distorting her time reports to misrepresent her daily starting time. While some of the evidence is sketchy, you know that Fox's time reports are false. Accompanied by an industrial relations representative, you decide to confront Fox directly in a disciplinary interview. However, before

---

DATE: April 14, 1991

TO: J. Hartwig

FROM: D. Curtis

SUBJECT: Written Warning

   On this date you were 30 minutes late to work with no justification for your tardiness. A similar offense occurred last Friday. At that time you were told that failure to report for work on schedule will not be condoned. I now find it necessary to tell you in writing that you must report to work on time. Failure to do so will result in your dismissal from employment. Please sign below that you have read and that you understand this warning.

[Name]   [Date]

FIGURE 14-3
Sample written warning of disciplinary action.

you can begin the meeting, Fox announces, "I'd appreciate it if a coworker of mine could be present during this meeting. If a coworker cannot be present, I refuse to participate." Your reaction to this startling request is to:

A Ask Fox which coworker she desires and reconvene the meeting once the employee is present.

B Deny her request and order her to participate or face immediate discipline for insubordination.

C Terminate the meeting with no further discussion.

D Ignore the request and proceed with the meeting, hoping that Fox will participate anyway.

E Inform Fox that, as her supervisor, you are a coworker and attempt to proceed with the meeting.

Unless your reaction was A or C, you have probably committed a violation of the National Labor Relations Act.[35]

In *NLRB v. J. Weingarten, Inc.*, the Supreme Court ruled that a *union* employee has the right to demand that a union representative be present at an investigatory interview that the employee reasonably believes may result in disciplinary action.[54] However, in *NLRB v. Sears, Roebuck and Co.* (1985), the court overturned an earlier decision, ruling that *Weingarten* rights do not extend to nonunion employees.[53] To summarize the Weingarten mandate:

1. The employee must *request* representation; the employer has no obligation to offer it voluntarily.

2. The employee must reasonably believe that the investigation may result in disciplinary action taken against him or her.

3. The employer is not obligated to carry on the interview or to justify its refusal to do so. The employer may simply cancel the interview and thus effectively disallow union or coworker representation.

4. The employer has no duty to bargain with any union representative during the interview.

If the National Labor Relations Board determines that these rights were violated and that an employee was subsequently disciplined for conduct that was the subject of the unlawful interview, the board will issue a "make-whole" remedy. This may include (1) back pay, (2) an order expunging from the employee's personnel records any notation of related discipline, or (3) a cease-and-desist order. To avoid these kinds of problems, top management must decide what company policy will be in such cases, communicate that policy to first-line supervisors, and give first-line supervisors clear and concise instructions regarding their responsibilities should an employee request representation at an investigatory interview.[35]

Having satisfied their legal burden, how should supervisors actually conduct the disciplinary interview? They must do *nine* things well:

1. Come to the interview with as many facts as possible. Check the employee's personnel file for previous offenses as well as for evidence of exemplary behavior and performance.

2. Conduct the interview in a quiet, private place. "Praise in public, discipline in private" is a good rule to remember. Whether the employee's attitude is truculent or contrite, recognize that he or she will be apprehensive. In contrast to other interviews, where your first objective is to dispel any fears and help the person relax, a "light touch" is inappropriate here.

3. Avoid aggressive accusations. State the facts in a simple, straightforward way. Be sure that any fact you use is accurate, and never rely on hearsay, rumor, or unconfirmed guesswork.

4. Be sure that the employee understands the rule in question and the reason it exists.

5. Allow the employee to make a full defense, even if you think he or she has none. If any point the employee makes has merit, tell him or her so and take it into consideration in your final decision.

6. Stay cool and calm; treat the subordinate as an adult. Never use foul language or touch the subordinate. Such behaviors may be misinterpreted or grossly distorted at a later date.

7. If you made a mistake, be big enough to admit it.

8. Consider extenuating circumstances and allow for honest mistakes on the part of the subordinate.

9. Even when corrective discipline is required, try to express confidence in the subordinate's worth as a person and ability to perform acceptably in the future. Rather than dwelling on the past, which you *cannot* change, focus on the future, which you *can*.

Employment-at-Will

For the more than 70 percent of U.S. workers who are not covered by a collective bargaining agreement or an individual employment contract, dismissal is an ever-present possibility. An *employment-at-will* is created when an employee agrees to work for an employer but there is no specification of how long the parties expect the agreement to last. Under a century-old common law in the United States, employment relationships of indefinite duration can, in general, be terminated at the whim of either party.[48] However, unlike the winners of most sex- or race-bias cases, who generally collect back pay only, successful victims of unjust dismissal can collect sizable punitive and compensatory damages from their former employers. Thus an analysis of 120 wrongful discharge cases that went to trial in California found that the average salary of fired employees was $36,254. Plaintiffs won 67.5 percent of their cases and were awarded an average of $646,855. About 40 percent of the awards were for punitive damages.[26]

Those who stand to gain the most tend to be lower- and middle-level professionals and managers not covered by collective bargaining agreements or the individual employment contracts frequently given to senior executives. As one labor lawyer noted, "It's the white male manager's discrimination law."[1]

In recent years, several important exceptions to the "at-will" doctrine have emerged. These exceptions provide important protections for workers. The first— and most important—is legislative. Federal laws limit an employer's right to terminate at-will employees for such reasons as age, race, sex, religion, national origin, union activity, reporting of unsafe working conditions, or physical handicap.[66] However, employment-at-will is primarily a matter of state law.[42]

Such suits are now permitted in 46 states, and in many of them courts have shown a willingness to apply traditional causes of action—such as defamation, fraud, intentional infliction of emotional distress, and invasion of privacy—to this area of employment law.[26,33]

State courts have carved out three judicial exceptions. The first is a *public policy exception*. That is, an employee may not be fired because he or she refuses to commit an illegal act, such as perjury or price-fixing. Second, when an employer has promised not to terminate an employee except for unsatisfactory job performance or other good cause, the courts will insist that the employer carry out that promise. This includes *implied* promises (such as oral promises and implied covenants of good faith and fair dealing) as well as explicit ones.[30] For example, in *Fortune v. National Cash Register Company*, a salesperson (Mr. Fortune) was fired after he sold a large quantity of cash registers. Under the terms of his contract, Mr. Fortune would not receive a portion of his commission until the cash registers were delivered. He claimed he was fired before delivery was made to avoid payment of the full $92,000 commission on the order. The court held that terminating Mr. Fortune solely to deprive him of his commissions would breach the covenant of good faith implied in every contract.[2]

The third exception allows employees to seek damages for outrageous acts related to termination, including character defamation. For example, in *Rulon-Miller v. IBM* an employee was fired for dating the manager of a competing firm. A California court ruled that the supervisor's actions in demanding that the employee choose between her job or her beau were severe enough to support an action for outrageous conduct.[42]

Another example of this exists in so-called retaliatory discharge cases, where a worker is fired for actions ranging from filing a workers' compensation claim to reporting safety violations to government agencies. The Supreme Court has ruled that where state law permits (as it does in 34 states), union as well as nonunion employees have the right to sue over their dismissals, even if they are covered by a collective bargaining contract that provides a grievance procedure and remedies.[76]

For some employers, however, relief is in sight. The California Supreme Court ruled in 1988 that most individuals suing their former employers for wrongful discharge can ask only for compensatory damages, such as lost wages. With very few exceptions (e.g., discrimination), they cannot seek punitive damages.[65] In Montana, the state Supreme Court upheld the state's Wrongful Discharge Act. That law limits remedies to no more than 4 years' worth of lost wages and benefits and excludes recovery for emotional distress. Punitive damages are prohibited in all but certain unusual cases of employer fraud or malice. The statute also prohibits judges from using expansive theories of personal injury or implied promises to allow awards.[49] On the other hand, courts in many states—notably Illinois, Massachusetts, Michigan, and New York—expressly permit punitive damages in certain instances.[26]

To avoid potential charges of unjust dismissal, managers should scrutinize each facet of the human resource management system. They should look, for example, at the following:

Recruitment. Beware of creating implicit or explicit contracts in recruitment advertisements. Ensure that no job duration is implied and that employment is not guaranteed or "permanent."

Interviewing. Phrases intended to entice a candidate into accepting a position, such as "employment security," "lifelong relationship" with the company, "permanent" hiring, and so forth, can create future problems.

Applications. Include a statement that describes the rights of the at-will employee, as well as those of the employer. However, do not be so strident that you scare off applicants.

Handbooks and manuals. A major source of company policy statements regarding "permanent" employment and discharge for "just cause" is the employee handbook. According to a growing number of state laws, such handbook language constitutes an *implied contract* for employment. Courts have upheld an employer's prerogative to refrain from making any promises to employees regarding how a termination will be conducted or the conditions under which they may be fired. However, if an employer does make such a promise of job security, whether implied verbally or in writing in an employment document or employee handbook, then the employer is bound by that promise.[25]

Performance appraisals. Include training and written instructions for all raters, and use systems that minimize subjectivity to the greatest extent possible. Give employees the right to read and comment on their appraisals, and require them to sign an acknowledgment that they have done so whether or not they agree with the contents of the appraisal.[47] Encourage managers to give "honest" appraisals; if an employee is not meeting minimum standards of performance, "tell it like it is" rather than leading the employee to believe that his or her performance is satisfactory.

Document employee misconduct and poor performance, and provide for a progressive disciplinary policy, thereby building a record establishing "good cause."[18]

Employment Contracts

Earlier we noted that employees with contracts (bargained collectively or individually) are not at-will employees. More and more executives, professionals, and even middle managers are demanding contracts. Thus a survey of 560 of the nation's largest companies revealed that 48 percent of them have written understandings with their high-ranking employees.[69] While getting a contract can be a wise career move, when is the proper time to ask for one—and how?

You should consider asking for a contract in any business where the competition for talent is intense, where ideas are at a premium, or whenever the conditions of your employment differ in unusual ways from a company's standard practices. A contract assures you of a job and a minimum salary for some period of time, usually 2 to 3 years, during which you agree not to quit. Other typical provisions include your title, compensation (salary, procedures for salary increases, bonuses), benefits, stock options, length of vacation, the circumstances under which you can be fired, severance pay, and, in some cases, no-compete agreements.[37,69]

No-compete agreements are most common in such highly competitive industries as computers, pharmaceuticals, toys, defense equipment, and electronics. However, whether or not a contract has been signed, executives are still required to maintain all trade secrets with which their employers have entrusted them. This obligation, often called a "fiduciary duty of loyalty," cannot keep the executive out of the job market, but it does provide the employer with legal recourse if an executive joins a competitor and tells all. Indeed, this is precisely what McDonald's claimed when it succeeded in muzzling a former market researcher.[61]

■ **COMPANY**   McLITIGATION
EXAMPLE

The former employee (we'll call him McEx) was an expert in market re-search. He quit to join a competitor a few years ago, taking with him a large batch of papers. McDonald's filed suit, alleging that he walked away with company secrets.

Before filing suit and within a few days of his leaving, McDonald's sent a letter to McEx warning him not to divulge any "confidential information" regarding activities such as marketing, advertising, training methods, profit margins, raw materials prices, selling prices, and operating procedures.

The letter further requested a meeting with McEx, during which he would be asked to return any written materials he had taken from McDonald's and also to sign an agreement not to divulge any company trade secrets to his new employer.

When McEx declined to attend the meeting, McDonald's promptly filed suit in McEx's new home state. The company managed to win a temporary restraining order that McEx says effectively meant he could not perform *any* market research for his new employer. He was thereafter relegated to less important work.

Finally, about 6 months after the suit was filed, the case was settled out of court. McEx agreed not to use information gained on the job with Mc-Donald's in his new job. But the issue had become academic. Disenchanted with his new nonjob and aware that his new employer was viewing him more as a problem than as an asset, McEx left his new job. He is now employed by another food chain, not involving fast-food restaurants.[61] In short, companies are now playing hard ball when it comes to the disclosure of trade secrets. For both parties, the stakes are high.

Increasingly, judges are finding that no-compete agreements go too far in re-straining employees. In some cases they are modifying terms to make them less restrictive (e.g., with respect to geographical boundaries or the length of time an employee is barred from competing). In others they are invalidating the agree-ments altogether, viewing them as illegal restraints of trade. While some kinds of no-compete pacts stand a better chance in court than others (e.g., those in which the seller of a business promises not to compete with the buyer), closer scru-tiny reflects a broader trend in which courts are viewing employee rights more favorably.[27]

Now back to employment contracts. In dealing with a prospective employer, do not raise the issue of a contract until you have been offered a job and have thoroughly discussed the terms of your employment. How do you broach the subject? Calmly. Say, for example, "I'd appreciate a letter confirming these ar-rangements." If the employer asks why, you might point out that both of you are used to putting business agreements on paper and that it's to your mutual benefit to keep all these details straight.[69]

Here are some tips on how to negotiate an employment contract:

1. Keep the tone upbeat. Don't use the words "I" and "you"; talk about "we"—like you're already aboard.
2. Decide beforehand on three or four "make or break" issues (e.g., salary, job assignment, location). These are your "need to haves." Also make a list of secondary issues, so-called "nice to haves" (e.g., company car, sign-on bonus).
3. Negotiate the entire package at one time. Don't keep coming back to nitpick.
4. Be flexible (except on your "make or break" issues); let the company win on some things.

Once you receive the proposed contract, have an attorney review it before you sign. All indications are that in the 1990s employment contracts will become more, not less, popular. As one executive recruiter noted: "We seem to be drifting toward a point where no executive will move without some form of legal protection" (ref. 69, p. 132).

Termination

Termination is one of the most difficult tasks a manager has to perform. As we learned in our discussion of employment-at-will, disgruntled former employees are winning about two-thirds of court cases contesting their dismissals. Clearly there is room for improvement on the part of managers. For those fired, the perception of inequity, of procedural injustice, is often what drives them to court.

Sometimes termination is done for disciplinary reasons, and sometimes for economic reasons (i.e., "downsizing"). It is not an infrequent occurrence, since some 2 million workers in the United States are fired every year, and that doesn't include large-scale layoffs.[26] With respect to layoffs, while the Plant Closing Law of 1988 requires employers of more than 100 workers to grant 60 days' written notice before closing a plant, or before laying off more than one-third of a workforce in excess of 150 people, very few firms provide any training to supervisors on *how* to conduct terminations.

While termination may be traumatic for the employee, it is often no less so for the boss. Faced with saying the words "Your services are no longer required," even the strongest person can get the "shakes," sleepless nights, and sweaty palms.[71] So how should termination be handled? Certainly not the way it was at one company that was trying to downsize. At 8:30 A.M. all employees were ordered to their offices. Between then and 10:30 A.M., like angels of death, managers accompanied by security guards knocked on doors, brusquely informed employees that their services were no longer required, gave affected employees a box in which to place their personal articles, and asked the employees to leave the premises within 15 minutes, accompanied by a security guard. Is this procedural justice? Certainly not.

As an alternative, more humane procedure, companies should familiarize all

THE TERMINATION CHECKLIST

DOCUMENTATION
_____ If the job is eliminated, gather supporting evidence of a company or department reduction in head-count.
_____ If poor performance is the reason, the file should contain copies of several successive poor appraisals that were transmitted to (and usually signed by) the candidate at the time they were prepared.

CLEARANCES
_____ Who needs to approve the termination?

PRIOR NOTICES
_____ Safeguards to prevent leaks to the public
_____ Key staff members
_____ Board members
_____ Key customers
_____ Regulatory agency officers

PRECAUTIONS FOR NEW LEAKS
_____ Ignore the leak
_____ Advance the date of termination to immediate
_____ Delay the termination with no comment

TERMS OF TERMINATION
_____ Resignation
_____ Transfer to special assignment
_____ Early retirement
_____ Outright termination

LEGAL PRECAUTIONS
_____ Salary
_____ Bonuses
_____ Benefits
_____ Other obligations
_____ Scientists and inventors
_____ No-compete agreements

PUBLIC ANNOUNCEMENTS
_____ Should it be a standard press release?
_____ What should the content of the statement be?

PERSONAL CONSIDERATIONS
_____ Medical data
_____ Significant dates
_____ Family circumstances
_____ Personal emotional state

FIGURE 14-4
The termination checklist. [_Source:_ D. H. Sweet (1989). Outplacement. In W. F. Cascio (ed.), _Human resource planning, employment, and placement._ Washington, DC: Bureau of National Affairs, pp. 246, 247.]

supervisors with company policies and provide a termination checklist to use when conducting dismissals. One such checklist is shown in Figure 14-4.

Before deciding to dismiss an employee, managers should conduct a detailed review of all relevant facts, including the employee's side of the story. To assure consistent treatment, the supervisor also should examine how similar cases have been handled in the past. Once the decision to terminate has been made, the termination interview should minimize trauma for the affected employee. Prior to conducting such an interview, be prepared to answer three basic questions: who, when, and where.

THE TERMINATION INTERVIEW
____ Think through details.
____ When? Not late on Friday.
____ Who? It's the line manager's responsibility.
____ Where? Best place is in a neutral area or the candidate's office.
____ Outplacement consultant on hand?
____ Termination letter prepared?

ORDERLY TRANSITIONS OF COMMITMENTS
____ Reassign internal assignments and projects.
____ External activities to be reassigned:
  • Customer servicing
  • Convention or professional meetings
  • Speeches and public relations commitments
  • Civic and professional commitments
  • Club memberships
  • Board memberships, e.g., of subsidiaries

REGROUPING THE STAFF
____ Announcement to immediate colleagues and support staff
____ What they are to be told
____ Transfer of assignments
____ References
____ Reassurances

TERMINATION LETTERS
____ Written evidence to verify the termination
____ Summary of important information the candidate may not have listened to, or remembered
____ Brief and business-like confirmation of the facts and the details
____ Include:
  • Termination date
  • Severance or bridging pay allowance
  • Vacation pay
____ Continuation of benefits:
  • Regular benefits
  • Special benefits, such as pension rights
____ Job search support:
  • Logistical
  • Financial
  • Outplacement
  • Transfer of responsibilities
  • Continuation of responsibilities
  • Return of company property
  • Legal documents
  • Conditions of termination?

Source: Reprinted with permission from James J. Gallagher, chairman, J. J. Gallagher Associates, New York, N.Y.

Who.   The responsibility for terminating rests with the manager of the individual who is to be released. No one else has the credibility to convey this difficult message.

When.   This decision may be crucial to the success of the termination process. First of all, consider personal situations—birthdays, anniversaries, family illnesses. Further, most experts agree that Friday is the worst day of the week for terminations. That leaves the employee with the entire weekend to brood before any positive action can be taken.[79]

Where.   Neutral territory—not the manager's or employee's office. The firing manager should arrange a neutral location so that each party is easily able to leave after the interview.

Following these activities, the firing manager should follow five rules for the termination interview:[71]

1. *Present the situation in a clear, concise, and final manner.* Don't confuse the message to be delivered, and don't drag it out. "Tom, no doubt you are aware that the organization has eliminated some jobs, and one of them is yours." Remember: Spend only a few minutes, don't make excuses, don't bargain, and don't compromise. Get to the point quickly and succinctly. As one outplacement executive noted: "It's not cruel to cut clean."[79]

2. *Avoid debates or a rehash of the past.* Arguments about past performance may only compound bad feelings that already exist. Don't shift responsibility; the person is your responsibility and you must accept that as a fact.

3. *Never talk down to the individual.* Your objective should be to remove as much of the emotion and trauma as possible. Emphasize that it's a situation that isn't working and that the decision is made. It's a business decision—don't make excuses or apologies. Be tactful, and by all means, avoid insulting (and unlawful) remarks, such as "At your age I'd be thinking of early retirement."

4. *Be empathetic, but not compromising.* "I'm sorry that this has to happen, but the decisions are made. We are going to provide assistance to you (or to each of the people affected)."

5. *What's the next step?* "I'm going to give you this letter outlining the severance arrangements. I suggest you take the rest of the day off and plan on being here tomorrow at 9 A.M. to talk with the benefits people. Also, we have engaged a very successful outplacement firm, and I would like to introduce you to Fred Martin, who, if you wish, will be working with you through your transition" (ref. 71, p. 56).

Be prepared for a variety of reactions, from disbelief, to silent acceptance, to rage. The key is to remain calm and focus on helping the employee confront the reality of the situation. This is best done by maintaining your distance and composure. It does no good to argue or cry along with the employee.

After terminations or layoffs, the work attitudes and behaviors of remaining employees ("survivors") may suffer. If the layoff (or its management, or both) is perceived to be unjust, survivors are likely to feel angry. In addition, they may feel guilty that they, rather than their laid-off coworkers, could have been dismissed just as easily. This layoff-induced stress, with its attendant feelings of anger, guilt, and job insecurity, can be reduced in two ways. One, provide extra social support (e.g., from coworkers and supervisors) to those survivors who are perceived as especially "at-risk." Two, organizations that provide outplacement support to those who are dismissed enjoy, as a secondary benefit, reduced post-layoff stress among survivors.[7,8]

Finally, public disclosure of termination practices (e.g., in the case of layoffs) may actually help displaced employees, since it assures potential employers that economic factors—not individual shortcomings—caused the dismissals.[72] Having examined a very public issue, termination, let us now turn our attention to a related issue, employee privacy.

EMPLOYEE PRIVACY AND ETHICAL ISSUES

Privacy refers to the interest that employees have in controlling the use that is made of their personal information and in being able to engage in behavior free from regulation or surveillance.[56] Attention centers on three main issues: the kind of information collected and retained about individuals, how that information is used, and the extent to which it can be disclosed to others. These issues often lead to ethical dilemmas for managers, that is, choice situations that have the potential to result in a breach of acceptable behavior.

But what is "acceptable" behavior? The difficulty lies in maintaining a proper balance between the common good and personal freedom, between the legitimate business needs of an organization and a worker's feelings of dignity and worth.[63] Although we cannot prescribe the *content* of ethical behavior across all conceivable situations, we can prescribe *processes* that may lead to an acceptable (and temporary) consensus among interested parties regarding an ethical course of action. In the remainder of this chapter, we will examine a number of areas that pose potential ethical dilemmas for employers and privacy concerns for employees or job applicants. Let us begin by considering fair information practice policies.

Fair Information Practices in the Computer Age

Federal government agencies are subject to the Privacy Act of 1974, under which individuals have three rights: (1) access to any personal records about them and the right to review their contents, copy any portions of them, and amend them to correct erroneous information; (2) the right to prevent the information in their files from being used for any purpose other than the particular purpose for which it was collected; and (3) the right to sue for damages that occur as a result of intentional action that violates any individual rights under the act.

Computerized tracking in the United States begins at age 2, when, under U.S. tax law, children claimed as dependents must apply for a Social Security number.[34] That number, in effect, becomes a national identifier, enabling records from different databases to be matched, using desktop computers to call up data banks.

Computers have an awesome power to track people's lives by digging through dozens of data banks and compiling what amounts to electronic dossiers. Unfortunately, computerized information jumps so quickly from agency to agency that untangling an error can be very difficult.[16] Thus safeguards to protect personal privacy are more important than ever. What should managers do?

First, *periodically and systematically review record-keeping practices* such as the following:

- The number and types of records maintained on employees, former employees, and applicants
- The specific information retained in each record
- The uses made of information in each type of record
- The disclosures made to parties outside the organization
- The extent to which individuals are aware and informed of such uses and disclosures of information about them

After reviewing their current practices, managers should *articulate, communicate, and implement fair information practice policies* by taking the following actions:

- Limit the collection of information about individuals to that which is relevant to specific decisions
- Inform individuals of the types of information being maintained and the uses to be made of it
- Adopt procedures to ensure the accuracy, timeliness, and completeness of such information
- Permit individuals to see, copy, correct, or amend records about themselves
- Take adequate security precautions to limit internal access to records (e.g., physical security, passwords, system audit trails, read/write authentication routines)
- Limit external disclosures of information, particularly those made without the individual's authorization
- Conduct regular reviews of compliance with these fair information practice policies.[10]

Companies that have taken such measures, such as IBM, Bank of America, AT&T, Cummins Engine, Avis, and TRW, report that they have not been overly costly, produced burdensome traffic in access demands, or reduced the general quality of their HR decisions. Furthermore, they receive strong employee approval for their policies when they ask about them on company attitude surveys. By matching words with deeds, companies such as these are weaving their concerns for employee privacy into the very fabric of their corporate cultures. As one CEO noted:

> You can't just write a code and hang it up on the wall . . . you have to keep reminding people what you stand for. Unless you stress that—especially with the emphasis in a corporation on making profits—it's not always clear to people which way management wants them to go. If more corporations would do this across America, we would raise the trust of the man-in-the-street that's been lost by business, government, and all institutions (ref. 78, p. 1F).

Assessment of Job Applicants and Employees

Decisions to hire, promote, train, or transfer are major events in individuals' careers. Frequently such decisions are made with the aid of tests, interviews, situational exercises, performance appraisals, and other assessment techniques. Developers and users of these instruments must be concerned with questions of fairness, propriety, and individual rights, as well as with other ethical issues.

Developers, if they are members of professional associations such as the American Psychological Association, the Society for Human Resource Management, or the Academy of Management, are bound by the ethical standards put forth by those bodies. Managers who use assessment instruments are subject to other ethical principles, beyond the general concerns for accuracy and equality of opportunity. These include:[46]

- Guarding against invasion of privacy
- Guaranteeing confidentiality
- Obtaining informed consent from employees and applicants before assessing them
- Respecting employees' rights to know (e.g., regarding test content, and the meaning, interpretation, and intended use of scores)
- Imposing time limitations on data (i.e., removing information that has not been used for HR decisions, especially if it has been updated)
- Using the most valid procedures available, thereby minimizing erroneous acceptances and erroneous rejections
- Treating applicants and employees with respect and consideration; for example, by standardizing procedures for all candidates

What can applicants do when confronted by a question that they believe is irrelevant or an invasion of privacy? Some may choose not to respond. However, research indicates that employers tend to view such nonresponse as an attemp to conceal facts that would reflect poorly on an applicant. Hence applicants (especially those who have nothing to hide) are ill-advised not to respond.[70] Clearly, it is the employer's responsibility to (1) know the kinds of questions that are being asked of candidates and (2) review the appropriateness and job relatedness of all such questions.

Employee Searches

This issue involves a careful balancing of an employer's right to manage its business and to implement reasonable work rules and standards (e.g., to curb theft and to improve security) against the privacy rights of employees. To avoid legal problems, employers should adhere *strictly* to the following guidelines:[56]

1. The search policy should be based on legitimate employer interests, such as prevention of theft, drinking on company property, and use, possession, or sale

of illegal drugs on company property. Employees (and unions) usually view reasons such as these as reasonable.

2. Be sure to include all types of searches (lockers, personal searches, purses, lunch boxes, etc.) in company policy. This will help to preclude an employee's claim of discriminatory treatment or invasion of privacy.

3. Provide adequate notice to employees (and to their unions, if appropriate) before implementing the policy.

4. Instruct those responsible for conducting the actual searches not to touch any employee or, if this is not possible, to touch only effects and pockets. This will provide a defense against an employee's claim of assault and battery.

5. If an employee is suspected of theft, conduct the search away from other employees and on company time.

Whenever searches are conducted, ensure that they are performed in a dignified and reasonable manner, with proper regard for each employee's rights to due process.

Whistle-Blowing

Research indicates that individuals can be conditioned to behave unethically (if they are rewarded for it), especially under increased competition,[55] but that the threat of punishment has a counterbalancing influence.[36] More important, when a formal or informal organizational policy is present that favors ethical behavior, ethical behavior tends to increase.[29]

Research with almost 8600 employees of 22 federal agencies and departments revealed that those who had observed alleged wrongdoing were more likely to "blow the whistle" if they:

- Were employed by organizations perceived by others to be responsive to complaints
- Held professional positions, had long service, and had positive reactions to their work
- Were recently recognized for good performance
- Were male (although race was unrelated to whistle-blowing)
- Were members of large work groups[51]

These findings are consistent with other research that has destroyed the myth that whistle-blowers are social misfits. A study of nearly 100 people who reported wrongdoing in public and private-sector organizations found that the average whistle-blower was a 47-year-old family man employed for 7 years before exposing his company's misdeeds.[21]

Despite retaliation, financial loss, and high emotional and physical stress,[32] there are at least two reasons why more whistle-blowers are likely to come forward in the future. One, some 30 states (and the federal government) now protect the jobs

IMPACT OF PROCEDURAL JUSTICE AND ETHICS ON PRODUCTIVITY, QUALITY OF WORK LIFE, AND THE BOTTOM LINE

As we have seen throughout this chapter, employees and former employees are very sensitive to the general issue of "justice on the job." On a broad range of issues, they expect to be treated justly, fairly, and with due process. Doing so certainly contributes to improved productivity and quality of work life, for grievances are both time-consuming and costly. On the other hand, organizations that disregard employee rights can expect two things: (1) to be hit with lawsuits and (2) to find courts and juries to be sympathetic to tales of employer wrongdoing. Employment-at-will cases illustrate this trend clearly. As for employers contesting such suits, one corporate attorney noted: "Even a victory isn't a victory because the [defendant's] attorneys' fees are at least $50,000 for a typical case".[4] As in so many other areas of employee relations, careful attention to procedural justice and ethical decision making yields direct as well as indirect benefits. The old adage, "an ounce of prevention is worth a pound of cure" says it all.

of workers who report wrongdoing by their companies.[43,74] Two, disclosure of fraud, waste, and abuse by federal contractors can lead to substantial financial gains by whistle-blowers. As a result of recent amendments to the federal False Claims Act of 1863, private citizens may sue a contractor for fraud on the government's behalf and share up to 30 percent of whatever financial recovery the government makes as a result of the charges. Thus when the government won $14.3 million from one of its contractors, Industrial Tectonics of Dexter, Michigan, the former Tectonics employee who filed the lawsuit laying out evidence of overcharging won a $1.4 million reward.[68]

Conclusion

Ethical behavior is not governed by hard and fast rules. Rather, it adapts and changes in response to social norms. This is nowhere more obvious than in human resource management. What was considered ethical in the 1950s and 1960s (deep-probing selection interviews; management prescriptions of standards of dress, ideology, and lifestyle; refusal to let employees examine their own personnel files) would be considered improper today. Indeed, as we have seen, growing concern for employee rights has placed organizational decision-making policies in the public domain. The beneficial effect of this, of course, is that it is sensitizing both employers and employees to new concerns.

To be sure, ethical choices are rarely easy. The challenge in managing human resources does not lie in the mechanical application of moral prescriptions, but rather in the process of creating and maintaining genuine relationships from which to address ethical dilemmas that cannot be covered by prescription.[10]

■ HUMAN RESOURCE MANAGEMENT IN ACTION
CONCLUSION

A RADICAL EXPERIMENT AT GE: HOURLY WORKERS CONTROL A GRIEVANCE REVIEW PANEL

Shortly after the procedure went into effect, a grievant took the first case to the panel. By policy, he was allowed to choose the names of four panelists of hourly workers at random and to put one name back, leaving three panelists of hourly workers to hear the case with the two managers.

The case was an intriguing one. It involved a job promotion that had been denied because of a rule prohibiting a person from downgrading to a lower-level job and then upgrading back to the same previous job within 6 months. The grievant felt that extenuating circumstances should have allowed him to bypass the 6-month rule.

After hearing all the evidence and investigating precedents, the panel ruled against the grievant. One of the hourly members of the panel said, "We sympathize with the guy, but a rule is a rule and it's the same for everyone." The message in that statement is that the panelists have taken their responsibility seriously.

Is the expanded grievance procedure with the review panel a cure-all for GE's employee relations concerns? Certainly not. But the company has proven itself correct in its belief that employees can be trusted to make wise decisions. As a result, both management and employees agree, the Columbia plant is now a better place in which to work.

SUMMARY

The broad theme of this chapter is "justice on the job." This includes procedural justice, due process, and ethical decision making. Each of these processes should guide the formulation of policy in matters involving dispute resolution (e.g.,

IMPLICATIONS FOR MANAGEMENT PRACTICE

Individual managers who disregard employee rights to procedural justice do so at their peril. If you are operating in a unionized setting, know the collective bargaining agreement inside and out. More important, follow the letter and spirit of its provisions. In nonunion settings, be sure that decisions about selection, assignment, promotion, discipline, and discharge are based on clear standards and recorded judgments that can be examined when a dispute arises. Provide explicit procedures for resolving conflicts and be sure that all employees know how to use them. Finally, treat all people with dignity and respect; think win-win rather than win-lose.

through union or nonunion grievance procedures), arbitration, discipline, employment contracts, and termination for disciplinary or economic reasons. Indeed, such concerns for procedural justice and due process form the basis for many challenges to the employment-at-will doctrine.

Two of the most important employment issues of our time are employee privacy and ethical decision making. Four areas that involve employee privacy are receiving considerable emphasis: fair information practice in the computer age, the assessment of job applicants and employees, employee searches, and whistle-blowing. Although it is not possible to prescribe the *content* of ethical behavior in each of these areas, *processes* that incorporate procedural justice can lead to an acceptable (and temporary) consensus among interested parties regarding an ethical course of action.

DISCUSSION QUESTIONS

14•1 Discuss the similarities and differences in these concepts: procedural justice, corporate due process, and ethical decisions about behavior.

14•2 What advice would you give to an executive who is about to negotiate an employment contract?

14•3 Advise top management on the procedures to follow in implementing a large-scale layoff.

14•4 How can a firm avoid lawsuits for employment-at-will?

14•5 What are some guidelines to follow in determining a reasonable compromise between a company's need to run its business and employee rights to privacy?

REFERENCES

1. A fight over the freedom to fire (1982, Sep. 20). *Business Week*, p. 116.
2. Bakaly, C. G., Jr., & Grossman, J. M. (1984, August). How to avoid wrongful discharge suits. *Management Review*, pp. 41–46.
3. Bandura, A. (1986). *Social foundations of thought and action: A social cognitive theory*. Englewood Cliffs, NJ: Prentice-Hall.
4. Barrett, A., cited in Schlender, B. R. (1988, Dec. 30). California ruling curtails damages in dismissal suits. *The Wall Street Journal*, p. B1.
5. Baum, L. (1986, June 16). Punishing workers with a day off. *Business Week*, p. 80.
6. Belohlav, J. (1983). Realities of successful employee discipline. *Personnel Administrator*, **28**(3), 74–77, 92.
7. Brockner, J. (1988). The effect of work layoffs on survivors: Research, theory, and practice. In B. M. Staw & L. L. Cummings (eds.), *Research in organizational behavior*, vol. 10. Greenwich, CT: JAI Press, pp. 213–255.
8. Brockner, J., Grover, S. L., & Blonder, M. D. (1988). Predictors of survivors' job involvement following layoffs: A field study. *Journal of Applied Psychology*, **73**, 436–442.
9. Business and the law (1987, March 30). *The New York Times*, p. D2.
10. Cascio, W. F. (1991). *Applied psychology in personnel management* (4th ed.). Englewood Cliffs, NJ: Prentice-Hall.

11. Cullen, J. B., Victor, B., & Stephens, C. (1989). An ethical weather report: Assessing the organization's ethical climate. *Organizational Dynamics*, **18**, 50–62.

12. Curtis, W., Smith, R., & Smoll, F. (1979). Scrutinizing the skipper: A study of leadership behaviors in the dugout. *Journal of Applied Psychology*, **64**, 391–400.

13. Dalton, D. R., & Todor, W. D. (1985). Gender and workplace justice: A field assessment. *Personnel Psychology*, **38**, 133–151.

14. Dalton, D. R., & Todor, W. D. (1981). Win, lose, draw: The grievance process in practice. *Personnel Administrator*, **26**(3), 25–29.

15. Dalton, D. R., Todor, W. D., & Owen, C. L. (1987). Sex effects in workplace justice outcomes: A field assessment. *Journal of Applied Psychology*, **72**, 156–159.

16. Davis, B. (1987, Aug. 20). Abusive computers. *The Wall Street Journal*, pp. 1, 12.

17. Drost, D. A., & O'Brien, F. P. (1983). Are there grievances against your non-union grievance procedure? *Personnel Administrator*, **28**(1), 36–42.

18. Engel, P. G. (1985, Mar. 18). Preserving the right to fire. *Industry Week*, pp. 39–40.

19. Ewing, J. B. (1989, Oct. 23). Corporate due process lowers legal costs. *The Wall Street Journal*, p. A14.

20. *Fall River Dyeing and Finishing Corp. v. N.L.R.B.* (1987). *Labor Law Reports*, Sn. 12, 333.

21. Farnsworth, C. H. (1987, Feb. 22). Survey of whistle blowers finds retaliation but few regrets. *The New York Times*, p. 22.

22. Fasman, Z. D., & Fischler, K. (1987). Labor relations consequences of mergers and acquisitions. *Employee Relations Law Journal*, **13**, 14–42.

23. Fossum, J. A. (1990). Employee and labor relations in an evolving environment. In J. A. Fossum (ed.), *Employee and labor relations*. Washington, DC: Bureau of National Affairs, pp. 4-1 to 4-22.

24. Franke, R., & Karl, J. (1978). The Hawthorne experiments: First statistical interpretation. *American Sociological Review*, **43**, 623–643.

25. Fulmer, W. E., & Casey, A. W. (1990). Employment at will: Options for managers. *Academy of Management Executive*, **4**(2), 102–107.

26. Geyelin, M. (1989, Sep. 7). Fired managers winning more lawsuits. *The Wall Street Journal*, p. B1.

27. Green, W. B. (1989, Jan. 11). Courts skeptical of "noncompete" pacts. *The Wall Street Journal*, p. B1.

28. Greenberg, J. (1987). Reactions to procedural injustice in payment distributions: Do the means justify the ends? *Journal of Applied Psychology*, **72**, 55–61.

29. Hegarty, W. H., & Sims, H. P., Jr. (1979). Organizational philosophy, policies, and objectives related to unethical decision behavior: A laboratory experiment. *Journal of Applied Psychology*, **64**, 331–338.

30. Heshizer, B. (1984). The implied contract exception to at-will employment. *Labor Law Journal*, **35**, 131–141.

31. Hill, M., Jr., & Sinicropi, A. V. (1980). *Evidence in arbitration*. Washington, DC: Bureau of National Affairs.

32. Hilts, P. J. (1991, March 22). Hero in exposing science hoax paid dearly. *The New York Times*, pp. A1, B6.

33. Hoerr, J. (1988, Mar. 28). It's getting harder to pass out pink slips. *Business Week*, p. 68.

34. Internal Revenue Service. (1991). *Publication 501: Exemptions, standard deduction, and filing information*. Washington, D.C.: U.S. Government Printing Office.

35. Israel, D. (1983). The Weingarten case sets precedent for co-employee representation. *Personnel Administrator*, **28**(2), 23–26.

36. Jansen, E., & Von Glinow, M. A. (1985). Ethical ambivalence and organizational reward systems. *Academy of Management Review*, **10**, 814–822.

37. Johnson, R. K. (1988, May). Employment contracts. *The Advisor*, pp. 6, 7.

38. Klaas, B. S. (1989). Managerial decision making about employee grievances: The impact of the grievant's work history. *Personnel Psychology*, **42**, 53–68.

39. Klaas, B. S., & Wheeler, H. N. (1990). Managerial decision making about employee discipline: A policy capturing approach. *Personnel Psychology*, **43**, 117–134.

40. Kotlowitz, A. (1987, Aug. 28). Labor's turn? *The Wall Street Journal*, pp. 1, 14.

41. Kotlowitz, A. (1987, Apr. 1). Grievous work. *The Wall Street Journal*, pp. 1, 12.

42. Koys, D. J., Briggs, S., & Grenig, J. (1987). State court disparity on employment-at-will. *Personnel Psychology*, **40**, 565–577.

43. Labor letter (1989, Apr. 25). *The Wall Street Journal*, p. A1.

44. Labor letter (1989, Nov. 14). *The Wall Street Journal*, p. A1.

45. Labor letter (1984, Feb. 7). *The Wall Street Journal*, p. 1.

46. London, M. & Bray, D. W. (1980). Ethical issues in testing and evaluation for personnel decisions. *American Psychologist*, **35**, 890–901.

47. Lorber, L. Z. (1984). Basic advice on avoiding employment-at-will troubles. *Personnel Administrator*, **29**(1), 59–62.

48. Lorber, L. Z., Kirk, J. R., Kirschner, K. H., & Handorf, C. R. (1984). *Fear of firing: A legal and personnel analysis of employment-at-will.* Alexandria, VA: ASPA.

49. *Meech v. Hillhaven West, Inc.*, 4 IER cases 737 (Mont. 1989).

50. Meyer, D., & Cooke, W. (1988). Economic and political factors in the resolution of formal grievances. *Industrial Relations*, **27**, 318–335.

51. Miceli, M. P., & Near, J. P. (1988). Individual and situational correlates of whistle-blowing. *Personnel Psychology*, **41**, 267–281.

52. Mills, D. Q. (1989). *Labor-management relations* (4th ed.). New York: McGraw-Hill.

53. *NLRB v. Sears Roebuck and Co.* (1985, Feb. 27). *Daily Labor Report*, **39**, D1–D5.

54. *NLRB v. Weingarten* (1974). 420 U.S. 251, 95 S. Ct. 959.

55. Nielsen, R. P. (1989). Changing unethical organizational behavior. *Academy of Management Executive*, **3**(2), 123–130.

56. Nobile, R. (1985). Employee searches in the workplace: Developing a realistic policy. *Personnel Administrator*, **30**(5), 89–98.

57. Noble, K. B. (1988, June 30). Unions limited in use of dues and fees. *The New York Times*, p. 13.

58. Oberle, R. L. (1978, January). Administering disciplinary actions. *Personnel Journal*, pp. 29–31.

59. Olson, F. C. (1984). How peer review works at Control Data. *Harvard Business Review*, **62**(6), 58–61.

60. O'Reilly, C. A., III, & Weitz, B. A. (1980). Managing marginal employees: The use of warnings and dismissals. *Administrative Science Quarterly*, **25**, 467–484.

61. Personal affairs (1983, June 6). *Forbes*, pp. 174, 178.

62. Pfeffer, J. (1981). Management as symbolic action: The creation and maintenance of meaning. In L. Cummings & B. Staw (eds.), *Research in Organizational Behavior*, vol. 3. Greenwich, CT: JAI Press.

63. Privacy (1988, Mar. 28). *Business Week*, pp. 61–68.

64. Reibstein, L. (1986, Dec. 3). More firms use peer review panel to resolve employees' grievances. *The Wall Street Journal*, p. 33.

65. Schlender, B. R. (1988, Dec. 30). California ruling curtails damages in dismissal suits. *The Wall Street Journal*, p. B1.

66. Spurgeon, Haney, & Howbert, P. A. (1985). *Ready, fire! (aim): A manager's primer in the law of terminations.* Colorado Springs, CO: Author.

67. Staudhar, P. D. (1976). Grievance arbitration in public employment. *The Arbitration Journal*, **31**, 116–124.

68. Stevenson, R. W. (1989, July 10). Workers who turn in bosses use law to seek big rewards. *The New York Times*, pp. 1, D3.

69. Stickney, J. (1984, December). Settling the terms of employment. *Money*, pp. 127, 128, 132.

70. Stone, D. L., & Stone, E. F. (1987). Effects of missing application-blank information on personnel selection decisions: Do privacy protection strategies bias the outcome? *Journal of Applied Psychology*, **72**, 452–456.

71. Sweet, D. H. (1989). *A manager's guide to conducting terminations.* Lexington, MA: Lexington Books.

72. Sweet, D. H. (1989). Outplacement. In W. F. Cascio (ed.), *Human resource planning, employment, and placement.* Washington, DC: Bureau of National Affairs, pp. 2-236 to 2-261.

73. Taking it to arbitration (1985, July 16). *The Wall Street Journal*, p. 1.

74. Wald, M. L. (1990, Mar. 11). Whistle-blowers in atomic plants to be aided. *The New York Times*, p. 28.

75. *Webster's new collegiate dictionary* (1976). Springfield, MA: Merriam-Webster.

76. Wermiel, S. (1988, June 7). Justices expand union workers' right to sue. *The Wall Street Journal*, p. 4.

77. Wesman, E. C., & Eischen, D. E. (1990). Due process. In J. A. Fossum (ed.), *Employee and labor relations.* Washington, DC: Bureau of National Affairs, pp. 4-82 to 4-133.

78. Williams, W. (1985, June 9). White-collar crime: Booming again. *The New York Times*, pp. 1F, 6F.

79. Youngblood, D. (1987, June 22). Supervisors offered guidelines to "humane" firing. *Rocky Mountain News*, p. 62.

A CONCEPTUAL VIEW OF HUMAN RESOURCE MANAGEMENT
STRATEGIC OBJECTIVES, ENVIRONMENTS, FUNCTIONS

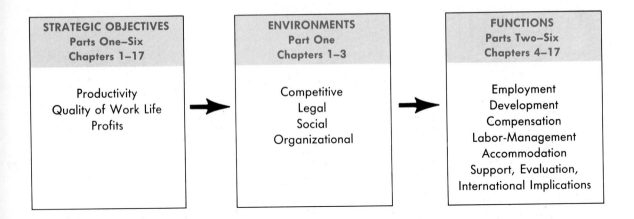

STRATEGIC OBJECTIVES
Parts One–Six
Chapters 1–17

Productivity
Quality of Work Life
Profits

ENVIRONMENTS
Part One
Chapters 1–3

Competitive
Legal
Social
Organizational

FUNCTIONS
Parts Two–Six
Chapters 4–17

Employment
Development
Compensation
Labor-Management
Accommodation
Support, Evaluation,
International Implications

RELATIONSHIP OF HRM FUNCTIONS TO HRM ACTIVITIES

FUNCTIONS	ACTIVITIES
PART 2 EMPLOYMENT	Job Analysis, Human Resource Planning, Recruiting, Staffing (Chapters 4–6)
PART 3 DEVELOPMENT	Orientation, Training, Performance Appraisal, Managing Careers (Chapters 7–9)
PART 4 COMPENSATION	Pay, Benefits, Incentives (Chapters 10–12)
PART 5 LABOR-MANAGEMENT ACCOMMODATION	Union Representation, Collective Bargaining, Procedural Justice, Ethics (Chapters 13, 14)
PART 6 SUPPORT, EVALUATION, INTERNATIONAL IMPLICATIONS	Job Safety and Health, Costs/Benefits of HRM Activities, International Dimensions of HRM (Chapters 15–17)

PART SIX

Support, Evaluation, and International Implications

This capstone section deals with three broad themes: organizational support for employees, evaluation of human resource management activities, and the international implications of human resource management activities. Chapter 15 examines key issues involved in employee safety and health, mental and physical. Chapter 16 presents the latest methods for assessing the costs and benefits of human resource management activities in six major areas. Finally, Chapter 17 considers key issues in international human resource management; given the rapid growth of multinational corporations, it is perhaps in this area more than in any other that employees and their families need special social and financial support from their firms.

Safety, Health, and Employee Assistance Programs

■ **HUMAN RESOURCE MANAGEMENT IN ACTION**

SUBSTANCE ABUSE ON THE JOB PRODUCES TOUGH POLICY CHOICES FOR MANAGERS*

Experts estimate that 5 to 10 percent of employees in any company have a substance abuse problem (alcohol or drugs) serious enough to merit treatment. The situation may be even worse. Thus in 1984 and 1985, unbeknown to employees and job applicants, Chevron Corp. carried out anonymous drug testing. About 30 percent of all applicants and 20 percent of all employees tested positive for illegal drug use.

What is an appropriate policy for managers to adopt in these circumstances? Certainly cost pressures are forcing some employers to reexamine their drug and alcohol treatment programs. After noting that costs for a 21-day detoxification program run from $4000 to $14,000, one health care professional commented, "People want to fire other people because they consume a lot of health-care dollars. Those of us in the . . . field are feeling

*Adapted from: Firms debate hard line on alcoholics, *The Wall Street Journal*, April 13, 1989, p. B1. Reprinted by permission of *The Wall Street Journal*, © 1989 Dow Jones & Company, Inc. All rights reserved worldwide.

[pressure]. We were feeling it before *Valdez*, and we'll feel it after. In terms of cutting their costs, they go for the most visible, and clearly the most visible are chemically dependent people."

Another professional in the field says that more hard-line companies simply demote people who have been in treatment. "They won't have a written policy, but they'll guide that person into a position of no strategic importance. If asked, the companies won't acknowledge it. They don't want the bad publicity of being a mean guy."

Buoying these hard-liners are some very public drug- and alcohol-related accidents of which the Exxon *Valdez* oil spill is probably the best known. According to federal regulators, the rate of railroad employees who failed drug or alcohol tests following accidents rose to 6 percent in the first 11 months of 1988, from 4.6 percent in 1986. More recently, three Northwest Airlines pilots were convicted of operating a commercial airliner while intoxicated. What should firms do? While dismissal and demotion are two obvious policy choices, rehabilitation is a third.

Among companies that endorse rehabilitation, however, there is considerable debate about whether employees should be returned to their jobs if they are successfully rehabilitated. Standard industry practice is to return people to their jobs after treatment. Exxon, however, bucked the industry trend following the wreck of its oil tanker Exxon *Valdez* (and the environmental disaster that followed). The ship's captain had been treated for alcoholism and returned to work. After the accident, a blood test revealed a high level of alcohol in his system. Exxon therefore adopted the policy that, following treatment, known alcohol and drug abusers won't be allowed to return to so-called critical jobs such as piloting a ship, flying a plane, or operating a refinery, although they will be given other jobs.

Those who favor returning people to work after rehabilitation argue that it is not only more humane, but also more effective. Refusing to return people to work—even in safety-sensitive positions—would be "short-sighted. It will make sure that no one who's an alcoholic ever gets help," according to the medical director of United Airlines (which regularly returns pilots to their jobs after treatment). "As ubiquitous a disease as alcoholism is, you have two choices: You either have practicing alcoholics in the cockpits, or you have recovering ones." Those who take a more hard-line attitude toward drug and alcohol abuse point out that many companies are thinking through their policies, wondering how much criticism from the community they can tolerate.

Challenges

1. What are some arguments for and against each of these policies: dismissal, demotion, return to the same job following rehabilitation, return to a different job following rehabilitation?

2. Should follow-up be required after rehabilitation? If so, how long should it last and what form should it take?

As the chapter opening vignette shows, managers face tough policy issues in the area of workplace health and safety. As we shall see, a combination of external factors (e.g., the spiraling cost of health care) and internal factors (e.g., new technology) are making these issues impossible to ignore. Here are some decisions that managers will have to grapple with:

QUESTIONS THIS CHAPTER WILL HELP MANAGERS ANSWER

1. What is the cost-benefit trade-off of adopting measures to enhance workplace safety and health?
2. What should an informed, progressive AIDS policy look like?
3. Does it make sound business sense to institute a worksite wellness program? If so, who should be allowed to participate?

This chapter begins by examining how social and legal policies on the federal and state levels have evolved on this issue, beginning with workers' compensation laws and culminating with the passage of the Occupational Safety and Health Act. The chapter then considers enforcement of the act, with special emphasis on the rights and obligations of management. It also examines prevailing approaches to job safety and health in other countries. Finally it considers the problems of AIDS and business, employee assistance programs, and corporate "wellness" programs. Underlying all these efforts is a conviction on the part of many firms that it is morally right to improve job safety and health—and that doing so will enhance the productivity and quality of work life of employees at all levels.

EXTENT AND COST OF SAFETY AND HEALTH PROBLEMS

Consider these startling facts. Every year in U.S. workplaces:[1]

- Roughly 1 of every 12 workers is injured or becomes ill on the job.[43]
- Almost 11,000 workers die in workplace accidents.
- 2 million workers are disabled.
- 137,000 new cases of disabling illness occur.
- 1.8 million workers suffer injuries involving lost workdays.
- 35 million workdays are lost.

This figure balloons to 75 million workdays lost when permanently disabling injuries that occurred in prior years are included.

The cost? A staggering $40 billion in lost wages, medical costs, insurance administration costs, and indirect costs. At the level of the individual firm, a Du Pont safety engineer determined that a disabling injury costs an average of $18,650. A company with 1000 employees could expect to have 27 lost-workday injuries per year. With a 4.5 percent profit margin, the company would need $11.3 million of sales to offset that cost.[59]

Regardless of one's perspective, social or economic, these are disturbing figures. In response, public policy has focused on two types of actions: *monetary compensation* for job-related injuries and *preventive measures* to enhance job safety and health. State-run workers' compensation programs and the federal Occupational Safety and Health Administration are responsible for implementing public policy in these areas. Let's examine each of them.

WORKERS' COMPENSATION: A HISTORICAL PERSPECTIVE

In the late nineteenth and early twentieth centuries, employers were relatively free to run their operations as they saw fit, whether or not the operations were safe. Employees injured on the job had to file lawsuits against their employers in order to receive *any* compensation for their injuries. Employers lost only when it could be proven that their negligence resulted in the injury. This rarely happened, and, in fact, workers rarely brought suit because it cost money to do so. Under common law the firm had certain defenses. It could not be held liable if it could show either (1) that an employee in accepting the job knew of the hazards or (2) that the worker, or even a fellow worker, had been negligent and in any way contributed to the accident.[71]

These views began to change only after major disasters in which many workers lost their lives. For example, state inspection of mines in Pennsylvania was first authorized in 1870 after a fire in an anthracite mine killed 109 miners. Mandatory safety regulations concerning fire escapes were instituted after the 1911 Triangle Shirtwaist Company fire, in which over 100 women in a crowded sweatshop died trying to escape the flames when the exit doors were locked.

Another new development was the introduction of workers' compensation laws by state governments in the early 1900s. Such laws are based on the principle of *liability without fault*, under which employers contribute to a fund providing compensation to employees involved in work-related accidents and injuries. The scale of benefits is related to the nature of the injury. The benefits are not provided because of liability or negligence on the part of the employer; rather, they are provided simply as a matter of social policy.[2] Since the premiums paid reflected the accident rate of the particular employer, states hoped to provide an incentive for firms to lower their premium costs by improving work conditions. The Supreme Court upheld the constitutionality of such laws in 1917, and by 1948 all states had adopted them in one form or another.[15]

For the more than 80 million workers, or 88 percent of the nation's workforce who are covered, workers' compensation provides three types of benefits: (1) payments to replace lost wages while an employee is unable to work, (2) payments to cover medical bills, and (3) if an individual is unable to return to his or her former occupation, financial support for retraining.[1,110] To replace lost wages, the legislation typically allows for some percentage of regular wages (60 to 67 percent) up to a maximum amount. However, the benefits actually received are often less than half of regular wages.[62]

By the 1960s it was becoming apparent that neither the workers' compensation laws nor state safety standards were acting to reduce occupational hazards. Evidence began to accumulate that there were health hazards (so-called silent killers) in the modern work environment that either had not been fully recognized previously or were not fully understood. Research on industrial disease was beginning to discover that even brief exposure to certain toxic materials in a work environment could produce disease, sterility, and high mortality rates. This new concern was dramatized by revelations of "black lung" (pneumoconiosis) among coal miners, of "brown lung" (byssinosis) among textile workers, and of the toxic and carcinogenic (cancer-causing) effects of substances such as vinyl chloride and asbestos in other work environments.

Today, stress-related awards account for nearly 14 percent of occupational disease claims, up from less than 5 percent just 8 years ago. Workers' compensation has also been awarded for certain adverse physiological reactions to computer monitors, such as eye strain.[77] Thus, in addition to *compensation* for work-related injuries, it became clear that a federally administered program of *prevention* of workplace health and safety hazards was essential. This concern culminated in the passage of the Williams-Steiger Occupational Safety and Health Act of 1970.

THE OCCUPATIONAL SAFETY AND HEALTH ACT

Purpose and Coverage

The purpose of the act is an ambitious one: "To assure so far as possible every working man and woman in the Nation safe and healthful working conditions and to preserve our human resources." Its coverage is equally ambitious, for the law extends to any business (regardless of size) that *affects* interstate commerce. Since almost any business affects interstate commerce, almost all businesses are included, for a total of about 75 million workers in 5 million workplaces.[104] Federal, state, and local government workers are excluded since the government cannot easily proceed against itself in the event of violations.

Administration

The 1970 act established three government agencies to administer and enforce the law:

- *The Occupational Safety and Health Administration* (OSHA) to establish and enforce the necessary safety and health standards
- *The Occupational Safety and Health Review Commission* (a three-member board appointed by the President) to rule on the appropriateness of OSHA's enforcement actions when they are contested by employers, employees, or unions

■ *The National Institute for Occupational Safety and Health* to conduct research on the causes and prevention of occupational injury and illness, to recommend new standards (based on this research) to the Secretary of Labor, and to develop educational programs

Safety and Health Standards

Under the law, each employer has a "general duty" to provide a place of employment "free from recognized hazards." Employers also have the "special duty" to comply with all standards of safety and health established under the act.

In setting safety and health standards, OSHA is required by Congress to adopt existing "consensus standards." Some of these were existing federal standards in industries such as mining, construction, and longshoring. Others had been developed over the years by organizations such as the American National Standards Institute and the National Fire Protection Association and by various trade associations such as the Associated General Contractors and the Manufacturing Chemists Association. Finally, labor unions, public interest groups, various states, and the National Institute for Occupational Safety and Health (NIOSH) have suggested new or revised OSHA standards. NIOSH, for example, has identified over 15,000 toxic substances based on its research.

To date, OSHA has issued a large number of detailed standards covering numerous environmental hazards. These include power tools, machine guards, compressed gas, materials handling and storage, and toxic substances such as asbestos, cotton dust, silica, lead, and carbon monoxide. While the majority of such standards were acknowledged as helpful and important, employers found some of them infuriatingly niggling. For example:

> (In a portable toilet) The building shall be of fly-tight construction, doors shall be self-closing. . . . The seat top shall be not less than 12 inches nor more than 16 inches above the floor.
>
> In response to numerous complaints, and in compliance with President Carter's orders that regulatory agencies get rid of their nuisance rules and standards, OSHA dropped 928 of its least important.[37,100]

Record-Keeping Requirements

A good deal of paperwork is required of employers under the act. Specifically:

■ A general log of each injury or illness (OSHA Form 200), shown in Figure 15-1

■ Supplementary records of each injury or illness (OSHA Form 101)

Employees are guaranteed access, on request, to Form 200 at their workplace, and the records must be retained for 5 years following the calendar year they cover.[100] The purpose of these reports is to identify where safety and health problems have

U.S. Department of Labor

For Calendar Year 19 _____   Page _____ of_____

Company Name

Establishment Name

Establishment Address

Form Approved
O.M.B. No. 1220-0029

Extent of and Outcome of INJURY						Type, Extent of, and Outcome of ILLNESS													
Fatalities	Nonfatal Injuries					Type of Illness							Fatalities	Nonfatal Illnesses					
Injury Related	Injuries With Lost Workdays				Injuries Without Lost Workdays	CHECK Only One Column for Each Illness (See other side of form for terminations or permanent transfers.)							Illness Related	Illnesses With Lost Workdays				Illnesses Without Lost Workdays
Enter DATE of death. Mo./day/yr.	Enter a CHECK if injury involves days away from work, or days of restricted work activity, or both.	Enter a CHECK if injury involves days away from work.	Enter number of DAYS away from work.	Enter number of DAYS of restricted work activity.	Enter a CHECK if no entry was made in columns 1 or 2 but the injury is recordable as defined above.	Occupational skin diseases or disorders	Dust diseases of the lungs	Respiratory conditions due to toxic agents	Poisoning (systemic effects of toxic materials)	Disorders due to physical agents	Disorders associated with repeated trauma	All other occupational illnesses	Enter DATE of death. Mo./day/yr.	Enter a CHECK if illness involves days away from work, or days of restricted work activity, or both.	Enter a CHECK if illness involves days away from work	Enter number of DAYS away from work.	Enter number of DAYS of restricted work activity.	Enter a CHECK if no entry was made in columns 8 or 9.
(1)	(2)	(3)	(4)	(5)	(6)	(a)	(b)	(c)	(d)	(e)	(f)	(g)	(8)	(9)	(10)	(11)	(12)	(13)

INJURIES

ILLNESSES

Certification of Annual Summary Totals By _____ Title _____ Date _____

OSHA No. 200   POST ONLY THIS PORTION OF THE LAST PAGE NO LATER THAN FEBRUARY 1.

FIGURE 15-1
OSHA Form 200, log and summary of occupational injuries and illnesses.

been occurring (if at all). Such information helps call management's attention to the problems, as well as that of an OSHA inspector, should he or she visit the workplace. The annual summary must be sent to OSHA directly, to help the agency determine which workplaces should receive priority for inspections.

OSHA Enforcement

In administering the act, OSHA inspectors have the right to enter a workplace and to conduct a compliance inspection. However, in the 1978 *Marshall v. Barlow's, Inc.* decision, the Supreme Court ruled that employers could require a search warrant before allowing the inspector onto company premises.[67] In practice, only about 3 percent of employers go that far, perhaps because the resulting inspection is likely to be especially "close."[24]

Since it is impossible for the roughly 1100 agency insepctors, or "coshos" (compliance safety and health officers), to visit the nation's 5 million workplaces, a system of priorities has been established. Coshos, most of whom are either safety engineers or industrial hygienists, assign top priority to workplaces where there is an imminent danger to worker health and safety or where a disaster involving deaths or accidents hospitalizing five or more employees has already occurred.

Second priority goes to investigating employee complaints that safety or health standards have been violated. Employers are prohibited from discriminating against employees who file such complaints, and an employee representative is entitled to accompany the cosho during the inspection.

Special inspection attention is also given to highly hazardous industries, such as marine cargo handling, roof and sheetmetal work, meat and meat products, lumber and wood products, and miscellaneous transportation equipment (such as mobile homes).[21] Finally, random inspections of workplaces of all sizes that do not fit into one of the preceding categories are common.[103] Such a prospect is an effective motivator for most employers to provide safe and healthful working environments.

Considerable emphasis has been given to OSHA's role of *enforcement*, but not much to its role of *consultation*. Employers in nearly every state who want help in recognizing and correcting safety and health hazards can get it from a free, on site consultation service funded by OSHA. The service is delivered by state governments or private-sector contractors using well-trained safety and/or health professionals (e.g., industrial hygienists). Primarily targeted for smaller businesses, this program is penalty-free and completely separate from the OSHA inspection effort. An employer's only obligation is a commitment to correct serious job safety and health hazards.

Penalties Fines are mandatory where serious violations are found. If a violation is willful (one in which an employer either knew that what was being done constituted a violation of federal regulations or was aware that a hazardous condition existed and made no reasonable effort to eliminate it), employers can be assessed a civil penalty of up to $70,000 for each violation (as of 1991). An employer who fails to correct a violation (within the allowed time limit) for which a citation has been issued can be fined up to $7000 for each day that the violation continues. Finally, as of 1991 a willful first violation involving the death of a worker can carry a criminal penalty as high as $70,000 and 6 months in prison. A second such conviction can mean up to $140,000 and a full year behind bars.[80] Needless to say, the legislators who enacted OSHA put real teeth into the law.

Appeals Employers can appeal citations, proposed penalties, and corrections they have been ordered to make through multiple levels of the agency, culminating with the Occupational Safety and Health Review Commission. The commission presumes the employer to be free of violations and puts the burden of proof on OSHA.[104] Further appeals can be pursued through the federal court system.

Role of the states Although OSHA is a federally run program, the act allows states to develop and to administer their own programs if they are approved by the Secretary of Labor. There are many criteria for approval, but the most important is that the state program must be judged "at least as effective" as the federal program. Currently 25 states and territories have approved plans in operation.

Workers' rights to health and safety Both unionized and nonunionized workers have walked off the job when subjected to unsafe working conditions.[74,109] In unionized firms, walkouts have occurred during the term of valid collective bargaining agreements that contained no-strike and grievance and/or arbitration clauses.[33] Are such walkouts legal? Yes, the Supreme Court has ruled, under certain circumstances. Consider the case of *Gateway Coal Co. v. United Mine Workers of America.*

UNSAFE CONDITIONS AT GATEWAY COAL

■ **COMPANY EXAMPLE**

As a result of line supervisors making false entries in their logs, the accumulation of gas significantly increased the probability of an explosion in the mine. The union called a meeting, during which members voted unanimously to refuse to work under those supervisors. That day the supervisors in question were suspended, but they subsequently returned to work despite the fact that criminal charges were pending against them.

The miners immediately walked off their jobs. When the company offered to submit the dispute to arbitration, the union refused. An injunction was issued, ordering the miners to return to work and to submit the dispute to arbitration. The employees honored the injunction and the case was submitted. The arbitrator ruled that retention of the supervisors did not present a health hazard.

The union appealed the issuance of the injunction to the Third Circuit Court of Appeals, which sided with the union. The court reasoned that if employees *believe* dangerous conditions exist, there is no reason to sub-ordinate their judgment to that of an arbitrator. Regardless of how impartial the arbitrator is, he or she is not staking his or her life on the outcome of the decision.

Gateway Coal appealed to the Supreme Court, which found that a work stoppage that is called to protect workers from "immediate danger" is au-thorized by Section 502 of the Taft-Hartley Act. The walkout cannot be stopped by an injunction, even when employees have agreed to a compre-hensive no-strike clause.

Reviews of case law in this area found the following precedents currently in force:[41,62]

- Objective evidence must be presented to support the claim that abnor-mally dangerous working conditions exist.
- If such evidence is presented, a walkout under Section 502 is legal *re-gardless* of the existence of a no-strike or arbitration clause.
- It is an unfair labor practice for an employer to interfere with activity protected under Section 502. This is true whether a firm is unionized or nonunionized.
- Expert testimony (e.g., by an industrial hygienist) is critically important in establishing the presence of abnormally dangerous working conditions.
- If a good-faith belief is not supported by objective evidence, then em-ployees who walk off the job are subject to disciplinary action.

OSHA's Impact

From its inception, OSHA has been both cussed and discussed, and its effectiveness in improving workplace safety and health has been questioned by the very firms it regulates.[38] Controversy has ranged from disagreements over the setting of health standards to inspection procedures.[90] Employers complain of excessively detailed and costly regulations ($25 billion in the agency's first 10 years), which, they believe, ignore workplace realities. OSHA has even been satirized in a video game called "Hard Hat Mack."

OSHA versus Hard Hat Mack The blue-collar blip, called Mack, is described as a "bona fide working-class hero" striving to build a high-rise building. Another blip, which spends the game going after the blue-collar blip, is described as a representative from OSHA. The game package says that the OSHA blip has a "crew cut, clipboard, and absolutely no sense of humor. The government sends a generous supply of these guys to cite you into oblivion."

Mack faces a lot of other obstacles, of course—falling rivets, runaway jackham-mers, and exposed wires. At advanced levels, a misstep on a girder can even send Mack tumbling into a portable toilet. But the OSHA blip is just as dangerous; if it catches him, Mack dies. Although the game has outraged some public officials,

OSHA took it in stride. In fact, the head of the agency wrote to the game's developer: "Let's be fair; Hard Hat Mack is a lot safer on the job with OSHA around."[72]

It is one thing for employers to cite the total cost of compliance, but a fair evaluation requires that we put this figure into perspective. Over a 10-year period, a $25 billion expenditure averages out to $2.5 billion per year in a trillion-dollar-per-year economy. This is about 7.5 percent of what workplace accidents have recently cost the nation annually.[1] Such "preventive" expenditures do not seem unreasonable.

During its first 10 years, organized labor generally praised OSHA for identifying and restricting exposure to health hazards that in 1970 were considered "part of the job" and for imposing safety protections and participatory rights for workers.[54] By the late 1980s, however, the praise faded to ridicule. Said the health and safety director of the Communications Workers of America: "OSHA's a creampuff. . . . Basically it's done nothing for workers."[102]

Small businesses have praised OSHA for delivering on its regulatory reform promises. Thus one survey of small businesses showed that 42.6 percent believed OSHA had shown the most positive change of all regulatory agencies. No other agency received more than 6 percent of the vote from this survey.[79]

OSHA's ability to improve workplace safety and health continues to be debated. On the one hand, investigations by Congress[14,102] and by outside researchers[35,68] have found that OSHA has made no significant, lasting reductions in lost workdays or injury rates. In the opinion of the AFL-CIO, this is due to a lack of enforcement of safety standards and regulations by OSHA. Directors of OSHA argue exactly the opposite: It's precisely because of better record keeping, brought about in part by stiff fines against companies levied by OSHA, that injury rates haven't shown a sustained decline.[48] Another reason is that employers try to improve their competitiveness at the expense of safety.[89] Here's an example.

MAINTAINING PRODUCTIVITY AT THE EXPENSE OF SAFETY

■ COMPANY EXAMPLE

Such a cost-benefit attitude may have contributed to the deaths of two pipe fitters at McDonnell Douglas Corporation's fighter-plane plant in St. Louis. The two died of chemical burns after a 6000-gallon tank they were filling with hydrofluoric acid overflowed. Said an official of the International Association of Machinists: "The safety rules weren't being enforced; sometimes it cuts into the profit" (ref. 91, p. 18).

The tank had no quantity indicator, and because a safety valve had been blowing out frequently, a solid rubber plug had been inserted "to avoid shutdowns." The men were not wearing chemical-proof suits or respirators, as safety rules require. OSHA cited the company for eight safety violations and proposed fines totalling $44,200. The company said it was reemphasizing safety practices.[91]

Despite these problems, even OSHA's critics have agreed that simply by calling attention to the problems of workplace safety and health, OSHA has caused a lot more *awareness* of these dangers than would otherwise have been the case. Management's willingness to correct hazards and to improve such vital environmental conditions as ventilation, noise levels, and machine safety is much greater now than it was before OSHA. Critics also agree that, because of OSHA and the National Institute for Occupational Safety and Health, we now know far more about such dangerous substances as vinyl chloride, PCBs, asbestos, cotton dust, and a host of other carcinogens. As a result, management has taken at least the initial actions needed to protect workers from them.

Finally, any analysis of OSHA's impact must consider the fundamental issue of the *causes* of workplace accidents. OSHA standards govern potentially unsafe *work conditions* that employees may be exposed to. There are no standards that govern potentially unsafe *employee behaviors*. And while employers may be penalized for failure to comply with safety and health standards, employees are subject to no such threat. Research suggests that the enforcement of OSHA standards, directed as it is to environmental accidents and illnesses, can hope *at best* to affect 25 percent of on-the-job accidents.[22] The remaining 75 percent require *behavioral* rather than *technical* modifications.

In short, a company's response to enforcement plays as important a role as the nature of the enforcement activities themselves. Simple examination of the frequency or severity of accidents reportable to OSHA over time fails to take into account the *process* of compliance, that is, what happened between inspections and subsequent accidents.[38] Shortly we will examine the kinds of preventive safety and health activities that do work, but first let's consider an approach to assessing the costs and benefits of occupational safety and health programs.

ASSESSING THE COSTS AND BENEFITS OF OCCUPATIONAL SAFETY AND HEALTH PROGRAMS

Employers frequently complain that there is no systematic method of quantifying costs and benefits when dealing with employee safety and health conditions. Technically that is true, but here is a behavior costing model that may provide a useful start.[36]

Let's begin by distinguishing *nondiscretionary* from *discretionary* safety and health expenditures. Federal, state, and local agencies require firms to comply with safety and health regulations. To comply, firms may have to purchase and install special equipment, such as machine guards, safety switch interlocks, and treaded, nonslip flooring. These costs are nondiscretionary. To do otherwise is to risk heavy fines and losses from liability and damage suits.

Beyond mere compliance, however, companies have a number of options regarding the degree to which they invest in employee safety and health. A motivational poster program (e.g., "Think Safety") is a token effort that requires minimal expense. Creation of a safety committee to encourage active employee involvement through meetings, plant inspections, and evaluation of employee complaints is more expensive. The highest-cost option includes regular safety training for all employees. The training may involve films, lectures by safety experts, or hands-on drills and demonstrations with safety and emergency apparatus. For each of these levels of safety and health programs, investment *costs* are measurable. They include the salaries and wages of employees participating in the program, the costs of outside services used, and the costs to implement the programs.

Unfortunately, the *benefits* to be derived from such programs cannot be traced as easily to the bottom line. Certainly the most quantifiable benefit resulting from the successful introduction of a safety and health program is a reduction in casualty and workers' compensation insurance rates. Less measurable benefits involve the *avoidance* of the "indirect" costs of an accident, including:

1. Cost of wages paid for time lost
2. Cost of damage to material or equipment
3. Cost of overtime work required by the accident
4. Cost of wages paid to supervisors while their time is required for activities resulting from the accident
5. Costs of decreased output of the injured worker after she or he returns to work
6. Costs associated with the time it takes for a new worker to learn the job
7. Uninsured medical costs borne by the company
8. Cost of time spent by higher management and clerical workers to investigate or to process workers' compensation forms

Prediction of these costs, and identification of trends in them, is very difficult. It must be done on the basis of historical information (to gauge trends) and judgment by managers (to assess the seriousness of accidents *avoided*). These concepts may be incorporated into a cost/benefit curve of the sort shown in Figure 15-2.

The shape of the curve will depend on the range of factors just discussed, and it may well be that cost/benefit relationships can be plotted for various hazard classifications in a particular plant or industry. As each preventive cost is added, additional savings or benefits accrue to some point of diminishing (economic) return. The word "economic" is in parentheses because there should be no limit to efforts to eliminate accident and health hazards. Like many other problems of the marketplace, safety and health programs involve what economists call "externalities"—the fact that all the social costs of production are not necessarily included on a firm's profit and loss statement. The employer does not suffer the worker's injury or disease and therefore lacks the full incentive to reduce it. As long as the outlays required for preventive measures are less than the social costs of disability among workers, higher fatality rates, and the diversion of medical resources, then the enforcement of safety and health standards is well worth it and society will benefit.[5,15]

ORGANIZATIONAL SAFETY AND HEALTH PROGRAMS

As noted earlier, accidents result from two broad causes: *unsafe work conditions* (physical and environmental) and *unsafe work behaviors*. Unsafe physical conditions

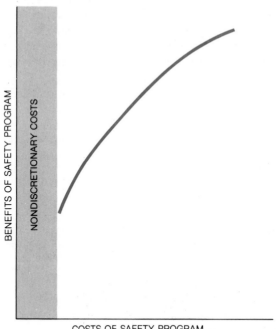

FIGURE 15-2
Safety cost/benefit
curve.

include defective equipment, inadequate machine guards, and lack of protective equipment. Examples of unsafe environmental conditions are noise, radiation, dust, fumes, and stress. In one study of work injuries, 50 percent resulted from unsafe work conditions, 45 percent resulted from unsafe work behaviors, and 5 percent were of indeterminate origin.[28] However, accidents often result from an *interaction* of unsafe conditions and unsafe acts. Thus if a particular operation forces a worker to lift a heavy part and twist to set it on a bench, then the operation itself forces the worker to perform the unsafe act. Telling the worker not to lift and twist at the same time will not solve the problem. The *unsafe condition itself* must be corrected, either by redesigning the flow of material or by providing the worker with a mechanical device for lifting.[45]

To eliminate, or at least to reduce, the number and severity of workplace accidents, a combination of management and engineering controls is essential. These are shown in Figure 15-3.

Engineering controls attempt to eliminate unsafe work conditions and to neutralize unsafe worker behaviors; management controls attempt to increase safe behaviors. Engineering controls involve some modification of the work environment: for example, installing a metal cover over the blades of a lawnmower to make it almost impossible for a member of a grounds crew to catch his or her foot in the blades.

Management's first duty is to formulate a safety policy. Its second duty is to implement and sustain this policy through a *loss control program*. Such a program

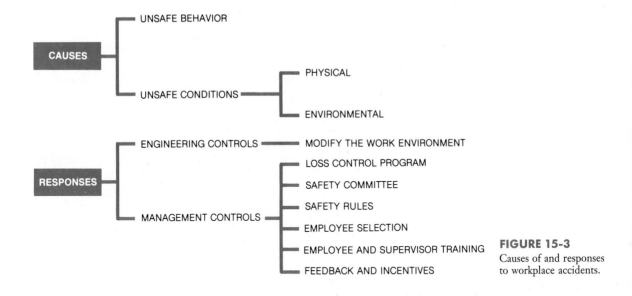

FIGURE 15-3
Causes of and responses to workplace accidents.

has four components: a safety budget, safety records, management's personal concern, and management's good example.[44]

To reduce the frequency of accidents, management must be willing to spend money and to budget for safety. As we have seen, accidents involve *direct* as well as *indirect* costs. Since the national average for indirect costs is 4 times higher than the average for direct costs, it is clear that money spent to improve safety is returned many times over through the control of accidents. Detailed analysis of accident reports, as well as management's personal concern (e.g., meeting with department heads over safety issues, on-site visits by top executives to discuss the need for safety, and publication of the company's accident record), keeps employees aware constantly of the need for safety.

Study after study has shown the crucial role that management plays in effective safety programs.[20,50,93] Such concern is manifest in a number of ways: appointment of a high-level safety officer, rewards to supervisors on the basis of the safety records of their subordinates, and comparison of safety results against preset objectives. Management's good example completes a loss control program. If hard hats are required at a particular operation, then executives should wear hard hats even if they are in business suits. If employees see executives disregarding safety rules or treating hazardous situations lightly by not conforming with regulations, then they will feel that they, too, have the right to violate the rules. In short, organizations show their concern for loss control by establishing a clear safety policy and by assuming the responsibility for its implementation.

Here are two examples, one illustrating management's concern for safety, the other illustrating management's lack of concern.

■ **COMPANY EXAMPLE**

MANAGEMENT CONCERN AFFECTS MINE SAFETY

In a comprehensive study, a National Academy of Sciences panel examined each of almost 40,000 coal mine injuries and deaths which occurred over a 2-year period and which involved the 19 largest underground coal producers. The panel also visited mines and interviewed safety experts, managers, and laborers. It found large and persistent differences in safety rates among the firms. Why? "We found the most important of these factors to be management's commitment, as reflected by the attention and resources it devotes to improving safety," said the panel. Other important factors, according to the panel, are *cooperation* between management and labor in safety programs, and the *quality* of safety training provided to employees and supervisors. Not to be overlooked, however, are *better laws and stricter enforcement*, especially by the federal government; *better safety technology*, such as roof supports and ventilation systems; and *improved knowledge of geological conditions* in underground mines.

Mines are safer today than even 10 years ago, and injuries tend to be less severe than they used to be, but still there are about 100 fatalities annually. This evidence indicates clearly that there should be no dilution or compromise to the safety effort.[61]

■ **COMPANY EXAMPLE**

CUTTING CORNERS IN THE MEATPACKING INDUSTRY

IBP, formerly known as Iowa Beef Processors, is the largest meatpacker in the United States. It operates 12 plants that employ 17,000 workers. In 1987 OSHA levied a $2.59 million fine against the company for failing willfully to report more than 1000 job-related injuries and illnesses over a 2-year period. Among the unreported injuries and illnesses cited by the agency were knife cuts and wounds, concussions, burns, hernias, and fractures.

OSHA determined that 1 week before it subpoenaed IBP's records, the company assembled 50 people to "revise" injury and illness logs. According to OSHA, IBP added more than 800 injuries and illnesses that had not been recorded when they occurred. How did OSHA know this to be true? Company workers had previously obtained the unrevised logs and had given them to agency investigators.[90]

In 1988 OSHA tacked on an additional $3.1 million in fines against IBP for requiring employees to perform repetitive motions that can cause nerve damage (carpal tunnel syndrome) that may cripple the hand or wrists so that the victim is unable to grip or pick up objects. The matter was settled in 1989, when IBP agreed to pay a reduced fine ($975,000), while establishing a model job redesign program to combat repetitive motion injuries.[98,105]

Role of the Safety Committee

Representation on the committee by employees, managers, and safety specialists can lead to much higher commitment to safety than might otherwise be the case. Indeed, merely establishing the committee indicates management's concern. Beyond that, however, the committee has important work to do:

- Recommend (or critique) safety policies issued by top management.
- Develop in-house safety standards and ensure compliance with OSHA standards.
- Provide safety training for employees and supervisors.
- Conduct safety inspections.
- Continually promote the theme of job safety through the elimination of unsafe conditions and unsafe behaviors.

As an example of recommendations that such a committee might make, consider some possible policies to reduce the incidence of repetitive-motion injuries that have afflicted not only meatpackers and pianists but also telephone and computer operators and supermarket checkout clerks who repeatedly slide customers' purchases over price scanners. Such policies include redesigning tools, equipment, and workstations to make the work easier; slowing production lines; training workers to recognize early symptoms of the disorder; rotating them among different jobs; and assigning them to slower, easier work after injuries occur.[52]

Safety Rules

Safety rules are important refinements of the general safety policies issued by top management. To be effective, they should make clear the consequences of not following the rules: for example, progressive discipline. Evidence indicates, unfortunately, that in many cases the rules are not obeyed. Take protective equipment, for example. OSHA standards require that employers *furnish* and that employees *use* suitable protective equipment (e.g., hard hats, goggles, face shields, earplugs, respirators) where there is a "reasonable probability" that injuries can be prevented by such equipment. However, as the following data show, "You can lead a horse to water, but you can't make him drink":[104]

- Hard hats were worn by only 16 percent of those workers who sustained head injuries, although 40 percent were required to wear them.
- Only 1 percent of workers suffering facial injuries were wearing facial protection.
- Only 23 percent of workers with foot injuries were wearing safety shoes or boots.
- Only 40 percent of workers with eye injuries were wearing protective equipment.

Perhaps the rules are not being obeyed because they are not being enforced. But it is also possible that they are not being obeyed because of flaws in employee selection practices, inadequate training, or because there is simply no incentive for doing so.

Employee Selection

To the extent that keen vision, dexterity, hearing, balance, and other physical or psychological characteristics make a critical difference between success and failure on a job, they should be used to screen applicants. However, there are two other factors that also relate strongly to accident rates among workers: *age* and *length of service*.[88,92] Regardless of length of service, the younger the employee, the higher the accident rate. In fact, accident rates are substantially higher during the *first month* of employment than in all subsequent time periods, regardless of age. And when workers of the same age are studied, accident rates decrease as length of service increases. Thus in mining, the disabling injury rate for miners 18 to 24 years of age is about 3 times that of miners over 45, and it is about twice that of miners between the ages of 25 and 45.[61] The same general pattern holds true in industries as diverse as retail trade, transportation and public utilities, and services. The lesson for managers is clear: *New worker equals high risk!*

Training for Employees and Supervisors

Accidents often occur because workers lack one vital tool to protect themselves: *information*. Consider the following data collected by the Bureau of Labor Statistics:[104]

- Nearly one out of every five workers injured while operating power saws received no safety training on the equipment.
- Of 724 workers hurt while using scaffolds, 27 percent had received no information on safety requirements for installing the kind of scaffold on which they were injured.
- Of 554 workers hurt while servicing equipment, 61 percent were not told about lockout procedures that prevent the equipment from being turned on inadvertently while it is being serviced.

In nearly every type of injury that researchers have studied, the same story is repeated over and over. Workers often do not receive the kind of safety information they need, *even on jobs that require them to use dangerous equipment*. This is unfortunate, but a problem that is just as serious occurs when safety practices that are taught in training are not reinforced back on the job. Regular feedback and incentives for compliance are essential.

Feedback and Incentives

Previous chapters have underscored the positive impact on the motivation of employees when they are given feedback and incentives to improve productivity. The same principles can also be used to improve safe behavior. Thus in one study of a wholesale bakery that was experiencing a sharp increase in work accidents, researchers developed a detailed coding sheet for observing safe and unsafe behaviors.

Observers then used the sheets to record systematically both safe and unsafe employee behaviors over a 25-week period before, during, and after a safety training program. Slides were used to illustrate both safe and unsafe behaviors. Trainees were also shown data on the percentage of safe behaviors in their departments, and a goal of 90 percent safe behaviors was established. Following all of this, the actual percentage of safe behaviors was posted in each department. Supervisors were trained to use positive reinforcement (praise) when they observed safe behaviors. In comparison to departments that received no training, workers in the trained departments averaged almost 24 percent more safe behaviors. Not only did employees react favorably to the program, but the company was able to maintain it. One year prior to the program, the number of lost-time injuries per million hours worked was 53.8. Even in highly hazardous industries, this figure rarely exceeds 35. One year after the program, it was less than 10.[56]

Similar results were found in a farm machinery manufacturing firm.[84] Behavioral safety rules were obeyed more when employees received frequent feedback concerning their performance in relation to an accepted standard. Although the implementation of a training session to teach employees exactly what was expected of them also resulted in a significant increase in performance, it did not produce optimum performance. Assigning employees specific, difficult, yet acceptable safety goals, and providing information concerning their performance in relation to these goals, produced the maximum reduction in lost-time injuries. The results of these studies suggest that training, goal setting, and feedback provide useful alternatives to disciplinary sanctions or extrinsic incentives (safety awards) to encourage compliance with the rules.

PROMOTING JOB SAFETY AND HEALTH: APPROACHES THAT WORK

An in-depth study of 27 heavy manufacturers within the foundry industry revealed four general types of responses to OSHA regulations:[38]

1. *Technical responses* include replacing or redesigning equipment, modifying physical workspaces, and providing worker protection (engineering controls).
2. *Information responses* refer to changes in the way that health and safety information is transmitted within the organization.
3. *Administrative responses* include changes in the authority structure or in policies and procedures with respect to safety and health (e.g., upgrading the safety function and shifting it from the engineering to the human resources department).
4. *External responses* refer to legal or political actions to change the enforcement of safety and health regulations.

When the types of responses to OSHA over a 7-year period were related statistically to the number of accidents 4 years later, the results indicated that OSHA was successful in generating all four types of responses through its inspection program. However, only certain kinds of responses actually reduced accidents. Of the four types, technical and administrative responses were the most effective, while external responses (as might be expected) were the least effective. In terms of administrative responses, the overall safety climate and the status of the safety function were key factors, as were the safety committee and the enforcement of safety rules.[38]

Job Safety and Health: What Are Companies Doing?

Now that we know which approaches to job safety and health work best, it seems appropriate to ask what companies are actually doing.

Tragic accidents like the gas leak in Bhopal, India (see the "International Application" below), and at the Soviet nuclear plant in Chernobyl have focused world attention and awareness on the critical importance of proper safety procedures.

Traditionally, managers tended to think of safety as an important issue in manufacturing. Yet the workforce today is losing manufacturing jobs to technology and service jobs, and it includes growing numbers of women. Many of the new jobs involve video display terminals (VDTs), semiconductor production, or exposure to chemicals. Some companies are proactively dealing with these new challenges.

Between 40 and 50 percent of the U.S. workforce deals with VDTs on a daily basis. Many users complain of a variety of syndromes, including blurred vision, eye strain, repetitive motion disorders, and muscular pains in the shoulder, back, or neck.[65] To deal with this, the St. Paul Companies, a large insurance company, recently introduced a program designed to teach VDT users relaxation techniques, workstation organization, and health awareness, including the need for regular eye checkups. The company reported significantly lowered technostress levels following the program.[77]

Another new technology that may produce adverse health consequences is semiconductor production, which involves acids and gases. Such consequences may include a higher rate of miscarriages among women who work in the production process and also higher rates of nausea, headaches, and rashes. Digital Equipment, AT&T, Intel, and Texas Instruments all have adopted policies that allow pregnant women to transfer out of production operations without sacrificing pay or seniority.[77]

Another thing that companies are doing is alerting workers exposed to high levels of chemicals or other possible causes of disease. The notification rules come under OSHA's "hazard communication" standard put into effect in 1988. The rules apply to about 575,000 hazardous chemicals and 320,000 manufacturing businesses, affecting 32 million workers.[19,40] They require *every* workplace in the country to identify and list hazardous chemicals being used ("from bleach to bowl cleaner"),[46] and to train employees in their use. Such "right-to-know" requirements have helped to avoid situations like the following.

For many office workers, video display terminals are essential tools.

RIGHT-TO-KNOW RULES IN THE CHEMICAL INDUSTRY

■ **COMPANY EXAMPLE**

Cathy Zimmerman, a 26-year-old lab technician at Hercules, Inc., in Wilmington, Delaware, was pouring chemicals last year when she noticed that the bottles were labeled "mutagen" and "teratogen." She went to her dictionary, which said that a mutagen can alter chromosomes and that a teratogen can cause malformations in fetuses. "I said, 'O, my God!'" she recalls. "When I saw that, I talked to my boss and told him I was scared. I didn't want to take a chance."

Mrs. Zimmerman, who is expecting her first child, has since been transferred to Hercules' flavoring division, where she works with less hazardous materials. But she hopes that a new right-to-know training program required by OSHA will prevent such surprises in the future. "With right-to-know, we'd have gone over it first, before it came into the lab," she says. "We didn't have that before."

Some employees are alarmed to discover that they have been working with certain hazardous chemicals. Others are overwhelmed by the detailed labeling, which they say makes it even harder to distinguish really dangerous materials. Meanwhile some businesses claim that fearful workers are demanding unnecessary and costly changes. At the same time, however, OSHA defends the measure, arguing that heightened awareness, and even anxiety, will help reduce work-related accidents. As one spokesperson for OSHA commented, "I'd rather be anxious and alive than calm and dead."[40]

In the United States there is considerable pressure to improve plant safety. Now let's consider the situation in other countries.

INTERNATIONAL APPLICATION: HEALTH AND SAFETY— THE RESPONSE BY GOVERNMENTS AND MULTINATIONAL FIRMS IN LESS DEVELOPED COUNTRIES

In 1984, 45 tons of lethal methyl isocyanate gas leaked from the Union Carbide (India) Ltd. pesticide plant in the central Indian city of Bhopal, killing more than 3400 people and injuring over 200,000 in history's worst industrial disaster. Subsequently two events occurred: (1) in 1989 the Indian Supreme Court ordered Union Carbide to pay $470 million in damages to victims of the disaster (although dissatisfied survivors could still file claims in the United States as well)[23]; and (2) India formed committees in every state to identify potential factory hazards, as government and public awareness of environmental hazards skyrocketed. However, the committees inspect only major factories, not the thousands of small chemical factories, many of which are illegal.

These two events both produced important consequences. U.S. multinational firms found out that liability for any Bhopal-like disaster could be decided in U.S. courts.[10] This, more than pressure from third-world governments, has forced companies to tighten safety procedures, upgrade plants, supervise maintenance more closely, and educate workers and communities in their far-flung empires.[30]

In India, despite the outcry against Union Carbide, the country continues to welcome foreign investment and technology. However, the government is insisting that it know more about the risks involved, including potential manufacturing hazards. New factories must carry out environmental impact studies and install safety equipment. As a government spokesman noted, "If there is a lesson to learn, it is when we buy black boxes we must know the entire consequences."[73]

In Mexico, a gas explosion at Pemex, the state-owned oil monopoly, killed at least 500 people and wounded thousands of others at about the same time as the Bhopal disaster. One year later, little had been done to improve the conditions that caused the explosion. After years of neglect and rampant pollution at Pemex facilities, the government was loathe to clamp down because that would focus attention on the main culprit: the Mexican government itself.[30]

Neither the Bhopal nor the Pemex incidents had any noticeable effect on multinational investment in Mexico. In fact, all the developing countries in one survey seem to rely on the multinationals, rather than on draconic new regulations, to prevent a repeat of Bhopal. This is true in South Korea, Taiwan, and Egypt, for example. Like Mexico, the biggest polluters in Egypt are government-owned. Many pesticide, fertilizer, dye, cement, and steel plants are in the suburbs of Cairo and Alexandria, the biggest population centers of overcrowded Egypt. Most of the factories are old and poorly maintained by the government, which owns them and has more pressing problems.[30] As these few examples make clear, in many of the less developed countries around the world, foreign investment is a political and economic issue, not a safety issue.

In at least one newly industrialized country, South Korea, government, management, and unions are becoming aware of the human cost of unsafe conditions. In 1989, 2 out of every 100 mine and factory workers were injured, and 26 out of every 100,000 were killed. (In the United States, the death rate is 10 per 100,000 workers.) In 1990, the death rate jumped 43 percent and the accident rate 3 percent. Twenty percent of Korean workers have suffered an accident. Yet government efforts to educate workers have fallen flat. Why? Many regard the wearing of welding masks or hard hats as unmanly.[87]

HEALTH HAZARDS AT WORK

The National Institute of Occupational Safety and Health has identified over 15,000 toxic substances, of which some 500 might require regulation as carcinogens (cancer-causing substances). The list of harmful chemical, physical, and biological hazards is a long one. It includes carbon monoxide, vinyl chloride, dusts, particulates, gases and vapors, radiation, excessive noise and vibration, and extreme temperatures. When present in high concentrations, these agents can lead to respiratory, kidney, liver, skin, neurological, and other disorders. Scary, isn't it?

There have been some well-publicized lawsuits against employers for causing occupational illnesses as a result of lack of proper safeguards or technical controls.[42] Thus in 1984 the U.S. Supreme Court ruled in the case of Karen Silkwood, a former laboratory analyst at a plutonium plant in Oklahoma, that the federal government's interest in nuclear safety didn't prevent a jury from awarding damages to Mrs. Silkwood's family for injuries arising out of exposure to radiation at her workplace.[66] And in a later decision, for example, a jury in Cleveland awarded $520,000 to a former government employee who sued the maker of a fire-proofing material that contained asbestos after she was diagnosed as having an asbestos-related disease. The woman had worked in the building for 12 years and sued the original seller of the material 3 years after that.[27]

The U.S. Supreme Court has ruled that the states can prosecute company officials under criminal statutes for endangering the health of employees, even if such hazards are also regulated by OSHA.[107] As of 1990, state supreme courts in Illinois, Michigan, and New York approved such suits.[66] Nevertheless, some of the criticism against employers is not fair. To prove negligence, it must be shown that management *knew* of the connection between exposure to the hazards and negative health consequences and that management *chose* to do nothing to reduce worker exposure. Yet few such connections were made until recent years. Even now, alternative explanations for the causes of disease or illness cannot be ruled out in many cases. Responsibility for regulation has been left to OSHA.

As an example of OSHA's preferred approach, consider its agreement with Asarco to control the exposure of steelworkers to lead.

■ **COMPANY EXAMPLE**

CONTROLLING LEAD EXPOSURE AT ASARCO

The agreement between OSHA and Asarco was designed to control worker exposure to lead through "feasible" controls and workplace practices at three Asarco smelters and a refinery. It resulted from lengthy discussions between the government, the company, and the United Steelworkers union.

OSHA's lead standard calls for, among other things, an air concentration of 50 micrograms (i.e., 50 millionths of a gram) per cubic meter. Under the agreement, Asarco will improve ventilation and provide filtered air for mobile equipment and certain rooms. The parties agreed that when the agreement expires, they will renew it and incorporate technological improvements in the monitoring of exposure to lead. In the meantime, OSHA retains its authority to inspect the facilities in response to serious accidents or complaints from employees.

The union strongly backed the whole idea; in fact, an industrial hygienist for the Steelworkers commented, "We get better control a whole lot faster than when we have to fight it out in a government review procedure. Frequently a judge winds up making a decision about how to control hazardous substances, and the judge probably hasn't been in the plant or isn't familiar with procedures and technical equipment used to control exposure levels."[4]

As this example illustrates, the primary emphasis to date has been on installing engineering controls that *prevent* exposure to harmful substances. In fact, in a sweeping move in 1989, OSHA established or toughened workplace exposure limits for 376 toxic chemicals. The new rules are expected to cost employers $788 million a year. While this figure might sound steep, consider that an estimated $25 billion is spent annually just to *treat* preventable cancer. The benefits? According to OSHA, the new limits should save nearly 700 lives a year and reduce work-related illnesses such as cancer, liver and kidney impairments, and respiratory and cardiovascular illnesses by about 55,000 cases a year.[51] But is cost-benefit analysis appropriate when lives are literally at stake?

The Supreme Court recognized this problem in its 1981 "Cotton Dust" decision. It held that OSHA need not balance the costs of implementing standards against the benefits expected. OSHA has to show only that it is *economically feasible* to implement the standards. The decision held that Congress had already decided the balance between costs and benefits in favor of the worker when it passed the law.[95] On one issue all parties agree: *The nature of cancer itself makes it virtually impossible for workers to protect themselves from exposure to cancer-causing substances.* In the absence of government-mandated exposure regulations, a few firms have instituted genetic screening for job applicants and genetic monitoring for employees.

Legal Implications of Genetic Screening and Monitoring

Genetic screening is a one-time test (via a blood or urine count) to determine whether a job applicant carries genetic traits that might predispose her or him to adverse health effects when exposed to certain chemicals. Genetic monitoring is the routine testing of employees who work with potentially toxic substances, to detect evidence of genetic impairment.[78] With today's technology, it is possible to screen individuals for very few diseases—emphysema, heart disease, hemophilia, and sickle-cell anemia.[81] Moreover, scientists have not yet been able to screen out such "confounders" as the age of the workers, prior illnesses, and above-average smoking or drinking. Hence it is impractical for businesses to begin widespread testing.[63]

Unfortunately, it appears that there is a potential contradiction between OSHA and Title VII of the 1964 Civil Rights Act with regard to genetic screening. Such screening may trigger lawsuits under Title VII because there is considerable evidence showing that genetic impairments differ as a function of ethnicity. If a charge of racial discrimination is filed against an employer based on the results of genetic screening, it is necessary to show the validity, or "business necessity," of such screening. However, given the present state of the science, validity evidence is unavailable. Furthermore, the demonstration of business necessity to support unequal hiring or promotion rates has been upheld *only on the basis of expected differences in job performance, not on the basis of the probability of contracting disease.*[78] To date, there are no legal precedents in this area.

On the other hand, the "general duty" clause of OSHA and specific standards that deal with the removal of employees from environments that are potentially damaging to them can be interpreted as sanctioning *any* practice that contributes to improvements in the health of workers. Consequently, if employers *fail* to take genetic-screening and genetic-monitoring information into account, they may be violating the spirit of OSHA. What can firms do? Policies similar to that of Dow Chemical are typical: "No employee, male or female, will knowingly be exposed to hazardous levels of material known to cause cancer or genetic mutations in humans." This is consistent with the Supreme Court's 1991 ruling regarding fetal protection policies (see discussion on pp. 80 and 81).[53,69]

Unfortunately, many hazardous jobs are high-paying. This situation is "unfortunate" because workers are understandably reluctant to transfer out of these jobs to avoid occupational exposures unless they are protected against loss of income. As we have seen, some companies have provided just such income protection for pregnant production workers who might be exposed to the toxic gases and liquids used to etch microscopic circuits onto silicon wafers.[6] In the past, some workers even went so far as to have themselves sterilized to protect their jobs.[11] It seems, then, that companies have two choices: Either guarantee transferees no loss of income, or else obtain signed, voluntary consent agreements from employees who choose to stay on hazardous jobs. While consent agreements will not absolve employers from liability under workers' compensation laws and civil disability suits, they may minimize the amount of punitive damages that employees are awarded.[76] Better yet, if at all possible, alter the workplace rather than the workforce. Eliminate the *causes* of biological impairment.

AIDS and Business

AIDS (acquired immune deficiency syndrome) is a medical time bomb. With 324,000 cases expected by the end of 1991, employers are fast having to deal with increasing numbers of AIDS victims in the workplace.[18] Consider these facts and prognoses about the disease:

- Employers' medical costs rose by 20 percent from 1988 to 1990, in part because of AIDS.[58]
- Non-AIDS public-health programs will be curtailed in cities hit hard by the epidemic.
- With no cure in sight for at least 20 years, the Public Health Service estimates that the AIDS medical bill may be as much as $16 billion by 1991. The U.S. Centers for Disease Control (CDC) estimates that 215,000 Americans will have died of the disease by the end of 1991.[12]
- The cost of treating an AIDS patient from diagnosis to death was $94,000 in 1987. This is higher than the average cost of treating leukemia, cancer of the digestive system, a heart attack, or paraplegia from an auto crash.[39]
- By 1991 AIDS is expected to be the leading cause of death for those aged 25 to 44. These are the people whose historically low rates of sickness and death help keep at least a loose lid on health-care and insurance costs and whose tax dollars subsidize government programs for children and the elderly.
- The cumulative costs of long-term disability payments to people with AIDS through 1995 are expected to exceed $2 billion.
- Life insurance policies already in force will generate AIDS-related life insurance claims of $50 billion through the end of the century—up from $200 million in 1986. In fact, the industry paid $1 billion in AIDS-related claims in 1989, up 70 percent from 1988.[16]
- Of all the economic costs of AIDS, the greatest by far is the productivity drain—an estimated $56 billion in 1991, representing 12 percent of the economic costs of all illness.[39]
- Jobs held by AIDS-affected persons are protected by the Americans with Disabilities Act of 1990. The act also prohibits discrimination against job applicants who have the disease.

Bank of America has developed a model corporate policy to deal with the AIDS problem at work. Its basic features include the following:

Assumption 1. AIDS is not a casually contagious disease, and there is little risk of transmission in the workplace. But given the irrational fear that AIDS often inspires, the best way to avoid a difficult and disruptive situation is to prepare and educate both management and employees before the first employee gets AIDS.

Assumption 2. An employee's health condition is personal and confidential. At Bank of America employees are not required to tell their managers that they have AIDS or other life-threatening illnesses. But they are assured that they can work with the human resources department to facilitate benefits and to discuss other illness-related concerns. (Human resources department personnel receive extensive training about AIDS.) Providing a supportive work environment for people with life-threatening illnesses not only helps them financially; it can even prolong their lives.

Policy. As long as employees with AIDS are able to meet acceptable performance standards—and their condition is not a threat to themselves or others—they should be treated like other employees. If warranted, the bank makes reasonable accommodations for the employee (such as flexible hours), as long as these do not hamper the business needs of the work unit.

Policy. Coworkers who wish to transfer may do so, although Bank of America found that such apprehension is usually based on lack of information. Since publishing its policy, the bank has not had any requests for transfer based on fear of a coworker's illness.

Policy. An employee who contracts AIDS should be encouraged to seek assistance from established community support groups for medical treatment and counseling. The bank has found that the best and most cost-effective way to treat employees with AIDS is through "case management" programs that provide for home or hospice care. Such flexible benefits coverage is a fairly recent development, but Bank of America has worked with its third-party insurers to provide it.

In short, Bank of America is playing an important role in AIDS-related education, support, and benefits for *all* its employess. In fact, its board and top-management committee's main concern is "Are we doing enough?"[70]

EMPLOYEE ASSISTANCE PROGRAMS

Another (brighter) side of the employee health issue is reflected in employee assistance programs (EAPs). Such programs represent an expansion of traditional work in occupational alcoholism treatment programs. From a handful of such programs begun in the 1940s (led by Du Pont), different schools of thought have emerged regarding the best way to treat alcoholism in industry, along with a diversity of treatment programs. As recently as 1959, only about 50 American companies were operating such programs.[89] As of 1989, there were over 14,000 such programs in the United States, and many others in Canada as well.[94]

Management's concern over the issue is understandable, for alcohol misuse by employees is costly in terms of productivity, time lost from work, and treatment. How prevalent is alcoholism and how costly is it? Unfortunately, while many figures are bandied about, a critical review of the development and reporting of knowledge about employee alcoholism treatment programs showed these estimates to be supported by limited empirical data.[106] Specifically, three problems remain. One, no study yet reported has determined whether employees diagnosed as alcoholic on the basis of job performance problems (e.g., absenteeism, poor judgment, erratic performance) are indeed alcoholics. Two, the impact of "constructive coercion" ("shape up or ship out") on *drinking behavior*—rather than on *work behavior*—has not been assessed adequately. Three, it is not at all clear that the diagnosis and treatment of drug abuse problems should be identical to that for alcoholism problems.[106] Nevertheless, drug abuse is no less insidious. It cuts across all job levels and types of organizations, and together with employee alcohol abuse, costs U.S. businesses an estimated $30.1 billion in annual productivity losses.[26]

Here is a profile of the "typical" recreational drug user in today's workforce. He or she:

- Was born between 1948 and 1965
- Is late 3 times as often as fellow employees
- Requests early dismissal or time off during work 2.2 times as often
- Has 2.5 times as many absences of 8 days or more
- Uses 3 times the normal level of sick benefits
- Is 5 times as likely to file a workers' compensation claim
- Is involved in accidents 3.6 times as often as other employees
- Is one-third less productive than fellow workers

A longitudinal study of 5,465 applicants for jobs with the U.S. Postal Service found that after an average of 1.3 years of employment, employees who had tested positive for illicit drugs had an absenteeism rate 59.3 percent higher than employees who had tested negative. Those who had tested positive also had a 47 percent higher rate of involuntary turnover than those who had tested negative. However, there was no relationship between drug-test results and measures of injury and accident occurrence.[75] This may not be true in other occupations, however.

Said a construction union leader in California, "Sometimes 90 percent of the crew's been doing uppers. I just leave the jobs when the guys are dopers. Would you want to work on a 4-story building knowing the guy with the blowtorch next to you is doing drugs?" (ref. 99, p. 55).

Traditionally, supervisory approaches to the alcoholism problem focused on two areas: *detection* and *referral*. Supervisors in the most successful programs were given training in how to identify the problem drinker (absenteeism, tardiness, changes in mood, hand trembling, and withdrawal from social contact). The next steps were: (1) confrontation, based on documented evidence of impaired work performance; (2) the offer of a rehabilitation program; and, as a last resort, (3) discipline up to and including discharge.[101]

A Broader Perspective

By its very title, "employee assistance program" signals a change both in application and in technique from the traditional occupational alcoholism treatment program. Modern EAPs extend services to all "troubled" employees. A troubled employee is *an individual who is confronted by unresolved personal or work-related problems.*[8] Such problems run the gamut from alcoholism, drug abuse, and high stress to marital, family, and financial problems. While some of these may originate "outside" the work context, they most certainly will have spillover effects to the work context.

In the traditional alcoholism treatment program, the supervisor had to look for symptoms of alcoholism and then diagnose the problem. Under an EAP, however, the supervisor is responsible *only* for identifying declining work performance. If normal corrective measures do not work, the supervisor confronts the employee with evidence of his or her poor performance and offers the EAP.

By using declining work performance or a particular disruptive incident as the *sole* basis for referral to the EAP, management is able to maintain high work standards and consistent practices. Employees know that participation in the program is voluntary. But they also know that continued poor work performance will result in disciplinary action and, ultimately, in termination. In the contemporary view, the supervisor need not become involved in the employee's personal problem—or even know what it is. Rather, *the supervisor's focus is on job performance, attitude, and productivity.* While supervisors may do some career counseling for lower-level employees (often as part of an annual performance appraisal), the results of a survey of major U.S. corporations indicated that supervisors very rarely get involved in any other type of counseling activity.[60]

Companies like Monsanto, Kodak, Xerox, and Kennecott Copper are instituting EAPs based on an awareness of their social responsibility. By offering assistance to troubled employees, the company promotes a positive climate of employee relations.[96] It also contributes to the employee's well-being and to his or her ability to function productively at work, at home, and in the community.

How Employee Assistance Programs Work

There are five steps involved in starting an EAP:[83]

1. *Develop a written statement* of the objectives of the program, consistent with organizational policy. Confirm the company's desire to offer help to employees with behavioral or medical problems, and emphasize that such help will be offered on a *personal and confidential* basis.

2. *Teach managers, supervisors, and union representatives what to do*—and what not to do—when they confront the troubled employee and when they use the program to resolve job performance problems.

3. *Establish procedures for referral* of the troubled employee to an in-house or to an outside professional who can take the time to assess what is wrong and arrange for treatment.

4. *Establish a planned program of communications* to employees to announce (and periodically to remind them) that the service is available, that it is confidential, and that other employees are using it.

5. *Continually evaluate* the program in terms of its stated objectives.

IMPACT OF SAFETY, HEALTH, AND EAPs ON PRODUCTIVITY, QUALITY OF WORK LIFE, AND THE BOTTOM LINE

We know that the technology is available to make workplaces safe and healthy for the nation's men and women. We also know that legislation can never substitute for managerial commitment to safe and healthy workplaces based on demonstrated economic and social benefits. The many examples of economic and social payoffs of job safety and rehabilitative or preventive health efforts presented in this chapter indicate clearly that productivity, QWL, and the bottom line all stand to gain. "You can pay me now, or pay me later" says it all.

With respect to step 2 above, employee confrontation, it is important to stress that any program that relies on a large and changing group of relatively untrained supervisors to handle the initial confrontation must expect a certain amount of performance failure. Some managers or supervisors may allow feelings of sympathy or concern to delay appropriate action. This is "killing with kindness." If the same manager suspected that the employee had symptoms of a heart attack or cancer, she or he would probably insist that the employee get an immediate checkup. Similarly, a union steward may be reluctant to confront a fellow union member in a way that may sound threatening. Both the supervisor and the steward need to be trained to recognize that they are helping, not hurting, the employee by referring her or him to the EAP.

Evaluation of Employee Assistance Programs

At the most basic level, the task of evaluation is counting—counting clients, counting interactions, counting dollars, counting hours, and so forth. The most difficult tasks of evaluation are deciding *what* things should be counted and developing routine *methods* for counting them. Managers should count the things that will provide the most useful feedback.[29]

Productivity, absenteeism, accidents, medical expenses, insurance premiums, turnover, and unemployment costs are obvious areas where savings might be realized.[17] Equally important are variables that also affect profit yet are difficult to quantify. These include, for example, the cost of poor management decisions, poor morale, work errors, "on-the-job absence," and most significantly the cost of doing nothing.

While EAPs run by outside firms cost from $12 to $35 per employee per year,[31] recent data on their effects are impressive. In one study, for example, 70 percent of the 17,743 employees who were referred to EAPs for alcoholism were back on the job and performing adequately.[97] Another study reported $2.74 saved for every $1 spent on the program.[55] And General Motors found that blue-collar workers who resolved their alcohol and drug abuse problems through an EAP filed only half as many grievances as they did before treatment.

EAPs have also been developed and applied in countries other than the United States, but exact transfer from one culture to another simply will not work. Rather, it is necessary to "fit" the EAP to the social, cultural, economic, and political climates of the countries in question.[7]

One final caution is in order. Often there is a "rush to evaluate" EAPs and other occupational programs. This can lead to premature claims of success or, equally likely, premature condemnation. *Beware of making strong statements about a program's impact at least until repeated evaluations have demonstrated the same findings for different groups of employees.*[29] Now let's look at how one firm evaluated its EAP.

BOTTOM-LINE IMPACT OF AN EMPLOYEE ASSISTANCE PROGRAM AT AT&T

■ **COMPANY EXAMPLE**

The study followed each of 110 employees for 22 months before and 22 months after their involvement with the company's EAP program.[32] The most significant conclusions were:

1. The age, sex ethnicity, and years of service of employees in the study reflected the actual characteristics of employees in the corporation. There was not a "typical" profile of an EAP client.

2. The corporation had a considerable investment in many of the employees who used the services of the EAP. In the group studied, 50 percent had over 11 years of service, and 77 percent were over the age of 30.

3. Location of the EAP within the medical department, combined with supervisors' use of job performance criteria for referrals, was effective. It instilled confidence in employees, and it provided an opportunity for them to receive comprehensive diagnosis and treatment. Troubled employees were identified in all diagnostic categories: alcohol and/or drug abuse, emotional problems, family and/or marital, and work-related difficulties.

4. Alcohol and drug abuse accounted for the highest percentage (42 percent) of employee problems. Emotional problems were the second-largest diagnostic category (39 percent), with family and work making up the remaining 19 percent. In terms of the *source* of referrals, 46 percent came from the medical department, 22 percent came from supervisors, 16 percent were self-referrals, and the remainder were referred by spouses or fellow employees.

5. The rate of rehabilitation or improvement for all cases was 86 percent. In the case of alcoholism, for example, *rehabilitation* was defined as 18 months of sustained sobriety. *Improvement* was defined as tangible efforts to overcome one's problem and participation in a rehabilitation program.

6. There was a significant decrease in accidents on and off the job, absenteeism, and visits to the medical department following EAP involvement. Among the 110 employees studied, there were 26 accidents resulting in 164

lost work days *before* participation in the EAP, but only 5 resulting in 19 lost days *after* participation in the EAP.

7. Among employees referred by their supervisors for poor performance, over 85 percent were no longer poor performers following EAP involvement. Prior to EAP involvement, these employees were in serious jeopardy of losing their jobs. Further, of this group, 41 percent were promoted during the post-investigation period.

8. Five variables for which objective dollar figures could be determined yielded a net savings from before to after EAP involvement (that is, over a 3.5-year period) of more than $790,000 (in 1990 dollars).

These variables were: *on-the-job accidents, incidental absences, disability absences, visits to medical,* and *anticipated losses* (i.e., savings resulting from rehabilitation of potentially lost employees). Chapter 16 describes the actual costing methods used by AT&T in greater detail; for now, note that the cost savings in these five areas are conservative since they do not include such hidden factors as the dollar value of improved productivity, employee morale, and more effective use of supervisory time. Since the effects of this EAP program were studied over a period of $3\frac{1}{2}$ years, the results are likely to be quite reliable.

CORPORATE HEALTH PROMOTION: THE CONCEPT OF "WELLNESS"

Consider these sobering facts:

- In 1960, per capita expenditures for medical care were $146. By 1990, as noted in Chapter 11, they averaged over $1800 per person. This is a record that promises to be broken every year.
- Business today pays half the nation's health-care bill. Common backaches alone cause a loss of 91 million workdays per year, for a total cost of more than $9 billion in lost productivity, disability payments, and lawsuits.[86]
- Business spends some $700 million per year to replace the 200,000 employees aged 45 to 65 who are killed or disabled by heart disease.

All of this means rising costs for health benefits, which now account for about 26 percent of corporate earnings.[108] Keep in mind that health plans do not promise good health. They simply pay for the cost of ill health and the associated rehabilitation.

Because 8 of the 10 leading causes of death are largely preventable, managers are beginning to look to *disease prevention* as one way to reduce health-care spending. The old saying "an ounce of prevention is worth a pound of cure" is certainly true when one compares the costs of a workshop to help employees stop smoking with the price tag on an average coronary bypass operation.[9]

Is it possible that health-care costs can be tamed through on-the-job exercise programs and health promotion efforts? Convinced that if people were healthier, they would be sick less often, over 500 corporations (including IBM, Control Data, Xerox, and Kimberly-Clark) are building jogging tracks, providing personalized risk-factor calculations, and improving workers' ways of handling stress. Do such programs work? In a moment we will consider that question, but first let's define our terms and look at the overall concept.

The process of corporate health promotion begins by promoting *health aware-ness*, that is, knowledge of the present and future consequences of behaviors and lifestyles and the risks they may present.[13] The objective of "wellness programs" is not to eliminate symptoms and disease; it is to help employees build lifestyles that will enable them to achieve their full physical and mental potential.[57] Wellness programs differ from EAPs in that *wellness focuses on prevention, while EAPs focus on rehabilitation*. Health promotion is a four-step process:[85]

1. Educate employees about health-risk factors—life habits or body characteristics that may increase the chances of developing a serious illness. For heart disease (the leading cause of death), some of these risk factors are: high blood pressure, cigarette smoking, high cholesterol levels, diabetes, a sedentary lifestyle, and obesity. Some factors, such as smoking, stress, and poor nutrition, are associated with many diseases.
2. Identify the health-risk factors that each employee faces.
3. Help employees eliminate or reduce these risks through healthier lifestyles and habits.
4. Help employees maintain their new, healthier lifestyles through self-monitoring and evaluation. The central theme of health promotion is "No one takes better care of you than you do."

To date, the most popular programs are smoking cessation, blood pressure control, cholesterol reduction, weight control and fitness, and stress management. In well-designed programs, 40 to 50 percent of employees can be expected to participate.[64] Here is a company example.

CONTROL DATA'S "STAY WELL" PROGRAM

■ COMPANY EXAMPLE

Control Data Corporation, with over $4 billion in annual sales, has an ambitious health promotion program. It is called "Stay Well," and it reaches 22,000 employees and their families in 14 cities. A key ingredient of the program is the recruitment of informal "opinion leaders" to promote the program at each plant. Stay Well includes physiological tests, computerized health-risk profiles, wellness education classes, and courses in lifestyle change. The lifestyle courses cover such areas as stress, fitness, weight control, nutrition, and smoking cessation.

Stay Well also features follow-up worker support groups to help make the lifestyle changes stick and employee task forces to promote health-enhancing changes in the workplace. Such task forces have won stretch breaks, showers, no-smoking areas, and fresh fruit in vending machines. Said the director of the company's health-care services division. "We want to produce cultural changes in the workplace. We want to change the norms of health-related behavior."[3]

A 4-year study of 15,000 Control Data employees showed dramatic relationships between employees' health habits and insurance claim costs. For example, people whose weekly exercise was equivalent to climbing fewer than five flights of stairs, or walking less than half a mile, spent 114 percent more on health claims than those who climbed at least 15 flights of stairs or walked 1.5 miles weekly. Health-care costs for obese people were 11 percent higher than those for thin ones. And workers who routinely failed to use seat belts spent 54 percent more days in the hospital than those who usually buckled up. Finally, people who smoked an average of one or more packs of cigarettes a day had 118 percent higher medical expenses than nonsmokers. This study was the first to tie health costs to workers' behavior. It was corroborated in another longitudinal study that appeared at about the same time.[82] Together, such results may form the basis for incentive programs to (1) improve workers' health habits and (2) reduce employees' contributions to health-insurance costs or increase their benefits.[47]

The success of Stay Well and its companion EAP has prompted Control Data to market them to other firms. Buyers for Stay Well include 3M and Northeastern Mutual Life Insurance. Philip Morris and the National Basketball Association are among the more than 35 organizations that have signed up for the company's EAP.

Evaluation: Do Wellness Programs Work?

Few controlled studies exist,[25] and the movement's doctrines remind some medical doctors of earlier measures that also seemed as unassailable as apple pie—annual physicals, annual Pap smears, and mass health screening. Unfortunately, none of these provided the huge health benefits that seemed almost guaranteed.

Wellness programs are especially difficult to evaluate, for at least six reasons:[17]

1. Health-related costs that actually decreased are hard to identify.
2. Program sponsors use different methods to measure and report costs and benefits.
3. Program effects may vary depending on *when* they are measured (immediate versus lagged effects).
4. Program effects may vary, depending on *how long* they are measured.
5. Few studies use control groups.

6. Data on effectiveness are limited in the choice of variables, estimation of the economic value of indirect costs and benefits, estimation of the timing and duration of program effects, and estimation of the present value of future benefits.

At a general level, four key questions need to be answered:

1. Do health promotion programs in fact eliminate or reduce health-risk factors?
2. Are these changes long-lasting?
3. If the changes are long-lasting, will illness and its subsequent costs be reduced?
4. Are the savings great enough to justify the expense?

The answers to the first two questions appear to be yes, based on a number of independent studies done during the 1980s.[34] A firm answer to the third question is not yet in, but the reduction in heart disease following the surgeon general's report on smoking suggests a cautious yes.

With respect to the fourth question, several studies have focused on costs that would have been incurred if a wellness program had not been available. This was the approach taken by the Adolph Coors Co. in evaluating its mammography (breast cancer) screening program. By calculating exactly how many examinations showed breast cancer in the early stages, Coors was able to calculate the costs avoided, assuming that without mammography the problem would have gone undetected and the cancer would have matured. Coors spent $232,500 to perform 2500 screenings and avoided $828,000 in health-care costs. This yielded a net savings of $595,500, or an ROI of greater than 3.5:1.[49] Other studies are of the "what if" variety. Here is one of the better "what ifs."

COST-BENEFIT ANALYSIS OF A COMPANY EXERCISE PROGRAM

■ **PRACTICAL EXAMPLE**

An analysis of 5000 employees' health risks in one firm indicated that the company could expect 210 heart attacks in the next 10 years. The risk analysis also showed that 80 percent, or 168, of these heart attacks could probably be prevented. Of these 168 preventable cases, one-third, or 56 employees, could be expected to take part in an exercise program. And one-third of the 56, or 19, of the expected heart attacks could be prevented by the exercise program.

The cost savings attributed to this exercise program would be the dollars *not* spent on medical care and disability benefits for the 19 heart attacks that were avoided. Assuming total medical-care costs of $65,000 per heart attack, on average,[39] plus $10,000 per heart attack in disability costs, each heart attack *avoided* saves the company $75,000 in direct expenses. The total saved by preventing 19 heart attacks would be over $1.4 million

($1,425,000). And that figure does not even include replacement costs and reduced productivity.[19] Analyses such as these make the "wellness" concept well worth looking into.

HUMAN RESOURCE MANAGEMENT IN ACTION
CONCLUSION

SUBSTANCE ABUSE ON THE JOB PRODUCES TOUGH POLICY CHOICES FOR MANAGERS

Given the amounts of time and money invested in employees, especially highly skilled knowledge workers, many firms try to rehabilitate those with substance abuse problems. But how do firms get "problem" employees into rehabilitation programs? The most popular approaches are self-referral and referral by family and friends. Among pilots who have gone through the airline industry's alcohol-rehabilitation program, in effect since 1973, 85 percent were turned in initially by family, friends, or coworkers.

According to the Air Line Pilots Association, one of the hallmarks of the industry's program is a willingness of people to turn in an alcoholic pilot. That willingness, in turn, depends on knowing that the pilot can return to work. If people know that by turning in a pilot they will also be taking away his or her livelihood, they may not do it.

The key to return to work, in the opinion of most professionals in the field of substance abuse, is follow-up, because substance abuse is a recurring disease. Prior to the Exxon *Valdez* accident, the company really had no systematic policy on how to handle employees after treatment. The company depended only on the judgments of local managers.

Under United's program, rehabilitated pilots are monitored for at least 2 years. During this time, the pilot is required to meet monthly with a committee comprised of counselors and representatives of both union and management in a kind of group therapy session with other recovering pilots. They may also be required to undergo periodic surprise alcohol or drug tests. United has never had an alcohol-related accident.

Although experts don't always agree on how long follow-up should last, programs most commonly require 6 months of intensive contact, such as weekly meetings, and a year after that of monthly contact. Longer-term follow-up may last as long as 4 years.

SUMMARY

Public policy regarding occupational safety and health has focused on state-run workers' compensation programs for job-related injuries and federally mandated

IMPLICATIONS FOR MANAGEMENT PRACTICE

In the coming years we can expect to see three developments in occupational safety and health:

1. More widespread promotion of OSHA's consultative role, particularly as small businesses recognize that this is a no-cost, no-penalty option available to them.
2. Wider use of cost-benefit analysis by regulatory agencies. Industry is demanding it, and Executive Order 12292 signed by President Reagan endorses it.
3. Broadening of the target group for EAPs and wellness programs, to include dependents and retirees.

The high costs of disabling injuries and occupational diseases, together with these three trends, suggest that the commitment of resources to enhance job safety and health makes good business sense *over and above* concerns for corporate social responsibility.

preventive measures to enhance job safety and health. OSHA enforces the provisions of the 1970 Occupational Safety and Health Act, under which employers have a "general duty" to provide a place of employment "free from recognized hazards." Employers also have the special duty to comply with all standards of safety and health established under the act. OSHA's effectiveness has been debated for over a decade, but it is important to note that workplace accidents can result either from *unsafe work conditions* or from *unsafe work behaviors*. OSHA can affect only unsafe work conditions. There are no standards that govern potentially unsafe employee behaviors.

A major concern of employers today is with the possible health hazards associated with new technology, such as video display terminals and semiconductors, with diseases related to radiation or carcinogenic substances that may have long latency periods, and with AIDS.

To date, OSHA has issued only 10 major health standards. Two reasons account for this: It is difficult to identify carcinogenic substances, and it is difficult to determine regulatory standards once they are identified. Management's first duty in this area is to develop a safety and health policy. Management's second duty is to implement and sustain the policy through a loss control program.

Employee assistance programs represent a brighter side of the health issue. Such programs offer assistance to all "troubled" employees. Under an EAP, supervisors need be concerned only with identifying declining work performance, not with involvement in employee problems. Treatment is left to professionals. Finally, health promotion, or "wellness," programs differ from EAPs in that their primary focus is on prevention, not rehabilitation. Like EAPs there is controversy over their relative worth, and like EAPs they hold considerable promise.

DISCUSSION QUESTIONS

15■1 Should OSHA's enforcement activities be expanded? Why or why not?

15■2 What advantages and disadvantages do you see with workers' compensation?

15■3 Discuss the relative effectiveness of engineering versus management controls to improve job safety and health.

15■4 You have just been named CEO of a company that manufactures athletic shoes. Outline a job safety and health program.

15■5 If the benefits of EAPs cannot be demonstrated to exceed their costs, should EAPs be discontinued?

15■6 Should organizations be willing to invest more money in employee wellness? Why or why not?

REFERENCES

1. *Accident facts* (1990). Chicago: National Safety Council.

2. Allen, R. E., & Keaveny, T. J. (1988). *Contemporary labor relations* (2d ed.). Reading, MA: Addison-Wesley.

3. American business is bullish on "Wellness" (1982, March 29). *Medical World News*, pp. 33–39.

4. Apcar, L. M. (1984, Feb. 1). OSHA signs union-backed Asarco plan to control steelworker exposure to lead. *The Wall Street Journal*, p. 7.

5. Ashford, N. A. (1976). *Crisis in the workplace: Occupational disease and injury*. Cambridge, MA: MIT Press.

6. AT&T bans pregnant women from toxic area. (1987, Jan. 14). *Denver Post*, p. 1E.

7. Balgopal, P. R., Ramanathan, C. S., & Patchner, M. A. (1987, December). *Employee assistance programs: A cross-cultural perspective*. Paper presented at the Conference on International Personnel and Human Resource Management, Singapore.

8. Berg, N. R., & Moe, J. P. (1979). Assistance for troubled employees. In D. Yoder & H. G. Heneman, Jr. (eds.), *ASPA handbook of personnel and industrial relations*. Washington, DC: BNA, pp. 1.59–1.77.

9. Bernstein, J. E. (1983, November). Handling health costs by reducing health risks. *Personnel Journal*, pp. 882–887.

10. Bhopal judge orders Union Carbide to pay $270 million in interim relief. (1987, Dec. 18). *The Wall Street Journal*, p. 4.

11. Bitter reaction (1979, Feb. 9). *The Wall Street Journal*, pp. 1, 33.

12. Blustein, P. (1987, May 18). The nation comes to grips with the widening problem of AIDS. *The Wall Street Journal*, p. 20.

13. Brennan, A. J. (1983). Worksite health promotion can be cost-effective. *Personnel Administrator*, **28**(4), 39–42.

14. Brooks, J. (1977). *Failure to meet commitments made in the Occupational Safety and Health Act*. Committee on government operations, 95th Congress of the United States, Washington, DC: USGPO.

15. Burtt, E. J. (1979). *Labor in the American economy*. New York: St. Martin's Press.

16. Business bulletin (1990, Dec. 6). *The Wall Street Journal*, p. A1.

17. Cascio, W. F. (1991). *Costing human resources: The financial impact of behavior in organizations* (3d ed.). Boston: PWS-Kent.

18. Chase, M. (1987, May 18). AIDS costs. *The Wall Street Journal*, pp. 1, 20.

19. *Chemical hazard communication* (1988). Washington, DC: U.S. Department of Labor, OSHA #3084 (revised).

20. Cohen, A. (1977). Factors in successful occupational safety programs. *Journal of Safety Research*, **9**, 168–178.
21. Computers behind increase in workplace injuries (1989, Dec. 4). *Denver Post*, p. 3D.
22. Cook, W. N., & Gautschi, F. H. (1981). OSHA plant safety programs and injury reduction. *Industrial Relations*, **20**(3), 245–257.
23. Damages for a deadly cloud (1989, Feb. 27). *Time*, p. 53.
24. Elliott, S. (1984, June 27). OSHA Region III Area Director, personal communication.
25. Falkenberg, L. E. (1987). Employee fitness programs: Their impact on the employee and the organization. *Academy of Management Review*, **12**, 511–522.
26. Farkas, G. M. (1989). The impact of federal rehabilitation laws on the expanding role of employee assistance programs in business and industry. *American Psychologist*, **44**, 1482–1490.
27. $520,000 awarded in an asbestos-related illness (1987, Oct. 8). *The New York Times*, p. A21.
28. Follmann, J. F., Jr. (1978). *The economics of industrial health*. New York: AMACOM.
29. Foote, A., & Erfurt, J. (1981, September–October). Evaluating an employee assistance program. *EAP Digest*, pp. 14–25.
30. Foreign firms feel the impact of Bhopal most (1985, Nov. 26). *The Wall Street Journal*, p. 24.
31. French, H. W. (1987, March 26). Helping the addicted worker. *The New York Times*, pp. 29, 34.
32. Gaeta, E., Lynn, R., & Grey, L. (1982, May–June). AT&T looks at program evaluation. *EAP Digest*, pp. 22–31.
33. *Gateway Coal Co. v. United Mine Workers of America* (1974). 1974 OSHD, Sn. 17,085. Chicago: Commerce Clearing House.
34. Gebhardt, D. L., & Crump, C. E. (1990). Employee fitness and wellness programs in the workplace. *American Psychologist*, **45**, 262–272.
35. Geyelin, M. (1989, April 28). Study faults federal effort to enforce worker safety. *The Wall Street Journal*, p. B1.
36. Ginter, E. M. (1979, May). Communications and cost-benefit aspects of employee safety. *Management Accounting*, pp. 24–32.
37. Gobbledygook out (1977, Dec. 6). *Miami Herald*, p. 17A.
38. Gricar, B. G., & Hopkins, H. D. (1983). How does your company respond to OSHA? *Personnel Administrator*, **28**(4), 53–57.
39. Harris, D. (1987, November). AIDS: We'll all pay. *Money*, pp. 109–134.
40. Hays, L. (1986, July 8). New rules on workplace hazards prompt intensified on-the-job training programs. *The Wall Street Journal*, p. 31.
41. Hoover, J. J. (1983). Workers have new rights to health and safety. *Personnel Administrator*, **28**(4), 47–51.
42. *Illinois v. Chicago Magnet Wire Corp.* (1990, Oct. 24) 126 Ill.2d 356, 534 N.E., 2d 962, 128 Ill.
43. Injuries on the job (1984, March 30). *USA Today*, p. 1B.
44. *Inside OSHA: The role of management in safety* (1975, Nov. 1). New York: Man and Manager, Inc.
45. *Inside OSHA: Supervisory participation in safety* (1975, Sep. 1). New York: Man and Manager, Inc.
46. Jacobs, S. L. (1988, Nov. 22). Small business slowly wakes to OSHA hazard rule. *The Wall Street Journal*, p. B2.
47. James, F. B. (1987, Apr. 14). Study lays groundwork for tying health costs to workers' behavior. *The Wall Street Journal*, p. 37.

48. Job-related injury-rate up; 6 million cases in 1987 (1988, Nov. 16). *Denver Post*, p. 2B.
49. Johnson, S. (1988, June). Breast screening's bottom line—lives saved. *Administrative Radiology*, p. 4.
50. Karr, A. R. (1989, Nov. 2). USX charged with violation of safety rules. *The Wall Street Journal*, p. A22.
51. Karr, A. R. (1989, Jan. 16). OSHA sets or toughens exposure limits on 376 toxic chemicals in workplace. *The Wall Street Journal*, p. C16.
52. Karr, A. R. (1988, Oct. 31). OSHA urges record penalty for meatpacker. *The Wall Street Journal*, p. A4.
53. Kilborn, P. (1990, Sept. 2). Manufacturer's policy, women's job rights clash. *Denver Post*, p. 2A.
54. Kirkland, L. (1980, July). OSHA: A 10-year success story. *AFL-CIO American Federationist*, pp. 1–4.
55. Klarreich, S. H., DiGiuseppe, R., & DiMattia, D. J. (1987). EAPs: Mind over myth. *Personnel Administrator*, **32**(2), 119–121.
56. Komaki, J., Barwick, K. D., & Scott, L. R. (1978). A behavioral approach to occupational safety: Pinpointing and reinforcing safe performance in a food manufacturing plant. *Journal of Applied Psychology*, **63**, 434–445.
57. Kreitner, R. (1982, May–June). Personal wellness: It's just good business. *Business Horizons*, pp. 28–35.
58. Labor letter (1990, Jan. 30). *The Wall Street Journal*, p. A1.
59. Labor letter (1987, April 14). *The Wall Street Journal*, p. 1.
60. LaVan, H., Mathys, N., & Drehmer, D. (1983). A look at the counseling practices of major U.S. corporations. *Personnel Administrator*, **28**(6), 76–81, 143–146.
61. Leary, W. E. (1982, Aug. 2). Management concern affects mine safety. *Denver Post*, p. 1C.
62. Ledvinka, J., & Scarpello, V. G. (1991). *Federal regulation of personnel and human resource management* (2d ed.). Boston: PWS-Kent.
63. Leib, J. (1987, July 6). Screening for genetic ills threatens to rile workplace. *Denver Post*, p. 1B.
64. List, W. (1987, May 15). Employee fitness pays dividends. *Toronto Globe and Mail*, p. D18.
65. Lorber, L. Z., & Kirk, R. J. (1987). *Fear itself: A legal and personnel analysis of drug testing, AIDS, secondary smoke, and VDTs*. Alexandria, VA: ASPA Foundation.
66. Marcus, A. D., & de Cordoba, J. (1990, Oct. 17). New York court rules employers can face charges in worker safety. *The Wall Street Journal*, p. B9.
67. *Marshall v. Barlow's, Inc.* (1978). 1978 OSHD, Sn. 22,735. Chicago: Commerce Clearing House.
68. McCaffrey, D. P. (1983). An assessment of OSHA's recent effects on injury rates. *Journal of Human Resources*, **18**(1), 131–146.
69. Meier, B. (1987, Feb. 5). Companies wrestle with threats to workers' reproductive health. *The Wall Street Journal*, p. 25.
70. Merritt, N. L. (1987, March 23). Bank of America's blueprint for a policy on AIDS. *Business Week*, p. 127.
71. Milkovich, G. T., & Newman, J. M. (1990). *Compensation* (3d ed.). Homewood, IL: BPI-Irwin.
72. Miller, J. (1983, Nov. 17). Is-nothing-sacred dept.: OSHA is the bad guy in this video game. *The Wall Street Journal*, p. 33.

73. Miller, M. (1985, Nov. 26). Words still speak louder than deeds: India hasn't come to grips with plant safety. *The Wall Street Journal*, p. 24.

74. *NLRB v. Jasper Seating Co.* (1988). CA 7, 129 LRRM 2337.

75. Normand, J., Salyards, S. D., & Mahoney, J. J. (1990). An evaluation of preemployment drug testing. *Journal of Applied Psychology*, **75**, 629–639.

76. Nothstein, G., & Ayres, J. (1981). Sex-based considerations of differentiation in the workplace: Exploring the biomedical interface between OSHA and Title VII. *Villanova Law Review*, **26**(2), 239–321.

77. Olian, J. D. (1990). Workplace safety and employee health. In J. A. Fossum (ed.), *Employee and labor relations*. Washington, DC: Bureau of National Affairs, pp. 4-218 to 4-285.

78. Olian, J. D., & Snyder, T. C. (1984). The implications of genetic testing. *Personnel Administrator*, **29**(1), 19–27.

79. OSHA chief leaves agency in limbo (1984, April–May). *NFIB Mandate*, p. 6.

80. OSHA penalties increased (1991, February). *Mountain States Employers Council Bulletin*, p. 2.

81. Otten, A. L. (1986, Feb. 24). Probing the cell. *The Wall Street Journal*, pp. 1, 41.

82. Parkes, K. R. (1987). Relative weight, smoking, and mental health as predictors of sickness and absence from work. *Journal of Applied Psychology*, **72**, 275–286.

83. Ray, J. S. (1982). Having problems with worker performance? Try an EAP. *Administrative Management*, **43**(5), 47–49.

84. Reber, R. A., & Wallin, J. A. (1984). The effects of training, goal setting, and knowledge of results on safe behavior: A component analysis. *Academy of Management Journal*, **27**, 544–560.

85. Reed, R. W. (1984, January). Is education the key to lower health care costs? *Personnel Journal*, pp. 40–46.

86. Renner, J. F. (1987, March–April). Wellness programs: An investment in cost containment. *EAP Digest*, pp. 49–53.

87. Risk capital: Korea suffers the highest rate of industrial accidents (1990, Sept. 11). *The Wall Street Journal*, p. A1.

88. Root, N. (1981). Injuries at work are fewer among older employees. *Monthly Labor Review*, **104**(3), 30–34.

89. Scanlon, W. (1983, May–June). Trends in EAPs: Then and now. *EAP Digest*, pp. 38–41.

90. Shabecoff, P. (1987, Oct. 11). Industry is split over disclosure of job dangers. *The New York Times*, p. 28.

91. Simison, R. L. (1986, March 18). Safety last. *The Wall Street Journal*, pp. 1, 18.

92. Siskind, F. (1982). Another look at the link between work injuries and job experience. *Monthly Labor Review*, **105**(2), 38–41.

93. Smith, M. J., Cohen, H. H., Cohen, A., & Cleveland, R. J. (1978). Characteristics of successful safety programs. *Journal of Safety Research*, **10**, 5–15.

94. Sperling, D. (1989, March 9). More employers help foot the detox bill. *USA Today*, p. 5D.

95. Stead, W. E., & Stead, J. G. (1983, January). OSHA's cancer prevention policy: Where did it come from and where is it going? *Personnel Journal*, pp. 54–60.

96. Stone, D. L., & Kotch, D. A. (1989). Individuals' attitudes toward organizational drug testing policies and practices. *Journal of Applied Psychology*, **74**, 518–521.

97. Substance abuse in the workplace (1987, June 20). *Hospitals*, pp. 68–73.

98. Swoboda, F. (1990, Jan. 12). OSHA targets repetitive motion injuries. *Washington Post*, p. A10.

99. Taking drugs on the job (1983, Aug. 22). *Newsweek*, pp. 52–58.

100. Thanks, Dr. Bingham (1978, Nov. 29). *The Wall Street Journal*, p. 22.

101. Trice, H. M., & Roman, P. M. (1978). *Spirits and demons at work* (2d ed.). Ithaca, NY: New York State School of Industrial and Labor Relations.

102. Trost, C. (1988, April 22). Occupational hazard: A much-maligned OSHA confronts rising demands with a reduced budget. *The Wall Street Journal Supplement*, p. 25R.

103. Trost, C. (1986, Jan. 8). OSHA to check safety at more firms in an expansion of inspection policy. *The Wall Street Journal*, p. 50.

104. U.S. Department of Labor (1983, March). *Program Highlights: Job safety and health*. Washington, DC: USGPO, Fact Sheet No. OSHA-83-01 (revised).

105. U.S. fines meatpacker $3.1 million over injuries (1988, May 12). *The New York Times*, p. A20.

106. Weiss, R. M. (1987). Writing under the influence: Science versus fiction in the analysis of corporate alcoholism programs. *Personnel Psychology*, **40**, 341–356.

107. Wermiel, S. (1989, Oct. 3). Justices let states prosecute executives for job hazards covered by U.S. law. *The Wall Street Journal*, p. A11.

108. Winslow, R. (1991, Jan. 29). Medical costs soar, defying firms' cures. *The Wall Street Journal*, p. B1.

109. *Whirlpool Corporation v. Marshall* (1981, Feb. 26). *Daily Labor Report*, Washington, DC: Bureau of National Affairs, pp. D3–D10.

110. Worker insurance evolution (1983, Dec. 6). *The New York Times*, pp. D1, D17.

Competitive Strategies, Human Resource Strategies, and the Financial Impact of Human Resource Management Activities

■ **HUMAN RESOURCE MANAGEMENT IN ACTION**

ATTITUDE SURVEY RESULTS: CATALYST FOR MANAGEMENT ACTIONS*

Attitude surveys can yield far more than a measure of morale. By relating specific management actions and styles to high employee turnover and lowered profitability, the results of an attitude survey in one company led to concrete directions for change. The changes implied improved productivity, quality of work life, and bottom-line financial gain.

The company is a nationwide retail operation with an exceptional record of growth and profitability. To staff its rapidly expanding management positions, the company hires large numbers of men and women as trainees in

---

*Adapted from: B. Goldberg and G. G. Gordon, Designing attitude surveys for management action, *Personnel Journal*, October 1978, pp. 546–549.

■

store management. However, despite attractive salaries and promotion opportunities, the company was having trouble retaining the new hires. Top management was at a loss to explain why. Turnover among store managers accelerated beyond the most recent hires; managers in whom the company invested considerable time and money were also quitting. Moreover, there was no apparent pattern to the turnover—some locations were experiencing a great deal, others very little.

Despite continued profitability, there was growing concern among top management that the level of turnover might be detrimental to the company's long-term success. The actual dollar outlay for the cost of turnover was only one aspect of the problem. An additional consideration was the possibility of poor public relations resulting from unhappy former employees. As a consumer-oriented company, the firm was concerned about its public image and the effect that a "bad employer" reputation could have on the patronage of its stores.

THE PROBLEM: TURNOVER VERSUS PROFITABILITY

As turnover worsened, the company conducted various statistical analyses and reviewed reports from field managers in an attempt to locate the source of the problem. Several theories were proposed, such as low pay and inconvenient scheduling of work, but none was supported by sufficient evidence to produce change. Indeed, most of the proposed solutions to the turnover problem (e.g., hire more employees to work fewer hours) were rejected because their anticipated costs would reduce company profitability.

Top management initially felt that high turnover was acceptable because it did not have much of an adverse effect on profits. In fact, many managers believed that turnover actually increased profitability because it kept overall salary costs down. Vacancies caused stores to operate understaffed until replacements were hired, and these new hires were paid lower salaries than their predecessors.

WHY AN ATTITUDE SURVEY?

Despite attempts to find it, the root cause of the turnover of store managers remained elusive. The problem could lie anywhere in the management system, in the types of employees hired, in how they were trained, in how they were managed, or in how their performance was rewarded.

Top management decided to conduct a broad survey among the store managers themselves to determine the cause of the high turnover. The survey's intent was not to determine how to improve morale and thereby to reduce turnover. It was to help management discover the factors contributing to turnover and the concrete and constructive actions that might reduce it. And, because top management believed that high turnover had a positive effect on profitability, another objective of the survey was to determine what could be done to reduce turnover without reducing profitability! This part of the survey yielded some very enlightening results.

DESIGNING THE SURVEY

The company first rank-ordered its profit centers in two ways — (1) according to turnover and (2) according to profitability — based on results for the most recent 12-month period. A questionnaire was developed through personal interviews with a number of store managers, and hypotheses were advanced concerning the relationship between the attitudes of store managers and turnover. The hypotheses produced further guides for questionnaire design; they also yielded an outline for subsequent data analyses.

The resulting questionnaire covered a broad range of management issues, including:

- Store characteristics (location and volume)
- Biographical characteristics of the store managers
- Recruitment and selection practices
- Training activities
- Working conditions
- Management climate
- Rewards system

The questionnaire was sent to every store manager then working in one of the profit centers identified earlier.

SURVEY RESULTS

The survey revealed significant differences in the ways store managers were selected, managed, and treated. It also identified a number of fundamental management practices that were counterproductive. For example, some higher-level supervisors never made field visits to work with their store managers.

However, the most revealing part of the survey results had to do with turnover and profitability. Many factors contributing to high turnover were also contributing to lower profitability. The survey revealed six critical areas of human resource management, all interrelated and each related to turnover and profitability.

Challenges

1. What are some of the advantages and disadvantages of a low turnover rate?

2. How can attitude surveys help orient managers toward more effective performance?

3. In the survey design phase, why do you think the company first ranked each store in terms of its profitability and turnover rate?

QUESTIONS THIS CHAPTER WILL HELP MANAGERS ANSWER

1. Does our firm's HR strategy follow from our firm's competitive business strategy?

2. What kinds of employee behaviors and HR activities should we encourage, given our firm's competitive business strategy?

3. How can management assess the costs and benefits of these employee behaviors and HR activities?

In business settings, it is hard to be convincing without data. If the data are developed systematically and comprehensively and are analyzed in terms of their strategic implications for the business or business unit, they are more convincing. The chapter opening vignette demonstrates how a systematic procedure (an attitude survey) designed to collect data on a broad range of management issues could be used to improve management practices. This chapter will first present several alternative competitive strategies and then identify the kinds of employee behaviors and human resource (HR) activities that are most consistent with each one. Then we shall discuss the need for audit and evaluation of HR activities and how HR research can help in this effort. Finally, we will present examples of methods used to assess the costs and benefits of HR activities in several key areas.

ORIENTATION

As emphasized earlier, the focus of this book is *not* on training HR specialists. Rather, the focus is on training line managers who must, by the very nature of their jobs, manage people and work with them to accomplish organizational objectives. Consequently, the purpose of this chapter is not how to measure the effectiveness of the human resources department; the purpose is to show how to align HR strategies with general business strategies and, having done so, to assess the costs and benefits of relevant HR activities. The methods can and should be used in cooperation with the human resources department. But they are not the exclusive domain of that department. They are general enough to be used by any manager in any department to measure the costs and benefits of employee behavior.

This is not to imply that dollars are the only barometer of the effectiveness of human resource activities. The payoffs from some activities, such as affirmative action and child care, must be viewed in a broader social context. Further, the firm's strategy and goals must guide the work of each business unit *and* of that unit's human resource management activities. For example, to emphasize its outreach efforts to the disadvantaged, a firm might adopt a conscious strategy to *train* workers for entry-level jobs, while *selecting* workers who already have the skills to perform higher-level jobs. To make the most effective use of the information that follows, it is important always to keep these points in mind.

Alternative Competitive Strategies

The means that firms use to compete for business in the marketplace and to gain competitive advantage are known as *competitive strategies*.[26] Competitive strategies may differ in a number of ways, including the extent to which firms emphasize innovation, quality enhancement, or cost reduction.[31] Moreover, there is growing recognition that the different types of strategies require different types of HR practices.[14] The important lesson for managers is that *human resources represent a competitive advantage that can increase profits when managed wisely.*

Because different types of HR practices are important under different competitive strategies, the assessment of outcomes associated with HR activities should focus on those activities that are most crucial to the implementation of the competitive strategy chosen. In a later section we will tie together competitive strategies and the HR activities most relevant to them, but first we need to describe each strategy.

Innovation strategy is used to develop products or services that differ from those of competitors. Its primary objective is to offer something new and different. Enhancing product or service quality is the primary objective of the *quality-enhancement strategy*. Finally, the objective of a *cost-reduction strategy* is to gain competitive advantage by being the lowest cost producer of goods or provider of services. Innovation strategy emphasizes managing people so that they work *differently*; quality-enhancement strategy emphasizes managing people so that they work *smarter*; and cost-reduction strategy emphasizes managing people so that they work *harder*.[31]

While it is convenient to think of these three competitive strategies as pure types applied to entire organizations, business units, or even functional specialties, reality is more complex. As the following statement illustrates, various combinations of the three strategies are often observed in practice.

As is well known, Ford Motor Co. has emphasized employee involvement since the early 1980s. In October 1978, Philip Caldwell, then president of Ford, made the following statement at a meeting of top executives: "Our strategy for the years ahead will come to nothing unless we ask for greater participation of our work force. Without motivated and concerned workers, we're not going to lower our costs as much as we need to—and we aren't going to get the product quality we need." (ref. 3, p. 391). Elements of both cost-reduction and quality-enhancement strategies are evident in Caldwell's statement.

Employee Behaviors and Human Resource Strategies Appropriate to Each Competitive Business Strategy

Innovation strategy Under a competitive strategy of innovation, the implications for managing people may include selecting highly skilled individuals, giving employees more discretion, using minimal controls, making greater investments in human resources, providing more resources for experimentation, allowing and even rewarding occasional failure, and appraising performance for its long-run implications. Innovative firms such as Hewlett-Packard, 3M, Raytheon, and PepsiCo illustrate this strategy.[31]

Because the innovation process depends heavily on individual expertise and creativity, employee turnover can have disastrous consequences.[17] Moreover, firms pursuing this strategy are likely to emphasize long-term needs in their training programs for managers, and to offer training to more employees throughout the organization.[15] HR strategy should therefore emphasize the use of highly valid selection and training programs and also the reduction of controllable turnover, especially among high performers who are not easy to replace.

The latter approach is being used more and more by firms who are trying to hang on to valued employees as they steer through bankruptcy reorganizations. Such "employee-retention plans" offer incentive bonuses for managers who stay for 1 or 2 years and who meet certain performance criteria. They also offer lucrative severance packages if jobs are cut. Federated Department Stores and Allied Stores, Campeau Corporation's U.S. retailing subsidiaries, used this approach, as did Braniff, L. J. Hooker, LTV, and Wickes Companies.[25] Although the programs are relatively new, early indications are that they work. Why do companies adopt them? Because it does little good for a firm to fight its way out of bankruptcy court if essential employees don't stay around to guide the restructured operations.[25]

Quality-enhancement strategy The profile of behaviors appropriate under this strategy includes: relatively repetitive and predictable behaviors; a longer-term focus; a modest amount of cooperative, interdependent behavior; a high concern for quality with a modest concern for quantity of output; a high concern with *how* goods or services are made or delivered; low risk-taking activity; and commitment to the goals of the organization.[31]

Quality enhancement typically involves greater commitment from employees and fuller use of their abilities. As a result, fewer employees may be needed to accomplish the same amount of work. This phenomenon has been observed at firms such as L. L. Bean, Corning Glass, Honda, and Toyota.[34]

It is well known that the gains in productivity that result from more valid selection or training programs can be expressed in various ways: in dollars, increases in output, decreases in hiring needs, or savings in payroll costs.[7] Since fewer workers *may* be needed after the implementation of more valid selection or training programs, managers may wish to focus on the change in staffing requirements (as well as the associated cost savings) as one outcome of a quality-enhancement strategy.

Since reliable and predictable behavior is important to the implementation of this strategy, another objective is to minimize absenteeism, tardiness, and turnover. Cost savings associated with any HR programs designed to control these undesirable behaviors should therefore be documented carefully. In a later section of this chapter, we will present methods for doing this.

Commitment to the goals of the organization, and flexibility to change, can both be increased by constant formal and informal training programs. Changes in commitment and flexibility can then be assessed by measuring employee attitudes over multiple time periods. Finally, other ways to signal concern for the long-term welfare of employees are by actively promoting day care, employee assistance programs, wellness, and smoking cessation programs.

In summary, to be consistent with a quality-enhancement strategy, HR strategy should focus on the use of highly valid selection and training programs, on promoting positive changes in employees' attitudes and in their lifestyles, and on decreasing absenteeism and controllable turnover. To assess the effectiveness of strategy implementation, managers must then examine costs and benefits in each of these areas.

Cost-reduction strategy Firms pursuing this strategy are characterized by tight fiscal and management controls, minimization of overhead, and pursuit of economies of scale. The primary objective is to increase productivity by decreasing the unit cost of output per employee. Strategies for reducing cost include reducing the number of employees; reducing wages; using part-time workers, subcontractors, or automation; changing work rules; and permitting flexibility in job assignments.[31]

The profile of employee behaviors under this strategy includes relatively repetitive and predictable behaviors, a comparatively short-term focus, primarily autonomous or individual activity, a modest concern for quality coupled with a high concern for quantity of output (goods or services), emphasis on results, low risk taking, and stability. In addition, there is minimal use of training and development.

Sometimes managements adopt cost-reduction strategies in rather desperate situations, as their firms struggle to survive. More commonly, though, cost reduction is used in combination with other strategies to keep companies prosperous. As an example, consider the response to international competition of Cummins Engine Co., a $2.5 billion manufacturer of diesel engines and related products and services headquartered in Columbus, Indiana. The company has about 22,000 employees worldwide, and its sales mix is 70 percent U.S. business and 30 percent international. It powers about 60 percent of the trucks on U.S. highways.

Cummins watched with deep concern throughout the 1970s as foreign competition won nearly 100 percent of the U.S. motorcycle market, 30 percent of the U.S. auto market, and a big chunk of the U.S. steel market—all in about 10 years. In the company's view, those gains in market share were mostly won fairly and squarely with better products, quality, prices, and responsiveness to the customer.[37] Those industries are close to Cummins's, and the company vowed to compete aggressively.

To do so, it focused on the variables of product, prices and costs, and performance. It spent nearly a billion dollars on product development through the 1980s—triple the company's market value in 1980! To meet world price levels, the company swore off price increases for 5 years. As for performance, managers at every level developed specific goals in the areas of quality, cost, and delivery and allocated them to work groups throughout the company. Every quarter the president provided videotaped progress reports to all employees.

What were the results? Financially, the company has lost no domestic business to international competition. Its domestic market share has grown, as has its success in international markets. As one executive noted: "We have experienced, and managed, a full range of human emotions during these years. . . . Our people have been stretched, pulled, and at times really shaken up trying to meet all these challenges; facilities have been closed as operations were consolidated, and many jobs were lost despite our successful efforts to create new ones. . . . This process, of course, continues . . . for it is a game—or war—that can be won but never finished." (ref. 37, p. 31).

HUMAN RESOURCES RESEARCH—THE BASIS FOR AUDIT AND EVALUATION OF HR ACTIVITIES

One of the classic functions of management is that of control. In a small business, managers are close to the scene of operations. They can see for themselves exactly what is happening. However, the need for management control becomes greater as managers are further removed from the scene of operations—as is the case in many firms that do business in multiple locations. As we have stressed, it is important for managers to assess the degree of "fit" between their firm's competitive strategies and its human resource strategies. Beyond that, it is important to conduct HR research—to assess the outcomes of the HR activities undertaken, and at different levels of analysis.

Types of Outcomes

Outcomes may be expressed in quantitative terms (e.g., cost-benefit analysis) or in qualitative terms (e.g., indicators of overall morale, job satisfaction, or reaction to a training program). Alone, each type of outcome is incomplete; both are necessary to describe the rich results of HR programs. Later on in this chapter, we will illustrate how quantitative outcomes can be determined. Now, however, let's consider a qualitative HR research tool that is becoming quite popular—the attitude survey.

To a large extent, the growing popularity of attitude surveys is due to an idea stressed in many popular books on management: that it is important to listen to employees. This idea has taken on added significance as more companies endure the organizational trauma of mergers and restructurings or adopt more participative management styles.

As employee surveys become more common, the range of issues on which opinions are solicited is expanding considerably. At Wells Fargo & Co. in San Francisco, for instance, employees have been asked about such things as the effectiveness of the bank's advertising, the quality of innovation of its products, and its responsibility to the community.

It is one thing to ask employees for their opinions—it shows that management is willing to listen. But surveys can backfire; employees become angry and resentful if their expectations are raised but management fails to react to their comments or complaints. When facing employees who feel that they are underpaid, for example, one manager noted that firms "had better be prepared with facts to tell them that their perception is incorrect or perhaps that there are reasons. That can get very sensitive."[27] As a result of its own survey, Hewlett-Packard found out that engineers were concerned about their lack of communication with peers in other units. After listening to the engineers at a postsurvey meeting, the company accelerated development of an electronic mail system.

After mergers and acquisitions, many companies try to move quickly to evaluate the morale of the evaluated company and to discover any differences in operating styles. Just 2 months after it acquired Crocker National Corp., for example, Wells Fargo surveyed 1500 Crocker employees. As a Wells Fargo vice president noted: "There's a lot of organizational change going on. . . . Wells Fargo was in a major downsizing, and now [there is] the acquisition. This helps us know what's going on . . . we really didn't know what the silent majority felt."[27]

Attitude surveys represent just one type of HR research tool. In addition, the wide availability of computerized employee databases makes it possible to answer a variety of other questions, such as factors that relate consistently to the retention of engineers, the productivity and turnover of salespeople, and the personal characteristics of employees who accept offers of early retirement. Finally, detailed, sophisticated research is being conducted on issues as diverse as the impact of plant shutdowns, worker participation in management decisions, worker ownership, and the social costs of unemployment and concession bargaining.[32] As these few examples show, the range of HR research topics, and the methods used to investigate them, are limited only by the imagination and ingenuity of the managers and researchers involved.

Level of Analysis

It is important to distinguish HR activities performed at the corporate level from those performed at the middle-management level or at the operating level.[35] At the corporate level, HR decisions involve the design of policies that meet an organization's strategic challenges, such as business objectives, corporate values or culture, technology, structure, and responses to constraints from the external environment (e.g., safety policies).

At the middle-management level, key HR decisions involve the design of systems or programs that are consistent with policy guidelines and will facilitate the cost-effective achievement of business goals. The primary objective is management control, and it is accomplished by assessing the cost-effectiveness of HR programs.

At the operating level, managers implement HR policies and programs, making decisions that affect the attraction, retention, and motivation of employees. This level includes the hands-on HR practices of line managers (e.g., to reduce absenteeism or controllable turnover) and the day-to-day services provided by the HR function (e.g., recruiting, staffing, training) that directly affect HR outcomes.

Assuming that a manager appreciates the need to align competitive and human resource strategies, and desires to assess the costs and benefits of the HR activities that are most relevant to the chosen strategy, how does he or she proceed? Let us begin by distinguishing human resource accounting from behavior costing.

Human Resource Accounting

In the mid-1960s the first attempts were made to account for the costs of human resource management activities. This accounting has come to be known generally as human resource accounting (HRA).

The first firm to report HRA results was the R. G. Barry Corp. of Columbus, Ohio, which did so in its 1967 annual report.[38] The company's objective was to report accurate estimates of the worth of the human assets in its employ. For each manager, costs were accumulated in five subsidiary accounts: (1) recruiting and acquisition, (2) formal orientation and training, (3) informal orientation and training, (4) experience, and (5) development. The costs for each manager were amortized over his or her expected working lifetime; unamortized costs (such as for a manager who leaves the company) were written off.

Valuing managers in this way is what accountants call the "asset model of accounting," which uses the historical cost of the asset. That is, the organization's investment in each manager—the asset—is measured by the expenses actually incurred—the historical cost—in developing each manager as an asset.

Such an approach considers only the investments made in managers and not the returns on those investments. This is one reason why asset models of HRA never caught on widely.[2,28]

A newer approach focuses on dollar estimates of the behaviors, such as the absenteeism, turnover, and job performance of managers. This approach does not measure the value of a manager as an asset, but rather the economic consequences of his or her behavior. This is an *expense model* of HRA.[22] It is the approach taken in this chapter to assessing the costs and benefits of the activities of all employees, managerial as well as nonmanagerial. We will apply standard cost accounting procedures to employee behavior. To do this, we must first identify each of the elements of behavior to which we can assign a cost; each behavioral cost element must be separate and mutually exclusive from another. To begin, let's define some key terms.

The Behavior Costing Approach

Contrary to popular belief, there are methods for determining the costs of employee behavior in *all* human resource management activities—behaviors associated with the attraction, selection, retention, development, and utilization of people in organizations. These costing methods are based on several definitions and a few necessary assumptions.

To begin, there are, as in any costing situation, controllable and uncontrollable costs, and there are direct and indirect measures of these costs.

Direct measures refer to actual costs, such as the accumulated, direct cost of recruiting.

Indirect measures do not deal directly with cost; they are usually expressed in terms of time, quantity, or quality.[11] In many cases indirect measures can be converted to direct measures. For example, if we know the length of time per preemployment interview plus the interviewer's hourly pay, it is a simple matter to convert time per interview into cost per interview.

Indirect measures have value in and of themselves, and they also supply part of the data needed to develop a direct measure. As a further example, consider the direct and indirect costs associated with mismanaged organizational stress, as shown in Table 16-1. The direct costs listed in the left column of Table 16-1 can all be expressed in terms of dollars. To see this, consider just two items: the costs associated with work accidents and grievances (Figure 16-1). Figure 16-1 presents just some of the direct costs associated with accidents; it is not meant to be exhaustive, and it does not include such items as lost time, replacement costs, "work to rule" by coworkers if they feel that the firm is responsible, the cost of the safety committee's investigation, and the costs associated with changing technology or job design to prevent future accidents. Items shown in the right column of Table 16-1 cannot be expressed as easily in dollar terms, but they are no less important, and the cost of these indirect items may in fact be far larger than the direct costs. Both direct and indirect costs, as well as benefits, must be considered in order to apply behavior costing methodology properly.

■ TABLE 16·1
DIRECT AND INDIRECT COSTS ASSOCIATED WITH MISMANAGED STRESS

Direct costs	Indirect costs
Participation and membership	**Loss of vitality**
Absenteeism	Low morale
Tardiness	Low motivation
Strikes and work stoppages	Dissatisfaction
Turnover	**Communication breakdowns**
Performance on the job	Decline in frequency of contact
Quality of productivity	Distortions of messages
Quantity of productivity	**Faulty decision making**
Grievances	**Quality of work relations**
Accidents	Distrust
Unscheduled machine downtime and repair	Disrespect
Material and supply overutilization	Animosity
Inventory shrinkages	**Opportunity costs**
Compensation awards	

Source: B. A. Macy & P. H. Mirvis, *Evaluation Review,* **6**(3), Figure 4-5, copyright © 1982 by Sage Publications, Inc. Reprinted by permission.

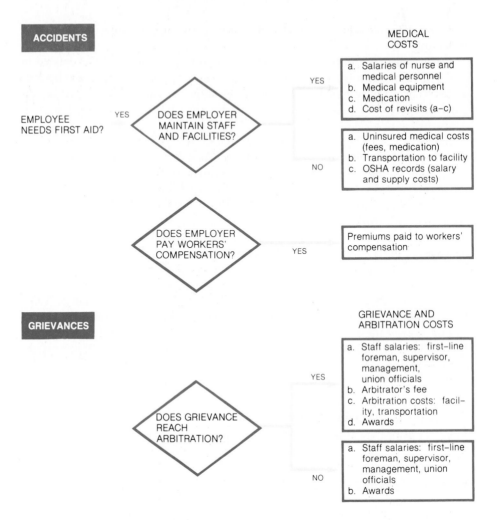

FIGURE 16-1
The costs of accidents
and grievances.

Controllable versus uncontrollable costs In any area of behavior costing, some types of costs are controllable through prudent HR decisions, while other costs are simply beyond the control of the organization. Consider employee turnover as an example. To the extent that people leave for reasons of "better salary," "more opportunity for promotion and career development," or "greater job challenge," the costs associated with turnover are somewhat controllable. That is, the firm can alter its human resource management practices to reduce the voluntary turnover. However, if the turnover is due to such factors as death, poor health, or spouse transfer, the costs are uncontrollable.

The point is that in human resource costing, our objective is not simply to *measure* costs but also to *reduce* the costs of human resources by devoting resources to the more "controllable" factors. To do this, we must do two things well:

1. Identify, for each HR decision, which costs are controllable and which are not.
2. Measure these costs at Time 1 (prior to some intervention designed to reduce controllable costs) and then again at Time 2 (after the intervention).

Hence the real payoff from determining the cost of employee behaviors lies in being able to demonstrate a financial gain from the wise application of human resource management methods.

The following six sections present both hypothetical and actual company examples of behavior costing in the areas of absenteeism, turnover, company-sponsored day care, employee assistance programs, selection, and training. Our focus will be limited *only* to behavior costing methods and practical examples of each. We will not deal with alternative human resource management approaches that might be used to reduce costs in each area: for example, to reduce the costs of employee absenteeism or turnover. These have been discussed elsewhere in the book.

COSTING EMPLOYEE ABSENTEEISM

In any human resource costing application, it is important first to define exactly what is being measured. From a business standpoint, *absenteeism is any failure of an employee to report for or to remain at work as scheduled, regardless of reason.* The term "as scheduled" is very significant, for this automatically excludes vacations, holidays, jury duty, and the like. It also eliminates the problem of determining whether an absence is "excusable" or not. Medically verified illness is a good example of this. From a business perspective, the employee is absent and is simply not available to perform his or her job; that absence will cost money. How much money? At General Motors, where daily absenteeism among the hourly work force often hovers around 15 percent, the annual tab is $1 billion.[23,24]

A flowchart (based on ref. 18) that shows how to estimate the total cost of employee absenteeism over any period is shown in Figure 16-2. To illustrate the computation of each cost element in Figure 16-2, let us use as an example a hypothetical 1800-employee firm called Mini-Mini-Micro Electronics; dollar figures are shown in Table 16-2. An item-by-item explanation of each of them follows.

Item 1: Total hours lost. If we assume a 2.1 percent monthly absenteeism rate (about average for manufacturing firms in 1990),[6] we can apply this figure to *total scheduled work hours.* Hours of *scheduled work time* per employee may be determined as follows:

2080 hours of work per year

−80 hours of vacation (2 weeks)

−40 hours (5 days) paid holidays

1. Compute total employee hours lost to absenteeism for the period.

2. Compute weighted average wage or salary/hr per absent employee.

3. Compute cost of employee benefits/hr per employee.

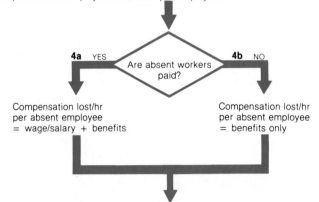

4a YES   Are absent workers paid?   **4b** NO

Compensation lost/hr
per absent employee
= wage/salary + benefits

Compensation lost/hr
per absent employee
= benefits only

5. Compute total compensation lost to absent employees [(1) × (4a) or (4b) as applicable].

6. Estimate total supervisory hours lost to employee absenteeism.

7. Compute average hourly supervisory salary + benefits.

8. Estimate total supervisory salaries lost to managing absenteeism problems [(6) × (7)].

9. Estimate all other costs incidental to absenteeism.

10. Estimate total cost of absenteeism [(5) + (8) + (9)].

11. Estimate total cost of absenteeism/employee [(10) ÷ Total no. of employees].

FIGURE 16-2

Total estimated cost of employee absenteeism. [*Source*: Wayne F. Cascio, *Costing human resources: The financial impact of behavior in organizations*, 3d ed. (1991). © PWS-Kent Publishing Co., Boston. Reprinted by permission of PWS-Kent Publishing Co., a division of Wadsworth, Inc.]

This equals 1960 hours of scheduled work time per employee × 1800 employees = 3,528,000 total scheduled work hours per year. If 2.1 percent of total scheduled work hours are lost to absenteeism, then a total of 3,528,000 × 0.021, or 74,088, hours are lost.

Item 2: Weighted average wage or salary per hour per absent employee. If a computerized system is available for employees to phone in a report of their

■ **TABLE 16·2**
COST OF EMPLOYEE ABSENTEEISM AT
MINI-MINI-MICRO ELECTRONICS

Item	Mini-Mini-Micro Electronics
1. Total hours lost to employee absenteeism for the period	74,088 hours
2. Weighted average wage or salary per hour per employee	$10.159 per hour
3. Cost of employee benefits per hour per employee	$3.556 per hour
4. Total compensation lost per hour per absent employee (a) If absent workers are paid (wage or salary plus benefits) (b) If absent workers are not paid (benefits only)	$13.715 per hour —
5. Total compensation lost to absent employees [total hours lost × 4(a) or 4(b), whichever applies]	$1,016,116.92
6. Total supervisory hours lost on employee absenteeism	8820 hours
7. Average hourly supervisory wage, including benefits	$18.225 per hour
8. Total supervisory salaries lost to managing problems of absenteeism (hours lost × average hourly supervisory wage — item 6 × item 7)	$160,744.50
9. All other costs incidental to absenteeism not included in the preceding items	$50,000
10. Total estimated cost of absenteeism — summation of items 5, 8, and 9	$1,226,861.42
11. Total estimated cost of absenteeism per employee: Total estimated costs ÷ total number of employees	$681.59 per employee absence

absence, then the exact wage or salary per hour per absent employee can be determined. If not, then the following procedure may be used:

Occupational group	Approx. percent of total absenteeism	Average hourly wage	Weighted average wage
Blue collar	0.55	$10.45	$ 5.747
Clerical	0.35	8.15	2.852
Management	0.10	15.60	1.560
Total weighted average pay per employee per hour			$10.159

Item 3: Cost of employee benefits per hour. We include the cost of benefits in our calculations because benefits consume, on average, more than a third of

total compensation (see Chapter 11). Ultimately we want to be able to calculate the total compensation lost due to absenteeism. Since our primary interest is in the cost of benefits per absentee, we take the weighted average hourly wage multiplied by benefits as a percentage of base pay. (If benefits differ as a function of union-nonunion or exempt-nonexempt status, then a weighted average benefit should be computed in the same manner as was done to compute a weighted average wage.) For Mini-Mini-Micro, this figure is

$$\$10.159 \times 35\% = \$3.556 \text{ per hour}$$

Item 4: Total compensation lost per hour per absent employee. This equals the weighted average hourly wage plus hourly cost of benefits (assuming that absent workers are paid). Some firms (e.g., Honda USA) do not pay absentees: "No work, no pay." In such instances, only the cost of benefits should be included in the estimate of total compensation lost per hour per absent employee. For Mini-Mini-Micro, the compensation lost per hour for each absent employee is

$$\$10.159 + \$3.556 = \$13.715$$

Item 5: Total compensation lost to absent employees. This is simply total hours lost multiplied by total compensation lost per hour:

$$74,088 \text{ hr} \times \$13.715/\text{hr} = \$1,016,116.92$$

Note that the first five items shown in Figure 16-2 refer to the costs associated with absentees themselves. The next three items refer to the firm's costs of *managing* employee absenteeism.

Item 6: Total supervisory hours lost in dealing with employee absenteeism. Three factors determine this lost time, which is the product of $A \times B \times C$, where:

A = Estimated average number of hours lost per supervisor per day managing absenteeism problems

The supervisor's time is "lost" because, instead of planning, scheduling, and troubleshooting productivity problems, he or she must devote time to nonproductive activities associated with managing absenteeism problems. The actual amount of time lost can be determined by having supervisors keep diaries indicating how they spend their time or by conducting structured interviews with experienced supervisors.

B = Total number of supervisors who deal with absenteeism problems

C = Total number of working days in the period for which absentee costs are being analyzed (including all shifts and weekend work).

For Mini-Mini-Micro Electronics, the data needed for this calculation are:

Estimate of A = 30 min, or 0.50 hr, per day

Estimate of B = 1800 employees (10%, or 180, are supervisors, and 40% of the 180, or 72, of the supervisors deal regularly with absenteeism problems)

Estimate of C = 245 days per year

$$\text{Supervisory hours lost in dealing with absensteeism} = 0.50 \text{ hr/day} \times 72 \text{ supervisors} \times 245 \text{ days/year}$$

$$= 8820 \text{ supervisory hours lost per year}$$

Item 7: Average hourly supervisory salary plus benefits. For those supervisors who deal regularly with absenteeism problems, assume that their average hourly salary is $13.50 plus 35 percent benefits ($4.725), or $18.225 per hour.

Item 8: Total cost of supervisory salaries lost to managing problems of absenteeism. To determine this cost, multiply the total supervisory hours lost by the total hourly supervisory salary:

8820 hr lost × $18.225/hr = $160,744.50

Item 9: All other absenteeism-related costs not included in items 1 through 8. Assume that Mini-Mini-Micro spends $50,000 per year in absenteeism-related costs that are not associated either with absentees or with supervisors. These costs are associated with elements such as overtime premiums, wages for temporary help, machine downtime, production losses, inefficient materials usage by temporary substitute employees, and, for very large organizations, permanent labor pools to "fill in" for absent workers.

Item 10: Total cost of employee absenteeism. This is the sum of the three costs determined thus far: costs associated with absent employees (item 5) plus costs associated with the management of absenteeism problems (item 8) plus other absenteeism-related costs (item 9). For Mini-Mini-Micro Electronics, this figure is

$1,016,116.92 + $160,744.50 + $50,000 = $1,226,861.42

Item 11: Per-employee cost of absenteeism. This is the total cost divided by 1800 employees, or $681.59.

Perhaps the first question management will ask upon seeing absenteeism cost figures is "What do they mean? Are we average, above average, or what?" Unfortunately, there are no industrywide figures on the costs of employee absenteeism. Certainly these costs will vary depending on the type of firm, the industry, and the level of employee that is absent (unskilled versus skilled or professional workers). Remember that the dollar figure just determined (we will call this the "Time 1" figure) becomes meaningful as a *baseline* from which to measure the financial gains realized as a result of a strategy to reduce absenteeism. At some later time (we will call this "Time 2"), the total cost of absenteeism should be measured again. The difference between the Time 2 figure and the Time 1 figure, minus the cost of implementing the strategy to reduce absenteeism, represents *net gain*.

Another question that often arises at this point is "Are these dollars real? Since supervisors are drawing their salaries anyway, what difference does it make if they have to manage absenteeism problems?" True, but what is the best possible gain from them for that pay? Let's compare two firms, A and B, identical in regard to all resources and costs—supervisors get paid the same, work the same hours, manage the same size staff, and produce the same kind of product. *But* absenteeism in A is very low, and in B it is very high. The paymasters' records show the same pay to supervisors, but the accountants show higher profits in A than in B. Why? Because the supervisors in firm A spend less time managing absenteeism problems. They are more productive because they devote their energies to planning, scheduling, and troubleshooting. Instead of putting in a 10- or 12-hour day (that the supervisors in firm B consider "normal"), they wrap things up after only 8 hours. In short, reducing the hours that supervisors must spend managing absenteeism problems has two advantages: (1) It allows supervisors to maximize their productivity, and (2) it reduces the stress and wear and tear associated with repeated 10- to 12-hour days, which in turn enhances the quality of work life of supervisors.

COSTING EMPLOYEE TURNOVER

Turnover may be defined as *any permanent departure beyond organizational boundaries*[19]—a broad and admittedly ponderous definition. Not included as turnover within this definition, therefore, are transfers within an organization and temporary layoffs. The rate of turnover in percent over any period can be calculated by the formula:

$$\frac{\text{Number of turnover incidents per period}}{\text{Average workforce size}} \times 100\%$$

Nationwide in 1990, for example, monthly turnover rates averaged about 1 percent, or 12 percent annually.[6] However, this figure most likely represents both controllable turnover (controllable by the organization) and uncontrollable turnover. Controllable turnover is "voluntary" by the employee, while uncontrollable turnover is "involuntary" (e.g., retirement, death, or spouse transfer). Furthermore, turnover may be *functional*, where the employee's departure produces a benefit for the organization, or *dysfunctional*, where the departing employee is someone the organization would like to retain.

High performers who are difficult to replace represent dysfunctional turnovers;

low performers who are easy to replace represent functional turnovers. The crucial issue in analyzing turnover, therefore, is not how many employees are leaving but the performance and replaceability of those who are leaving versus those who are staying.[20]

In costing employee turnover, first we determine the total cost of all turnover, and then we estimate the percentage of that amount representing controllable, dysfunctional turnover—resignations that represent a net loss to the firm and that the firm could have prevented. Thus, if total turnover costs $1 million, and 50 percent is controllable and dysfunctional, then $500,000 is our Time 1 baseline measure. To demonstrate the net financial gain associated with the strategy adopted prior to Time 2, the total gain at Time 2, say $700,000, minus the cost of implementing the strategy to reduce turnover, say $50,000, must be compared to the cost of turnover at Time 1 ($500,000). In this example, the net gain to the firm is $150,000. Now let's see how the total cost figure is derived.

Components of Turnover Costs

There are three broad categories of costs in the basic turnover costing model: separation costs, replacement costs, and training costs. In this section, we present only the cost elements that comprise each of these three broad categories. (See ref. 8 for more detailed formulas.)

Separation costs There are four cost elements in separation costs. These are:

Exit interview, including the cost of the interviewer's time and the cost of the terminating employee's time.

Administrative functions related to termination: for example, removal of the employee from payroll, termination of benefits, and turn-in of company equipment.

Separation pay, if applicable.

Increased unemployment tax. Such an increase may come from either or both of two sources. First, in states that base unemployment tax rates on each company's turnover rate, high turnover will lead to a higher unemployment tax rate. Suppose a company with a 10 percent annual turnover rate was paying unemployment tax at a rate of 5 percent on the first $7000 of each employee's wages in 1990. But in 1991, because its turnover rate jumped to 15 percent, the company's unemployment tax rate may increase to 5.5 percent. Second, replacements for those who leave will result in extra unemployment tax being paid. Thus a 500-employee firm with no turnover during the year will pay the tax on the first $7000 (or whatever the state maximum is) of each employee's wages. The same firm with a 20 percent annual turnover rate will pay the tax on the first $7000 of the wages of 600 employees.

The sum of these four cost elements represents the total separation costs for the firm.

Replacement costs The eight cost elements associated with replacing employees who leave include:

Communicating job availability

Preemployment administrative functions: for example, accepting applications and checking references

Entrance interview, or perhaps multiple interviews

Testing and/or other types of assessment procedures

Staff meetings, if applicable, to determine if replacements are needed, to recheck job analyses and job specifications, to pool information on candidates, and to reach final hiring decisions

Travel and moving expenses: travel for all applicants and travel plus moving expenses for all new hires

Postemployment acquisition and dissemination of information: for example, all the activities associated with in-processing new employees

Medical examinations, if applicable, either performed in-house or contracted out

The sum of these eight cost elements represents the total cost of replacing those who leave.

Training costs This third component of turnover costs includes three elements:

Informational literature (e.g., an employee handbook)

Instruction in a formal training program

Instruction by employee assignment (e.g., on-the-job training)

The sum of these three cost elements represents the total cost of training replacements for those who leave.

Two points should be noted: First, if there is a formal orientation program, the per-person costs associated with replacements for those who left should be included in the first cost element, *informational literature*. This cost should reflect the per-person, amortized cost of developing the literature, not just its delivery. Do not include the total cost of the orientation program unless 100 percent of the costs can be attributed to employee turnover.

Second, probably the major cost associated with employee turnover, *reduced productivity during the learning period*, is generally not included along with the cost elements *instruction in a formal training program* and *instruction by employee assignment*. The reason for this is that formal work-measurement programs are not often found in employment situations. Thus it is not possible to calculate accurately the dollar value of the loss in productivity during the learning period. If such a program does exist, then by all means include this cost. For example, a major brokerage firm did a formal work-measurement study of this problem and reported the results shown in Table 16-3. The bottom line in all of this is that we want to be con-

■ **TABLE 16·3**
PRODUCTIVITY LOSS OVER EACH THIRD OF THE LEARNING PERIOD FOR FOUR JOB CLASSIFICATIONS

Classification	Weeks in learning period	Productivity loss during learning		
		1	2	3
Management and partners	24	75%	40%	15%
Professionals and technicians	16	70	40	15
Office and clerical	10	60	40	15
Broker trainees	104	85	75	50

Note: The learning period for the average broker trainee is 2 years, although the cost to the firm is generally incurred only in the first year. It is not until the end of the second year that the average broker trainee is fully productive.

servative in our training cost figures so that we can defend every number we generate.

The sum of the three component costs—separation, replacement, and training—represents the total cost of employee turnover for the period in question. Other factors could also be included in our tally, such as the uncompensated performance differential between leavers and their replacements, but that is beyond the scope of this book. For more on this, see ref. 8.

Remember, *the purpose of measuring turnover costs is to improve management decision making.* Once turnover figures are known, managers have a sound basis for choosing between current turnover costs and instituting some type of turnover reduction program (e.g., job enrichment, realistic job previews).

As examples, consider the results Corning, Inc., found when it tallied *only* its out-of-pocket expenses for turnover, such as interview costs and hiring bonuses. That number, $16 to $18 million annually, led to investigations into the causes of turnover and, in turn, to new policies on flexible scheduling and career development.[33]

Merck & Company, the pharmaceutical giant, found that, depending on the job, turnover costs were 1.5 to 2.5 times the annual salary paid.[33] In the retail automobile industry, the cost of turnover averages over $18,000 per salesperson.[1] Finally (in 1990 dollars), at a major brokerage firm the cost per terminating employee was almost $7000,[9] and the cost per terminating store manager at a large retail department store chain was $10,000.[36] Obviously, there are opportunities in this area for enterprising managers to make significant bottom-line contributions to their organizations.

Many firms today are pursuing a quality-enhancement strategy. In an effort to maintain reliable and predictable behavior by employees, the firms are taking steps to minimize absenteeism and controllable turnover. One of the most popular approaches for doing this is company-sponsored day care.

ASSESSING THE COSTS AND BENEFITS OF COMPANY-SPONSORED DAY CARE

Union Bank recently opened a new profit center in Los Angeles. This one, how-ever, doesn't lend money or manage money. It takes care of children. Union Bank, 77 percent owned by the Bank of Tokyo, provided the day-care facility with a $105,000 subsidy. In return, it saved the bank as much as $232,000.[33] Here's how.

The bank conducted a before-and-after study. That is, by comparing absentee-ism, turnover, and maternity leave time a year before the center opened to the same data a year after the center opened, researchers gained more control over the comparison statistics. They compared 87 users of the center, a control group of 105 employees with children of similar ages who used other day-care operations, and employees as a whole.

Savings in turnover totaled $63,000 to $157,000, based on the fact that turnover among center users was 2.2 percent, compared with 9.5 percent in the control group and 18 percent throughout the bank. Another $35,000 was saved in lost days' work. Users of the center were absent an average of 1.7 days less than the control group, and their maternity leaves were 1.2 weeks shorter than those for other employees. Finally, the bank added a bonus of $40,000 in free publicity, based on estimates of media coverage of the center. The conclusion: The bank's day-care center saves (conservatively) between $138,000 and $232,000 per year. As one executive commented: "This isn't a touchy-feely kind of program. It's as much a management tool as it is an employee benefit."[33]

Another approach that firms are using to foster innovation and quality enhance-ment is the employee assistance program (EAP). In our next section we consider how one firm assessed its costs and benefits.

THE COSTS AND BENEFITS OF AN EMPLOYEE ASSISTANCE PROGRAM

As noted in Chapter 15, AT&T examined the impact of its EAP for 110 employees 22 months pre- and postinvolvement.[12] Unfortunately, many of the variables as-sociated with cost savings either are difficult to measure in terms of dollars saved (e.g., the impact on productivity and morale) or are not accessible to researchers. At AT&T, savings formulas could not be developed in all areas where behavioral changes were reported. To be conservative, *estimates were not used*. In areas where savings formulas could be developed, cost figures on *actual* company expenditures were used. This process resulted in a cost analysis of five variables: on-the-job accidents, incidental absences (1 to 7 days), disability absences, employee visits to the medical department, and "anticipated" losses that did not occur. The study did not include the cost of creating the EAP or training the supervisors and staff personnel. Despite the fact that the study is old, it remains one of the best-controlled evaluations to date. Dollar costs have been updated to account for inflation (using the average annual change in the Consumer Price Index from 1978 to 1990). There is, of course, no guarantee that the figures below reflect *actual* cost savings in 1991.

On-the-Job Accidents

The only accidents considered were those that involved lost work time. The cost per accident, $5360, is the actual company cost for expenses, including administrative costs, medical expenses, replacement costs, and disability expenses under law. Lost-productivity costs and lost-time costs are not included in this figure. As the following data indicate, the reduction in the cost of accidents for EAP clients following their involvement in the program was $112,560.

	No. of accidents	Cost per accident	Total cost	Difference
Before EAP	26	$5360	$139,360	
After EAP	5	$5360	26,800	$112,560

Incidental Absences

The data used in this analysis were supplied by the corporate controller's department. The costs represent the average daily amount charged to departments based on gender and on management or nonmanagement status. The costs were then multiplied by the number of days absent for each category. The actual savings to AT&T, $43,325, is the difference between the cost of pre- and post-EAP incidental absenteeism for the employees studied.

	Pre-EAP			Post-EAP		
Category	Days	Average salary	Cost	Days	Average salary	Cost
Male management	101	$250	$25,250	35	$250	$ 8,750
Male nonmanagement	209	90	18,810	31	90	2,790
Female management	50	161	8,050	5	161	805
Female nonmanagement	61	89	5,429	21	89	1,869
Totals	421		$57,539	92		$14,214

Difference in cost pre- and post-EAP: $57,539 − $14,214 = $43,325.

Disability Absence

Disability absences do not include incidental absence days. The average daily amount charged to each department for disability absence was $147. This figure does not include hospital, medical, or surgical costs; replacement costs; or lost productivity resulting from absence.

	Pre-EAP	Post-EAP
Total days	1531	192
Cost @ $147 per day:	$225,057	$28,224

Difference pre- and post-EAP: $196,833

Savings of $196,833 were realized as a result of a reduction in disability absence from before to after program participation. However, the cost for disability days incurred as a result of EAP hospitalizations (980 days × $147 per day, or $144,060) must also be taken into account. Subtracting out these costs ($196,833 − $144,060) still yields a net savings of $52,733 in disability absences.

Visits to the Medical Department

Costs in this category were based on all recorded visits as indicated by the medical file of each client. In 1990 dollars, it costs $97, on average, per visit to the medical department. This figure included only the actual costs of operating the medical department and not the cost of time away from the job. As the figures below indicate, $36,762 was saved following the EAP as a result of fewer visits to the medical department.

	Number of visits	Average cost per visit	Total cost	Cost savings
Pre-EAP	818	$97	$79,346	
Post-EAP	439	97	42,583	$36,763

Anticipated Losses

There were 44 employees referred to the EAP who were in danger of losing their jobs. In all cases, progressive discipline leading toward dismissal had been initiated by management. Of the 44 referred to the EAP, four employees were actually dismissed. The other 40 were retained, and their job performance improved significantly. In fact, 41 percent of them were promoted during the postinvestigation period.

The human resources department reported that the average replacement cost to the company for each employee lost was $3766. This figure, multiplied by the 40 employees retained, yielded a savings of $150,640. These are not really out-of-pocket costs to the firm. Nevertheless, they represent savings because they are costs not incurred—given the success of the EAP with respect to the retention of the 40 employees who were not dismissed because their performance improved.

In addition, the training organization reported average training costs of $532 for 2 days of training per year for each nonmanagement employee, and $800 for 3 days of training per year for each management employee. The 40 employees retained represented a cumulative total of 113 years of service for nonmanagement employees and 421 years of service for management employees. Savings as a result of training investments were $396,916. These calculations are shown as follows:

$$\frac{44 \text{ potentially lost employees}}{\text{referred to EAP}} - 4 \text{ actually lost} = \frac{40 \text{ remaining}}{\text{on payroll}}$$

Average company investment in employment and training

$$\$3766 \text{ replacement cost} \times 40 = \$150,640$$

$$\frac{\$532/\text{year training cost per}}{\text{nonmanagement employee}} \times 113 \text{ total years of service} = \$60,116$$

$$\frac{\$800/\text{year training cost per}}{\text{management employee}} \times 421 \text{ total years of service} = \$336,800$$

$$\text{Total savings} = \$547,556$$

This amount does not include administrative time, lost productivity, or reduced morale.

Summary of Savings

The costs and benefits associated with improved performance on five key variables indicated a substantial financial gain associated with EAP treatment of employee medical and/or behavioral problems. Net savings are shown below.

On-the-job accidents	$112,560
Incidental absence	43,325
Disability absence	52,773
Visits to medical	36,763
Anticipated losses	547,556
Total savings	$792,977

Clearly the program was worth the effort financially as well as socially. Costing out net benefits associated with an EAP also illustrates the point that the economic consequences of employee behavior can be determined for any human resource management activity.

THE COSTS AND BENEFITS OF EMPLOYEE SELECTION PROGRAMS

Of all the aspects of human resource management, the opportunity for the greatest cost-benefit payoff will come from hiring the best available candidates and not hiring less than the best available candidates. By using accurate (that is, valid) predictors of actual job performance, a firm can have meaningful measures of candidates who will perform well as employees and candidates who are unlikely to perform well. Further, candidates who are predicted to be "high-caliber" employees and are hired will derive more from a training program.

Benefits also accrue to the candidates selected as a result of accurate matching of their abilities and interests with job requirements. Hence valid employee selection programs enhance the quality of their work lives. Placing a skilled electronics worker into an unskilled production job is just one example of such a mismatch. We do no favors to any applicant by mismatching his or her individual capabilities and interests with job requirements.

Unfortunately, the dollar payoffs associated with valid selection programs are unknown in many firms because the firms simply do not know how to assess them. This issue was discussed briefly in Chapter 6. Let us begin here by reviewing the factors that determine the dollar gain in productivity associated with any selection procedure, as shown in Table 16-4.

The net payoff (utility), in dollars, expected to result from the use of any selection procedure(s) can be determined from the following formula:

$$\Delta U = (2) \times (3) \times (4) \times (6) - [(2) \times (7)/(5)] \tag{16-1}$$

In words, the formula is:

$$
\begin{array}{c}
\text{Dollar} \\
\text{gain in} \\
\text{productivity}
\end{array}
=
\begin{array}{c}
\text{number} \\
\text{of} \\
\text{selectees}
\end{array}
\times
\begin{array}{c}
\text{validity of} \\
\text{the selection} \\
\text{procedure}
\end{array}
\times
\begin{array}{c}
\text{variability in} \\
\text{job performance} \\
\text{in dollars per year}
\end{array}
$$

$$
\times
\begin{array}{c}
\text{average score} \\
\text{of selectees on} \\
\text{the selection} \\
\text{procedure}
\end{array}
-
\left(
\begin{array}{c}
\text{number of} \\
\text{selectees}
\end{array}
\times
\begin{array}{c}
\text{cost to fill} \\
\text{one vacancy}
\end{array}
\right)
$$

The technical details involved in actually computing the utility of a selection procedure are beyond the scope of this chapter. (See ref. 8 for an in-depth discussion.) In this section, therefore, our objective is simply to illustrate the kinds of economic returns that organizations can expect from the use of valid selection procedures. We will do so by presenting the results of two real-world studies—one in the public sector and one in the private sector of the economy.

Study 1 used Equation 16-1 to estimate the economic impact of a valid test (the Programmer Aptitude Test) if it were used to select new computer programmers for 1 year in the federal government.[29] Results indicated that the average gain in productivity per new programmer was $6680 per year. Since the average computer programmer in the federal government stays for 9.69 years, the average gain over that time is $64,729.

But wait—a dollar received in 9.69 years is certainly worth less than a dollar received today. To take account of that fact, dollars received in the future must be discounted back to the present (e.g., by estimating the rate of inflation over 9.69 years). In addition, firms must pay corporate taxes and allow for variable costs (i.e., costs that rise or fall with productivity, such as sales commissions). Although taxes and variable costs do not apply to the federal government jobs in Study 1, taking discounting, taxes, and variable costs into account could lower estimates

■ **TABLE 16·4**
FACTORS THAT DETERMINE DOLLAR PAYOFFS
FROM SELECTION PROCEDURES

Factor	Dimension	Technical name
1. Total gain in dollars over random selection	Dollars	Utility (ΔU)
2. How many people are hired	Number of employees	Number of selectees (N_s)
3. How accurately the procedure(s) forecast which applicants will be the most productive employees	Correlation coefficient (varies from -1 to $+1$)	Validity (r_{xy})
4. How much individual applicants differ in productivity (that is, the variability in job performance in dollars)	Dollars per year	Standard deviation of job performance (SD_y)
5. The percentage of applicants selected	Percent in decimal form	Selection ratio (SR)
6. The average score on the predictor(s) achieved by selectees	A scale from -3 to $+3$	$\bar{Z}_x$
7. The cost of the selection procedure(s)	Dollars	C

from Equation 16-1 by as much as 70 percent.[4,5] Nevertheless, since the federal government hires an average of 618 new programmers every year, these results indicate that millions of dollars in lost productivity can be saved by using valid selection procedures just in this one occupation.

Study 2 investigated the impact of an assessment center on management performance at American Telephone & Telegraph Co.[10] The payoff associated with first-level management assessment, given that 1116 managers were selected and that their average tenure as first-level managers was 4.4 years, was over $13 million. Even after adjusting for the effects of discounting, taxes, and variable costs, the gains in improved performance were still estimated (conservatively) at over $4 million for this one group.

What can we learn from these results? The payoffs associated with the use of valid selection procedures may far exceed those associated with any other HR activity. Moreover, the technology is now available for an organization of *any* size to demonstrate this.[16]

COSTING THE EFFECTS OF TRAINING ACTIVITIES

As noted in Chapter 7, we assess the results of training to determine whether it is worth the cost. Training valuation (meaning in financial terms) is not easy, but the technology to do it is available and well developed.[7] A manager may have to value training in two types of situations: one in which only *indirect* measures of dollar outcomes are available, and one in which *direct* measures of dollar outcomes are available.

Indirect measures of training outcomes are more common than direct measures. That is, many studies of training outcomes report improvements in job performance or decreases in errors, scrap, and waste. Relatively few studies report training outcomes directly in terms of dollars gained or saved. Using a variation of Equation 16-1, indirect measures often can be converted into estimates of the dollar impact of training,[30] but as was the case with the utility of selection, such technical details are beyond the scope of this chapter. Let us therefore focus on a study that examined the impact of training on sales performance.

Direct Measures of Training Outcomes

When direct measures of the dollar outcomes of training are available, then standard valuation methods are appropriate. The following study valued the results of a behavior-modeling training program (see Chapter 7 for a fuller description of behavior modeling) for sales representatives in relation to the program's effects on sales performance.[21]

Study design A large retailer conducted a behavior-modeling program in two departments, Large Appliances and Radio/TV, within 14 of its stores in one large metropolitan area. The 14 stores were matched into seven pairs in terms of size, location, and market characteristics. Stores with unusual characteristics that could affect their overall performance, such as declining sales or recent changes in management, were not included in the study.

The training program was then introduced in seven stores, one in each of the matched pairs, and not in the other seven stores. Other kinds of ongoing sales training programs were provided in the control group stores, but the behavior-modeling approach was used only in the seven experimental-group stores. In the experimental-group stores, 58 sales associates received the training, and their job performance was compared to that of 64 sales associates in the same departments in the control-group stores.

As in most sales organizations, detailed sales records for each individual were kept on a continuous basis. These records included total sales as well as hours worked on the sales floor. Since all individuals received commissions on their sales and since the value of the various products sold varied greatly, it was possible to compute a job performance measure for each individual in terms of average commissions per hour worked.

There was considerable variation in the month-to-month sales performance of each individual, but sales performance over 6-month periods was more stable. In fact, the average correlation between consecutive sales periods of 6 months each was about .80 (where 1.00 equals perfect agreement). Hence the researchers decided to compare the sales records of participants for 6 months before the training program was introduced with the results achieved during the same 6 months the following year, after the training was concluded. All sales promotions and other programs in the stores were identical, since these were administered on an areawide basis.

The training program itself The program focused on specific aspects of sales situations, such as "approaching the customer," "explaining features, advantages, and benefits," and "closing the sale." The usual behavior-modeling procedure was followed. First the trainers presented *guidelines* (or "learning points") for handling each aspect of a sales interaction. Then the trainees *viewed a videotaped situation* in which a "model" sales associate followed the guidelines in carrying out that aspect of the sales interaction with a customer. The trainees then *practiced* the same situation in role-playing rehearsals. Their performance was *reinforced* and shaped by their supervisors, who had been trained as their instructors.

Study results Of the original 58 trainees in the experimental group, 50 were still working as sales associates 1 year later. Four others had been promoted during the interim, and 4 others had left the company. In the control group stores, only 49 of the original 64 were still working as sales associates 1 year later. Only 1 had been promoted, and 14 others had left the company. Thus the behavior-modeling program may have had a substantial positive effect on turnover since only about 7 percent of the trained group left during the ensuing year, in comparison to 22 percent of those in the control group. (This result had not been predicted.)

Figure 16-3 presents the changes in average per-hour commissions for participants in both the trained and untrained groups from the 6-month period before the training was conducted to the 6-month period following the training. Note in Figure 16-3 that the trained and untrained groups did not have equal per-hour commissions at the start of the study. While the *stores* that members of the two groups worked in were matched at the start of the study, *sales commissions* were not. Sales associates in the trained group started at a lower point than did sales

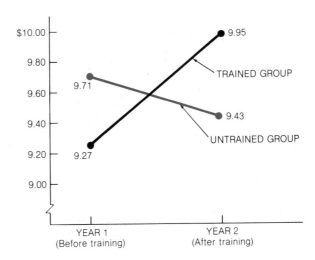

FIGURE 16-3
Changes in per-hour commissions before and after the behavior modeling training program.

IMPACT OF HUMAN RESOURCE MANAGEMENT ACTIVITIES ON PRODUCTIVITY, QUALITY OF WORK LIFE, AND THE BOTTOM LINE

There is a rapidly growing awareness in the business community of the need for HR research. Indeed, there is a growing consensus among managers in many industries that the future success of their firms may depend more on the skill with which human problems are handled than on the degree to which their firms maintain leadership in technical areas. Awareness alone will not improve productivity. Rather, to quote Thomas A. Edison, it will be a matter of "99 percent perspiration and 1 percent inspiration." There are no quick-fix solutions; as General Motors found in the gradual turnaround of its problem plants at Tarrytown and Lordstown, when HR research results get translated into operating management practices, everybody wins. Labor-management relations improve, productivity goes up, quality goes up, profitability goes up, reworks go down, and the quality of work life becomes more tolerable.

The head of Mazda Motor Corporation captured the essence of HRM when he said: "The most important element in management is the human being," whatever his or her job happens to be. Another executive went a step further, saying, "The corporation that is not in the business of human development may not be in any business. At least not for long."[13]

associates in the untrained group. Average per-hour commissions for the trained group increased over the year from $9.27 to $9.95 ($12.62 to $13.54 in 1990 dollars); average per-hour commissions for the untrained group declined over the year from $9.71 to $9.43 ($13.21 to $12.83 in 1990 dollars). In other words, the trained sales associates increased their average earnings by about 7 percent, whereas those who did not receive the behavior-modeling training experienced a 3 percent decline in average earnings. This difference was statistically significant. Other training outcomes were also assessed (e.g., trainee attitudes, supervisory behaviors), but, for our purposes, the most important lesson was that the study provided objective evidence to indicate the dollar impact of the training on increased sales.

The program also had an important secondary effect on turnover. Since all sales associates are given considerable training (which represents an extensive investment of time and money), it appears that the behavior modeling contributed to *cost savings* in addition to *increased sales*. As noted in the previous discussion of turnover costs, an accurate estimate of these cost savings requires that the turnovers be separated into controllable and uncontrollable because training can affect only controllable turnover.

Finally, the use of objective data as criterion measures in a study of this kind does entail some problems. As pointed out earlier, the researchers found that a 6-month period was required to balance out the month-to-month variations in sales performance resulting from changing work schedules, sales promotions, and similar influences that affected individual results. It also took some vigilance to ensure that the records needed for the study were kept in a consistent and conscientious manner in each store. According to the researchers, however, these problems were not great in relation to the usefulness of the study results. "The evidence that the training program had a measurable effect on sales was certainly more convincing in demonstrating the value of the program than would be merely the opinions of participants that the training was worthwhile" (ref. 21, p. 761).

■ **HUMAN RESOURCE MANAGEMENT IN ACTION**
CONCLUSION

ATTITUDE SURVEY RESULTS: CATALYST FOR MANAGEMENT ACTIONS

The survey highlighted six areas of human resource management that were related to effective company performance in terms of turnover and profitability:

1. *Recruitment and selection.* High-profit locations were recruiting many more management trainees from among the nonmanagement employees already working for the company. Hence the high-profit locations were getting store manager trainees who already had experience and an understanding of what the job entailed.

2. *Training.* Classroom instruction was rated favorably by everyone and was not a factor in turnover. The training that did make a difference was *on-the-job training.* Store managers in high-profit, low-turnover areas reported that they received better in-store training than did their counterparts in lower profitability areas.

3. *Staffing.* Keeping management staff at a minimum was not producing greater profits. It was producing overworked and disenchanted managers who could neither run their stores effectively nor provide the training found to be so important for new store managers. Less effective profit centers had fewer managers, who worked many more hours, had fewer days off, and were bothered more frequently at home about work-related matters when they had a scheduled day off.

4. *Performance management.* Managers in the high-profit, low-turnover areas received performance reviews on a quarterly basis. Store managers throughout the system who received performance reviews less than quarterly wanted to see them conducted more often. In addition, everyone expressed a desire for more informal feedback from superiors about their performance.

A second aspect of performance management and control was regular store visits by higher-level supervisors. Supervisors in high-profit areas visited their stores more frequently than did their counterparts in low-profit areas.

5. *Climate.* Job security in this company's environment was not associated with compensation or with promotion opportunities. However, it was

associated with the needs of the store managers to be treated fairly, to be kept informed, and to have superiors available when needed to help the store managers solve their problems. In less effective profit centers, store managers saw their superiors as less competent at handling problems, they had less confidence that their superiors would back them up in their actions, and they felt that their superiors neglected them in terms of the frequency of store visits and formal performance reviews. They also indicated that they were more apt to hear things first through the grapevine rather than directly from their superiors.

6. *Management style.* The areas described thus far all point to some basic differences in how the store managers were being managed in different parts of the company. These distinctions became clearer when comparisons were made between high- and low-turnover centers that were highly profitable. In fact, two styles of management seemed to result in high profitability. In high-profit, low-turnover centers, store managers felt that they worked in a delegative and supportive climate, with a strong emphasis on performance and the control of performance; however, these emphases were balanced by a demonstrated concern for the store managers and their needs. In contrast, high-profit, high-turnover areas were characterized as directive and overcontrolling in style; strong emphasis was placed on the achievement of bottom-line results *without* a comparable emphasis on the personal and developmental needs of the store managers.

TOP MANAGEMENT'S RESPONSE TO THE SURVEY FINDINGS

Based on the survey results, top management established a task force to deal with the problems identified. The task force recommended 28 specific actions with time frames for accomplishment that varied from 1 month to 1 year. These actions ranged from close enforcement of staffing guidelines to development of an improved in-store training package. In time, as expected, turnover began to trend downward.

This study illustrates two important aspects of ensuring the effectiveness of an attitude survey as a management tool. First, the survey dealt with the operational aspects of working life in the company, and it focused on issues over which top management had some control. Hence top management found it an easy task to translate survey findings into direct actions. Second, an attitude survey's credibility with top management rests squarely on its ability to demonstrate that *the results are important in some meaningful business sense.* In the present study, the message that provoked significant actions was the proof that if certain management practices were adopted, greater profitability *and* reduced turnover could be expected.

While it is not always possible to relate survey results directly to profits (as it was here), it is possible to approach any survey from the perspective of how the results can contribute to organizational effectiveness. This perspective is a key step in establishing the credibility of the survey.

IMPLICATIONS FOR MANAGEMENT PRACTICE

Many managers do not realize the magnitude of their firm's investment in employees until they adopt a systematic framework for costing human resources. However, to be most useful, such a framework must include three key steps:

1. Understand your organization's, department's, and operating unit's competitive strategies—innovation, quality enhancement, cost reduction, or some combination of these.
2. Make sure that HR activities are consistent with your chosen competitive strategy. For example, if innovation is the objective, don't skimp on training and development activities.
3. Use behavior costing methods to assess the costs and benefits of the HR activities that are most relevant to your chosen competitive strategy.

SUMMARY

In assessing the costs and benefits of HR activities, managers must first understand the competitive strategies of their organizations, departments, and operating units. Three possible strategies are innovation, quality enhancement, and cost reduction. The next task is to align HR strategy with competitive strategy, and to emphasize the kinds of employee behaviors that are most appropriate to the chosen strategy. In order to assess the outcomes of HR activities, HR research (which includes both qualitative and quantitative outcomes) may be conducted at corporate, middle management, or operating levels.

One approach to HR research that is growing in popularity is called behavior costing. To apply behavior costing methodology properly, both direct and indirect costs must be considered. However, our objective is not simply to *measure* these costs; it is also to *reduce* them by devoting resources to those costs that are controllable. We discussed behavior costing methods in six key areas of employee behavior: absenteeism, turnover, company-sponsored day care, employee assistance programs, employee selection, and employee training.

Assessing the costs and benefits of human resource management activities is just one aspect of the broader subject of HR research. The objective of HR research is to contribute to the development and application of improved solutions to employee relations problems and to the more effective use of people in organizations. When HR research results that are targeted on operational problems get translated into practice, everybody wins.

DISCUSSION QUESTIONS

16•1 Discuss three controllable and three uncontrollable costs associated with absenteeism.

16•2 Why should efforts to reduce turnover focus only on controllable costs?

16•3 What is the difference between direct and indirect costs?

16•4 Discuss the HR activities that are most relevant to the following competitive strategies: innovation, quality enhancement, and cost reduction.

16▪5 As a top manager faced with the task of allocating 100 percent of the resources available for employee selection and/or training, what percentage would you allocate to each function? What factors influenced your decision?

16▪6 If attitude surveys are to be taken seriously by management, what key issues should be considered in their design, implementation, and evaluation?

REFERENCES

1. Ashbach, N. W. (1989, April). *The cost of turnover in the retail automobile industry.* Unpublished manuscript, Executive MBA Program, University of Colorado.
2. Baker, G. M. N. (1974). The feasibility and utility of human resource accounting. *California Management Review,* **16**(4), 17–23.
3. Banas, P. A. (1988). Employee involvement: A sustained labor/management initiative at the Ford Motor Company. In J. P. Campbell and R. J. Campbell (eds.), *Productivity in organizations.* San Francisco: Jossey-Bass, pp. 388–416.
4. Boudreau, J. W. (1983). Economic considerations in estimating the utility of human resource productivity improvement programs. *Personnel Psychology,* **36**, 551–576.
5. Boudreau, J. W. (1988). Utility analysis. In L. Dyer (ed.), *Human resource management: Evolving roles and responsibilities.* Washington, DC: Bureau of National Affairs, pp. 1-125 to 1-186.
6. *Bulletin to Management* (1990, 2d Quarter). Washington, DC: Bureau of National Affairs.
7. Cascio, W. F. (1989). Using utility analysis to assess training outcomes. In I. L. Goldstein (ed.), *Training and development in organizations.* San Francisco: Jossey-Bass, pp. 63–88.
8. Cascio, W. F. (1991). *Costing human resources: The financial impact of behavior in organizations* (3rd ed.). Boston: PWS-Kent.
9. Cascio, W. F. (1983, August). One year's turnover costs in a major brokerage firm. In M. Quaintance (chair), *Cost analyses of human resource interventions: Are they worth it?* Symposium conducted at the meeting of the American Psychological Association, Anaheim, CA.
10. Cascio, W. F., & Ramos, R. A. (1986). Development and application of a new method for assessing job performance in behavioral/economic terms. *Journal of Applied Psychology,* **71**, 20–28.
11. Fitz-enz, J. (1984). *How to measure human resources management.* New York: McGraw-Hill.
12. Gaeta, E., Lynn, R., & Grey, L. (1982, May–June). AT&T looks at program evaluation. *EAP Digest,* pp. 22–31.
13. Gilmour, A. D. (1988). Changing times in the automotive industry. *Academy of Management Executive,* **2**(1), 23–28.
14. Jackson, S. E., & Schuler, R. S. (1990). Human resource planning. *American Psychologist,* **45**, 223–239.
15. Jackson, S. E., Schuler, R. S., & Rivero, J. C. (1989). Organizational characteristics as predictors of personnel practices. *Personnel Psychology,* **42**, 727–736.
16. Jacobs, R., & Baratta, J. E. (1989). Tools for staffing decisions: What can they do? What do they cost? In W. F. Cascio (ed.), *Human resource planning, employment, and placement.* Washington, DC: Bureau of National Affairs, pp. 2-159 to 2-199.

17. Kanter, R. M. (1985, Winter). Supporting innovation and venture development in established companies. *Journal of Business Venturing*, **1**, 47–60.

18. Kuzmits, F. E. (1979). How much is absenteeism costing *your* organization? *Personnel Administrator*, **24**(6), 29–33.

19. Macy, B. A., & Mirvis, P. H. (1983). Assessing rates and costs of individual work behaviors. In S. E. Seashore, E. E. Lawler, P. H. Mirvis, & C. Camann (eds.), *Assessing organizational change*. New York: Wiley, pp. 139–177.

20. Martin, D. C., & Bartol, K. M. (1985). Managing turnover strategically. *Personnel Administrator*, **30**(11), 63–73.

21. Meyer, H. H., & Raich, M. S. (1983). An objective evaluation of a behavior modeling training program. *Personnel Psychology*, **36**, 755–761.

22. Mirvis, P. H., & Macy, B. A. (1976). Measuring the quality of work and organizational effectiveness in behavioral-economic terms. *Administrative Science Quarterly*, **21**, 212–226.

23. Patterson, G. A. (1990, Aug. 24). GM offers to boost benefits for workers laid off but proposes no job guarantees. *The Wall Street Journal*, p. A2.

24. People (1984, April 14). *Rocky Mountain News*, p. 2.

25. Pollock, E. J. (1990, March 20). Beleaguered firms dangle lures to retain employees. *The Wall Street Journal*, pp. B1, B2.

26. Porter, M. E. (1985). *Competitive advantage*. New York: Free Press.

27. Reibstein, L. (1986, Oct. 27). A finger on the pulse. Companies expand use of employee surveys. *The Wall Street Journal*, p. 27.

28. Scarpello, V., & Theeke, H. A. (1989). Human resource accounting: A measured critique. *Journal of Accounting Literature*, **8**, 265–280.

29. Schmidt, F. L., Hunter, J. E., McKenzie, R. C., & Muldrow, T. W. (1979). Impact of valid selection procedures on workforce productivity. *Journal of Applied Psychology*, **64**, 609–626.

30. Schmidt, F. L., Hunter, J. E., & Pearlman, K. (1982). Assessing the economic impact of personnel programs on workforce productivity. *Personnel Psychology*, **35**, 333–347.

31. Schuler, R. S., & Jackson, S. E. (1987). Linking competitive strategies with human resource management practices. *Academy of Management Executive*, **1**(3), 207–219.

32. Serrin, W. (1985, Aug. 10). Labor center filling a data vacuum. *The New York Times*, p. 62.

33. Solomon, J. (1988, Dec. 29). Companies try measuring cost savings from new types of corporate benefits. *The Wall Street Journal*, p. B1.

34. Taylor, A., III. (1990, Nov. 19). Why Toyota keeps getting better and better and better. *Fortune*, pp. 66–79.

35. Tsui, A. S., & Gomez-Mejia, L. R. (1988). Evaluating human resource effectiveness. In L. Dyer (ed.), *Human resource management: Evolving roles and responsibilities*. Washington, DC: Bureau of National Affairs, pp. 1-187 to 1-227.

36. Weekley, J., & Champagne, B. (1983). *Employee turnover costs in the Zale division*. Unpublished manuscript, Zale Corporation, Irving, TX.

37. White, B. J. (1988). The internationalization of business: One company's response. *Academy of Management Executive*, **2**(1), 29–32.

38. Woodruff, R. C., Jr. (1970). Human resources accounting. *Canadian Chartered Accountant*, **97**, 156–161.

CHAPTER 17

International Dimensions of Human Resource Management

■ HUMAN RESOURCE MANAGEMENT IN ACTION

A DAY IN THE LIFE OF TOMORROW'S MANAGER*

6:10 A.M.: The year is 2010 and another Monday morning has begun for Linda Smith. The marketing VP for a major U.S. appliance manufacturer is awakened by her computer alarm. She saunters to her terminal to check the weather outlook in Madrid, Spain, where she'll fly late tonight, and to send an electronic voice message to a supplier in Thailand.

Meet the manager of the future, a different breed from her contemporary counterparts. She lives in an international business world shaped by competition, collaboration, and corporate diversity. Comfortable with technology, she's been logging on to computers since she was 7 years old. A literature honors student with a joint MBA-advanced communications degree, the 38-year old joined her current employer 4 years ago after stints at two other corporations—one abroad—and a marketing consulting firm. Now she oversees offices in a score of countries on four continents.

---

*Adapted from C. Hymowitz, Day in the life of tomorrow's manager, *The Wall Street Journal*, March 20, 1989, p. B1. Reprinted by permission of *The Wall Street Journal*, © 1989 Dow Jones & Company, Inc. All rights reserved worldwide.

Is this realistic? Absolutely, say chief executives and management consultants. Tomorrow's manager will have to know how to operate in an anytime, anyplace universe. They may land on London time and leave on Tokyo time. While managers who aren't cost conscious and productive won't survive any better in the future than they do now, in the future they'll also have to be more flexible, more responsive, and smarter. Managers will have to be nurturers and teachers, instead of police officers and watchdogs.

7:20 A.M.: Ms. Smith and her husband, who heads his own architecture firm, organize the home front before darting to the supertrain. They leave instructions for their computer to call the housecleaning service as well as gourmet carryout service that will prepare dinner for eight guests Saturday. And they quickly review schedules for their two small daughters with their nanny.

On the train during a speedy 20-minute commute from suburb to city, Linda Smith checks her electronic mailbox and also reads her favorite trade magazine via her laptop computer.

The jury is still out on how dual-career couples will juggle high-pressure work and personal lives. While some experts predict that the frenetic pace will only quicken, others believe that more creative uses of flexible schedules as well as technological advances in communications and travel will allow more balance. Said one expert: "In the past, nobody cared if your staff had heart attacks, but in tomorrow's knowledge-based economy we'll be judged more on how well we take care of people."

Challenges

1. What kinds of employee relations, compensation, and career management issues will Linda Smith encounter at the office?
2. Given the globalization of companies, will managers intent on rising to the top still be judged largely on how well they articulate ideas and work with others?

---

1. What factors should I consider in "sizing-up" managers, employees, and customers from a different culture?
2. What should be the components of expatriate recruitment, selection, orientation, and training strategies?
3. How should an expatriate compensation package be structured?
4. What special issues deserve attention in the repatriation of overseas employees?

QUESTIONS THIS CHAPTER WILL HELP MANAGERS ANSWER

Increasingly, the world is becoming a "global village" as multinational investment continues to grow. All the human resource management issues that have been discussed to this point are interrelated conceptually and operationally and are particularly relevant in the international context: human resource planning, recruitment, selection, orientation, training and development, career management, compensation, and labor relations. In examining all these issues, as well as considering the special problems of repatriation (the process of reentering one's native culture after being absent from it), this chapter thus provides a capstone to the book. As usual, numerous practical examples will illustrate important issues.

THE MULTINATIONAL COMPANY: A FACT OF MODERN ORGANIZATIONAL LIFE

In order to maintain a leadership position in any one developed country, any business, whether large or small, increasingly has to attain and hold leadership positions in all developed markets worldwide. It has to be able to do research, to design, to develop, to engineer, to manufacture in any part of the developed world, and to export from any developed country to any other. It has to go transnational.[21]

The vehicle for doing this is often not an acquisition or a financial transaction, but what the Germans call a "community of interest": an international alliance, a collaboration between two or more multinational companies developed to let them jointly pursue a common goal. However, alliances cover only *some* of the activities of the partners. The partners therefore maintain their individual identities and engage in other activities, separate from those of the alliance. As an example, consider the joint venture between Chrysler and Mitsubishi, called Diamond Star Corp., in Normal, Illinois. The plant, managed by Mitsubishi, produces the Plymouth Laser and the Eagle Talon for Chrysler Motors and the Eclipse for Mitsubishi.

This characteristic distinguishes an international alliance from an international merger or acquisition, in which the identities and activities of the partners are fully merged. Such alliances may take several forms; for example, joint ventures, marketing and distribution agreements, research and development partnerships, or licensing agreements.[13] In the opinion of many, such alliances are an essential component of global business strategy.[53,69,71]

One reason that leadership in any one developed market increasingly requires leadership in all is that the developed world has become one in terms of technology. All developed countries are equally capable of doing everything, doing it equally well, and doing it equally fast. All developed countries also share instant information. Companies can therefore compete just about everywhere the moment that economic conditions give them a substantial price advantage. In an age of sharp and violent currency fluctuations, this means that a leader must be able to innovate, to produce, and to market in every area of the developed world—or else be defenseless against foreign competition should currency exchange rates shift sharply.[21] Besides, when customers vote with their pocketbooks, they leave the trappings of nationalism behind.[53]

In this emerging economic order, foreign investment by the world's leading corporations is a fact of modern organizational life. Today foreign investment is viewed not just as an opportunity for U.S. companies investing abroad but also as an opportunity for other countries to develop subsidiaries in the United States and elsewhere. Thus during the 1980s some 2000 European companies entered into alliances with U.S. firms.[13] Foreign owners now control more than 12 percent of U.S. manufacturing assets and employ 3 million U.S. workers.[45] Before proceeding further, let's define some terms that will be used throughout the chapter:[29]

> A *multinational company (MNC)* is a firm with substantial investment outside its home country in plant (as a rule, 20 percent or more of its total plant investment) and management. Such a company operates across national borders and claims its legitimacy from its effective use of assets to serve its far-flung customers.
>
> An *expatriate* or *foreign-service employee* is a generic term applied to anyone working outside her or his home country with a planned return to that or a third country.
>
> *Home country* is the expatriate's country of residence.
>
> *Host country* is the country in which the expatriate is working.
>
> A *third-country national* is an expatriate who has transferred to an additional country while working abroad. A German working for a U.S. firm in Spain is a third-country national.

One of the most important determinants of a company's success in an international venture is *the quality of its executives*. In the words of one international executive, "Virtually any type of international problem, in the final analysis, is either created by people or must be solved by people. Hence, having the right people in the right place at the right time emerges as the key to a company's international growth. If we are successful in solving that problem, I am confident we can cope with all others" (Dueer, in ref. 30, p. 61).

Growth of MNCs

Do you recognize these firms? More than 46 percent of their total revenue comes from overseas operations: Exxon, Mobil, IBM, Dow Chemical, Coca-Cola, National Cash Register, Pan Am, Gillette, Citicorp, and Chase Manhattan.[63] Notice how the firms include major sectors of the economy—oil, computers, chemicals, electronics, consumer goods, airlines, and banking. This is no accident. Since World War II there has been a major increase in the number of U.S. executives and technical specialists employed outside the United States, a trend that has accompanied the growth of the MNC. At present, about 100,000 companies do business overseas, including 25,000 firms with foreign office affiliates, and 3500 major multinational companies. One-third of U.S. profits come from international business, and one-sixth of the nation's jobs are created by foreign trade.[64]

Foreigners hold top management positions in one-third of large U.S. firms and in one-fourth of European-based firms. They are even more conspicuous in third-world, developing countries. Thus a study of four large European MNCs (among the 60 largest in Europe) revealed that 80 percent of all international transfers were into developing countries, and only 20 percent into Europe or North America. In 60 to 70 percent of all transfers, the companies were not able to find qualified local individuals. Most of the executives transferred had special technical expertise in fields such as engineering, agriculture, medicine, or accounting and finance.[26]

It should be clear by now that today's world economy is governed by an entirely new set of rules, and that to compete effectively firms must abandon such outdated assumptions and behaviors as these:

- Believing that there is "one best way" to approach all problems or that for each problem there is only "one best answer"
- Attending only to immediate short-term problems and issues, focusing on details, seeing only the parts and not the whole, ignoring the long-term, failing to put problems in a context, and losing sight of the objectives of the overall organization and the entire economy
- Failing to be aware of the implicit and unstated assumptions that have guided individual behavior and organizational policies in the past, and failing to change them when they are no longer appropriate in the current environment[47]

To take an example of the "one best way" approach, many U.S. executives were surprised to find out how well Japanese ways worked at Nissan's car and truck plant in Smyrna, Tennessee. The plant features Japanese-style quality controls (small work groups with a big say in problem solving, job rotation every 2 hours, and statistical quality control techniques), just-in-time delivery of parts, and widespread use of industrial robots. Painting is done with West German technology, using robots from Norway. Fiber-optic communications, developed by U.S. aerospace firms, monitor 3000 points in the paint process. The result? After producing 500,000 vehicles, the plant showed two things: (1) U.S. workers are just as productive and skilled as the Japanese, and (2) the plant is one of the most efficient, highest-quality plants in the world.[33]

As the United States lost market share and jobs in important industries like steel, autos, and electronics, both labor and management in many firms grudgingly acknowledged that they had to change, that they could not continue doing business as usual. They had to "reach out" to the broader world at large. Thus, as we saw in Chapter 12, many ideas for managing the General Motors Saturn plant were borrowed from around the world as a result of plant visits by the Group of 99, a team of Saturn workers who traveled 2 million miles to visit some 160 pioneering enterprises, including Hewlett-Packard, McDonald's, Volvo, Kawasaki, and Nissan.[31] As is well known, all these firms have operations in many countries around the globe. It is also well known that when expatriates staff overseas operations, costs can be astronomical.

Costs of Overseas Executives

One of the first lessons that MNCs learn is that it is far cheaper to hire competent host-country nationals (if they are available) than to send their own executives overseas, for foreign-service employees typically cost *3 to 5 times* their annual home-country salaries.[1,43] Table 17-1 illustrates some of these costs.

Even for executives who do not relocate overseas, daily allowances are high: For example, relative to a $225 daily living allowance in Washington, DC (in 1990 dollars), costs are 37 percent higher in London, 60 percent higher in Geneva, and 82 percent higher in Tokyo.[67] Of course, these costs fluctuate with international exchange rates relative to the U.S. dollar. On top of the high costs, there is a high failure rate among overseas personnel—an average of 30 percent over all locations and even higher in developing countries.[66] For all levels of employees, the costs of mistaken expatriation include the costs of initial recruitment, relocation expenses, premium compensation, repatriation costs (i.e., costs associated with re-settling the expatriate), replacement costs, and the tangible costs of poor job performance.[17] When an overseas assignment does not work out, it *still* costs a company, on average, 2.5 times the employee's base salary.[14]

Although the costs of expatriates are considerable, there are also compensating benefits to multinational firms. In particular, overseas postings allow managers to develop international experience outside of their home countries—the kind of experience needed to compete successfully in the global economy that we now live in.

■ **TABLE 17·1**
TYPICAL U.S. EXPATRIATE COMPENSATION PACKAGE (ANNUAL EXPENSE): MARRIED AND ONE CHILD

Category	U.S. compensation	Overseas compensation
Base salary	$70,000	$70,000
Overseas incentive		7,500
Hardship		5,000
Housing differential		25,000
Furniture		8,000
Utilities differential		12,000
Car and driver		10,000
Cost-of-living adjustment		2,000
Club membership		500
Education		5,000
Total	$70,000	$145,000
U.S. tax	15,000	15,000
Net annual compensation	$55,000	$130,000

Note: A complete expatriate package also includes the following: (1) annual transportation to the United States for home leave, (2) storage of U.S. household goods, (3) shipment of some goods to the foreign location, (4) U.S. auto disposal, (5) U.S. house management, (6) interim living, (7) travel to new assignment and return, and (8) annual tax equalization.
Source: M. A. Conway, Manage expatriate expenses for capital returns, *Personnel Journal*, July 1987, p. 69.

Nevertheless, it is senseless to send people abroad who do not know what they are doing overseas and cannot be effective in the foreign culture. As the manager of international human resources at Hewlett-Packard remarked, "When you are sending someone abroad to work on an important agreement, it is terribly important that they have as much information as possible about how to do business in that country. The cost of training is inconsequential compared to the risk of sending inexperienced or untrained people" (ref. 18, p. 47).

For all these reasons, companies need to consider the impact of culture on international human resource management. But what is culture? *Culture* refers to characteristic ways of doing things and behaving that people in a given country or region have evolved over time. It helps people make sense of their part of the world, and provides them with an identity. Thus their part of the world is foreign only to strangers, not to those who live there.

THE ROLE OF CULTURAL UNDERSTANDING IN INTERNATIONAL MANAGEMENT PRACTICE

Managers who have no appreciation for cultural differences are *ethnocentric*. They believe in the inherent superiority of their own group and culture, and they tend to look down on those considered "foreign." Rather than accepting differences as legitimate, they view and measure alien cultures in terms of their own.

In contrast, *cosmopolitan* managers are sensitive to cultural differences, respect the distinctive practices of others, and make allowances for such factors when communicating with representatives of different cultural groups. Recognizing that culture and behavior are relative, they are more tentative, and less absolute, in their interactions with others.[32]

Such cultural understanding can minimize "culture shock," and allow managers to be more effective with employees and customers. The first step in this process is to increase one's general awareness of differences across cultures, for they deeply affect human resource management practices.

HUMAN RESOURCE MANAGEMENT PRACTICES AS A CULTURAL VARIABLE

Particularly when business does not go well, Americans returning from overseas assignments tend to blame the local people, calling them irresponsible, unmotivated, or downright dishonest.[11] Such judgments are pointless, for many of the problems are a matter of fundamental cultural differences that profoundly affect how different people view the world and operate in business. This section presents a systematic framework, 10 broad classifications, that will help managers assess any culture and examine its people systematically. It does not consider every aspect of culture, and by no means is it the only way to analyze culture. Rather, it is a useful beginning for cultural understanding. The framework is comprised of the following 10 factors.[32]

Sense of self and space

Dress and appearance

Food and eating habits

Communication and language

Time and time sense

Relationships

Values and norms

Beliefs and attitudes

Work motivation and practices

Mental processes and learning

Sense of Self and Space

Self-identity may be manifested by humble bearing in some places, or by macho behavior in others. Some (e.g., the United States) may promote independence and creativity, while others (e.g., Japan) emphasize group cooperation and conformity. Americans have a sense of space that requires more distance between people, while Latins and Vietnamese want to get much closer. Each culture has its own unique ways of doing things.

Dress and Appearance

This includes outward garments as well as body decorations. Many cultures wear distinctive clothing—the Japanese kimono, the Indian turban, the Polynesian sarong, the "organization-man-or-woman" look of business, and uniforms that distinguish wearers from everybody else. Cosmetics are more popular and accepted in some cultures than in others, as is cologne or after-shave lotion among men.

Food and Eating Habits

The manner in which food is selected, prepared, presented, and eaten often differs by culture. Most major cities have restaurants that specialize in the distinctive cuisine of various cultures—everything from Asian to Zambian. Utensils also differ, ranging from bare hands to chop sticks to full sets of cutlery. Knowledge of food and eating habits often provides insights into customs and culture.

Communication: Verbal and Nonverbal

The axiom "Words mean different things to different people" is especially true in cross-cultural communication. When an American says she is "tabling" a proposition, it is generally accepted that it will be put off. In England, "tabling" means to discuss something now. Translations from one language to another can generate even more confusion as a result of differences in style and context. Coca-Cola found this out when it began marketing its soft-drink products in China.

The traditional Coca-Cola trademark took on an unintended translation when shopkeepers added their own calligraphy to the company name. "Coca-Cola," pronounced "ke kou ke la" in one Chinese dialect, translates as "bite the wax tadpole." Reshuffling the pronunciation to "ko kou ko le" is roughly translated to mean "may the mouth rejoice."[64]

In many cultures, directness and openness are not appreciated. An open person may be seen as weak and untrustworthy, and directness can be interpreted as abrupt and hostile behavior. Providing specific details may be seen as insulting to one's intelligence. Written contracts may suggest that a person's word is not good.

Nonverbal cues may also mean different things. In the United States, one who does not look someone in the eye arouses suspicion and is called "shifty-eyed." In some other countries, however, looking one in the eye is perceived as aggression.[18] Just as communication skills are key ingredients for success in U.S. business, such skills are also basic to success in international business. There is no compromise on this issue; ignorance of local customs and communications protocol is a high-risk strategy.

Time and Time Sense

To Americans, time is money. We live by schedules, deadlines, and agendas; we hate to be kept waiting, and we like to "get down to business" quickly. In many countries, however, people simply will not be rushed. They arrive late for appointments, and business is preceded by hours of social rapport. People in a rush are thought to be arrogant and untrustworthy.[18]

In the United States, the most important issues are generally discussed first when making a business deal. In Ethiopia, however, the most important things are taken up last. While being late seems to be the norm for business meetings in Latin America, the reverse is true in Sweden, where prompt efficiency is the watchword.[64] The lesson for Americans doing business overseas is clear: *Be flexible about time and realistic about what can be accomplished.* Adapt to the process of doing business in any particular country.

Relationships

Cultures designate human and organizational relationships by age, sex, status, and family relationships, as well as by wealth, power, and wisdom.[32] Relationships between and among people vary by category—in some cultures the elderly are honored, in others they are ignored. In some cultures women must wear veils and act deferentially; in others the female is considered the equal, if not the superior, of the male.

In some cultures (e.g., Japan, Korea, and to some extent the United States and Great Britain) *where* one went to school may affect one's status. Often lifelong relationships are established among individuals who attended the same school. In other cultures (e.g., Switzerland), one's rank in the military may affect one's job level and prospects for promotion. Finally, the issue of nepotism is viewed very differently in different parts of the world. While most U.S. firms frown upon the practice of hiring or contracting work directly with family members, in Latin America or Arab countries, it only makes sense to hire someone you can trust.[18]

Values and Norms

From its value system, a culture sets norms of behavior, or what some call "local customs." International managers ignore them at their peril. For example, consider the impact of values and norms on negotiating styles.

BARGAINING WITH THE JAPANESE*

■ **PRACTICAL EXAMPLE**

The knot tightens in the Western businessman's stomach as he peers glumly at the Japanese negotiating team across the table. The executive's flight leaves early tomorrow. His home office has been pressing him to complete a deal quickly. But although the talks have dragged on for days, the key issues have barely been discussed. "What is this?" the frustrated businessman wonders. "Don't these people know that time is money?"

Such questions arise frequently when Western executives confront the Japanese. Foreigners eager to do business must often endure endless rounds of what seem to be aimless talks, dinners, and drinks. Still, they have little choice but to put up with the ceremony if they hope to gain access to Japan's vast domestic market.

The exotic set of rituals seen during negotiations is the face Japan presents to the world of business. Japanese negotiators are exquisitely polite

---

*Adapted from: The negotiation waltz, *Time*, Aug. 1, 1983, pp. 41, 42.

and agonizingly vague, yet at the same time they are determined to win the best possible deal. Perhaps the most striking feature of this system of bargaining is the huge amount of time it consumes. One Australian attorney offers the following rule of thumb: *Allow 5 times as long as usual when doing business in Japan.*

Japanese companies negotiate slowly because everyone from junior management to major shareholders must approve a deal, in keeping with the national tradition of consensus. Startled Western executives may therefore find themselves confronting negotiating teams of 10 to 15 Japanese. Moreover, this may be only the beginning. The faces can change from session to session as new experts are added for different topics.

The Japanese are usually minutely well informed about their prospective partners. Said one former official of British Leyland who worked on a joint agreement with Honda, "The Japanese negotiators seemed to know more about our labor and managerial problems than we did."

At first the Japanese seem to have remarkably little interest in the business at hand. Their conversation is likely to dwell at length on social and family concerns rather than on products and prices. They stress personal relations because they are interested in the long-term implications of an agreement. Western executives, on the other hand, may tend to look more at the shorter term. Said one expert, "The American feeling is that it's the horse buyer's fault if he fails to ask whether a horse is blind; . . . for the Japanese, however, a deal is more of a discussion of where mutual interests lie" (ref. 49, p. 42).

GUIDELINES FOR NEGOTIATING WITH THE JAPANESE

Experts on Japanese business methods offer the following guidelines for foreign negotiators:[49]

1. Women should not be part of any formal talks. Japanese women are all but barred from the management of big companies, and the important after-hours socializing in Japan is exclusively stag. (Understandably, this is difficult for American professional women to accept.)

2. Do not send anyone under 35 to conduct negotiations. Said a U.S. manager with a high-tech firm, "You are insulting the Japanese by sending a young man to deal with a senior executive, who is likely to be 65."

3. Be wary of mistaking Japanese politeness for agreement. A Japanese negotiator may frequently nod and say "hai" (yes) during talks. But the word also is used to let the listener know that the conversation is being followed, as with the English "uh-huh" or "I see." In short, "yes" does not always mean "yes."

4. Japanese negotiators may confuse outsiders by lapsing into silence to mull a point. Western businesspeople may then jump into that pool of

silence, much to their regret. Thus the head of a Japanese firm did nothing when a contract from International Telephone and Telegraph (ITT) was presented for his signature. The ITT manager then hastily sweetened the deal by $250,000. If he had waited just a few more minutes, he would have saved the company a quarter of a million dollars.

5. Evasiveness is another characteristic of Japanese negotiators. They hate to be pinned down, and they often suppress their views out of deference to their seniors. Add to this the Japanese tendency to tell listeners what they seem to want to hear, and a foreign negotiator can easily go astray.[49]

To be successful, a visiting executive never lets on what he is really thinking, he has unending patience, and he is unfailingly polite. In short, he acts very Japanese.

Beliefs and Attitudes

To some degree, religion expresses the philosophy of a people about important facets in life. While Western culture is largely influenced by Judeo-Christian traditions, and Middle Eastern culture by Islam, Oriental and Indian cultures are dominated by Buddhism, Confucianism, Taoism, and Hinduism. In cultures where a religious view of work still prevails, work is viewed as an act of service to God and people and is expressed in a moral commitment to the job or quality of effort. In Japan, the cultural loyalty to family is transferred to the work organization. It is expressed in work-group participation, communication, and consensus.[32]

T. Fujisawa, cofounder of Honda Motor Co., once remarked, "Japanese and American management is 95 percent the same, and differs in all important respects." In other words, while organizations are becoming more similar in terms of structure and technology, people's behavior within those organizations continues to reveal culturally based dissimilarities.[2] One area where this is apparent is in orientation. The Japanese and Europeans look to long-term accomplishments; Americans tend to stress short-term results. Each has its advantages and disadvantages. The U.S. approach translates into management styles that can be very exciting and dynamic but narrow in range and shallow in strategy. On the other hand, since Japanese and European managers tend to be less opportunistic, they sometimes miss out on fast-breaking opportunities.[28]

Work Motivation and Practices

Knowledge of what motivates workers in a given culture, combined with (or based on) a knowledge of what they think matters in life, is critical to the success of the international manager. Europeans pay particular attention to *power and status*, which results in more formal management and operating styles in comparison to the *informality* found in the United States. In the United States individual *initiative and achievement* are rewarded, but in Japan managers are encouraged to seek *consensus* before acting, and employees work as teams. In one comparison of motivating factors for middle-aged Japanese and American business managers, the Japanese showed more interest in advancement, money, and forward striving. Since these characteristics tend to be closely associated with success, it may be that achievement and advancement motivation are driving forces behind Japanese productivity, and "team" action only their method for disciplining and rewarding it.[34] When a similar survey was conducted among German workers, 48 percent said higher income is the key motivating factor for them, followed by opportunities for promotion (25 percent), and more independence (25 percent).[23]

The determinants of work motivation may not be all that different in developing countries. In Zambia, for example, work motivation seems to be determined by six factors: the nature of the work itself, opportunities for growth and advancement, material and physical provisions (i.e., pay, benefits, job security, favorable physical work conditions), relations with others, fairness or unfairness in organizational practices, and personal problems. The effect of personal problems is totally negative. That is, *their presence impairs motivation, but their absence does not enhance it.*[44]

Mental Processes and Learning

Linguists, anthropologists, and other experts who have studied this issue have found vast differences in the ways that people think and learn in different cultures. While some cultures favor abstract thinking and conceptualization, others prefer rote memory and learning. Chinese, Japanese, and Korean written languages are based on ideograms or "word pictures." On the other hand, English is based on precise expression using words. Western cultures stress linear thinking and logic, that is, A then B then C then D. Among Arabic and Oriental cultures, however, nonlinear thinking prevails. This has direct implications for negotiation processes. That is, A may be followed by C; then back to B and on to D. Such an approach, in which issues are treated as independent and not linked by sequence, can be confusing and frustrating to Westerners because it does not appear "logical." What can we conclude from this? What seems to be universal is that each culture has a reasoning process, but each manifests the process in its own distinctive way.[32] Managers who do not understand or appreciate such differences may conclude (erroneously and to their detriment) that certain cultures are "inscrutable."

There are three important lessons to be learned from this brief overview of cross-cultural differences.[29] One, it is critically important that managers of MNCs *guard against exportation of headquarters-country bias.* As we have seen, the human resource management approach that works well in the headquarters country might be totally out of step in another country. Managers who bear responsibility for international operations need to understand the cultural differences inherent in the management systems of the countries in which their firms do business. Two, *think in global terms.* We live in a world where a worldwide allocation of physical and human resources is necessary for continued survival. Three, *recognize that no country has all the answers.* Flexible work hours, quality circles, and various inno-vative approaches to productivity have arisen outside the United States. Effective multinational managers must not only think in global terms but must also be able to synthesize the best management approaches to deal with the complex problems at hand.

HUMAN RESOURCE MANAGEMENT ACTIVITIES OF MNCs

Before we consider recruitment, selection, training, and other international human resource management issues, it is important that we address a fundamental ques-tion: Is this subject worthy of study in its own right? The answer is yes, for two reasons—scope and risk exposure.[48] In terms of scope, there are at least five im-portant differences between domestic and international operations. International operations have:

1. More functions, such as taxation and coordination of dependents
2. More heterogeneous functions, such as coordination of multiple-salary currencies
3. More involvement in the employee's personal life, such as housing, health, education, and recreation
4. Different approaches to management, since the population of expatriates and locals varies
5. More complex external influences, such as from societies and governments

Heightened risk exposure is a second distinguishing characteristic of interna-tional human resource management. Companies are vulnerable to a variety of legal issues in each country, and the human and financial consequences of a mistake in the international arena are much more severe. On top of that, terrorism is now an ever-present risk for executives overseas. Indeed, it is estimated that MNCs spend 1 to 2 percent of their revenues on protection against terrorism.[20] This has had an important effect on how people are prepared for and moved to and from international assignment locations. In light of these considerations, it seems rea-sonable to ask, "Why do people accept overseas assignments?" Why do they go? When people agree to uproot themselves from their native lands, permanently or temporarily, more than finances have to be taken into account. Psychological and social issues must also be considered. A study of 135 middle-level American ex-patriate managers revealed two primary underlying factors in their decisions to accept a foreign assignment: increased pay and career mobility.[46]

As we have seen, companies often "sweeten the pot" considerably for their overseas personnel. But what about career mobility? An overseas assignment should enhance an executive's career, not dead end it. At firms such as Allied-Signal, General Electric, and Rohm & Haas, overseas exposure is a desirable, if not in-dispensable, requirement for senior management positions.[40] "Global strategy means global executives" (ref. 1, p. 72). Yet two studies concluded that in many companies, foreign assignments carry more risks than rewards. Why? Lack of training and support for employees and their families, loss of visibility from headquarters, and lack of systematic efforts to reabsorb repatriated managers back into the domestic corporate culture.[40] Results like these should serve as a red flag to companies, indicating a need for careful attention to the HR management aspects of international assignments.

Organizational Structure

Successful expatriate managers must be able to balance local conditions and cultures with home-office desires. From the perspective of strategic management, the fundamental problem is to keep the strategy, structure, and human resource dimensions of the organization in direct alignment.[4] These problems are compounded, of course, in international joint ventures, characterized by multiple ownership and multinational affiliations.[59] Research indicates that organizational structure can facilitate communications in this environment, thus increasing the expatriate's effectiveness.

A basic issue, however, is centralized versus decentralized control. Centralized control is more common when parent firms wish to retain power, and it is also more common among West European and Japanese firms than among U.S. multinationals. Decentralized structures are more common when subsidiaries are less dependent on parent firms for resources such as management talent, technology, and marketing expertise.[20]

In actuality, MNCs do not have to choose between centralization and decentralization. Instead, they may use a combination of approaches, centralizing management decisions in strategic areas, such as R&D and finance, and decentralizing operational functions such as marketing and human resources.[20] Lloyd's Bank International has established procedures to address this need specifically. Branch offices must operate within broad policies, and home-office personnel must make regular inspections to ensure that these policies are being followed; at the same time, there has been an effort to build a high degree of flexibility into the system.[59]

Human Resource Planning

This issue is particularly critical for MNCs, for they need to analyze both the local *and* international external labor markets as well as their own internal labor markets in order to estimate the supply of people with the skills required at some time in the future.

Six other key issues in international HR planning include:[20]

1. Identifying top management potential early
2. Identifying critical success factors for future international managers
3. Providing developmental opportunities
4. Tracking and maintaining commitments to individuals in international career paths

5. Tying strategic business planning to HR planning and vice versa
6. Dealing with multiple business units while attempting to achieve globally and regionally focused (e.g., European, Asian) strategies.

In North America and Europe, national labor markets can usually supply the skilled technical and professional people needed. However, developing countries are characterized by severe shortages of qualified managers and skilled workers and by great surpluses of people with little or no skill, training, or education.[56] The bottom line for MNCs operating in developing countries is that they must be prepared to develop required skills among their own employees.

Recruitment

Broadly speaking, MNCs follow three basic models in the recruitment of executives: (1) They may select from the national group of the parent company only, (2) they may recruit only from within their own country and the country where the branch is located, or (3) they may adopt an international perspective and emphasize the unrestricted use of all nationalities.[59] Each of these strategies has both advantages and disadvantages.

Ethnocentrism: home-country executives only This strategy may be appropriate during the early phases of international expansion, because firms at this stage are concerned with transplanting a part of the business that has worked in their home country. Hence, detailed knowledge of that part is critical to success. On the other hand, a policy of ethnocentrism, of necessity, implies blocked promotional paths for local executives. And if there are many subsidiaries, home-country nationals must recognize that their foreign service may not lead to faster career progress. Finally, there are cost disadvantages to ethnocentrism as well as increased tendencies to *impose* the management style of the parent company.[30]

Limiting recruitment to home- and host-country nationals only This may result from acquisition of local companies. In Japan, for instance, where the labor market is tight, most people are reluctant to switch firms. Thus, use of a local partner may be extremely important. Hiring nationals has other advantages as well. It eliminates language barriers, expensive training periods, and cross-cultural adjustment problems of managers and their families. It also allows MNCs to take advantage of (lower) local salary levels while still paying a premium to attract high-quality employees.

Yet these advantages are not without cost. Local managers may have difficulty bridging the gap between the subsidiary and the parent company, for the business experience to which they have been exposed may not have prepared them to work as part of a multinational enterprise.[30] Finally, consideration of *only* home- and host-country nationals may result in the exclusion of some very able executives.

Geocentrism: seek the best person for the job regardless of nationality At first glance it may appear that this strategy is optimal and most consistent with the underlying MNC philosophy. Yet there are potential problems. Such a policy can be *very* expensive, it would take a long time to implement, and it requires a great deal of centralized control over managers and their career patterns. To implement such a policy effectively, MNCs must make it very clear that cross-national service is important to the firm and that it will be rewarded. They also must foster actively a policy of open career opportunities for top management positions. In view of these requirements, is it really any surprise that so few MNCs have developed a truly international executive cadre? Let's now consider a very serious problem that confronts many executives offered overseas assignments.

■ PRACTICAL EXAMPLE

JOB AID FOR SPOUSES OF OVERSEAS EXECUTIVES*

In half of all U.S. families, both husband and wife hold jobs. By 1995, according to the U.S. Department of Labor, more than 81 percent of married women aged 35 to 44 will be employed or seeking work. Here is a scenario likely to become more and more common in the future. A company offers a promotion overseas to a promising executive. But the executive's spouse has a flourishing career in the United States. What should the company—and the couple—do?

Employers and employees are wrestling with this dilemma more often these days. As noted in Chapter 9, job aid for the so-called trailing spouse is already a popular benefit for domestic transfers. Now, on a limited basis, some employers are also providing informal job help to the spouses of international transferees.

HR officers may try to find a job for the spouse within the company, press a spouse's current employer for a foreign post, provide job leads through customers and suppliers, or plow through costly government red tape to get work permits. This kind of aid usually occurs in industries like banking, financial services, pharmaceuticals, and computers, all of which have significant numbers of high-level women executives.

Despite company efforts, it is often very difficult to place spouses abroad. Where there are language barriers or barriers of labor laws, tradition, or underemployment, it can be almost impossible. Certain Mideast nations frown on women working or even driving. Moreover, an international assignment can slow a spouse's professional progress and sometimes stir resentment. And when both husband and wife work for the same employer, nepotism rules can interfere with the pursuit of their careers overseas because one is more likely to have to supervise the other. For example, a Citibank lending officer decided to get married just before the bank moved him to a small, 40-person office in Maracaibo, Venezuela. His wife, also a Citibank lending officer, had to go on unpaid leave.

*Adapted from: J. S. Lublin, More spouses receive help in job searches when executives take positions overseas, *The Wall Street Journal*, Jan. 26, 1984, p. 29. Reprinted by permission of *The Wall Street Journal*, © 1984 Dow Jones & Company, Inc. All rights reserved worldwide.

Sensitive about the employment of more women, many companies are considering expansion of their informal job assistance for spouses of employees transferred abroad. Consultants and spouses of executives who have lived abroad are convinced that employers *could* provide additional guidance. They also say that businesses should not penalize aspiring managers who reject foreign transfers because of their mate's career needs. In fact, many experts believe that spousal income loss will be *the* overseas compensation issue of the 1990s and the single most important factor determining an executive's decision to accept or reject an overseas position.[1,54] Recognizing this problem, North American Philips Corp. offers an alternative to work. Instead, it pays a yearly sum for the spouse to attend school—whether or not the spouse worked before.[1]

Despite all the obstacles, overseas assignments for dual-career couples can work out—but it may require some "creative juggling" by both employers and employees. Thus an electronics company sought to recruit a marketing executive for a Hong Kong post, but his wife, a financial services corporation executive, lacked any job prospects. At the urging of an executive recruiter, the electronics company hired the woman for a 4-month project to promote a new product. It also helped start her career as a marketing consultant with introductions to the Hong Kong business community.[42]

International Staffing

There are two important guidelines in this area: (1) Do not assume that a job requires the same skills from one location to another, and (2) do not underestimate the effect of the local culture and physical environment on the candidate.[10] In many cultures, tribal and family norms take precedence over technical qualifications in hiring employees. African managers often hire relatives and members of their tribes.[56] Likewise, in India, Korea, and Latin America, family connections are frequently more important than technical expertise. For an expatriate, technical competence along with other factors, such as the ability to relate well to others, may increase her or his chances of successful performance abroad.[65]

Selection criteria for international jobs cover five areas: *personality, skills, attitudes, motivation, and behavior.*[70] Personality traits related to success include: perseverance and patience (for when everything falls apart); initiative (because no one will be there to indicate what one should try next); and flexibility (to accept and to try new ways).

Highly developed technical skills, of course, provide the basic rationale for selecting a person to work overseas. In addition, however, candidates should possess skills in communication (home- and host-country languages, verbal, nonverbal, and written);[55] interpersonal relations (in developing countries, native people will simply walk off the job rather than continue to work with disagreeable outsiders); and stress management (to overcome the inevitable "culture shock"—frustration,

■ TABLE 17·2
INTERVIEW WORKSHEET FOR INTERNATIONAL CANDIDATES

Motivation
- Investigate reasons and degree of interest in wanting to be considered.
- Determine desire to work abroad, verified by previous concerns such as personal travel, language training, reading, and association with foreign employees or students.
- Determine whether the candidate has a realistic understanding of what working and living abroad requires.
- Determine the basic attitudes of the spouse toward an overseas assignment.

Health
- Determine whether any medical problems of the candidate or his or her family might be critical to the success of the assignment.
- Determine whether he or she is in good physical and mental health, without any foreseeable change.

Language ability
- Determine potential for learning a new language.
- Determine any previous language(s) studied or oral ability (judge against language needed on the overseas assignment).
- Determine the ability of the spouse to meet the language requirements.

Family considerations
- How many moves has the family made in the past among different cities or parts of the United States?
- What problems were encountered?
- How recent was the last move?
- What is the spouse's goal in this move?
- What are the number of children and the ages of each?
- Has divorce or its potential, death of a family member, etc., weakened family solidarity?
- Will all the children move? Why or why not?
- What are the location, health, and living arrangements of grandparents and the number of trips normally made to their home each year?
- Are there any special adjustment problems that you would expect?
- How is each member of the family reacting to this possible move?
- Do special educational problems exist within the family?

Resourcefulness and initiative
- Is the candidate independent; can he or she make and stand by his or her decisions and judgments?
- Does he or she have the intellectual capacity to deal with several dimensions simultaneously?

Source: D. M. Noer, *Multinational People Management*, Washington, DC: Bureau of National Affairs, 1975, pp. 55–57.

conflict, anxiety, and feelings of alienation—that accompanies overseas assignments).

Tolerant attitudes toward people who may differ significantly in race, creed, color, values, personal habits, and customs are essential for success in overseas work. People who look down smugly on other cultures as inferior to their own simply will not make it overseas.

High motivation has long been acknowledged as a key ingredient for success in missionary work. Who, for example, can forget the zeal of the Protestant missionaries in the book *Hawaii*, by James Michener, as they set out from their native New England? While motivation is often difficult to assess reliably, at the very

■ **TABLE 17·2**
INTERVIEW WORKSHEET FOR INTERNATIONAL CANDIDATES (*Cont.*)

Resourcefulness and initiative (continued)

- Is he or she able to reach objectives and produce results with whatever personnel and facilities are available, regardless of the limitations and barriers that might arise?
- Can the candidate operate without a clear definition of responsibility and authority on a foreign assignment?
- Will the candidate be able to explain the aims and company philosophy to the local managers and workers?
- Does he or she possess sufficient self-discipline, and self-confidence to overcome difficulties or handle complex problems?
- Can the candidate work without supervision?
- Can the candidate operate effectively in a foreign environment without normal communications and supporting services?

Adaptability

- Is the candidate sensitive to others, open to the opinions of others, cooperative, and able to compromise?
- What are his or her reactions to new situations, and efforts to understand and appreciate differences?
- Is he or she culturally sensitive, aware, and able to relate across the culture?
- Does the candidate understand his or her own culturally derived values?

- How does the candidate react to criticism?
- What is his or her understanding of the U.S. government system?
- Will he or she be able to make and develop contacts with his or her peers in the foreign country?
- Does he or she have patience when dealing with problems?
- Is he or she resilient; can he or she bounce back after setbacks?

Career planning

- Does the candidate consider the assignment anything other than a temporary overseas trip?
- Is the move consistent with his or her progression and that planned by the company?
- Is his or her career planning realistic?
- What is the candidate's basic attitude toward the company?
- Is there any history or indication of interpersonal problems with this employee?

Financial

- Are there any current financial and/or legal considerations that might affect the assignment, e.g., house purchase, children and college expenses, car purchases?
- Are financial considerations negative factors, i.e., will undue pressures be brought to bear on the employee or his or her family as a result of the assignment?

least, firms should try to eliminate from consideration those who are only looking to get out of their own country for a change in scenery.

The last criterion is behavior—especially concern for other members of a group, tolerance for ambiguity, displays of respect, and nonjudgmental behavior. These characteristics may be determined from tests or interviews. Research indicates that U.S. psychological tests can be used by MNCs in many countries, but the content as well as the administration of the tests may need to be adapted to the culture in which they are to be used.[5,36]

With regard to interviews, Table 17-2 provides a checklist of areas to probe in selecting candidates for international assignments. Note the section on "language ability." In a recent survey, almost two-thirds of 100 top managers of MNCs indicated that in their future selection decisions for international assignments, a command of foreign languages would be prized. As one manager noted: "We wonder how a manager can assess business opportunities in a foreign country if he does not speak the language and has little knowledge of the culture. . . . Management by walking around, visiting foreign operations, and keeping in touch by telephone is not enough."[24]

A final issue involves government regulation of staffing activities in foreign countries. In several western European countries, for example, employment offices are operated by the government, and private agencies are not permitted. And in countries such as Holland, Poland, and Sweden, prospective employees have the right to prior knowledge of psychological tests. If they so choose, they can insist that test results not be reported to an employer. In fact, in Sweden, employer, union, peers, and subordinates all participate in the entire selection process for managers—from job analysis to the hiring or promotion decision.[19] These kinds of HR practices and regulations may require that U.S. MNCs radically modify their human resource and industrial relations policies to operate successfully overseas.

Orientation

Orientation is particularly important in overseas assignments, both before departure and after arrival. Formalized orientation efforts—for example, elaborate audiovisual presentations for the entire family, supplemented by presentations by representatives of the country and former expatriates who have since returned to the United States—are fine, to a point. Such approaches try to provide a comprehensive picture of the new environment, its opportunities, inconveniences, and essential differences. However, unless firms recognize that these "differences" are not the same for everybody in the audience of prospective expatriates, their orientation efforts are doomed.[17] Instead of trying to convey the "truth about Tokyo," overseas orientation programs should make quite clear that employees and family members will each experience their *own* Tokyos. No matter what they may have heard or read, each of their experiences will be unique.

Another important aspect of overseas orientation that is sometimes overlooked is the company's culture at the overseas site.[17] Its ways of doing things, its expectations from employees and their families, and its differences in the ways jobs are done may all differ from U.S. practices. Failure to include such information only exacerbates the ensuing culture shock upon arrival.

In fact, there may be three separate phases to orientation:[17] The first is called *initial orientation*, and it may last as long as 2 full days. Key components are:

- *Cultural briefing.* Traditions, history, government, economy, living conditions, clothing and housing requirements, health requirements, and visa applications. (Drugs get a lot of coverage, both for adults and for teenagers—whether they use drugs or not. Special emphasis is given to the different drug laws in foreign

IMPACT OF MNC HUMAN RESOURCE MANAGEMENT ON PRODUCTIVITY, QUALITY OF WORK LIFE, AND THE BOTTOM LINE

The impact of effective (or ineffective) recruitment, selection, orientation, training and development, compensation, and industrial relations practices are magnified when overseas assignments are involved. The *downside* risk associated with poor performance (regardless of cause) and reduced morale of subordinates is huge, given the costs (roughly 3 to 5 times annual salary) associated with sending managers abroad. On the other hand, there is potential for great gains in productivity and QWL, the incumbent's as well as her or his subordinates', and, consequently, bottom-line profits when the processes discussed in this chapter are implemented properly.

countries. Alcohol use also gets special attention when candidates are going to Moslem countries, such as Saudi Arabia.)

- *Assignment briefing.* Length of assignment, vacations, salary and allowances, tax consequences, and repatriation policy.
- *Relocation requirements.* Shipping, packing, or storage; and home sale, rental, or acquisition.

During this time, it is important that employees and their families understand that there is no penalty attached to changing their minds about accepting the proposed assignment. It is better to bail out early than reluctantly to accept an assignment to be regretted later.

The second phase is *predeparture orientation*, which may last another 2 or 3 days. Its purpose is to make a more lasting impression on employees and their families and to remind them of material that may have been covered months earlier. Topics covered at this stage include:

- Introduction to the language
- Further reinforcement of important values, especially open-mindedness
- Enroute, emergency, and arrival information

The introduction to the language is important, for facility with the host country's language sets up an immediate rapport. Indeed, many foreign business people consider it a compliment for an expatriate to be able to converse in their language. Yet it often takes months, sometimes years, to master a foreign language. As is often the case, U.S. multinationals can learn from the practices of their overseas counterparts. British Petroleum uses outside facilities, such as Berlitz, for this purpose. For senior-level appointments to exotic locations, the duration of the language training is generally 6 weeks, followed by further tutoring upon arrival in the destination country. Spouses are also encouraged to take language training, to facilitate faster adaptation overseas.[65]

The final aspect of overseas orientation is *arrival orientation*. Upon arrival, employees and their families should be met by assigned company sponsors. This phase of orientation usually takes place on three levels:

- *Orientation toward the environment.* Language, transportation, shopping, and other subjects that—depending on the country—may be understandable only through actual experience.
- *Orientation toward the work unit and fellow employees.* Often a supervisor or a delegate from the work unit will introduce the new employee to his or her fellow workers, discuss expectations of the job, and share his or her own initial experiences as an expatriate. The ultimate objective, of course, is to relieve the feelings of strangeness or tension that the new expatriate feels.
- *Orientation to the actual job.* This may be an extended process that focuses on cultural differences in the way a job is done. Only when this process is complete, however, can we begin to assess the accuracy and wisdom of the original selection decision.

Cross-Cultural Training and Development

In a recent study of MNCs, 68 percent of U.S. firms that responded had no training programs *at all* for expatriate managers. Yet the same study found that rigorous selection and training procedures predicted success as an expatriate in U.S., western European, and Japanese multinationals! In the U.S. sample, the most important reasons for expatriate failure were: inability of the manager's spouse to adjust abroad and the manager's own failure to adjust to the different physical and cultural environment. Furthermore, U.S. expatriates had a higher failure rate than either Japanese or Europeans.[65]

To provide a deeper understanding of the relationship between lack of training and expatriate failure, consider the results of a recent survey on training needs for expatriate managers of U.S. companies doing business in Beijing. The results were clear. First, the formal aspects of the business and economic systems in China were viewed as less important than the behavioral factors—the "intangibles." Chinese language ability ranked very high. People with the greatest business experience—not necessarily those with the best Chinese language skills—all said that knowledge of the language was essential. Chinese negotiating style and Chinese social practices also received high marks. In short, China training should deal specifically with the interaction of Chinese cultural, political, and economic forces with the practicalities of the business environment.[68] It should also aim to develop "creative" survival skills. Indeed, there really are only three tasks set out for the executive headed for a foreign country: surviving, coping, and, finally, succeeding.[25]

However, to survive, cope, and succeed, managers need training in three areas: the culture, the language, and assistance with practical, day-to-day matters.[20] A recent review of research in this area found that cross-cultural training has a positive impact on the individual's development of skills, on his or her adjustment to the cross-cultural situation, and on his or her performance in such situations.[6] These results suggest that sending a manager overseas without training is like sending David to meet Goliath without even a sling shot.

To a very great extent, expatriate failure rates can be attributed to the culture shock that usually occurs 4 to 6 months after arrival in the foreign country. The symptoms are not pleasant: homesickness, boredom, withdrawal, a need for excessive amounts of sleep, compulsive eating or drinking, irritability, exaggerated cleanliness, marital stress, family tension and conflict (involving children), hostility toward host-country nationals, loss of ability to work effectively, and physical ailments of a psychosomatic nature.[14]

To be sure, many of the common stresses of everyday living become amplified when a couple is living overseas with no support other than from a spouse. To deal with these potential problems, spouses are taught to recognize stress symptoms in one another, and they are counseled to be supportive. One exercise, for example, is for the couples periodically to list what they believe causes stress in their mates, what the other person does to relieve it, and what they themselves do to relieve it. Then they compare lists.[14]

A model of international training and development Figure 17-1 provides a "road map" for the kinds of training and development activities that MNCs might undertake. This kind of guidance is essential, because in the glitter and glow of the many training techniques available, it is easy to lose sight of the forest for the trees.

Regardless of the specific method used, cross-cultural training may be conducted on two levels: academic and interpersonal.[29] Academic training uses books, maps, films, and discussions of the history, culture, and socioeconomic patterns of the host country. Interpersonal training is more direct, for it is the actual (or simulated) *experience* of living in the host country. Research indicates that the most effective cross-cultural training programs use both types, for they build on each other.[22] Here is how one company uses interpersonal training.

JOB SWAPS AT MOLEX ENHANCE INTERNATIONAL UNDERSTANDING*

■ **COMPANY EXAMPLE**

Eighteen shop-floor employees of a manufacturer of electrical components, Molex, Inc., in Ireland, Japan, and the United States recently swapped jobs; they discovered quickly that their way of doing things is not necessarily best or easiest. The 18 employees, 6 from each country, were given 10-day working holidays in a foreign country to see how similar operations are being done elsewhere.

---

*Adapted from: How Molex swaps jobs for international understanding, *Management Review*, July 1985, p. 35.

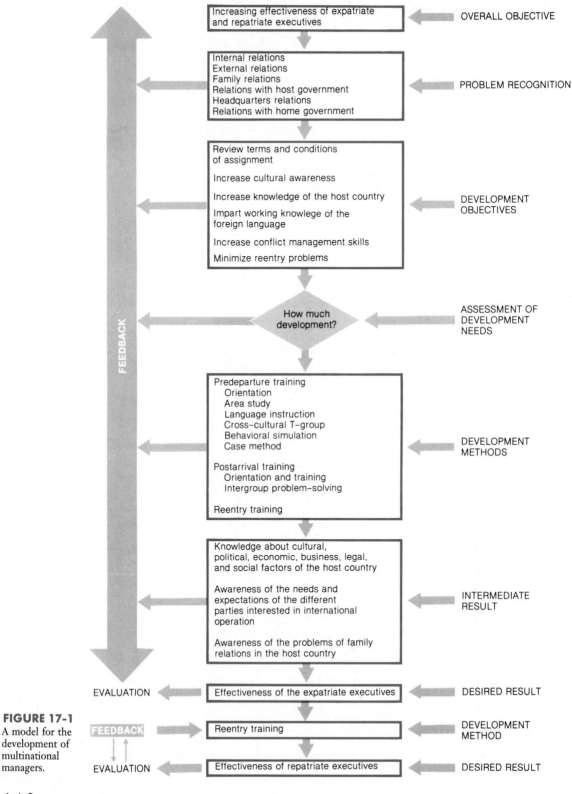

FIGURE 17-1
A model for the development of multinational managers.

640

The employees performed the same job in the foreign plant as they did in their own country, and they were each paid their regular wages. All expenses were paid by the sponsoring plant. Participants were chosen by draw. However, to be considered, they must have been with the company at least 3 years. Participation was voluntary.

U.S. employees who visited Molex Japan came home with much admiration for their Japanese colleagues. They were particularly impressed with their dedication and attention to quality. Visitors to Molex Shannon in Ireland were impressed with the plant layout and the appearance of the machines and the facility. They were also impressed with the speed and efficiency of the work performed by their Irish colleagues.

The U.S. workers also came back with an idea for redesigning one of the U.S. plant's work areas to reduce the need for continual bending. The Japanese picked up several useful tips from the Americans on how to operate their machines more efficiently. The employees also exchanged ideas and little tricks on stocking materials, loading machines, loading hoppers, and sorting runners.

Said one executive, "Employees are more willing to accept new ideas and accept hard facts from other shop-floor employees than from management, we found." The $48,000 exercise also gives the employees a greater feeling of pride. "They now feel they are part of a much larger, worldwide organization. They have also come to understand that by having subsidiary companies overseas we are not taking jobs from Americans, as they previously argued, but rather [we] are creating jobs. They now recognize that we do things here in the United States in support of our manufacturing operations overseas to serve overseas markets. And that we are becoming a stronger company and protecting U.S. jobs as a result."

Integration of Training and Business Strategy

The multinational firm must have a continuing, long-range program of management development that is integrated with its global strategy and business planning. It needs to work constantly toward broadening the experience and outlook of all of its executives.[7,30] These ideas are best illustrated by an example.

Emhart Corp., which makes and markets worldwide a line of hardware and machinery, concluded that its future growth would be outside the United States. To instill a global orientation in all its managers, domestic and international, the company undertook a large-scale management development program on the general theme of "global competitiveness." The program had five objectives:

1. To help manage the transition from domestic company to global competitor
2. To build a global business perspective
3. To identify factors critical to global business success

4. To assess the company's own competitive position
5. To build working relationships across decentralized businesses

To accomplish these objectives, the training covered topics such as the following:

- The world in the year 2000—political, social, and economic dimensions
- The dynamics of global trade
- Operations in a global business—global marketing, manufacturing, sourcing, and design
- Factors that distinguish successful from unsuccessful global competitors

Such a program is obviously long-term in orientation and broad in scope. Although results of the program may not manifest themselves for years, the program itself represents a reasonable attempt to link training design with business strategy.

International Compensation

Compensation policies can produce some of the most intense internal conflicts within an MNC. They can also influence the pattern of promotion that executives seek within the firm. Overpaid posts in peripheral foreign activities, for example, might attract executive talent away from more important, but lower-paid, posts in the mainstream of the firm's development. Few other areas in international human resource management demand as much top-management attention as does compensation.

The principal problem is straightforward: *Salary levels for the same job differ among countries in which an MNC operates.* Compounding this problem is the fact that fluctuating exchange rates require constant attention in order to maintain constant salary rates in U.S. dollars.[12]

Ideally, an effective international compensation policy should meet the following objectives:

- Attract and retain employees who are qualified for overseas service.
- Facilitate transfers between foreign affiliates and between home-country and foreign locations.
- Establish and maintain a consistent relationship between the compensation of employees of all affiliates, both at home and abroad.
- Maintain compensation that is reasonable in relation to the practices of leading competitors.[30]

It is important that a worldwide compensation system be established within each MNC so that cultural variables can be dealt with systematically. The following two principles have helped establish such systems in many MNCs:

Home-country concept All expatriates are tied to their respective home-country payrolls regardless of where they are working. Doing so provides, in essence, a cultural frame of reference within which to make compensation decisions. Also, it keeps the overseas employee thinking in terms of her or his home-country compensation values. This can help make repatriation less traumatic.

Modular approach This approach breaks the compensation package down into its separate elements, and, relative to home-country and host-country laws, modifies those elements so that the expatriate neither loses nor gains. Specific "modules" of the compensation package are therefore set up to balance out the total package. The philosophy underlying this approach is to keep the employee "whole" in terms of home-country purchasing power.[29]

In analyzing the international compensation package, there are two major components: direct salary payments (with their associated tax consequences) and indirect payments in the form of (1) benefits and (2) adjustments and incentives. Let's consider each of these.

Salaries To be competitive, MNCs normally follow local salary patterns in each country. Is there any other alternative? A firm that tried to maintain the same salary levels in all countries would "cost itself out" of markets where lower salary levels prevail, and it would be unable to attract managers in high-salary countries. To deal with this problem, one approach is to establish base salaries relative to those of the home country (this is the *home-country concept*) and then to add to these various types of premiums (See Table 17-1). One of the most common is the *foreign-service premium*, which typically ranges from 10 to 30 percent or more of base pay.[1] Some companies offer this premium tax-free. Its purpose also varies. In MNCs that take a modular approach to international compensation, it represents a combination of compensation for living away from the home country plus an inducement to accept an overseas assignment. In this case, the percentage is usually low. However, in MNCs that intend the expatriation premium to compensate for *all* overseas problems, it is much higher.

Another adjustment usually made in international compensation is *income tax equalization* with the home country. Its objective is to ensure that when the expatriate is assigned overseas, she pays neither more nor less tax than she would have paid had she remained in her home country. This is an important part of the compensation package, for under the Tax Reform Act of 1986, U.S. citizens working abroad can exclude up to $70,000 per year of foreign income from U.S. taxes. Tax liability for income above $70,000 (salary, bonuses, and allowances) is largely academic for U.S. residents covered by a company tax equalization program.[51]

In addition, Americans are allowed to deduct from their income the amount they pay for housing overseas above a base housing cost—currently $7322.[61] This is a big break, considering, for example, that apartments designed for expatriates in Hong Kong can cost as much as $7000 to $8000 per month (in 1991 dollars)![62]

Benefits These may vary drastically from one country to another. For example, in Europe it is common for employees to get added compensation in proportion to the number of family members or unpleasant working conditions. In Japan, a supervisor whose weekly salary is only $500 (in 1991 dollars) may also get benefits that include family income allowances, housing or housing loans, subsidized vacations, year-end bonuses that can equal 3 months' pay, and profit sharing.[30]

MNCs commonly handle benefits coverages in terms of the "best of both worlds" benefits model.[29] Figure 17-2 illustrates the approach. Wherever possible, the expatriate is given home-country benefits coverages. However, in areas such as disability insurance, where there may be no home-country plan, the employee may join the host-country plan.

Another benefit provided by most U.S. multinationals is the *cost-of-living allowance* (COLA). Its purpose is to provide for the difference in living costs (that is, the costs of goods, services, and currency realignments) between the home country and the host country. COLAs may include any one or more of the following components:

- *Housing allowance*
- *Education allowance* to pay for schools, uniforms, and other educational expenses that would not have been incurred had the expatriate remained in the United States
- *Income tax equalization allowance* (as described earlier)
- *Hardship pay*, which is usually a percentage of base pay provided as compensation for living in a culturally deprived area—one with no schools, transportation, or entertainment[62]
- *Hazardous-duty pay* to compensate for living in an area where physical danger is present, such as a war zone

Such a premium can be as high as 25 percent of base pay in some Middle Eastern and African countries.[67]

- *Home leave*—commonly one trip every year to the expatriate's home country for the entire family. Hardship posts normally include more frequent travel for rest and relaxation.
- *School allowance*—as a rule, companies will pay for private schooling for the children of their expatriates.[1]

Finally, it is common practice for companies to pay for security guards in many overseas locations, such as the Middle East, the Philippines, and Indonesia.

Pay adjustments and incentives In the United States adjustments in individual pay levels are based, to a great extent, on how well people do their jobs, as reflected in a performance appraisal. In most areas of the third world, however, objective measures for rating employee or managerial performance are uncommon. Social

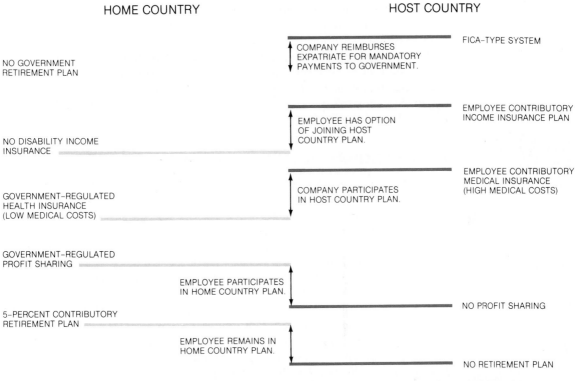

FIGURE 17-2
Best-of-both-worlds benefits model.

status is based on characteristics such as age, religion, ethnic origin, and social class. Pay differentials that do not reflect these characteristics will not motivate workers. For example, consider Japan. Rewards are based less on the nature of the work performed or individual competence than on seniority and personal characteristics such as age, education, or family background. A pay system based on individual job performance would not be acceptable since group performance is emphasized, and the effect of individual appraisal would be to divide the group.[58] Needless to say, exportation of U.S. performance appraisal practices to these kinds of cultures can have disastrous effects.

Despite such differences, research indicates that there also are important similarities in reward allocation practices across cultures. The most universal of these seems to be the equity norm, according to which rewards are distributed to group members based on their contributions.[38]

When implementing performance appraisal overseas, therefore, first determine the *purpose* of the appraisal. Second, whenever possible, set standards of performance against quantifiable assignments, tasks, or objectives. Third, allow more time to achieve results abroad than is customary in the domestic market. Fourth, keep the objectives flexible and responsive to potential market and environmental contingencies.[35] More and more U.S. MNCs that are exploring strategic compensation approaches at home are beginning to adopt similar approaches for their senior executives worldwide. They are beginning to introduce local and regional performance criteria into these plans, and they are attempting to qualify the plans under local tax laws. Why are they doing this? To create stronger linkages between executives' performance and long-term business goals and strategies, to extend equity ownership to key executives (through stock options), and in many instances to provide tax benefits.[8,9]

MULTINATIONAL COLLECTIVE BARGAINING

Labor relations structures, laws, and practices vary considerably among countries. Unions may or may not exist. Management or government may dictate terms and conditions of employment. Labor agreements may or may not be contractual obligations. Management may conclude agreements with unions that have little or no membership in a plant, or with nonunion groups that wield more bargaining power than the established unions. And principles and issues that are relevant in one context may not be in others: for example, seniority in layoff decisions, or even the concept of a layoff.[27,39]

In general, unions may constrain the choices of MNCs in three ways: (1) by influencing wage levels to the extent that cost structures may become noncompetitive, (2) by limiting the ability of MNCs to vary employment levels at their own discretion, and (3) by hindering or preventing global integration of MNCs (i.e., by forcing them to develop parallel operations in different countries).[20]

One of the most intriguing aspects of international labor relations is multinational collective bargaining. Unions have found MNCs particularly difficult to deal with in terms of union power and difficult to penetrate in terms of union representation.[41,52] Here are some of the special problems that MNCs present to unions:

1. While national unions tend to follow the development of national companies, union expansion typically cannot follow the expansion of a company across national boundaries, with the exception of Canada. Legal differences, feelings of nationalism, and differences in union structure and industrial relations practices are effective barriers to such expansion.[3]

2. The nature of foreign investment by MNCs has changed. In the past, MNCs tended to invest in foreign sources of raw materials. As a result, the number of processing and manufacturing jobs in the home country may actually have increased. However, in recent years there has been a shift toward the development of parallel, or nearly parallel, operations in other countries. Foreign investment of this type threatens union members in the home country with loss of jobs or with a slower rate of growth of jobs, especially if their wages are higher than those of workers in the host country. This threat is especially serious to U.S. union members, whose wages may be higher than those of workers in other countries.[3]

3. When an MNC has parallel operations in other locations, the firm's ability to switch production from one location shut down by a labor dispute to another

location is increased. This, of course, assumes that the same union does not represent workers at each plant or that, if different unions are involved, they do not coordinate their efforts and strike at the same time. Another assumption is that the various plants are sufficiently parallel that their products are interchangeable.

One solution to the problems that MNCs pose for union members is multinational collective bargaining. For this to work, though, requires coordination of efforts and the cooperation of unions. What is called for is an "international union" with the centralization of authority characteristic of U.S. national unions. Yet two persistent problems stand in the way of such an international union movement:[41]

1. National and local labor leaders would have to be willing to relinquish their autonomy to an international level. This is a major stumbling block because the local union or enterprise union is essentially an autonomous organization.

2. Political and philosophical differences pose a further barrier to any international union movement. For example, a French labor leader committed to a communist form of economic organization is unlikely to yield authority willingly to an international union patterned after the United Auto Workers or any other union committed to the capitalist economic system. Conversely, the leaders of the United Auto Workers are unlikely to relinquish their autonomy to a communist international labor union.

As an example of the difficulties such cooperation poses, consider the role of labor unions in the New Europe (the 12-member European Community unified into a common market for goods, services, capital, and labor in 1992). To the unions the issue is clear: It's a question of jobs, pay, and standard of living. The threat to organized labor is clear, for higher unemployment is almost certain in the early stages of a more efficient Europe. To protect its interests, the German trucking industry lodged protests against the proposed deregulation of their industry. Why? Because deregulation would allow more efficient Dutch truckers to operate freely inside Germany. Prospects for a unified "European union" that might negotiate with employers are weak.

How have multinational collective bargaining efforts worked? Research indicates that such bargaining efforts have typically placed little pressure on management. When labor has been successful in attaining its objectives, this has usually been due to some action by a critical national union. However, that union would probably have engaged in the same action without multinational union coordination and cooperation.[3]

Alternative Union Strategies

Since the prospects for effective multinational collective bargaining by unions are not very promising, unions must consider alternative strategies. These include:

- Independent bargaining by unions with an MNC within each country
- Securing legislation to protect union members' jobs within each country
- Attempting to coordinate multinational collective bargaining

In 1976, the adoption of a set of voluntary guideines by the Organization for Economic Cooperation and Development (OECD) regarding a "code of conduct" for MNCs provided a skeletal structure on which unions could base claims for, and enhance the credibility of, multinational collective bargaining.[11] OECD member countries (most of Europe plus the United States, Canada, Japan, Australia, and New Zealand) account for 20 percent of the world's population, 60 percent of its industrial output, and 70 percent of its trade.[11] The voluntary guidelines cover the following areas: disclosure of information, competition, financing, taxation, employment and industrial relations, and science and technology. Business interests are represented before the OECD through the Business and Industry Advisory Committee, and labor's interests are represented by the Trade Union Advisory Committee (TUAC). The TUAC consists of national trade union centers, such as the AFL-CIO in the United States, the Federation of German Trade Unions in West Germany, and the Trade Union Congress in the United Kingdom. Certainly the OECD guidelines provide a good start toward the development of an international framework for industrial relations. But they are no panacea, as the following company example illustrates.

■ **COMPANY EXAMPLE**

POWER TACTICS IN MULTINATIONAL UNION-MANAGEMENT RELATIONS

On arriving for work one Valentine's Day, the 500 employees of Hyster Company's forklift truck factory in Irvine, Scotland, were taken to a meeting run by Hyster's chief executive, William Kilkenny. He was fresh in from the head offices in Portland, Oregon, bearing big new plans for Irvine. With a British government grant, he disclosed, Hyster was set to invest $60 million in the plant. It was prepared to reorganize and expand. It was willing to close two production lines at its Dutch factory and move them to Scotland. Irvine would gain 1000 jobs. In return, Hyster wanted a sacrifice. Workers would have to take a pay cut of 14 percent, managers 18 percent. They had, Kilkenny told them, 48 hours to decide.

On the following morning, each employee received a letter from the company. "Hyster," it said, "is not convinced at this time that Irvine is the best of the many alternatives open to it. It has not made up its mind. The location of the plant to lead Europe is still open."

At the bottom of the page there was a ballot. A yes or a no was called for. Only 11 people voted no.

Workers complained that they had no warning, no consultation. Said one, "It was industrial rape—do or else." Hyster's workers in Irvine have no union, but the vote might have been no different if they did. The most powerful union in Europe is no match for a company run out of Portland. A union is concerned with the workers in its country; a multinational corporation knows no bounds.

Plant managers within an MNC could easily tell their Swiss workers, as the managers of one reputedly did, that new work was going to the lower-paid British, tell the British that production was being passed to the more efficient French, and tell the French that the MNC was creating jobs for the highly cooperative Swiss. MNCs rarely tell their scattered workers everything. Workers of different nationalities rarely tell each other anything. In an age when information is power, they lack both.

A day after its Scottish staff accepted a pay cut, Hyster telexed the news to its plant manager in Holland. It was his first official word of Hyster's "decision," which turned out to include the firing of a number of Dutch workers and his own early retirement.

Dutch law calls for consultation about such things, and the plant union took Hyster to court. There, a judge ordered Hyster to discuss its strategy with members of the factory works council. It did, revealing the sliver of its corporate plan that applied to them. The union did not like it and went to court again.

A long legal battle could have cost dearly, so Hyster struck a deal: The workers would drop the suit, and the company would not transfer production for 3 years. Now the Scottish workforce is off balance again, despite Hyster's assurance that its expansion will go through.

COMPANY VIEW

Hyster's managing director in Europe is an American. But he is fighting a different war. "We're battling the Japanese," he says. "They've captured an alarmingly large share of the European market. To counter them, we have to produce a cost-effective forklift truck, and to do that, we've implemented a worldwide restructuring program. That required some very tough decisions. Given the circumstances, we've made every effort to communicate effectively with our employees."

UNION VIEW

Said one union leader, "What they call decentralized industrial relations means isolation for us. Without a multinational union you're at the mercy of a company like this." International unions have set up about 50 worker groups representing the car makers, the electronics companies, and the oil and chemicals industries. Their aim is to collect and exchange information. To date, however, not one MNC has agreed to meet with any of them. The MNCs are playing "hard ball," and they wield considerable power in international labor relations.[50]

REPATRIATION

The problems of repatriation, for those who succeed abroad as well as for those who do not, have been well documented. *All* repatriates experience some degree of anxiety in three areas: personal finances, reacclimation to the U.S. lifestyle, and readjustment to the corporate structure.[15] They also worry about the future of their careers and the location of their U.S. assignments.[16] Precisely the same issues were found in a study of Japanese expatriates who returned to Japan.[10]

Financially, repatriates face the loss of the foreign-service premium and the effect of inflation on home purchases. Having become accustomed to foreign ways, upon reentry they often find home-country customs strange and, at the extreme, even annoying. Finally, many repatriates complain that their assignments upon return to their home country were mundane and lacked status and authority, in comparison to their overseas positions.[15] Possible solutions to these problems fall into three areas: planning, career management, and compensation.

Planning

Both the expatriation assignment and the repatriation move should be examined as parts of an integrated whole—not as unrelated events in the individual's career.[15] To do this, a firm agreement must be reached *prior* to expatriation about the specific job assignment overseas, the term of the assignment, the compensation package for the assignment, and the position, level, and location to which the employee will return.[1] Increasingly, MNCs are seeking to improve their human resource planning and also to implement it on a worldwide basis. Careful inclusion of expatriation and repatriation moves in this planning will help reduce uncertainty and the fear that accompanies it.[15]

Career Management

Some MNCs appoint a "career sponsor" to look out for the expatriate's career interests while she or he is abroad to keep the expatriate abreast of company developments. The development of global electronic mail networks certainly has made that job faster and easier than it used to be. Sponsors also must be sensitive to the "job shock" the expatriate may suffer when she or he gets back and must be trained to counsel the returning employee (and her or his family as well) until resettlement is deemed complete.[37]

To accelerate this process, some firms assemble a group of former expatriates to give advice and offer insights based on their own experiences.[57]

Compensation

Loss of a monthly premium to which the expatriate has been accustomed is a severe shock financially, whatever the rationale. To overcome this problem, some firms have replaced the monthly foreign-service premium with a one-time "mo-

IMPLICATIONS FOR MANAGEMENT PRACTICE

No one has discovered a single best way to manage. But before a company can build an effective management team, it must understand thoroughly its own culture, the other cultures in which it does business, and the challenges and rewards of blending the best of each.

In the immediate future, there will certainly be international opportunities for managers at all levels, particularly those with the technical skills needed by developing countries. In the longer run, each MNC may have its own "foreign legion," a cadre of sophisticated international executives drawn from many countries.[59] There is a bright future for managers with the cultural flexibility to be sensitive to the values and aspirations of foreign countries.

Finally, there is one thing of which we can be certain. Talent—social, managerial, and technical—is needed to make MNCs go. Competent human resource management practices can find that talent, recruit it, select it, train and develop it, motivate it, reward it, and profit from it. This will be the greatest challenge of all in the years to come.

bility premium" (e.g., 3 months' pay) for each move—overseas, back home, or to another overseas assignment. MNCs are also providing low-cost loans or other financial assistance so that expatriates can get back into their hometown housing markets at a level at least equivalent to what they left. Finally, there is a strong need for financial counseling for repatriates. Such counseling has the psychological advantage of demonstrating to repatriates that the company is willing to help with the financial problems that they may encounter in uprooting their families once again to bring them home.[15]

■ HUMAN RESOURCE MANAGEMENT IN ACTION
CONCLUSION

A DAY IN THE LIFE OF TOMORROW'S MANAGER

8:15 A.M.: In her high-tech office that doubles as a conference room, Ms. Smith reviews the day's schedule with her executive assistant. (Traditional secretaries vanished a decade earlier.) Then it's on to her first meeting: a conference via video screen between her division's chief production manager in Cincinnati and a supplier near Munich.

While today's managers spend most of their time conferring with bosses and subordinates in their own companies, tomorrow's managers will be intimately hooked to suppliers and customers and will be well versed in competitors' strategies.

10:30 A.M.: At a staff meeting, Ms. Smith finds herself refereeing between two subordinates who disagree vehemently on how to promote a new appliance. One, an Asian manager, suggests that a fresh campaign begin much sooner than envisioned. The other, a European, wants to hold off until results of a test market are received later that week.

Linda Smith quickly recognizes that this is a cultural, not strategic, clash, pitting a let's-do-it-now, analyze-it-later approach against a more cautious style. She makes them aware that they're not really far apart, and the European manager agrees to move swiftly.

By 2010 managers will have to handle greater cultural diversity with subtle human relations skills. Managers will have to understand that employees don't think alike about such basics as handling confrontation, or even what it means to do a good day's work.

12:10 P.M.: Lunch is in Ms. Smith's office today, giving her time to take a video lesson in conversational Japanese. She already speaks Spanish fluently and wants to master at least two more languages. After 20 minutes, she moves to her computer to check her company's latest political-risk assessment on Spain. The report indicates that while recent student unrest is not anti-American, she decides to have a bodyguard meet her at the Madrid airport anyway.

Technology will provide managers with easy access to more data than they can possibly use. The challenge will be to synthesize the data to make effective decisions.

2:20 P.M.: Two of Ms. Smith's top lieutenants complain that they and others on her staff feel that a bonus payment for a recent project wasn't divided equitably. Bluntly, they note that while Ms. Smith received a hefty $20,000 bonus, her 15-member staff had to split $5,000 and they threaten to defect. Smith quickly calls her boss, who says he'll think about increasing the bonus for staff members.

With skilled technical and professional managers likely to be in short supply, tomorrow's managers will have to share more authority with their subordinates and, in some cases, pay them as much or more than the managers themselves earn.

While yielding more to their employees, managers in their thirties in 2010 may find their own climb up the corporate ladder stalled by superiors—older baby boomers who don't want to retire. Nevertheless, despite the globalization of companies and the speed of overall change, some things will stay the same. Managers intent on rising to the top will still be judged largely on how well they articulate ideas and work with others. In addition, different corporate cultures will still encourage and reward different qualities—for example, risk taking versus caution and predictability.

6 P.M.: Before heading to the airport, Ms. Smith uses her videophone to give her daughters a good-night kiss and to talk about the next day's schedule with her husband. Learning that he must take an unexpected trip himself the next evening, she promises to catch the SuperConcord home in time to put the kids to sleep herself.

SUMMARY

Foreign investment by the world's leading corporations is a fact of modern organizational life. For American executives transferred overseas, the opportunities are great, but the risks of failure (roughly 3 in 10) are considerable. This is because there are fundamental cultural differences that affect how different people view the world and operate in business. The lesson for MNCs is clear: Guard against the exportation of home-country bias, think in global terms, and recognize that no country has all the answers.

Recruitment for overseas assignments is typically based on one of the three basic models: (1) ethnocentrism, (2) limiting recruitment to home- and host-country nationals, or (3) geocentrism. Selection is based on five criteria: personality, skills, attitudes, motivation, and behavior. Orientation for expatriates and their families often takes place in three stages: initial, predeparture, and postarrival. Cross-cultural training may be academic (books, films, discussions) or interpersonal (the actual or simulated experience of living in the host country), but to be most effective it should be integrated with the firm's long-range global strategy and business planning. International compensation presents special problems since salary levels differ among countries. To be competitive, MNCs normally follow local salary patterns in each country. Expatriates, however, receive various types of premiums (foreign service, tax equalization, and COLAs) in addition to their base salaries. Benefits are handled in terms of the best-of-both-worlds model. An overseas assignment is not complete until repatriation problems have been resolved; these fall into three areas: personal finances, reacclimation to the U.S. lifestyle, and readjustment to the corporate structure. Finally, since MNCs operate across national boundaries while unions typically do not, the balance of power clearly rests with management in the multinational arena.

DISCUSSION QUESTIONS

17•1 What advice would you give to a prospective expatriate regarding the application of his management style in Japan?

17•2 Discuss the special problems that women face in overseas assignments.

17•3 How can the balance of power between management and labor be restored in international labor relations?

17•4 Describe the conditions necessary in order for a geocentric recruitment policy to work effectively.

17•5 What are some key cultural differences that need to be addressed by MNCs operating across national boundaries?

17•6 Should foreign language proficiency be required for executives assigned overseas? Why or why not?

REFERENCES

1. Adkins, L. (1990, October–November). Innocents abroad? *World Trade*, pp. 70–76.
2. Adler, N. J., Doktor, R., & Redding, S. G. (1986). From the Atlantic to the Pacific century: Cross-cultural management reviewed. *Journal of Management*, **12**, 295–318.

3. Allen, R., & Keaveny, T. (1988). *Contemporary labor relations* (2d ed.). Reading, MA: Addison-Wesley.

4. Bartlett, C. A. (1986). Building and managing the transnational: The new organizational challenge. In M. E. Porter (ed.), *Competition in global industries*. Boston: Harvard Business School Press, pp. 367–404.

5. Birnbaum, P. H., Farh, J. L., & Wong, G. Y. Y. (1986). The job characteristics model in Hong Kong. *Journal of Applied Psychology*, **71**, 598–605.

6. Black, J. S., & Mendenhall, M. (1990). Cross-cultural training effectiveness: A review and a theoretical framework for future research. *Academy of Management Review*, **15**, 113–136.

7. Blocklyn, P. L. (1989). Developing the international executive. *Personnel*, **66**(3), 44–47.

8. Brooks, B. J. (1988). Long-term incentives: International executives need them too. *Personnel*, **65**(8), 40–42.

9. Brooks, B. J. (1987, May). Trends in international executive compensation. *Personnel*, pp. 67–70.

10. Browning, E. S. (1986, May 6). Unhappy returns: After living abroad, Japanese find it hard to adjust back home. *The Wall Street Journal*, pp. 1, 24.

11. Campbell, D. C., & Rowan, R. L. (1983). *Multinational enterprises and the OECD industrial relations guidelines*. Philadelphia: Industrial Research Unit, The Wharton School, University of Pennsylvania.

12. Capdevielle, P. (1989). International comparisons of hourly compensation costs. *Monthly Labor Review*, **112**(6), 10–12.

13. Cascio, W. F., & Serapio, M. G., Jr. (1991, Winter). Human resources systems in an international alliance: The undoing of a done deal? *Organizational Dynamics*, 63–74.

14. Chronis, P. G. (1983, Feb. 6). They're learning how to live overseas . . . in Boulder. *Denver Post*, pp. 1C, 8–9C.

15. Clague, L., & Krupp, N. B. (1978). International personnel: The repatriation problem. *Personnel Administrator*, **23**(4), 29–33, 45.

16. Coming home (1987, Nov. 16). *The Wall Street Journal*, p. 33.

17. Conway, M. A. (1984). Reducing expatriate failure rates. *Personnel Administrator*, **29**(7), 31–38.

18. Copeland, L. (1984). Making costs count in international travel. *Personnel Administrator*, **29**(7), 47–51.

19. de Wolff, C. J., & Shimmin, S. (1976). The psychology of work in Europe: A review of a profession. *Personnel Psychology*, **29**(2), 175–196.

20. Dowling, P. J., & Schuler, R. S. (1990). *International dimensions of human resource management*. Boston: PWS-Kent.

21. Drucker, P. F. (1987, Aug. 25). The transnational economy. *The Wall Street Journal*, p. 38.

22. Earley, P. C. (1987). International training for managers: A comparison of documentary and interpersonal methods. *Academy of Management Journal*, **30**, 685–698.

23. Employee motivation in Germany (1989, March). *Manpower Argus*, no. 246, p. 6.

24. Fowler, E. (1987, Jan. 1). Many U.S. firms fail to post the right man overseas. *International Herald Tribune*, p. 13.

25. Frankenstein, J. (1985, Aug. 14). How China turns businessmen into basket cases. *Asian Wall Street Journal*, p. 8.

26. Galbraith, J., & Elstrom, A. (1976, Summer). International transfer of managers— Some important policy considerations. *Columbia Journal of World Business*, **11**, 44–55.

27. Gaugler, E. (1988). HR management: An international comparison. *Personnel*, **65**(8), 24–30.
28. George, W. W. (1983). How Honeywell takes advantage of national cultural differences. *Management Review*, **72**(9), 30–31.
29. Gilroy, E. B., Noer, D. M., & Spoor, J. E. (1979). Personnel administration in the multinational/transnational corporation. In D. Yoder & H. G. Heneman, Jr. (eds.), *ASPA handbook of personnel and industrial relations*. Washington, DC: Bureau of National Affairs, chap. 1.7.
30. Greene, W. E., & Walls, G. D. (1984). Human resources: Hiring internationally. *Personnel Administrator*, **29**(7), 61–66.
31. Gwynne, S. C. (1990, Oct. 29). The right stuff. *Time*, pp. 74–84.
32. Harris, P. R., & Moran, R. T. (1990). *Managing cultural differences* (3d ed.). Houston: Gulf Publishing.
33. Hillkirk, J. (1987, Oct. 28). Nissan gears up in USA. *USA Today*, p. 4B.
34. Howard, A., Shudo, K., Umeshima, M. (1983). Motivation and values among Japanese and American managers. *Personnel Psychology*, **36**(4), 883–898.
35. Howard, C. G. (1987). Out of sight—Not out of mind. *Personnel Administrator*, **32**(6), 82–90.
36. Hulin, C. L., & Mayer, L. J. (1986). Psychometric equivalence of a translation of the Job Descriptive Index into Hebrew. *Journal of Applied Psychology*, **71**, 83–94.
37. Kendall, D. W. (1981). Repatriation: An ending and a beginning. *Business Horizons*, **24**(6), 21–25.
38. Kim, K. I., Park, H. J., & Suzuki, N. (1990). Reward allocations in the United States, Japan, and Korea: A comparison of individualistic and collectivistic cultures. *Academy of Management Journal*, **33**, 188–198.
39. Kujawa, D. (1982). International labor relations. In I. Walter & T. Murray (eds.), *Handbook of international business*. New York: Wiley.
40. Labor letter (1990, Jan. 16). *The Wall Street Journal*, p. A1.
41. Levine, M. J. (1988). Labor movements and the multinational corporation: A future for collective bargaining? *Employee Relations Law Journal*, **13**, 382–403.
42. Lublin, J. S. (1984, Jan. 26). More spouses receive help in job searches when executives take positions overseas. *The Wall Street Journal*, p. 29.
43. Luck-Nunke, B. (1984). Recruiting European nationals to return to their home countries. *Personnel Administrator*, **29**, 41–45.
44. Machungwa, P. D., & Schmitt, N. (1983). Work motivation in a developing country. *Journal of Applied Psychology*, **68**(1), 31–42.
45. McWhirter, W. (1989, Oct. 9). I came, I saw, I blundered. *Time*, pp. 72, 73.
46. Miller, E. L., & Cheng, J. (1978). A closer look at the decision to accept an overseas position. *Management International Review*, **4**, 25–33.
47. Mitroff, I. I., & Mohrman, S. A. (1987). The slack is gone: How the United States lost its competitive edge in the world economy. *Academy of Management Executive*, **1**, 65–70.
48. Morgan, P. V. (1986). International HRM: Fact or fiction? *Personnel Administrator*, **31**(9), 43–47.
49. Negotiation waltz (1983, Aug. 1). *Time*, pp. 41–42.
50. Newman, B. (1983, Nov. 30). Border dispute: Single-country unions of Europe try to cope with multinationals. *The Wall Street Journal*, pp. 1, 22.
51. Northrup, B. (1987, Feb. 27). Planning for '87: The impact abroad. *The Wall Street Journal*, pp. 17D, 18D.

52. Northrup, H. R., & Rowan, R. L. (1979). *Multinational collective bargaining attempts: The record, the cases, and the prospects.* Philadelphia: Industrial Research Unit, The Wharton School, University of Pennsylvania.

53. Ohmae, K. (1989, March–April). The global logic of strategic alliances. *Harvard Business Review*, pp. 143–154.

54. Overman, S. (1989, October). Shaping the global workplace. *Personnel Administrator*, pp. 41–44, 101.

55. Ronen, S. (1989). Training the international assignee. In I. L. Goldstein (ed.), *Training and development in organizations.* San Francisco: Jossey-Bass, pp. 417–453.

56. Safavi, F. (1981). A model of management education in Africa. *Academy of Management Review*, **6**(2), 319–331.

57. Savich, R. S., & Rodgers, W. (1988). Assignment overseas: Easing the transition before and after. *Personnel*, **65**(8), 44–48.

58. Sekimoto, M. (1983). Performance appraisal in Japan, past and future. *The Industrial/ Organizational Psychologist*, **20**(4), 52–58.

59. Shahzad, N. (1984). The American expatriate manager. *Personnel Administrator*, **29**(7), 23–30.

60. Shenkar, O., & Zeira, Y. (1987). Human resources management in international joint ventures: Directions for research. *Academy of Management Review*, **12**, 546–557.

61. Siner, R. C. (1986, Dec. 30). Americans abroad: Possible tax problems. *International Herald Tribune*, p. 1.

62. Stone, R. J. (1986, January). Pay and perks for overseas executives. *Personnel Journal*, pp. 64–69.

63. The 100 largest U.S. multinationals (1987, July 27). *Forbes*, pp. 152–156.

64. Thorsberg, F. (1984, June 17). Culture gap hurts American workers overseas. *Honolulu Star Bulletin & Advertiser*, p. B-5.

65. Tung, R. L. (1988). *The new expatriates.* Cambridge, MA: Ballinger.

66. Tung, R. L. (1987). Expatriate assignments: Enhancing success and minimizing failure. *Academy of Management Executive*, **1**, 117–125.

67. U.S. Department of Labor (1990, July). *U.S. Department of State indexes of living costs abroad, quarters allowances, and hardship differentials.* Washington, DC: USGPO, SupDoc no. L2.101:990–993.

68. Wall, J. A. (1990). Managers in the people's Republic of China. *Academy of Management Executive*, **4**(2), 19–32.

69. Weihrich, H. (1990). Europe 1992: What the future may hold. *Academy of Management Executive*, **4**(2), 7–17.

70. Willis, H. L. (1984). Selection for employment in developing countries. *Personnel Administrator*, **29**(7), 53–58.

71. Wysocki, B., Jr. (1990, Mar. 26). Cross-border alliances become favorite way to crack new markets. *The Wall Street Journal*, pp. A1, A6.

Illustration Credits

Fig. 4-4 Reprinted by permission from the Position Analysis Questionnaire. Copyright © 1969 by Purdue Research Foundation. All rights reserved.

Fig. 4-5 Reprinted by permission of Control Data Business Advisors, 1985.

Figs. 4-10, 4-11 L. J. Reypert, "Succession planning in the Ministry of Transportation and Communications, Province of Ontario," *Human Resource Planning*, 4, 1981, pp. 153, 154.

Fig. 7-3 From I. L. Goldstein, *Training: Program Development and Evaluation*. Copyright © 1974 by Wadsworth Publishing Company, Inc. Reprinted by permission of the publisher, Brooks/Cole Publishing Company, Monterey, CA.

Fig. 7-4 K. L. Vinton, A. O. Clark, and J. W. Seybolt, "Assessment of training needs for supervisors," *Personnel Administrator*, November 1983, p. 49. Reprinted by permission. Copyright 1983, The American Society for Personnel Administration, 606 North Washington Street, Alexandria, VA 22314.

Fig. 8-6 F. J. Landy and J. L. Farr, *Police Performance Appraisal*, Department of Justice, 1975. Used by permission of the authors.

Fig. 10-4 Hay Associates. Used by permission.

Fig. 12-3 Copyright © 1975 by the Regents of the University of California. Reprinted from J. R. Hackman, G. Oldham, R. Janson, and K. Purdy, *California Management Review*, XVII, p. 62, by permission of the Regents.

Fig. 13-2 R. L. Miller, "Preparation for negotiations," copyright January 1978, p. 38. Reprinted with the permission of *Personnel Journal*, Costa Mesa, CA. All rights reserved.

Fig. 15-2 E. M. Ginter, "Communications and cost-benefit aspects of employee safety," *Management Accounting*, May 1979, p. 26. Used by permission of the publisher.

Fig. 16-1 J. C. Quick and J. D. Quick. *Organizational Stress and Preventative Management*, McGraw-Hill, 1984, p. 87. B. A. Macy and P. H. Mirvis, "Organizational change efforts: Methodologies for assessing organization effectiveness and program costs versus benefits," *Evaluation Review*, 6(3), 1982, pp. 301–372. Copyright © 1982 by Sage Publications, Inc. Reprinted by permission.

Fig. 16-3 H. H. Meyer and M. S. Raich, "An objective evaluation of a behavior modeling training program," *Personnel Psychology*, 36, 1983, p. 759. Used by permission of the publisher.

Fig. 17-1 A. Rahim, "A model for developing key expatriate executives," copyright April 1983. Reprinted with the permission of *Personnel Journal*, Costa Mesa, CA. All rights reserved.

Fig. 17-2 D. M. Noer, *Multinational People Management*, The Bureau of National Affairs, Inc., Washington, DC, 1975, p. 120.

Photo Credits

Page 4: Courtesy of McDonald's. **Page 35:** UPI/Bettmann Newsphotos. **Page 72:** AP/Wide World. **Page 106:** UPI/Bettmann Newsphotos. **Page 159:** Courtesy of Novosad and Co., Inc. **Page 189:** Randy Matusow. **Page 321:** Richard Wood/The Picture Cube. **Page 424:** Andrew Sacks/Time Magazine. **Page 492:** Courtesy of New United Motor. **Page 559:** Gerard Fritz/Monkmeyer. **Page 624:** Liu Heung Sh'ing/Woodfin Camp & Associates.

Name Index

Subject Index